Labor Economics

Sixth Edition

George J. Borjas
Harvard University

McGraw-Hill
Irwin

LABOR ECONOMICS, SIXTH EDITION

Published by McGraw-Hill, a business unit of The McGraw-Hill Companies, Inc., 1221 Avenue of the Americas, New York, NY 10020. Copyright © 2013 by The McGraw-Hill Companies, Inc. All rights reserved. Printed in the United States of America. Previous editions © 2010, 2008, and 2005. No part of this publication may be reproduced or distributed in any form or by any means, or stored in a database or retrieval system, without the prior written consent of The McGraw-Hill Companies, Inc., including, but not limited to, in any network or other electronic storage or transmission, or broadcast for distance learning.

Some ancillaries, including electronic and print components, may not be available to customers outside the United States.

This book is printed on acid-free paper.

1 2 3 4 5 6 7 8 9 0 DOC/DOC 1 0 9 8 7 6 5 4 3 2

ISBN   978-0-07-352320-0
MHID   0-07-352320-8

Vice President & Editor-in-Chief: *Brent Gordon*
Vice President of Specialized Publishing: *Janice M. Roerig-Blong*
Publisher: *Douglas Reiner*
Sponsoring Editor: *Daryl C. Bruflodt*
Marketing Coordinator: *Colleen P. Havens*
Lead Project Manager: *Jane Mohr*
Design Coordinator: *Brenda A. Rolwes*
Cover Designer: *Studio Montage, St. Louis, Missouri*
Cover Image: *© Imagestate Media RF*
Buyer: *Kara Kudronowicz*
Media Project Manager: *Balaji Sundararaman*
Compositor: *Laserwords Private Limited*
Typeface: *10/12 Times New Roman*
Printer: *R.R. Donnelley*

All credits appearing on page or at the end of the book are considered to be an extension of the copyright page.

Library of Congress Cataloging-in-Publication Data

Borjas, George J.
  Labor economics / George J. Borjas. — 6th ed.
    p. cm.
  ISBN 978-0-07-352320-0 (alk. paper)
  1. Labor economics. 2. Labor market—United States. I. Title.
  HD4901.B674 2013
  331—dc23
                                        2011038722

About the Author

George J. Borjas

George J. Borjas is the Robert W. Scrivner Professor of Economics and Social Policy at the John F. Kennedy School of Government, Harvard University. He is also a research associate at the National Bureau of Economic Research. Professor Borjas received his Ph.D. in economics from Columbia University in 1975.

Professor Borjas has written extensively on labor market issues. He is the author of several books, including *Wage Policy in the Federal Bureaucracy* (American Enterprise Institute, 1980), *Friends or Strangers: The Impact of Immigrants on the U.S. Economy* (Basic Books, 1990), and *Heaven's Door: Immigration Policy and the American Economy* (Princeton University Press, 1999). He has published more than 125 articles in books and scholarly journals, including the *American Economic Review,* the *Journal of Political Economy,* and the *Quarterly Journal of Economics.*

Professor Borjas was elected a Fellow of the Econometric Society in 1998, and a Fellow of the Society of Labor Economics in 2004. In 2011, Professor Borjas was awarded the IZA Prize in Labor Economics. He was an editor of the *Review of Economics and Statistics* from 1998 to 2006. He also has served as a member of the Advisory Panel in Economics at the National Science Foundation and has testified frequently before congressional committees and government commissions.

To Sarah, Timothy, and Rebecca

Preface to the Sixth Edition

The original motivation for writing *Labor Economics* grew out of my years of teaching labor economics to undergraduates. After trying out many of the textbooks in the market, it seemed to me that students were not being exposed to what the essence of labor economics was about: to try to *understand* how labor markets work. As a result, I felt that students did not really grasp *why* some persons choose to work, while other persons withdraw from the labor market; *why* some firms expand their employment at the same time that other firms are laying off workers; or *why* earnings are distributed unequally in most societies.

The key difference between *Labor Economics* and competing textbooks lies in its philosophy. I believe that knowing the *story* of how labor markets work is, in the end, more important than showing off our skills at constructing elegant models of the labor market or remembering hundreds of statistics and institutional details summarizing labor market conditions at a particular point in time.

I doubt that many students will (or should!) remember the mechanics of deriving a labor supply curve or the way that the unemployment rate is officially calculated 10 or 20 years after they leave college. However, if students could remember the *story* of the way the labor market works—and, in particular, that workers and firms respond to changing incentives by altering the amount of labor they supply or demand—the students would be much better prepared to make informed opinions about the many proposed government policies that can have a dramatic impact on labor market opportunities, such as a "workfare" program requiring that welfare recipients work or a payroll tax assessed on employers to fund a national health care program or a guest worker program that grants tens of thousands of entry visas to high-skill workers. The exposition in this book, therefore, stresses the *ideas* that labor economists use to understand how the labor market works.

The book also makes extensive use of labor market statistics and reports evidence obtained from hundreds of research studies. These data summarize the stylized facts that a good theory of the labor market should be able to explain, as well as help shape our thinking about the way the labor market works. The main objective of the book, therefore, is to survey the field of labor economics with an emphasis on *both* theory and facts. The book relies much more heavily on "the economic way of thinking" than competing textbooks. I believe this approach gives a much better understanding of labor economics than an approach that minimizes the story-telling aspects of economic theory.

Requirements

The book uses economic analysis throughout. *All* of the theoretical tools are introduced and explained in the text. As a result, the only prerequisite is that the student has some familiarity with the basics of microeconomics, particularly supply and demand curves. The exposure acquired in the typical introductory economics class more than satisfies this prerequisite. All other concepts (such as indifference curves, budget lines, production functions, and isoquants) are motivated, defined, and explained as they appear in our story. The book does not make use of any mathematical skills beyond those taught in high school algebra (particularly the notion of a slope).

Labor economists also make extensive use of econometric analysis in their research. Although the discussion in this book does not require any prior exposure to econometrics, the student will get a much better "feel" for the research findings if they know a little about how labor economists manipulate data to reach their conclusions. The appendix to Chapter 1 provides a simple (and very brief) introduction to econometrics and allows the student to visualize how labor economists conclude, for instance, that wealth reduces labor supply, or that schooling increases earnings. Additional econometric concepts widely used in labor economics—such as the difference-in-differences estimator or instrumental variables—are introduced in the context of policy-relevant examples throughout the text.

Changes in the Sixth Edition

Users of the textbook reacted favorably to the substantial rearrangement of material (mainly of labor supply) that I carried out in the previous edition. The Sixth Edition continues this new tradition by further tightening up the discussion on labor supply so that the chapter now contains material that can be roughly done in a week of lectures. In order to maintain the labor supply discussion at a tractable length (and in keeping with my philosophy that textbooks are not meant to be encyclopedias), some material that had been a staple in earlier editions is now omitted (specifically, the models of household fertility and household specialization).

The Sixth Edition continues and expands other traditions established in earlier editions. In particular, the text has a number of new detailed policy applications in labor economics and uses the evidence reported in state-of-the-art research articles to illustrate the many uses of modern labor economics. As before, the text makes frequent use of such econometric tools as the difference-in-differences estimator and instrumental variables—tools that play a central role in modern research in labor economics. In fact, the Sixth Edition introduces students to yet another tool in our econometric arsenal, the method of fixed effects—a technique that is widely used to ensure that the empirical analysis is indeed holding "other things equal."

Most important, a number of users of the textbook have repeatedly requested a more technical presentation of some of the basic models of labor economics. To accommodate this request, I have written a Mathematical Appendix that appears at the end of the textbook. This appendix presents a mathematical version of some of the canonical models in labor economics, including the neoclassical model of labor-leisure choice, the model of labor demand, a derivation of Marshall's rules of derived demand, and the schooling model.

It is very important to emphasize that the Mathematical Appendix is an "add-on." None of the material in this appendix is a prerequisite to reading or understanding any of the discussion in the 12 core chapters of the textbook. Instructors who like to provide a more technical derivation of the various models can use the appendix as a takeoff point for their own discussion and presentation. This is the first time that such an appendix appears in the textbook, so I would particularly welcome any suggestions or reactions that would be useful in the presentation and organization of the material in the next edition (including suggestions for additional models that should be discussed).

Among the specific applications included in the Sixth Edition are:

1. Several new "Theory at Work" boxes. The sidebars now include a discussion of the impact of weather on the consumption of leisure, the link between the human capital

of kindergarteners and their socioeconomic outcomes decades later, how the exodus of renowned Jewish scientists from Nazi Germany affected the productivity of the doctoral students they left behind, the economic consequences of political discrimination in Hugo Chavez's Venezuela, the link between teachers' unions and student outcomes, and a discussion of the long-run consequences of graduating from school during a recession.

2. A careful updating of all the data tables presented in the text, and particularly the data on unemployment trends in the United States since the financial crisis of 2008.

3. An introduction to the method of fixed effects by noting how this methodology is used to estimate the key parameter that summarizes how a worker reacts to wage changes in a model of labor supply over the life cycle.

4. An expanded discussion of the "new" monopsony literature, including estimates of the labor supply elasticity at the firm level.

As in previous editions, each chapter contains "Web Links," guiding students to Websites that provide additional data or policy discussions. There is an updated list of "Selected Readings" that include both standard references in a particular area and recent applications. Finally, the Sixth Edition adds one additional end-of-chapter problem in each chapter.

Organization of the Book

The instructor will find that this book is much shorter than competing labor economics textbooks. The book contains an introductory chapter, plus 11 substantive chapters. If the instructor wished to cover all of the material, each chapter could serve as the basis for about a week's worth of lectures in a typical undergraduate semester course. Despite the book's brevity, the instructor will find that all of the key topics in labor economics are covered. The discussion, however, is kept to essentials as I have tried very hard not to deviate into tangential material, or into 10-page-long ruminations on my pet topics.

Chapter 1 presents a brief introduction that exposes the student to the concepts of labor supply, labor demand, and equilibrium. The chapter uses the "real-world" example of the Alaskan labor market during the construction of the oil pipeline to introduce these concepts. In addition, the chapter shows how labor economists contrast the theory with the evidence, as well as discusses the limits of the insights provided by both the theory and the data. The example used to introduce the student to regression analysis is drawn from "real-world" data—and looks at the link between differences in mean wages across occupations and differences in educational attainment as well as the "female-ness" of occupations.

The book begins the detailed analysis of the labor market with a detailed study of labor supply and labor demand. Chapter 2 examines the factors that determine whether a person chooses to work and, if so, how much, while Chapter 3 examines the factors that determine how many workers a firm wants to hire. Chapter 4 puts together the supply decisions of workers with the demand decisions of employers and shows how the labor market "balances out" the conflicting interests of the two parties.

The remainder of the book extends and generalizes the basic supply-demand framework. Chapter 5 stresses that jobs differ in their characteristics, so that jobs with unpleasant working conditions may have to offer higher wages in order to attract workers. Chapter 6 stresses that workers are different because they differ either in their educational attainment or in the amount of on-the-job training they acquire. These human capital investments help determine the economy's wage distribution. Chapter 7 discusses how changes in the rate of return to skills in the 1980s and 1990s changed the wage distribution in many industrialized economies, particularly in the United States. Chapter 8 describes a key mechanism that allows the labor market to balance out the interests of workers and firms, namely labor turnover and migration.

The final section of the book discusses a number of distortions and imperfections in labor markets. Chapter 9 analyzes how labor market discrimination affects the earnings and employment opportunities of minority workers and women. Chapter 10 discusses how labor unions affect the relationship between the firm and the worker. Chapter 11 notes that employers often find it difficult to monitor the activities of their workers, so that the workers will often want to "shirk" on the job. The chapter discusses how different types of pay incentive systems arise to discourage workers from misbehaving. Finally, Chapter 12 discusses why unemployment can exist and persist in labor markets.

The text uses a number of pedagogical devices designed to deepen the student's understanding of labor economics. A chapter typically begins by presenting a number of stylized facts about the labor market, such as wage differentials between blacks and whites or between men and women. The chapter then presents the story that labor economists have developed to understand why these facts are observed in the labor market. Finally, the chapter extends and applies the theory to related labor market phenomena. Each chapter typically contains at least one lengthy application of the material to a major policy issue, as well as several boxed examples showing the "Theory at Work."

The end-of-chapter material also contains a number of student-friendly devices. There is a chapter summary describing briefly the main lessons of the chapter; a "Key Concepts" section listing the major concepts introduced in the chapter (when a key concept makes its first appearance, it appears in **boldface**). Each chapter includes "Review Questions" that the student can use to review the major theoretical and empirical issues, a set of 15 problems that test the students' understanding of the material, as well as a list of "Selected Readings" to guide interested students to many of the standard references in a particular area of study. Each chapter then ends with "Web Links," listing Web sites that can provide more detailed information about particular issues.

The supplementary material for the textbook includes a Web site that contains much of the material that students would ordinarily find in a Study Guide (**www.mhhe.com/ borjas6e**), a *Solutions Manual* that gives detailed answers to all of the end-of-chapter problems, PowerPoint presentations that instructors can adapt and edit to fit their own lecture style and organization, a *Test Bank* that includes 30 multiple choice questions per chapter, and a digital image library. Instructors should contact their McGraw-Hill sales representative to obtain access to both the *Solutions Manual* and the PowerPoint presentation.

Acknowledgments

I am grateful to the many colleagues who have graciously provided me with data from their research projects. These data allow me to present the intuition and findings of many empirical studies in a way that is accessible to students who are just beginning their study of labor economics. I have also benefited from countless e-mail messages sent by users of the textbook—both students and instructors. These messages often contained very valuable suggestions, most of which found their way into the Sixth Edition. I strongly encourage users to contact me (gborjas@harvard.edu) with any comments or changes that they would like to see included in the next revision. I am grateful to Robert Lemke of Lake Forest College, who updated the Web site for this edition, helped me expand the menu of end-of-chapter problems, and collaborated in the *Solutions Manual* and *Test Bank;* and Michael Welker, Franciscan University of Steubenville, who created the PowerPoint presentation for the Sixth Edition. I am particularly grateful to many friends and colleagues who have generously shared some of their research data so that I could summarize and present it in a relatively simple way throughout the textbook, including David Autor, William Carrington, John Friedman,Barry Hirsch, Lawrence Katz, Alan Krueger, David Lee, and Solomon Polachek. Finally, I have benefited from the comments and detailed reviews made by many colleagues on the earlier editions. These colleagues include:

Ulyses Balderas
Sam Houston State University

Laura Boyd
Denison University

Lawrence Boyd
University of Hawaii, West Oahu

Kristine Brown
University of Illinois–Champaign

John Buck
Jacksonville University

Darius Conger
Ithaca College

Jeffrey DeSimone
University of Texas Arlington

Richard Dibble
New York Institute Technology

Andrew Ewing
University of Washington

Julia Frankland
Malone University

Steffen Habermalz
Northwestern University

Mehdi Haririan
Bloomsburg University of Pennsylvania

Masanori Hashimoto
Ohio State University–Columbus

James Hill
Central Michigan University

Jessica Howell
California State University–Sacramento

Sarah Jackson
Indiana University of Pennsylvania–Indiana

Thomas Kniesner
Syracuse University

Cory Koedel
University of Missouri–Columbia

Myra McCrickard
Bellarmine University

Elda Pema
Naval Postgraduate School

Esther Redmount
Colorado College

Jeff Sarbaum
University of North Carolina–Greensboro

Martin Shields
Colorado State University

Todd Steen
Hope College

Erdal Tekin
Georgia State University

Alejandro Velez
Saint Mary's University

Elizabeth Wheaton
Southern Methodist University

Janine Wilson
University of California–Davis

All editions of this book have been dedicated to my children. I began work on the first edition shortly before they began to arrive and the 6th edition is being published while my children are in college. It has been a most interesting and rewarding time. I am truly lucky and grateful to have been able to experience it.

Contents in Brief

Contents

Chapter 1

Introduction to Labor Economics

Observations always involve theory.

—Edwin Hubble

Most of us will allocate a substantial fraction of our time to the labor market. How we do in the labor market helps determine our wealth, the types of goods we can afford to consume, with whom we associate, where we vacation, which schools our children attend, and even the types of persons who find us attractive. As a result, we are all eager to learn how the labor market works. **Labor economics** studies how labor markets work.

Our interest in labor markets arises not only from our personal involvement, however, but also because many social policy issues concern the labor market experiences of particular groups of workers or various aspects of the employment relationship between workers and firms. The policy issues examined by modern labor economics include

1. Why did the labor force participation of women rise steadily throughout the past century in many industrialized countries?
2. What is the impact of immigration on the wage and employment opportunities of native-born workers?
3. Do minimum wages increase the unemployment rate of less-skilled workers?
4. What is the impact of occupational safety and health regulations on employment and earnings?
5. Are government subsidies of investments in human capital an effective way to improve the economic well-being of disadvantaged workers?
6. Why did wage inequality in the United States rise so rapidly after 1980?
7. What is the impact of affirmative action programs on the earnings of women and minorities and on the number of women and minorities that firms hire?
8. What is the economic impact of unions, both on their members and on the rest of the economy?

9. Do generous unemployment insurance benefits lengthen the duration of spells of unemployment?

10. Why did the unemployment rate in the United States begin to approach the typically higher unemployment rate of European countries after 2008?

This diverse list of questions clearly illustrates why the study of labor markets is intrinsically more important and more interesting than the study of the market for butter (unless one happens to be in the butter business!). Labor economics helps us understand and address many of the social and economic problems facing modern societies.

1-1   An Economic Story of the Labor Market

This book tells the "story" of how labor markets work. Telling this story involves much more than simply recounting the history of labor law in the United States or in other countries and presenting reams of statistics summarizing conditions in the labor market. After all, good stories have themes, characters that come alive with vivid personalities, conflicts that have to be resolved, ground rules that limit the set of permissible actions, and events that result inevitably from the interaction among characters.

The story we will tell about the labor market has all of these features. Labor economists typically assign motives to the various "actors" in the labor market. We typically view workers, for instance, as trying to find the best possible job and assume that firms are trying to make money. Workers and firms, therefore, enter the labor market with different objectives—workers are trying to sell their labor at the highest price and firms are trying to buy labor at the lowest price.

The types of economic exchanges that can occur between workers and firms are limited by the set of ground rules that the government has imposed to regulate transactions in the labor market. Changes in these rules and regulations would obviously lead to different outcomes. For instance, a minimum wage law prohibits exchanges that pay less than a particular amount per hour worked; occupational safety regulations forbid firms from offering working conditions that are deemed too risky to the worker's health. The deals that are eventually struck between workers and firms determine the types of jobs that are offered, the skills that workers acquire, the extent of labor turnover, the structure of unemployment, and the observed earnings distribution. The story thus provides a theory, a framework for understanding, analyzing, and predicting a wide array of labor market outcomes.

The underlying philosophy of the book is that modern economics provides a useful story of how the labor market works. The typical assumptions we make about the behavior of workers and firms, and about the ground rules under which the labor market participants make their transactions, suggest outcomes often corroborated by the facts observed in real-world labor markets. The study of labor economics, therefore, helps us understand and predict why some labor market outcomes are more likely to be observed than others.

Our discussion is guided by the belief that learning the story of how labor markets work is as important as knowing basic facts about the labor market. The study of facts without theory is just as empty as the study of theory without facts. Without understanding how labor markets work—that is, without having a theory of why workers and firms pursue some employment relationships and avoid others—we would be hard-pressed to predict the impact on the labor market of changes in government policies or changes in the demographic composition of the workforce.

A question often asked is which is more important—ideas or facts? The analysis presented throughout this book stresses that "ideas *about* facts" are most important. We do not study labor economics so that we can construct elegant theories of the labor market, or so that we can remember how the official unemployment rate is calculated and that the unemployment rate was 6.9 percent in 1993. Rather, we want to understand which economic and social factors generate a certain level of unemployment, and why.

The main objective of this book is to survey the field of labor economics with an emphasis on *both* theory and facts: where the theory helps us understand how the facts are generated and where the facts can help shape our thinking about the way labor markets work.

1-2   The Actors in the Labor Market

Throughout the book, we will see that there are three leading actors in the labor market: workers, firms, and the government.[1]

As workers, we receive top casting in the story. Without us, after all, there is no "labor" in the labor market. We decide whether to work or not, how many hours to work, how much effort to allocate to the job, which skills to acquire, when to quit a job, which occupations to enter, and whether to join a labor union. Each of these decisions is motivated by the desire to *optimize,* to choose the best available option from the various choices. In our story, therefore, workers will always act in ways that maximize their well-being. Adding up the decisions of millions of workers generates the economy's labor supply not only in terms of the number of persons who enter the labor market, but also in terms of the quantity and quality of skills available to employers. As we will see many times throughout the book, persons who want to maximize their well-being tend to supply more time and more effort to those activities that have a higher payoff. The **labor supply curve,** therefore, is often upward sloping, as illustrated in Figure 1-1.

The hypothetical labor supply curve drawn in the figure gives the number of engineers that will be forthcoming at every wage. For example, 20,000 workers are willing to supply their services to engineering firms if the engineering wage is $40,000 per year. If the engineering wage rises to $50,000, then 30,000 workers will choose to be engineers. In other words, as the engineering wage rises, more persons will decide that the engineering profession is a worthwhile pursuit. More generally, the labor supply curve relates the number of person-hours supplied to the economy to the wage that is being offered. The higher the wage that is being offered, the larger the labor supplied.

Firms co-star in our story. Each firm must decide how many and which types of workers to hire and fire, the length of the workweek, how much capital to employ, and whether to offer a safe or risky working environment to its workers. Like workers, firms in our story also have motives. In particular, we will assume that firms want to maximize profits. From the firm's point of view, the consumer is king. The firm will maximize its profits by

---

[1] In some countries, a fourth actor can be added to the story: trade unions. Unions may organize a large fraction of the workforce and represent the interests of workers in their bargaining with employers as well as influence political outcomes. In the United States, however, the trade union movement has been in decline for several decades. By 2010, only 6.9 percent of private-sector workers were union members.

FIGURE 1-1   Supply and Demand in the Engineering Labor Market

The labor supply curve gives the number of persons who are willing to supply their services to engineering firms at a given wage. The labor demand curve gives the number of engineers that the firms will hire at that wage. Labor market equilibrium occurs where supply equals demand. In equilibrium, 20,000 engineers are hired at a wage of $40,000.

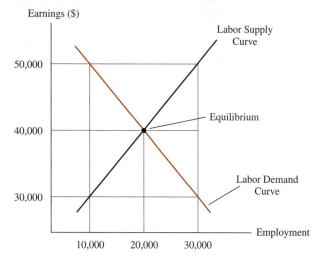

making the production decisions—and hence the hiring and firing decisions—that best serve the consumers' needs. In effect, the firm's demand for labor is a **derived demand,** a demand derived from the desires of consumers.

Adding up the hiring and firing decisions of millions of employers generates the economy's labor demand. The assumption that firms want to maximize profits implies that firms will want to hire many workers when labor is cheap but will refrain from hiring when labor is expensive. The relation between the price of labor and how many workers firms are willing to hire is summarized by the downward-sloping **labor demand curve** (also illustrated in Figure 1-1). As drawn, the labor demand curve tells us that firms in the engineering industry want to hire 20,000 engineers when the wage is $40,000 but will hire only 10,000 engineers if the wage rises to $50,000.

Workers and firms, therefore, enter the labor market with conflicting interests. Many workers are willing to supply their services when the wage is high, but few firms are willing to hire them. Conversely, few workers are willing to supply their services when the wage is low, but many firms are looking for workers. As workers search for jobs and firms search for workers, these conflicting desires are "balanced out" and the labor market reaches an **equilibrium.** In a free-market economy, equilibrium is attained when supply equals demand.

As drawn in Figure 1-1, the equilibrium wage is $40,000 and 20,000 engineers will be hired in the labor market. This wage-employment combination is an equilibrium because it balances out the conflicting desires of workers and firms. Suppose, for example, that the engineering wage were $50,000—above equilibrium. Firms would then want to hire only 10,000 engineers, even though 30,000 engineers are looking for work. The excess number of job applicants would bid down the wage as they compete for the few jobs available.

Suppose, instead, that the wage were $30,000—below equilibrium. Because engineers are cheap, firms want to hire 30,000 engineers, but only 10,000 engineers are willing to work at that wage. As firms compete for the few available engineers, they bid up the wage.

There is one last major player in the labor market, the government. The government can tax the worker's earnings, subsidize the training of engineers, impose a payroll tax on firms, demand that engineering firms hire two black engineers for each white one hired, enact legislation that makes some labor market transactions illegal (such as paying engineers less than $50,000 annually), and increase the supply of engineers by encouraging their immigration from abroad. All these actions will change the equilibrium that will eventually be attained in the labor market. Government regulations, therefore, help set the ground rules that guide exchanges in the labor market.

The Trans-Alaska Oil Pipeline

In January 1968, oil was discovered in Prudhoe Bay in remote northern Alaska. The oil reserves were estimated to be greater than 10 billion barrels, making it the largest such discovery in North America.[2]

There was one problem with the discovery—the oil was located in a remote and frigid area of Alaska, far from where most consumers lived. To solve the daunting problem of transporting the oil to those consumers who wanted to buy it, the oil companies proposed building a 48-inch pipeline across the 789-mile stretch from northern Alaska to the southern (and ice-free) port of Valdez. At Valdez, the oil would be transferred to oil supertankers. These huge ships would then deliver the oil to consumers in the United States and elsewhere.

The oil companies joined forces and formed the Alyeska Pipeline Project. The construction project began in the spring of 1974, after the U.S. Congress gave its approval in the wake of the 1973 oil embargo. Construction work continued for three years and the pipeline was completed in 1977. Alyeska employed about 25,000 workers during the summers of 1974 through 1977, and its subcontractors employed an additional 25,000 workers. Once the pipeline was built, Alyeska reduced its pipeline-related employment to a small maintenance crew.

Many of the workers employed by Alyeska and its subcontractors were engineers who had built pipelines across the world. Very few of these engineers were resident Alaskans. The remainder of the Alyeska workforce consisted of low-skill labor such as truck drivers and excavators. Many of these low-skill workers were resident Alaskans.

The theoretical framework summarized by the supply and demand curves can help us understand the shifts in the labor market that *should* have occurred in Alaska as a result of the Trans-Alaska Pipeline System. As Figure 1-2 shows, the Alaskan labor market was initially in an equilibrium represented by the intersection of the demand curve D_0 and the supply curve S_0. The labor demand curve tells us how many workers would be hired in the Alaskan labor market at a particular wage, and the labor supply curve tells us how many workers are willing to supply their services to the Alaskan labor market at a particular wage. A total of E_0 Alaskans were employed at a wage of w_0 in the initial equilibrium.

---

[2] This discussion is based on the work of William J. Carrington, "The Alaskan Labor Market during the Pipeline Era," *Journal of Political Economy* 104 (February 1996): 186–218.

FIGURE 1-2   The Alaskan Labor Market and the Construction of the Oil Pipeline

The construction of the oil pipeline shifted the labor demand curve in Alaska from D_0 to D_1, resulting in higher wages and employment. Once the pipeline was completed, the demand curve reverted back to its original level and wages and employment fell.

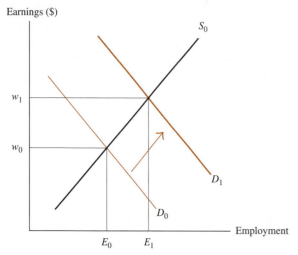

The construction project clearly led to a sizable increase in the demand for labor. Figure 1-2 illustrates this shift by showing the demand curve moving outward from D_0 to D_1. The outward shift in the demand curve implies that—at any given wage—Alaskan employers were looking for more workers.

This theoretical framework immediately implies that the shift in demand moved the Alaskan labor market to a new equilibrium, one represented by the intersection of the new demand curve and the original supply curve. At this new equilibrium, a total of E_1 persons were employed at a wage of w_1. The theory, therefore, predicts that the pipeline construction project would increase *both* employment and wages. As soon as the project was completed, however, and the temporary need for construction workers disappeared, the demand curve would have shifted back to its original position at D_0. In the end, the wage would have gone back down to w_0 and E_0 workers would be employed. In short, the pipeline construction project should have led to a temporary increase in both wages and employment during the construction period.

Figure 1-3 illustrates what *actually* happened to employment and earnings in Alaska between 1968 and 1983. Because Alaska's population grew steadily for some decades, Alaskan employment also rose steadily even before the oil discovery in Prudhoe Bay. The data clearly show, however, that employment "spiked" in 1975, 1976, and 1977 and then went back to its long-run growth trend in 1977. The earnings of Alaskan workers also rose substantially during the relevant period. After adjusting for inflation, the monthly earnings of Alaskan workers rose from an average of $2,648 in the third quarter of 1973 to $4,140 in the third quarter of 1976, an increase of 56 percent. By 1979, the real earnings of Alaskan workers were back to the level observed prior to the beginning of the pipeline construction project.

FIGURE 1-3

Wages and Employment in the Alaskan Labor Market, 1968–1984

Source: William J. Carrington, "The Alaskan Labor Market during the Pipeline Era," *Journal of Political Economy* 104 (February 1996): 199.

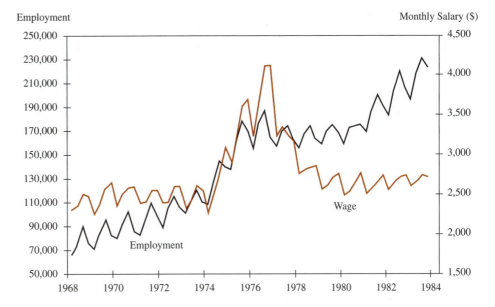

It is worth noting that the temporary increase in earnings and employment occurred because the supply curve of labor is upward sloping, so that an outward shift in the demand curve moves the labor market to a point further up on the supply curve. As we noted earlier, an upward-sloping supply curve implies that more workers are willing to work when the wage is higher. It turns out that the increase in labor supply experienced in the Alaskan labor market occurred for two distinct reasons. First, a larger fraction of Alaskans were willing to work when the wage increased. In the summer of 1973, about 39 percent of Alaskans were working. In the summers of 1975 and 1976, about 50 percent of Alaskans were working. Second, the rate of population growth in Alaska accelerated between 1974 and 1976—because persons living in the lower 48 states moved to Alaska to take advantage of the improved economic opportunities offered by the Alaskan labor market (despite the frigid weather conditions there). The increase in the rate of population growth, however, was temporary. Population growth reverted back to its long-run trend soon after the pipeline construction project was completed.

1-3 Why Do We Need a Theory?

We have just told a simple story of how the Trans-Alaska Pipeline System affected the labor market outcomes experienced by workers in Alaska—and how each of the actors in our story played a major role. The government approved the pipeline project despite the environmental hazards involved; firms who saw income opportunities in building the pipeline increased their demand for labor; and workers responded to the change in demand by increasing the quantity of labor supplied to the Alaskan labor market. We have, in effect, constructed a simple theory or **model** of the Alaskan labor market. Our model is characterized by an upward-sloping labor supply curve, a downward-sloping labor demand curve, and the assumption that an equilibrium is eventually attained that resolves the conflicts between workers and firms. As we have just seen, this model predicts that the construction of the oil pipeline would temporarily increase wages and employment in the Alaskan labor market. Moreover, this prediction is testable—that is, the predictions about wages and employment can be compared with what actually happened to wages and employment. It turns out that the supply-demand model passes the test; the data are consistent with the theoretical predictions.

Needless to say, the model of the labor market illustrated in Figure 1-2 does not do full justice to the complexities of the Alaskan labor market. It is easy to come up with many factors and variables that our simple model ignored and that could potentially influence the success of our predictions. For instance, it is possible that workers care about more than just the wage when they make labor supply decisions. The opportunity to participate in such a challenging or cutting-edge project as the construction of the Trans-Alaska Pipeline could have attracted engineers at wages lower than those offered by firms engaged in more mundane projects—despite the harsh working conditions in the field. The theoretical prediction that the construction of the pipeline project would increase wages would then be incorrect because the project could have attracted more workers at lower wages.

If the factors that we have omitted from our theory play a crucial role in understanding how the Alaskan labor market operates, we might be wrongly predicting that wages and employment would rise. If these factors are only minor details, our model captures the essence of what goes on in the Alaskan labor market and our prediction would be valid.

We could try to build a more complex model of the Alaskan labor market, a model that incorporates every single one of these omitted factors. Now that would be a tough job! A completely realistic model would have to describe how millions of workers and firms interact and how these interactions work themselves through the labor market. Even if we knew how to accomplish such a difficult task, this "everything-but-the-kitchen-sink" approach would defeat the whole purpose of having a theory. A theory that mirrored the real-world labor market in Alaska down to the most minute detail might indeed be able to explain all the facts, but it would be as complex as reality itself, cumbersome and incoherent, and thus would not at all help us understand how the Alaskan labor market works.

There has been a long debate over whether a theory should be judged by the realism of its assumptions or by the extent to which it finally helps us understand and predict the labor market phenomena we are interested in. We obviously have a better shot at predicting labor market outcomes if we use more realistic assumptions. At the same time, however, a theory that mirrors the world too closely is too clumsy and does not isolate what *really* matters. The "art" of labor economics lies in choosing which details are essential to the story and which details are not. There is a trade-off between realism and simplicity, and good economics hits the mark just right.

As we will see throughout this book, the supply-demand framework illustrated in Figure 1-1 often isolates the key factors that motivate the various actors in the labor market. The model provides a useful way of organizing our thoughts about how the labor market works. The model also gives a solid foundation for building more complex and more realistic models of the labor market. And, most important, the model works. Its predictions are often consistent with what is observed in the real world.

The supply-demand framework predicts that the construction of the Alaska oil pipeline would have temporarily increased employment and wages in the Alaskan labor market. This prediction is an example of **positive economics.** Positive economics addresses the relatively narrow "What is?" questions, such as, What is the impact of the discovery of oil in Prudhoe Bay, and the subsequent construction of the oil pipeline, on the Alaskan labor market? Positive economics, therefore, addresses questions that can, in principle, be answered with the tools of economics, without interjecting any value judgment as to whether the particular outcome is desirable or harmful. Much of this book is devoted to the analysis of such positive questions as, What is the impact of the minimum wage on unemployment? What is the impact of immigration on the earnings of native-born workers? What is the impact of a tuition assistance program on college enrollment rates? What is the impact of unemployment insurance on the duration of a spell of unemployment?

These positive questions, however, beg a number of important issues. In fact, some would say that these positive questions beg *the* most important issues: *Should* the oil pipeline have been built? *Should* there be a minimum wage? *Should* the government subsidize college tuition? *Should* the United States accept more immigrants? *Should* the unemployment insurance system be less generous?

These broader questions fall in the realm of **normative economics,** which addresses much broader "What should be?" questions. By their nature, the answers to these normative questions require value judgments. Because each of us probably has different values, our answers to these normative questions may differ *regardless* of what the theory or the facts tell us about the economic impact of the oil pipeline, the disemployment effects of the minimum wage, or the impact of immigration on the economic well-being of native workers.

Normative questions force us to make value judgments about the type of society we wish to live in. Consider, for instance, the impact of immigration on a particular host country. As we will see in subsequent chapters, the supply-demand framework implies that an increase in the number of immigrants lowers the income of competing workers but raises the income of the firms that hire the immigrants by even more. On net, therefore, the receiving country gains. Moreover, because (in most cases) immigration is a voluntary supply decision, it also makes the immigrants better off.

Suppose, in fact, that the evidence for a particular host country was completely consistent with the model's predictions. In particular, the immigration of 10 million workers improved the well-being of the immigrants (relative to their well-being in the source countries); reduced the income of native workers by, say, $25 billion annually; and increased the incomes of capitalists by $40 billion. Let's now ask a normative question: *Should* the host country admit 10 million more immigrants?

This normative question cannot be answered solely on the basis of the theory or the facts. Even though total income in the host country has increased by $15 billion, there also has been a redistribution of wealth. Some persons are worse off and others are better off. To answer the question of whether the country should continue to admit immigrants, one has to decide whose economic welfare the country should care most about: that of immigrants, who are made better off by immigration; that of native workers, who are made worse off; or that of the capitalists who own the firms, who are made better off. One might even bring into the discussion the well-being of the people left behind in the source countries, who are clearly affected by the emigration of their compatriots. It is clear that any policy discussion of this issue requires clearly stated assumptions about what constitutes the "national interest," about who matters more. In the end, therefore, normative judgments about the costs and benefits of immigration depend on our values and ideology.

Many economists often take a "fall-back" position when these types of problems are encountered. Because the immigration of 10 million workers increases the *total* income in the host country by $15 billion, it is possible to redistribute income in the postimmigration economy so that every person in that country is made better off. A policy that can *potentially* improve the well-being of everyone in the economy is said to be "efficient"; it increases the size of the economic pie available to the country. The problem, however, is that this type of redistribution seldom occurs; the winners typically remain winners and the losers remain losers. Our answer to a normative question, therefore, will force each of us to confront the trade-off that we are willing to make between efficiency and distributional issues. In other words, normative questions force us to compare the value that we attach to an increase in the size of the economic pie with the value that we attach to a change in how the pie is split.

As a second example, we will see that the supply-demand framework predicts that unionization transfers wealth from firms to workers, but that unionization also shrinks the size of the economic pie. Suppose that the facts unambiguously support these theoretical implications: unions increase the total income of workers by, say, $40 billion, but the country as a whole is poorer by $20 billion. Let's now ask a normative question: *Should* the government pursue policies that discourage workers from forming labor unions?

Again, our answer to this normative question depends on how we contrast the gains accruing to the unionized workers with the losses accruing to the employers who must pay higher wages and to the consumers who must pay higher prices for union-produced goods.

The lesson from this discussion should be clear. As long as there are winners and losers—and most government policies inevitably leave winners and losers in their wake—neither the theoretical implications of economic models nor the facts are sufficient to answer the normative question of whether a particular policy is desirable. Throughout this book, therefore, we will find that economic analysis is very useful for framing and answering positive questions but is much less useful for addressing normative questions.

Despite the fact that economists cannot answer what many would consider to be the "big questions," there is an important sense in which framing and answering positive questions is crucial for any policy discussion. Positive economics tells us how particular government policies affect the well-being of different segments of society. Who are the winners, and how much do they gain? Who are the losers, and how much do they lose?

The adoption of a particular policy requires that these gains and losses be compared and that some choice be made as to who matters more. In the end, any informed policy discussion requires that we be fully aware of the price that has to be paid when making particular choices. The normative conclusion that one might reach may well be affected by the magnitude of the costs and benefits associated with the particular policy. For example, the distributional impact of immigration (that is, redistributing income from workers to firms) could easily dominate the normative discussion if immigration generated only a small increase in the size of the economic pie. The distributional impact, however, would be less relevant if it was clear that the size of the economic pie was greatly enlarged by immigration.

1-4   The Organization of the Book

The book begins by considering how persons decide whether to enter the labor market and how many hours to work (Chapter 2). This chapter helps us understand why workers differ in their attachment to the labor market, how our labor supply decisions interact with those of family members, and how we allocate our time over the life cycle.

We then turn to a description of the firm's hiring decisions (Chapter 3). Firms wish to maximize profits and will hire only those workers who add sufficiently to the firm's revenue. We shall discuss the factors that motivate firms to create and destroy jobs.

Chapter 4 explores in detail the interaction of supply and demand in the labor market and the implications of equilibrium. We will then begin to generalize the supply-demand framework by relaxing some of the key assumptions of the basic model. We know, for example, that not all jobs are alike; some jobs offer nice working conditions; other jobs offer very unpleasant conditions (Chapter 5). We also know that not all workers are alike; some workers choose to acquire a substantial amount of human capital, but other workers do not (Chapters 6 and 7).

The final section of the book analyzes various features of modern labor markets, including labor mobility (Chapter 8), labor market discrimination (Chapter 9), unionization (Chapter 10), the nature of incentive pay (Chapter 11), and unemployment (Chapter 12).

Summary

- Labor economics studies how labor markets work. Important topics addressed by labor economics include the determination of the income distribution, the economic impact of unions, the allocation of a worker's time to the labor market, the hiring and firing decisions of firms, labor market discrimination, the determinants of unemployment, and the worker's decision to invest in human capital.

- Models in labor economics typically contain three actors: workers, firms, and the government. It is typically assumed that workers maximize their well-being and that firms maximize profits. Governments influence the decisions of workers and firms by imposing taxes, granting subsidies, and regulating the "rules of the game" in the labor market.

- A good theory of the labor market should have realistic assumptions, should not be clumsy or overly complex, and should provide empirical implications that can be tested with real-world data.

- The tools of economics are helpful for answering positive questions. The information thus generated may help in making policy decisions. The answer to a normative question, however, typically requires that we impose a value judgment on the desirability of particular economic outcomes.

Review Questions

1. What is labor economics? Which types of questions do labor economists analyze?
2. Who are the key actors in the labor market? What motives do economists typically assign to workers and firms?
3. Why do we need a theory to understand real-world labor market problems?
4. What is the difference between positive and normative economics? Why are positive questions easier to answer than normative questions?

Web Links

A number of Web sites publish data and research articles that are very valuable to labor economists.

The Bureau of Labor Statistics (BLS) is the government agency responsible for calculating the monthly unemployment rate as well as the Consumer Price Index. Their Web site contains a lot of information on many aspects of the U.S. labor market, as well as comparable international statistics: stats.bls.gov.

The Bureau of the Census reports detailed demographic and labor market information: www.census.gov.

The Statistical Abstract of the United States is an essential book that is available online. It is published annually and contains detailed information on many aspects of the U.S. economy: www.census.gov/statab/www.

The Organization for Economic Cooperation and Development (OECD) reports statistics on labor market conditions in many advanced economies: www.oecd.org.

The National Bureau of Economic Research (NBER) publishes a working paper series that represents the frontier of empirical research in economics. Their web site also contains a number of widely used data sets. The working papers and data can be accessed and downloaded by students and faculty at many universities: www.nber.org.

IZA is a Bonn-based research institute that conducts labor research. Their discussion paper series provides up-to-date research on labor issues in many countries: www.iza.org.

Appendix

An Introduction to Regression Analysis

Labor economics is an empirical science. It makes extensive use of **econometrics,** the application of statistical techniques to study relationships in economic data. For example, we will be addressing such questions as

1. Do higher levels of unemployment benefits lead to longer spells of unemployment?
2. Do higher levels of welfare benefits reduce work incentives?
3. Does going to school for one more year increase a worker's earnings?

The answers to these three questions ultimately depend on a correlation between pairs of variables: the level of unemployment compensation and the duration of unemployment spells; the level of welfare benefits and the labor supply; educational attainment and wages. We also will want to know not only the *sign* of the correlation, but the *size* as well. In other words, by how many weeks does a $50 increase in unemployment compensation lengthen the duration of unemployment spells? By how many hours does an increase of $200 per month in welfare benefits reduce the labor supply of workers? And by how much our earnings increase if we get a college education?

Although this book does not use econometric analysis in much of the discussion, the student can better appreciate both the usefulness *and* the limits of empirical research by knowing how labor economists manipulate the available data to answer the questions we are interested in. The main statistical technique used by labor economists is **regression analysis.**

An Example

It is well known that there are sizable differences in wages across occupations. We are interested in determining why some occupations pay more than others. One obvious factor that determines the average wage in an occupation is the level of education of workers in that occupation.

It is common in labor economics to conduct empirical studies of earnings by looking at the logarithm of earnings, rather than the actual level of earnings. There are sound theoretical and empirical reasons for this practice, one of which will be described shortly. Suppose there is a linear equation relating the average log wage in an occupation (log w) to the mean years of schooling of workers in that occupation (s). We write this line as

$$\log w = \alpha + \beta s \qquad\qquad \textbf{(1-1)}$$

The variable on the left-hand side—the average log wage in the occupation—is called the **dependent variable.** The variable on the right-hand side—average years of schooling in the occupation—is called the **independent variable.** The main objective of regression analysis is to obtain numerical estimates of the coefficients α and β by using actual data on the mean log wage and mean schooling in each occupation. It is useful, therefore, to spend some time interpreting these **regression coefficients.**

Equation (1-1) traces out a line, with intercept α and slope β; this line is drawn in Figure 1-4. As drawn, the regression line makes the sensible assumption that the slope β is positive, so wages are higher in occupations where the typical worker has more schooling. The intercept α gives the log wage that would be observed in an occupation where workers have zero years of schooling. Elementary algebra teaches us that the slope of a line is given by the change in the vertical axis divided by the corresponding change in the horizontal axis or

$$\beta = \frac{\text{Change in log wage}}{\text{Change in years of schooling}} \qquad\qquad \textbf{(1-2)}$$

Put differently, the slope β gives the change in the log wage associated with a one-year increase in average schooling. *It is a mathematical fact that a small change in the log wage approximates the percent change in the wage.* For example, if the difference in the mean log wage between two occupations is 0.051, we can interpret this statistic as indicating that there is approximately a 5.1 percent wage difference between the two occupations. This property is one of the reasons why labor economists typically conduct studies of salaries using the logarithm of the wage; they can then interpret changes in this quantity as a percent change in the wage. This mathematical property of logarithms implies that the coefficient β can be interpreted as giving the percent change in earnings resulting from a one-year increase in schooling.

To estimate the parameters α and β, we first need to obtain data on the average log wage and average years of schooling by occupation. These data can be easily calculated using the Annual Demographic Supplement of the Current Population Surveys. These data, collected

FIGURE 1-4
**The Regression
Line**

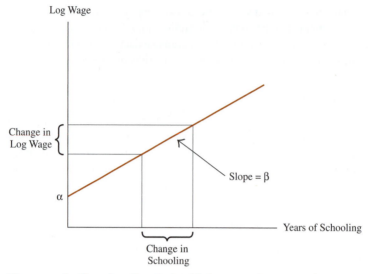

The regression line gives the relationship between the average log wage
rate and the average years of schooling of workers across occupations.
The slope of the regression line gives the change in the log wage resulting from a one-year change in years of schooling. The intercept gives the
log wage for an occupation where workers have zero years of schooling.

in March of every year by the Bureau of Labor Statistics, contain a lot of information about
employment conditions and salaries for tens of thousands of workers. One can use the
data to compute the average log hourly wage and the average years of schooling for men
working in each of 45 different occupations. The resulting data are reported in Table 1-1.
To give an example, the typical man employed as an engineer had a log wage of 3.37 and
15.8 years of schooling. In contrast, the typical man employed as a construction laborer
had a log wage of 2.44 and 10.5 years of schooling.

The plot of the data presented in Figure 1-5 is called a **scatter diagram** and describes
the relation found between the average log wage and the average years of schooling in the
real world. The relation between the two variables does not look anything like the regression line that we hypothesized. Instead, it is a scatter of points. Note, however, that the
points are not randomly scattered on the page, but instead have a noticeable upward-sloping
drift. The raw data, therefore, suggest a positive correlation between the log wage and
years of schooling, but nothing as simple as an upward-sloping line.

We have to recognize, however, that education is not the only factor that determines the
average wage in an occupation. There is probably a great deal of error when workers report
their salary to the Bureau of Labor Statistics. This measurement error disperses the points
on a scatter diagram away from the line that we believe represents the "true" data. There
also might be other factors that affect average earnings in any given occupation, such as
the average age of the workers or perhaps a variable indicating the "female-ness" of the
occupation. After all, it often is argued that jobs that are predominantly done by men (for
example, welders) tend to pay more than jobs that are predominantly done by women (for
example, kindergarten teachers). All of these extraneous factors would again disperse our
data points away from the line.

TABLE 1-1   Characteristics of Occupations, 2001

Source: Annual Demographic Files of the Current Population Survey, 2002.

Occupation	Mean Log Hourly Wage of Male Workers	Mean Years of Schooling for Male Workers	Female Share (%)
Administrators and officials, public administration	3.24	15.7	52.4
Other executives, administrators, and managers	3.29	14.9	42.0
Management-related occupations	3.16	15.4	59.4
Engineers	3.37	15.8	10.7
Mathematical and computer scientists	3.36	15.6	32.2
Natural scientists	3.22	17.4	34.2
Health diagnosing occupations	3.91	19.8	31.2
Health assessment and treating occupations	3.23	16.2	86.2
Teachers, college and university	3.17	18.8	44.7
Teachers, except college and university	2.92	16.5	75.8
Lawyers and judges	3.72	19.7	29.3
Other professional specialty occupations	2.90	15.9	54.0
Health technologists and technicians	2.76	14.2	83.1
Engineering and science technicians	2.97	13.8	26.0
Technicians, except health, engineering, and science	3.30	15.4	48.5
Supervisors and proprietors, sales occupations	2.96	13.9	37.6
Sales representatives, finance and business services	3.39	15.1	44.7
Sales representatives, commodities, except retail	3.14	14.4	25.4
Sales workers, retail and personal services	2.61	13.4	64.0
Sales-related occupations	2.93	14.8	72.4
Supervisors, administrative support	2.94	13.8	61.2
Computer equipment operators	2.91	13.8	57.1
Secretaries, stenographers, and typists	2.75	13.8	98.0
Financial records, processing occupations	2.67	14.2	92.9
Mail and message distributing	2.87	13.2	41.9
Other administrative support occupations, including clerical	2.66	13.4	79.2
Private household service occupations	2.46	10.6	96.0
Protective service occupations	2.80	13.6	18.7
Food service occupations	2.23	11.4	60.0
Health service occupations	2.38	13.2	89.1
Cleaning and building service occupations	2.37	11.2	48.2
Personal service occupations	2.55	13.4	80.4
Mechanics and repairers	2.81	12.6	5.2
Construction trades	2.74	11.9	2.4
Other precision production occupations	2.82	12.3	22.5
Machine operators and tenders, except precision	2.62	11.8	35.2
Fabricators, assemblers, inspectors, and samplers	2.65	12.0	36.2
Motor vehicle operators	2.59	12.1	12.7
Other transportation occupations and material moving	2.68	11.8	6.3
Construction laborer	2.44	10.5	3.9
Freight, stock, and material handlers	2.44	12.0	30.4
Other handlers, equipment cleaners, and laborers	2.42	11.3	28.0
Farm operators and managers	2.52	12.9	20.5
Farm workers and related occupations	2.29	9.9	18.5
Forestry and fishing occupations	2.70	12.0	3.7

FIGURE 1-5 The Scatter Diagram Relating Wages and Schooling by Occupation, 2001

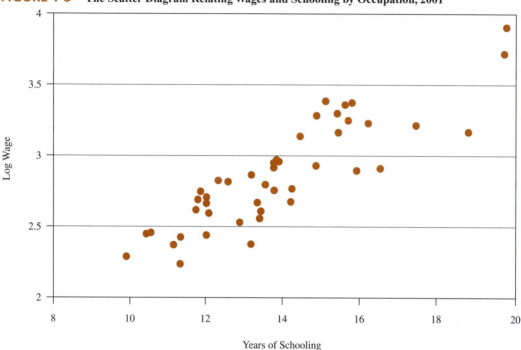

The objective of regression analysis is to find the *best* line that goes through the scatter diagram. Figure 1-6 redraws our scatter diagram and inserts a few of the many lines that we could draw through the scatter. Line *A* does not represent the general trend very well; after all, the raw data suggest a positive correlation between wages and education, yet line *A* has a negative slope. Both lines *B* and *C* are upward sloping, but they are both a bit "off"; line *B* lies above all of the points in the scatter diagram and line *C* is too far to the right.

The **regression line** is the line that best summarizes the data.[3] The formula that calculates the regression line is included in every statistics and spreadsheet software program. If we apply the formula to the data in our example, we obtain the regression line

$$\log w = 0.869 + 0.143s \qquad (1\text{-}3)$$

This estimated regression line is superimposed on the scatter diagram in Figure 1-7.

We interpret the regression line reported in equation (1-3) as follows. The estimated slope is positive, indicating that the average log wage is indeed higher in occupations where workers are more educated. The 0.143 slope implies that each one-year increase in the mean schooling of workers in an occupation raises the wage by approximately 14.3 percent.

---

[3] More precisely, the regression line is the line that minimizes the sum of the square of the vertical differences between every point in the scatter diagram and the corresponding point on the line. As a result, this method of estimating the regression line is called *least squares*.

FIGURE 1-6 Choosing among Lines Summarizing the Trend in the Data

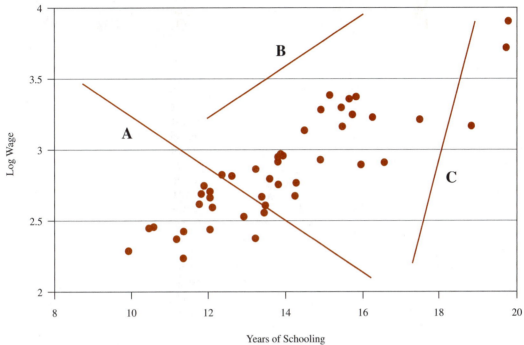

There are many lines that can be drawn through the scatter diagram. Lines *A*, *B*, and *C* provide three such examples. None of these lines "fit" the trend in the scatter diagram very well.

The intercept indicates that the log wage would be 0.869 in an occupation where the average worker had zero years of schooling. We have to be very careful when we use this result. After all, as the raw data reported in Table 1-1 show, no occupation has a workforce with zero years of schooling. In fact, the smallest value of s is 9.9 years. The intercept is obtained by extrapolating the regression line to the left until it hits the vertical axis. In other words, we are using the regression line to make an out-of-sample prediction. It is easy to get absurd results when we do this type of extrapolation: After all, what does it mean to say that the typical person in an occupation has no schooling whatsoever? An equally silly extrapolation takes the regression line and extends it to the right until, say, we wish to predict what would happen if the average worker had 25 years of schooling. Put simply, it is problematic to predict outcomes that lie outside the range of the data.

"Margin of Error" and Statistical Significance

If we plug the data reported in Table 1-1 into a statistics or spreadsheet program, we will find that the program reports many more numbers than just the intercept and the slope of a regression line. The program also reports what are called **standard errors,** or a measure of the statistical precision with which the coefficients are estimated. When poll results are reported in newspapers or on television, it is said, for instance, that 52 percent of the

FIGURE 1-7 The Scatter Diagram and the Regression Line

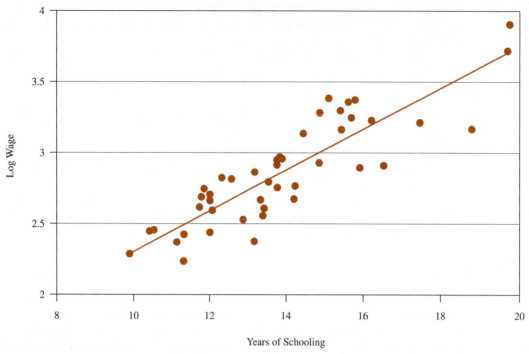

Years of Schooling

population believes that tomatoes should be bigger and redder, with a margin of error of plus or minus 3 percent. We use standard errors to calculate the margin of error of our estimated regression coefficients.

In our data, it turns out that the standard error for the intercept α is 0.172 and that the standard error for the slope β is 0.012. *The margin of error that is used commonly in econometric work is twice the standard error.* The regression thus allows us to conclude that a one-year increase in average schooling increases the log wage by 0.143, plus or minus 0.024 (or twice the standard error of 0.012). In other words, our data suggest that a one-year increase in schooling increases the average wage in an occupation by as little as 11.9 percent or by as much as 16.7 percent. Statistical theory indicates that the *true* impact of the one-year increase in schooling lies within this range with a 95 percent probability. We have to allow for a margin of error because our data are imperfect. Our data are measured with error, extraneous factors are being omitted, and our data are typically based on a random sample of the population.

The regression program will also report a **t statistic** for each regression coefficient. The *t* statistic helps us assess the **statistical significance** of the estimated coefficients. The *t* statistic is defined as

$$t \text{ statistic} = \frac{\text{Absolute value of regression coefficient}}{\text{Standard error of regression coefficient}} \qquad \textbf{(1-4)}$$

If a regression coefficient has a *t* statistic above the "magic" number of 2, the regression coefficient is said to be significantly different from zero. In other words, it is very likely that the true value of the coefficient is not zero, so there is some correlation between the two variables that we are interested in. If a t statistic is below 2, the coefficient is said to be insignificantly different from zero, so we cannot conclude that there is a correlation between the two variables of interest.

Note that the t statistic associated with our estimated slope is 11.9 (or $0.143 \div 0.012$), which is certainly above 2. Our estimate of the slope is significantly different from zero. Therefore, it is extremely likely that there is indeed a positive correlation between the average log wage in an occupation and the average schooling of workers.

Finally, the statistical software program will typically report a number called the **R-squared.** This statistic gives the fraction of the dispersion in the dependent variable that is "explained" by the dispersion in the independent variable. The R-squared of the regression reported in equation (1-3) is 0.762. In other words, 76.2 percent of the variation in the mean log wage across occupations can be attributed to differences in educational attainment across the occupations. Put differently, our very simple regression model seems to do a very good job at explaining why engineers earn more than construction laborers—it is largely because one group of workers has a lot more education than the other.

Multiple Regression

Up to this point, we have focused on a regression model that contains only one independent variable, mean years of schooling. As noted above, the average log wage of men in an occupation will probably depend on many other factors. The simple correlation between wages and schooling implied by the regression model in equation (1-3) could be confounding the effect of some of these other variables. To isolate the relationship between the log wage and schooling (and avoid what is called omitted variable bias), it is important to control for differences in other characteristics that also might generate wage differentials across occupations.

To provide a concrete example, suppose we believe that occupations that are predominantly held by men tend to pay more—for given schooling—than occupations that are predominantly held by women. We can then write an expanded regression model as

$$\log w = \alpha + \beta s + \gamma p \qquad (1\text{-}5)$$

where the variable p gives the percent of workers in an occupation that are women. As before, $\log w$ and s give the log wage and mean years of schooling of *men* working in that occupation.

We now wish to interpret the coefficients in this **multiple regression** model—a regression that contains more than one independent variable. Each coefficient in the multiple regression measures the impact of a particular variable on the log wage, *other things being equal.* For instance, the coefficient β gives the change in the log wage resulting from a one-year increase in mean schooling, holding constant the relative number of women in the occupation. Similarly, the coefficient γ gives the change in the log wage resulting from a one-percentage-point increase in the share of female workers, holding constant the average schooling of the occupation. Finally, the intercept α gives the log wage in a fictional occupation that employs only men and where the typical worker has zero years of schooling.

The last column in Table 1-1 reports the values of the female share p for the various occupations in our sample. It is evident that the representation of women varies significantly across occupations: 75.8 percent of teachers below the university level are women, as compared to only 5.2 percent of mechanics and repairers. Because we now have two independent variables, our scatter diagram is three dimensional. The regression "line," however, is now the plane that best fits the data in this three-dimensional space. If we plug these data into a computer program to estimate the regression model in equation (1-5), the estimated regression line is given by

$$\log w = 0.924 + 0.150s - 0.003p \qquad R\text{-squared} = 0.816 \qquad \textbf{(1-6)}$$
$$(0.154) \; (0.011) \;\; (0.001)$$

where the standard error of each of the coefficients is reported in parentheses below the coefficient.

Note that a one-year increase in the occupation's mean schooling raises weekly earnings by approximately 15.0 percent. In other words, if we compare two occupations that have the same female share but differ in years of schooling by one year, workers in the high-skill occupation earn 15 percent more than workers in the low-skill occupation.

Equally important, we find that the percent female in the occupation has a statistically significant negative impact on the log wage. In other words, men who work in predominantly female occupations earn less than men who work in predominantly male occupations—even if both occupations have the same mean schooling. The regression coefficient, in fact, implies that a 10-percentage-point increase in the female share lowers the average earnings of an occupation by 3.0 percent.

Of course, before we make the tempting inference that this empirical finding is proof of a "crowding effect"—the hypothesis that discriminatory behavior crowds women into relatively few occupations and lowers wages in those jobs—we need to realize that there are many other factors that determine occupational earnings. The multiple regression model can, of course, be expanded to incorporate many more independent variables. As we will see throughout this book, labor economists put a lot of effort into defining and estimating regression models that isolate the correlation between the two variables of interest *after controlling for all other relevant factors*. Regardless of how many independent variables are included in the regression, however, all the regression models are estimated in essentially the same way: The regression line best summarizes the trends in the underlying data.

Key Concepts

dependent variable *13*
derived demand, *4*
econometrics *12*
equilibrium, *4*
independent variable 13
labor demand curve, *4*
labor economics, *1*

labor supply curve, *3*
model, *7*
multiple regression *19*
normative economics, *9*
positive economics, *8*
regression analysis *13*
regression coefficients *13*

regression line *15*
R-squared *19*
scatter diagram *14*
significance *18*
statistical *18*
standard errors *16*
t statistic *18*

Chapter 2

Labor Supply

It's true hard work never killed anybody, but I figure, why take the chance?

—*Ronald Reagan*

Each of us must decide whether to work and, once employed, how many hours to work. At any point in time, the economywide labor supply is given by adding the work choices made by each person in the population. Total labor supply also depends on the fertility decisions made by earlier generations (which determine the size of the current population).

The economic and social consequences of these decisions vary dramatically over time. In 1948, 84 percent of American men and 31 percent of American women aged 16 or over worked. By 2010, the proportion of working men had declined to 64 percent, whereas the proportion of working women had risen to 54 percent. Over the same period, the length of the average workweek in a private-sector production job fell from 40 to 34 hours.[1] These labor supply trends have surely altered the nature of the American family as well as greatly affected the economy's productive capacity.

This chapter develops the framework that economists use to study labor supply decisions. In this framework, individuals seek to maximize their well-being by consuming goods (such as fancy cars and nice homes) and leisure. Goods have to be purchased in the marketplace. Because most of us are not independently wealthy, we must work in order to earn the cash required to buy the desired goods. The economic trade-off is clear: If we do not work, we can consume a lot of leisure, but we have to do without the goods and services that make life more enjoyable. If we do work, we will be able to afford many of these goods and services, but we must give up some of our valuable leisure time.

The model of labor-leisure choice isolates the person's wage rate and income as the key economic variables that guide the allocation of time between the labor market and leisure activities. In this chapter, we first use the framework to analyze "static" labor supply

---

[1] These statistics were obtained from the U.S. Bureau of Labor Statistics Web site: www.bls.gov/data/home.htm.

decisions, the decisions that affect a person's labor supply at a point in time. We will also extend the basic model to explore how the timing of leisure activities changes over the life cycle.

This economic framework not only helps us understand why women's work propensities rose and hours of work declined, but also allows us to address a number of questions with important policy and social consequences. For example, do welfare programs reduce incentives to work? Does a cut in the income tax rate increase hours of work? And what factors explain the rapid growth in the number of women who choose to participate in the labor market?

2-1 Measuring the Labor Force

On the first Friday of every month, the Bureau of Labor Statistics (BLS) releases its estimate of the unemployment rate for the previous month. The unemployment rate statistic is widely regarded as a measure of the overall health of the U.S. economy. In fact, the media often interpret the minor month-to-month blips in the unemployment rate as a sign of either a precipitous decline in economic activity or a surging recovery.

The unemployment rate is tabulated from the responses to a monthly BLS survey called the *Current Population Survey* (CPS). In this survey, nearly 50,000 households are questioned about their work activities during a particular week of the month (that week is called the reference week). Almost everything we know about the trends in the U.S. labor force comes from tabulations of CPS data. The survey instrument used by the CPS also has influenced the development of surveys in many other countries. In view of the importance of this survey in the calculation of labor force statistics both in the United States and abroad, it is useful to review the various definitions of labor force activities that are routinely used by the BLS to generate its statistics.

The CPS classifies all persons aged 16 or older into one of three categories: the *employed,* the *unemployed,* and the residual group that is said to be *out of the labor force.* To be employed, a worker must have been at a job with pay for at least 1 hour or worked at least 15 hours on a nonpaid job (such as the family farm). To be unemployed, a worker must either be on a temporary layoff from a job or have no job but be actively looking for work in the four-week period prior to the reference week.

Let E be the number of persons employed and U the number of persons unemployed. A person participates in the **labor force** if he or she is either employed or unemployed. The size of the labor force (LF) is given by

$$LF = E + U \qquad\qquad \textbf{(2-1)}$$

Note that the vast majority of employed persons (those who work at a job with pay) are counted as being in the labor force regardless of how many hours they work. The size of the labor force, therefore, does not say anything about the "intensity" of work.

The **labor force participation rate** gives the fraction of the population (P) that is in the labor force and is defined by

$$\text{Labor force participation rate} = \frac{LF}{P} \qquad\qquad \textbf{(2-2)}$$

The **employment rate** gives the fraction of the population that is employed, or

$$\text{Employment rate} = \frac{E}{P} \qquad \text{(2-3)}$$

Finally, the **unemployment rate** gives the fraction of labor force participants who are unemployed:

$$\text{Unemployment rate} = \frac{U}{LF} \qquad \text{(2-4)}$$

The Hidden Unemployed

The BLS calculates an unemployment rate based on a subjective measure of what it means to be unemployed. To be considered unemployed, a person must either be on temporary layoff or claim that he or she has "actively looked for work" in the past four weeks. Persons who have given up and stopped looking for work are not counted as unemployed, but are considered to be "out of the labor force." At the same time, some persons who have little intention of working at the present time may claim to be "actively looking" for a job in order to qualify for unemployment benefits.

The unemployment statistics, therefore, can be interpreted in different ways. During the severe recession that began in 2009, for instance, it is often argued that the official unemployment rate (that is, the BLS statistic) understates the depths of the recession and economic hardships. Because it is so hard to find work, many laid-off workers have become discouraged with their futile job search activity, dropped out of the labor market, and stopped being *counted as* unemployed. It is then argued that this army of **hidden unemployed** should be added to the pool of unemployed workers so that the unemployment problem is significantly worse than it appeared from the BLS data.[2]

Some analysts have argued that a more objective measure of aggregate economic activity may be given by the employment rate. The employment rate simply indicates the fraction of the population at a job. This statistic has the obvious drawback that it lumps together persons who say they are unemployed with persons who are classified as being out of the labor force. Although the latter group includes some of the hidden unemployed, it also includes many individuals who have little intention of working at the present time (for example, retirees, women with small children, and students enrolled in school).

A decrease in the employment rate could then be attributed to either increases in unemployment or unrelated increases in fertility or school enrollment rates. It is far from clear, therefore, that the employment rate provides a better measure of fluctuations in economic activity than the unemployment rate. We shall return to some of the questions raised by the ambiguity in the interpretation of the BLS labor force statistics in Chapter 12.

---

[2] If one included the hidden unemployed as measured by the BLS (which counts persons who are out of the labor force because they are "discouraged over job prospects") as well as persons who are only "marginally attached" to the labor force, the unemployment rate in March 2011 would have increased from the official 8.8 percent to 15.7 percent.

2-2   Basic Facts about Labor Supply

This section summarizes some of the key trends in labor supply in the United States.[3] These facts have motivated much of the research on labor supply conducted in the past three decades. Table 2-1 documents the historical trends in the labor force participation rate of men. There was a slight fall in the labor force participation rates of men in the twentieth century, from 80 percent in 1900 to 72 percent by 2009. The decline is particularly steep for men near or above age 65, as more men choose to retire earlier. The labor force participation rate of men aged 45 to 64, for example, declined by 11 percentage points between 1950 and 2009, while the participation rate of men over 65 declined from 46 to 22 percent over the same period. Moreover, the labor force participation rate of men in their prime working years (ages 25 to 44) also declined, from 97 percent in 1950 to 91 percent in 2009. Note, however, that the labor force participation rate of men in their retirement years has begun to increase in the past 20 years.[4]

As Table 2-2 shows, there also has been a huge increase in the labor force participation rate of women. At the beginning of the century, only 21 percent of women were in the labor force. As late as 1950, even after the social and economic disruptions caused by two world wars and the Great Depression, only 29 percent of women were in the labor force. During the past 50 years, however, the labor force participation rate of women has increased dramatically. By 2009, almost 60 percent of all women were in the labor force.

TABLE 2-1   **Labor Force Participation Rates of Men, 1900–2009**

Sources: U.S. Bureau of the Census, *Historical Statistics of the United States, Colonial Years to 1970,* Washington, DC: Government Printing Office, 1975; U.S. Bureau of the Census, *Statistical Abstract of the United States,* Washington, DC: Government Printing Office, various issues.

Year	All Men	Men Aged 25–44	Men Aged 45–64	Men Aged over 65
1900	80.0	94.7	90.3	63.1
1920	78.2	95.6	90.7	55.6
1930	76.2	95.8	91.0	54.0
1940	79.0	94.9	88.7	41.8
1950	86.8	97.1	92.0	45.8
1960	84.0	97.7	92.0	33.1
1970	80.6	96.8	89.3	26.8
1980	77.4	93.0	80.8	19.0
1990	76.4	93.3	79.8	16.3
2000	74.7	93.1	78.3	17.5
2009	72.0	91.0	80.8	21.9

[3] For more detailed discussions of the trends in labor supply in the United States and in other countries, see John H. Pencavel, "Labor Supply of Men: A Survey," in Orley C. Ashenfelter and Richard Layard, editors, *Handbook of Labor Economics,* vol. 1, Amsterdam: Elsevier, 1986, pp. 3–102; and Mark R. Killingsworth and James J. Heckman, "Female Labor Supply: A Survey," in ibid., pp. 103–204. See also Mark R. Killingsworth, *Labor Supply,* Cambridge: Cambridge University Press, 1983.

[4] See Tammy Schirle, "Why Have the Labor Force Participation Rates of Older Men Increased since the Mid-1990s?" *Journal of Labor Economics* 26 (October 2008): 549–594.

TABLE 2-2   **Labor Force Participation Rates of Women, 1900–2009**

Sources: U.S. Bureau of the Census, *Historical Statistics of the United States, Colonial Years to 1970,* Washington, DC: Government Printing Office, 1975, p. 133; and U.S. Department of Commerce, *Statistical Abstract of the United States, 2011,* Washington, DC: Government Printing Office, 2011, Table 596.

Year	All Women	Single Women	Married Women	Widowed, Divorced, or Separated
1900	20.6	43.5	5.6	32.5
1910	25.4	51.1	10.7	34.1
1930	24.8	50.5	11.7	34.4
1940	25.8	45.5	15.6	30.2
1950	29.0	46.3	23.0	32.7
1960	34.5	42.9	31.7	36.1
1970	41.6	50.9	40.2	36.8
1980	51.5	64.4	49.9	43.6
1990	57.5	66.7	58.4	47.2
2000	60.2	69.0	61.3	49.4
2009	59.2	64.2	61.4	49.3

It is worth noting that the increase in female labor force participation was particularly steep among married women. Their labor force participation rate almost doubled in recent decades, from 32 percent in 1960 to 61.4 percent in 2009.

These dramatic shifts in labor force participation rates were accompanied by a sizable decline in average hours of work per week. Figure 2-1 shows that the typical person employed in production worked 55 hours per week in 1900, 40 hours in 1940, and just under 34 hours in 2010.[5]

There exist sizable differences in the various dimensions of labor supply across demographic groups at a particular point in time. As Table 2-3 shows, men not only have larger participation rates than women, but are also less likely to be employed in part-time jobs. Only 6 percent of working men are in part-time jobs, as compared to 16 percent of working women. The table also documents a strong positive correlation between labor supply and educational attainment for both men and women. In 2010, 92 percent of male college graduates and 80 percent of female college graduates were in the labor force, as compared to only 74 and 48 percent of male and female high school dropouts, respectively. There are also racial differences in labor supply, with white men having higher participation rates and working more hours than black men.

Finally, the decline in average weekly hours of work shown in Figure 2-1 was accompanied by a substantial increase in the number of hours that both men and women devote to leisure activities. It has been estimated that the number of weekly leisure hours increased by 6.2 hours for men and 4.9 hours for women between 1965 and 2003.[6]

[5] An interesting study of the trends in the length of the workday is given by Dora L. Costa, "The Wage and the Length of the Work Day: From the 1890s to 1991," *Journal of Labor Economics* 18 (January 2000): 156–181. She finds that low-wage workers had the longest workday at the beginning of the twentieth century. By the 1990s, however, this trend was reversed and high-wage workers had the longest workday. See also Peter Kuhn and Fernando Lozano, "The Expanding Workweek? Understanding Trends in Long Work Hours among U.S. Men, 1979–2006," *Journal of Labor Economics* 26 (April 2008): 311–343.

[6] Mark Aguiar and Erik Hurst, "Measuring Trends in Leisure: Allocation of Time over Five Decades," *Quarterly Journal of Economics* 122 (August 2007): 969–1006.

FIGURE 2-1   Average Weekly Hours of Work of Production Workers, 1900–2010

Sources: The pre-1947 data are drawn from Ethel Jones, "New Estimates of Hours of Work per Week and Hourly Earnings, 1900–1957," *Review of Economics and Statistics* 45 (November 1963): 374–385. Beginning in 1947, the data are drawn from U.S. Department of Labor, Bureau of Labor Statistics, *Employment, Hours, and Earnings from the Current Employment Statistics Survey,* "Table B-7. Average Weekly Hours of Production or Nonsupervisory Workers on Private Nonfarm Payrolls by Industry Sector and Selected Industry Detail": www.bls.gov/ces/cesbtabs.htm.

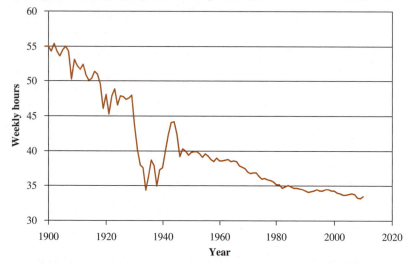

TABLE 2-3   Labor Supply in the United States, 2010 (persons aged 25–64)

Source: U.S. Bureau of Labor Statistics, *Current Population Survey*, March 2010. The average number of hours worked is calculated in the subsample of workers. The percent of workers in part-time jobs refers to the proportion working fewer than 30 hours per week.

	Labor Force Participation Rate		Annual Hours of Work		Percent of Workers in Part-Time Jobs	
	Men	Women	Men	Women	Men	Women
All persons	85.4	72.4	2,031	1,797	5.8	15.5
Educational attainment:						
Less than 12 years	74.0	48.2	1,763	1,617	9.4	18.5
12 years	83.1	68.2	1,949	1,755	5.8	15.8
13–15 years	85.6	75.0	2,030	1,771	6.2	16.3
16 years or more	91.6	80.4	2,182	1,878	4.6	14.1
Age:						
25–34	89.9	74.5	1,930	1,749	7.0	14.4
35–44	91.6	76.1	2,084	1,798	4.3	15.8
45–54	86.9	76.5	2,089	1,853	4.6	14.2
55–64	70.5	60.8	2,015	1,777	8.0	18.6
Race:						
White	86.2	74.0	2,079	1,799	5.3	16.6
Black	77.2	71.9	1,934	1,832	6.3	10.9
Hispanic	87.4	65.9	1,879	1,739	7.5	14.9

The data presented in this section provide the basic "stylized facts" that have moti-vated much of the work on the economics of labor supply. As we will see below, the evi-dence suggests that changes in the economic environment—particularly in wage rates and incomes—can account for many of the observed shifts in labor supply.

2-3   The Worker's Preferences

The framework that economists typically use to analyze labor supply behavior is called the **neoclassical model of labor-leisure choice.** This model isolates the factors that determine whether a particular person works and, if so, how many hours she chooses to work. By isolating these key factors, we can tell a simple "story" that explains and helps us understand many of the stylized facts discussed above. More important, the theory lets us predict how changes in economic conditions or in government policies will affect work incentives.

The representative person in our model receives satisfaction both from the consump-tion of goods (which we denote by C) and from the consumption of leisure (L). Obvi-ously, the person consumes many different types of goods during any given period. To simplify matters, we aggregate the dollar value of all the goods that the person consumes and define C as the total dollar value of all the goods that the person purchases during the period. For example, if the person spends \$1,000 weekly on food, rent, car payments, movie tickets, and other items, the variable C would take on the value of \$1,000. The variable L gives the number of hours of leisure that a person consumes during the same time period.

Utility and Indifference Curves

The notion that individuals get satisfaction from consuming goods and leisure is summa-rized by the **utility function:**

$$U = f(C, L) \qquad \qquad \textbf{(2-5)}$$

The utility function transforms the person's consumption of goods and leisure into an index U that measures the individual's level of satisfaction or happiness. This index is called *utility.* The higher the level of index U, the happier the person. We make the sensible assumption that buying more goods or having more leisure hours both increase the person's utility. In the jargon of economics, C and L are "goods," not "bads."

Suppose that a person is consuming \$500 worth of consumption goods and 100 hours of leisure weekly (point Y in Figure 2-2). This particular consumption basket yields a particu-lar level of utility to the person, say 25,000 utils. It is easy to imagine that different com-binations of consumption goods and hours of leisure might yield the same level of utility. For example, the person might say that she would be indifferent to consuming \$500 worth of goods and 100 hours of leisure or consuming \$400 worth of goods and 125 hours of lei-sure. Figure 2-2 illustrates the many combinations of C and L that generate this particular level of utility. The locus of such points is called an **indifference curve**—and all points along this curve yield 25,000 utils.

FIGURE 2-2   **Indifference Curves**

Points X and Y lie on the same indifference curve and yield the same level of utility (25,000 utils); point Z lies on a higher indifference curve and yields more utility.

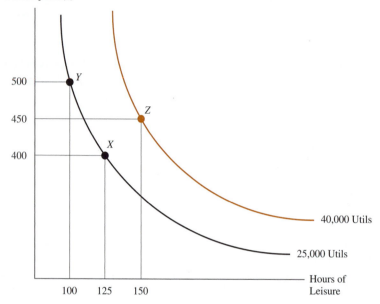

Consumption ($)

x-axis labels: 100, 125, 150, Hours of Leisure
y-axis labels: 400, 450, 500
curve labels: 40,000 Utils, 25,000 Utils
points: Y (100, 500), Z (150, 450), X (125, 400)

Suppose that the person were instead consuming $450 worth of goods and 150 hours of leisure (point Z in the figure). This consumption basket would put the person on a higher indifference curve, yielding 40,000 utils. We can then construct an indifference curve for this level of utility. In fact, we can construct an indifference curve for every level of utility. As a result, the utility function can be represented graphically in terms of a family (or a "map") of indifference curves.

Indifference curves have four important properties:

1. *Indifference curves are downward sloping.* We assumed that individuals prefer more of both C and L. If indifference curves were upward sloping, a consumption basket with more C and more L would yield the same level of utility as a consumption basket with less C and less L. This clearly contradicts our assumption that the individual likes both goods and leisure. The only way that we can offer a person a few more hours of leisure, and still hold utility constant, is to take away some of the goods.

2. *Higher indifference curves indicate higher levels of utility.* The consumption bundles lying on the indifference curve that yields 40,000 utils are preferred to the bundles lying on the curve that yields 25,000 utils. To see this, note that point Z in the figure must yield more utility than point X, simply because the bundle at point Z allows the person to consume more goods and leisure.

3. *Indifference curves do not intersect.* To see why, consider Figure 2-3, where indifference curves are allowed to intersect. Because points X and Y lie on the same indifference curve, the individual would be indifferent between the bundles X and Y. Because points Y and Z

FIGURE 2-3   **Indifference Curves Do Not Intersect**

Points *X* and *Y* yield the same utility because they are on the same indifference curve; points *Y* and *Z* also should yield the same utility. Point *Z*, however, is clearly preferable to point *X*.

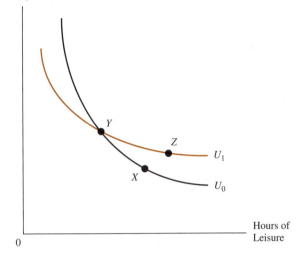

Consumption ($)

Hours of Leisure

0

lie on the same indifference curve, the individual would be indifferent between bundles *Y* and *Z*. The person would then be indifferent between *X* and *Y*, and between *Y* and *Z*, so that she should also be indifferent between *X* and *Z*. But *Z* is clearly preferable to *X*, because *Z* has more goods and more leisure. Indifference curves that intersect contradict our assumption that individuals like to consume both goods and leisure.

4. *Indifference curves are convex to the origin.* The convexity of indifference curves does not follow from either the definition of indifference curves or the assumption that both goods and leisure are "goods." The convexity reflects an additional assumption about the shape of the utility function. It turns out (see problem 1 at the end of the chapter) that indifference curves must be convex to the origin if we are ever to observe a person sharing her time between work and leisure activities.

The Slope of an Indifference Curve

What happens to a person's utility as she allocates one more hour to leisure or buys an additional dollar's worth of goods? The **marginal utility** of leisure is defined as the change in utility resulting from an additional hour devoted to leisure activities, holding constant the amount of goods consumed. We denote the marginal utility of leisure as MU_L. Similarly, we can define the marginal utility of consumption as the change in utility if the individual consumes one more dollar's worth of goods, holding constant the number of hours devoted to leisure activities. We denote the marginal utility of consumption by MU_C. Because we have assumed that both leisure and the consumption of goods are desirable activities, the marginal utilities of leisure and consumption must be positive numbers.

As we move along an indifference curve, say from point *X* to point *Y* in Figure 2-2, the slope of the indifference curve measures the rate at which a person is willing to give up some leisure time in return for additional consumption, *while holding utility constant.* Put differently, the slope tells us how many additional dollars' worth of goods it would take to "bribe" the person into giving up some leisure time. It can be shown that the slope of an indifference curve equals[7]

$$\frac{\Delta C}{\Delta L} = -\frac{MU_L}{MU_C} \qquad\qquad \textbf{(2-6)}$$

The absolute value of the slope of an indifference curve, which is also called the **marginal rate of substitution (MRS) in consumption,** is the ratio of marginal utilities.

The assumption that indifference curves are convex to the origin is essentially an assumption about how the marginal rate of substitution changes as the person moves along an indifference curve. Convexity implies that the slope of an indifference curve is steeper when the worker is consuming a lot of goods and little leisure, and that the curve is flatter when the worker is consuming few goods and a lot of leisure. As a result, the absolute value of the slope of an indifference curve declines as the person "rolls down" the curve. The assumption of convexity, therefore, is equivalent to an assumption of *diminishing* marginal rate of substitution.

Differences in Preferences across Workers

The map of indifference curves presented in Figure 2-2 illustrates the way a *particular* worker views the trade-off between leisure and consumption. Different workers will typically view this trade-off differently. In other words, some persons may like to devote a great deal of time and effort to their jobs, whereas other persons would prefer to devote most of their time to leisure. These interpersonal differences in preferences imply that the indifference curves may look quite different for different workers.

Figure 2-4 shows the indifference curves for two workers, Cindy and Mindy. Cindy's indifference curves tend to be very steep, indicating that her marginal rate of substitution takes on a very high value (see Figure 2-4*a*). In other words, she requires a sizable monetary bribe (in terms of additional consumption) to convince her to give up an additional hour of leisure. Cindy obviously likes leisure, and she likes it a lot. Mindy, on the other hand, has flatter indifference curves, indicating that her marginal rate of substitution takes on a low value (see Figure 2-4*b*). Mindy, therefore, does not require a large bribe to convince her to give up an additional hour of leisure.

Interpersonal differences in the "tastes for work" are obviously important determinants of differences in labor supply in the population. Workers who like leisure a lot (like Cindy) will tend to work few hours. And workers who do not attach a high value to their leisure time (like Mindy) will tend to be workaholics.

---

[7] To show that the slope of an indifference curve equals the ratio of marginal utilities, suppose that points X and Y in Figure 2-2 are very close to each other. In going from point X to point Y, the person is giving up ΔL hours of leisure, and each hour of leisure she gives up has a marginal utility of MU_L. Therefore, the loss in utility associated with moving from X to Y is given by $\Delta L \times MU_L$. The move from X to Y also involves a gain in utility. After all, the worker is not just giving up leisure time; she is consuming an additional ΔC dollars' worth of goods. Each additional dollar of consumption increases utility by MU_C units. The total gain in utility is given by $\Delta C \times MU_C$. By definition, all points along an indifference curve yield the same utility. This implies that the loss in moving from point X to point Y must be exactly offset by the gain, or $(\Delta L \times MU_L) + (\Delta C \times MU_C) = 0$. Equation (2-6) is obtained by rearranging terms.

FIGURE 2-4 Differences in Preferences across Workers

(*a*) Cindy's indifference curves are relatively steep, indicating that she requires a substantial bribe to give up an additional hour of leisure. (*b*) Mindy's indifference curves are relatively flat, indicating that she attaches a much lower value to her leisure time.

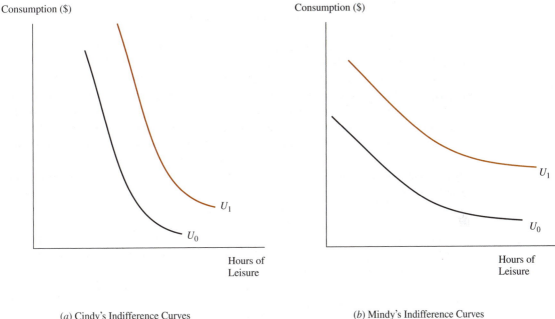

(*a*) Cindy's Indifference Curves   (*b*) Mindy's Indifference Curves

For the most part, economic models gloss over these interpersonal differences in preferences. The reason for this omission is that differences in tastes, although probably very important, are hard to observe and measure. It would be extremely difficult, if not impossible, to conduct surveys that would attempt to measure differences in indifference curves across workers. Moreover, the reliance on interpersonal differences in tastes provides an easy way out for anyone who wishes to explain why different workers behave differently. After all, one could simply argue that different behavior patterns between any two workers arise because worker *A* likes leisure more than worker *B,* and there would be no way of proving whether such a statement is correct or not.

Economic models instead stress the impact of variables that are much more easily observable—such as wages and incomes—on the labor supply decision. Because these variables can be observed and measured, the predictions made by the model about which types of persons will tend to work more are testable and refutable.

2-4   The Budget Constraint

The person's consumption of goods and leisure is constrained by her time and by her income. Part of the person's income (such as property income, dividends, and lottery prizes) is independent of how many hours she works. We denote this "nonlabor income" by *V.* Let *h* be the number of hours the person will allocate to the labor market during the period and w be the hourly wage rate. The person's **budget constraint** can be written as

$$C = wh + V \qquad\qquad (2\text{-}7)$$

In words, the dollar value of expenditures on goods (C) must equal the sum of labor earnings (wh) and nonlabor income (V).[8]

As we will see, the wage rate plays a central role in the labor supply decision. Initially, we assume that the wage rate is constant *for a particular person,* so the person receives the same hourly wage regardless of how many hours she works. In fact, the "marginal" wage rate (that is, the wage rate received for the last hour worked) generally depends on how many hours a person works. Persons who work over 40 hours per week typically receive an overtime premium, and the wage rate in part-time jobs is often lower than the wage rate in full-time jobs.[9] For now, we ignore the possibility that a worker's marginal wage may depend on how many hours she chooses to work.

Given the assumption of a constant wage rate, it is easy to graph the budget constraint. The person has two alternative uses for her time: work or leisure. The total time allocated to each of these activities must equal the total time available in the period, say T hours per week, so that $T = h + L$. We can then rewrite the budget constraint as

$$C = w(T - L) + V \qquad\qquad (2\text{-}8)$$

or

$$C = (wT + V) - wL$$

This last equation is in the form of a line, and the slope is the negative of the wage rate (or $-w$).[10] The **budget line** is illustrated in Figure 2-5. Point E in the graph indicates that if the person decides not to work at all and devotes T hours to leisure activities, she can still purchase V dollars' worth of consumption goods. Point E is the *endowment point.* If the person is willing to give up one hour of leisure, she can then move up the budget line and purchase an additional w dollars' worth of goods. In fact, each additional hour of leisure that the person is willing to give up allows her to buy an additional w dollars' worth of goods. In other words, each hour of leisure consumed has a price, and the price is given by the wage rate. If the worker gives up all her leisure activities, she ends up at the intercept of the budget line and can buy $(wT + V)$ dollars' worth of goods.

The consumption and leisure bundles that lie below the budget line are available to the worker; the bundles that lie above the budget line are not. The budget line, therefore, delineates the frontier of the worker's **opportunity set**—the set of all the consumption baskets that a particular worker can afford to buy.

---

[8] The specification of the budget constraint implies that the worker does not save in this model. The worker spends all of her income in the period under analysis.

[9] Shelly Lundberg, "Tied Wage-Hours Offers and the Endogeneity of Wages," *Review of Economics and Statistics* 67 (August 1985): 405–410. There are also jobs, such as volunteer work, where the observed wage rate is zero; see Richard B. Freeman, "Working for Nothing: The Supply of Volunteer Labor," *Journal of Labor Economics* 15 (January 1997): S140–S166.

[10] Recall that the equation for a line relating the variables y and x is given by $y = a + bx,$ where a is the intercept and b is the slope.

FIGURE 2-5   **The Budget Line Is the Boundary of the Worker's Opportunity Set**

Point *E* is the endowment point, telling the person how much she can consume if she does not enter the labor market. The worker moves up the budget line as she trades off an hour of leisure for additional consumption. The absolute value of the slope of the budget line is the wage rate.

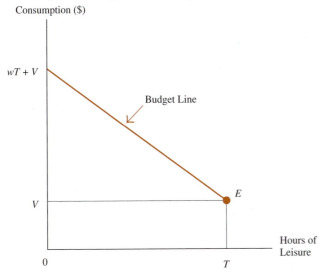

2-5   The Hours of Work Decision

We make one important assumption about the person's behavior: she wishes to choose the particular combination of goods and leisure that maximizes her utility. This means that the person will choose the level of goods and leisure that lead to the highest possible level of the utility index *U*—given the limitations imposed by the budget constraint.

Figure 2-6 illustrates the solution to this problem. As drawn, the budget line *FE* describes the opportunities available to a worker who has $100 of nonlabor income per week, faces a market wage rate of $10 per hour, and has 110 hours of nonsleeping time to allocate between work and leisure activities (assuming she sleeps roughly 8 hours per day).

Point *P* gives the optimal bundle of consumption goods and hours of leisure chosen by the utility-maximizing worker. The highest indifference curve attainable places her at point *P* and gives her U^* units of utility. At this solution, the worker consumes 70 hours of leisure per week, works a 40-hour workweek, and buys $500 worth of goods weekly. The worker would obviously prefer to consume a bundle on indifference curve U_1, which provides a higher level of utility. For example, the worker would prefer to be at point *Y*, where she works a 40-hour workweek and can purchase $1,100 worth of consumption goods. Given her wage and nonlabor income, however, the worker could never afford this consumption bundle. In contrast, the worker could choose a point such as *A*, which lies on the budget line, but she would not do so. After all, point *A* gives her less utility than point *P*.

The optimal consumption of goods and leisure for the worker, therefore, is given by the point where the budget line is tangent to the indifference curve. This type of solution is called an *interior solution* because the worker is not at either corner of the opportunity set (that is, at point *F*, working all available hours, or at point *E*, working no hours whatsoever).

FIGURE 2-6   An Interior Solution to the Labor-Leisure Decision

A utility-maximizing worker chooses the consumption-leisure bundle given by point *P*, where the indifference curve is tangent to the budget line.

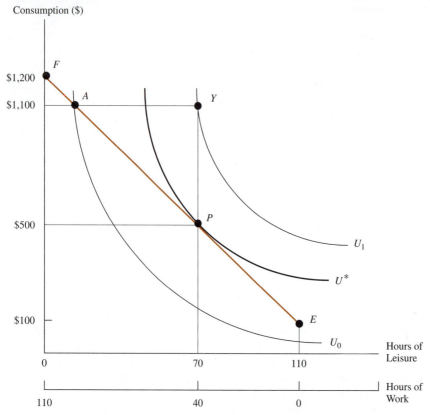

Interpreting the Tangency Condition

At the optimal point *P*, the budget line is tangent to the indifference curve. In other words, the slope of the indifference curve equals the slope of the budget line. This implies that[11]

$$\frac{MU_L}{MU_C} = w \qquad \text{(2-9)}$$

At the chosen level of consumption and leisure, the marginal rate of substitution (the rate at which a person is willing to give up leisure hours in exchange for additional consumption) equals the wage rate (the rate at which the market allows the worker to substitute one hour of leisure time for consumption).

---

[11] Although the slope of the indifference curve and the slope of the budget line are both negative numbers, the minus signs cancel out when the two numbers are set equal to each other, resulting in the condition reported in equation (2-9).

The economic intuition behind this condition is easier to grasp if we rewrite it as

$$\frac{MU_L}{w} = MU_C \qquad\qquad\qquad \textbf{(2-10)}$$

The quantity MU_L gives the additional utility received from consuming an extra hour of leisure. This extra hour costs w dollars. The left-hand side of equation (2-10), therefore, gives the number of utils received from spending an additional dollar on leisure. Because C is defined as the dollar value of expenditures on consumption goods, MU_C gives the number of utils received from spending an additional dollar on consumption goods. The tangency solution at point P in Figure 2-6 implies that the last dollar spent on leisure activities buys the same number of utils as the last dollar spent on consumption goods. If this equality did not hold (so that, for example, the last dollar spent on consumption buys more utils than the last dollar spent on leisure), the worker would not be maximizing utility. She could rearrange her consumption plan so as to purchase more of the commodity that yields more utility for the last dollar.

What Happens to Hours of Work When Nonlabor Income Changes?

We wish to determine what happens to hours of work when the worker's nonlabor income V increases. The increase in V might be triggered by the payment of higher dividends on the worker's stock portfolio or perhaps because some distant relatives had named the worker as the beneficiary in their will.

Figure 2-7 illustrates what happens to hours of work when the worker has an increase in V, *holding the wage constant*.[12] Initially, the worker's nonlabor income equals $100 weekly, which is associated with endowment point E_0. Given the worker's wage rate, the budget line is then given by F_0E_0. The worker maximizes utility by choosing the bundle at point P_0. At this point, the worker consumes 70 hours of leisure and works 40 hours.

The increase in nonlabor income to $200 weekly shifts the endowment point to E_1, so that the new budget line is given by F_1E_1. Because the worker's wage rate is being held constant, the slope of the budget line originating at point E_1 is the same as the slope of the budget line that originated at point E_0. An increase in nonlabor income that holds the wage constant expands the worker's opportunity set through a parallel shift in the budget line.

The increase in nonlabor income allows the worker to jump to a higher indifference curve, such as point P_1 in Figure 2-7. Increases in nonlabor income necessarily make the worker better off. After all, the expansion of the opportunity set opens up many additional opportunities for the worker. Figure 2-7a draws point P_1 so that the additional nonlabor income increases both expenditures on consumption goods and the number of leisure hours consumed. As a result, the length of the workweek falls to 30 hours. Figure 2-7b draws point P_1 so that the additional nonlabor income reduces the demand for leisure hours, increasing the length of the workweek to 50 hours. The impact of the change in nonlabor income (holding wages constant) on the number of hours worked is called an **income effect.**

---

[12] This type of theoretical exercise is called *comparative statics,* and is one of the main tools of economic theory. The methodology isolates how the outcomes experienced by a particular individual respond to a change in the value of one of the model's parameters. In this subsection, we are using the methodology to predict what should happen to labor supply when the worker's nonlabor income increases.

FIGURE 2-7 The Effect of a Change in Nonlabor Income on Hours of Work

An increase in nonlabor income leads to a parallel, upward shift in the budget line, moving the worker from point P_0 to point P_1. (a) If leisure is a normal good, hours of work fall. (b) If leisure is an inferior good, hours of work increase.

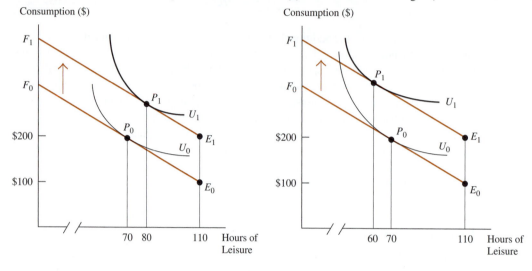

(a) Leisure Is a Normal Good   (b) Leisure Is an Inferior Good

Both panels in Figure 2-7 draw "legal" indifference curves. Both panels have indifference curves that are downward sloping, do not intersect, and are convex to the origin. It seems, therefore, that we cannot predict how an increase in nonlabor income affects hours of work unless we make an additional restriction on the shape of indifference curves. The additional restriction we make is that leisure is a "normal" good (as opposed to leisure being an "inferior" good).

We define a commodity to be a normal good when increases in income, holding the prices of all goods constant, increase its consumption. A commodity is an inferior good when increases in income, holding prices constant, decrease its consumption. Low-priced subcompact cars, such as the ill-fated Yugo, for instance, are typically thought of as inferior goods, whereas BMWs are typically thought of as normal goods. In other words, we would expect the demand for Yugos to decline as nonlabor income increased, and the demand for BMWs to increase.

If we reflect on whether leisure is a normal or an inferior good, most of us would probably reach the conclusion that leisure activities are a normal good. Put differently, if we were wealthier, we would surely demand a lot more leisure. We could then visit Aspen in December, Rio in February, and exotic beaches in the South Pacific in the summer.

Because it seems reasonable to assume that leisure is a normal good and because there is some evidence (discussed below) supporting this assumption, our discussion will focus on this case. The assumption that leisure is a normal good resolves the conflict between the two panels in Figure 2-7 in favor of the panel on the left-hand side. An increase in V then raises the demand for leisure hours and thus reduces hours of work. *The income effect, therefore, implies that an increase in nonlabor income, holding the wage rate constant, reduces hours of work.*

FIGURE 2-8   The Effect of a Change in the Wage Rate on Hours of Work

A change in the wage rate rotates the budget line around the endowment point *E*. A wage increase moves the worker from point *P* to point *R,* and can either decrease or increase hours of work.

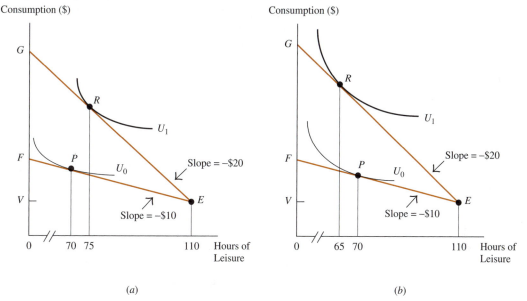

(a)   (b)

What Happens to Hours of Work When the Wage Changes?

Consider a wage increase from $10 to $20 an hour, holding nonlabor income *V* constant. The wage increase rotates the budget line around the endowment point, as illustrated in Figure 2-8. The rotation of the budget line shifts the opportunity set from *FE* to *GE*. It should be obvious that a wage increase does not change the endowment point: the dollar value of the goods that can be consumed when one does not work is the same regardless of whether the wage rate is $10 or $20 an hour.

The two panels presented in Figure 2-8 illustrate the possible effects of a wage increase on hours of work. In Figure 2-8a, the wage increase shifts the optimal consumption bundle from point *P* to point *R*. At the new equilibrium, the individual consumes more leisure (the increase is from 70 to 75 hours), so that hours of work fall from 40 to 35 hours.

Figure 2-8b, however, illustrates the opposite result. The wage increase again moves the worker to a higher indifference curve and shifts the optimal consumption bundle from point *P* to point *R*. This time, however, the wage increase reduces leisure hours (from 70 to 65 hours), so the length of the workweek increases from 40 to 45 hours. It seems, therefore, that we cannot make an unambiguous prediction about an important question without making even more assumptions.

The reason for the ambiguity in the relation between hours of work and the wage rate is of fundamental importance and introduces a set of tools and ideas that play a central role in all of economics. Both panels in Figure 2-8 show that, regardless of what happens to hours of work, a wage increase expands the worker's opportunity set. Put differently, a worker has more opportunities when she makes $20 an hour than when she makes $10 an hour. We know that an increase in income increases the demand for all normal goods, including leisure. The increase in the wage thus increases the demand for leisure, which reduces hours of work.

But this is not all that happens. The wage increase also makes leisure more expensive. When the worker earns $20 an hour, she gives up $20 every time she decides to take an hour off. As a result, leisure time is a very expensive commodity for high-wage workers and a relatively cheap commodity for low-wage workers. High-wage workers should then have strong incentives to cut back on their consumption of leisure activities. A wage increase thus reduces the demand for leisure and increases hours of work.

This discussion highlights the essential reason for the ambiguity in the relation between hours of work and the wage rate. A high-wage worker wants to enjoy the rewards of her high income, and hence would like to consume more leisure. The same worker, however, finds that leisure is very expensive and that she simply cannot afford to take time off from work.

These two conflicting forces are illustrated in Figure 2-9a. As before, the initial wage rate is $10 per hour. The worker maximizes her utility by choosing the consumption bundle given by point P, where she is consuming 70 hours of leisure and works 40 hours per week. Suppose the wage increases to $20. As we have seen, the budget line rotates and the new consumption bundle is given by point R. The worker is now consuming 75 hours of leisure and working 35 hours. As drawn, the person is working fewer hours at the higher wage.

It helps to think of the move from point P to point R as a two-stage move. The two stages correspond exactly to our discussion that the wage increase generates two effects: It increases the worker's income and it raises the price of leisure. To isolate the income effect, suppose we draw a budget line that is parallel to the old budget line (so that its slope is also –$10), but tangent to the new indifference curve. This budget line (DD) is also illustrated in Figure 2-9a, and generates a new tangency point Q.

FIGURE 2-9 **Decomposing the Impact of a Wage Change into Income and Substitution Effects**
An increase in the wage rate generates both income and substitution effects. The income effect (the move from point P to point Q) reduces hours of work; the substitution effect (the move from Q to R) increases hours of work.

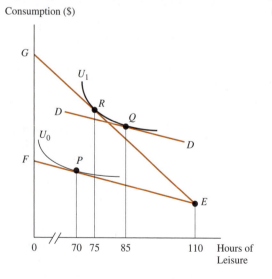

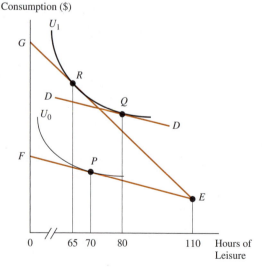

(a) Income Effect Dominates   (b) Substitution Effect Dominates

The move from initial position *P* to final position *R* can then be decomposed into a first-stage move from *P* to *Q* and a second-stage move from *Q* to *R*. It is easy to see that the move from point *P* to point *Q* is an income effect. In particular, the move from *P* to *Q* arises from a change in the worker's income, holding wages constant. The income effect isolates the change in the consumption bundle induced by the additional income generated by the wage increase. Because both leisure and goods are normal goods, point *Q* must lie to the northeast of point *P* (so that more is consumed of both goods and leisure). The income effect thus increases the demand for leisure (from 70 to 85 hours) and reduces hours of work by 15 hours per week.

The second-stage move from *Q* to *R* is called the **substitution effect.** It illustrates what happens to the worker's consumption bundle as the wage increases, holding utility constant. By moving along an indifference curve, the worker's utility or "real income" is held fixed. The substitution effect thus isolates the impact of the increase in the price of leisure on hours of work, holding real income constant.

The move from point *Q* to point *R* illustrates a substitution away from leisure time and toward consumption of other goods. In other words, as the wage rises, the worker devotes less time to expensive leisure activities (from 85 to 75 hours) and increases her consumption of goods. Through the substitution effect, therefore, the wage increase reduces the demand for leisure and increases hours of work by 10 hours. *The substitution effect implies that an increase in the wage rate, holding real income constant, increases hours of work.*

As drawn in Figure 2-9*a*, the decrease in hours of work generated by the income effect (15 hours) exceeds the increase in hours of work associated with the substitution effect (10 hours). The stronger income effect thus leads to a negative relationship between hours of work and the wage rate. In Figure 2-9*b*, the income effect (again the move from point *P* to point *Q*) decreases hours of work by 10 hours, whereas the substitution effect (the move from *Q* to *R*) increases hours of work by 15 hours. Because the substitution effect dominates, there is a positive relationship between hours of work and the wage rate.

The reason for the ambiguity in the relationship between hours of work and the wage rate should now be clear. As the wage rises, a worker faces a larger opportunity set and the income effect increases her demand for leisure and decreases labor supply. As the wage rises, however, leisure becomes more expensive and the substitution effect generates incentives for that worker to switch away from the consumption of leisure and instead consume more goods. This shift frees up leisure hours and thus increases hours of work.

To summarize the relation between hours of work and the wage rate:

- An increase in the wage rate increases hours of work if the substitution effect dominates the income effect.
- An increase in the wage rate decreases hours of work if the income effect dominates the substitution effect.

2-6   To Work or Not to Work?

Our analysis of the relation between nonlabor income, the wage rate, and hours of work assumed that the person worked both before and after the change in nonlabor income or the wage. Hours of work then adjusted to the change in the opportunity set. But what factors motivate a person to enter the labor force in the first place?

The implication that our demand for leisure time responds to its price is not very surprising. When the wage rate is high, we will find ways of minimizing the use of our valuable time, such as contact a ticket broker and pay very high prices for concert and theater tickets, rather than stand in line for hours to buy a ticket at face value. We will often hire a nanny or send our children to day care, rather than withdraw from the labor market. And we will consume many pre-prepared meals and order pizza or take-out Chinese food, rather than engage in lengthy meal preparations.

It turns out that our allocation of time responds to economic incentives even when there are no easy substitutes available, such as when we decide how many hours to sleep. Sleeping takes a bigger chunk of our time than any other activity, including market work. The typical man sleeps 56.0 hours per week, whereas the typical woman sleeps 56.9 hours per week. Although most persons think that how long we sleep is biologically (and perhaps even culturally) determined, recent research suggests that, to some extent, sleep time also can be viewed as simply another activity that responds to economic incentives. As long as some minimum biological threshold for the length of a sleeping spell is met, the demand for sleep time seems to respond to changes in the price of time.

In particular, there is a negative correlation between a person's earnings capacity and the number of hours spent sleeping. More highly educated persons, for example, sleep less—an additional four years of school decreases sleep time by about one hour per week. Similarly, a 20 percent wage increase reduces sleep time by 1 percent, or about 34 minutes per week. When the wage is high, therefore, even dreaming of a nice, long vacation in a remote island becomes expensive.

Source: Jeff E. Biddle and Daniel S. Hamermesh, "Sleep and the Allocation of Time," *Journal of Political Economy* 98 (October 1990): 922–943.

To illustrate the nature of the work decision, consider Figure 2-10. The figure draws the indifference curve that goes through the endowment point E. This indifference curve indicates that a person who does not work at all receives U_0 units of utility. The woman, however, can choose to enter the labor market and trade some of her leisure time for earnings that will allow her to buy consumption goods. The decision of whether to work or not boils down to a simple question: Are the "terms of trade"—the rate at which leisure can be traded for additional consumption—sufficiently attractive to bribe her into entering the labor market?

Suppose initially that the person's wage rate is given by w_{low} so that the woman faces budget line GE in Figure 2-10. No point on this budget line can give her more utility than U_0. At this low wage, the person's opportunities are quite meager. If the worker were to move from the endowment point E to any point on the budget line GE, she would be moving to a lower indifference curve and be worse off. For example, at point X the woman gets only U_G utils. At wage w_{low}, therefore, the woman chooses not to work.

In contrast, suppose that the wage rate was given by w_{high}, so that the woman faces budget line HE. It is easy to see that moving to any point on this steeper budget line would increase her utility. At point Y, the woman gets U_H utils. At the wage w_{high}, therefore, the woman is better off working.

In sum, Figure 2-10 indicates that the woman does not enter the labor market at low wage rates (such as w_{low}), but does enter the labor market at high wage rates (such as w_{high}). As we rotate the budget line from wage w_{low} to wage w_{high}, we will typically encounter a wage rate, call it $\tilde{w}$, that makes her indifferent between working and not working. We call $\tilde{w}$ the

FIGURE 2-10 The Reservation Wage

If the person chooses not to work, she can remain at the endowment point E and get U_0 units of utility. At a low wage (w_{low}), the person is better off not working. At a high wage (w_{high}), she is better off working. The reservation wage is given by the slope of the indifference curve at the endowment point.

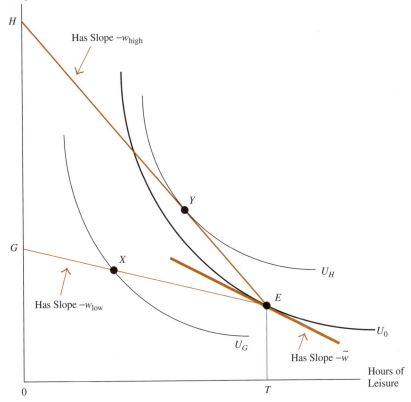

reservation wage. The reservation wage gives the minimum increase in income that would make a person indifferent between remaining at the endowment point E and working that first hour. In Figure 2-10, the reservation wage is given by the absolute value of the slope of the indifference curve at point E.

The definition of the reservation wage implies that the person will not work at all if the market wage is less than the reservation wage; and the person will enter the labor market if the market wage exceeds the reservation wage. The decision to work, therefore, is based on a comparison of the market wage, which indicates how much employers are willing to pay for an hour of work, and the reservation wage, which indicates how much the worker requires to be bribed into working that first hour.

The theory obviously implies that a high reservation wage makes it less likely that a person will work. The reservation wage will typically depend on the person's tastes for work, which helps to determine the slope of the indifference curve, as well on many other factors. For instance, the assumption that leisure is a normal good implies that the reservation wage rises as nonlabor income increases.[13] Because workers want to consume more leisure as nonlabor income increases, a larger bribe will be required to convince a wealthier person to enter the labor market.

Holding the reservation wage constant, the theory also implies that high-wage persons are more likely to work. A rise in the wage rate, therefore, increases the labor force participation rate of a group of workers. As we shall see, this positive correlation between wage rates and labor force participation rates helps explain the rapid increase in the labor force participation rate of women observed in the United States and in many other countries in the past century.[14]

In sum, the theory predicts a positive relation between the person's wage rate and her probability of working. It is of interest to contrast this strong prediction with our earlier result that a wage increase has a theoretically ambiguous effect on hours of work, depending on whether the income or substitution effect dominates.

The disparity between these two results arises because an increase in the wage generates an income effect *only if the person is already working.* A person working 40 hours per week will surely be able to consume many more goods when the wage is $20 per hour than when the wage is $10 per hour. This type of wage increase makes leisure more expensive (so that the worker wants to work more) *and* makes the person wealthier (so that the worker wants to work less). In contrast, if the person is not working at all, an increase in the wage rate has no effect on her real income. The amount of goods that a nonworker can buy is independent of whether her potential wage rate is $10 or $20 an hour. An increase in the wage of a nonworker, therefore, does not generate an income effect. The wage increase simply makes leisure time more expensive and hence is likely to draw the nonworker into the labor force.

2-7   The Labor Supply Curve

The predicted relation between hours of work and the wage rate is called the **labor supply curve.** Figure 2-11 illustrates how a person's labor supply curve can be derived from the utility-maximization problem that we solved earlier.

The left panel of the figure shows the person's optimal consumption bundle at a number of alternative wage rates. As drawn, the wage of $10 is the person's reservation wage, the wage at which she is indifferent between working and not working. This person, therefore, supplies zero hours to the labor market at any wage less than or equal to $10. Once the wage rises above $10, the person chooses to work some hours. For example, she works

---

[13] Try to prove this statement by drawing a vertical line through the indifference curves in Figure 2-6. By moving up this vertical line, we are holding constant hours of leisure. Because of their convexity, the indifference curves will get steeper as we move to higher indifference curves.

[14] The modern analysis of labor force participation decisions within an economic framework began with the classic work of Jacob Mincer, "Labor Force Participation of Married Women," in H. Gregg Lewis, editor, *Aspects of Labor Economics,* Princeton, NJ: Princeton University Press, 1962, pp. 63–97. An important study that stresses the comparison between reservation and market wages is given by James J. Heckman, "Shadow Prices, Market Wages and Labor Supply," *Econometrica* 42 (July 1974): 679–694.

20 hours when the wage is $13; 40 hours when the wage if $20; and 30 hours when the wage is $25. Note that, as drawn, the figure implies that substitution effects dominate at lower wages and that income effects dominate at higher wages.

The right panel of the figure traces out the labor supply curve, the relation between the optimal number of hours worked and the wage rate. Initially, the labor supply curve is positively sloped as hours and wages move together. Once the wage rises above $20, however, the income effect dominates and hours of work decline as the wage rises, creating a segment of the labor supply curve that has a negative slope. The type of labor supply curve illustrated in Figure 2-11*b* is called a *backward-bending* labor supply curve because it eventually bends around and has a negative slope.

We can use the utility-maximization framework to derive a labor supply curve for every person in the economy. The labor supply curve in the aggregate labor market is then given by adding up the hours that all persons in the economy are willing to work at a given wage. Figure 2-12 illustrates how this "adding up" is done in an economy with two workers, Alice and Brenda. Alice has reservation wage $\tilde{w}_A$; Brenda has a higher reservation wage $\tilde{w}_B$. It should

FIGURE 2-11 Deriving a Labor Supply Curve for a Worker

The labor supply curve traces out the relationship between the wage rate and hours of work. At wages below the reservation wage ($10), the person does not work. At wages higher than $10, the person enters the labor market. The upward-sloping segment of the labor supply curve implies that substitution effects are stronger initially; the backward-bending segment implies that income effects may dominate eventually.

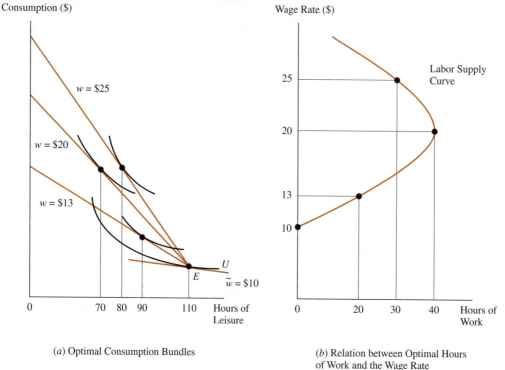

(a) Optimal Consumption Bundles

(b) Relation between Optimal Hours of Work and the Wage Rate

FIGURE 2-12 Derivation of the Market Labor Supply Curve from the Supply Curves of Individual Workers

The market labor supply curve "adds up" the supply curves of individual workers. When the wage is below $\tilde{w}_A$, no one works. As the wage rises, Alice enters the labor market. If the wage rises above $\tilde{w}_B$, Brenda enters the market.

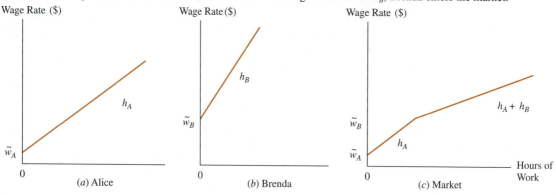

(a) Alice

(b) Brenda

(c) Market

be clear that no one would work if the wage is below $\tilde{w}_A$, and that only Alice would work if the wage is between $\tilde{w}_A$ and $\tilde{w}_B$. At wages higher than $\tilde{w}_B$, market labor supply is given by the total number of hours worked by Alice and Brenda, or $h_A + h_B$. The labor supply curve in the market, therefore, is obtained by adding up the supply curves of all workers *horizontally*.

To measure the responsiveness of hours of work to changes in the wage rate, we define the **labor supply elasticity** as

$$\sigma = \frac{\text{Percent change in hours of work}}{\text{Percent change in wage rate}} = \frac{\Delta h/h}{\Delta w/w} = \frac{\Delta h}{\Delta w} \cdot \frac{w}{h} \quad \textbf{(2-11)}$$

The labor supply elasticity gives the percentage change in hours of work associated with a 1 percent change in the wage rate. The sign of the labor supply elasticity depends on whether the labor supply curve is upward sloping ($\Delta h/\Delta w$ (0) or downward sloping ($\Delta h/\Delta w < 0$), and, hence, is positive when substitution effects dominate and negative when income effects dominate. Hours of work are more responsive to changes in the wage the greater the absolute value of the labor supply elasticity.

To see how the labor supply elasticity is calculated, consider the following example. Suppose that the worker's wage is initially $10 per hour and that she works 1,900 hours per year. The worker gets a raise to $20 per hour, and she decides to work 2,090 hours per year. This worker's labor supply elasticity can then be calculated as

$$\sigma = \frac{\text{Percent change in hours of work}}{\text{Percent change in wage rate}} = \frac{10\%}{100\%} = 0.1 \quad \textbf{(2-12)}$$

When the labor supply elasticity is less than one in absolute value, the labor supply curve is said to be *inelastic*. In other words, there is relatively little change in hours of work for a given change in the wage rate. If the labor supply elasticity is greater than one in absolute value—indicating that hours of work are greatly affected by the change in the wage—the labor supply curve is said to be *elastic*. It is obvious that labor supply is inelastic in the numerical example in equation (2-12). After all, a doubling of the wage (a 100 percent increase) raised labor supply by only 10 percent.

2-8 Estimates of the Labor Supply Elasticity

Few topics in applied economics have been as thoroughly researched as the empirical relationship between hours of work and wages. We begin our review of this literature by focusing on the estimates of the labor supply elasticity for men. Since most prime-age men participate in the labor force, the typical study uses the sample of working men to correlate a particular person's hours of work with his wage rate and nonlabor income. In particular, the typical regression model estimated in these studies is

$$h_i = \beta w_i + \gamma V_i + \text{Other variables} \quad \textbf{(2-13)}$$

where h_i gives the number of hours that person i works; w_i gives his wage rate; and V_i gives his nonlabor income. The coefficient β measures the impact of a one-dollar wage increase on hours of work, holding nonlabor income constant; and the coefficient measures the impact of a one-dollar increase in nonlabor income, holding the wage constant. The neoclassical model of labor-leisure choice implies that the sign of the coefficient β depends on whether income or substitution effects dominate. In particular, β is negative if income effects dominate and positive if substitution effects dominate. The estimate of the coefficient β can be used to calculate the labor supply elasticity defined by equation (2-11). Assuming leisure is a normal good, the theory also predicts that the coefficient γ should be negative because workers with more nonlabor income consume more leisure.

There are almost as many estimates of the labor supply elasticity as there are empirical studies in the literature. As a result, the variation in the estimates of the labor supply elasticity is enormous. Some studies report the elasticity to be zero; other studies report it to be large and negative; still others report it to be large and positive. There have been some attempts to determine which estimates are most credible.[15] These surveys conclude that the elasticity of the male labor supply is roughly around −0.1. In other words, a 10 percent increase in the wage leads, on average, to a 1 percent decrease in hours of work for men. In terms of the decomposition into income and substitution effects, there is some consensus that a 10 percent increase in the wage increases hours of work by about 1 percent because of the substitution effect, but also leads to a 2 percent decrease because of the income effect. As predicted by the theory, therefore, the substitution effect is positive.

Three key points are worth noting about the −0.1 "consensus" estimate of the labor supply elasticity. First, it is negative, so income effects dominate. The dominance of income effects is often used to explain the decline in hours of work between 1900 and 2000 that we documented earlier in this chapter. In other words, the secular decline in hours of work can be attributed to the income effects associated with rising real wages.[16] Second, the labor supply curve is inelastic. Hours of work for men do not seem to be very responsive to changes in the wage. In fact, one would not be stretching the truth too far if one were to claim that the male labor supply elasticity is essentially zero. This result should not be too surprising since most prime-age men work a full workweek every week of the year.[17]

[15] A recent survey of the labor supply literature is given by Richard Blundell and Thomas MaCurdy, "Labor Supply: A Review of Alternative Approaches," in Orley C. Ashenfelter and David Card, editors, *Handbook of Labor Economics*, vol. 3A, Amsterdam: Elsevier, 1999, pp. 1559–1695. Many of the large positive elasticities reported in the literature are found in studies that attempt to estimate the impact of changes in income tax rates on labor supply. A good survey of this literature is given by Jerry A. Hausman, "Taxes and Labor Supply," in Alan J. Auerbach and Martin Feldstein, editors, *Handbook of Public Economics*, vol. 1, Amsterdam: Elsevier, 1985, pp. 213–263. Recent research, however, suggests that a more careful specification of the econometric model used to estimate how taxes affect labor supply yields a labor supply response that is much weaker and closer in line with the consensus estimate of −0.1; see Thomas MaCurdy, David Green, and Harry Paarsch, "Assessing Empirical Approaches for Analyzing Taxes and Labor Supply," *Journal of Human Resources* 25 (Summer 1990): 415–490; James P. Ziliak and Thomas J. Kniesner, "The Effect of Income Taxation on Consumption and Labor Supply," *Journal of Labor Economics* 23 (October 2005): 769–796.

[16] Thomas J. Kniesner, "The Full-Time Workweek in the United States: 1900–1970," *Industrial and Labor Relations Review* 30 (October 1976): 3–15; and John Pencavel, "A Cohort Analysis of the Association between Work Hours and Wages among Men," *Journal of Human Resources* 37 (Spring 2002): 251–274. In recent years, hours of work have begun to rise for highly educated men, high-wage men. This increase may be due to a strong substitution effect caused by a rapidly rising real wage; see Peter Kuhn and Fernando Luzano, "The Expanding Workweek? Understanding Trends in Long Work Hours among U.S. Men, 1979–2006," *Journal of Labor Economics* 26 (April 2008): 311–343.

[17] Recall, however, that the labor force participation rate of men fell throughout much of the twentieth century. For a study of this trend, see Chinhui Juhn, "The Decline of Male Labor Market Participation: The Role of Market Opportunities," *Quarterly Journal of Economics* 107 (February 1992): 79–121.

And, third, it is important to keep in mind that this is the "consensus" estimate of the labor supply elasticity for prime-age men. The available evidence suggests that the labor supply elasticity probably differs greatly between men and women and between younger and older workers.

Problems with the Estimated Elasticities

Why is there so much variation in the estimates of the labor supply elasticity across studies? It turns out that much of the empirical research in this area is marred by a number of statistical and measurement problems. In fact, each of the three variables that are crucial for estimating the labor supply model—the person's hours of work, the wage rate, and nonlabor income—introduces difficult problems into the estimation procedure.

Hours of Work

What precisely do we mean by hours of work when we estimate a labor supply model: is it hours of work per day, per week, or per year? The elaborate theoretical apparatus that we have developed does not tell us what the span of the time period should be. It turns out, however, that the observed responsiveness of hours of work to a wage change depends crucially on whether we look at a day, a week, or a year.[18] Not surprisingly, the labor supply curve becomes more elastic the longer the time period over which the hours-of-work variable is defined, so labor supply is almost completely inelastic if we analyze hours of work per week, but it is a bit more responsive if we analyze hours of work per year. Our conclusion that the labor supply elasticity is around −0.1 is based on studies that look at variation in annual hours of work.

There is also substantial measurement error in the hours-of-work measure that is typically reported in survey data.[19] Workers who are paid by the hour know quite well how many hours they worked last week; after all, their take-home pay depends directly on the length of the workweek. Many of us, however, are paid an annual salary and we make little (if any) effort to track exactly how many hours we work in any given week. When we are asked how many hours we work per week, many of us will respond "40 hours" because that is the easy answer. Actual hours of work, however, may have little to do with the mythical 40-hour workweek for many salaried workers. As we will see shortly, this measurement error introduces a bias into the estimation of the labor supply elasticity.

The Wage Rate

The typical salaried worker is paid an annual salary, regardless of how many hours she puts into her job. It is customary to define the wage rate of salaried workers in terms of the average wage, the ratio of annual earnings to annual hours worked. This calculation transmits any measurement errors in the reported measure of hours of work to the wage rate.

---

[18] See Finis Welch, "Wages and Participation," *Journal of Labor Economics* 15 (January 1997): S77–S103; and Chinhui Juhn, Kevin M. Murphy, and Robert H. Topel, "Why Has the Natural Rate of Unemployment Increased over Time?" *Brookings Papers on Economic Activity* 2 (1991): 75–126.

[19] John Bound, Charles Brown, Greg Duncan, and Willard Rogers, "Evidence on the Validity of Cross-Sectional and Longitudinal Labor Market Data," *Journal of Labor Economics* 12 (July 1994): 345–368.

Theory at Work
WORK AND LEISURE IN EUROPE AND THE UNITED STATES

In 1960, hours of work and labor force participation rates were roughly similar or higher in European countries than in the United States. The labor force participation rate of men was around 92 percent in the United States, as compared to 92 to 95 percent in France, Germany, or Italy. Similarly, the typical employed person worked around 2,000 hours per year in each of the countries.

By 2000, there was a huge gap in the work effort of the typical person in Europe vis-'a-vis the United States. The male labor force participation rate was just over 85 percent in the United States, as compared to 80 percent in Germany and 75 percent in France or Italy. Similarly, annual hours of work per employed person had fallen to 1,800 hours in the United States, but had fallen even further to about 1,400 hours in Germany, 1,500 hours in France, and 1,600 hours in Italy.

Although it is now frequently alleged that European "culture" explains why Europeans work less than Americans, this hypothesis is not informative. After all, that same "culture" led to a very different outcome—Europeans working at least as much as Americans—only a few decades ago.

Recent research concludes that a small number of observable factors tend to explain the differential work and leisure trends between the United States and western European countries. Part of these differences result from the much higher European tax rates on earned income. In Germany and Belgium, for example, the marginal tax rate on earned income is between 60 and 70 percent, while in France and Italy, it is greater than 50 percent. These tax rates contrast with the roughly 35 percent marginal tax rate in the United States. The higher tax rate generates substitution effects in European countries that reduce the incentive to work.

It turns out, however, that these tax rate differentials may not be sufficiently large to explain the huge differences in labor supply. European labor market regulations, and particularly those policies advocated by labor unions in declining European industries to "share work," seem to explain the bulk of the labor supply differences. Despite their stated objective of spreading out the available work among a large number of potential workers, these work-sharing policies did not increase employment. Instead, they increased the returns to leisure as an ever-larger fraction of the population began taking longer vacations. The "social multiplier" effect of a larger return to leisure activity seems to have had a much wider social impact on the work decisions of potential workers in many European countries.

Source: Alberto Alesina, Edward Glaeser, and Bruce Sacerdote, "Work and Leisure in the U.S. and Europe: Why So Different?" *NBER Macro Annual*, 2005: 1–64.

To illustrate the problem introduced by these measurement errors, suppose that a worker overreports her hours of work. Because of the way the wage rate is constructed (that is, as the ratio of annual earnings to annual hours of work), the denominator of this ratio is too big and we estimate an artificially low wage rate. High reported hours of work are then associated with low wage rates, generating a spurious negative correlation between hours and average wages. Suppose instead that the worker underreports her hours of work. The constructed wage rate is then artificially high, again generating a spurious negative correlation between hours of work and the wage. As a result, measurement error tends to exaggerate the importance of income effects. In fact, there is evidence that correcting for measurement error in hours of work greatly reduces the magnitude of the income effect.[20]

Even in the absence of measurement error, there is an important conceptual problem in defining the wage rate as the ratio of annual earnings to hours of work for salaried workers.

[20] George J. Borjas, "The Relationship between Wages and Weekly Hours of Work: The Role of Division Bias," *Journal of Human Resources* 15 (Summer 1980): 409–423.

The correct price of leisure in the neoclassical model of labor-leisure choice is the marginal wage, the increase in earnings associated with an additional hour of work. The relevant marginal wage for salaried workers may have little to do with the average wage earned per hour.

Finally, a researcher attempting to estimate the labor supply model quickly encounters the serious problem that the wage rate is not observed for people who are not working. However, a person who is out of the labor market does *not* have a zero wage rate. All that we really know is that this person's wage is below the reservation wage. Many empirical studies avoid the problem of calculating the wages of nonworkers by simply throwing the nonworkers out of the sample that is used for calculating the labor supply elasticity.

This procedure, however, is fundamentally flawed. The decision of whether to work depends on a comparison of market wages and reservation wages. Persons who do not work have either very low wage rates or very high reservation wages. The sample of workers (or of nonworkers), therefore, is not a random sample of the population. Because most of the econometric techniques and statistical tests that have been developed specifically assume that the sample under analysis is a random sample, these techniques cannot be used to analyze the labor supply behavior of a sample that only includes workers. As a result, the estimated labor supply elasticities are not calculated correctly. This problem is typically referred to as "selection bias."[21]

Nonlabor Income

We would ideally like V to measure that part of the worker's income stream that has nothing to do with how many hours he works. For most people, however, the current level of nonlabor income partly represents the returns to past savings and investments. Suppose that some workers have a "taste for work." The shape of their indifference curves is such that they worked long hours, had high labor earnings, and were able to save and invest a large fraction of their income in the past. These are precisely the workers who will have high levels of nonlabor income today. If a worker's taste for work does not change over time, these are also the workers who will tend to work more hours today. The correlation between nonlabor income and hours of work will then be positive, simply because persons who have large levels of nonlabor income are the persons who tend to work many hours.

In fact, some studies in the literature report that workers who have more nonlabor income work more hours. This finding would suggest either that leisure is an inferior good or that the biases introduced by the correlation between tastes for work and nonlabor income are sufficiently strong to switch the sign of the estimated income effect. More careful studies that account for the correlation between "tastes for work" and nonlabor income find that increases in nonlabor income do indeed reduce hours of work.[22]

---

[21] A number of sophisticated statistical techniques have been developed to handle the self-selection problem. These techniques typically involve estimating labor supply functions that include not only the wage rate and nonlabor income as independent variables but also the predicted probability that a person is working. See James J. Heckman, "Sample Selection Bias as a Specification Error," *Econometrica* 47 (January 1979): 153–162; and James J. Heckman, "Sample Selection Bias as a Specification Error with an Application to the Estimation of Labor Supply Functions," in James P. Smith, editor, *Female Labor Supply: Theory and Estimation,* Princeton, NJ: Princeton University Press, 1980, pp. 206–248.

[22] James P. Smith, "Assets and Labor Supply," in Smith, editor, *Female Labor Supply: Theory and Estimation,* pp. 166–205.

2-9   Labor Supply of Women

Table 2-4 documents the growth of the female labor force in a number of countries between 1980 and 2003.[23] These statistics suggest two key results. There are substantial differences across countries in women's labor force participation rates. In Italy, for instance, fewer than half of women aged 15 to 64 participated in the labor force in 2003; in the United States and Canada, the participation rate hovered around 70 percent. These differences can probably be attributed to differences in economic variables and cultural factors, as well as the institutional framework in which labor supply decisions are being made.

Despite the international differences in the level of labor force participation, the data also reveal that these countries experienced a common trend: rising female labor force participation during the past few decades. The participation rate of women increased from 40 to 47 percent in Italy between 1980 and 2003; from 55 to 64 percent in Japan; and from 33 to 50 percent in Greece.

In the United States, the participation rate has grown over time both for a particular group of female workers and across cohorts of workers.[24] In other words, the participation rate of a given birth cohort of women increases as the women get older (past the childbearing years). For example, the participation rate of women born around

TABLE 2-4

International Differences in Female Labor Force Participation Rate (women aged 15–64)

Source: U.S. Bureau of the Census, *Statistical Abstract of the United States, 2006,* Washington, DC: Government Printing Office, Table 1343.

Country	1980	1990	2003
Australia	52.7	62.1	66.4
Canada	57.8	67.6	70.4
France	54.4	57.8	62.0
Germany	52.8	56.7	64.0
Greece	33.0	43.6	50.2
Ireland	36.3	43.8	56.2
Italy	39.6	45.9	46.8
Japan	54.8	60.3	64.2
Korea, South	—	51.2	54.3
Mexico	33.7	—	42.4
New Zealand	44.6	63.0	67.6
Portugal	54.3	62.9	67.2
Spain	32.2	41.2	50.7
Sweden	74.1	80.4	75.0
Turkey	—	36.7	26.9
United Kingdom	58.3	66.5	67.8
United States	59.7	68.5	71.7

[23] A survey of these international trends is given by Jacob Mincer, "Intercountry Comparisons of Labor Force Trends and of Related Developments: An Overview," *Journal of Labor Economics* 3 (January 1985 Supplement): S1–S32.

[24] James P. Smith and Michael P. Ward, "Time-Series Growth in the Female Labor Force," *Journal of Labor Economics* 3 (January 1985, Part 2): S59–S90; and Claudia Goldin, "Life-Cycle Labor-Force Participation of Married Women: Historical Evidence and Implications," *Journal of Labor Economics* 7 (January 1989): 20–47.

1930 was 27.7 percent when they were 30 years old and rose to 58.0 percent when they were 50 years old. Equally important, there has been a substantial increase in labor force participation across cohorts, with more recent cohorts having larger participation rates. At age 30, for example, women born around 1950 had a participation rate of 61.6 percent, more than twice the participation rate of women born in 1930 at an equivalent point in the life cycle.

Our theoretical discussion highlights the role of changes in the wage rate as a key determinant of the increase in female labor force participation. In particular, as the wage increases, nonworking women have an incentive to reduce the time they allocate to the household sector and are more likely to enter the labor market.[25] In fact, the real wage of women increased substantially in most countries. Between 1960 and 1980, the real wage of women grew at an annual rate of 6.2 percent for Australian women, 4.2 percent for British women, 5.6 percent for Italian women, and 2.1 percent for American women. The across-country relationship between the increase in labor force participation rates and the increase in the real wage is illustrated in Figure 2-13. Even without the use of sophisticated econometrics, one can see that labor force participation rates grew fastest in those developed countries that experienced the highest increase in the real wage.

FIGURE 2-13   **Cross-Country Relationship between Growth in Female Labor Force and the Wage, 1960–1980**

Source: Jacob Mincer, "Intercountry Comparisons of Labor Force Trends and of Related Developments: An Overview," *Journal of Labor Economics* 3 (January 1985, Part 2): S2, S6.

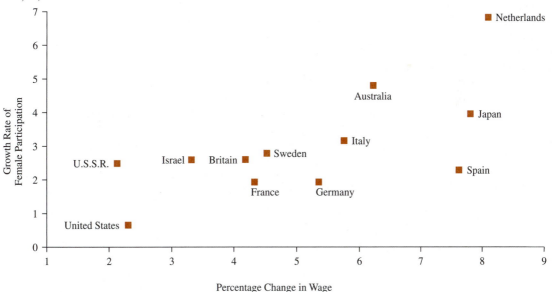

[25] Recall that the theory implies that a wage increase does not generate an income effect for nonworkers. The only impact of a wage increase on this group of persons is to increase the price of leisure and to make it more likely that they will now enter the labor force.

The labor force participation decision is based on a comparison of the market wage with the reservation wage. Hence, the increase in the labor force participation rates of women could be due not only to a rise in the market wage but also to a decline in women's reservation wages. It is likely that an increase in the number of children raises a woman's reservation wage and reduces the probability that the woman will work. In fact, if a woman has children under the age of six, her probability of working falls by nearly 20 percentage points.[26] Between 1950 and 2000, the total lifetime fertility of the average adult woman declined from 3.3 to 2.1 children, so the reduction in fertility probably contributed to the increase in female labor force participation.[27] It is also likely, however, that the rise in the market wage, which increased female participation rates, also made childbearing a very expensive household activity. As a result, some of the causation runs in the opposite direction: women participate more not because they have fewer children; rather, they have fewer children because the rising wage induces them to reduce their time in the household sector and enter the labor market.[28]

More generally, the model suggests that women's labor supply may be more responsive to wage changes than men's labor supply. Note that a wage increase makes household production relatively less valuable at the same time that it increases the price of leisure. Therefore, a wage increase would encourage a person to substitute time away from household production and toward market work. A rise in the real wage will then draw many women out of the household production sector and move them into the market sector. Because very few men specialized in household production in earlier decades, such a transition would have been relatively rare among men.

Female labor force participation rates also are influenced by technological changes in the process of household production. There have been remarkable time-saving technological advances in household production, including stoves, washing machines, and the microwave oven. As a result, the amount of time required to produce many household commodities was cut drastically in the twentieth century, freeing up the scarce time for leisure activities and for work in the labor market. A large difference in the marginal product of household time between the husband and the wife makes it likely that one of the two spouses will specialize in the household sector. The technological advances in household production probably reduced the gap in household productivity between the two spouses, lessening the need for specialization and further contributing to the increase in female labor force participation rates.

The economic model should not be interpreted as saying that *only* wage rates, reductions in fertility, and technological advances in household production are responsible for the huge increase in labor force participation of married women in this century. Changes in cultural and legal attitudes toward working women, as well as the social and economic disruptions brought about by two world wars and the Great Depression, also played a role.

[26] John Cogan, "Married Women's Labor Supply: A Comparison of Alternative Estimation Procedures," in Smith, editor, *Female Labor Supply: Theory and Estimation,* p. 113.

[27] U.S. Bureau of the Census, *Statistical Abstract of the United States,* Washington, DC: Government Printing Office, various issues.

[28] Joshua D. Angrist and William N. Evans, "Children and Their Parents' Labor Supply: Evidence from Exogenous Variation in Family Size," *American Economic Review* 88 (June 1998): 450–477.

A fascinating example is that unmarried young women living in states that granted them an early right to obtain oral contraceptives (i.e., the pill) without parental consent experienced a faster increase in labor force participation rates.[29] However, the evidence indicates that economic factors *do* matter and that a significant part of the increase in the labor force participation of married women can be understood in terms of the changing economic environment. It has been estimated that about 60 percent of the total growth in the female labor force between 1890 and 1980 can be attributed to the rising real wage of women.[30]

In recent years, technological changes in the labor market have allowed an increasing number of workers to do much of their work at home, further changing labor supply incentives. A recent study, in fact, reports that women who find it expensive to enter the labor market—such as women with small children—have strong incentives to use their home as their work base.[31] For example, only 15 percent of all women aged 25–55 who worked in a traditional "onsite" setting had children under the age of six. In contrast, 30 percent of "home-based" workers had children under the age of six. The prevalence of home-based work will likely rise as firms discover and adopt new technologies that allow them to outsource much of their work to other sites.

Many studies have attempted to estimate the responsiveness of women's hours of work to changes in the wage rate. Unlike the consensus estimate of the labor supply elasticity for prime-age men (that is, an elasticity on the order of -0.1), most studies of female labor supply find a *positive* relationship between a woman's hours of work and her wage rate, so substitution effects dominate income effects among working women. Recent studies that control for the selectivity bias arising from estimating labor supply models in the nonrandom sample of working women, however, tend to indicate that the size of the female labor supply elasticity may not be very large, perhaps on the order of 0.2.[32] A 10 percent increase in the woman's wage, therefore, increases her hours of work by about 2 percent.

Because of the huge changes in female labor supply witnessed in recent decades, there is a perception that female labor supply is more elastic than male labor supply. It is important to stress, however, that this perception is mostly due to the fact that female labor force

[29] Martha J. Bailey, "More Power to the Pill: The Effect of Contraceptive Freedom on Women's Life Cycle Labor Supply," *Quarterly Journal of Economics* 121 (February 2006): 289–320. See also Claudia Goldin, *Understanding the Gender Gap: An Economic History of American Women,* New York: Oxford University Press, 1990.

[30] Smith and Ward, "Time-Series Growth in the Female Labor Force"; Goldin, *Understanding the Gender Gap,* pp. 122–138; and Claudia Goldin, "The Role of World War II in the Rise of Women's Employment," *American Economic Review* 81 (September 1991): 741–756. More recent work finds the very rapid increase in labor force participation rates among successive cohorts of American women can only be explained if the rise in the real wage of women was accompanied by a reduction in the cost of raising children. See Orazio Attanasio, Hamish Low, and Virginia Sánchez-Marcosn, "Explaining Changes in Female Labor Supply in a Life-Cycle Model," *American Economic Review* 98 (September 2008): 1517–1552.

[31] Linda N. Edwards and Elizabeth Field-Hendrey, "Home-Based Work and Women's Labor Force Decisions," *Journal of Labor Economics* 20 (January 2002): 170–200.

[32] See Thomas Mroz, "The Sensitivity of an Empirical Model of Married Women's Hours of Work to Economic and Statistical Assumptions," *Econometrica* 55 (July 1987): 765–800; Francine D. Blau and Lawrence M. Kahn, "Changes in the Labor Supply of Married Women: 1980–2000," *Journal of Labor Economics* 25 (July 2007): 393–438; and Bradley T. Haim, "The Incredible Shrinking Elasticities: Married Female Labor Supply, 1978–2002," *Journal of Human Resources* 42 (Fall 2007): 881–918.

participation rates are very responsive to changes in the wage. Among working women, however, there is growing evidence that women's hours of work, like those of men, are not very responsive to changes in the wage. Put differently, female labor supply mainly responds to economic factors at the margin of deciding whether or not to work, rather than at the margin of deciding how many hours to work once in the labor force.

The evidence also suggests that the labor force participation rates and hours of work of married women respond to changes in the husband's wage. A 10 percent increase in the husband's wage lowers the participation rate of women by 5.3 percentage points and reduces the hours that working wives allocate to the labor market by 1.7 percent. There is little evidence, however, that the husband's labor supply is affected by the wife's wage rate.[33] Overall, the empirical studies show some support for the notion that the family's labor supply decisions are jointly made by the various family members, with female labor supply being particularly responsive to changes in the husband's wage.

2-10   Policy Application: Welfare Programs and Work Incentives

The impact of income maintenance programs, such as Aid to Families with Dependent Children (AFDC) or Temporary Assistance for Needy Families (TANF), on the work incentives of recipients has been hotly debated since the days when the United States declared a war on poverty in the mid-1960s. In fact, much of the opposition to welfare programs was motivated by the conjecture that these programs encourage recipients to "live off the dole" and foster dependency on public assistance. The perception that welfare does not work and that the so-called War on Poverty was lost found a sympathetic ear among persons on all sides of the political spectrum and led to President Clinton's promise to "end welfare as we know it."[34] This political consensus culminated in the enactment of the Personal Responsibility and Work Opportunity Reconciliation Act (PRWORA) in August 1996. The welfare reform legislation imposed lifetime limits on the receipt of various types of welfare programs, tightened eligibility requirements for most families, and mandated that many benefit-receiving families engage in work-related activities.

Cash Grants and Labor Supply

To illustrate how welfare programs can alter work incentives, let's begin by considering a simple program that grants eligible persons a cash grant. In particular, suppose that eligible persons (such as unmarried women with children) are given a cash grant of, say, $500 per month as long as they remain outside the labor force. If these persons enter the labor market, the government officials immediately assume that the women no longer need public assistance and the women are dropped from the welfare rolls (regardless of how much they earned).

---

[33] Orley Ashenfelter and James J. Heckman, "The Estimation of Income and Substitution Effects in a Model of Family Labor Supply," *Econometrica* 42 (January 1974): 73–85; and Shelly Lundberg, "Labor Supply of Husbands and Wives: A Simultaneous Equation Approach," *Review of Economics and Statistics* 70 (May 1988): 224–235.

[34] Charles Murray, *Losing Ground: American Social Policy, 1950–1980,* New York: Basic Books, 1984; and David T. Ellwood, *Poor Support: Poverty in the American Family,* New York: Basic Books, 1988. A survey of the academic studies that assess the impact of these programs is given by Robert Moffitt, "Incentive Effects of the U.S. Welfare System: A Review," *Journal of Economic Literature* 30 (March 1992): 1–61.

FIGURE 2-14 Effect of a Cash Grant on Work Incentives

A take-it-or-leave-it cash grant of $500 per month moves the worker from point P to point G, and encourages the worker to leave the labor force.

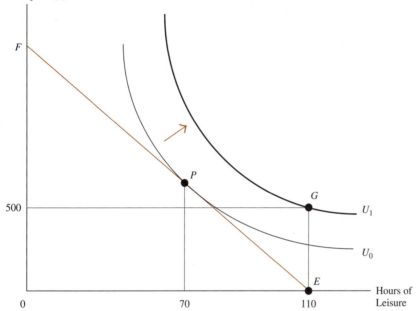

The impact of the cash grant on work incentives is illustrated in Figure 2-14. In the absence of the program, the budget line is given by FE and leads to an interior solution at point P, in which the person consumes 70 hours of leisure and works 40 hours.

For simplicity, assume that the woman does not have any nonlabor income. The introduction of a cash grant of $500 to nonworkers then introduces point G into the opportunity set. At this point, the woman can purchase $500 worth of consumption goods if she participates in the welfare program and does not work. Once the woman enters the labor market, however, the welfare grant is taken away and the opportunity set switches back to the original budget line FE.

The existence of the cash grant at point G can greatly reduce work incentives. As drawn, the woman attains a higher level of utility by choosing the corner solution at point G (that is, the welfare solution) than by choosing the interior solution at point P (that is, the work solution).

This type of "take-it-or-leave-it" cash grant can induce many workers to drop out of the labor market. In fact, it should be clear that low-wage women are most likely to choose the welfare solution. An improvement in the endowment point (from point E to point G) increases the worker's reservation wage, reducing the likelihood that a low-wage person will enter the labor market.

It is important to emphasize that welfare programs do not lower the labor force participation rates of low-wage workers because these workers lack a "work ethic." After all, we have implicitly assumed that the preferences of low-wage workers (as represented by the family of indifference curves) are identical to the preferences of high-wage workers.

Rather, the welfare program reduces the work incentives of low-wage workers because it is these workers who are most likely to find that the economic opportunities provided by the welfare system are better than those available in the labor market.

The Impact of Welfare on Labor Supply

In view of the extreme disincentive effects of the program illustrated in Figure 2-14, social assistance programs typically allow welfare recipients to remain in the labor force. Although welfare recipients can work, the amount of the cash grant is often reduced by some specified amount for every dollar earned in the labor market. Prior to 1996, for example, the AFDC grant was reduced by 67 cents for every dollar that the woman earned in the labor market (during the first four months that the woman was on welfare).[35]

It is instructive to describe with a numerical example how this type of welfare program alters the person's opportunity set. Suppose that, if the woman does not work at all and goes on welfare, her monthly income is $500 (assuming that she does not have any other non-labor income). For the purposes of this example, suppose that the government takes away 50 cents from the cash grant for every dollar earned in the labor market. This means that, if the woman works one hour at a wage of $10, her labor earnings increase by $10 but her grant is reduced by $5. Her total income, therefore, is $505. If she decides to work two hours, her labor earnings are $20 but her grant is reduced by $10. Total income would then be $510. Every additional hour of work increases income by only $5. Under the guise of reducing the size of the welfare grant, the government is actually taxing the welfare recipient's wage at a 50 percent rate. Therefore, it becomes important to differentiate between the woman's *actual* wage rate (which is $10 an hour) and the *net* wage (which is only $5 an hour).

Figure 2-15 illustrates the budget line created by this type of welfare program. In the absence of the program, the budget line is given by *FE* and the woman would choose the consumption bundle given by point *P*. She would then consume 70 hours of leisure and work 40 hours.

The welfare program shifts the budget line in two important ways. Because of the $500 monthly grant when the woman does not work, the endowment point changes from point *E* to point *G*. The program also changes the slope of the budget line. We have seen that the reduction of the grant by 50 cents for every dollar earned in the labor market is equivalent to a 50 percent tax on her earnings. The relevant slope of the budget line, therefore, is the net wage rate. Hence the welfare program cuts the (absolute value of the) slope by half, from $10 to $5. The budget line associated with the welfare program is then given by *HG*.

As drawn, when given the choice between the budget line *FE* and the budget line *HG*, the woman opts for the welfare system and chooses the consumption bundle given by point *R*. She consumes 100 hours of leisure and works 10 hours. Even this liberal "workfare" program, therefore, seems to have work disincentives because she works fewer hours than she would have worked in the absence of welfare.

[35] The taxation scheme implicit in the pre-1996 AFDC program was actually quite peculiar. During the first four months of a welfare spell, the welfare recipient was allowed to keep the first $90 earned per month (this amount was called the "earnings disregard"), but any additional earnings were taxed at a 67 percent tax rate. After being on welfare for four months, the earnings disregard was still $90 per month, but additional earnings were taxed at a 100 percent rate. An exhaustive description of the parameters of all means-tested entitlement programs in the United States is given by the Committee on Ways and Means, U.S. House of Representatives, *Overview of Entitlement Programs, Green Book,* Washington, DC: Government Printing Office, various issues.

FIGURE 2-15 **Effect of a Welfare Program on Hours of Work**

A welfare program that gives the worker a cash grant of $500 and imposes a 50 percent tax on labor earnings reduces work incentives. In the absence of welfare, the worker is at point *P.* The income effect resulting from the program moves the worker to point *Q;* the substitution effect moves the worker to point *R.* Both income and substitution effects reduce hours of work.

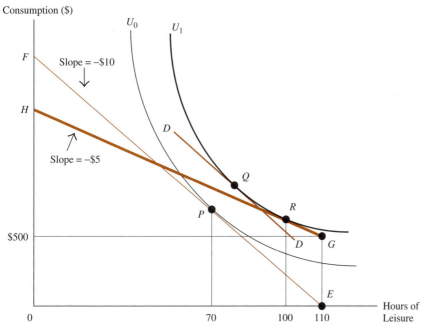

In fact, we can demonstrate that a welfare program that includes a cash grant and a tax on labor earnings *must* reduce hours of work. In particular, point *R* must be to the right of point *P.* To see why, draw a hypothetical budget line parallel to the pre-welfare budget line, but tangent to the new indifference curve. This line is labeled *DD* in Figure 2-15. It is easy to see that the move from point *P* to point *Q* is an income effect and represents the impact of the cash grant on hours of work. This income effect increases the demand for leisure. In other words, point *Q* must be to the right of point *P.*

The move from point *Q* to point *R* represents the substitution effect induced by the 50 percent tax on labor earnings, and point *R* must be to the right of point *Q.* The tax cuts the price of leisure by half for welfare recipients. As a consequence, the welfare recipient will demand even more leisure.

This stylized example vividly describes the work incentive problems introduced by welfare programs. If our model adequately represents how persons make their work decisions, it is impossible to formulate a relatively generous welfare program without substantially reducing work incentives. Awarding cash grants to recipients, as welfare programs unavoidably do, reduces both the probability of a person working and the number of hours worked by those who remain on the job. In addition, efforts to recover some of the grant money from working welfare recipients effectively impose a tax on work activities. This tax reduces the price of leisure and further lowers the number of hours that the welfare recipient will work.

The study of how welfare programs affect work incentives shows how the basic framework provided by the neoclassical model of labor-leisure choice is a point of departure that can be used to analyze more complex situations. By specifying in more detail how a person's opportunities are affected by government policies, we can easily adapt the model to analyze important social questions. The beauty of the economic approach is that we do not need different models to analyze labor supply decisions under alternative government policies or social institutions. In the end, we are always analyzing the *same* model—how workers allocate their limited time and money so as to maximize their utility—but we keep feeding the model more detail about the person's opportunity set.

Welfare Reform and Labor Supply

As we saw earlier, the theory predicts that welfare programs create work disincentives. In fact, many of the studies that studied the impact of the pre-1996 welfare programs typically found that the AFDC program reduced labor supply by 10 to 50 percent from the level of work effort that would have been found in the absence of the program, and the values of the labor supply elasticities generally fell in line with the consensus estimates described above.[36]

On August 22, 1996, President Clinton signed into law the welfare reform legislation that fundamentally changed the welfare system of the United States. A key provision in the legislation gave states a great deal of freedom in setting eligibility rules and benefit levels for many assistance programs.[37] For example, California now allows a TANF recipient to earn up to $225 per month without affecting the size of the welfare benefit, but any additional earnings are taxed at a 50 percent rate. In contrast, Illinois taxes all labor earnings at a 33 percent rate, while Mississippi applies a 100 percent tax rate on any labor earnings above $90 per month.

Many studies have used this variation across states to determine the impact of welfare programs on labor supply and many other variables, including the size of the welfare population itself. One difficult problem with the studies that evaluate the welfare reform legislation is that the period immediately following the enactment of PRWORA coincided with a historic economic boom in the United States. As a result, it has been difficult to determine how much of the decline in the size of the welfare caseload (from 4.4 million families receiving TANF in August 1996 to 2.2 million in June 2000) can be attributed to the economic boom and how much can be attributed to the changes in welfare policy.[38]

---

[36] For example, see Hilary Williamson Hoynes, "Welfare Transfers in Two-Parent Families: Labor Supply and Welfare Participation under AFDC-UP," *Econometrica* 64 (March 1996): 295–332. This literature is reviewed by Alan B. Krueger and Bruce D. Meyer, "Labor Supply Effects of Social Insurance," in Alan Auerbach and Martin Feldstein, editors, *Handbook of Public Economics,* Vol. 4, Amsterdam: North-Holland, 2002; and Robert A. Moffitt, "Welfare Programs and Labor Supply," in Alan Auerbach and Martin Feldstein, editors, *Handbook of Public Economics,* Vol. 4, Amsterdam: North-Holland, 2002.

[37] For a detailed discussion of the state differences in the TANF program and of the available research, see Robert A. Moffitt, "The Temporary Assistance for Needy Families Program," in Robert A. Moffitt, *Means-Tested Transfer Programs in the United States,* Chicago: University of Chicago Press, 1993, pp. 291–363.

[38] Robert F. Schoeni and Rebecca Blank, "What Has Welfare Reform Accomplished? Impacts on Welfare Participation, Employment, Poverty, Income, and Family Structure," National Bureau of Economic Research Working Paper No. 7627, March 2000; Jeffrey Grogger, "The Effects of Time Limits, the EITC, and Other Policy Changes on Welfare Use, Work, and Income among Female-Headed Families," *Review of Economics and Statistics* 85 (May 2003): 394–408.

Many states have conducted large-scale experiments. In the typical experiment, a group of randomly chosen families is offered a particular set of program parameters and benefits, while other families are offered a different set. By investigating the variation in labor supply among the different groups of families, it is possible to determine if labor supply responds to the financial incentives implied by the program parameters. These experiments often confirm the theoretical predictions.[39] One well-known experiment, the Minnesota Family Investment Program, allowed women to keep some of the cash benefits even if their earnings were relatively high (about 140 percent of the poverty line). The results of this experiment indicated that reducing the tax on labor earnings indeed encouraged the welfare recipients to work more.

There also has been a lot of interest in determining the impact of "time limits" on welfare participation. A key provision of PRWORA limits the amount of time that families can receive federal assistance to 60 months over their lifetimes, and many states have used their authority to set even shorter time limits.

The presence of time limits introduces interesting strategic choices for an eligible family: a family may choose to "bank" its benefits in order to maintain eligibility further into the future. Federal law permits welfare payments only to families that have children younger than 18 years of age. As a result, the family's choice of whether to receive assistance today (and use up some of its 60 eligible months) or to save its eligibility for a later period depends crucially on the age of the youngest child. Families with older children might as well use up their benefits now since it is unlikely that they can qualify for benefits some years into the future. In contrast, families with younger children have a longer time span over which they must allow for the possibility that they will require assistance, and they have an incentive not to use up the 60 months of lifetime benefits too soon.

The evidence strongly confirms this interesting insight. Time limits have the greatest effect on welfare participation rates of families with small children. All other things equal, the presence of time limits reduces the welfare participation of families where the youngest child is 3 years old by about 8 percentage points relative to the welfare participation of families where the youngest child is 10 years old.[40]

2-11 Policy Application: The Earned Income Tax Credit

An alternative approach to improving the economic status of low-income persons is given by the Earned Income Tax Credit (EITC). This program began in 1975 and has been expanded substantially since. By 2007, the EITC was the largest cash-benefit entitlement program in the United States, granting nearly $40 billion to low-income households.

To illustrate how the EITC works, consider a household composed of a working mother with two qualifying children. In 2005, for example, this woman could claim a tax credit of up to 40 percent of her earnings as long as she earned less than $11,000 per year, resulting in

[39] See Jeffrey Grogger; Lynn A. Karoly, and Jacob Alex Klerman, *Consequences of Welfare Reform: A Research Synthesis,* Santa Monica, CA: The Rand Corporation, July 2002; and Rebecca Blank, "Evaluating Welfare Reform in the U.S.," *Journal of Economic Literature* 40 (December 2002): 1105–1166.

[40] Jeffrey Grogger, "Time Limits and Welfare Use," *Journal of Human Resources* 39 (Spring 2004): 405–424; and Jeffrey Grogger and Charles Michalopoulos, "Welfare Dynamics under Time Limits," *Journal of Political Economy* 111 (June 2003): 530–554.

FIGURE 2-16   The EITC and the Budget Line (not drawn to scale)

In the absence of the tax credit, the budget line is given by *FE*. The EITC grants the worker a credit of 40 percent on labor earnings as long she earns less than $11,000. The credit is capped at $4,400. The worker receives this maximum amount as long as she earns between $11,000 and $14,370. The tax credit is then phased out gradually. The worker's net wage is 21.06 cents below her actual wage whenever she earns between $14,370 and $35,263.

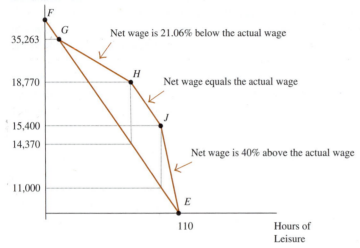

a maximum credit of $4,400. This maximum credit would be available as long as she earned between $11,000 and $14,370. After reaching the $14,370 threshold, the credit would begin to be phased out. In particular, each additional dollar earned reduces the credit by 21.06 cents. This formula implies that the credit completely disappears once the woman earns $35,263.

Figure 2-16 illustrates how the EITC introduces a number of "kinks" into the worker's opportunity set. The figure assumes that the worker does not have any nonlabor income. In the absence of the EITC, the worker faces the straight budget line given by *FE*. The EITC changes the net wage associated with an additional hour of work. As long as the worker earns less than $11,000 per year, the worker can claim a tax credit of up to 40 percent of earnings. Suppose, for instance, that the wage rate is $10 an hour and that the worker decides to work only one hour during the entire year. She can then file a tax return that would grant her a $4 tax credit. Therefore, the EITC implies that the worker's net wage is $14, a 40 percent raise. This 40 percent tax credit makes the budget line steeper, as illustrated by the segment *JE* in Figure 2-16.

If the woman earns $11,000, she receives the maximum tax credit, or $4,400. In fact, she is eligible for this maximum credit as long as she earns anywhere between $11,000 and $14,370. As long as the worker is in this range, therefore, the EITC does not change the net wage. It simply generates an increase in the worker's income of $4,400—as illustrated by the segment *HJ* in Figure 2-16, which illustrates that the EITC generates a pure income effect in this range of the program.

Once the worker's annual earnings exceed $14,370, the EITC is phased out at a rate of 21.06 cents for every dollar earned. Suppose, for example, that the worker earns exactly $14,370 and decides to work an additional hour at $10 an hour. The tax credit is then cut back by about $2.11, implying that the worker's net wage is only $7.89 an hour. The EITC, therefore, acts like a wage cut, flattening out the budget line, as illustrated by segment *GH* in Figure 2-16. Once the worker earns $35,263 during the year, she no longer qualifies for the EITC and her budget line reverts back to the original budget line (as in segment *FG*).

This detailed illustration of how the EITC works illustrates how government programs change the worker's opportunity set, creating strangely shaped budget lines with a number of kinks. These kinks can have important effects on the worker's labor supply decision.

So how does the EITC affect labor supply? The various panels of Figure 2-17 illustrate a number of possibilities. In Figure 2-17*a*, the worker would not be in the labor force in the absence of the EITC program (she maximizes her utility by being at the endowment point *P*). The increase in the net wage associated with the EITC draws the woman into the labor force, and she maximizes her utility by moving to point *R*. The reason for the increased propensity to work should be clear from our previous discussion. The EITC increases the net wage for nonworkers, making it more likely that the labor market can match their reservation wages and, hence, encouraging these persons to join the labor force. The theory, therefore, has a clear and important prediction: the EITC should increase the labor force participation rate in the targeted groups.

In Figure 2-17*b*, the person would be in the labor force even if the EITC were not in effect (at point *P*). This worker's annual income implies that the EITC generates an income effect—without affecting the net wage. The worker maximizes her utility by moving to point *R*, and she would be working fewer hours.

Finally, in Figure 2-17*c*, the person would work a large number of hours in the absence of the EITC (at point *P*). The EITC cuts her net wage, and she maximizes her utility by cutting hours and moving to the kink at point *R*.

The theory, therefore, suggests that the EITC has two distinct effects on labor supply. First, the EITC increases the number of labor force participants. Because the tax credit is granted only to persons who work, more persons will enter the labor force to take advantage of this program. Second, the EITC may change the number of hours worked by persons who would have been in the labor force even in the absence of the program. As drawn in the various panels of Figure 2-17, the EITC motivated workers to work fewer hours—but the change in the net wage generates both income and substitution effects and the impact of the EITC on hours worked will depend on the relative importance of these two effects.

The available evidence confirms the theoretical prediction that the EITC draws many new persons into the labor force.[41] Some of this evidence is summarized in Table 2-5. The Tax Reform Act of 1986 substantially expanded the benefits available through the EITC. The theory suggests that this legislative change should have increased the labor force participation rates of the targeted groups. Consider the population of unmarried women in the United States. Those who have at least one child potentially qualify for the EITC (depending on how much they earn), whereas those without children do not qualify. Table 2-5 shows that the labor force participation rate of the eligible women increased from 72.9 percent to 75.3 percent before and after the 1986 tax reform went into effect, an increase of 2.4 percentage points.

---

[41] V. Joseph Hotz and John Karl Scholz, "The Earned Income Tax Credit," in Robert A. Moffitt, editor, *Means-Tested Transfer Programs in the United States,* Chicago: University of Chicago Press, 2003; and Nada Eissa and Hilary W. Hoynes, "Behavioral Responses to Taxes: Lessons from the EITC and Labor Supply," *Tax Policy and the Economy* 20(2006): 74–110.

FIGURE 2-17   **The Impact of the EITC on Labor Supply**
The EITC shifts the budget line, and will draw new workers into the labor market. In (a), the person enters the labor market by moving from point P to point R. The impact of the EITC on the labor supply of persons already in the labor market is less clear. In the shifts illustrated in (b) and (c), the worker reduced hours of work.

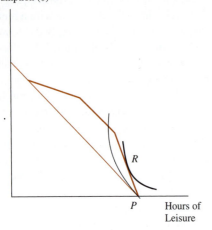

(a) EITC Draws Worker into Labor Market

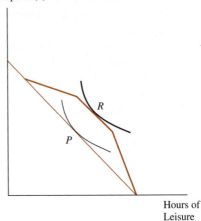

(b) EITC Reduces Hours of Work

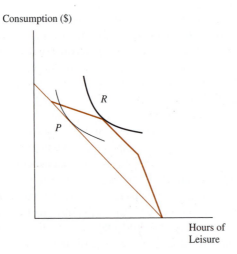

(c) EITC Reduces Hours of Work

TABLE 2-5   **The Impact of the Earned Income Tax Credit on Labor Force Participation**

Source: Nada Eissa and Jeffrey B. Liebman, "Labor Supply Response to the Earned Income Tax Credit," *Quarterly Journal of Economics* 111 (May 1996): 617.

	Participation Rate before Legislation (%)	Participation Rate after Legislation (%)	Difference (%)	Difference-in-Differences (%)
Treatment group—eligible for the EITC:				
Unmarried women with children	72.9	75.3	2.4	
Control group—not eligible for the EITC:				2.4
Unmarried women without children	95.2	95.2	0.0	

Before one can conclude that this change in labor force participation rates can be attributed to the EITC, one must consider the possibility that other factors might account for the 2.4 percentage point increase in labor force participation rates observed during that period. A booming economy, for instance, could have easily drawn more women into the labor market even in the absence of the EITC. Or there could exist long-run demographic and social trends that might account for the increasing propensity for these women to enter the labor force.

As in the typical experiment conducted in the natural sciences, we need a "control group"—a group of workers that would have experienced the same types of macroeconomic or demographic changes but that were not "injected" with the benefits provided by the EITC. Such a group could be the group of unmarried women without children. It turns out that their labor force participation did not change at all as a result of the Tax Reform Act of 1986—it stood at 95.2 percent both before and after the tax reform legislation.

The impact of the EITC on labor force participation, therefore, can be calculated by comparing the trend in the "treatment group"—the unmarried women with children—with the trend in the "control group"—the unmarried women without children. The labor force participation rate changed by 2.4 percentage points in the treatment group and by 0 percentage points in the control group. One can then estimate the net impact of the EITC on labor force participation by taking a "difference-in-differences": 2.4 percentage points minus 0 percentage points, or 2.4 percentage points.

This methodology for uncovering the impact of specific policy changes or economic shocks on labor market outcomes is known as the **difference-in-differences estimator** and has become very popular in recent years. The approach provides a simple way of measuring how particular events can alter labor market opportunities. At the same time, however, it is important to recognize that the validity of the conclusion depends crucially on our having chosen a correct control group that nets out the impact of *all* other factors on the trends that we are interested in.[42]

It is worth concluding by remarking briefly on the labor supply consequences of the two distinct approaches that we have discussed for subsidizing disadvantaged workers. The typical welfare program uses a "cash grant"—granting income grants to persons who do not or cannot work. As we have seen, these grants can greatly reduce work incentives

[42] Marianne Bertrand, Esther Duflo, and Sendhil Mullainathan, "How Much Should We Trust Differences-in-Differences Estimates?" *Quarterly Journal of Economics* 119 (February 2004): 249–275.

and make it more likely that program participants do not enter the labor force. The earned income tax credit, in contrast, subsidizes work. It does not provide a cash grant, and instead increases the net wage for nonworkers who enter the labor force. As a result, it can greatly increase work incentives and make it more likely that eligible recipients work.

2-12   Labor Supply over the Life Cycle

Up to this point, our model of labor supply analyzes the decisions of whether to work and how many hours to work from the point of view of a worker who allocates his time in a single time period and who ignores the fact that he will have to make similar choices continuously over many years. In fact, because consumption and leisure decisions are made over the entire working life, workers can "trade" some leisure time today in return for additional consumption tomorrow. For instance, a person who devotes a great deal of time to his job today can save some of the additional earnings and use these savings to increase his consumption of goods in the future.

As we will see in Chapter 6, a great deal of evidence suggests that the typical worker's age-earnings profile—the worker's wages over the life cycle—has a predictable path: wages tend to be low when the worker is young; they rise as the worker ages, peaking at about age 50; and the wage rate tends to remain stable or decline slightly after age 50. The path of this typical age-earnings profile is illustrated in Figure 2-18a. This age-earnings profile implies that the price of leisure is relatively low for younger and older workers and is highest for workers in their prime-age working years.

Consider how the worker's labor supply should respond to the wage increase that occurs between ages 20 and 30, or to the wage decline that might occur as the worker nears retirement age. It is important to note that these types of wage changes are part of the aging process *for a given worker.* A change in the wage along the worker's wage profile is called an "evolutionary" wage change, for it indicates how the wages of a particular worker evolve over time. It is crucial to note that an evolutionary wage change has no impact whatsoever on the worker's total *lifetime income.* The worker fully expects his wage to go up as he matures and to go down as he gets closer to retirement. As a result, an evolutionary wage change alters the price of leisure—but does not alter the value of the total opportunity set available to the worker over his life cycle. To be more precise, suppose we know that our life cycle age-earnings profile takes on the precise shape illustrated in Figure 2-18a. The fact that our wage rises slightly from age 37 to age 38 or declines slightly from age 57 to age 58 does not increase or decrease our lifetime wealth. We already expected these evolutionary wage changes to occur and they have already been incorporated in the calculation of lifetime wealth.

Suppose then that the wage falls as a worker nears retirement age, and consider the following question: Would the worker be better off by working a lot of hours at age 50 and consuming leisure in his sixties, or would the worker be better off by working relatively few hours at age 50 and devoting a great deal of time to his job in his sixties?

The worker will clearly find it worthwhile to work more hours at age 50, invest the money, and buy consumption goods and leisure at some point in the future when the wage is lower and leisure is not as expensive. After all, this type of labor supply decision would increase the worker's lifetime wealth; it gives him a much larger opportunity set than would be available if he were to work many hours in his sixties (when the wage is low) and consume many hours of leisure in his fifties (when the wage is high).

FIGURE 2-18   **The Life Cycle Path of Wages and Hours for a Typical Worker**

(*a*) The age-earnings profile of a typical worker rises rapidly when the worker is young, reaches a peak at around age 50, and then wages either stop growing or decline slightly. (*b*) The changing price of leisure over the life cycle implies that the worker will devote relatively more hours to the labor market when the wage is high and fewer hours when the wage is low.

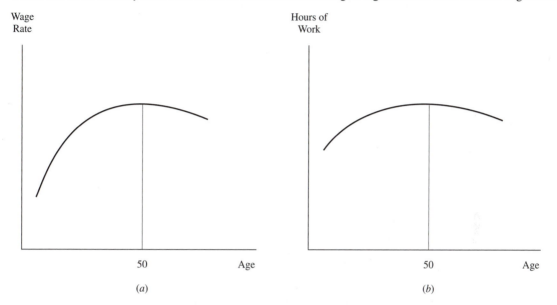

A very young worker faces the same type of situation. His wage is relatively low—and he will find it optimal to consume leisure activities when he is very young, rather than in his thirties and forties, when the price of those leisure activities will be very high. The argument, therefore, suggests that we will generally find it optimal to concentrate on work activities in those years when the wage is high and to concentrate on leisure activities in those years when the wage is low.[43]

In the end, this approach to life cycle labor supply decisions implies that hours of work and the wage rate should move together over time *for a particular worker,* as illustrated in Figure 2-18*b*. This implication differs strikingly from our earlier conclusion that a wage increase generates both income and substitution effects, and that there could be a negative relationship between wages and hours of work if income effects dominate. This important difference between the models (that is, the one-period "static" model considered in the previous sections and the life cycle model presented here) arises because the two models mean very different things by a change in the wage. In the one-period model, an increase in the wage expands the worker's opportunity set and hence creates an income effect that increases the demand for leisure. In the life cycle model, an evolutionary wage change—the wage change that workers expect as they age—does not change the total lifetime income available to a *particular* worker, and leaves the lifetime opportunity set intact.

[43] A detailed exposition of the model is given by James J. Heckman, "Life Cycle Consumption and Labor Supply: An Explanation of the Relationship between Income and Consumption over the Life Cycle," *American Economic Review* 64 (March 1974): 188–194.

FIGURE 2-19 **Hours of Work over the Life Cycle for Two Workers with Different Wage Paths**

Joe's wage exceeds Jack's at every age. Although both Joe and Jack work more hours when the wage is high, Joe works more hours than Jack only if the substitution effect dominates. If the income effect dominates, Joe works fewer hours than Jack.

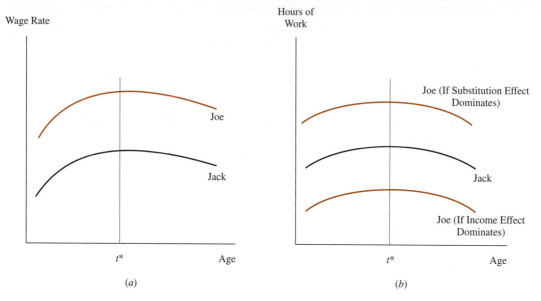

In contrast, if we were to compare two workers, say Joe and Jack, with different age-earnings profiles, the difference in hours of work between these two workers would be affected by both income and substitution effects. As illustrated in Figure 2-19a, Joe's wage exceeds Jack's at every age. Both Joe and Jack should work more hours when wages are high. Their life cycle profiles of hours of work are illustrated in Figure 2-19b. We do not know, however, which of the two workers allocates more hours to the labor market. In particular, even though Joe has a higher wage and finds leisure to be a very expensive commodity, he also has a higher lifetime income and will want to consume more leisure. The difference in the level of the two wage profiles, therefore, generates an income effect. If these income effects are sufficiently strong, Joe's hours-of-work profile will lie below Jack's; if substitution effects dominate, Joe will work more hours than Jack at every age.

The life cycle approach suggests a link not only between wages and hours of work, but also between wages and labor force participation rates. As we saw earlier in the chapter, the labor force participation decision depends on a comparison of the reservation wage to the market wage. In each year of the life cycle, therefore, the worker will compare the reservation wage to the market wage. Suppose initially that the reservation wage is roughly constant over time. The person is then more likely to enter the labor market in periods when the wage is high. As a result, participation rates are likely to be low for young workers, high for workers in their prime working years, and low again for older workers.

The participation decision, however, also depends on how reservation wages vary over the life cycle. The reservation wage measures the bribe required to enter the labor market. For instance, the presence of small children in the household increases the value of time in

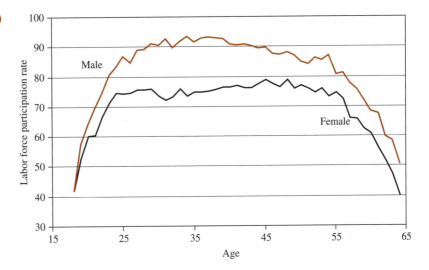

FIGURE 2-20

Labor Force Participation Rates over the Life Cycle, 2010

Source: U.S. Bureau of Labor Statistics, *Annual Demographic Supplement of the Current Population Surveys,* 2010.

the nonmarket sector for the person most responsible for child care and, hence, also would increase the reservation wage. Therefore, it is not surprising to find that some married women participate in the labor force intermittently. They work prior to the arrival of the first child, withdraw from the labor market when the children are small and need full-time care, and return to the labor market once the children enroll in school.

The key implication of the analysis can be easily summarized: A person will work few hours in those periods of the life cycle when the wage is low and will work many hours in those periods when the wage is high. The evidence on age-earnings profiles suggests that the wage is relatively low for young workers, increases as the worker matures and accumulates various types of skills, and then may decline slightly for older workers. The model then suggests that the profile of hours of work over the life cycle will have exactly the same shape as the age-earnings profile: hours of work increase as the wage rises and decline as the wage falls. The theoretical prediction that people allocate their time over the life cycle so as to take advantage of changes in the price of leisure is called the **intertemporal substitution hypothesis.**

Evidence

The available evidence suggests that both labor force participation rates and hours of work respond to evolutionary wage changes. Figure 2-20 illustrates the relationship between labor force participation rates and age in the United States. Male participation rates peak when men are between 25 and 45 years old and begin to decline noticeably after age 45. In contrast, female participation rates, probably because of the impact of child-raising activities on the participation decision, do not peak until women are around 45 years old.

Overall, the trends illustrated in the figure are consistent with the theoretical prediction that participation rates should be highest when the wage is high (that is, when workers are in their thirties and forties). The decline in labor force participation rates

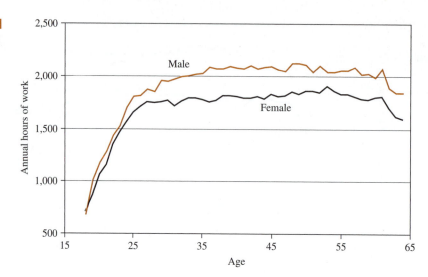

FIGURE 2-21
Hours of Work over the Life Cycle, 2010

Source: U.S. Bureau of Labor Statistics, *Annual Demographic Supplement of the Current Population Surveys,* 2010.

observed after age 55, however, is much too steep to be explained by the wage decline that is typically observed as workers near retirement age. The rapid decline in participation rates at older ages may be health related and, as we will see later in this chapter, also may be attributable to the work disincentive effects of various retirement and disability insurance programs.

Figure 2-21 illustrates the actual relationship between hours of work and age. As with participation rates, hours of work among working men rise rapidly until about age 30, peak at ages 35 to 45, and begin to decline at age 50. During the prime working years, men work about 2,100 hours annually. In contrast, hours of work among working women do not peak until age 50 (probably because some younger women work in part-time jobs while they have small children in the household).

Many studies have attempted to estimate the responsiveness of hours of work to changes in the wage over the life cycle.[44] These studies typically use a longitudinal sample of workers (that is, a data set where each person in the sample is followed over time) to estimate how a given worker adjusts his or her hours of work to the evolutionary wage changes that occur as the worker ages. The intertemporal substitution hypothesis implies that the correlation between changes in hours of work and changes in the wage should be positive: As a worker ages, an increase in the wage rate should increase hours of work.

---

[44] Thomas E. MaCurdy, "An Empirical Model of Labor Supply in a Life-Cycle Setting," *Journal of Political Economy* 89 (December 1981): 1059–1085. See also Joseph G. Altonji, "Intertemporal Substitution in Labor Supply: Evidence from Micro Data," *Journal of Political Economy* 94 (June 1986, Part 2): S176–S215; Joseph V. Hotz, Kinn Kydland, and Guilherme Sedlacek, "Intertemporal Preferences and Labor Supply," *Econometrica* 56 (March 1988): 335–360; and Casey Mulligan, "Substitution over Time: Another Look at Life Cycle Labor Supply," *NBER Macroeconomics Annual* 13 (1998): 75–134.

Taxi drivers in New York City typically pay a fixed fee to lease their cab for a prespecified period, such as a day or week. The driver is responsible for buying gas and for some of the car maintenance. As part of the leasing contract, the cabbie can keep whatever fare income he generates as he cruises the city streets. Every time he leases a cab, therefore, he faces an important labor supply decision: How long should he keep on looking for additional fares?

The work shift of a typical Manhattan cabbie surveyed in a recent study lasted 6.9 hours, of which only about 4.6 hours were actually spent driving a passenger. The rest of the time was spent cruising for a fare or taking a break. The total income during the shift was $161, so that the average hourly wage rate was around $23.

This average wage rate, however, probably masks a great deal of variation in the rewards to working an additional hour. The marginal wage rate probably depends greatly on the weather and on the time of the day and day of the week. For example, there may be many potential passengers on a rainy Friday afternoon, as New Yorkers leave their offices early to prepare for the weekend.

The theory of intertemporal labor substitution implies that the typical cabbie should be willing to work a longer shift when he expects the city streets to be busy and full of potential passengers and to take leisure on those hours and days that are expected to be slower. It is not surprising, therefore, that there are relatively few cabs cruising the streets at 2 a.m. on a Monday morning. In fact, a recent study shows that cabbies respond to the changed economic situations during the day and during the week in a way that is consistent with the theory: They drive a longer shift when the marginal wage rate is higher.

Sources: Henry S. Farber, "Is Tomorrow Another Day? The Labor Supply of New York City Cabdrivers," *Journal of Political Economy* 113 (February 2005): 46–82; and Colin Camerer, Linda Babcock, George Loewenstein, and Richard Thaler, "Labor Supply of New York City Cabdrivers: One Day at a Time," *Quarterly Journal of Economics* 112 (May 1997): 407–441.

The data illustrated in Figure 2-21 clearly indicate that hours of work increase early on in the life cycle and decline as retirement age approaches. The data, however, also reveal that hours of work are "sticky" over a long stretch of the working life. For example, annual hours worked by men barely budge between the ages of 35 and 50, despite the fact that the wage rises substantially during this period. Because hours of work tend to be sticky, many studies conclude that the response of hours of work to evolutionary wage changes is small: a 10 percent increase in the wage leads to less than a 1 percent increase in hours of work. Therefore, labor supply over the life cycle (as defined by hours of work per year) may not be very responsive to changes in the wage.[45]

Estimation of Life Cycle Models

The estimation of the intertemporal labor supply elasticity—the crucial parameter that determines how hours of work evolve in the life cycle model of the labor-leisure choice—helped introduce what has become a very useful econometric technique into the labor

---

[45] It is important to stress, however, that there is a lot of debate over the validity of this conclusion. The magnitude of the labor supply response to life cycle changes in the wage (called the *intertemporal elasticity of substitution*) has important implications in macroeconomics. Some macroeconomic models require sizable intertemporal elasticities to explain the behavior of employment over the business cycle. As a result, there is heated disagreement over the evidence suggesting that the intertemporal elasticity is small.

economics literature.[46] The economic model states that we should be tracking a specific individual over the lifetime so that we can observe how his hours of work change from year to year as a response to year-to-year wage changes. Suppose that we have a longitudinal data set that allows us to observe a particular worker i twice, say, at the ages of 40 and 41. Let H_{it} give his hours of work at age t, and w_{it} gives his wage rate at that age. It is easy to see that one can difference the data for each individual estimate the following regression model across the sample of different workers:

$$\Delta H_{it} = \sigma \Delta w_{it} + \text{Other variables} \qquad \textbf{(2-14)}$$

where ΔH_{it} gives the year-to-year change in hours of work and Δw_t gives the year-to-year change in the worker's wages. The coefficient σ would be related to the intertemporal labor supply elasticity because it measures the change in hours of work for a given person resulting from a particular change in his wage rate.

The statistically interesting part of the problem arises when one observes the same person for more than two periods. Suppose, for example, that we have a sample containing 1,000 workers and that each worker in our data is observed over a period of 20 years. Although one could imagine differencing the data a number of times, there exists a statistically easier procedure that effectively does the same thing. In particular, we would stack all the 20 observations for a particular worker across all workers. The new regression model, therefore, would have 20,000 observations. We would then estimate the following regression model on this stacked data set:

$$H_{it} = \sigma w_{it} + \alpha_1 F_1 + \alpha_2 F_2 + \ldots + \alpha_{1000} F_{1000} + \text{Other variables} \qquad \textbf{(2-15)}$$

where F_1 is a "dummy variable" set equal to one if that observations refers to person 1, and zero otherwise; F_2 is another dummy variable set equal to one if that observation refers to person 2, and zero otherwise; and so on. In effect, the regression model in equation (2-15) includes a dummy variable for each person in the data, and there would be 1,000 such dummy variables.

The set of dummy variables $(F_1, \ldots, F_{1000})$ are called **fixed effects,** because they indicate that hours of work for worker i, for whatever reasons, has a fixed factor that determines the person's hours of work on a permanent basis, even apart from year-to-year wage fluctuations. Put differently, the set of individual-specific fixed effects included in the regression model in equation (2-15) controls for any factors that are specific to persons and allows us to concentrate on measuring how wage changes affect changes in hours of work for a specific person. In fact, it can be shown that if each worker in our data were only observed twice, the method of including fixed effects in the regression model would be numerically identical to the common-sense differencing of all of the variables illustrated in equation (2-15).

---

[46] See Thomas E. MaCurdy, "An Empirical Model of Labor Supply in a Life-Cycle Setting," *Journal of Political Economy* 89 (December 1981): 1059–1085. See also Richard Blundell, Costas Meghir, and Pedro Neves, "Labour Supply and Intertemporal Substitution," *Journal of Econometrics* 59 (September 1993): 137–160; and David Card, "Intertemporal Labor Supply: An Assessment," in Christopher A. Sims, editor, *Advances in Econometrics: Sixth World Congress*, vol. II, Cambridge: Cambridge University Press, 1994, pp. 49–80.

The elasticities of intertemporal substitution estimated by the method of fixed effects tend to be positive, but numerically small. As noted above, many of the estimates suggest that the elasticity is around 0.1, indicating that a year-to-year wage increase of 10 percent would increase annual hours of work by only about 1 percent.

The statistical method of fixed effects has become a commonly used empirical technique in the toolkit of modern labor economics. It is easy to see why: There are obviously many person-specific factors that affect how many hours we work. Some of us are workaholics, and some of us would rather watch *Jersey Shore*. Our tastes for work are, to a large extent, fixed; they are a part of who we are. The individual-specific fixed effects help control for these idiosyncratic differences among workers and allow us to focus on what is most important in terms of the economic models: how changes in economic opportunities for a given worker affect the labor supply of that worker.

Labor Supply over the Business Cycle

Not only does labor supply respond to changes in economic opportunities over a worker's life cycle, but the worker also may adjust his labor supply to take advantage of changes in economic opportunities induced by business cycles. Do recessions motivate many persons to enter the labor market in order to "make up" the income of family members who have lost their jobs? Or do the unemployed give up hope of finding work in a depressed market and leave the labor force altogether?

The **added worker effect** provides one possible mechanism for a relation between the business cycle and the labor force participation rate. Under this hypothesis, so-called secondary workers who are currently out of the labor market (such as young persons or mothers with small children) are affected by the recession because the main breadwinner becomes unemployed or faces a wage cut. As a result, family income falls and the secondary workers get jobs to make up the loss. The added worker effect thus implies that the labor force participation rate of secondary workers has a countercyclical trend (that is, it moves in a direction opposite to the business cycle): it rises during recessions and falls during expansions.

The relationship between the business cycle and the labor force participation rate also can arise because of the **discouraged worker effect.** The discouraged worker effect argues that many unemployed workers find it almost impossible to find jobs during a recession and simply give up. Rather than incur the costs associated with fruitless job search activities, these workers decide to wait out the recession and drop out of the labor force. As a result of the discouraged worker effect, the labor force participation rate has a procyclical trend: it falls during recessions and increases during expansions.

Of course, the business cycle will generate both added workers and discouraged workers. The important question, therefore, is which effect dominates empirically. This question is typically addressed by correlating the labor force participation rate of a particular group with the aggregate unemployment rate, a summary measure of aggregate economic activity. If the added worker effect dominates, the correlation should be positive because the deterioration in economic conditions encourages more persons to enter the labor market. If the discouraged worker effect dominates, the correlation should be negative because the high level of unemployment in the economy convinces many workers to "give up" on their job searches and drop out of the labor market. There is overwhelming evidence that the correlation between the labor force participation rates of many groups and the aggregate unemployment rate is negative, so the discouraged worker effect dominates.[47]

Because the discouraged worker effect dominates the correlation between labor force participation and the business cycle, the official unemployment rate reported by the Bureau of Labor Statistics (BLS) might be too low. Recall that the BLS defines the unemployment rate as the ratio of persons who are unemployed to persons who are in the labor force (that is, the employed plus the unemployed). If an unemployed person becomes discouraged and leaves the labor force, he or she is no longer actively looking for work and, hence, will no longer be counted among the unemployed. As a result, the official unemployment rate may greatly understate the unemployment problem in the aggregate economy during severe recessions. However, the argument that the discouraged workers should be included in the unemployment statistics is open to question.[48] Some of these discouraged workers may be "taking advantage" of the relatively poor labor market conditions to engage in leisure activities.

As we saw earlier, the life cycle model of labor supply suggests that some workers choose to allocate time to the labor market during certain periods of the life cycle and to consume leisure during other periods. The real wage typically rises during expansions (when the demand for labor is high) and declines during recessions (when the demand for labor slackens). We would then expect the labor force participation rate to be high at the peak of economic activity and to decline as economic conditions worsen. The procyclical trend in the labor force participation rate then arises not because workers give up hope of finding jobs during recessions but because it is not worthwhile to work in those periods when the real wage is low. In an important sense, therefore, the so-called discouraged workers are doing precisely what the life cycle model of labor supply suggests that they should do: allocate their time optimally over the life cycle by consuming leisure when it is cheap to do so. As a result, the pool of hidden unemployed should not be part of the unemployment statistics. We will discuss the implications of this controversial hypothesis in more detail in Chapter 12.

Job Loss and the Added Worker Effect

It is worth emphasizing that the business cycle is not the only economic shock that can generate added worker and discouraged worker effects. A family's economic stability—and the distribution of labor supply within the household—also will be affected by any random events that create job instability for primary earners in the household, such as unforeseen plant closings and other types of job displacement.

---

[47] Jacob Mincer, "Labor Force Participation and Unemployment: A Review of Recent Evidence," in R. A. Gordon and M. S. Gordon, editors, *Prosperity and Unemployment,* New York: Wiley, 1966, pp. 73–112; and Shelly Lundberg, "The Added Worker Effect," *Journal of Labor Economics* 3 (January 1985): 11–37.

[48] This argument is developed at length in the influential article by Robert E. Lucas and Leonard Rapping, "Real Wages, Employment, and Inflation," *Journal of Political Economy* 77 (October 1969): 721–754.

Theory at Work
WEATHER AND LEISURE

Most of us look forward to days when we can take off some time from work and just relax. In an ideal world, on such days the weather would cooperate: It would be sunny and warm, and we would be totally free to enjoy our favorite activities, whether they be playing volleyball on the beach, sitting down in our backyard, or strolling down a shop-filled avenue.

Unfortunately, the weather does not always cooperate. As Mark Twain famously said, "Everybody talks about the weather, but nobody does anything about it." Well, it turns out that although our actions cannot affect the weather, we *can* react to the weather in our area and take actions that minimize the adverse impact that bad weather would have had on our planned leisure activities.

The life cycle version of the neoclassical labor-leisure model predicts that individuals work more in those periods when the rewards to working are the greatest. If the weather interferes with leisure activities—for example, making a day at the beach much less pleasant—then it would be optimal for a person to work more on that day and postpone the day at the beach until a day when the sun cooperates.

It turns out that working men do adjust their work-leisure activities in accordance with this very intuitive prediction of the life cycle model. Suppose a "rainy day"

occurs when there is precipitation of at least 0.1 inch in the local area. Holding other factors constant, including a person's education, age, and average weather patterns in the region of the country where the worker lives, a rainy day increases the time allocated to working activities by 29 minutes per day, while it reduces the time allocated to leisure activities by 25 minutes per day. In other words, the typical male worker will adjust his time over the working week to account for local weather fluctuations, working more on those days when the weather makes leisure activities less pleasant and consuming more leisure activities on those days when it is worth consuming.

Surprisingly, these very intuitive empirical patterns are not found among working women. One potential explanation of the gender difference may be that men are more likely to participate in sports activities during their leisure hours. But it is unclear if this conjecture accounts for the entire gender difference.

Sources: Marie Connolly, "Here Comes the Rain Again: Weather and the Intertemporal Substitution of Leisure," *Journal of labor Economics* 24 (January 2008): 73–100; see also Jorge Gonzalez-Chapela, "On the Price of Recreation Goods as a Determinant of Male Labor Supply," *Journal of Labor Economics* 25 (October 2007): 795–824.

Recent research shows that intra-household responses in labor supply play an important role in attenuating earnings losses caused by layoffs and plant closings. It is documented, for instance, that there is a sizable positive labor supply response by the wife to the husband's unexpected job loss, and that this supply increase can compensate for over 25 percent of the loss in family income.[49] Interestingly, the evidence also indicates that much of the potential increase in the wife's labor supply will be "crowded out" by the presence of the unemployment insurance system. In other words, the government-provided assistance to the unemployed husband greatly reduces the need for the wife to enter the labor market in response to the husband's job loss.

---

[49] Melvin Stephens, "Worker Displacement and the Added Worker Effect," *Journal of Labor Economics* 20 (July 2002): 504–537; see also Julie Berry Cullen and Jonathan Gruber, "Does Unemployment Insurance Crowd Out Spousal Labor Supply," *Journal of Labor Economics* 18 (July 2000): 546–572.

2-13 Policy Application: The Decline in Work Attachment among Older Workers

As noted earlier, there has been a marked drop in labor force participation among older men. It is hard to argue that the increasing propensity for early retirement is linked to the deteriorating health of this particular age group. After all, at the same time that their labor market attachment was weakening, the life expectancy of white men aged 50 rose from 22 to 29.2 years between 1939 and 2007.[50]

Part of the declining labor force participation of older workers may be attributable to an increase in pension benefits. The fraction of men who were covered by pension programs other than Social Security rose from 26 percent in 1950 to 66 percent in 1990. Not surprisingly, there is a strong link between the availability of private pension plans and the labor force participation of older men. For example, the probability that men aged 58 to 63 work falls by 18 percentage points if they have private pension plans.[51]

Many studies have attempted to determine if the increased generosity of the Social Security system is also partly responsible for the move toward early retirement. After accounting for inflation, Social Security benefits increased by about 20 percent during the early 1970s. Moreover, during the 1980s, a period when real wages fell for many workers, real Social Security benefits (which are indexed to the inflation rate) remained roughly constant. Despite the substantial increase in a worker's "Social Security wealth" (or the total value of the Social Security benefits that the worker can expect to receive over his lifetime), the available evidence does not strongly support the argument that increases in Social Security benefits explain a large part of the decline in the participation rates of older persons. In fact, the evidence suggests that at most 15 percent of the decline in participation rates of older workers can be attributed to the increase in Social Security retirement benefits.[52]

Some studies instead argue that an important part of the decline in the labor market attachment of older workers in the United States can be attributed to the work disincentives created by the Social Security Disability Program. In the United States, workers who become disabled are eligible to receive disability payments for as long as the disability lasts. The monthly disability benefit equals the Social Security retirement benefits that the worker would have received had he or she continued working until age 65, *regardless of the worker's age at the time the disability occurred.*

[50] U.S. Bureau of the Census, *Statistical Abstract of the United States,* Washington, DC: Government Printing Office, various issues.

[51] Alan Gustman and Thomas Steinmeier, "Partial Retirement and the Analysis of Retirement Behavior," *Industrial and Labor Relations Review* 37 (April 1984): 403–415; and Edward P. Lazear, "Pensions as Severance Pay," in Zvi Bodie and John Shoven, editors, *Financial Aspects of the United States Pension System,* Chicago: University of Chicago Press, 1983.

[52] Alan B. Krueger and Jörn-Steffen Pischke, "The Effect of Social Security on Labor Supply: A Cohort Analysis of the Notch Generation," *Journal of Labor Economics* 10 (October 1992): 412–437. See also Gary Burtless, "Social Security, Unanticipated Benefit Increases, and the Timing of Retirement," *Review of Economic Studies* 53 (October 1986): 781–805.

Theory at Work

THE NOTCH BABIES

Audrey was born in March 1916 and her sister Edith was born in June 1917. They both began working at the same book bindery in southern California in October 1957. They both worked continuously at this firm and received the same pay until they retired. When the younger sister Edith turned 65, both Edith and Audrey went to the Social Security office to claim their benefits. Because Audrey had worked for about 18 months past her 65th birthday, she expected to receive slightly higher benefits. It turned out, however, that Audrey received $624.40 per month, whereas Edith received only $512.60 per month.

This real-life example illustrates the decline in economic opportunities experienced by the so-called notch babies, the cohort of persons born between 1917 and 1921, in their retirement years. Because of a 1977 legislative change in the formulas used to calculate Social Security benefits, the notch cohort received substantially lower benefits than earlier cohorts. As the experience of Audrey and Edith illustrates, a worker born in 1917 can receive about 20 percent less Social Security income than a worker born in 1916 with essentially the same job and earnings history.

The hypothesis that an increase in Social Security benefits reduces labor force participation rates must imply that a substantial decrease in benefits (like the one experienced by the notch babies) should increase labor force participation rates. It turns out, however, that the labor force participation rate of the notch babies is not markedly higher than the participation rate of other birth cohorts. The "natural experiment" arising from the legislative creation of the notch babies, therefore, suggests that increases in Social Security wealth can only explain a minor part of the decline in the labor force participation rates of older workers.

Sources: Alan B. Krueger and Jörn-Steffen Pischke, "The Effect of Social Security on Labor Supply: A Cohort Analysis of the Notch Generation," *Journal of Labor Economics* 10 (October 1992): 412–437.

Many workers would like to claim that they are disabled in order to enjoy the leisure activities associated with early retirement. As a result, the eligibility requirements for the disability program are harsh and strictly enforced. Workers applying for disability benefits must often be certified as being disabled by government-picked physicians; there is a waiting period of five months before the worker can apply for disability benefits; and the worker cannot be employed in "gainful activities" (defined as a job where the worker earns more than $500 per month).

There is heated disagreement over whether the disability program has contributed to the decline in the labor force participation of older workers. Some studies have claimed that practically the entire decline in labor force participation rates among men aged 55 to 64 can be attributed to the disability program.[53] Other researchers, however, cast doubt

[53] Donald Parsons, "The Decline in Male Labor Force Participation," *Journal of Political Economy* 88 (February 1980): 117–134. See also John Bound and Timothy Waidmann, "Disability Transfers, Self-Reported Health, and the Labor Force Attachment of Older Men: Evidence from the Historical Record," *Quarterly Journal of Economics* 107 (November 1992): 1393–1420; David H. Autor and Mark G. Duggan, "The Rise in the Disability Rolls and the Decline in Unemployment," *Quarterly Journal of Economics* 118 (February 2003): 157–205; and Dan Black, Kermit Daniel, and Seth Sanders, "The Impact of Economic Conditions on Participation in Disability Programs: Evidence from the Coal Boom and Bust," *American Economic Review* 92 (March 2002): 27–50.

on these findings. One recent study, for example, examined the labor supply decisions of the disability applicants who are rejected by the government.[54] Because of the strict eligibility requirements, the government rejects nearly half of the claims. If these rejected claims were mainly attempts by workers to misuse the program, one might expect that the rejected workers would return to the labor force once they learned that they cannot "get away" with this early retirement strategy. It turns out, however, that fewer than half of the rejected applicants go back to work after the final (and adverse) determination of their case. This result has been interpreted as indicating that the men who receive disability benefits would not have been in the labor force even in the absence of such a program.

Despite these criticisms, there remains a strong suspicion that the disability program has much to do with the increase in early retirement. Perhaps the most convincing evidence is provided by a recent study of the Canadian experience.[55] In the United States, the disability program is a federal program, which implies that eligibility and benefit levels are the same throughout the entire country. In Canada, there are two programs: the Quebec Pension Program (QPP) covers only persons residing in Quebec and the Canada Pension Program (CPP) covers persons residing in the rest of Canada. Although these two systems are similar in many ways, benefits in the QPP rose faster in the 1970s and 1980s. By 1986, the QPP was substantially more generous than the CPP. In January 1987, the CPP raised its benefit levels to bring the two programs to parity.

Table 2-6 provides a difference-in-differences analysis of the impact of this change in benefit levels on the labor supply of the affected population. The top rows of the table show that benefit levels in the rest of Canada increased by $2,642 (Canadian dollars) between

TABLE 2-6 **The Impact of Disability Benefits on Labor Supply in Canada**

Source: Jonathan Gruber, "Disability Insurance Benefits and Labor Supply," *Journal of Political Economy* 108 (December 2000): 1175.

	Before	After	Difference	Difference-in-Differences
Annual benefits:				
Canada Pension Program	$5,134	$7,776	$2,642	$1,666
Quebec Pension Program	6,876	7,852	976	
Percent of men aged 45–59 not employed last week:				
Treatment group: CPP	20.0%	21.7%	1.7%	2.7%
Control group: QPP	25.6	24.6	−1.0	

[54] John Bound, "The Health and Earnings of Rejected Disability Insurance Applicants," *American Economic Review* 79 (June 1989): 482–503.

[55] Jonathan Gruber, "Disability Insurance Benefits and Labor Supply," *Journal of Political Economy* 108 (December 2000): 1162–1183.

1986 and 1987, as compared to only an increase of $976 in Quebec. As a result of the policy shift, the average disability benefit in the rest of Canada increased by $1,666 more than the increase experienced by persons residing in Quebec.

The bottom rows of the table document how this increased generosity affected labor supply. The fraction of men aged 45–59 who did not work fell from 25.6 to 24.6 in Quebec (a decrease of 1.0 percentage point), likely reflecting changes in aggregate economic activity over the period. In contrast, the proportion of comparable men residing outside Quebec who did not work *rose* from 20.0 to 21.7 percent, an increase of 1.7 percentage points. The difference-in-differences estimator (or $1.7 - (-1.0)$) implies that the increased generosity of the disability program increased the proportion of men who did not work by 2.7 percentage points. It seems, therefore, that generous disability benefits do indeed reduce the labor supply of men nearing retirement age.

The Social Security Earnings Test

Many workers who consider themselves retired continue to work, perhaps in a part-time job. In the United States, for example, nearly 20 percent of "retired" persons also hold a job.

Until 2000, the Social Security system had a provision, known as the **Social Security earnings test,** that presumably discouraged Social Security recipients from working. In the year 2000, for example, retirees between the ages of 65 and 69 who received Social Security benefits could have earned up to $17,000 per year without affecting their retirement benefits.[56] If earnings exceeded this threshold, the government reduced the size of the Social Security benefit. In particular, $1 of Social Security benefits was withheld for every $3 earned *above* the exempt amount, so that workers who earned more than $17,000 implicitly faced a 33 percent tax rate. The earnings test did not apply to workers who were 70 or older. In 2000, the earnings test was eliminated and retired workers are now free to work and collect Social Security benefits without any penalty on their benefits.

It was often claimed that the earnings test discouraged retirees from participating in the labor force. It turns out, however, that these claims were not justified. Figure 2-22 shows how the earnings test could affect work incentives. Suppose that the retiree receives $10,000 in Social Security benefits per year (and that he does not have any other nonlabor income). Let us now construct the budget line facing this worker under the Social Security system in effect in the year 2000. The endowment point E in the figure indicates that if the retiree does not work, he could purchase $10,000 worth of goods. If the retiree works a few hours (at a wage of w dollars), he can increase the value of his consumption bundle, as illustrated by the segment FE of the budget line.

At point F in the figure, the retiree earns the maximum allowed by the Social Security Administration before Social Security benefits are reduced, so he can consume $27,000 worth of goods (the $10,000 Social Security benefits plus $17,000 in labor earnings). If the retiree keeps on working, however, the marginal wage rate is no longer w, but $w(1 - 0.33)$,

[56] See Leora Friedberg, "The Labor Supply Effects of the Social Security Earnings Test," *Review of Economics and Statistics* 82 (February 2000): 48–63; and Steven J. Haider and David S. Loughran, "The Effect of the Social Security Earnings Test on Male Labor Supply: New Evidence from Survey and Administrative Data," *Journal of Human Resources* 43 (Winter 2008): 57–87.

FIGURE 2-22   **The Impact of the Social Security Earnings Test on Hours of Work**

The Social Security earnings test (which taxes retirees when they earn more than $17,000 per year) generates the budget "line" *HGFE*. The repeal of the earnings test moves retirees to budget line *H'E*. The first retiree (worker 1) would not change his hours of work; the second retiree would reduce his hours; and the third retiree might increase or decrease his hours, depending on whether substitution or income effects dominate.

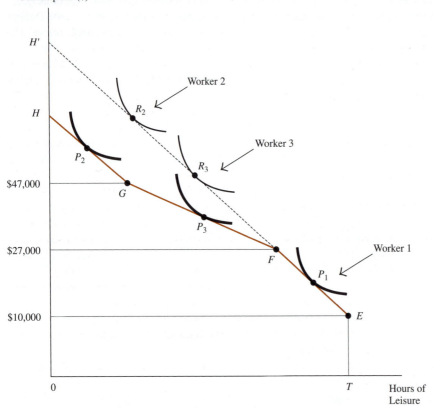

flattening out the budget line, and generating segment *FG*. Finally, if the retiree earns more than $47,000, the retiree forfeits his entire Social Security benefits, and the slope of the budget line reverts back to its original slope.[57] The earnings test thus generates the budget "line" *HGFE* in Figure 2-22.

It is of interest to ask if the elimination of the earnings test would increase the labor supply of older workers. The elimination of the test would allow the retiree to face budget line *H'E,* instead of *HGFE*. As is evident in Figure 2-22, there are three potential effects of the

[57] The first $17,000 of earnings for this retiree is exempt from the Social Security tax, so that only $30,000 of wage income is subject to the tax. Because Social Security benefits are reduced by $1 for every $3 of taxable income, the entire Social Security benefit of a worker who earns $47,000 is taxed away. The consumption basket available to this worker is illustrated by point G in Figure 2-22. He has $47,000 available for consumption (or $10,000 in Social Security benefits + $47,000 in wage income − $10,000 in Social Security taxes).

earnings test on work incentives. The first worker (worker 1 in the figure) has indifference curves that place him at point P_1, where he works very few hours, regardless of whether there is an earnings test. Obviously, this retiree will not be affected by the elimination of the earnings test. The second worker's indifference curves place him at point P_2, indicating strong "tastes for work." This person allocates many hours to the labor market even though it means he has to forfeit his Social Security benefits. Interestingly, removing the earnings test for this worker is equivalent to an increase in the person's wealth, moving the worker from point P_2 to point R_2. This income effect induces the retiree to consume more leisure hours, thus *reducing* work hours.

Finally, the third worker is a retiree who works a "medium" number of hours. This person has not entirely forfeited his Social Security benefits and faces a 33 percent tax rate on labor earnings. The repeal of the earnings test moves this worker from point P_3 to point R_3. In other words, this worker effectively gets a wage increase when the earnings test is repealed. As such, the worker will experience both an income and a substitution effect. The income effect will motivate the worker to consume more leisure and work fewer hours; the substitution effect induces the worker to consume fewer leisure hours and work more hours. As drawn, the substitution effect dominates.

Overall, the theory suggests that the elimination of the Social Security earnings test is unlikely to substantially increase labor supply among retirees. A few studies have examined the labor supply consequences of repealing the earnings test. The evidence confirms the theoretical expectation: the labor supply effects of the repeal tended to be small.[58]

Summary

- The reservation wage is the wage that makes a person indifferent between working and not working. A person enters the labor market when the market wage rate exceeds the reservation wage.

- Utility-maximizing workers allocate their time so that the last dollar spent on leisure activities yields the same utility as the last dollar spent on goods.

- An increase in nonlabor income reduces hours of work of workers.

- An increase in the wage generates both an income and a substitution effect among persons who work. The income effect reduces hours of work; the substitution effect increases hours of work. The labor supply curve, therefore, is upward sloping if substitution effects dominate and downward sloping if income effects dominate.

- An increase in nonlabor income reduces the likelihood that a person enters the labor force. An increase in the wage increases the likelihood that a person enters the labor force.

- The labor supply elasticity is on the order of -0.1 for men and $+0.2$ for women.

- Welfare programs create work disincentives because they provide cash grants to participants as well as tax those recipients who enter the labor market. In contrast, credits on earned income create work incentives and draw many nonworkers into the labor force.

[58] Jae G. Song and Joyce Manchester, "New Evidence on Earnings and Benefit Claims Following Changes in the Retirement Earnings Test in 2000," *Journal of Public Economics* 91 (April 2007): 669–700.

Key Concepts

added worker effect, 71	indifference curve, 27	marginal utility, 29
budget constraint, 32	intertemporal substitution	neoclassical model of
budget line, 32	hypothesis, 67	labor-leisure choice, 27
discouraged worker	labor force, 22	opportunity set, 32
effect, 71	labor force participation	reservation wage, 41
difference-in-differences	rate, 22	Social Security earnings
estimator, 63	labor supply curve, 42	test, 77
employment rate, 23	labor supply elasticity, 44	substitution effect, 39
fixed effects, 70	marginal rate of	unemployment rate, 23
hidden unemployed, 23	substitution (MRS) in	utility function, 27
income effect, 35	consumption, 30	

Review Questions

1. What happens to the reservation wage if nonlabor income increases, and why?
2. What economic factors determine whether a person participates in the labor force?
3. How does a typical worker decide how many hours to allocate to the labor market?
4. What happens to hours of work when nonlabor income decreases?
5. What happens to hours of work when the wage rate falls? Decompose the change in hours of work into income and substitution effects.
6. What happens to the probability that a particular person works when the wage rises? Does such a wage increase generate an income effect?
7. Why do welfare programs create work disincentives?
8. Why does the earned income tax credit increase the labor force participation rate of targeted groups?
9. Why have average hours worked per week declined?
10. Why did the labor force participation rate of women increase so much in the past century?
11. Why does a worker allocate his or her time over the life cycle so as to work more hours in those periods when the wage is highest? Why does the worker not experience an income effect during those periods?
12. What is the added worker effect? What is the discouraged worker effect?
13. What factors account for the secular decline in labor force participation rates among older workers in the United States?

Problems

2-1. How many hours will a person allocate to leisure activities if her indifference curves between consumption and goods are concave to the origin?

2-2. What is the effect of an increase in the price of market goods on a worker's reservation wage, probability of entering the labor force, and hours of work?

2-3. Tom earns $15 per hour for up to 40 hours of work each week. He is paid $30 per hour for every hour in excess of 40. Tom faces a 20 percent tax rate and pays $4 per hour in child care expenses for each hour he works. Tom receives $80 in child support payments each week. There are 168 hours in the week. Graph Tom's weekly budget line.

2-4. Cindy gains utility from consumption C and leisure L. The most leisure she can consume in any given week is 168 hours. Her utility function is $U(C, L) = C \times L$. This functional form implies that Cindy's marginal rate of substitution is C/L. Cindy receives $630 each week from her great-grandmother—regardless of how much Cindy works. What is Cindy's reservation wage?

2-5. You can either take a bus or drive your car to work. A bus pass costs $5 per week, whereas driving your car to work costs $60 weekly (parking, tolls, gas, etc.). You spend half an hour less on a one-way trip in your car than on a bus. How would you prefer to travel to work if your wage rate is $10 per hour? Will you change your preferred mode of transportation if your wage rate rises to $20 per hour? Assume you work five days a week and time spent riding on a bus or driving a car does not directly enter your utility.

2-6. Shelly's preferences for consumption and leisure can be expressed as

$$U(C, L) = (C - 200) \times (L - 80)$$

This utility function implies that Shelly's marginal utility of leisure is $C - 200$ and her marginal utility of consumption is $L - 80$. There are 168 hours in the week available to split between work and leisure. Shelly earns $5 per hour after taxes. She also receives $320 worth of welfare benefits each week regardless of how much she works.

a. Graph Shelly's budget line.

b. What is Shelly's marginal rate of substitution when L = 100 and she is on her budget line?

c. What is Shelly's reservation wage?

d. Find Shelly's optimal amount of consumption and leisure.

2-7. Explain why a lump-sum government transfer can entice some workers to stop working (and entices no one to start working) while the earned income tax credit can entice some people who otherwise would not work to start working (and entices no one to stop working).

2-8. In 1999, 4,860 TANF recipients were asked how many hours they worked in the previous week. In 2000, 4,392 of these recipients were again subject to the same TANF rules and were again asked their hours of work during the previous week. The remaining 468 individuals were randomly assigned to a "Negative Income Tax" (NIT) experiment that gave out financial incentives for welfare recipients to work and subjected them to its rules. Like the other group, they were asked about their hours of work during the previous week. The data from the experiment are contained in the table below.

a. What effect did the NIT experiment have on the employment rate of public assistance recipients? Develop a standard difference-in-differences table to support your answer.

b. What effect did the NIT experiment have on the weekly hours worked of public assistance recipients who worked positive hours during the survey week? Develop a standard difference-in-differences table to support your answer.

	Total Number of Recipients	Number of Recipients Who Worked at Some Time in the Survey Week		Total Hours of Work by All Recipients in the Survey Week	
		1999	2000	1999	2000
TANF	4,392	1,217	1,568	15,578	20,698
NIT	468	131	213	1,638	2,535
Total	4,860	1,348	1,781	17,216	23,233

2-9. Consider two workers with identical preferences, Phil and Bill. Both workers have the same life cycle wage path in that they face the same wage at every age, and they know what their future wages will be. Leisure and consumption are both normal goods.

    a. Compare the life cycle path of hours of work between the two workers if Bill receives a one-time, unexpected inheritance at the age of 35.

    b. Compare the life cycle path of hours of work between the two workers if Bill had always known he would receive (and, in fact, does receive) a one-time inheritance at the age of 35.

2-10. Under current law, most Social Security recipients do not pay federal or state income taxes on their Social Security benefits. Suppose the government proposes to tax these benefits at the same rate as other types of income. What is the impact of the proposed tax on the optimal retirement age?

2-11. A worker plans to retire at the age of 65, at which time he will start collecting his retirement benefits. Then there is a sudden change in the forecast of inflation when the worker is 63 years old. In particular, inflation is now predicted to be higher than it had been expected so that the average price level of market goods and wages is now expected to be higher. What effect does this announcement have on the person's preferred retirement age

    a. If retirement benefits are fully adjusted for inflation?

    b. If retirement benefits are not fully adjusted for inflation?

2-12. Presently, there is a minimum and maximum social security benefit paid to retirees. Between these two bounds, a retiree's benefit level depends on how much she contributed to the system over her work life. Suppose Social Security was changed so that everyone aged 65 or older was paid $12,000 per year regardless of how much she earned over her working life or whether she continued to work after the age of 65. How would this likely affect hours worked of retirees?

2-13. Over the last 100 years, real household income and standards of living have increased substantially in the United States. At the same time, the total fertility rate, the average number of children born to a woman during her lifetime, has fallen in the United States from about three children per woman in the early twentieth century to about two children per woman in the early twenty-first century. Does this suggest that children are inferior goods?

2-14. Consider a person who can work up to 80 hours each week at a pretax wage of $20 per hour but faces a constant 20 percent payroll tax. Under these conditions, the worker maximizes her utility by choosing to work 50 hours each week. The government proposes a negative income tax whereby everyone is given $300 each week and anyone can supplement her income further by working. To pay for the negative income tax, the payroll tax rate will be increased to 50 percent.

    a. On a single graph, draw the worker's original budget line and her budget line under the negative income tax.

    b. Show that the worker will choose to work fewer hours if the negative income tax is adopted.

    c. Will the worker's utility be greater under the negative income tax?

2-15. The absolute value of the slope of the consumption-leisure budget line is the after-tax wage, *w*. Suppose some workers earn *w* for up to 40 hours of work each week and then earn 2*w* for any hours worked thereafter (called overtime). Other workers may earn *w* for up to 40 hours of work each week and then only earn 0.5*w* thereafter as working more than 40 hours requires getting a second job, which pays an hourly wage less than their primary job. Both types of workers experience a "kink" in their consumption-leisure budget line.

    a. Graph in general terms the budget line for each type of worker.

    b. Which type of worker is likely to work up to the point of the kink, and which type of worker is likely to choose a consumption-leisure bundle far away from the kink?

Selected Readings

David H. Autor and Mark G. Duggan, "The Rise in the Disability Rolls and the Decline in Unemployment," *Quarterly Journal of Economics* 118 (February 2003): 157–205.

Gary S. Becker, "A Theory of the Allocation of Time," *Economic Journal* 75 (September 1965): 493–517.

Stacy Dickert-Conlin and Amitabh Chandra, "Taxes and the Timing of Births," *Journal of Political Economy* 107 (February 1999): 161–177.

Nada Eissa and Jeffrey B. Liebman, "Labor Supply Response to the Earned Income Tax Credit," *Quarterly Journal of Economics* 111 (May 1996): 605–637.

Jeffrey Grogger and Charles Michalopoulos, "Welfare Dynamics under Time Limits," *Journal of Political Economy* 111 (June 2003): 530–554.

James J. Heckman, "Life Cycle Consumption and Labor Supply: An Explanation of the Relationship between Income and Consumption over the Life Cycle," *American Economic Review* 64 (March 1974): 188–194.

James J. Heckman, "Sample Selection Bias as a Specification Error with an Application to the Estimation of Labor Supply Functions," in James P. Smith, editor, *Female Labor Supply: Theory and Estimation.* Princeton, NJ: Princeton University Press, 1980, pp. 206–248.

Thomas E. MaCurdy, "An Empirical Model of Labor Supply in a Life-Cycle Setting," *Journal of Political Economy* 89 (December 1981): 1059–1085.

Jacob Mincer, "Labor Force Participation of Married Women," in H. Gregg Lewis, editor, *Aspects of Labor Economics.* Princeton, NJ: Princeton University Press, 1962, pp. 63–97.

Robert A. Moffitt, "Welfare Programs and Labor Supply," in Alan J. Auerbach and Martin Feldstein, editors, *Handbook of Public Economics,* vol. 4. Amsterdam: Elsevier, 2006.

Web Links

The Bureau of Labor Statistcs publishes a detailed description of how it defines and measures the concepts of labor force and unemployment: stats.bls.gov/cps/cps_htgm.htm.

The Social Security Administration publishes many documents that provide not only a detailed description of the system, but also such facts as the most popular names given to babies born in a particular calendar year and a calculator that predicts Social Security benefits for a particular worker: www.ssa.gov/.

Chapter 3

Labor Demand

The laborer is worthy of his hire.

—*The Gospel of St. Luke*

The last chapter analyzed the factors that determine how many workers choose to enter the labor market and how many hours those workers are willing to rent to employers. Labor market outcomes, however, depend not only on the willingness of workers to supply their time to work activities, but also on the willingness of firms to hire those workers. We now turn, therefore, to a discussion of the demand side of the labor market.

The hiring and firing decisions made by firms create and destroy many jobs at any time. During a typical year in the 1980s, for instance, nearly 9 percent of jobs in the U.S. manufacturing industry were newly created and 11 percent of existing jobs vanished. Our analysis of labor demand begins by recognizing that firms do not hire workers simply because employers want to see "bodies" filling in various positions in the firm. Rather, firms hire workers because consumers want to purchase a variety of goods and services. In effect, firms are the middlemen that hire workers to produce those goods and services. The firm's labor demand—just like the firm's demand for other inputs in the production process such as land, buildings, and machines—is a "derived demand," derived from the wants and desires of consumers.

Despite the apparent similarity between the factors that determine the firm's demand for labor and the firm's demand for other inputs in the production process, economists devote a great deal of their time to the separate study of labor demand. After all, workers *do* differ from other inputs in a number of important ways. All of us are keenly interested in the characteristics of the firms that rent our services for eight hours a day. Some firms provide working conditions and social opportunities that are quite amenable, whereas working conditions in other firms may be appalling. The determinants of the demand for labor also have important social and political implications. In fact, many of the central questions in economic policy involve the number of workers that firms employ and the wage that they offer those workers. Such diverse policies as minimum wages, employment subsidies, and restrictions on an employer's ability to fire or lay off workers are attempts to regulate various aspects of the firm's labor demand.

3-1   The Production Function

We begin the study of labor demand by specifying the firm's **production function.** The production function describes the technology that the firm uses to produce goods and services. For simplicity, we initially assume that there are only two factors of production (that is, two inputs in the production process): the number of employee-hours hired by the firm (E) and capital (K), the aggregate stock of land, machines, and other physical inputs. We write the production function as

$$q = f(E, K) \qquad \textbf{(3-1)}$$

where q is the firm's output. The production function specifies how much output is produced by any combination of labor and capital.

The definition of the labor input makes two assumptions that are very restrictive. First, the number of employee-hours E is given by the product of the number of workers hired times the average number of hours worked per person. By focusing on the product E, rather than on its two separate components, we are assuming that the firm gets the same output when it hires 10 workers for an eight-hour day as when it hires 20 workers for a four-hour shift. To simplify the presentation, we will ignore the distinction between the number of workers hired and the number of hours worked throughout much of this chapter, and we will simply refer to the labor input E as the number of workers hired by the firm.

Second, the production function assumes that different types of workers can somehow be aggregated into a single input that we call "labor." In fact, workers are very heterogeneous. Some workers are college graduates, while others are high school dropouts; some have a lot of labor market experience, whereas others are new entrants. In short, some workers probably make a much larger contribution to the firm's output than other workers.

We will see, however, that it is useful to first derive the firm's labor demand by ignoring these complications. The simpler model provides a solid understanding of how firms make their hiring decisions. Later in the chapter we build upon this foundation to allow for a more general specification of the production technology.

Marginal Product and Average Product

The most important concept associated with the firm's production function is that of marginal product. The **marginal product of labor** (which we denote by MP_E) is defined as the change in output resulting from hiring an additional worker, holding constant the quantities of all other inputs. Similarly, the **marginal product of capital** (or MP_K) is defined as the change in output resulting from a one-unit increase in the capital stock, holding constant the quantities of all other inputs. We assume that the marginal products of both labor and capital are positive numbers, so that hiring either more workers or more capital leads to more output.

It is easy to understand how we calculate the marginal product of labor by using a numerical example. Table 3-1 summarizes the firm's production when it hires different numbers of workers, *holding capital constant.* If the firm hires one worker, it produces 11 units of output. The marginal product of the first worker hired, therefore, is 11 units. If the firm hires two workers, production rises to 27 units of output, and the marginal product of the second worker is 16 units.

TABLE 3-1 Calculating the Marginal and Average Product of Labor (Holding Capital Constant)

Number of Workers Employed	Output (Units)	Marginal Product (Units)	Average Product (Units)	Value of Marginal Product ($)	Value of Average Product ($)
0	0	—	—	—	—
1	11	11	11.0	22	22.0
2	27	16	13.5	32	27.0
3	47	20	15.7	40	31.3
4	66	19	16.5	38	33.0
5	83	17	16.6	34	33.2
6	98	15	16.3	30	32.7
7	111	13	15.9	26	31.7
8	122	11	15.3	22	30.5
9	131	9	14.6	18	29.1
10	138	7	13.8	14	27.6

Note: The calculations for the value of marginal product and the value of average product assume that the price of the output is $2.

Figure 3-1 graphs the data in our example to illustrate the assumptions that are typically made about the shape of the production function. Figure 3-1a shows the total product curve. This curve describes what happens to output as the firm hires more workers. The total product curve is obviously upward sloping.

FIGURE 3-1   The Total Product, the Marginal Product, and the Average Product Curves
(a) The total product curve gives the relationship between output and the number of workers hired by the firm (holding capital fixed). (b) The marginal product curve gives the output produced by each additional worker, and the average product curve gives the output per worker.

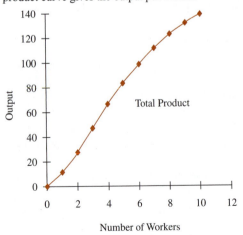

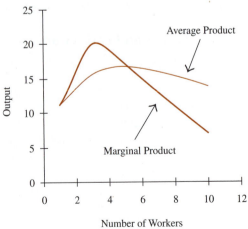

(a)   (b)

The marginal product of labor is the slope of the total product curve—that is, the rate of change in output as more workers are hired. The shape of the total product curve, therefore, has important implications for the marginal product curve, which is illustrated in Figure 3-1*b*. In our numerical example, output first rises at an increasing rate as more workers are hired. This implies that the marginal product of labor is rising, perhaps because of the initial gains resulting from assigning workers to specific tasks. Eventually, output increases at a decreasing rate. In other words, the marginal product of labor begins to decline, so that the next worker hired adds less to the firm's output than a previously hired worker. In our example, the marginal product of the third worker hired is 20 units, but the marginal product of the fourth worker is 19 units, and that of the fifth worker declines further to 17 units.

The assumption that the marginal product of labor eventually declines follows from the **law of diminishing returns.** Recall that the marginal product of labor is defined in terms of a *fixed* level of capital. The first few workers hired may increase output substantially because the workers can specialize in narrowly defined tasks. As more and more workers are added to a fixed capital stock (that is, to a fixed number of machines and a fixed amount of land), the gains from specialization decline and the marginal product of workers declines. We will assume that the law of diminishing returns operates over some range of employment. In fact, we will see that unless the firm eventually encounters diminishing returns, it will want to expand its employment indefinitely.

We define the **average product** of labor (or AP_E) as the amount of output produced by the typical worker. This quantity is defined by $AP_E = q/E$. In our numerical example, the firm produces 66 units of output when it hires four workers, so the average product is 16.5 units. Figure 3-1*b* illustrates the relationship between the marginal product and the average product curves. An easy-to-remember rule describing the geometric relationship between these two curves is: *the marginal curve lies above the average curve when the average curve is rising, and the marginal curve lies below the average curve when the average curve is falling.* This implies that the marginal curve intersects the average curve at the point where the average curve peaks (which happens at five workers in our example). It should be clear that the assumption of diminishing returns also implies that the average product of labor curve will eventually decline.

Profit Maximization

To analyze the hiring decisions made by the firm, we make an assumption about the firm's behavior. In particular, the firm's objective is to maximize its profits. The firm's profits are given by

$$\text{Profits} = pq - wE - rK \qquad (3\text{-}2)$$

where p is the price at which the firm can sell its output, w is the wage rate (that is, the cost of hiring an additional worker), and r is the price of capital.

In this chapter, we assume that the firm is a small player in the industry. As a result, the price of the output p is unaffected by how much output this particular firm produces and sells, and the prices of labor (w) and capital (r) are also unaffected by how much labor and capital the firm hires. From the firm's point of view, therefore, all of these prices are constants, beyond its control. A firm that cannot influence prices is said to be a **perfectly competitive firm.** Because a perfectly competitive firm cannot influence prices, such a firm maximizes profits by hiring the "right" amount of labor and capital.

3-2 The Employment Decision in the Short Run

Define the *short run* as a time span that is sufficiently brief that the firm cannot increase or reduce the size of its plant or purchase or sell physical equipment. In the short run, therefore, the firm's capital stock is fixed at some level K_0.

The firm can then determine the additional output produced by each worker by reading the numbers off the marginal product curve. For example, Figure 3-1 indicates that the eighth worker hired increases the firm's output by 11 units. To obtain the dollar value of what each additional worker produces, we can multiply the marginal product of labor times the price of the output. This quantity is called the **value of marginal product** of labor and is given by

$$VMP_E = p \times MP_E \qquad\qquad (3\text{-}3)$$

The value of marginal product of labor is the dollar increase in revenue generated by an additional worker—holding capital constant. Suppose the price of the output equals $2. The eighth worker hired would then contribute $22 to the firm's revenue.

The value of marginal product curve is illustrated in Figure 3-2 (and the underlying data are reported in Table 3-1). Because the value of marginal product equals the marginal product of labor times the (constant) price of the output, the value of marginal product curve is simply a "blown-up" version of the marginal product curve. The law of diminishing returns then implies that the dollar gains from hiring additional workers eventually decline.

We define the **value of average product** of labor as

$$VAP_E = p \times AP_E \qquad\qquad (3\text{-}4)$$

The value of average product gives the dollar value of output per worker. Because both the value of marginal product and the value of average product curves are blown-up versions

FIGURE 3-2 The Firm's Hiring Decision in the Short Run

A profit-maximizing firm hires workers up to the point where the wage rate equals the value of marginal product of labor. If the wage is $22, the firm hires eight workers.

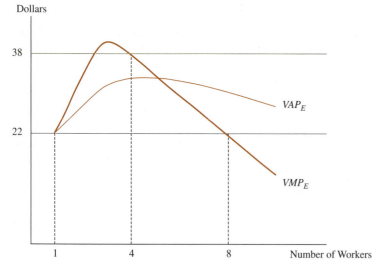

of the underlying marginal product and average product curves, the geometric relationship between the marginal and average curves in Figure 3-2 is identical to the relationship we discussed earlier.

How Many Workers Should the Firm Hire?

The competitive firm can hire all the labor it wants at a constant wage of *w* dollars. Suppose the wage in the labor market is $22. As illustrated in Figure 3-2, a profit-maximizing firm will then hire eight workers. At this level of employment, the value of marginal product of labor equals the wage rate *and* the value of marginal product curve is downward sloping, or

$$VMP_E = w \quad \text{and} \quad VMP_E \text{ is declining} \qquad \text{(3-5)}$$

In other words, at the point where the firm maximizes profits, the marginal gain from hiring an additional worker equals the cost of that hire, and it does not pay to further expand the firm because the value of hiring more workers is falling.

The intuition for this result is as follows: Suppose the firm decides to hire only six workers. If the firm hired the seventh worker, it would get more in additional revenues than it would pay out to that worker (the value of marginal product of the seventh worker is $26 and the wage is only $22). A profit-maximizing firm, therefore, will want to expand and hire more labor. If the firm were to hire more than eight workers, however, the value of marginal product would be lower than the cost of the hire. Suppose, for instance, that the firm wants to hire the ninth worker. It would cost $22 to hire this worker, even though her value of marginal product is only $18. From a profit-maximizing point of view, therefore, it is not worth hiring more than eight workers.

Note that Figure 3-2 also indicates that the wage also would equal the value of marginal product if the firm hired just one worker. At that point, however, the value of marginal product curve is upward sloping. It is easy to see why hiring just one worker does not maximize profits. If the firm hired another worker, the second worker hired would contribute even more to the firm's revenue than the first worker.

This argument shows why the law of diminishing returns plays such an important role in the theory. If VMP_E kept rising, the firm would maximize profits by expanding indefinitely. It would then be difficult to maintain the assumption that the firm's decisions do not affect the price of output or the price of labor and capital. In effect, the law of diminishing returns sets limits on the size of the firm.

It is also worth stressing that the profit-maximizing condition requiring that the wage equal the value of marginal product of labor *does not say* that the firm should set the wage equal to the value of marginal product. After all, the competitive firm has no influence over the wage, and, hence, the firm cannot "set" the wage equal to anything. All the firm can do is set its employment level so that the value of marginal product of labor equals the predetermined wage.

Finally, it is worth considering the firm's hiring decision if the competitive wage were very high, such as $38 in Figure 3-2. At this wage, it would seem that the firm should hire four workers, where the wage equals the value of marginal product. If the firm hired four workers, however, the value of the average product of labor ($32) would be less than the wage. Because the per-worker contribution to the firm is less than the wage, the firm loses money and leaves the market. The only points on the value of marginal product curve that are relevant for the firm's hiring decision are the ones that lie on the downward-sloping portion of the curve *below* the point where the VAP_E curve intersects the VMP_E curve. For convenience, we will restrict our attention to this particular segment of the VMP_E curve.

FIGURE 3-3   **The Short-Run Demand Curve for Labor**

Because marginal product eventually declines, the short-run demand curve for labor is downward sloping. A drop in the wage from \$22 to \$18 increases the firm's employment. An increase in the price of the output shifts the value of marginal product curve upward and increases employment.

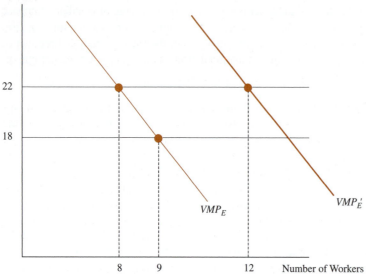

The Short-Run Labor Demand Curve for a Firm

We can now derive the short-run **demand curve for labor.** This demand curve tells us what happens to the firm's employment as the wage changes, holding capital constant. The construction of the short-run labor demand curve is presented in Figure 3-3, which draws the relevant downward-sloping portion of the firm's value of marginal product curve, or VMP_E. Initially, the wage is \$22 and the firm hires eight workers. If the wage falls to \$18, the firm hires nine workers. The short-run demand curve for labor, therefore, is given by the value of marginal product curve. Because the value of marginal product of labor declines as more workers are hired, it must be the case that a fall in the wage increases the number of workers hired.

The position of the labor demand curve depends on the price of the output. Because the value of marginal product is given by the product of output price and marginal product, the short-run demand curve shifts up if the output becomes more expensive. For example, suppose that the output price increases, shifting the value of marginal product curve in Figure 3-3 from VMP_E to VMP_E'. If the wage were \$22, the increase in output price raises the firm's employment from 8 to 12 workers. Therefore, there is a positive relation between short-run employment and output price. Finally, recall that the short-run demand curve holds capital constant at some level K_0. We would have derived a different short-run labor demand curve if we had held the capital stock constant at a different level K_1. The relationship between the value of marginal product of labor and the level of the capital stock is discussed below.[1]

---

[1] Note that the position of the labor demand curve also depends on the productive efficiency of workers. Suppose, for instance, that a technological advance such as a "work-hard pill" makes workers much more productive. The short-run labor demand curve would then shift up because the value of marginal product of each worker rises.

The Short-Run Labor Demand Curve in the Industry

We have derived the short-run labor demand curve for a single firm. We obviously can apply the same approach and derive a short-run labor demand curve for every firm in the industry, the group of firms that produce the same output. It would seem that the industry's labor demand curve can be obtained by adding up *horizontally* the demand curves of the individual firms. For example, suppose that every firm in the industry hires 15 workers when the wage is $20, but increases its employment to 30 workers when the wage falls to $10. It would seem that one could get the industry demand curve by simply summing up the employment across firms. If there were two firms in the industry, one might conclude that this industry hires 30 workers when the wage is $20 and 60 workers when the wage falls to $10.

This approach, however, is incorrect because it ignores the fact that the labor demand curve for a firm takes the price of the output *as given*. Each firm in a perfectly competitive industry is small enough that it cannot influence prices. But if all firms in the industry take advantage of the lower wage by increasing their employment, there would be a great deal more output in the industry and this would imply that the price of the output would fall. As a result, if all firms expand their employment, the value of marginal product (or output price times marginal product) also falls, and the labor demand curve of each individual firm shifts slightly to the left. Employment in this industry would then expand less than would have been the case if we just added up the demand curves of individual firms.

Figure 3-4 illustrates this point for an industry with two identical firms. As shown in Figure 3-4*a,* each firm hires 15 workers when the wage is $20 and 30 workers when the wage falls to $10. The sum of these two demand curves is illustrated in Figure 3-4*b* by the curve *DD.* It is impossible, however, for every firm in the industry to expand its employment without lowering the price of the output. As a result, the demand curve for each firm shifts back slightly, so that at the lower wage of $10, each firm hires only 28 workers. The industry, therefore, employs 56 workers at the lower wage. The "true" industry labor demand curve is then given by *TT.* This curve, which accounts for the fact that the price of the output adjusts if all firms expand, is steeper than the industry demand curve one would obtain by just summing horizontally the demand curves of individual firms.

We use an elasticity to measure the responsiveness of employment in the industry to changes in the wage rate. The short-run **elasticity of labor demand** is defined as the percentage change in short-run employment (E_{SR}) resulting from a 1 percent change in the wage:

$$\delta_{SR} = \frac{\text{Percent change in employment}}{\text{Percent change in the wage}} = \frac{\Delta E_{SR}/E_{SR}}{\Delta w/w} = \frac{\Delta E_{SR}}{\Delta w} \cdot \frac{w}{E_{SR}} \quad (3\text{-}6)$$

Because the short-run demand curve for labor is downward sloping, it must be the case that the elasticity is negative. In our example, we saw that the industry hires 30 workers when the wage is $20 and hires 56 workers if the wage falls to $10. The short-run elasticity is:

$$\delta_{SR} = \frac{\text{Percent change in employment}}{\text{Percent change in the wage}} = \frac{(56-30)/30}{(10-20)/20} = -1.733 \quad (3\text{-}7)$$

FIGURE 3-4   The Short-Run Demand Curve for the Industry

Each firm in the industry hires 15 workers when the wage is $20. If the wage falls to $10, each firm now wants to hire 30 workers. If all firms expand, the supply of the output in the industry increases, reducing the price of the output and reducing the value of marginal product, so the labor demand curve of each individual firm shifts slightly to the left. At the lower price of $10, each firm then hires only 28 workers. The industry demand curve is not given by the horizontal sum of the firm's demand curves (*DD*), but takes into account the impact of the industry's expansion on output price (*TT*).

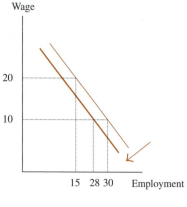

(*a*) Individual Firms

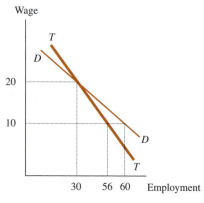

(*b*) Industry

Labor demand is said to be elastic if the absolute value of the elasticity of the labor demand curve is greater than one. Labor demand is said to be inelastic if the absolute value of the elasticity is less than one.

An Alternative Interpretation of the Marginal Productivity Condition

The requirement that firms hire workers up to the point where the value of marginal product of labor equals the wage gives the firm's "stopping rule" in its hiring decision—that is, the rule that tells the firm when to stop hiring. This hiring rule is also known as the **marginal productivity condition.** An alternative and more familiar way of describing profit-maximizing behavior refers to the stopping rule for the firm's output: A profit-maximizing firm should produce up to the point where the cost of producing an additional unit of output (or **marginal cost**) equals the revenue obtained from selling that output (or **marginal revenue**).

   This condition is illustrated in Figure 3-5. The marginal cost (*MC*) curve is upward sloping—as the firm expands, costs increase at an increasing rate. For a competitive firm, the revenue from selling an additional unit of output is given by the constant output price p. The equality of price and marginal cost occurs at output q^*. If the firm were to produce fewer than q^* units of output, it would increase its profits by expanding production. After all, the revenue from selling an extra unit of output exceeds the costs of producing that unit. In contrast, if the firm were to produce more than q^* units, it would increase its profits by shrinking. The marginal cost of producing these units exceeds the marginal revenue.

FIGURE 3-5   The Firm's Output Decision

A profit-maximizing firm produces up to the point where the output price equals the marginal cost of production. This profit-maximizing condition is the same as the one requiring firms to hire workers up to the point where the wage equals the value of marginal product.

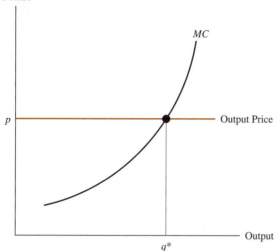

It turns out that the profit-maximizing condition equating price and marginal cost (which gives the optimal level of output) is identical to the profit-maximizing condition equating the wage and the value of marginal product of labor (which gives the optimal number of workers). Recall that MP_E tells us how many units of output an additional worker produces. Suppose, for instance, that $MP_E = 5$. This implies that it takes one-fifth of a worker to produce one extra unit of output. More generally, if one additional worker produces MP_E units of output, then $1/MP_E$ worker will produce one unit of output. Each of these workers gets paid a wage of w dollars. Hence, the cost of producing an extra unit of output is equal to

$$MC = w \times \frac{1}{MP_E} \tag{3-8}$$

The condition that the firm produces up to the point where marginal cost equals price can then be written as

$$w \times \frac{1}{MP_E} = p \tag{3-9}$$

By rearranging terms in equation (3-9), we obtain the marginal productivity condition $w = p \times MP_E$. In short, the condition telling the profit-maximizing firm when to stop producing output is exactly the same as the condition telling the firm when to stop hiring workers.

Criticisms of Marginal Productivity Theory

A commonly heard criticism of marginal productivity theory is that it bears little relation to the way employers actually make hiring decisions. Most employers have probably never heard of the concept of the value of marginal product—let alone ask their personnel managers to conduct detailed and complex calculations that equate this quantity to the wage rate and thereby determine how many workers they should hire.

Proponents of the theory do not take this criticism seriously. One obvious response to the criticism is that if some employers did not behave the way that marginal productivity theory says they should behave, those employers would not last long in the marketplace. Only the fittest— that is, the most profitable—survive in the competitive market. And if a particular employer is not hiring workers optimally, some other firm will undercut the inefficient employer.

One also could argue that the value of the theory of marginal productivity does not necessarily depend on the validity of the assumptions—or on whether it provides a "realistic" depiction of the labor market. Babe Ruth and Willie Mays, for example, most likely did not study and memorize the physics that dictate how a baseball reacts to being hit by a wooden bat and how Newton's laws of motion determine how the ball travels through the air. Nevertheless, they clearly learned and intuitively understood—through innate ability and acquired skills—the implications of these laws for hitting a home run. In other words, Babe Ruth and Willie Mays surely *acted as if* they knew all the relevant laws of physics.

In the same vein, employers probably do not know how to solve the mathematical equations that equate the value of marginal product to the wage rate. Nevertheless, the pressures of a competitive market have forced them to learn the rules of thumb implied by those equations: how to make the hiring decisions that ensure that they can make money and that their business will survive. In short, employers in a competitive labor market must *act as if* they know and obey the implications of marginal productivity theory.

3-3   The Employment Decision in the Long Run

In the long run, the firm's capital stock is not fixed. The firm can expand or shrink its plant size and equipment. Therefore, in the long run, the firm maximizes profits by choosing both how many workers to hire and how much plant and equipment to invest in.

Isoquants

An **isoquant** describes the possible combinations of labor and capital that produce the same level of output. Isoquants, therefore, describe the production function in exactly the same way that indifference curves describe a worker's utility function. Figure 3-6 illustrates the isoquants associated with the production function $q = f(E, K)$. The isoquant labeled q_0 gives all the capital-labor combinations that produce exactly q_0 units of output, and the isoquant labeled q_1 gives all the capital-labor combinations yielding q_1 units.

Figure 3-6 illustrates the properties of these constant-output curves:

1. Isoquants must be downward sloping.
2. Isoquants do not intersect.
3. Higher isoquants are associated with higher levels of output.
4. Isoquants are convex to the origin.

FIGURE 3-6   Isoquant Curves

All capital-labor combinations that lie along a single isoquant produce the same level of output. The input combinations at points X and Y produce q_0 units of output. Input combinations that lie on higher isoquants produce more output.

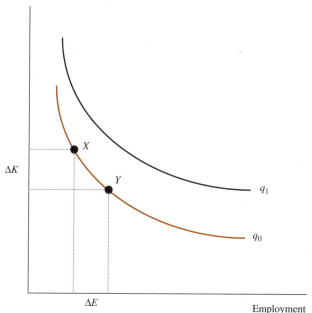

These properties of isoquants correspond exactly to the properties of indifference curves. Finally, just as the slope of an indifference curve is given by the negative of the ratio of marginal utilities, the slope of an isoquant is given by the negative of the ratio of marginal products. In particular:[2]

$$\frac{\Delta K}{\Delta E} = -\frac{MP_E}{MP_K} \qquad (3\text{-}10)$$

The absolute value of this slope is called the **marginal rate of technical substitution.** The assumption that isoquants are convex to the origin is an assumption about how the marginal rate of technical substitution changes as the firm switches from capital to labor. In particular, the convexity assumption implies *diminishing* marginal rate of technical substitution (or a flatter isoquant) as the firm substitutes more labor for capital.

[2] To prove this, let's calculate the slope of the isoquant between points X and Y in Figure 3-6 (assuming that points X and Y are very close to each other). In going from point X to point Y, the firm hires ΔE more workers, and each of these workers produces MP_E units of output. Hence, the gain in output is given by the product $\Delta E \times MP_E$. In going from point X to point Y, however, the firm is also getting rid of ΔK units of capital. Each of these units has a marginal product of MP_K. The decrease in output is then given by $\Delta K \times MP_K$. Because output is the same at all points along the isoquant, the gain in output resulting from hiring more workers must equal the reduction in output resulting from cutting the capital stock, so that $(\Delta E \times MP_E) + (\Delta K \times MP_K) = 0$. Equation (3-10) is obtained by rearranging the terms in this equation.

FIGURE 3-7   Isocost Lines

All capital-labor combinations that lie along a single isocost curve are equally costly. Capital-labor combinations that lie on a higher isocost curve are more costly. The slope of an isoquant equals the ratio of input prices $(-w/r)$.

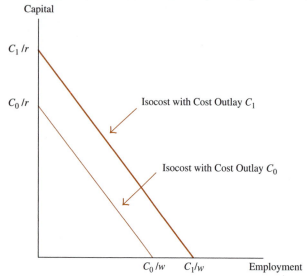

Isocosts

The firm's costs of production, which we denote by C, are given by

$$C = wE + rK \qquad \text{(3-11)}$$

Let's consider how the firm can spend a particular amount of money, call it C_0. The firm could decide to hire only capital, in which case it could hire C_0/r units of capital (where r is the price of capital), or it could hire only labor, in which case it would hire C_0/w workers. The line connecting all the various combinations of labor and capital that the firm could hire with a cost outlay of C_0 dollars is called an **isocost** line, and is illustrated in Figure 3-7.

A number of properties of isocost lines are worth noting. In particular, note that the isocost line gives the menu of different combinations of labor and capital that are equally costly. Second, higher isocost lines imply higher costs. Figure 3-7 illustrates the isocost lines associated with cost outlays C_0 and C_1, where $C_1 > C_0$. Finally, one can easily derive the slope of an isocost line by rewriting equation (3-11) as

$$K = \frac{C}{r} - \frac{w}{r}E \qquad \text{(3-12)}$$

This equation is of the form $y = a + bx$, with intercept C/r and slope $-w/r$. The slope of the isocost line, therefore, is the negative of the ratio of input prices.

Cost Minimization

A profit-maximizing firm that is producing q_0 units of output obviously wants to produce these units at the lowest possible cost. Figure 3-8 illustrates the solution to this cost-minimization problem. In particular, the firm chooses the combination of labor and

FIGURE 3-8   The Firm's Optimal Combination of Inputs

A firm minimizes the costs of producing q_0 units of output by using the capital-labor combination at point P, where the isoquant is tangent to the isocost. All other capital-labor combinations (such as those given by points A and B) lie on a higher isocost curve.

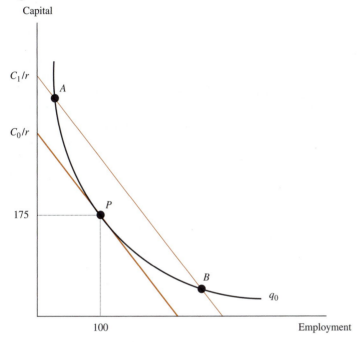

capital (100 workers and 175 machines) given by point P, where the isocost is tangent to the isoquant. At point P, the firm produces q_0 units of output at the lowest possible cost because it uses a capital-labor combination that lies on the lowest possible isocost. The firm can produce q_0 units of output using other capital-labor combinations, such as point A or B on the isoquant. This choice, however, would be more costly because it places the firm on a higher isocost line (with a cost outlay of C_1 dollars).

At the cost-minimizing solution P, the slope of the isocost equals the slope of the isoquant, or

$$\frac{MP_E}{MP_K} = \frac{w}{r} \qquad\qquad \textbf{(3-13)}$$

Cost minimization, therefore, requires that the marginal rate of technical substitution equal the ratio of prices. The intuition behind this condition is easily grasped if we rewrite it as

$$\frac{MP_E}{w} = \frac{MP_K}{r} \qquad\qquad \textbf{(3-14)}$$

The last worker hired produces MP_E units of output for the firm at a cost of w dollars. If the marginal product of labor is 20 units and the wage is \$10, the ratio MP_E/w implies that the last dollar spent on labor yields two units of output. Similarly, the ratio MP_K/r gives the output yield of the last dollar spent on capital. Cost-minimization requires that the last dollar spent on labor yield as much output as the last dollar spent on capital. In other words, the last dollar spent on each input gives the same "bang for the buck."

The hypothesis that firms minimize the cost of producing a particular level of output is often confused with the hypothesis that firms maximize profits. It should be clear that if we constrain the firm to produce q_0 units of output, the firm must produce this level of output in a cost-minimizing way in order to maximize profits. Profit-maximizing firms, therefore, will always use the combination of labor and capital that equates the ratio of marginal products to the ratio of input prices. This condition alone, however, does not describe the behavior of profit-maximizing firms. After all, the equality of ratios in equation (3-13) was derived by *assuming* that the firm was going to produce q_0 units of output, regardless of any other considerations. A profit-maximizing firm will not choose to produce just any level of output. Rather, a profit-maximizing firm will choose to produce the *optimal* level of output—that is, the level of output that maximizes profits, where the marginal cost of production equals the price of the output (or q^* units in Figure 3-5).

Therefore, the condition that the ratio of marginal products equals the ratio of prices does not tell us everything we need to know about the behavior of profit-maximizing firms in the long run. We saw earlier that for a given level of capital—*including the optimal level of capital*—the firm's employment is determined by equating the wage with the value of marginal product of labor. By analogy, the profit-maximizing condition that tells the firm how much capital to hire is obtained by equating the price of capital (r) and the value of marginal product of capital VMP_K. Therefore, long-run profit maximization also requires that labor and capital be hired up to the point where

$$w = p \times MP_E \quad \text{and} \quad r = p \times MP_K \qquad \textbf{(3-15)}$$

These profit-maximizing conditions imply cost minimization. Note that the ratio of the two marginal productivity conditions in equation (3-15) implies that the ratio of input prices equals the ratio of marginal products.[3]

3-4 The Long-Run Demand Curve for Labor

We can now determine what happens to the firm's long-run demand for labor when the wage changes. We initially consider a firm that produces q_0 units of output. We assume that this output is *the* profit-maximizing level of output, in the sense that, at that level of production, output price equals marginal cost. A profit-maximizing firm will produce this output at the lowest cost possible, so it uses a mix of labor and capital where the ratio of marginal products equals the ratio of input prices. The wage is initially equal to w_0. The optimal combination of inputs for this firm is illustrated in Figure 3-9, where the firm uses 75 units of capital and 25 workers to produce the q_0 units of output. Note that the cost outlay associated with producing this level of output equals C_0 dollars.

Suppose the market wage falls to w_1; how will the firm respond? The absolute value of the slope of the isocost line is equal to the ratio of input prices (or w_1/r), so the isocost line

---

[3] To restate the point, profit maximization implies cost minimization, but cost minimization need not imply profit maximization.

FIGURE 3-9 **The Impact of a Wage Reduction, Holding Constant Initial Cost Outlay at C_0**
A wage reduction flattens the isocost curve. If the firm were to hold the initial cost outlay constant at C_0 dollars, the isocost would rotate around C_0 and the firm would move from point P to point R. A profit-maximizing firm, however, will not generally want to hold the cost outlay constant when the wage changes.

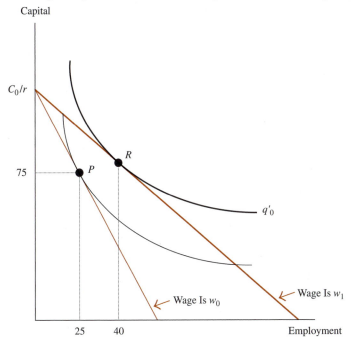

will be flattened by the wage cut. Because of the resemblance between the wage change in Figure 3-9 and the wage change in the neoclassical model of labor-leisure choice that we discussed in Chapter 2, there is a strong inclination to duplicate the various steps of our earlier geometric analysis.

We have to be extremely careful when drawing the new isocost line, however, because *the obvious way of shifting the isocost line is also the wrong way of shifting it.* As illustrated in Figure 3-9, we may want to shift the isocost by rotating it around the original intercept C_0/r. If this rotation of the isocost line were "legal," the firm would move from point P to point R. The wage reduction increases the firm's employment from 25 to 40 workers and increases output from q_0 to q'_0 units.

Although we are tempted to draw Figure 3-9, the analysis is simply wrong! The rotation of the isocost around the original intercept C_0/r implies that the firm's cost outlay is being held constant, at C_0 dollars. *There is nothing in the theory of profit maximization to require that the firm incur the same costs before and after the wage change.* The long-run constraints of the firm are given by the technology (as summarized by the production function) and by the constant price of the output and other inputs (p and r). In general, the firm will not maximize its profits by constraining itself to incur the same costs before and after a wage change.

FIGURE 3-10   **The Impact of a Wage Reduction on the Output and Employment of a Profit-Maximizing Firm**
(*a*) A wage cut reduces the marginal cost of production and encourages the firm to expand (from producing 100 to 150 units). (*b*) The firm moves from point *P* to point *R*, increasing the number of workers hired from 25 to 50.

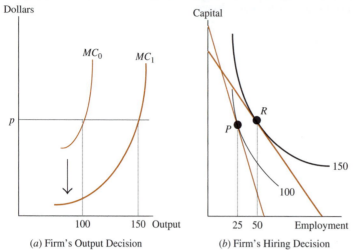

(*a*) Firm's Output Decision   (*b*) Firm's Hiring Decision

Will the Firm Expand if the Wage Falls?

The decline in the wage will typically cut the marginal cost of producing the firm's output.[4] In other words, it is cheaper to produce an additional unit of output when labor is cheap than when labor is expensive. We then expect that the drop in the wage would encourage the firm to expand production. Figure 3-10*a* shows the impact of this reduction in marginal cost on the firm's scale (that is, on the size of the firm). Because the marginal cost curve drops from MC_0 to MC_1, the wage cut encourages the firm to produce 150 units of output rather than 100 units.

Therefore, the firm will "jump" to a higher isoquant, as illustrated in Figure 3-10*b*. As noted earlier, the total cost of producing 150 units of output need not be the same as the cost of producing only 100 units. As a result, the new isocost line need not originate from the same point in the vertical axis as the old isocost line. We do know, however, that a profit-maximizing firm will produce the 150 units of output efficiently; that is, this output will be produced using the cost-minimizing mix of labor and capital. The optimal mix of inputs, therefore, is given by the point on the higher isoquant where the isoquant is tangent to a new isocost line, which has a slope equal to w_1/r (and hence is flatter than the original isocost line). The solution is given by point *R* in Figure 3-10*b*.

As drawn, the firm's employment increases from 25 to 50 workers. We will see below that the firm will *always* hire more workers when the wage falls. The positioning of point *R* in Figure 3-10*b* also implies that the firm will use more capital. We will see below that

---

[4] It can be shown that the marginal cost of production falls when the inputs used in the production process are "normal" inputs—in the sense that the firm uses more labor and more capital as it expands, holding the prices of labor and capital constant. The key result of the theory—that the long-run labor demand curve is downward sloping—also holds even if labor were an inferior input.

FIGURE 3-11 **The Long-Run Demand Curve for Labor**

The long-run demand curve for labor gives the firm's employment at a given wage and is downward sloping.

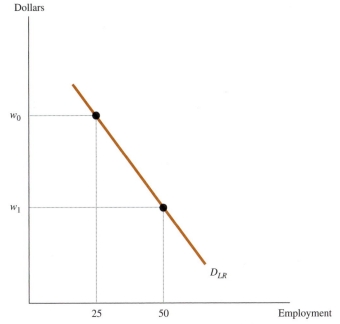

this need not always be the case. In general, a wage cut can either increase or decrease the amount of capital demanded.

The long-run demand curve for labor (or D_{LR}) is illustrated in Figure 3-11. At the initial wage of w_0, the firm hired 25 workers. When the wage fell to w_1, the firm hired 50 workers. We will now show that the long-run demand curve for labor must be downward sloping.

Substitution and Scale Effects

In our derivation of a worker's labor supply curve, we decomposed the impact of a wage change on hours of work into income and substitution effects. This section uses a similar decomposition to assess the impact of a wage change on the firm's employment. In particular, the wage cut reduces the price of labor relative to that of capital. The decline in the wage encourages the firm to readjust its input mix so that it is more labor intensive (and thus takes advantage of the now-cheaper labor). In addition, the wage cut reduces the marginal cost of production and encourages the firm to expand. As the firm expands, it wants to hire even more workers.

These two effects are illustrated in Figure 3-12. The firm is initially at point P, where it faces a wage equal to w_0, produces 100 units of output, and hires 25 workers. When the wage falls to w_1, the firm moves to point R, producing 150 units of output and hiring 50 workers.

It is useful to view the move from point P to point R as a two-stage move. In the first stage, the firm takes advantage of the lower price of labor by expanding production. In the second stage, the firm takes advantage of the wage change by rearranging its mix of inputs (that is, by switching from capital to labor), *while holding output constant.*

FIGURE 3-12 Substitution and Scale Effects

A wage cut generates substitution and scale effects. The scale effect (the move from point P to point Q) encourages the firm to expand, increasing the firm's employment. The substitution effect (from Q to R) encourages the firm to use a more labor-intensive method of production, further increasing employment.

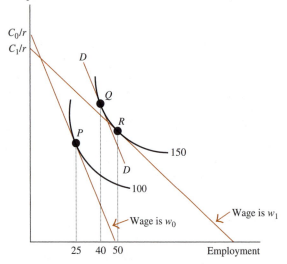

To conduct this decomposition, Figure 3-12 introduces a new isocost line, labeled DD. This isocost line is tangent to the new isoquant (which produces 150 units of output), but is parallel to the isocost that the firm faced before the wage reduction. In other words, the absolute value of the slope of the DD isocost is equal to w_0/r, the original price ratio. The tangency point between this new isocost and the new isoquant is given by point Q.

We define the move from point P to point Q as the **scale effect.** The scale effect indicates what happens to the demand for the firm's inputs as the firm expands production. As long as capital and labor are "normal inputs," the scale effect increases both the firm's employment (from 25 to 40 workers) and the capital stock.[5]

In addition to expanding its scale, the wage cut encourages the firm to adopt a different method of production, one that is more labor intensive to take advantage of the now-cheaper labor. The **substitution effect** indicates what happens to the firm's employment as the wage changes, holding output constant, and is given by the move from Q to R in Figure 3-12. Holding output constant at 150 units, the firm adopts a more labor-intensive input mix, substituting away from capital and toward labor. As drawn, the substitution effect raises the firm's employment from 40 to 50 workers. Note that the substitution effect *must* decrease the firm's demand for capital.

Both the substitution and scale effects induce the firm to hire more workers as the wage falls. As drawn, Figure 3-12 indicates that the firm hires more capital when the wage falls, so that the scale effect (which increases the demand for capital) outweighs the substitution effect (which reduces the demand for capital). The firm would use less capital if the substitution effect dominated the scale effect.

[5] Note that the definition of normal inputs is analogous to that of normal goods in Chapter 2.

As usual, we use the concept of an elasticity to measure the responsiveness of changes in long-run employment (E_{LR}) to changes in the wage. The long-run elasticity of labor demand is given by

$$\delta_{LR} = \frac{\text{Percentage change in employment}}{\text{Percentage change in the wage}} = \frac{\Delta E_{LR}/E_{LR}}{\Delta w/w} = \frac{\Delta E_{LR}}{\Delta w} \cdot \frac{w}{E_{LR}} \quad \textbf{(3-16)}$$

Because the long-run labor demand curve is downward sloping, the long-run elasticity of labor demand is negative.

An important principle in economics states that consumers and firms can respond more easily to changes in the economic environment when they face fewer constraints. Put differently, extraneous constraints prevent us from fully taking advantage of the opportunities presented by changing prices. In terms of our analysis, this principle implies that the long-run demand curve for labor is more elastic than the short-run demand curve for labor, as illustrated in Figure 3-13. In the long run, firms can adjust both capital and labor and can fully take advantage of changes in the price of labor. In the short run, the firm is "stuck" with a fixed capital stock and cannot adjust its size easily.

Estimates of the Labor Demand Elasticity

Many empirical studies attempt to estimate the elasticity of labor demand.[6] Given our earlier discussion of the problems encountered in estimating the labor supply elasticity, it should not be too surprising that there is a huge range of variation in the estimates of the labor demand elasticity. Although most of the estimates indicate that the labor demand curve is downward sloping, the range of the estimates is very wide.

FIGURE 3-13   **The Short- and Long-Run Demand Curves for Labor**

In the long run, the firm can take full advantage of the economic opportunities introduced by a change in the wage. As a result, the long-run demand curve is more elastic than the short-run demand curve.

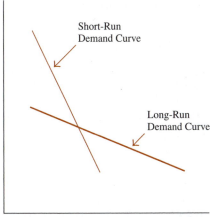

Dollars

Short-Run
Demand Curve

Long-Run
Demand Curve

Employment

[6] An encyclopedic survey of this literature is given by Daniel S. Hamermesh, *Labor Demand,* Princeton, NJ: Princeton University Press, 1993.

Theory at Work

CALIFORNIA'S OVERTIME REGULATIONS AND LABOR DEMAND

The Fair Labor Standards Act of 1938 requires that covered workers be paid 1.5 times the wage for any hours worked in excess of 40 hours per week. Unlike most states, California imposes additional regulations on overtime pay. Workers in California must be paid 1.5 times the wage for any hours worked in excess of 8 hours per *day*—even if they work fewer than 40 hours during the week. Before 1974, California's legislation applied only to female workers. After 1980, the legislation covers both men and women.

The theory of labor demand makes a clear prediction about how this legislation should affect the probability that California's workers work more than eight hours per day. In particular, the probability that *men* work more than eight hours per day in California should have declined between the 1970s and the 1980s—as the overtime-per-day regulation was extended to cover men and employers switched to cheaper methods of production.

Table 3-2 shows that 17.1 percent of California's working men worked more than eight hours per day in 1973. By 1985, only 16.9 percent of working men worked more than eight hours per day.

Before we can attribute this slight reduction in the length of the workday to the increasing coverage of the overtime legislation, we need to know what would have happened to the length of the workday for California's men in the absence of the legislation. In other words, we need a control group. One possible control group is the working men in other states—men whose workday was unaffected by the change in California's policies. It turns out that the fraction of men in other states working more than eight hours per day *rose* during the same period, from 20.1 to 22.8 percent. The "difference-in-differences" estimate of the impact of California's overtime legislation was a substantial reduction of 2.9 percentage points on the probability of working more than eight hours per day. Alternatively, the control group could be California's working women—who had always been covered by the legislation. The probability that their workday lasted more than eight hours also rose during the period, from 4.0 to 7.2 percent. Again, the difference-in-differences approach implies that California's overtime legislation reduced the probability that working men worked more than eight hours per day by 3.4 percentage points.

TABLE 3-2   Employment Effects of Overtime Regulation in California

Source: Daniel S. Hamermesh and Stephen J. Trejo, "The Demand for Hours of Labor: Direct Estimates from California," *Review of Economics and Statistics* 82 (February 2000): 38–47.

| | Treatment Group | Control Group | |
	Men in California (%)	Men in Other States (%)	Women in California (%)
Workers working more than 8 hours per day in			
1973	17.1	20.1	4.0
1985	16.9	22.8	7.2
Difference	−0.2	2.7	3.2
Difference-in-differences	—	**−2.9**	**−3.4**

Despite the dispersion in the estimates of the short-run labor demand elasticity, there is some consensus that the elasticity lies between −0.4 and −0.5. In other words, a 10 percent increase in the wage reduces employment by perhaps 4 to 5 percentage points in the short run. The evidence also suggests that the estimates of the long-run labor demand elasticity cluster around −1, so the long-run labor demand curve is indeed more elastic than the short-run curve. In the long run, a 10 percent change in the wage leads to a 10 percent change in employment. About one-third of the long-run elasticity can be attributed to the substitution effect and about two-thirds to the scale effect.

3-5   The Elasticity of Substitution

The size of the firm's substitution effect depends on the curvature of the isoquant. Two extreme situations are illustrated in Figure 3-14. In Figure 3-14*a*, the isoquant is a straight line, with a slope equal to –0.5. In other words, output remains constant whenever the firm lays off two workers and replaces them with one machine. This "rate of exchange" between labor and capital is the same regardless of how many workers or how much capital the firm already has. The marginal rate of technical substitution is constant when the isoquant is a line. Whenever any two inputs in production can be substituted at a constant rate, the two inputs are called **perfect substitutes.**[7]

The other extreme is illustrated in Figure 3-14*b*. The right-angled isoquant implies that using 20 workers and 5 machines yields q_0 units of output. If we hold capital constant at five units, adding more workers has no impact on output. Similarly, if we hold labor

FIGURE 3-14   **Isoquants When Inputs Are Either Perfect Substitutes or Perfect Complements**

Capital and labor are perfect substitutes if the isoquant is linear (so that two workers can always be substituted for one machine). The two inputs are perfect complements if the isoquant is right-angled. The firm then gets the same output when it hires 5 machines and 20 workers as when it hires 5 machines and 25 workers.

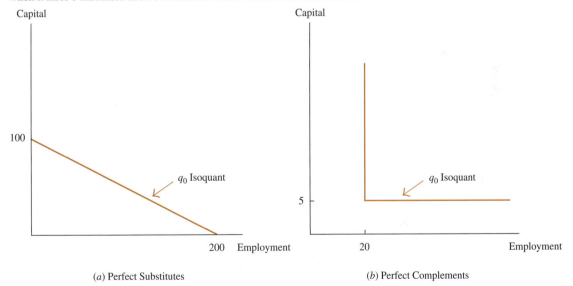

(*a*) Perfect Substitutes   (*b*) Perfect Complements

[7] Note that our definition of perfect substitution does *not* imply that the two inputs have to be exchanged on a one-to-one basis; that is, one machine hired for each worker laid off. Our definition implies only that the rate at which capital can be replaced for labor is constant.

constant at 20 workers, adding more machines has no impact on output. A firm that does not wish to throw away money has only one recipe for producing q_0 units of output: use 20 workers and 5 machines! When the isoquant between any two inputs is right-angled, the two inputs are called **perfect complements**.

The substitution effect is very large when labor and capital are perfect substitutes. When the isoquant is linear, the firm minimizes the costs of producing q_0 units of output by hiring either 100 machines or 200 workers, depending on which of these two alternatives is cheaper. If the prices of the inputs change sufficiently, the firm will jump from one extreme to the other.

In contrast, there is no substitution effect when the two inputs are perfect complements. Because there is only one recipe for producing q_0 units of output, a change in the wage does not alter the input mix at all. The firm must always use 20 workers and 5 machines to produce q_0 units of output, regardless of the price of labor and capital.

In between these two extremes, there are a great number of substitution possibilities, depending on the curvature of the isoquant. The more curved the isoquant, the smaller the size of the substitution effect. To measure the curvature of the isoquant, we typically use a number called the **elasticity of substitution.** The elasticity of substitution between capital and labor (holding output constant) is defined by

$$\text{Elasticity of substitution} = \frac{\text{Percent change in } (K/E)}{\text{Percent change in } (w/r)} \qquad \textbf{(3-17)}$$

The elasticity of substitution gives the percentage change in the capital/labor ratio resulting from a 1 percent change in the relative price of labor. As the relative price of labor increases, the substitution effect tells us that the capital/labor ratio increases (that is, the firm gets rid of labor and replaces it with capital). The elasticity of substitution, therefore, is defined so that it is a positive number. It turns out that the elasticity of substitution is zero if the isoquant is right-angled, as in Figure 3-14b, and is infinite if the isoquant is linear, as in Figure 3-14a. The size of the substitution effect, therefore, directly depends on the magnitude of the elasticity of substitution.

3-6   Policy Application: Affirmative Action and Production Costs

There has been a great deal of debate about the economic impact of affirmative action programs in the labor market. These programs typically "encourage" firms to alter the race, ethnicity, or gender of their workforce by hiring relatively more of those workers who have been underrepresented in the firm's hiring in the past. A particular affirmative action plan, for instance, might require that the firm hire one black worker for every two workers hired.

Our theory of how firms choose the optimal mix of inputs in the production process helps us understand the nature of the debate over the employment impact of these programs. To simplify the discussion, suppose there are two inputs in the production process: black workers and white workers. In this example, therefore, we will ignore the role that capital plays in the firm's production. This simplification allows us to represent the firm's hiring choices in terms of the two-dimensional isocosts and isoquants that we derived in

FIGURE 3-15 Affirmative Action and the Costs of Production

(*a*) The discriminatory firm chooses the input mix at point *P*, ignoring the cost-minimizing rule that the isoquant be tangent to the isocost. An affirmative action program can force the firm to move to point *Q*, resulting in more efficient production and lower costs. (*b*) A color-blind firm is at point *P*, hiring relatively more whites because of the shape of the isoquants. An affirmative action program increases this firm's costs.

Black Labor

Black Labor

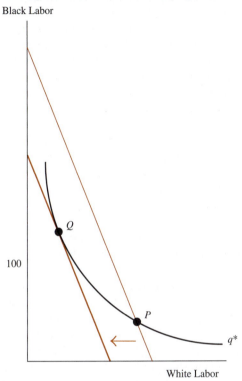

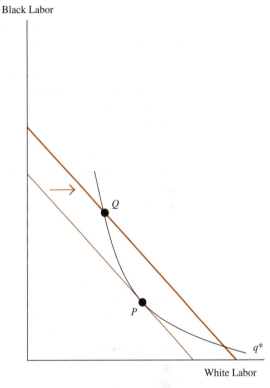

(*a*) Affirmative Action Reduces
Costs of Discriminatory Firm

(*b*) Affirmative Action Increases
Costs of Color-Blind Firm

the earlier sections. Suppose further that black and white workers are not perfect substitutes in production, so that the isoquants between these two groups have the usual convex shape, as illustrated in Figure 3-15*a*. The two groups of workers might have different productivities because they might differ in the amount and quality of educational attainment, or because they might have been employed in different occupations and hence are entering this firm with different types of job training.

A competitive firm can hire as many black workers as it wants at the going wage of w_B and can hire as many white workers as it wants at the going wage of w_W. A firm is "color-blind" if the race of the workers does not enter the hiring decision at all. A profit-maximizing color-blind firm would then want to produce q^* units of output in the most efficient way possible, where the isoquant is tangent to the isocost. This hiring mix is illustrated by point Q in Figure 3-15*a*.

Suppose, however, that the firm discriminates against black workers. In other words, the firm's management gets disutility from hiring blacks and would rather see whites filling most jobs in the firm. The firm's prejudice alters its hiring decision. A discriminatory firm will not want to be at point Q, but instead will choose an input mix that has more white workers and fewer black workers to produce the same q^* units of output, such as point P in the figure.

Note that employment discrimination moves the firm *away* from the input mix where the isoquant is tangent to the isocost. The prejudiced firm has simply decided that it is going to ignore the cost-minimizing rule because that rule generates the "wrong" color mix for the firm's workforce. As a result, the input mix chosen by the firm (or point P) is no longer a point where the isoquant is tangent to the isocost. After all, the slope of the isocost is given by the ratio of wage rates (or $-w_W/w_B$), and a competitive firm cannot influence wages. Therefore, point P does not lie on the lowest isocost that would allow the firm to produce q^* units of output, and the prejudiced firm uses an input combination that costs *more* than the input combination it would have chosen had it been a color-blind firm. Our theoretical framework, therefore, leads to a very simple—*and surprising*—conclusion: Discrimination is not profitable.[8]

Suppose that the government forces the firm to adopt an affirmative action program that mandates the firm hire relatively more blacks. This policy moves the firm's employment decision closer to the input mix that a color-blind firm would have chosen. In fact, if the government fine-tunes the employment quota "just right," it could force the discriminatory firm to hire the same input mix as a color-blind firm (or point Q).

This type of affirmative action policy has two interesting consequences. First, the firm's workforce has relatively more blacks. And, second, because it costs less to produce a particular level of output, the firm is more profitable.[9] In short, this type of affirmative action policy leads to a more efficient allocation of resources. The reason is that discriminatory firms are ignoring the underlying economic fundamentals. In particular, they disregard the information provided by the cost of hiring black and white workers when they make their hiring decisions, and instead go with their "feelings." Affirmative action policies would then force discriminatory firms to pay more attention to prices.

Before we conclude that the widespread adoption of affirmative action programs would be a boon to a competitive economy, it is important to recognize that the example illustrated in Figure 3-15a adopted a particular prism through which to view the world. In particular, the analysis assumed that the competitive firm *is* prejudiced, so that the firm's hiring decisions are affected by discrimination.

Needless to say, there is an alternative point of view, one that leads to very different implications. Suppose, in particular, that firms in the labor market do not discriminate at all against black workers. And suppose further that the shape of the firm's isoquants is such

---

[8] This conclusion was first derived in Gary S. Becker, *The Economics of Discrimination,* Chicago: University of Chicago Press, 1957. Chapter 9 presents a much more detailed discussion of discrimination in the labor market. In this section, we use the context of discrimination to show how our approach to modeling the firm's employment decision can inform us about the nature of the debate over many policy-relevant issues.

[9] Because the affirmative action program increases the demand for black workers and reduces the demand for white workers, the program also will tend to equalize the wages of black and white workers in the labor market.

that the firm hires relatively fewer black workers, even if blacks and whites are equally costly. This situation is illustrated in Figure 13-15b, where the slope of the isocost is minus one. The color-blind profit-maximizing firm then chooses the input mix at point *P* in the figure, where the isoquant is tangent to the isocost and the firm is producing output *q** in the cheapest way possible. Because of productivity differences between the two groups, this color-blind firm hires a workforce that has many white workers and relatively few black workers.

Suppose the government again mandates that firms hire relatively more blacks. This policy forces the firm to move from point *P,* the cost-minimizing solution, to point *Q,* a point where the isoquant is not tangent to the isocost. Therefore, this affirmative action program increases the firm's costs of production.

It is clear, therefore, that the "initial conditions" assumed in the exercise determine the inferences that one draws about the labor market impact of affirmative action programs. If one assumes that the typical competitive firm discriminates against black workers, an affirmative action program forces the firm to pay more attention to the economic fundamentals and increases the firm's profits. In contrast, if one assumes that the typical firm does not discriminate, an affirmative action program may substantially reduce the profitability of competitive firms and perhaps drive many of them out of business.[10]

As this discussion shows, our perception about the "real world" can greatly influence the position that we take in the debate over the labor market impacts of affirmative action. This fact reinforces the importance of couching the debate in the context of the empirical evidence about the existence and prevalence of labor market discrimination. As we will see in Chapter 9, labor economists have made a great deal of progress in trying to understand the factors that encourage firms to take race into account when they make hiring decisions and have derived widely used methodologies to measure the extent of labor market discrimination.

3-7   Marshall's Rules of Derived Demand

The famous **Marshall's rules of derived demand** describe the situations that are likely to generate elastic labor demand curves in a particular industry.[11] In particular:

* *Labor demand is more elastic the greater the elasticity of substitution.* This rule follows from the fact that the size of the substitution effect depends on the curvature of the isoquant. The greater the elasticity of substitution, the more the isoquant looks like a straight line, and the more "similar" labor and capital are in the production process. This allows the firm to easily substitute labor for capital as the wage increases.

[10] The evidence on whether affirmative action programs increase or reduce the firm's costs is inconclusive. See Jonathan Leonard, "Anti-Discrimination or Reverse Discrimination? The Impact of Changing Demographics, Title VII, and Affirmative Action on Productivity," *Journal of Human Resources* 19 (Spring 1984): 145–174; and Peter Griffin, "The Impact of Affirmative Action on Labor Demand: A Test of Some Implications of the Le Chatelier Principle," *Review of Economics and Statistics* 74 (May 1992): 251–260. A good survey of the literature is given by Harry Holzer and David Neumark, "Assessing Affirmative Action," *Journal of Economic Literature* 38 (September 2000): 483–568.

[11] The mathematical appendix presents a partial derivation of these rules. For a more technical, but complete derivation, see Hamermesh, *Labor Demand.*

- *Labor demand is more elastic the greater the elasticity of demand for the output.* When the wage rises, the marginal cost of production increases. A wage increase, therefore, raises the industry's price and reduces consumers' demand for the product. Because less output is being sold, firms cut employment. The greater the reduction in consumer demand (that is, the more elastic the demand curve for the output), the larger the cut in employment and the more elastic the industry's labor demand curve.

- *Labor demand is more elastic the greater labor's share in total costs.* Suppose labor is a relatively "important" input in the production process, in the sense that labor's share of total costs is large. This situation might occur, for example, when production is very labor intensive, as with a firm using highly trained craftspeople to produce expensive handmade ornaments. In this case, even a small increase in the wage rate would substantially increase the marginal cost of production. This increase in marginal cost raises the output price and induces consumers to cut back on their purchases of the ornaments. Firms, in turn, would cut back on employment substantially. In contrast, if labor is "unimportant," so that labor makes up only a small share of total costs, a wage increase has only a small impact on marginal cost, on the price of the output, and on consumer demand. There is little need for the firm's employment to shrink.[12]

- *The demand for labor is more elastic the greater the supply elasticity of other factors of production, such as capital.* We have assumed that firms can hire as much capital as they want at the constant price r. Suppose there is a wage increase and firms want to substitute from labor to capital. If the supply curve of capital is inelastic, so that the price of capital increases substantially as more and more capital is hired, the economic incentives for moving along an isoquant are greatly reduced. In other words, it is not quite as profitable to get rid of labor and employ capital instead. The demand curve for labor, therefore, is more elastic the easier it is to increase the capital stock (that is, the more elastic the supply curve of capital).

An Application of Marshall's Rules: Union Behavior

The behavior of labor unions illustrates how Marshall's rules can help us understand various aspects of the labor market. Consider a competitive firm that is initially nonunion. The firm hires 1,000 workers at the going wage. A union wants to organize the firm's workers,

---

[12] Actually, Marshall's third rule holds only when the absolute value of the elasticity of product demand exceeds the elasticity of substitution. The reason for this exception follows from the fact that we can arbitrarily make the labor input ever less important by redefining it in seemingly irrelevant ways. For example, we can subdivide the labor input of craftspeople producing ornaments into the various inputs of Irish craftspeople, Italian craftspeople, Mexican craftspeople, and so on. Each of these new labor inputs would obviously make up a very small fraction of total costs, but it is incorrect to say that the demand curve for Irish craftspeople is less elastic than the demand curve for all craftspeople. As we redefine the labor input into ever smaller subpopulations, the elasticity of substitution among the various inputs rises (is there any difference in productivity between the typical Irish and Italian craftsperson?). Marshall's third rule, therefore, holds only when the elasticity of substitution is sufficiently small (in effect, the various labor inputs used by the firm are not essentially the same input broken up into arbitrary categories). This clarification of the exception to Marshall's third rule was contributed by George J. Stigler, *The Theory of Price*, 3rd ed., New York: Macmillan, 1966, p. 244. A detailed discussion of the exception to Marshall's third rule is given by Saul D. Hoffman, "Revisiting Marshall's Third Law: Why Does Labor's Share Interact with the Elasticity of Substitution to Decrease the Elasticity of Labor Demand," *Journal of Economic Education*, 40, no. 4 (2009): 437–445.

and promises the workers that collective bargaining will increase the wage substantially. Because the firm's labor demand curve is downward sloping, the firm may respond to the higher wage by moving up its demand curve and cutting back employment. The union's organizing drive then has a greater chance of being successful when the demand curve for labor is inelastic. After all, an inelastic demand curve ensures that employment is relatively stable even if the workers get a huge wage increase. In other words, the workers would not have to worry about employment cutbacks if they voted for the union. It is in the union's best interests, therefore, to take whatever actions are available to lower the firm's elasticity of demand.

In view of this fact, it is not surprising that unions often resist technological advances that increase the possibilities of substituting between labor and capital. The typesetters' unions, for example, long objected to the introduction of computerized typesetting equipment in the newspaper industry. This type of behavior is an obvious attempt to reduce the value of the elasticity of substitution. A smaller elasticity of substitution reduces the size of the substitution effect and makes the demand curve for labor more inelastic.

Similarly, unions want to limit the availability of goods that compete with the output of unionized firms. For example, the United Auto Workers (UAW) was a strong supporter of policies that made it difficult for Japanese cars to crack into the U.S. market. If the UAW obtained a huge wage increase for its workers, the price of American-made cars would rise substantially. This price increase would drive many potential buyers toward foreign imports. If the union could prevent the entry of Toyotas, Nissans, and Hondas into the American marketplace, consumers would have few alternatives to buying a high-priced American-made car. It is in the union's interests, therefore, to reduce the elasticity of product demand by limiting the variety of goods that are available to consumers.

Marshall's rules also imply that unions are more likely to be successful when the share of labor costs is small. Unions can then make high wage demands without raising the marginal cost (and hence the price) of the output very much. In fact, there is evidence that unions that organize small groups of workers such as electricians or carpenters tend to be very successful in getting sizable wage increases.[13] Because these specialized occupations make up a small fraction of total labor costs, the demand curve for these workers is relatively inelastic.

Finally, unions often attempt to raise the price of other inputs, particularly nonunion labor. For example, the Davis-Bacon Act requires that contractors involved in publicly financed projects pay the "prevailing wage" to construction workers.[14] Not surprisingly, the prevailing wage is typically defined as the union wage, even if the contractor hires nonunion labor. This type of regulation raises the cost of switching from union labor to other inputs. Union support of prevailing wage laws, therefore, can be interpreted as an attempt to make the supply of other factors of production more inelastic and hence reduce the elasticity of demand for union labor.

---

[13] These unions are typically called "craft unions," in contrast to the "industrial unions" that unionize all workers in a given industry (like the UAW).

[14] For a review of the economic impact of "prevailing wage" policies, see Robert Goldfarb and John Morrall, "The Davis-Bacon Act: An Appraisal of Recent Studies," *Industrial and Labor Relations Review* 34 (January 1981): 191–206; and A. J. Tieblot, "A New Evaluation of Impacts of Prevailing Wage Law Repeal," *Journal of Labor Research* 7 (Spring 1996): 297–322.

3-8   Factor Demand with Many Inputs

Although we have assumed that the production function has only two inputs—labor and capital—we can easily extend the theory to account for more realistic production processes. There are clearly many different types of workers (such as skilled and unskilled) and many different types of capital (such as old machines and new machines). The production technology is then described by the production function:

$$q = f(x_1, x_2, x_3, \ldots, x_n) \qquad \text{(3-18)}$$

where x_i denotes the quantity of the ith input that is used in production. As before, the production function tells us how much output is produced by any combination of the inputs. We can define the marginal product of the ith input, or MP_i as the change in output resulting from a one-unit increase in that input, holding constant the quantities of all other inputs.

We can use this production function to derive the short- and long-run demand curves for a particular input. It will still be true that a profit-maximizing firm hires the ith input up to the point where its price (or w_i) equals the value of marginal product of that input:

$$w_i = p \times MP_i \qquad \text{(3-19)}$$

All of the key results derived in the simpler case of a two-factor production function continue to hold. The short-run and long-run demand curves for each input are downward sloping; the long-run demand curve is more elastic than the short-run demand curve; and a wage change generates both a substitution effect and a scale effect.

One common empirical finding is that the labor demand for unskilled workers is more elastic than for skilled workers.[15] In other words, for any given percentage increase in the wage, the cut in employment will be larger for unskilled workers than for skilled workers. An interesting interpretation of this result is that employment is inherently more unstable for unskilled workers than for skilled workers. As various economic shocks shift the wage of the two types of workers, the number of workers demanded will fluctuate significantly among unskilled workers, but much less so among skilled workers.

The presence of many inputs in the production process raises the possibility that the demand for input i might increase when the price of input j increases, but might fall when the price of input k increases. To measure the sensitivity in the demand for a particular input to the prices of other inputs, we define the **cross-elasticity of factor demand** as

$$\text{Cross-elasticity of factor demand} = \frac{\text{Percent change in } x_i}{\text{Percent change in } w_j} \qquad \text{(3-20)}$$

The cross-elasticity of factor demand gives the percentage change in the demand for input i resulting from a 1 percent change in the wage of input j.

The sign of the cross-elasticity in equation (3-20) provides one definition of whether any two inputs are substitutes or complements in production. If the cross-elasticity is positive, so that the demand for input i increases when the wage of input j rises, the two inputs i and j are said to be substitutes in production. After all, the increase in w_j increases the demand for input i at the same time that it reduces the demand for input j. The two inputs

---

[15] Hamermesh, *Labor Demand,* Chapter 3.

FIGURE 3-16   **The Demand Curve for a Factor of Production Is Affected by the Prices of Other Inputs**

The labor demand curve for input i shifts when the price of another input changes. (a) If the price of a substitutable input rises, the demand curve for input i shifts up. (b) If the price of a complement rises, the demand curve for input i shifts down.

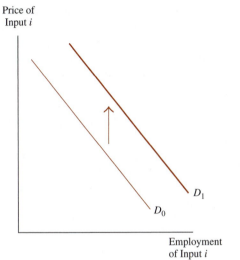

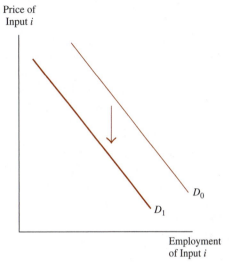

(a) Demand Curve Shifts Up When the Price
of a Substitute Increases

(b) Demand Curve Shifts Down When the
Price of a Complement Increases

are substitutes because they respond in different ways to the change in the wage; the firm is getting rid of the more expensive input and replacing it with the relatively cheaper input.

If the cross-elasticity of factor demand is negative, the demand for input i falls as a result of the increase in w_j, and inputs i and j are said to be complements in production. The inputs are complements when they both respond in exactly the same way to a rise in w_j. Put differently, the two inputs "go together."

Figure 3-16 illustrates this definition of substitutes and complements in terms of shifting demand curves. In Figure 3-16a, the demand curve for input i shifted up when the price of input j increased. In this case, the two inputs are substitutes. As input j became more expensive, employers substituted toward input i. Hence the demand curve for input i shifted up. In Figure 3-16b, the demand curve for input i shifted down when the price of input j rose. In other words, the demand for both inputs fell when input j became more expensive. The two inputs go together in production and are, therefore, complements.

A number of empirical studies suggest that unskilled labor and capital are substitutes, and that skilled labor and capital are complements.[16] In other words, as the price of machines

---

[16] Zvi Griliches, "Capital-Skill Complementarity," *Review of Economics and Statistics* 51 (November 1969): 465–468. See also Ann P. Bartel and Frank Lichtenberg, "The Comparative Advantage of Educated Workers in Implementing New Technology," *Review of Economics and Statistics* 69 (February 1987): 1–11; and Claudia Goldin and Lawrence F. Katz, "The Origins of Technology-Skill Complementarity," *Quarterly Journal of Economics* 113 (August 1998): 693–732. Although there is some debate over the validity of this finding, the evidence makes a strong case that, at the very least, skilled workers and capital are much more complementary (or less substitutable) than unskilled workers and capital.

falls, employers substitute away from unskilled workers. In contrast, as the price of machines falls and employers increase their use of capital equipment, the demand for skilled workers rises because skilled workers and capital equipment "go together." It has been found that a 10 percent fall in the price of capital reduces the employment of unskilled workers by 5 percent and increases the employment of skilled workers by 5 percent.[17]

This result has come to be known as the **capital-skill complementarity hypothesis.** This hypothesis has important policy implications. It suggests that subsidies to investments in physical capital (such as an investment tax credit) will have a differential impact on different groups of workers. Because an investment tax credit lowers the price of capital to the firm, it increases the demand for capital, reduces the demand for unskilled workers, and increases the demand for skilled workers. An investment tax credit, therefore, spurs investment in the economy, but also worsens the relative economic conditions of less-skilled workers. The capital-skill complementarity hypothesis also suggests that technological progress—such as the substantial reduction in the price of computing power in the 1980s and 1990s—can have a substantial impact on income inequality, again because it increases the demand for skilled workers and reduces the demand for unskilled workers.

3-9   Overview of Labor Market Equilibrium

We have analyzed the factors that encourage workers to supply a particular number of hours to the labor market and that encourage firms to demand a particular number of workers. The labor market is the place where the workers looking for jobs and the firms looking for workers finally meet each other and compare wage and employment offers. The interaction between workers and firms that occurs in the labor market determines the **equilibrium** wage and employment levels: the wage and employment levels that "balance" the number of hours that workers wish to work with the number of employee-hours that firms wish to employ. In this section, we briefly describe this equilibrium. Chapter 4 analyzes the properties of labor market equilibrium in greater detail.

Figure 3-17 illustrates the labor demand and labor supply curves in a particular labor market. As drawn, the supply curve slopes up, so that we are assuming that substitution effects dominate income effects. The demand curve is negatively sloped. The equilibrium wage and employment levels in this market are given by the point where the supply and demand curves intersect. A total of E^* workers are employed and each receives the market wage of w^*. To see why this intersection represents a labor market equilibrium, suppose that workers were getting paid a wage of w_{high}, which is above the equilibrium wage. At this wage, the demand curve indicates that firms are only willing to hire E_D workers, and the supply curve indicates that E_S workers are looking for work. A wage above the equilibrium level, therefore, implies that there is a surplus of workers competing for the few available jobs. This competition puts downward pressure on the wage. When the wage is above the equilibrium level, therefore, the competition for jobs drives down the wage.

If firms were offering a wage below the equilibrium level, such as w_{low} in Figure 3-17, the situation would be exactly reversed. Employers want to hire a lot of workers, but few persons are willing to work at the going wage. The competition among employers for the

[17] Kim Clark and Richard B. Freeman, "How Elastic Is the Demand for Labor?" *Review of Economics and Statistics* 62 (November 1980): 509–520.

FIGURE 3-17   Wage and Employment Determination in a Competitive Market

In a competitive labor market, equilibrium is attained at the point where supply equals demand. The "going wage" is w* and E* workers are employed.

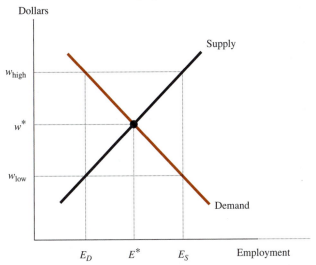

few available workers puts upward pressure on the wage and moves the wage up toward equilibrium.

Once the labor market attains the equilibrium wage, the conflicting wishes of employers and workers have been balanced. At this wage, the number of workers who are looking for work exactly equals the number of workers that employers want to hire. In the absence of any other economic shocks, the equilibrium level of the wage and employment can then persist indefinitely.

3-10   Policy Application: The Employment Effects of Minimum Wages

The U.S. federal government introduced mandatory minimum wages in the labor market in 1938 as one of the provisions of the Fair Labor Standards Act (FLSA).[18] In 1938, the nominal minimum wage was set at 25 cents an hour, and only 43 percent of nonsupervisory workers were covered by the minimum wage provisions of the FLSA. Workers in such industries as agriculture and intrastate retail services were exempt from the legislation. As Figure 3-18 shows, the nominal minimum wage has been adjusted at irregular intervals in the past six decades. The wage floor was increased to $5.85 an hour in 2007, and it now stands at $7.25 an hour. The coverage of the minimum wage also has been greatly expanded. Most workers who are not employed by state or local governments are now covered by the legislation.

[18] Other provisions of the FLSA include an overtime premium for persons who work more than 40 hours a week and regulations on the use of child labor.

FIGURE 3-18   **Minimum Wages in the United States, 1938–2010**

Source: U.S. Bureau of the Census, *Statistical Abstract of the United States,* Washington, DC: Government Printing Office, various issues; U.S. Bureau of the Census, *Historical Statistics of the United States, Colonial Times to 1970,* Washington, DC: Government Printing Office, 1975; and U.S. Bureau of Labor Statistics, *Employment and Earnings,* Washington, DC: Government Printing Office, January 2006.

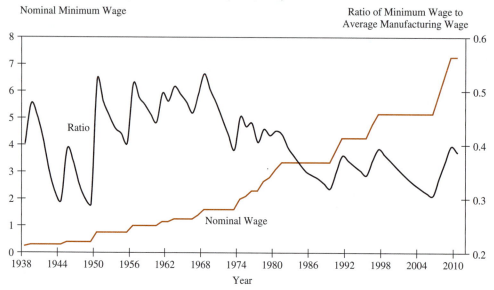

Figure 3-18 illustrates an important characteristic of minimum wages in the United States: They have not been indexed to inflation or productivity growth. As a result, the *real* minimum wage declines between the time that the nominal floor is set and the next time that Congress raises it. For instance, the minimum wage was set at $3.35 per hour in 1981, or 42 percent of the average wage in manufacturing. In 1989, the nominal minimum wage was still $3.35 per hour, but this wage was only 32 percent of the average wage in manufacturing. The "ratcheting" in the real minimum suggests that the economic impact of minimum wages declines the longer it has been since it was last raised.

Figure 3-19 illustrates the standard model economists use to analyze the impact of the minimum wage on employment.[19] Initially, the competitive labor market is in equilibrium at wage level w^* and employment E^*. The government imposes a minimum wage of $\overline{w}$. Let's assume initially that this minimum wage has universal coverage, so that all workers in the labor market are affected by the legislation, and that the penalties associated with paying less than the minimum wage are sufficiently stiff that employers comply with the legislation.

Once the government sets the wage floor at $\overline{w}$, firms move up the labor demand curve and employment falls to $\overline{E}$. As a result of the minimum wage, therefore, some workers ($E^* - \overline{E}$) are displaced from their current jobs and become unemployed. In addition, the higher wage encourages additional persons to enter the labor market. In fact, E_S workers would like to be employed, so an additional $E_S - E^*$ workers enter the labor market, cannot find jobs, and are added to the unemployment rolls.

[19] The standard model was first presented in George J. Stigler, "The Economics of Minimum Wage Legislation," *American Economic Review* 36 (June 1946): 358–365.

FIGURE 3-19   The Impact of the Minimum Wage on Employment

A minimum wage set at $\overline{w}$ forces employees to cut employment (from E^* to $\overline{E}$). The higher wage also encourages ($E_S - E^*$) additional workers to enter the market. The minimum wage, therefore, creates unemployment.

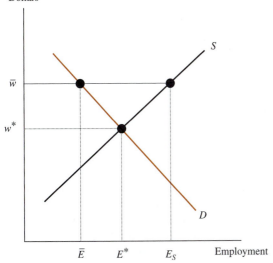

Therefore, a minimum wage creates unemployment both because some previously employed workers lose their jobs and because some workers who did not find it worthwhile to work at the competitive wage find it worthwhile to work at the higher minimum. The unemployment rate, or the ratio of unemployed workers to labor market participants, is given by $(E_S - \overline{E})/E_S$. This unemployment persists because the participants in the labor market have no incentives to alter their behavior: Firms do not wish to hire more workers *and* unemployed workers want to work at the minimum wage. The unemployment rate clearly depends on the level of the minimum wage, as well as on the elasticities of labor supply and labor demand. It is easy to verify that the unemployment rate is larger the higher the minimum wage and the more elastic the demand and supply curves.

Presumably, minimum wages are imposed so as to raise the income of the least skilled workers in the economy, for whom the competitive wage would be relatively low. As a result of the minimum wage, however, these workers now become particularly vulnerable to layoffs. The unskilled workers who are lucky enough to retain their jobs benefit from the legislation. The minimum wage, however, provides little consolation to the unskilled workers who lose their jobs.

Compliance with the Minimum Wage Law

This standard model of the impact of minimum wages assumes that all firms comply with the legislation. There seems to be a great deal of noncompliance with the minimum wage law. In 2006, for example, when the minimum wage stood at $5.15 an hour, 2.2 percent of workers earned $5.15 or less per hour, and 75.8 percent of these workers were paid less than $5.15.[20]

[20] U.S. Bureau of the Census, *Statistical Abstract of the United States, 2008,* Washington, DC: Government Printing Office, 2008, Table 631; see Orley Ashenfelter and Robert S. Smith, "Compliance with the Minimum Wage Law," *Journal of Political Economy* 87 (April 1979): 333–350.

The reason for this very high rate of noncompliance is that firms caught breaking the law face only trivial penalties. When a minimum wage violation is detected by one of the enforcement agents in the Employment Standards Administration of the Department of Labor, the government typically attempts to negotiate a settlement between the firm and the affected workers. As part of the settlement, the firm agrees to pay the workers the difference between the minimum wage and the actual wage for the last two years of work. Apart from the recovery of back pay, punitive damages are rare.

In effect, firms that break the law and are caught by the government received an interest-free loan. They can delay paying a portion of their payroll for up to two years. Moreover, firms that break the law and are not caught (which probably include the vast majority of cases) can continue hiring workers at the competitive wage. The greater the degree of noncompliance with the legislation, the smaller the employment cut resulting from the minimum wage and the lower the unemployment rate.

The Covered and Uncovered Sectors

The model summarized in Figure 3-19 also assumes that all workers are covered by the legislation. As noted above, only 43 percent of nonsupervisory workers in the economy were in the covered sector when the FLSA was first enacted. The size of the covered sector, however, has increased over time, so that the legislation now covers most workers.

To see how the adverse employment effects of minimum wages may be moderated by less-than-universal coverage, consider the labor markets illustrated in Figure 3-20.[21] There are two sectors in the economy, the covered sector in Figure 3-20a and the uncovered sector in Figure 3-20b. Prior to the imposition of a minimum wage, there exists a single equilibrium wage, w^*, in both markets (determined by the intersection of the supply curve S_C and the demand curve D_C in the covered sector, and the intersection of S_U and D_U in the uncovered sector). The minimum wage is imposed only on workers employed in the industries that comprise the covered sector. Workers employed in the uncovered sector are left to the mercy of the market and will receive the competitive wage.

Once the minimum wage is imposed on the covered sector, the wage rises to $\overline{w}$ and some workers lose their jobs. Covered sector employment falls to $\overline{E}$ and there are $E_C - \overline{E}$ displaced workers in the covered sector. Many of the displaced workers, however, can migrate to the uncovered sector and find work there. If some of these workers migrate to jobs in the uncovered sector, the supply curve in this sector shifts to S'_U (as illustrated in Figure 3-20b). As a result, the uncovered sector wage declines and the number of workers employed in the uncovered sector increases from E_U to E'_U.

However, this is not the only possible type of migration. After all, some workers initially employed in the uncovered sector might decide that it is worthwhile to quit their low-paying jobs and hang around in the covered sector until a minimum-wage job opens up. If many workers in the uncovered sector take this course of action, the direction of migration would then be from the uncovered to the covered sector. The supply curve in the uncovered sector would shift to S''_U in Figure 3-20b, *raising* the uncovered sector wage.

[21] Finis Welch, "Minimum Wage Legislation in the United States," in Orley Ashenfelter and James Blum, editors, *Evaluating the Labor-Market Effects of Social Programs,* Princeton: Princeton University Press, 1976; and Jacob Mincer, "Unemployment Effects of Minimum Wages," *Journal of Political Economy* 84 (August 1976): S87–S104.

FIGURE 3-20 The Impact of Minimum Wages on the Covered and Uncovered Sectors

If the minimum wage applies only to jobs in the covered sector, the displaced workers might move to the uncovered sector, shifting the supply curve to the right and reducing the uncovered sector's wage. If it is easy to get a minimum-wage job, workers in the uncovered sector might quit their jobs and wait in the covered sector until a job opens up, shifting the supply curve in the uncovered sector to the left and raising the uncovered sector's wage.

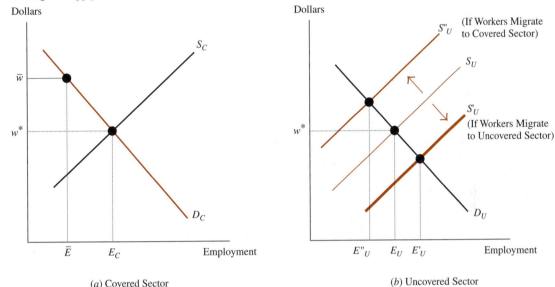

(a) Covered Sector   (b) Uncovered Sector

The analysis in Figure 3-20 shows how the free entry and exit of workers in and out of labor markets can equilibrate real wages in an economy *despite* the intentions of policy makers. In fact, if workers could migrate from one sector to the other very easily (that is, costlessly), one would expect that migration would continue as long as workers expected one of the sectors to offer a higher wage. The migration of workers across the two sectors would stop when the *expected* wage was equal across sectors.

To see this, let's calculate how much income a worker who enters the covered sector can expect to take home. Let π be the probability that a worker who enters the covered sector gets a job there, so that $1 - \pi$ is the probability that a worker in the covered sector is unemployed. If the worker lands a minimum-wage job, he gets wage $\overline{w}$; if he does not land a job, he has no income (ignoring any unemployment compensation). The wage that a person who enters the covered sector can actually expect to get is then given by

$$\text{Expected wage in covered sector} =$$
$$[\pi \times \overline{w}] + [(1 - \pi) \times 0] = \pi\overline{w} \qquad \textbf{(3-21)}$$

or a weighted average of the minimum wage $\overline{w}$ and zero.

The worker's alternative is to enter the uncovered sector. The wage in the uncovered sector is set by competitive forces and equals w_U. Because there is no unemployment in the uncovered sector, this wage is a "sure thing" for workers in that sector. Workers will move to whichever sector pays the higher expected wage. If the covered sector pays a higher expected wage than the uncovered sector, the flow of workers to minimum-wage jobs will lower the probability of getting a job, increase the length of unemployment spells, and decrease the expected wage. In contrast, if the wage is higher in the uncovered sector, the migration of workers to that sector shifts the supply curve outward and lowers the competitive wage w_U. As a result, the free migration of workers across sectors should eventually lead to

$$\pi \overline{w} = w_U \tag{3-22}$$

so that the expected wage in the covered sector equals the for-sure wage in the uncovered sector.

The discussion suggests that factors that influence the probability of landing a minimum-wage job help determine the direction of the migration flow between the two sectors. Suppose that workers who get a minimum-wage job keep it for a long time. It is then difficult for a person who has just entered the covered sector to obtain a job. An unemployed worker, therefore, quickly recognizes that she is better off working in the uncovered sector where wages are lower, but jobs are available. If the persons who hold minimum-wage jobs are footloose (so that there is a lot of turnover in these jobs), there is a high chance of getting a minimum-wage job, encouraging many workers to queue up for job openings in the covered sector.

Evidence

The simplest economic model of the minimum wage predicts that as long as the demand curve for labor is downward sloping, an increase in the minimum wage should decrease employment of the affected groups. A large empirical literature attempts to determine if this is, in fact, the case. Many of the empirical studies focus on the impact of minimum wages on teenagers, a group that is clearly affected by the legislation.[22] In 2003, about 10 percent of workers between the ages of 16 and 19 earned the minimum wage or less, as compared to only 1.7 percent of workers over the age of 25.[23]

A comprehensive survey of these studies concludes that the elasticity of teenage employment with respect to the minimum wage is probably between −0.1 and −0.3.[24] In other words, a 10 percent increase in the minimum wage lowers teenage employment by between 1 and 3 percent. Although this elasticity might seem small, it can have numerically

---

[22] See Finis Welch and James Cunningham, "Effects of Minimum Wages on the Level and Age Composition of Youth Employment," *Review of Economics and Statistics* 60 (February 1978): 140–145; Robert Meyer and David Wise, "The Effects of the Minimum Wage on the Employment and Earnings of Youth," *Journal of Labor Economics* 1 (January 1983): 66–100; Alison Wellington, "Effects of the Minimum Wage on the Employment Status of Youths: An Update," *Journal of Human Resources* 26 (Winter 1991): 27–47; and Richard V. Burkhauser, Kenneth A. Couch, and David C. Wittenburg, "A Reassessment of the New Economics of the Minimum Wage Literature with Monthly Data from the Current Population Survey," *Journal of Labor Economics* 18 (October 2000): 653–680.

[23] U.S. Bureau of the Census, *Statistical Abstract of the United States, 2002,* Washington, DC: Government Printing Office, 2002, Table 627.

[24] Charles Brown, "Minimum Wages, Employment, and the Distribution of Income," in Orley C. Ashenfelter and David Card, editors, *Handbook of Labor Economics,* vol. 3B, Amsterdam: Elsevier, 1999, pp. 2101–2163. Many studies also examine the impact of the minimum wage in other countries. Recent examples include Linda Bell, "The Impact of Minimum Wages in Mexico and Colombia," *Journal of Labor Economics* 15 (July 1997): S102–S135; Richard Dickens, Stephen Machin, and Alan Manning, "The Effects of Minimum Wages on Employment: Theory and Evidence from Britain," *Journal of Labor Economics* 17 (January 1999): 1–22; and Zadia M. Feliciano, "Does the Minimum Wage Affect Employment in Mexico?" *Eastern Economic Journal* 24 (Spring 1998): 165–180.

important effects. For example, between 1990 and 1991, the minimum wage rose from $3.35 to $4.25, or a 27 percent increase. If the elasticity of teenage employment with respect to the minimum wage is −0.15, the minimum wage increase reduced teenage employment by about 4 percent, or roughly 240,000 teenagers.[25] A quarter million displaced workers may not necessarily be a "numerically trivial" impact.

The long-standing consensus that the minimum wage has adverse employment impacts on the most susceptible workers has come under attack in recent years. The "consensus" elasticity estimates of −0.1 and −0.3 were typically obtained by looking at the time-series relation between the employment of teenagers and the minimum wage. In effect, these studies correlate teenage employment in a particular year with some measure of the real minimum wage, after adjusting for other variables that could potentially affect teenage employment in that year. The estimated elasticities, however, are extremely sensitive to the time period over which the correlation is estimated. During some time periods, the elasticity estimate is quite small (nearly zero), while if one estimates the same correlation over other time periods, one obtains a much more negative elasticity.[26]

A number of studies in the 1990s introduced a different methodology for estimating the employment effects of minimum wages by carrying out case studies that trace out the employment effects of specific minimum-wage increases on specific industries or sectors. These studies often conclude that many of the recent increases in the minimum wage have not had *any* adverse employment effects. One of these studies surveyed a large number of fast-food restaurants in Texas prior to (December 1990) and after (July 1991) the imposition of the $4.25 minimum wage.[27] Fast-food restaurants are a major employer of youths in the United States, and the minimum wage presumably should have a particularly strong effect on youth employment in that industry. It turns out, however, that there was little change in employment in these establishments, and, if anything, many of the restaurants actually increased their employment.

The "revisionist" evidence also seems to suggest that teenage employment is not affected when states enact a minimum wage that is higher than the federal level. In July 1988, two years prior to the increase in the federal minimum wage, California raised its minimum from $3.35 to $4.25 an hour. Prior to the increase, about 50 percent of California's teenagers earned less than $4.25 an hour, so that many teenagers were obviously affected by the

---

[25] There also exists a subminimum wage. Employers can pay teenage workers 85 percent of the minimum wage in the first three months of the job, as long as the worker is engaged in on-the-job training activities. This provision of the legislation reduces the price of younger unskilled workers relative to the price of older unskilled workers. Employers might then reevaluate their existing mix of labor inputs in order to take advantage of the now-cheaper youth workforce. However, only about 1 percent of employers use the subminimum wage; see David Card, Lawrence F. Katz, and Alan B. Krueger, "Employment Effects of Minimum and Subminimum Wages: Panel Data on State Minimum Wage Laws," *Industrial and Labor Relations Review* 47 (April 1994): 487–497.

[26] John F. Kennan, "The Elusive Effect of Minimum Wages," *Journal of Economic Literature* 33 (December 1993): 1950–65.

[27] Lawrence F. Katz and Alan B. Krueger, "The Effect of the Minimum Wage on the Fast-Food Industry," *Industrial and Labor Relations Review* 46 (October 1992): 6–21; see also David Card and Alan B. Krueger, *Myth and Measurement: The New Economics of the Minimum Wage,* Princeton, NJ: Princeton University Press, 1995.

state-mandated raise. Nevertheless, it seems as if California teenagers did not suffer any employment loss when the higher state minimum wage went into effect.[28]

The best-known case study analyzes the impact of the minimum wage in New Jersey and Pennsylvania.[29] On April 1, 1992, New Jersey increased its minimum wage to $5.05 per hour, the highest minimum wage in the United States, but the neighboring state of Pennsylvania did not follow suit and kept the minimum wage at $4.25, the federally mandated minimum. The New Jersey–Pennsylvania comparison provides a "natural experiment" that can be used to assess the employment impacts of minimum wage legislation.

Suppose, for example, that one contacts a large number of fast-food establishments (such as Wendy's, Burger King, KFC, and Roy Rogers) on *both* sides of the New Jersey–Pennsylvania state line prior to and after the New Jersey minimum went into effect. The restaurants on the western side of the state line (that is, in Pennsylvania) were unaffected by the New Jersey minimum wage, so employment in these restaurants should have changed only because of changes in economic conditions such as seasonal shifts in consumer demand for fried chicken and hamburgers. Employment in restaurants on the eastern side of the state line (that is, in New Jersey) were affected both by the increase in the legislated minimum as well as by changes in economic conditions. By comparing the employment change in the restaurants on both sides of the border, one can then "net out" the effect of changes in economic conditions and isolate the impact of the minimum wage on employment. In effect, one can use the difference-in-differences technique to measure the employment effect of minimum wages.

Table 3-3 summarizes the key results of this influential study. It turns out that the fast-food restaurants on the New Jersey side of the border did not experience a decline in employment relative to the restaurants on the Pennsylvania side of the border. In fact, employment in New Jersey actually *increased* relative to employment in Pennsylvania. The typical fast-food restaurant in New Jersey hired 0.6 more worker after the minimum wage increase than it did before the increase. At the same time, however, the macroeconomic trends in the fast-food

TABLE 3-3   **The Employment Effect of Minimum Wages in New Jersey and Pennsylvania**

Source: David Card and Alan B. Krueger, "Minimum Wages and Employment: A Case Study of the Fast-Food Industry in New Jersey and Pennsylvania," *American Economic Review* 84 (September 1994), Table 3.

	Employment in Typical Fast-Food Restaurant (in full-time equivalents)	
	New Jersey	Pennsylvania
Before New Jersey increased the minimum wage	20.4	23.3
After New Jersey increased the minimum wage	21.0	21.2
Difference	0.6	−2.1
Difference-in-differences	**2.7**	

[28] David Card, "Do Minimum Wages Reduce Employment? A Case Study of California, 1987–89," *Industrial and Labor Relations Review* 46 (October 1992): 38–54. Card's findings have been challenged by David Neumark and William Wascher, "State-Level Estimates of Minimum Wage Effects: New Evidence and Interpretations from Disequilibrium Methods," *Journal of Human Resources* 37 (Winter 2002): 35–62.

[29] David Card and Alan B. Krueger, "Minimum Wages and Employment: A Case Study of the Fast-Food Industry in New Jersey and Pennsylvania," *American Economic Review* 84 (September 1994): 772–793.

industry led to a decline in employment of about 2.1 workers in Pennsylvania—a state that was unaffected by the minimum wage increase. The difference-in-differences estimate of the impact of the minimum wage on employment, therefore, was an *increase* of about 2.7 workers in the typical fast-food restaurant. Needless to say, if correct, this line of research raises important questions about how labor economists think about the economic impact of minimum wages.

We are beginning to understand why the recent evidence based on specific case studies differs so sharply from the time-series evidence that dominated the earlier literature, and why the implications of our simple—and sensible—supply-and-demand framework seem to be so soundly rejected by the case-study data.[30]

One plausible reason is that the adverse effect of the minimum wage on employment is relatively small. It might then be hard to detect this effect in a rapidly changing economic environment. In other words, the "true" impact of the minimum wage on employment is negative, but small. As a result, sampling errors lead researchers to find either small positive or small negative effects.

It also has been convincingly shown that the survey data used in the New Jersey–Pennsylvania study contained a lot of measurement error and that this noise in the data generated correspondingly noisy estimates of the labor demand elasticity. In fact, if one replicates the study using the administrative employment data actually reported by the establishments, as opposed to the survey data collected by researchers, the employment effect of the minimum wage in the New Jersey–Pennsylvania experiment turns negative, and the estimated elasticity is within the consensus range of -0.1 to -0.3.[31]

An equally serious conceptual problem with the New Jersey–Pennsylvania case study is that the focus on employment trends in fast-food restaurants could easily provide a myopic and misleading picture of the employment effects of minimum wages. After all, these establishments might use a production technology where the number of workers is relatively fixed (one worker per grill, one worker per cash register, and so on). As a result, the minimum wage might not reduce employment in existing restaurants, but might discourage the national chain from opening additional restaurants (as well as accelerate the closing of marginally profitable restaurants). Moreover, economies of scale might also "shelter" fast-food restaurants from the minimum wage. The minimum wage would then accelerate the decline of the smaller and less competitive "mom-and-pop" restaurants and fast-food restaurants might even "thrive" as a result of the minimum wage.

The before-and-after comparisons of employment in affected firms also are affected by the *timing* of these comparisons. Employers may not change their employment exactly on the date that the law goes into effect, but may instead adjust their employment slowly as they take into account the mandated increase in their labor costs. In fact, a careful study of the impact of minimum wages in the Canadian labor market shows that the employment effects of the minimum wage are smallest when one compares employment just before and

[30] An excellent and comprehensive survey of the recent literature is given by David Neumark and William Wascher, "Minimum Wages and Employment," *Foundations and Trends in Microeconomics 3* (2007): 1–182. A potential explanation that is commonly offered in the literature is that fast-food restaurants have some degree of market power when hiring workers, so that the labor market is not competitive. This explanation will be discussed in more detail in Chapter 4

[31] David Neumark and William Wascher, "Minimum Wages and Employment: A Case Study of the Fast-Food Industry in New Jersey and Pennsylvania, Comment," *American Economic Review* 90 (December 2000): 1362–1396.

just after the increase in the minimum wage takes effect, and becomes more negative the longer the period over which the employment data are observed.[32]

The evidence from the New Jersey–Pennsylvania case study is also inconsistent with how restaurants shift their prices in response to minimum wage increases. The restaurant industry hires a large number of low-skill workers, so increases in the minimum age would likely lead to a significant increase in the costs of production. In a competitive market, the presumed reduction in employment caused by the minimum wage would lead to less output in the marketplace. This cut in supply should increase the prices charged by these establishments. A careful study of price changes in the "food away from home" component of the Consumer Price Index between 1995 and 1997 shows that increases in the federal

[32] See Michael Baker, Dwayne Benjamin, and Shuchita Stanger, "The Highs and Lows of the Minimum Wage Effect: A Time-Series Cross-Section Study of the Canadian Law," *Journal of Labor Economics* 17 (April 1999): 318–350.

and/or state minimum wages during the period increased prices in the restaurant industry. A 10 percent increase in the minimum wage roughly corresponds with a half-percent increase in restaurant prices.[33]

Finally, a few recent studies have revisited the time-series framework that dominated the earlier literature and have concluded that there is indeed a negative correlation between increases in the federal minimum wage and changes in teenage employment. One careful study looked at the time series of teenage employment over the 1954–1993 period and estimated that the elasticity of teenage 2010 employment with respect to the minimum wage is between -0.3 and -0.5.[34]

Is the Minimum Wage an Effective Antipoverty Program?

The minimum wage increases the wage for workers at the bottom of the wage distribution but may reduce employment opportunities for some of those workers. The trade-off between wage increases and potential employment losses raises questions about the effectiveness of the minimum wage as an antipoverty tool. This trade-off could be overlooked if the employment losses are "small," and if the benefits from the higher minimum wage accrued mainly to poor persons. But recent studies raise doubts about the effectiveness of the minimum wage as an antipoverty tool by noting that the main beneficiaries of the minimum wage are workers in better-off households.[35]

The minimum wage in the United States rose from $3.35 to $4.25 an hour between 1989 and 1992. In 1990, only about 7.1 percent of the workers in the labor force earned between $3.35 and $4.25 an hour and, hence, could potentially benefit from the increase in the minimum wage. Many of these workers, however, are teenagers from households that are not poor. The relatively low wage earned by these teenagers in 1990 has little to do with the economic status of their families and their own long-run economic opportunities. It turns out that only about 19 percent of the increase in income generated by the higher minimum wage accrued to poor households—households with annual incomes below the poverty line—and more than 50 percent of the income increase went to households with incomes that were at least twice the poverty threshold. The evidence, therefore, suggests that even if

[33] Daniel Aaronson, Eric French, and James MacDonald, "The Minimum Wage, Restaurant Prices, and Labor Market Structure," *Journal of Human Resources* 43 (Summer 2008): 688–720.

[34] Nicolas Williams and Jeffrey A. Mills, "The Minimum Wage and Teenage Employment: Evidence from Time Series," *Applied Economics* 33 (February 2001): 285–300; see also Walter J. Wessels, "Does the Minimum Wage Drive Teenagers Out of the Labor Force," *Journal of Labor Research* 26 (Winter 2005): 169–176; and David Neumark and William Wascher, "Minimum Wages, Labor Market Institutions, and Youth Employment: A Cross-National Analysis," *Industrial and Labor Relations Review* 57 (January 2004): 223–248.

[35] Richard V. Burkhauser, Kenneth A. Couch, and David C. Wittenburg, "'Who Gets What' from Minimum Wage Hikes: A Re-estimation of Card and Krueger's Distributional Analysis in Myth and Measurement: The New Economics of the Minimum Wage," *Industrial and Labor Relations Review* 49 (April 1996): 547–552; and David Neumark, Mark Schweitzer, and William Wascher, "The Effects of Minimum Wages on the Distribution of Family Income: A Nonparametric Approach," *Journal of Human Resources* 40 (Fall 2005): 867–894. An excellent discussion of the conceptual issues involved in using the minimum wage as an antipoverty tool is given by Richard V. Burkhauser, Kenneth A. Couch, and Andrew J. Glenn, "Public Policies for the Working Poor: The Earned Income Tax Credit versus Minimum Wage Legislation," *Research in Labor Economics* 15 (1996): 65–109.

the minimum wage has few adverse employment effects, it is not an effective way of combating poverty in the United States. For the most part, the benefits accrue to workers who are not at the bottom of the distribution of *permanent* income opportunities.

The Living Wage

Nearly 100 cities in the United States have enacted "living wage" ordinances. These laws typically set minimum wages that are far above the federal minimum and cover municipal employees or workers in firms that have business dealings with the city. As of December 2002, the living wage was $8.70 (per hour) in Ann Arbor, MI; $10.25 in Boston, MA; $10.86 in New Haven, CT; and $10.36 in San Jose, CA.

Although the living wage ordinances are relatively recent, a number of studies have already attempted to measure the impact of this type of minimum wage on wages and employment in the affected localities.[36] Few workers are covered by this type of legislation, so one might suspect that it would be difficult to detect any economic impact of the higher local minimum wage. Moreover, it is difficult to evaluate the impact of a living wage ordinance in a particular locality since it is unclear what the "control group" should be. Perhaps localities that choose to enact living wage ordinances are localities that have employment and economic conditions that are quite different from those of other localities.

One recent study does a particularly good job at trying to estimate the impact of living wages by defining the control group as the sample of cities that attempted to pass living wage ordinances, but where the attempt failed due to legal constraints.[37] Baton Rouge and Salt Lake City, for instance, passed living wages ordinances, but state law blocked each city's efforts. Similarly, a judge ruled that the St. Louis living wage ordinance was unconstitutional.

The comparison of employment trends in cities where the living wage ordinance was successful with those in cities where the ordinance eventually failed or was derailed shows that living wages do indeed raise the average wage level in the city, but they have adverse employment effects. An analysis of nearly 100 living wage ordinances indicated that the presence of a living wage ordinance in a locality reduced the probability of employment for persons in the bottom decile of the wage distribution, with the employment elasticity being around -0.1.

3-11   Adjustment Costs and Labor Demand

The model of labor demand derived in this chapter assumes that firms instantly adjust their employment when the economic environment changes. A firm wishing to adjust the size of its workforce, however, will typically find that it is costly to make quick changes. A firm laying off a large number of workers, for instance, will certainly incur substantial costs when the experience and knowledge of those workers vanish from the production line. A firm wishing to expand employment will find that hiring additional workers might be equally costly: the firm will have to process the job applicants through the personnel office

---

[36] The literature is surveyed by Scott Adams and David Neumark, "The Economic Effects of Living Wage Laws: A Provisional Review," *Urban Affairs Review* 40 (November 2004): 210–245. A nice example of is given by Larry D. Singell Jr. and James R. Terborg, "Employment Effects of Two Northwest Minimum Wage Initiatives," *Economic Inquiry* 45 (January 2007): 40–55.

[37] Scott Adams and David Neumark, "The Effects of Living Wage Laws: Evidence from Failed and Derailed Living Wage Campaigns," *Journal of Urban Economics* 58 (September 2005): 177–202.

FIGURE 3-21   Asymmetric Variable Adjustment Costs

Changing employment quickly is costly, and these costs increase at an increasing rate. If government policies prevent firms from firing workers, the costs of trimming the workforce will rise even faster than the costs of expanding the firm.

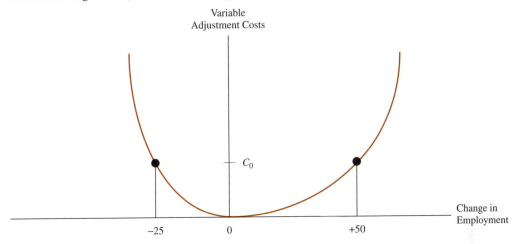

and train the new workers. The expenditures that firms incur as they adjust the size of their workforce are called **adjustment costs.**

There are two types of adjustment costs: *variable* adjustment costs and *fixed* adjustment costs. Variable adjustment costs depend on the number of workers that the firm is going to hire or fire. For example, the costs of training new workers obviously depend on whether the firm hires 1 or 10 workers. In contrast, fixed adjustment costs do not depend on how many workers the firm is going to hire or fire. Some of the expenses incurred in running a personnel office are independent of the number of job applicants or of the number of pink slips that the office might be processing.

Let's initially consider the firm's employment decisions in the presence of variable adjustment costs. Figure 3-21 illustrates one possible shape for the firm's variable adjustment cost curve. It costs the firm C_0 dollars to hire an additional 50 workers. It also costs the firm C_0 dollars to fire 25 workers. As drawn, it costs more to fire than to hire. This asymmetry might arise because of government policies that mandate employers to provide severance pay for workers who are laid off.

The variable adjustment cost curve illustrated in Figure 3-21 also incorporates the important assumption that the adjustment costs rise at an increasing rate, regardless of whether the firm is contracting or expanding. In other words, the marginal cost of adjustment (that is, the costs associated with hiring or firing an additional worker) is higher for the 50th worker hired than for the 25th worker hired. Similarly, the costs associated with handing out the 25th pink slip are lower than the costs associated with handing out the 50th pink slip.

It is easy to describe what happens to the firm's employment as the firm attempts to hire or fire additional workers in the presence of variable adjustment costs. Suppose, for instance, that the price of the output increases and that the firm expects this price increase to continue indefinitely. We know that the increase in output price will induce the firm to increase its employment from, say, 100 workers to 150 workers. Because it is costly to make an immediate transition to a new equilibrium, the firm will proceed slowly in hiring

FIGURE 3-22   The Slow Transition to a New Labor Equilibrium When a Firm Faces Variable Adjustment Costs

Variable adjustment costs encourage the firm to adjust the employment level slowly. The expansion from 100 to 150 workers might occur more rapidly than the contraction from 100 to 50 workers if government policies "tax" firms that cut employment.

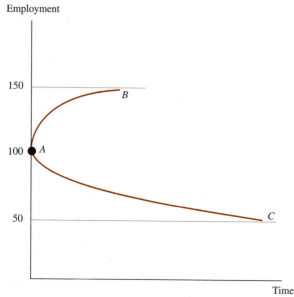

the additional workers, as illustrated by the adjustment path *AB* in Figure 3-22. A profit-maximizing firm will find that it is not worthwhile to hire all the additional workers immediately because the costs resulting from hiring a large number of workers at the same time exceed the costs incurred when hiring just a few workers at a time.

The same kind of slow adjustment occurs if the firm faces a decrease in output price. The firm would then like to cut employment from its initial level of 100 workers to 50 workers. Laying off too many workers at once, however, is disruptive, and the greater the number of layoffs, the higher the marginal cost of adjustment. The firm, therefore, will cut employment slowly, as illustrated by the adjustment path *AC* in Figure 3-22. As drawn, the firm is much slower in cutting employment than in adding workers. This asymmetry might arise if government mandates make it difficult for firms to trim their workforce.

Consider now the case where all of the adjustment costs are fixed and suppose that the firm is now hiring 100 workers, but, in response to an increase in output price, it would like to switch to a higher employment level of 200 workers. The instant the firm makes *any* change in its employment (whether adding 1 or 100 workers), the firm incurs this fixed adjustment cost. The firm then has two options. It can either choose to remain at its current employment level of 100 workers or adjust its employment to 200 workers. It does not pay for the firm to adjust its employment slowly because the fixed adjustment costs will be incurred regardless of how many additional workers the firm actually hires. If the firm is going to adjust its employment, it might as well adjust to the optimal level immediately.

The firm's decision will depend on which alternative yields higher profits. If the profits earned by maintaining the size of the workforce at 100 workers exceed the profits earned by adjusting to 200 workers (and bearing the fixed adjustment cost), the firm will shy away from adjusting its labor force. When fixed adjustment costs are sizable, therefore, employment changes in the firm will be sudden and large, if they occur at all.

The two types of adjustment costs, therefore, have very different implications for the dynamics of employment in the labor market. If variable adjustment costs are important, employment changes occur slowly as firms stagger their hiring and firing decisions to avoid the high costs incurred when making large changes in the size of the workforce. If fixed adjustment costs dominate, the firm will either remain at its current employment level or switch immediately to a different employment level.

The available evidence suggests that both variable and fixed adjustment costs play an important role in determining labor demand. In particular, variable adjustment costs might account for as much as 5 percent of the total wage bill in the early 1980s.[38] Because of these adjustment costs, it might take up to six months for the firm to adjust halfway to its optimal employment level when its economic environment changes. This result suggests that firms are continuously moving toward equilibrium, and that the firm's scale is not "what it should be" in the long run. As a result of variable adjustment costs, it has been estimated that the firm's output is typically off by about 2 percent from its desired output level. The evidence also indicates that many firms incur sizable fixed adjustment costs. A careful study of employment trends in the auto industry, for example, reveals that these firms change their employment suddenly by very large quantities, rather than gradually as implied by variable adjustment costs.[39]

The Impact of Employment Protection Legislation

To enhance the job security of workers, many developed countries have enacted legislation that imposes substantial costs on firms that initiate layoffs. For instance, Germany requires that firms notify the government before layoffs are announced, and many other countries mandate that firms offer severance pay to laid-off workers. Our analysis suggests that these policies influence the employment decisions of firms because they increase the costs of adjustment associated with layoffs. In particular, these policies would be expected to slow down the rate at which workers are laid off and may prevent layoffs altogether (if the policies substantially increase the fixed costs of adjustment). It is important to note, however, that these policies *also* discourage firms from hiring new workers during an economic expansion (because firms know that it will be difficult to lay off the workers when economic conditions worsen).

The evidence suggests that these job security provisions have an impact both on employment fluctuations and on labor demand. European countries that impose higher costs on layoffs (such as severance pay) have smaller fluctuations in employment over the

[38] Ray Fair, "Excess Labor and the Business Cycle," *American Economic Review* 75 (March 1985): 239–45; Jon Fay and James Medoff, "Labor and Output over the Business Cycle," *American Economic Review* 75 (September 1985): 638–55; and Ana Aizcorbe, "Procyclical Labor Productivity, Increasing Returns to Labor, and Labor Hoarding in U.S. Auto Assembly Plant Employment," *Economic Journal* 102 (1992): 860–873.

[39] Daniel S. Hamermesh, "Labor Demand and the Structure of Adjustment Costs," *American Economic Review* 79 (September 1989): 674–689; see also Paola Rota, "Estimating Labor Demand with Fixed Costs," *International Economic Review* 45 (February 2004): 25–48.

business cycle.[40] At the same time, however, mandating that employers pay three months' severance pay to laid-off workers with more than 10 years of seniority reduces the aggregate employment rate by about 1 percent.

The United States does not have a comprehensive job security law, except for the very weak advance notification legislation enacted in 1988. The Worker Adjustment and Retraining Notification Act (WARN) requires firms that employ at least 100 workers to give both their workers and local government officials a 60-day advance warning before closing down or initiating large-scale layoffs. The legislation, however, does not require that firms compensate laid-off workers (as is the case in many European countries).[41]

Even before the enactment of this legislation, there had been a steady erosion of the "employment-at-will" doctrine that long dominated the employment relationship in the U.S. nonunion sector, mainly because of the increasing volume of successful litigation by dismissed workers. For instance, there is some evidence that the weakening of the employment-at-will doctrine has reduced employment (by perhaps as much as 5 percent) in affected industries and states.[42] The weakening of the employment-at-will doctrine also encouraged many employers to switch from using long-term employees to temporary workers. Around 20 percent of the growth in the size of the temporary help services industry between 1973 and 1995 can be linked to this substitution.[43]

It is also worth adding that employment protection legislation affects not only the demand for labor, but also the amount of effort that workers supply to their jobs. In Italy, for example, it is difficult to fire workers after the 12th week of employment. A recent study examined the absentee rates of workers prior to and after this crucial point in their tenure.[44] Not surprisingly, workers are much more likely to be absent from their jobs after the

[40] Edward Lazear, "Job Security Provisions and Employment," *Quarterly Journal of Economics* 105 (August 1990): 699–726. See also Katharine G. Abraham and Susan N. Houseman, *Job Security in America: Lessons from Germany,* Washington, DC: Brookings Institute, 1993; Ronald Ehrenberg and George Jakubson, *Advance Notice Provisions in Plant Closing Legislation,* Kalamazoo, MI: W. E. Upjohn Institute, 1988; Marc A. Van Audenrode, "Short-Time Compensation, Job Security, and Employment Contracts: Evidence from Selected OECD Countries," *Journal of Political Economy* 102 (February 1994): 76–102; and John T. Addison and Jean-Luc Grosso, "Job Security and Employment: Revised Estimates," *Industrial Relations* 35 (October 1996): 585–603. A good survey of the literature is given by John T. Addison and Paulino Teixeira, "The Economics of Employment Protection," *Journal of Labor Research* 24 (Winter 2003): 85–129.

[41] The evidence suggests that the advance notice legislation has not been very effective; see John T. Addison and McKinley L. Blackburn, "The Worker Adjustment and Retraining Notification Act," *Journal of Economic Perspectives* 8 (Winter 1994): 181–190.

[42] James Dertouzos and Lynn Karoly, "Labor Market Responses to Employer Liability," The RAND Corporation, 1990; see also Alan B. Krueger, "The Evolution of Unjust Dismissal Legislation in the United States," *Industrial and Labor Relations Review* 44 (July 1991): 644–660.

[43] David H. Autor, "Outsourcing at Will: The Contribution of Unjust Dismissal Doctrine to the Growth of Employment Outsourcing," *Journal of Labor Economics* 21 (January 2003): 1–42; and David H. Autor, John J. Donahue III, and Stephen J. Schwab, "The Costs of Wrongful-Discharge Laws," *Review of Economics and Statistics* 88, no. 2 (2006): 211–231.

[44] Andrea Ichino and Regina T. Riphahn, "The Effect of Employment Protection on Worker Effort: Absenteeism during and after Probation," *Journal of the European Economic Association* 3 (March 2005): 120–143.

employment protection kicks in. This supply effect of employment protection legislation, of course, further increases the costs of employment and inevitably has feedback effects on the firm's willingness to hire additional workers.

The Distinction between Workers and Hours

Throughout this chapter, we have explicitly assumed that a change in the firm's labor demand is essentially a change in the number of workers that it hires. The firm, however, can adjust the number of employee-hours it wants by either changing the number of workers or changing the length of the workweek. The distinction between workers and hours is crucial in evaluating the impact of some employment policies. For example, the cost of employer-provided health insurance typically depends on the number of bodies employed. An increase in health insurance premiums would then discourage the firm from adding to its workforce. In contrast, legislation mandating employers to pay an overtime premium mainly affects the cost of lengthening the workweek.

The standard analysis of these issues starts by noting that workers and hours can play different roles in the production process.[45] In other words, an employer can use different combinations of workers and hours to produce the same output. Suppose, however, that the firm incurs a fixed cost of F dollars whenever the firm hires an additional worker. These fixed costs of hiring might include the cost of processing the person through the personnel office, training expenses, and government-mandated benefits such as health and pension programs. Once hired, the hourly wage rate is w dollars. The firm's demand for an additional hour of work will then cost only w dollars if that hour of work is conducted by a person who is already employed by the firm, but will cost $F + w$ dollars if that hour of work is conducted by a newly hired person.

What happens to the trade-off between hours and bodies when the firm faces an increase in the fixed costs of hiring (such as the imposition of a per-worker tax on firms to fund a national health insurance program)? When the fixed cost F increases, a substitution effect is generated. The firm would like to substitute away from the more expensive input (bodies) to the cheaper input (hours). In other words, the firm adjusts to the mandated increase in hiring cost by both lengthening the workweek and laying off workers. The increase in the fixed cost of hiring also generates a scale effect. Because the marginal cost of production rises, the firm contracts and will want to hire both fewer workers and fewer hours.

The evidence indicates that firms do substitute between workers and hours as the relative costs of the two factors of production change. It has been estimated that an increase in the overtime premium from time-and-a-half to double time may substantially change the number of full-time workers that the firm wishes to hire.[46] There is also evidence that employers prefer to hire full-time workers (rather than part-time workers) when the fixed

[45] The distinction between workers and hours is stressed by Sherwin Rosen, "Short-Run Employment Variation on Class-I Railroads in the U.S., 1947–63," *Econometrica* 36 (July–October 1968): 511–529; and Martin Feldstein, "Specifications of the Labor Input in the Aggregate Production Function," *Review of Economic Studies* 34 (October 1967): 375–386.

[46] Ronald G. Ehrenberg, "The Impact of the Overtime Premium on Employment and Hours in U.S. Industry," *Western Economic Journal* 9 (June 1971): 199–207.

Theory at Work
WORK-SHARING IN GERMANY

Many European countries experienced large unemployment rates in the 1990s. In France, the unemployment rate remained above 10 percent for much of that decade. In Germany, the unemployment rate has hovered around 9 percent since 1994. The persistence of this unemployment gave rise to the theory that unemployment can be reduced by sharing the available work among the many potential workers. In other words, more jobs would be created if the government mandated a reduction in the standard number of straight-time hours that the typical worker could work.

Several countries adopted this theory and reduced the length of the standard workweek. In 2000, for example, the French government mandated a reduction in the workweek from 39 to 35 hours. In Germany, the unions negotiated sizable reductions on an industry-by-industry basis. In the metalworking and printing sectors, for instance, the standard workweek fell from 40 to 36 hours between 1984 and 1994.

The concept of work-sharing can have an important unintended consequence—and may actually further *reduce* the demand for labor—because it ignores the fundamentals of economic theory. A reduction in the standard workweek imposes yet more constraints on the firm's decision of whether to hire an additional worker. After all, an employer who planned to use the new

workers for a 40-hour workweek at the straight-time wage will now have to pay an overtime premium after 35 hours. In effect, the reduction in the standard workweek may actually increase the average wage associated with hiring a new worker. As a result, employers who find it optimal to staff their factories with workers hired for a 40-hour shift find that the mandated reduction in the workweek increases the cost of hiring an additional worker. As a result, the employer will cut down on the number of hours demanded per worker *and* on the number of workers hired.

This is precisely what happened in Germany. The reduction in the standard workweek reduced the average number of hours worked weekly and increased the average wage rate—but total employment declined. Put differently, work-sharing held weekly income relatively constant for those lucky workers who remained at a job, but increased the number of persons without a job.

Sources: Jennifer Hunt, "Has Work-Sharing Worked in Germany?" *Quarterly Journal of Economics* 114 (February 1999): 117–148; see also Bruno Crépon and Francis Kramarz, "Employed 40 Hours or Not Employed 39: Lessons from the 1982 Mandatory Reduction of the Workweek," *Journal of Political Economy* 110 (December 2002): 1355–1389; and Phillippe Askenazy, "A Primer on the 35-Hour in France, 1997–2007," IZA Discussion Paper No. 3402, 2008.

costs of hiring are substantial.[47] For example, the employment of part-time workers in Great Britain fell substantially after the enactment of legislation that expanded employment protection for these workers.[48]

Job Creation and Job Destruction

As firms adjust to changes in the economic environment, new jobs are born and old jobs die. One of the most enduring "factoids" about the American economy is that most new jobs are created by small firms, which are often perceived to be the sole engine of economic growth. The Small Business Administration, for example, claims that "the term, 'Great American

[47] Mark Montgomery, "On the Determinants of Employer Demand for Part-Time Workers," *Review of Economics and Statistics* 70 (February 1988): 112–117; and Ronald G. Ehrenberg, Pamela Rosenberg, and Jeanne Li, "Part-Time Employment in the United States," in Robert Hart, editor, *Employment, Unemployment and Labor Utilization,* Boston: Unwin Hyman, 1988, pp. 256–281.

[48] Richard Disney and Erica M. Szyszczak, "Protective Legislation and Part-Time Employment in Britain," *British Journal of Industrial Relations* 22 (March 1984): 78–100.

Job Machine,' is appropriately applied to American small business," and President Clinton's 1993 State of the Union Address asserted that "because small business has created such a high percentage of all the new jobs in our nation over the last 10 or 15 years, our plan includes the boldest targeted incentives for small business in history."[49]

As our analysis of adjustment costs suggests, small firms would have an advantage in creating jobs if they could respond to favorable changes in the marketplace much faster than bigger firms (that is, if small firms face lower adjustment costs when creating new jobs). It also might be that small businesses have carved out a niche in the fastest-growing areas of the economy, or that the law of diminishing returns prevents large firms from expanding and hiring more workers.

A number of studies of the U.S. manufacturing sector conclusively show that a great deal of job creation and job destruction is *going on at the same time*. For example, in a typical year, nearly 11.3 percent of manufacturing jobs disappear, whereas nearly 9.2 percent of manufacturing jobs are newly created.[50] The annual net loss of jobs in the manufacturing sector was on the order of 2 percent.

The research also indicates that small firms are not the engines of employment growth that they are widely believed to be (at least in the manufacturing sector). Instead, large firms account for most newly created and newly destroyed manufacturing jobs.[51] In fact, firms with at least 500 workers account for 53 percent of all new jobs created and 56 percent of all jobs destroyed. Moreover, newly created jobs tend to last longer if they are created in larger firms. In particular, the probability that a newly created job still exists after one year is 76 percent for large firms and 65 percent for small firms. This is not surprising because large firms tend to be more stable; they create jobs that have a higher probability of surviving. Despite the popular mythology, therefore, it seems that large firms account for most of the new jobs in the U.S. manufacturing sector, and they create jobs that tend to be longer lasting.

3-12   Rosie the Riveter as an Instrumental Variable

A great deal of the state-of-the-art research done by labor economists involves trying to estimate labor demand and labor supply curves for particular groups. The findings reached by these studies are often used to predict how particular labor market shocks or policy changes will alter earnings and employment opportunities for workers and firms.

The typical effort to estimate a labor demand curve starts by observing data on employment and wages in a particular labor market—for example, the employment and wages of women. Figure 3-23 shows how the observed employment and wage data can be generated

---

[49] These quotes are drawn from Steven J. Davis, John Haltiwanger, and Scott Schuh, "Small Business and Job Creation: Dissecting the Myth and Reassessing the Facts," *Business Economics* 29 (July 1994): 13–21. See also David Neumark, Brandon Wall, and Junfu Zhang, "Do Small Businesses Create More Jobs? New Evidence for the United States from the National Establishment Time Series," *Review of Economics and Statistics* 93 (February 2011): 16–29.

[50] Steven J. Davis, John Haltiwanger, and Scott Schuh, *Job Creation and Destruction,* Cambridge, MA: MIT Press, 1996. See also Christian Belzil, "Job Creation and Job Destruction, Worker Reallocation, and Wages," *Journal of Labor Economics* 18 (April 1985): 183–203; and Simon Burgess, Julia Lane, and David Stevens, "Job Flows, Worker Flows, and Churning," *Journal of Labor Economics* 18 (July 2000): 473–502.

[51] Davis, Haltiwanger, and Schuh, "Small Business and Job Creation: Dissecting the Myth and Reassessing the Facts."

FIGURE 3-23 **Shifts in Labor Supply and Labor Demand Curves Generate the Observed Data on Wages and Employment**

The market is initially in equilibrium at point P, and we observe wage w_0 and employment E_0. If only the supply curve shifts, we can observe w_1 and E_1, and the available data would then allow us to trace out the labor demand curve. However, if both the supply and demand curves shift, we then observe w_2 and E_2, and the available data trace out the curve ZZ, which does not provide any information about the shape of the underlying labor demand curve.

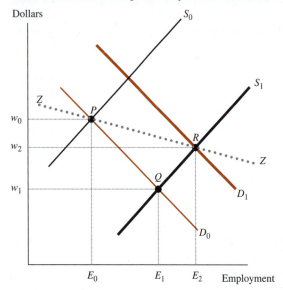

by our theory. Initially, the labor market is in equilibrium at point P, yielding wage w_0 and employment E_0. Suppose that the supply curve of women shifts to the right. The new equilibrium would be at point Q, yielding wage w_1 and employment E_1. The data we would observe consist of the pair of wages (w_0 and w_1) and the pair of employment statistics (E_0 and E_1). Figure 3-23 shows that these data can be used to essentially trace out (or *identify*) the labor demand curve. In other words, if we could observe a real-world situation where the only curve that shifted was the supply curve, the resulting data on wages and employment would allow us to estimate the labor demand elasticity.

Naturally, in most real-world situations, both the supply curve and the demand curve are shifting at the same time. When both curves shift, the new equilibrium would be at a point like R, with wage w_2 and employment E_2. The data we now observe consist of the pair of wages (w_0 and w_2) and the pair of employment statistics (E_0 and E_2). These data would allow us to trace out the curve ZZ in the figure, a curve that provides no information whatsoever about either the labor supply elasticity or the labor demand elasticity. When the two curves are moving at the same time, therefore, the resulting data on wages and employment do not help us identify the underlying structure of the labor market. Put differently, the resulting data (that is, the line ZZ) could not be used to predict how a particular policy shift (for example, an increase in the demand for high-tech workers by NASA) would affect wages and employment in the high-tech sector.

The "trick" for estimating the labor demand elasticity, therefore, is to find a situation where some underlying factor is shifting the supply curve but is leaving the demand curve fixed. In an econometric framework, we call a variable that shifts one of the curves and not the other an **instrument** or an **instrumental variable.** The availability of an instrument for supply lets us then use the **method of instrumental variables** to estimate the labor demand elasticity.[52]

A recent study provides a simple (and instructive) illustration of how particular historical events generate instruments that can be used to estimate the labor demand curve.[53] Nearly 16 million men were mobilized to serve in the Armed Forces during World War II, and around 73 percent of them were sent overseas. This shrinking in the number of male workers drew many women into the civilian labor force for the first time, giving rise to the stereotype of Rosie the Riveter, a woman who aided the war effort by performing "men's work." In 1940, only 28 percent of women over the age of 15 participated in the labor force. By 1945, the female participation rate was over 34 percent. Although many of these women left the labor force after the war, nearly half of them stayed, permanently increasing the number of working women by 1950 above what it would have been.[54]

To understand how the method of instrumental variables can be used in this context to estimate the labor demand curve for female labor, it is important to get a better sense of the historical circumstances. In October 1940, the Selective Service Act began a mandatory national draft registration for all men aged 21–35. By 1947, when the draft finally ended, six separate registrations had been mandated, eventually requiring all men aged 18–64 to register. After each of these registrations, the local draft boards used lotteries to determine the order in which registrants were called to active duty.

The local draft boards were authorized to grant draft deferments to particular groups of men. These deferments were typically based on a man's marital and parental status and on whether he had skills that were essential to civilian production. Farmers, for instance, were typically deferred because food was obviously needed to support the war effort. Because of these deferments, men living in farm states were substantially less likely to be drafted than men living in more urban states like New York or Massachusetts. In addition, because most military units were segregated during the war, relatively few blacks were drafted, and the geographic distribution of the black population created even more geographic differences in mobilization rates. Table 3-4 reports the mobilization rate for the various states, defined as the proportion of registered men aged 18–44 who served in the military between 1940 and 1945. The interstate variation is substantial. The rate was 41 percent in Georgia, 50 percent in California, and 55 percent in Massachusetts.

The mobilization rate provides the instrument that shifts the supply curve of female labor differently in different states. After all, Rosie would be more likely to become a riveter in those states where draft boards sent a larger fraction of men into active duty. As Figure 3-24*a* shows,

[52] Analogously, an instrument that shifted only the demand curve would allow us to estimate the labor supply elasticity.

[53] Daron Acemoglu, David H. Autor, and David Lyle, "Women, War and Wages: The Effect of Female Labor Supply on the Wage Structure at Midcentury," *Journal of Political Economy* 112 (June 2004): 497–551.

[54] Claudia Goldin, "The Role of World War II in the Rise of Women's Work," *American Economic Review* 81 (September 1991): 741–756.

TABLE 3-4   Mobilization Rate of Men and Changes in Female Wages and Employment, 1939–1949

Source: Daron Acemoglu, David H. Autor, and David Lyle, "Women, War and Wages: The Effect of Female Labor Supply on the Wage Structure at Midcentury," *Journal of Political Economy* 112 (June 2004): 497–551. The mobilization rate gives the proportion of men aged 18–44 who served in the military between 1940 and 1945; the percent change in female employment gives the log change in the total number of nonfarm weeks worked by women aged 14–64; the percent change in the female wage gives the (deflated) change in the log weekly wage of women employed full time multiplied by 100.

State	Mobilization Rate (%)	Change in Female Employment (%)	Change in Female Wage (%)	State	Mobilization Rate (%)	Change in Female Employment (%)	Change in Female Wage (%)
Alabama	43.6	20.3	81.0	New Jersey	49.7	24.3	35.7
Arkansas	43.6	19.2	79.5	New Mexico	47.8	51.1	50.6
Arizona	49.4	70.2	38.4	New York	48.4	24.9	33.7
California	50.0	65.7	31.3	North Carolina	42.1	23.3	51.6
Colorado	49.7	54.5	50.2	North Dakota	41.8	−12.5	51.8
Connecticut	49.4	27.9	34.5	Ohio	47.8	32.4	41.1
Delaware	46.9	39.4	24.6	Oklahoma	49.0	25.9	55.1
Florida	47.7	35.2	69.9	Oregon	53.1	66.5	42.3
Georgia	41.2	16.7	65.2	Pennsylvania	52.6	31.9	37.9
Idaho	49.8	53.3	58.1	Rhode Island	54.1	27.8	28.6
Illinois	47.6	26.2	42.0	South Carolina	42.7	31.1	80.0
Indiana	45.3	31.6	48.3	South Dakota	42.2	6.5	52.5
Iowa	45.3	2.9	51.2	Tennessee	44.9	19.5	52.4
Kansas	49.0	18.8	55.6	Texas	46.0	48.5	66.8
Kentucky	45.2	15.1	51.1	Utah	52.8	56.9	35.3
Louisiana	43.5	19.5	69.4	Vermont	47.3	21.9	62.6
Maine	50.3	19.1	38.4	Virginia	44.7	34.5	56.1
Maryland	46.9	22.1	48.9	Washington	52.4	72.8	39.2
Massachusetts	54.5	24.8	26.9	West Virginia	48.4	27.3	47.5
Michigan	45.3	39.1	48.6	Wisconsin	43.3	27.3	44.4
Minnesota	46.8	23.9	47.5	Wyoming	48.9	36.2	39.6
Mississippi	43.7	2.2	73.0				
Missouri	45.5	13.2	48.2				
Montana	49.4	10.1	44.2				
Nebraska	46.3	30.4	49.0				
New Hampshire	53.0	20.1	41.8				

there is a strong positive correlation between the 1939–49 growth in female employment and the state's mobilization rate. The regression line (with standard errors in parentheses) is

$$\text{Percent change in female employment} = -94.56 + 2.62 \text{ Mobilization rate} \tag{3-23}$$
$$\quad (31.88) \quad (0.67)$$

This regression equation implies that a 1 point increase in the mobilization rate increased female labor supply by 2.62 percent.

It also turns out that the interstate differences in mobilization rates are strongly correlated with the wage growth experienced by female workers. Figure 3-24*b* shows a strong negative

FIGURE 3-24 **The Impact of Wartime Mobilization of Men on Female Labor Supply and Wages**

(*a*) Mobilization Rate and Changes in Female Employment, by State

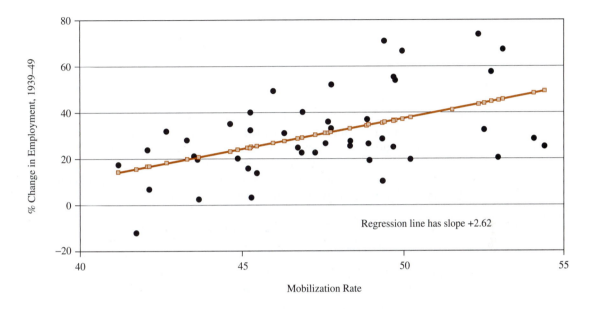

(*b*) Mobilization Rate and Changes in Female Wages, by State

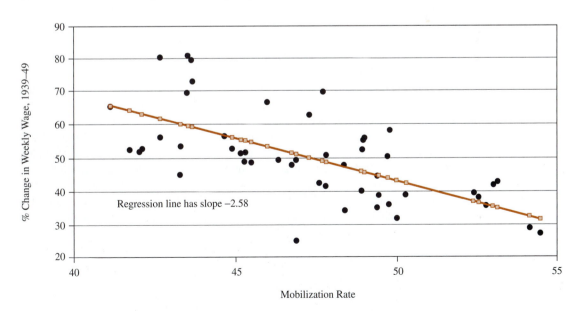

relation between the 1939–49 percent change in the female wage and the mobilization rate. In other words, female wages grew least in those states where a larger proportion of men went off to war. In fact, the regression line relating these two variables is

$$
\begin{aligned}
\text{Percent change in female wage} &= \\
171.69 &- 2.58 \text{ Mobilization rate} \\
(21.45)\ &(0.45)
\end{aligned}
\tag{3-24}
$$

The slope coefficient of this regression line indicates that a 1 point increase in the mobilization rate is associated with a 2.58 percent drop in the female wage.

The regression models reported in equations (3-23) and (3-24) can now be used to estimate the labor demand elasticity. The data tell us that for every 1 point increase in the male mobilization rate, female employment increased by 2.62 percent and female wages fell by 2.58 percent. Put differently, a historical event that reduced the female wage by 2.58 percent was associated with a 2.62 percent increase in female employment. Therefore, the labor demand elasticity is given by the ratio of these two numbers, or

$$
\delta = \frac{\text{Percent change in female employment}}{\text{Percent change in female wage}} = \frac{2.62}{-2.58} = -1.02 \tag{3-25}
$$

The historical experience of female wages and employment during World War II thus suggests that the labor demand elasticity for women is around -1.0.

The methodological approach summarized visually in Figures 3-24a and 3-24b can be expanded to control for other factors that might shift the labor supply or labor demand curves differently in different states, such as the educational attainment and age distribution of female workers. Although this multivariate approach cannot be easily illustrated, the method of instrumental variables relies on the same basic logic: the availability of an instrument that shifts only the labor supply curve allows us to use the resulting data on wages and employment to trace out the labor demand curve.

The discussion also illuminates the main weakness of the instrumental variable approach: The legitimacy of the entire exercise hinges on finding a *valid* instrument, a variable that shifts only one of the curves in the supply-demand framework. A great deal of the disagreement over the interpretation of many empirical results in labor economics often hinges on whether the researcher is using a valid instrument that allows her to trace out or identify either the labor supply or the labor demand curve. The ratio in equation (3-25) is a labor demand elasticity only if interstate differences in the mobilization rate generated interstate differences in female labor supply but did not generate interstate differences in female labor demand. As we have seen, the labor demand curve is given by the value of marginal product curve. The mobilization rate would then be a valid instrument only if it is uncorrelated with both interstate differences in the price level and interstate differences in female productivity.

Summary

- In the short run, a profit-maximizing firm hires workers up to the point where the wage equals the value of marginal product of labor.
- In the long run, a profit-maximizing firm hires each input up to the point where the price of the input equals the value of marginal product of the input. This condition implies that the optimal input mix is one in which the ratio of marginal products of labor and capital equals the ratio of input prices.
- In the long run, a decrease in the wage generates both substitution and scale effects. Both of these effects spur the firm to hire more workers.
- Both the short-run and long-run demand curves for labor are downward sloping, but the long-run demand curve is more elastic than the short-run curve.
- The short-run labor demand elasticity may be on the order of -0.4 to -0.5. The long-run elasticity is on the order of -1.
- Capital and skilled workers are complements in the sense that an increase in the price of capital reduces the demand for skilled workers. Capital and unskilled workers are substitutes in the sense that an increase in the price of capital increases the demand for unskilled workers.
- The imposition of a minimum wage on a competitive labor market creates unemployment because some workers are displaced from their jobs and because new workers enter the labor market hoping to find one of the high-paying (but scarce) jobs.
- The elasticity of teenage employment with respect to the minimum wage is on the order of -0.1 to -0.3.
- The presence of variable adjustment costs implies that firms adjust their employment slowly when the wage changes. If fixed adjustment costs are important, employment changes in the firm are large and sudden, if they occur at all.
- An instrument is a variable that shifts either the supply or demand curve. The variation caused by this shock can be used to estimate the labor demand or labor supply elasticity.

Key Concepts

adjustment costs, *127*
average product, *87*
capital-skill complementarity hypothesis, *114*
cross-elasticity of factor demand, *112*
demand curve for labor, *90*

elasticity of labor demand, *91*
elasticity of substitution, *106*
equilibrium, *114*
instrument, *135*
instrumental variable, *135*
isocost, *96*
isoquant, *94*

law of diminishing returns, *87*
marginal cost, *92*
marginal product of capital, *85*
marginal product of labor, *85*
marginal productivity condition, *92*

Review Questions

1. Why does a profit-maximizing firm hire workers up to the point where the wage equals the value of marginal product? Show that this condition is identical to the one that requires a profit-maximizing firm to produce the level of output where the price of the output equals the marginal cost of production.

2. Why is the short-run demand curve for labor downward sloping?

3. What mix of inputs should be used to produce a given level of output?

4. Suppose the firm is hiring labor and capital and that the ratio of marginal products of the two inputs equals the ratio of input prices. Does this imply that the firm is maximizing profits? Why or why not?

5. Suppose the wage increases. Show that in the long run the firm will hire fewer workers. Decompose the employment change into substitution and scale effects.

6. What factors determine the elasticity of the industry's labor demand curve?

7. What is the capital-skill complementarity hypothesis?

8. Show how the minimum wage creates unemployment in a competitive market.

9. Discuss the impact of the minimum wage when there are two sectors in the economy: the covered sector (which is subject to the minimum wage) and the uncovered sector (which is not).

10. Summarize the evidence regarding the impact of the minimum wage on employment.

11. How does the firm adjust its employment if it is costly to hire and fire workers?

12. Explain how and why the method of instrumental variables allows us to estimate the labor demand elasticity.

Problems

3-1. Suppose there are two inputs in the production function, labor and capital, and these two inputs are perfect substitutes. The existing technology permits one machine to do the work of three workers. The firm wants to produce 100 units of output. Suppose the price of capital is $750 per machine per week. What combination of inputs will the firm use if the weekly salary of each worker is $300? What combination of inputs will the firm use if the weekly salary of each worker is $225? What is the elasticity of labor demand as the wage falls from $300 to $225?

3-2. Figure 3-18 in the text shows the ratio of the federal minimum wage to the average hourly manufacturing wage.

   a. Describe how this ratio has changed from the 1950s to the 1990s. What might have caused this apparent shift in fundamental economic behavior in the United States?

   b. This ratio fell steadily from 1968 to 1974 and again from 1980 to 1990, but the underlying dynamics of the minimum wage and the average manufacturing wage were different during the two time periods. Explain.

3-3. Union A wants to represent workers in a firm that would hire 20,000 workers if the wage rate is $12 and would hire 10,000 workers if the wage rate is $15. Union B wants to represent workers in a firm that would hire 30,000 workers if the wage rate is $20 and would hire 33,000 workers if the wage rate is $15. Which union is likely to organize?

3-4. Consider a firm for which production depends on two normal inputs, labor and capital, with prices w and r, respectively. Initially the firm faces market prices of $w = 6$ and $r = 4$. These prices then shift to $w = 4$ and $r = 2$.

   a. In which direction will the substitution effect change the firm's employment and capital stock?

   b. In which direction will the scale effect change the firm's employment and capital stock?

   c. Can we say conclusively whether the firm will use more or less labor? More or less capital?

3-5. What happens to employment in a competitive firm that experiences a technology shock such that at every level of employment its output is 200 units per hour greater than before?

3-6. What type of instrumental variable is needed to estimate the labor supply elasticity? Can you think of any historical instances that would allow for this?

3-7. Suppose a firm purchases labor in a competitive labor market and sells its product in a competitive product market. The firm's elasticity of demand for labor is -0.4. Suppose the wage increases by 5 percent. What will happen to the amount of labor hired by the firm? What will happen to the marginal productivity of the last worker hired by the firm?

3-8. A firm's technology requires it to combine 5 person-hours of labor with 3 machine-hours to produce 1 unit of output. The firm has 15 machines in place and the wage rate rises from $10 per hour to $20 per hour. What is the firm's short-run elasticity of labor demand?

3-9. In a particular industry, labor supply is $E_S = 10 + w$ and labor demand is $E_D = 40 - 4w$, where E is the level of employment and w is the hourly wage.

   a. What are the equilibrium wage and employment if the labor market is competitive? What is the unemployment rate?

   b. Suppose the government sets a minimum hourly wage of $8. How many workers would lose their jobs? How many additional workers would want a job at the minimum wage? What is the unemployment rate?

3-10. Suppose the hourly wage is $10 and the price of each unit of capital is $25. The price of output is constant at $50 per unit. The production function is

$$f(E,K) = E^{1/2}K^{1/2}$$

so that the marginal product of labor is

$$MP_E = (1/2)(K/E)^{1/2}$$

If the current capital stock is fixed at 1,600 units, how much labor should the firm employ in the short run? How much profit will the firm earn?

3-11. Table 630 of the 2008 *U.S. Statistical Abstract* reports the federal nominal (current dollar) hourly minimum wages from 1960 through 2009. Use the consumer price index in Table 702 to create the real hourly minimum wages from 1960 through 2009 using year 2000 dollars. Under which president did the nominal minimum wage increase the most? the least? Under which president did the real minimum wage increase the most? the least?

3-12. How does the amount of unemployment created by an increase in the minimum wage depend on the elasticity of labor demand? Do you think an increase in the minimum wage will have a greater unemployment effect in the fast-food industry or in the lawn-care/landscaping industry?

3-13. Which one of Marshall's rules suggests why labor demand should be relatively inelastic for public school teachers and nurses? Explain.

3-14. Draw on a single graph the time to transition to a new labor equilibrium when a firm faces variable adjustment costs for the following two firms.

   a. A trucking firm currently employs 100 drivers. If the economy enters an expansionary period, the firm would like to employ 120 drivers for the foreseeable future. If the economy enters a contractionary period, the firm would like to employ 80 drivers for the foreseeable future. There are few regulations in the hiring and firing of truck drivers.

   b. A liberal arts college currently employs 100 professors—70 of whom are tenured, 20 of whom are on a tenure-track position, and 10 of whom are instructors not on a tenure track. (An assistant professor with a tenure-track position will eventually either be denied tenure and asked to leave the college or be granted tenure. Tenured faculty can only be released by the college if the professor engages in improper behavior or if the college faces extreme financial problems.) If the economy enters an expansionary period, the college would like to employ 120 professors for the foreseeable future. If the economy enters a contractionary period, the college would like to hire 80 professors for the foreseeable future. Legally it is very difficult to remove tenured professors, even during bad economic times. It is also very difficult to find (and hire) many high-quality professors during good economic times. Finally, almost all of the college's professors must be tenured or on a tenure-track position in order to satisfy student and parent demands that the college employ high-quality professors.

3-15. Consider a production model with two inputs—domestic labor (E_{Dom}) and foreign labor (E_{For}). The market is originally in equilibrium in that

$$\frac{MP_{E_{\text{Dom}}}}{w_{\text{Dom}}} = \frac{MP_{E_{\text{For}}}}{w_{\text{For}}}$$

Then a wage shock occurs to cause a substantial amount of outsourcing. Specifically, as a result of the shock, E_{Dom} falls considerably while E_{For} increases considerably.

   a. Show that the shock either increased the domestic wage or decreased the foreign wage, at least relatively.

   b. In the years following the shock, what are three (significantly different) policies that the domestic country could employ if it wanted to reverse the outflow of labor?

Selected Readings

Daron Acemoglu, David H. Autor, and David Lyle, "Women, War and Wages: The Effect of Female Labor Supply on the Wage Structure at Midcentury," *Journal of Political Economy* 112 (June 2004): 497–551.

David H. Autor, "Outsourcing at Will: The Contribution of Unjust Dismissal Doctrine to the Growth of Employment Outsourcing," *Journal of Labor Economics* 21 (January 2003): 1–42.

David Card and Alan B. Krueger, "Minimum Wages and Employment: A Case Study of the Fast-Food Industry in New Jersey and Pennsylvania," *American Economic Review* 84 (September 1994): 772–793.

Alida J. Castillo-Freeman and Richard B. Freeman, "When the Minimum Wage Really Bites: The Effect of the U.S.-Level Minimum on Puerto Rico," in George J. Borjas and Richard B. Freeman, editors, *Immigration and the Work Force: Economic Consequences for the United States and Source Areas.* Chicago: University of Chicago Press, 1992, pp. 177–211.

Bruno Crépon and Francis Kramarz, "Employed 40 Hours or Not Employed 39: Lessons from the 1982 Mandatory Reduction of the Workweek," *Journal of Political Economy* 110 (December 2002): 1355–1389.

Claudia Goldin and Lawrence F. Katz, "The Origins of Technology-Skill Complementarity," *Quarterly Journal of Economics* 113 (August 1998): 693–732.

Daniel S. Hamermesh and Stephen J. Trejo, "The Demand for Hours of Labor: Direct Estimates from California," *Review of Economics and Statistics* 82 (February 2000): 38–47.

Andrea Ichino and Regina T. Riphahn, "The Effect of Employment Protection on Worker Effort: Absenteeism during and after Probation," *Journal of the European Economic Association* 3 (March 2005): 120–143.

David Neumark and William Wascher, "Minimum Wages and Employment," *Foundations and Trends in Microeconomics* 3 (2007): 1–182.

Web Links

The Department of Labor's Web site contains a detailed description of the provisions in the Federal Labor Standards Act (FLSA): www.dol.gov/esa/whd/flsa.

Many nonprofit organizations have strong policy positions on the minimum wage and maintain informative Web sites. Two (very different) examples are the Employment Policies Institute (www.epionline.org) and the Coalition on Human Needs (www.chn.org).

Chapter 4

Labor Market Equilibrium

Order is not pressure which is imposed on society from without, but an equilibrium which is set up from within.

—*José Ortega y Gasset*

Workers prefer to work when the wage is high, and firms prefer to hire when the wage is low. Labor market equilibrium "balances out" the conflicting desires of workers and firms and determines the wage and employment observed in the labor market. By understanding how equilibrium is reached, we can address what is perhaps the most interesting question in labor economics: Why do wages and employment go up and down?

This chapter analyzes the properties of equilibrium in a perfectly competitive labor market. We will see that if markets are competitive and if firms and workers are free to enter and leave these markets, the equilibrium allocation of workers to firms is efficient; the sorting of workers to firms maximizes the total gains that workers and firms accumulate by trading with each other. This result is an example of Adam Smith's justly famous **invisible hand theorem,** wherein labor market participants in search of their own selfish goals attain an outcome that no one in the market consciously sought to achieve. The implication that competitive labor markets are efficient plays an important role in the framing of public policy. In fact, the impact of many government programs is often debated in terms of whether the particular policy leads to a more efficient allocation of resources or whether the efficiency costs are substantial.

We also will analyze the properties of labor market equilibrium under alternative market structures, such as monopsonies (where there is only one buyer of labor) and monopolies (where there is only one seller of the output). Each of these market structures generates an equilibrium with its own unique features. Monopsonists, for instance, generally hire fewer workers and pay less than competitive firms.

Finally, the chapter uses a number of policy applications—such as taxes, subsidies, and immigration—to illustrate how government policies shift the labor market to a different equilibrium, thereby altering the economic opportunities available to both firms and workers.

4-1 Equilibrium in a Single Competitive Labor Market

We have already briefly discussed how a competitive labor market attains equilibrium. We now provide a more detailed discussion of the properties of this equilibrium. Figure 4-1 illustrates the familiar graph showing the intersection of labor supply (S) and labor demand (D) curves in a competitive market. The supply curve gives the total number of employee-hours that agents in the economy allocate to the market at any given wage level; the demand curve gives the total number of employee-hours that firms in the market demand at that wage. Equilibrium occurs when supply equals demand, generating the competitive wage w^* and employment E^*. The wage w^* is the market-clearing wage because any other wage level would create either upward or downward pressures on the wage; there would be too many jobs chasing the few available workers or too many workers competing for the few available jobs.

Once the competitive wage level is determined in this fashion, each firm in this industry hires workers up to the point where the value of marginal product of labor equals the competitive wage. The first firm hires E_1 workers; the second firm hires E_2 workers; and so on. The total number of workers hired by all the firms in the industry must equal the market's equilibrium employment level, E^*.

FIGURE 4-1 **Equilibrium in a Competitive Labor Market**

The labor market is in equilibrium when supply equals demand; E^* workers are employed at a wage of w^*. In equilibrium, all persons who are looking for work at the going wage can find a job. The triangle P gives the producer surplus; the triangle Q gives the worker surplus. A competitive market maximizes the gains from trade, or the sum $P + Q$.

Dollars

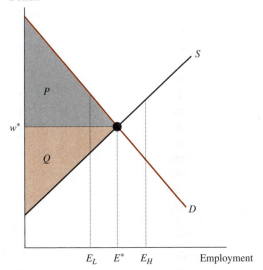

As Figure 4-1 shows, there is no unemployment in a competitive labor market. At the market wage w^*, the number of persons who want to work equals the number of workers firms want to hire. Persons who are not working are also not looking for work *at the going wage*. Of course, many of these persons would enter the labor market if the wage rose (and many would withdraw if the wage fell).

Needless to say, a modern industrialized economy is continually subjected to many shocks that shift both the supply and demand curves. It is unlikely, therefore, that the labor market actually ever reaches a stable equilibrium—with wages and employment remaining at a constant level for a long time. Nevertheless, the concept of labor market equilibrium remains useful because it helps us understand why wages and employment seem to go up or down in response to particular economic or political events. As the labor market reacts to a particular shock, wages and employment will tend to move toward their new equilibrium level.

Efficiency

Figure 4-1 also shows the benefits that accrue to the national economy as workers and firms trade with each other in the labor market. In a competitive market, E^* workers are employed at a wage of w^*. The total revenue accruing to the firm can be easily calculated by adding up the value of marginal product of the first worker, the second worker, and all workers up to E^*. This sum, in effect, gives the value of the total product produced by all workers in a competitive equilibrium. Because the labor demand curve gives the value of marginal product, it must be the case that the area under the labor demand curve gives the value of total product. Each worker receives a wage of w^*. Hence, the profits accruing to firms, which we call **producer surplus,** are given by the area of the triangle P.[1]

---

[1] To simplify the discussion, assume that labor is the only factor in the production function.

Workers also gain. The supply curve gives the wage required to bribe additional workers into the labor market. In effect, the height of the supply curve at a given point measures the value of the marginal worker's time in alternative uses. The difference between what the worker receives (that is, the competitive wage w^*) and the value of the worker's time outside the labor market gives the gains accruing to workers. This quantity is called **worker surplus** and is given by the area of the triangle Q in Figure 4-1.

The total **gains from trade** accruing to the national economy are given by the sum of producer surplus and worker surplus, or the area $P + Q$. *The competitive market maximizes the total gains from trade accruing to the economy.* To see why, consider what the gains would be if firms hired more than E^* workers, say E_H. The "excess" workers have a value of marginal product that is less than their value of time elsewhere. In effect, these workers are not being efficiently used by the labor market; they are better off elsewhere. Similarly, consider what would happen if firms hired too few workers, say E_L. The "missing" workers have a value of marginal product that exceeds their value of time elsewhere, and their resources would be more efficiently used if they worked.

The allocation of persons to firms that maximizes the total gains from trade in the labor market is called an **efficient allocation.** A competitive equilibrium generates an efficient allocation of labor resources.

4-2 Competitive Equilibrium across Labor Markets

The discussion in the previous section focused on the consequences of equilibrium in a *single* competitive labor market. The economy, however, typically consists of many labor markets, even for workers who have similar skills. These labor markets might be differentiated by region (so that we can talk about the labor market in the Northeast and the labor market in California), or by industry (the labor market for production workers in the automobile industry and the labor market for production workers in the steel industry).

Suppose there are two regional labor markets in the economy, the North and the South. We assume that the two markets employ workers of similar skills so that persons working in the North are perfect substitutes for persons working in the South. Figure 4-2 illustrates the labor supply and labor demand curves in each of the two labor markets (S_N and D_N in the North, and S_S and D_S in the South). For simplicity, the supply curves are represented by vertical lines, implying that supply is perfectly inelastic within each region. As drawn, the equilibrium wage in the North, w_N, exceeds the equilibrium wage in the South, w_S.

Can this wage differential between the two regions persist and represent a true competitive equilibrium? No. After all, workers in the South see their northern counterparts earning more. This wage differential encourages southern workers to pack up and move north, where they can earn higher wages and presumably attain a higher level of utility. Employers in the North also see the wage differential and realize that they can do better by moving to the South. After all, workers are equally skilled in the two regions, and firms can make more money by hiring cheaper labor.

If workers can move across regions freely, the migration flow will shift the supply curves in both regions. In the South, the supply curve for labor would shift to the left (to S'_S) as southern workers leave the region, raising the southern wage. In the North, the supply curve would shift to the right (to S'_N) as the southerners arrived, depressing the northern wage. If there were free

FIGURE 4-2 **Competitive Equilibrium in Two Labor Markets Linked by Migration**

The wage in the northern region (w_N) exceeds the wage in the southern region (w_S). Southern workers want to move north, shifting the southern supply curve to the left and the northern supply curve to the right. In the end, wages are equated across regions (at w^*). The migration of workers reduces the gains from trade in the South by the size of the shaded trapezoid in the southern labor market, and increases the gains from trade in the North by the size of the larger shaded trapezoid in the northern labor market. Migration increases the total gains from trade in the national economy by the triangle ABC.

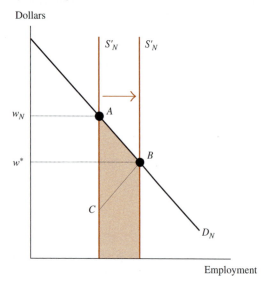

(a) The Northern Labor Market

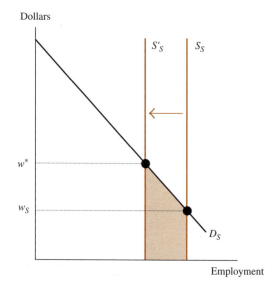

(b) The Southern Labor Market

entry and exit of workers in and out of labor markets, the national economy would eventually be characterized by a single wage, w^*.

Note that wages across the two labor markets also would be equalized if firms (instead of workers) could freely enter and exit labor markets. When northern firms close their plants and move to the South, the demand curve for northern labor shifts to the left and lowers the northern wage, whereas the demand curve for southern labor shifts to the right, raising the southern wage. The incentives for firms to move across markets evaporate once the regional wage differential disappears. As long as either workers or firms are free to enter and exit labor markets, therefore, a competitive economy will be characterized by a single wage.[2]

Efficiency Revisited

The "single wage" property of a competitive equilibrium has important implications for economic efficiency. Recall that, in a competitive equilibrium, the wage equals the value of marginal product of labor. As firms and workers move to the region that provides the

[2] A study of whether a labor market can be considered competitive is given by Stephen Machin and Alan Manning, "A Test of Competitive Labor Market Theory: The Wage Structure among Care Assistants in the South of England," *Industrial and Labor Relations Review* 57 (April 2004): 371–385.

best opportunities, they eliminate regional wage differentials. Therefore, workers of given skills have the same value of marginal product of labor in all markets.

The allocation of workers to firms that equates the value of marginal product across markets is also the sorting that leads to an efficient allocation of labor resources. To see why, suppose that a benevolent dictator takes over the economy and that this dictator has the power to dispatch workers across regions. In making allocation decisions, suppose this benevolent dictator has one overriding objective: to allocate workers to those places where they are most productive. When the dictator first takes over, he faces the initial situation illustrated in Figure 4-2, where the competitive wage in the North (w_N) exceeds the competitive wage in the South (w_S). Note that this wage gap implies that the value of marginal product of labor is greater in the North than in the South.

The dictator picks a worker in the South at random. What should he do with this worker? Because the dictator wants to place this worker where he is most productive, the worker is dispatched to the North. In fact, the dictator will keep reallocating workers to the northern region as long as the value of marginal product of labor is greater in the North than in the South. The law of diminishing returns implies that as the dictator forces more and more people to work in the North, the value of marginal product of northern workers declines and the value of marginal product of southern workers rises. The dictator will stop reallocating persons when the labor force consists only of persons whose value of marginal product exceeds the value of their time outside the labor market *and* when the value of marginal product is the same in all labor markets.

It is also easy to see how migration leads to an efficient allocation of resources by calculating the gains from trade in the labor market. Because the supply curves in Figure 4-2 are perfectly inelastic (implying that the value of time outside the labor market is zero), the total gains from trade are given by the area under the demand curve up to the equilibrium level of employment. The migration of workers out of the South reduces the total gains from trade in the South by the shaded area of the trapezoid in the southern labor market. The migration of workers into the North increases the total gains from trade in the North by the shaded area of the trapezoid in the northern labor market. A comparison of the two trapezoids reveals that the area of the northern trapezoid exceeds the area of the southern trapezoid by the size of the triangle *ABC,* implying that the total gains from trade in the national economy increase as a result of worker migration.

The surprising implication of our analysis should be clear: *Through an "invisible hand," workers and firms that search selfishly for better opportunities accomplish a goal that no one in the economy had in mind: an efficient allocation of resources.*

Convergence of Regional Wage Levels

There is a great deal of interest in determining whether regional wage differentials in the United States (as well as in other countries) narrow over time, as implied by our analysis of labor market equilibrium. Many empirical studies suggest that there is indeed a tendency toward convergence.[3]

---

[3] Robert J. Barro and Xavier Sala-i-Martin, "Convergence across States and Regions," *Brookings Papers on Economic Activity* (1991): 107–158; and Olivier Jean Blanchard and Lawrence F. Katz, "Regional Evolutions," *Brookings Papers on Economic Activity* 1 (1992): 1–61.

FIGURE 4-3 Wage Convergence across States

Source: Olivier Jean Blanchard and Lawrence F. Katz, "Regional Evolutions," *Brookings Papers on Economic Activity* 1 (1992): 1–61.

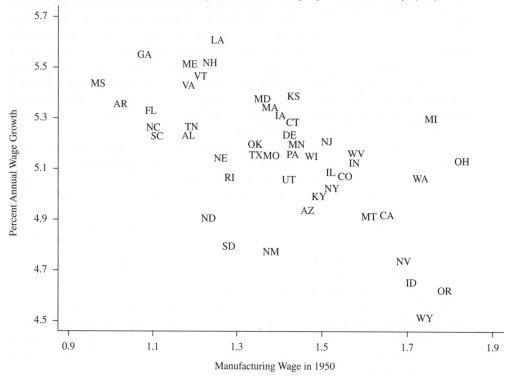

Figure 4-3 summarizes the key data underlying the study of wage convergence across states in the United States. The figure relates the annual growth rate in the state's manufacturing wage between 1950 and 1990 to the initial wage level in 1950. There is a strong negative relationship between the rate of wage growth and the initial wage level so that the states with the lowest wages in 1950 subsequently experienced the fastest wage growth. It has been estimated that about half the wage gap across states disappears in about 30 years. The evidence indicates, therefore, that wage levels do converge over time—although it may take a few decades before wages are equalized across markets.

Wage convergence also is found in countries where the workforce is less mobile, such as Japan. A study of the Japanese labor market indicates that wage differentials across prefectures (a geographic unit roughly comparable to a large U.S. county) disappear at about the same rate as interstate wage differentials in the United States: half of the regional differences vanish within a generation.[4]

---

[4] Robert J. Barro and Xavier Sala-i-Martin, "Regional Growth and Migration: A Japan–United States Comparison," *Journal of the Japanese and International Economies* 6 (December 1992): 312–346. Other international studies of wage convergence within regions of a country include Christer Lundh, Lennart Schon, and Lars Svensson, "Regional Wages in Industry and Labour Market Integration in Sweden, 1861–1913," *Scandinavian Economic History Review* 53 (2005): 71–84; and Joan R. Roses and Blanca Sanchez-Alonso, "Regional Wage Convergence in Spain 1850–1930," *Explorations in Economic History* 41 (October 2004): 404–425.

Of course, the efficient allocation of workers across labor markets and the resulting wage convergence are not limited to labor markets within a country, but also might occur when we compare labor markets across countries. Many recent studies have attempted to determine if international differences in per capita income are narrowing.[5] Much of this work is motivated by a desire to understand why the income gap between rich and poor countries seems to persist.

The empirical studies typically conclude that when one compares two countries with roughly similar endowments of human capital (for example, the educational attainment of the population), the wage gap between these countries narrows over time, with about half the gap disappearing within a generation. This result, called "conditional" convergence (because it compares countries that are already similar in terms of the human capital endowment of the workforce), does not necessarily imply that there will be convergence in income levels between rich and poor countries. The wage gap between rich and poor countries can persist for much longer periods because the very low levels of human capital in poor countries do not permit these countries to be on the same growth path as the wealthier countries.

The rate of convergence in income levels across countries plays an important role in the debate over many crucial policy issues. Consider, for instance, the long-term effects of the North American Free Trade Agreement (NAFTA). This agreement permits the unhampered transportation of goods (but not of people) across international boundaries throughout much of the North American continent (Canada, the United States, and Mexico).

In 2000, per capita GDP in the United States was over three times as large as that in Mexico. Our analysis suggests that NAFTA should eventually reduce the huge income differential between Mexico and the United States. As U.S. firms move to Mexico to take advantage of the cheaper labor, the demand curve for Mexican labor shifts out and the wage differential between the two countries will narrow. Our discussion suggests that U.S. workers who are most substitutable with Mexican workers will experience a wage cut as a result of the increase in trade. At the same time, however, American consumers will gain from the increased availability of cheaper goods. In short, NAFTA will likely create distinct groups of winners and losers in the American economy. In fact, the available evidence suggests that manufacturing firms are now finding the Mexican labor market to be relatively expensive.[6]

Although NAFTA inevitably affects the distribution of income across the three countries, our analysis of labor market efficiency implies that the *total* income of the countries in the free-trade zone is maximized when economic opportunities are equalized across countries. In other words, the equalization of wages across the three signatories of NAFTA increases the size of the economic pie available to the entire region. *In principle,* the additional wealth can be redistributed to the population of the three countries so as to make

[5] Robert J. Barro, "Economic Growth in a Cross-Section of Countries," *Quarterly Journal of Economics* 105 (May 1990): 501–526; N. Gregory Mankiw, David Romer, and David N. Weil, "A Contribution to the Empirics of Economic Growth," *Quarterly Journal of Economics* 107 (May 1991): 407–437; and Xavier Sala-i-Martin, "The World Distribution of Income: Falling Poverty and . . . Convergence, Period," *Quarterly Journal of Economics* 121 (May 2006): 351–397.

[6] Elisabeth Malkin, "Manufacturing Jobs Are Exiting Mexico," *New York Times,* November 5, 2002.

everyone in the region better off. This link between free trade and economic efficiency is typically the essential point emphasized by economists when they argue in favor of more open markets.[7]

4-3 Policy Application: Payroll Taxes and Subsidies

We can easily illustrate the usefulness of the supply and demand framework by considering a government policy that shifts the labor demand curve. In the United States, some government programs are funded partly through a payroll tax assessed on employers. In 2011, firms paid a tax of 6.2 percent on the first $106,800 of a worker's annual earnings to fund the Social Security system and an additional tax of 1.45 percent on all of a worker's annual earnings to fund Medicare.[8] In other countries, the payroll tax on employers is even higher. In Germany, for example, the payroll tax is 17.2 percent; in Italy, it is 21.2 percent; and in France, it is 25.3 percent.[9]

What happens to wages and employment when the government assesses a payroll tax on employers? Figure 4-4 answers this question. Prior to the imposition of the tax, the labor demand curve is given by D_0 and the supply of labor to the industry is given by S. In the competitive equilibrium given by point A, E_0 workers are hired at a wage of w_0 dollars.

Each point on the demand curve gives the number of workers that employers wish to hire at a particular wage. In particular, employers are willing to hire E_0 workers if each worker costs w_0 dollars. To simplify the analysis, consider a very simple form of payroll tax. In particular, the firm will pay a tax of $1 for every employee-hour it hires. In other words, if the wage is $10 an hour, the total cost of hiring an hour of labor will be $11 ($10 goes to the worker and $1 goes to the government). Because employers are only willing to pay a *total* of w_0 dollars to hire the E_0 workers, the imposition of the payroll tax implies that employers are now only willing to pay a wage rate of $w_0 - 1$ dollars to the workers in order to hire E_0 of them.

The payroll tax assessed on employers, therefore, leads to a downward parallel shift in the labor demand curve to D_1, as illustrated in Figure 4-4. The new demand curve reflects the wedge that exists between the *total* amount that employers must pay to hire a worker and the amount that workers actually receive from the employer. In other words, employers take into account the *total* cost of hiring labor when they make their hiring decisions— so that the amount that they will want to pay to workers has to shift down by $1 in order to cover the payroll tax. The payroll tax moves the labor market to a new equilibrium (point B in the figure). The number of workers hired declines to E_1. The equilibrium wage rate—that is, the wage rate actually *received* by workers—falls to w_1, but the *total* cost of hiring a worker rises to $w_1 + 1$.

---

[7] A detailed discussion of the impact of trade on labor markets is given by George Johnson and Frank Stafford, "The Labor Market Implications of International Trade," in Orley C. Ashenfelter and David Card, editors, *Handbook of Labor Economics,* vol. 3B, Amsterdam: Elsevier, 1999, pp. 2215–2288.

[8] Workers are also assessed a similar tax on their earnings, so the total tax payment is 15.3 percent on the first $106,800 of salary, and a 2.9 percent tax on wages above $106,800.

[9] U.S. Bureau of the Census, *Statistical Abstract of the United States, 2012.* Washington, DC: Government Printing Office, 2011, Table 1361.

FIGURE 4-4   The Impact of a Payroll Tax Assessed on Firms

A payroll tax of $1 assessed on employers shifts down the demand curve (from D_0 to D_1). The payroll tax cuts the wage that workers receive from w_0 to w_1 and increases the cost of hiring a worker from w_0 to $w_1 + 1$.

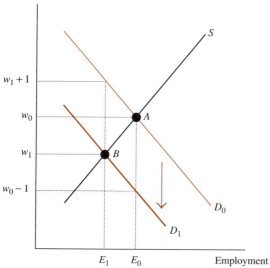

It is worth noting that even though the legislation clearly states that employers must pay the payroll tax, the labor market shifts part of the tax to the worker. After all, the cost of hiring a worker rises at the same time that the wage received by the workers declines. In a sense, therefore, firms and workers "share" the costs of the payroll tax.

A Tax Assessed on Workers

The political debate over payroll taxes often makes it appear that workers are better off when the payroll tax is assessed on the firm, rather than on the worker. In short, there seems to be an implicit assumption that most workers would rather see the payroll tax imposed on firms, whereas most firms would rather see the payroll tax imposed on workers. It turns out, however, that this assumption represents a complete misunderstanding of how a competitive labor market works. *It does not matter whether the tax is imposed on workers or firms.* The impact of the tax on wages and employment is the same regardless of how the legislation is written.

Suppose, for instance, that the $1 tax on every hour of work had been assessed on workers rather than employers. What would the resulting labor market equilibrium look like?

The labor supply curve gives the wage that workers require to supply a particular number of hours to the labor market. In Figure 4-5, workers are willing to supply E_0 hours when the wage is w_0 dollars. The government now mandates that workers pay the government $1 for every hour they work. Workers, however, still want to take home w_0 dollars if they supply E_0 hours. In order to supply these many hours, therefore, the workers will now want a payment of $w_0 + 1$ dollars from the employer. In effect, the payroll tax assessed on workers shifts the supply curve up by one dollar to S_1. The payroll tax imposed on workers, therefore, creates a wedge between the amount that workers must receive from their employers if they are to offer their services in the labor market and the amount that workers get to take home.

FIGURE 4-5   The Impact of a Payroll Tax Assessed on Workers

A payroll tax assessed on workers shifts the supply curve to the left (from S_0 to S_1). The payroll tax has the same impact on the equilibrium wage and employment regardless of who it is assessed on.

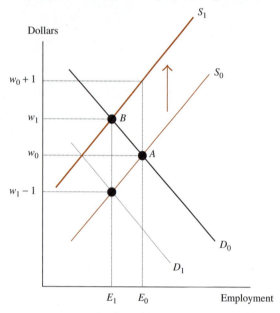

The labor market equilibrium then shifts from A to B. At the new equilibrium, workers receive a wage of w_1 dollars from the employer, and total employment falls from E_0 to E_1. Note, however, that because the worker must pay a \$1 tax per hour worked, the actual after-tax wage of the worker falls from w_0 to $w_1 - 1$.

The payroll tax assessed on the worker, therefore, leads to the same types of changes in labor market outcomes as the payroll tax assessed on firms. Both taxes reduce the take-home pay of workers, increase the cost of an hour of labor to the firm, and reduce employment. In fact, one can show that the \$1 payroll tax will have *exactly* the same numerical effect on wages and employment regardless of who bears the legal responsibility of paying for it. To see this, note that if the \$1 payroll tax had been assessed on firms, the demand curve in Figure 4-5 would have shifted down by \$1 (see the curve D_1 in the figure). The labor market equilibrium generated by the intersection of this demand curve and the original supply curve (S_0) is the same as the labor market equilibrium that resulted when the tax was assessed on workers. If the tax were assessed on firms, the worker would receive a wage of $w_1 - 1$, and the firm's total cost of hiring a worker would be w_1.

This result illustrates a principle that is worth remembering: The true incidence of the payroll tax (that is, who pays what) has little to do with the way the tax law is written or the way the tax is collected. In the end, the true incidence of the tax is determined by the way the competitive market operates. Even though a payroll tax assessed on the firm shifts down the demand curve, it has the same labor market impact as a revenue-equivalent payroll tax assessed on workers (which shifts up the supply curve).

FIGURE 4-6 **The Impact of a Payroll Tax Assessed on Firms with Inelastic Supply**

A payroll tax assessed on the firm is shifted completely to workers when the labor supply curve is perfectly inelastic. The wage is initially w_0. The \$1 payroll tax shifts the demand curve to D_1, and the wage falls to $w_0 - 1$.

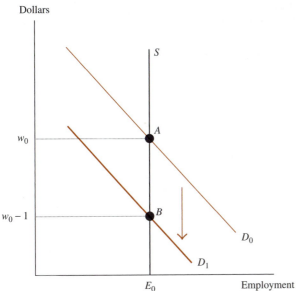

When Will the Payroll Tax Be Shifted Completely to Workers?

In one extreme case, the payroll tax is shifted entirely to workers. Suppose that the tax is assessed on the firm and that the supply curve of labor is perfectly inelastic, as illustrated in Figure 4-6. A total of E_0 workers are employed in this market regardless of the wage. As before, the imposition of the payroll tax shifts the demand curve down by \$1. Prior to the tax, the equilibrium wage was w_0. After the tax, the equilibrium wage is $w_0 - 1$. The more inelastic the supply curve, therefore, the greater the fraction of the payroll taxes that workers end up paying.

As we saw in Chapter 2, labor supply curves for men are inelastic. It would not be surprising, therefore, if most of the burden of payroll taxes is indeed shifted to workers. Although there is some disagreement regarding the exact amount of this shift, some studies suggest that workers, through a lower competitive wage, pay for as much 90 percent of payroll taxes.[10]

---

[10] Daniel S. Hamermesh, "New Estimates of the Incidence of the Payroll Tax," *Southern Economic Journal* 45 (February 1979): 1208–1219; Charles Beach and Frederick Balfour, "Estimated Payroll Tax Incidence and Aggregate Demand for Labour in the United Kingdom," *Econometrica* 50 (February 1983): 35–48; Jonathan Gruber, "The Incidence of Payroll Taxation: Evidence from Chile," *Journal of Labor Economics* 15 (July 1997, Part 2): S102–S135; Kevin Lang, "The Effect of the Payroll Tax on Earnings: A Test of Competing Models of Wage Determination," National Bureau of Economic Research Working Paper No. 9537, February 2003; and Patricia M. Anderson and Bruce D. Meyer, "Unemployment Insurance Tax Burdens and Benefits: Funding Family Leave and Reforming the Payroll Tax," *National Tax Journal* 59 (March 2006): 77–95.

FIGURE 4-7   Deadweight Loss of a Payroll Tax

(a) In a competitive equilibrium, E_0 workers are hired at a wage of w_0. The triangle P gives the producer surplus and Q gives the worker surplus. The total gains from trade equal $P + Q$. (b) The payroll tax reduces employment to E_1; raises the cost of hiring to w_{TOTAL}; and reduces the worker's take-home pay to w_{NET}. The triangle P^* gives the producer surplus; the triangle Q^* gives the worker surplus; and the rectangle T gives the tax revenues. The net loss to society, or deadweight loss, is given by the triangle DL.

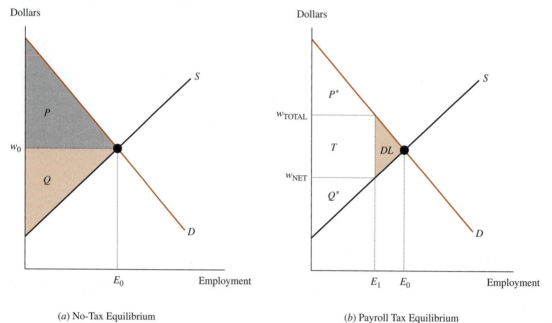

(a) No-Tax Equilibrium   (b) Payroll Tax Equilibrium

Deadweight Loss

Because payroll taxes typically increase the cost of hiring a worker, these taxes reduce total employment—regardless of whether the tax is imposed on workers or firms. The after-tax equilibrium, therefore, is inefficient because the number of workers employed is not the number that maximizes the total gains from trade in the labor market.

Figure 4-7a illustrates again the total gains from trade accruing to the national economy in the absence of a payroll tax. The total gains from trade are given by the sum of producer surplus and worker surplus, or the area $P + Q$.

Figure 4-7b shows what happens to this gain when the government imposes a payroll tax. As we have seen, it does not matter if the payroll tax is imposed on firms or imposed on workers. In either case, employment declines to E_1; the cost of hiring a worker rises to w_{TOTAL}; and the worker's take-home pay falls to w_{NET}. The producer surplus is now given by the smaller triangle P^*; the worker surplus is given by the smaller triangle Q^*; and the tax revenues accruing to the government are given by the rectangle T. The total gains from trade are given by the sum of the new producer surplus and the new worker surplus, as well as the tax revenues. After all, the government will redistribute these tax revenues in some fashion and someone will benefit from the government's expenditures. Table 4-1 summarizes the relevant information.

TABLE 4-1
Welfare
Implications of
a Payroll Tax

	No-Tax Equilibrium	Payroll Tax Equilibrium
Producer surplus	P	P^*
Worker surplus	Q	Q^*
Tax revenues	—	T
Total gain from trade	$P + Q$	$P^* + Q^* + T$
Deadweight loss	—	DL

The comparison of Figure 4-7*a* and Figure 4-7*b* yields an important conclusion. The imposition of the payroll tax reduces the total gains from trade. There is a triangle, *DL,* that represents the **deadweight loss** (or *excess burden*) of the tax. Note that the deadweight loss measures the value of gains forgone because the tax forces employers to cut employment below the efficient level and has nothing to do with the cost of enforcing or collecting the payroll tax. The deadweight loss arises because the tax prevents some workers who were willing to work from being hired by employers who were willing to hire them. These forgone deals were beneficial to society because the worker's value of marginal product exceeded the worker's value of time outside the labor market.[11]

Employment Subsidies

The labor demand curve is shifted not only by payroll taxes but also by government subsidies designed to encourage firms to hire more workers. An employment subsidy lowers the cost of hiring for firms. In the typical subsidy program, the government grants the firm a tax credit, say of $1, for every person-hour it hires. Because this subsidy reduces the cost of hiring a person-hour by $1, it shifts the demand curve up by that amount, as illustrated in Figure 4-8. The new demand curve (D_1) gives the price that firms are willing to pay to hire a particular number of workers after they take account of the employment subsidy. Labor market equilibrium shifts from point *A* to point *B.* At the new equilibrium, there is more employment (from E_0 to E_1). In addition, the subsidy increases the wage that workers actually receive (from w_0 to w_1), and *reduces* the wage that firms actually have to pay out of their own pocket (from w_0 to $w_1 - 1$).

The labor market impact of these subsidies can be sizable and will obviously depend on the elasticities of the labor supply and the labor demand curve. For instance, if the labor supply elasticity is 0.3 and the labor demand elasticity is -0.5, it has been estimated that a subsidy that reduces the cost of hiring by 10 percent would increase the wage by 4 percent and increase employment by 2 percent.[12]

The largest employment subsidy program in U.S. history, the New Jobs Tax Credit (NJTC), began soon after the recession of 1973–1975 and was in effect from mid-1977 through 1978. The NJTC gave firms a tax credit of 50 percent on the first $4,200 paid to a worker, as long as the firm's total wage bill rose by more than 2 percent over the

---

[11] A detailed discussion of the deadweight loss arising from various types of government regulations is given by James R. Hines Jr., "Three Sides of Harberger Triangles," *Journal of Economic Perspectives* 13 (Spring 1999): 167–188.

[12] Lawrence F. Katz, "Wage Subsidies for the Disadvantaged," in Richard B. Freeman and Peter Gottschalk, editors, *Generating Jobs,* New York: Russell Sage Press, 1998, pp. 21–53.

FIGURE 4-8 The Impact of an Employment Subsidy

An employment subsidy of $1 per worker hired shifts up the demand curve, increasing employment. The wage that workers receive rises from w_0 to w_1. The wage that firms actually pay falls from w_0 to $w_1 - 1$.

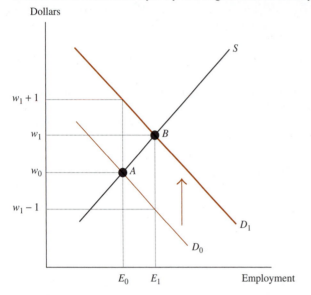

previous year. The firm could claim no more than $100,000 as a tax credit for any given year. Because only the first $4,200 of earnings were eligible for a credit, this program was designed to encourage the employment of low-wage workers.

A survey of the evidence concludes that the NJTC increased employment in the subsample of firms that were aware of the program, generating about 400,000 permanent new jobs.[13] The total cost of the tax credit to the U.S. Treasury was roughly $4.5 billion, so each new job cost taxpayers an average of $11,250.

It turns out, however, that only 27 percent of small firms were even aware of the NJTC's existence and that only 6 percent of firms actually made use of the tax credits. Because of the limited participation of firms, it is possible that only a small fraction of the employment increase can be directly attributed to the NJTC. After all, firms that had plans to expand and hire more workers had the most incentive to learn about the program and to make use of the tax credits. In other words, employment would have risen among the firms that ended up being the beneficiaries of the NJTC even if the program had not been in effect.

The Targeted Jobs Tax Credit (TJTC), which began in 1978, offers subsidies (lasting two years) to firms that hire workers from specific groups. These groups include ex-convicts, persons receiving general assistance, and Vietnam veterans. Originally, the TJTC provided

---

[13] Jeffrey Perloff and Michael Wachter, "The New Jobs Tax Credit—An Evaluation of the 1977–78 Wage Subsidy Program," *American Economic Review* 69 (May 1979): 173–179; John Bishop, "Employment in Construction and Distribution Industries: The Impact of the New Jobs Tax Credit," in Sherwin Rosen, editor, *Studies in Labor Markets,* Chicago, IL: University of Chicago Press, 1981; and Mark R. Killingsworth, "Substitution and Output Effects on Labor Demand: Theory and Policy Applications," *Journal of Human Resources* 20 (Winter 1985): 142–152.

a tax credit amounting to 50 percent of first-year and 25 percent of second-year wages (up to $6,000) for employers who hired individuals in the targeted groups. Few employers seem to have been aware of the existence of this program, and the evidence does not suggest that this particular type of targeted tax credit greatly increased the employment of targeted groups.[14] One possible explanation for the failure of targeted tax credits to increase employment is that employers may attach a stigma to targeted workers and will shy away from them. The impact of this type of discrimination on the firm's demand for labor is discussed at length in Chapter 9.

Employer Sanctions as a Payroll Tax

The number of illegal immigrants residing in the United States has risen dramatically in recent years. According to the Department of Homeland Security, 11.6 million illegal immigrants lived in the United States as of January 2006.[15]

The 1986 Immigration Reform and Control Act (IRCA) makes it illegal for employers to "knowingly hire" illegal immigrants. Under this legislation, employers who hire these unauthorized workers are subject to potential penalties and fines. Employers who disobey the law are liable for fines that, for first-time offenders, range from $250 to $2,000 per illegal alien hired. Criminal penalties can be imposed on repeated violators when there is a "pattern and practice" of hiring illegal aliens. These penalties include a fine of $3,000 per illegal alien, and up to six months in prison.

Partly because of lax enforcement, IRCA has obviously not hampered the growth of the illegal immigrant population in the United States. As a result, some states have moved to fill the void by enacting legislation that penalizes employers who hire illegal immigrants within the state. Beginning on January 1, 2008, for example, after a second offense, Arizona penalizes employers who hire illegal immigrants with the ultimate "death sentence": by simply revoking the employer's license to operate a business within the state of Arizona.

A number of studies examine the labor market impact of the employer sanctions introduced by IRCA.[16] A central idea in these studies is that employer sanctions act as a "tax" on employers. In other words, employer sanctions increase the cost of hiring a worker. After all, there is some probability that a hired worker is unauthorized to work in the

[14] John H. Bishop and Mark Montgomery, "Does the Targeted Jobs Tax Credit Create Jobs at Subsidized Firms?" *Industrial Relations* 32 (Fall 1993): 289–306. An extensive discussion of how tax policy affects human capital investments is given by Pedro Carneiro and James J. Heckman, "Human Capital Policy," in James J. Heckman and Alan B. Krueger, *Inequality in America: What Role for Human Capital Policies?* Cambridge, MA: MIT Press, 2003; see also J. Michael Orszag and Dennis J. Snower, "Designing Employment Subsidies," *Labour Economics* 10 (October 2003): 557–572.

[15] Michael Hoefer, Nancy Rytina, and Christopher Cambell, "Estimates of the Unauthorized Immigrant Population Residing in the United States: January 2006," Office of Immigration Statistics, Department of Homeland Security, August 2007, available at http://www.dhs.gov/xlibrary/assets/statistics/publications/ill_pe_2006.pdf.

[16] See Deborah A. Cobb-Clark, Clinton R. Shiells, and B. Lindsay Lowell, "Immigration Reform: The Effects of Employer Sanctions and Legalization on Wages," *Journal of Labor Economics* 13 (July 1995): 472–498; and J. Edward Taylor and Dawn Thilmany, "Labor Turnover, Farm Labor Contracts, and IRCA's Impact on the California Farm Labor Market," *American Journal of Agricultural Economics* 75 (May 1993): 350–360. An international comparison of various employer sanction programs is given by Philip Martin and Mark Miller, "Employer Sanctions: French, German, and US Experiences," International Migration Branch, International Labour Office, Geneva, 2000.

United States, and there is some probability that the employer will be caught and fined for this illegal hiring. In a competitive labor market, this fine is like a payroll tax that shifts the demand curve downwards as in Figure 4-4. Using this perspective, therefore, employer sanctions would *reduce* employment and *lower* wages in a competitive labor market. It would seem, therefore, that the group of workers that the employer sanctions are presumably trying to protect (namely, the "legal" or authorized workforce) is paying for the government's attempt to penalize employers that hire unauthorized aliens.

On reflection, however, it should be evident that viewing employer sanctions as a payroll tax introduces two crucial assumptions into the discussion that may not be correct. First, the application of Figure 4-4 in the employer sanctions context assumes that employers do not know the legal status of the workers they hire with certainty—which is why the "tax" is imposed on every worker hired. Second, the labor supply curve is assumed to remain fixed so that the number of unauthorized aliens in the labor market does not respond to the imposition of employer sanctions.

The assumption that employers do not know the legal status of potential new hires does not correctly describe how many of the newer state-specific employer sanction statutes in the United States operate. Some of these laws, for example, encourage an employer to use an electronically based program to authenticate whether a new hire is, in fact, legally entitled to work in the country. The E-Verify program is an "Internet-based system operated by the Department of Homeland Security (DHS) in partnership with the Social Security Administration (SSA) that allows participating employers to electronically verify the employment eligibility of their newly hired employees."[17] In other words, the E-Verify program allows an employer to (quickly and cheaply) determine whether a job applicant is legally entitled to work in the United States simply by checking the Social Security number reported by the applicant against the federal government's database.

Arizona's employer sanction legislation explicitly declares that the use of the E-Verify program relieves the employer from all legal liability if they were to mistakenly hire an unauthorized alien. From the perspective of an Arizona employer, as long as the E-Verify system authenticates the employment eligibility of a job applicant, the employer may proceed with the hiring even if it turns out that the electronic authentication was mistaken and that the job applicant was indeed an unauthorized alien. As a result, there is no "tax" associated with possible detection from hiring unauthorized workers as long as the employer abides by the results of the E-Verify program. Put differently, the Arizona employer sanction program would not lower the wage of the "legal" workforce since, by definition, anyone who "passes" the E-Verify test is considered to be an authorized worker.[18]

Second, the assumption that the labor supply of unauthorized aliens does not respond to the employer sanctions seems to be false in the Arizona context. Newspaper reports have noted that, even at this early stage, Arizona's program has already induced a decline in the

---

[17] The U.S. Department of Homeland Security maintains a Web site that provides information about the E-Verify program at http://www.dhs.gov/ximgtn/programs/gc_1185221678150.shtm.

[18] There is one hiring cost imposed by the Arizona employer sanction program that would indeed act as a "payroll" tax in a competitive labor market—namely, the cost that employers must incur to conduct the electronic check of Social Security numbers. The available evidence, however, suggests that this cost (on a per-worker basis) is numerically trivial.

number of unauthorized aliens choosing to settle in that state.[19] The laws of supply and demand would then presumably imply that such a cut in supply increases employer competition for the remaining workers, *raising* the wage of authorized workers.

4-4 Policy Application: Payroll Taxes versus Mandated Benefits

The government can ensure that workers receive particular benefits by mandating that firms provide those benefits to their workers. In the United States, for example, the federal government mandates that employers keep the workplace safe or provide workers' compensation insurance to their workers. How do such **mandated benefits** affect labor market outcomes in terms of wages and employment?

To illustrate the basic theory, it is useful to think in terms of a specific mandated benefit; for example, the provision of spinach pie to workers during the lunch hour. Although this example might sound a bit far-fetched, it is quite useful for understanding how the labor market consequences of government mandates differ from those of payroll taxes—regardless of whether the mandate requires firms to provide spinach pie or health insurance.

Figure 4-9a illustrates how the government mandate affects labor market equilibrium.[20] The initial equilibrium is at point P, with wage w_0 and employment E_0. Suppose that the mandated provision of spinach pie costs C dollars per worker. The mandated provision of this benefit results in a parallel downward shift of the demand curve to D_1, where the vertical difference between the two demand curves is C dollars. After all, the firm is willing to hire E_0 workers only if the per-worker total cost of employment is w_0. The mandated provision of spinach pie implies that the firm is now willing to pay each of the E_0 workers a wage of $w_0 - C$.

Consider initially the case where workers despise spinach pie—regardless of what the government says about its nutritional values. The government may mandate the firm to provide the benefit; the firms in the industry may indeed serve up a slice of spinach pie at lunchtime; but no one can force the workers to eat it. The workers simply take their slice and quickly dispose of it in the trash can. As a result, workers attach no value whatsoever to this particular benefit. The new labor market equilibrium would then be at point Q, where firms spend a total of $w_1 + C$ dollars to hire a worker (w_1 for the wage and C for the pie), and employment falls to E_1. Note that the equilibrium resulting from a government mandate where workers attach no value to the mandated benefit is what we would have observed if the government had instead enacted a payroll tax of C dollars.

However, it is possible that the typical worker appreciates the nutritional content of the spinach pie, finds it quite tasty, and values the mandated benefit. In particular, suppose that each worker in the industry values the provision of the spinach pie at B dollars, where $B < C$. In other words, workers are willing to pay somewhat less for the spinach pie than what it costs firms to provide it. The fact that the spinach pie makes workers better off implies that the mandated benefit affects not only the demand curve, but also the supply curve. The initial

[19] "Arizona Seeing Signs of Flight by Immigrants," *New York Times,* February 12, 2008.

[20] See Lawrence H. Summers, "Some Simple Economics of Mandated Benefits," *American Economic Review* 79 (May 1989): 177–183, for a more detailed discussion of the labor market consequences of mandated benefits.

FIGURE 4-9 The Impact of a Mandated Benefit

(a) It costs firms C dollars to provide a mandated benefit, shifting the demand curve from D_0 to D_1. Workers value the benefit only by B dollars, so the supply curve shifts down by less. Employment at the new equilibrium (point R) is higher than would have been the case if the firm had been assessed a payroll tax of C dollars (point Q), but lower than in a no-tax equilibrium (point P). (b) When the cost of providing the mandate equals the worker's valuation, the resulting equilibrium replicates the competitive no-tax equilibrium in terms of employment, total cost of hiring workers, and total compensation received by workers.

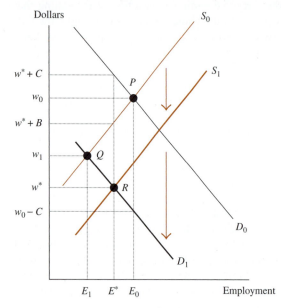

(a) Cost of Mandate Exceeds Worker's Valuation

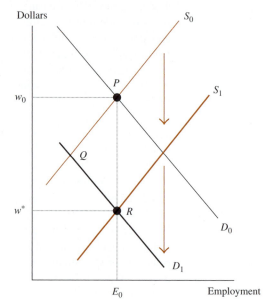

(b) Cost of Mandate Equals Worker's Valuation

supply curve S_0 in Figure 4-9a indicates that E_0 workers are willing to work as long as each receives a *total* compensation of w_0 dollars. Because workers value the spinach pie at B dollars, the E_0 workers are now willing to work as long as firms pay them a wage of $w_0 - B$. In effect, the mandated benefit leads to a parallel downward shift of the supply curve by B dollars, leading to the new supply curve S_1.

Because it is costly to provide the spinach pie and because workers value this pie, the new labor market equilibrium is given by the intersection of the new supply and demand curves (point R), so that E^* workers are employed at the new equilibrium. One important result of the analysis is that although employment falls from E_0 to E^*, it falls by less than it would have fallen if the government had instead imposed a payroll tax of C dollars on firms; in that case, employment would have dropped from E_0 to E_1.

The new equilibrium wage is w^*. But this wage does not represent the value of the employment package from the perspective of either workers or firms. It costs the firm $w^* + C$ dollars to hire a worker; and the worker values the compensation package at $w^* + B$ dollars. In contrast to the initial competitive equilibrium, workers receive less compensation and firms face higher costs. However, in contrast to the payroll tax equilibrium, both firms and workers are better off—workers earn higher compensation and firms face lower costs.

There is one special case that is of interest. Suppose that the mandated provision of a spinach pie costs C dollars to the firm *and* that workers value this pie at C dollars. In other words, workers value the mandated benefit at the same rate that it costs to provide this benefit (so that $B = C$). Figure 4-9*b* illustrates this situation. The supply curve and the demand curve both shift down by *exactly* the same amount (that is, C dollars). At the new equilibrium (point R), employment is still E_0. Similarly, workers value their compensation package at $w^* + C$, and the firm's cost is $w^* + C$. This quantity equals the competitive wage w_0.

The analysis of mandated benefits, therefore, reveals an important property of competitive labor market equilibrium. As long as the mandated benefit provides some value to workers, the mandated benefit is preferable to a payroll tax because it leads to a smaller cut in employment. Put differently, the government mandate reduces the deadweight loss arising from the reduced employment caused by the payroll tax. In fact, if the cost of providing the mandated benefit is exactly equal to the value that workers attach to this benefit, the mandated benefit does not create any such deadweight loss, as firms end up hiring exactly the same number of workers that would have been hired in a competitive equilibrium at exactly the same cost.

Health Insurance as a Mandated Benefit

In the United States, nearly two-thirds of persons below the age of 65 are covered by employer-provided health insurance, and nearly 16 percent do not have any health insurance coverage at all. There is a heated debate about whether employers should be required to provide health insurance to all their workers. Our discussion of payroll taxes and mandated benefits clearly suggests that mandated increases in health insurance premiums could have significant effects in the labor market, including changes in the market wage and in the number of workers employed.

A recent study estimates the magnitude of the labor market effects associated with health-related increases in hiring costs.[21] Beginning around 2000, partly because of a substantial increase in malpractice payments, the premiums for physician malpractice insurance soared, which, in turn, greatly increased the cost of employer-provided health insurance. Since 2000, for example, the cost of employer-provided health insurance has risen by nearly 60 percent, even though the type and scope of the coverage were unchanged. These increases vary greatly across states, suggesting that one can use the state variation in malpractice payments as an instrument in a model that attempts to identify how increases in the cost of employer-provided health insurance premiums affect wages and employment.

It has been estimated that a 10 percent increase in health insurance premiums reduces the probability of employment by 1.2 percentage points, reduces the number of hours worked by 2.4 percent, and lowers the wage of workers with employed-provided health insurance by just over 2 percent. In short, the implementation of any new health insurance mandate can easily have significant repercussions on the labor market.

As an example, consider President Clinton's Health Care Reform proposal (prepared in 1993 by a task force headed by his wife, Hillary Clinton). The Clinton proposal would have required employers to pay for a large fraction of the health insurance premium of

[21] Katherine Baicker and Amitabh Chandra, "The Labor Market Effects of Rising Health Insurance Premiums," *Journal of Labor Economics* 3 (July 2006): 609–634.

their workers. In particular, firms would have had to pay 80 percent of the costs of health insurance premiums for their workforce, with the total employer contributions being capped at 7.9 percent of the firm's payroll. Firms that employed fewer than 50 workers would have had their contributions capped at lower levels, sometimes as low as 3.5 percent of payroll.

Had it been enacted, the Clinton proposal would have been a new payroll tax on employers who did not currently provide health insurance to their workers or who provided "substandard" programs. As such, the program would have had sizable disemployment effects. In addition, because part of the tax is shifted to workers, wages would have fallen.

Our discussion suggests that the impact of payroll taxes on both employment and wages depends on the elasticities of both labor supply and labor demand. A back-of-the-envelope calculation suggests that if the labor supply curve has an elasticity of 0.2 and the labor demand curve has an elasticity of -1, the Clinton plan would have reduced employment by 517,000 jobs and the annual earnings of the workers who were currently uninsured would have fallen by at least $1,000.[22]

The Clinton Health Care Reform proposal would likely have had many other impacts on the labor market. For example, small firms would clearly have hesitated before expanding their workforce to more than 50 workers, while firms currently employing just over 50 workers would likely have contracted (or subdivided) as they searched for ways of minimizing their financial burden.

4-5 Policy Application: The Labor Market Impact of Immigration

We now consider how government policies that restrict or favor large-scale immigration shift the supply curve and alter labor market outcomes. Because of major policy changes, the United States witnessed a major resurgence in immigration after 1965. In the 1950s, for example, only about 250,000 immigrants entered the country annually. Since 2000, over 1 million legal and illegal immigrants are entering the country annually. These sizable supply shifts reignited the debate over immigration policy in the United States.[23]

There also has been a resurgence of large-scale immigration in many other developed countries. According to the United Nations, 3.1 percent of the world's population (or approximately 214 million people) now reside in a country where they were not born.[24] By 2010, the fraction of foreigners in the country's population was 13.1 percent in Germany, 10.7 percent in France, 13.5 percent in the United States, 21.3 percent in Canada, and 23.2 percent in Switzerland. Perhaps the key issue in the immigration debate

---

[22] Alan B. Krueger, "Observations on Employment-Based Government Mandates, with Particular Reference to Health Insurance," in Lewis Solmon and Alec Levenson, editors, *Labor Markets, Employment Policy and Job Creation,* Boulder, CO: Westview Press, 1994.

[23] A good summary of the socioeconomic characteristics of immigrants in the U.S. labor market is given by Abraham T. Mosisa, "The Role of Foreign-Born Workers in the U.S. Economy," *Monthly Labor Review* 125 (May 2002): 3–14.

[24] United Nations, Department of Economic and Social Affairs. Trends in International Migrant Stock: The 2008 Revision, http://esa.un.org/migration/p2k0data.asp

FIGURE 4-10   The Short-Run Impact of Immigration When Immigrants and Natives Are Perfect Substitutes
Because immigrants and natives are perfect substitutes, the two groups are competing in the same labor market.
Immigration shifts out the supply curve. As a result, the wage falls from w_0 to w_1, and total employment increases from
N_0 to E_1. Note that, at the lower wage, there is a decline in the number of natives who work, from N_0 to N_1.

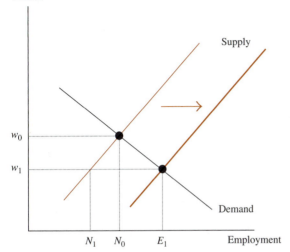

in most receiving countries concerns the impact of immigrants on the labor market opportunities of native-born workers.[25]

The simplest model of immigration assumes that immigrants and natives are perfect substitutes in production. In other words, immigrants and natives have the same types of skills and are competing for the same types of jobs. The impact of immigration on this labor market in the short run—with capital held fixed—is illustrated in Figure 4-10. As immigrants enter the labor market, the supply curve shifts out, increasing total employment from N_0 to E_1 and reducing wages (from w_0 to w_1). Note that fewer native-born workers are willing to work at this lower wage, so the employment of native workers actually falls, from N_0 to N_1. In a sense, immigrants "take jobs away" from natives by reducing the native wage and convincing some native workers that it is no longer worthwhile to work.

The short-run impact of immigration when native workers and immigrants are perfect substitutes, therefore, is unambiguous. As long as the demand curve is downward sloping and capital is fixed, an increase in immigration will move the economy down the demand curve, reducing the wage and employment of native-born workers.

Of course, the assumption that native workers and immigrants are perfect substitutes is questionable. It may be that immigrant and native workers are not competing for the same types of jobs. For instance, immigrants may be particularly adept at some types of labor-intensive agricultural production. This frees up the more skilled native workforce to

[25] An excellent description of the academic debate over how to measure the labor market impact of immigration and how this discussion has influenced the U.S. policy debate is given by Roger Lowenstein, "The Immigration Equation," *New York Times Magazine,* July 9, 2006.

FIGURE 4-11   **The Short-Run Impact of Immigration When Immigrants and Natives Are Complements**
If immigrants and natives are complements, they are not competing in the same labor market. The labor market in this figure denotes the supply and demand for native workers. Immigration makes natives more productive, shifting out the demand curve even though capital is fixed. This leads to a higher native wage and to an increase in native employment.

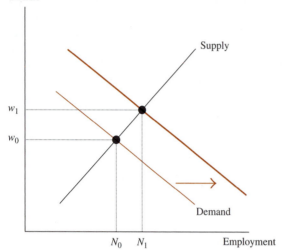

perform tasks that make better use of their human capital. The presence of immigrants increases native productivity because natives can now specialize in tasks that are better suited to their skills. Immigrants and natives thus *complement* each other in the labor market.

If the two groups are complements in production, an increase in the number of immigrants raises the marginal product of natives, shifting up the demand curve for native-born workers. As Figure 4-11 shows, this increase in native productivity raises the native wage from w_0 to w_1. Moreover, some natives who previously did not find it profitable to work now see the higher wage rate as an additional incentive to enter the labor market, and native employment also rises from N_0 to N_1.

Short-Run versus Long-Run Effects

Suppose that immigrants and natives are perfect substitutes. In the short run, immigrants lower the wage but raise the returns to capital. After all, employers can now hire workers at a lower wage. Over time, the increased profitability of firms will inevitably attract capital flows into the marketplace, as old firms expand and new firms open up shop to take advantage of the lower wage. This increase in the capital stock, therefore, will shift the demand curve for labor to the right and will tend to attenuate the negative impacts of the initial labor supply shock.

The crucial question is: By how much will the demand curve shift to the right in the long run? If the demand curve were to shift just a little, the competing native workers would still receive lower wages. If, on the other hand, the demand curve were to shift to the right dramatically, the negative wage effects might disappear.

The extent of the rightward shift in the labor demand curve depends on the technology underlying the production function. To illustrate, suppose that the aggregate production function in the receiving country can be described by the well-known Cobb-Douglas production function:

$$q = AK^{\alpha}L^{1-\alpha} \tag{4-1}$$

where A is a constant and α is a parameter that lies between 0 and 1. Note that this Cobb-Douglas production function has the property that the aggregate economy in the receiving country has constant returns to scale: if we double labor and double capital, we double output. There is strong evidence suggesting that the aggregate U.S. economy can be reasonably described by the type of production technology specified in equation (4-1).[26]

The theory of factor demand in a competitive labor market implies that the price of capital (which equals the rate of return to capital) is given by the value of marginal product of capital and that the wage is given by the value of marginal product of labor. For simplicity, suppose that the price of the output is set arbitrarily equal to $1. Using elementary calculus, it is then easy to show that the value of marginal product equations for capital and labor are given by

$$r = \$1 \times \alpha AK^{\alpha-1}L^{1-\alpha} \tag{4-2}$$

$$w = \$1 \times (1 - \alpha)AK^{\alpha}L^{-\alpha} \tag{4-3}$$

A little algebraic manipulation shows that we can rewrite these two equations as

$$r = \alpha A \left(\frac{K}{L}\right)^{\alpha-1} \tag{4-4}$$

$$w = (1 - \alpha)A \left(\frac{K}{L}\right)^{\alpha} \tag{4-5}$$

The short-run effect of immigration is simply to increase the number of workers in the economy. Examination of equations (4-4) and (4-5) will show that this increase in the number of workers will raise the rate of return to capital r and will lower the wage w.

Over time, the higher rate of return to capital will induce an increase in the size of the capital stock K. Suppose that, in the long run, after all the capital adjustments that could have taken place have taken place, the rate of return to capital falls back to its "normal" level. This argument implies that the rate of return to capital is fixed in the long run at a value of r. But equation (4-4) clearly illustrates that the only way that the rate of return to capital can be fixed in the long run is if the capital-labor ratio (K/L) also is fixed in the long run. In other words, if immigration increases the number of workers by, say, 20 percent, then the capital stock also must increase by 20 percent in the long run.

This theoretical insight has very interesting (and important) implications for the labor market impact of immigration in the long run. Consider equation (4-5). If the capital-labor ratio is constant in the long run, equation (4-5) clearly shows that *the wage also must be*

---

[26] Daniel S. Hamermesh, *Labor Demand*, Princeton, NJ: Princeton University Press, 1993.

FIGURE 4-12   The Long-Run Impact of Immigration When Immigrants and Natives Are Perfect Substitutes

Because immigrants and natives are perfect substitutes, the two groups are competing in the same labor market. Immigration initially shifts out the supply curve. As a result, the wage falls from w_0 to w_1. Over time, capital expands as firms take advantage of the cheaper workforce, shifting out the labor demand curve. If the aggregate production function has constant returns to scale, it must be the case that, after all capital adjustments have taken place, the wage is back at its initial level of w_1. In addition, the long-run level of native employment is exactly what it was prior to the immigrant influx.

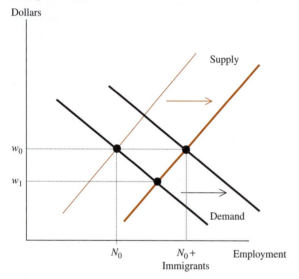

constant in the long run. In other words, immigration lowers the wage initially; over time, the capital stock increases as employers take advantage of the cheaper workforce; but, in the end, the capital stock completely adjusts to bring the economy back to where it began, with the same rate of return to capital and the same wage rate!

It is worth emphasizing that this theoretical prediction does *not* hinge on the assumption that the aggregate production function is Cobb-Douglas. The conclusion that immigration will have no long-run labor market impacts in the receiving country will hold whenever the aggregate production function has constant returns to scale.

The long-run effects are illustrated in Figure 4-12. The labor market is initially in equilibrium at a wage of w_0 and N_0 natives are employed at that wage. In the short run, the supply curve shifts to the right and the wage falls to w_1. In the long run, the demand curve also shifts to the right—and it must shift by a sufficient amount to bring the labor market back to its pre-immigration equilibrium. In the end, the wage is again equal to w_0. Note that, at this wage, the same number of native workers is employed as was employed prior to the immigrant influx.

We do not know how long it takes for the long run to arrive. It is unlikely that the capital stock adjusts instantaneously. We showed in Chapter 3, for example, that costs of adjustments create frictions in the speed with which employers adjust to various shocks. But the long run may not take as long as Keynes implied in his famous quip: "In the long run, we are all dead." The key lesson from the theory is that immigration will have an adverse wage impact on competing native workers over some time period, and this impact will weaken as the economy adjusts to the immigrant influx.

Spatial Correlations

The discussion suggests a simple way to determine empirically if immigrants and natives are complements or substitutes in production. If they are substitutes, the earnings of native workers should be lower if they reside in labor markets where immigrants are in abundant supply. If they are complements, native earnings should be higher in those labor markets where immigrants tend to cluster.

Much of the empirical research that attempts to determine how immigration alters the economic opportunities of native workers is based on this implication of the theoretical analysis. These studies typically compare native earnings in cities where immigrants are a substantial fraction of the labor force (for example, Los Angeles or New York) with native earnings in cities where immigrants are a relatively small fraction (such as Pittsburgh or Nashville). The cross-city correlations estimated between wages and immigration are called *spatial correlations*. Of course, native wages would vary among labor markets even if immigration did not exist. The validity of the analysis, therefore, hinges crucially on the extent to which all the other factors that generate dispersion in native wages across cities can be controlled for when estimating a spatial correlation. These factors include geographic differences in the skills of natives, regional wage differentials, and variations in the level of economic activity. In terms of the fixed effects methodology introduced in Chapter 2, these empirical studies often include fixed effects for each city. As a result, the wage impact of immigration is being estimated by "differencing" the data within each city and observing how a city's wage responds to changes in the number of immigrants settling in that city.

There has been a remarkable consensus in the many studies that estimate these spatial correlations.[27] The spatial correlation is probably slightly negative, so the native wage is somewhat lower in those labor markets where immigrants tend to reside. But the magnitude of this correlation is often very small. The evidence thus suggests that immigrants seem not to have much of an impact on the labor market opportunities of native workers.

It is often argued that African Americans are the one group whose economic progress is most likely to be hampered by the entry of immigrants into the United States.[28] The available evidence from the across-city studies, however, does not seem to support this claim.

[27] Jean B. Grossman, "The Substitutability of Natives and Immigrants in Production," *Review of Economics and Statistics* 54 (November 1982): 596–603; Joseph G. Altonji and David Card, "The Effects of Immigration on the Labor Market Outcomes of Less-Skilled Natives," in John M. Abowd and Richard B. Freeman, editors, *Immigration, Trade, and the Labor Market,* Chicago: University of Chicago Press, 1991, pp. 201–234; and Robert J. LaLonde and Robert H. Topel, "Labor Market Adjustments to Increased Immigration," in John M. Abowd and Richard B. Freeman, editors, *Immigration, Trade, and the Labor Market,* Chicago: University of Chicago Press, 1991, pp. 267–299. The evidence is surveyed in George J. Borjas, "The Economics of Immigration," *Journal of Economic Literature* 32 (December 1994): 1667–1717; Rachel M. Friedberg and Jennifer Hunt, "The Impact of Immigration on Host Country Wages, Employment and Growth," *Journal of Economic Perspectives* 9 (Spring 1995): 23–44; and David Card, "Is the New Immigration Really So Bad?" *Economic Journal* 115 (November 2005): F300–F323. Recent research also uses the cross-city comparison methodology to examine the impact of immigration on consumer prices; see Patricia Cortes, "The Effect of Low-Skilled Immigration on U.S. Prices: Evidence from CPI Data," *Journal of Political Economy* 116 (June 2008): 381–422.

[28] See Daniel S. Hamermesh and Frank Bean, editors, *Help or Hindrance? The Economic Implications of Immigration for African-Americans,* New York: Russell Sage Press, 1998, for a collection of studies that analyze the impact of immigration on the economic well-being of black natives.

On the contrary, some studies report that African Americans residing in cities with relatively large numbers of immigrants actually have slightly higher wages than those residing in other labor markets.

The Mariel Boatlift

On April 20, 1980, Fidel Castro declared that Cuban nationals wishing to move to the United States could leave freely from the port of Mariel. By September 1980, about 125,000 Cubans, mostly low-skill workers, had chosen to undertake the journey. The demographic impact of the *Marielitos* on Miami's population and labor force was sizable. Almost overnight, Miami's labor force had unexpectedly grown by 7 percent. An influential study, however, indicates that the trend of wages and employment opportunities for Miami's population, including its African-American population, was barely affected by the Mariel flow.[29] The economic trends in Miami between 1980 and 1985, in terms of wage levels and unemployment rates, were similar to those experienced by such cities as Atlanta, Houston, and Los Angeles, cities that did not experience the Mariel flow.

Table 4-2 summarizes the evidence. In 1979, prior to the Mariel flow, the black unemployment rate in Miami was 8.3 percent. This unemployment rate rose to 9.6 percent by 1981, after the Mariel flow. Before we conclude that the Marielitos were responsible for this 1.3 percentage point increase in black unemployment in Miami, however, we have to determine what was happening in comparable cities, cities that did not experience the Mariel flow. It turns out that black unemployment was rising even faster in the control group, from 10.3 to 12.6 percent (or an increase of 2.3 points)—probably because macroeconomic conditions were worsening during that period. If anything, therefore, it seems that the Mariel flow actually slowed down the rise in black unemployment, so that the difference-in-differences calculation (or 1.3–2.3) suggests that the Mariel flow was responsible for a 1.0 percentage point *decline* in the black unemployment rate.[30]

TABLE 4-2 Immigration and the Miami Labor Market

Sources: The Mariel flow data are drawn from David Card, "The Impact of the Mariel Boatlift on the Miami Labor Market," *Industrial and Labor Relations Review* 43 (January 1990), p. 251. The data for the Mariel flow that did not happen are drawn from Joshua D. Angrist and Alan B. Krueger, "Empirical Strategies in Labor Economics," in Orley C. Ashenfelter and David Card, editors, *Handbook of Labor Economics*, vol. 3A, Amsterdam: Elsevier, 1999, Table 7. The comparison cities are Atlanta, Houston, Los Angeles, and Tampa–St. Petersburg.

	The Mariel Flow		The Mariel Flow That Did Not Happen	
	Before	**After**	**Before**	**After**
Unemployment rate of blacks in				
Miami	8.3	9.6	10.1	13.7
Comparison cities	10.3	12.6	11.5	8.8
Difference-in-differences	**−1.0**		**+6.3**	

[29] David Card, "The Impact of the Mariel Boatlift on the Miami Labor Market," *Industrial and Labor Relations Review* 43 (January 1990): 245–257.

[30] It is important to point out, however, that the margin of error around this calculation is quite large, so one cannot confidently conclude that the difference-in-differences estimate is statistically different from zero.

The conclusion that even large and unexpected immigrant flows do not seem to adversely affect local labor market conditions seems to be confirmed by the experience of other countries. For instance, 900,000 persons of European origin returned to France within one year after the independence of Algeria in 1962, increasing France's labor force by about 2 percent. Nevertheless, there is no evidence that this increase in labor supply had a sizable impact on the affected labor markets.[31] Similarly, when Portugal lost the African colonies of Mozambique and Angola in the mid-1970s, nearly 600,000 persons returned to Portugal, increasing Portugal's population by almost 7 percent. The *retornados* did not seem to have a large impact on the Portuguese economy.[32]

Natural Experiments: Proceed with Caution

The Mariel study provides an excellent example of the difference-in-differences methodology: measuring the impact of immigration by comparing what happened in the labor market of interest (that is, the treated group) with what happened in labor markets that were not penetrated by immigrants (the control group). Recent research, however, has raised some questions about the interpretation of the evidence generated by these natural experiments—at least in the context of immigration.

In 1994, economic and political conditions in Cuba were ripe for the onset of a new boatlift of refugees into the Miami area, and thousands of Cubans began the hazardous journey. To prevent the refugees from reaching the Florida shore, the Clinton administration ordered the Navy to redirect all the refugees toward the American military base in Guantanamo. As a result, few of the potential migrants were able to migrate to Miami.

One can replicate the methodological design of the Mariel study by comparing Miami's labor market conditions—relative to those of control cities—before and after "the Mariel boatlift that didn't happen."[33] It turns out that this nonevent *had* a substantial adverse impact on the unemployment rate of Miami's black workers. The black unemployment rate in Miami rose from 10.1 to 13.7 percent between 1993 and 1995 (see again Table 4-2), as compared to a decline from 11.5 to 8.8 percent in a set of comparison cities. The difference-in-differences methodology [or $3.6 - (-2.7)$] would then indicate that the unemployment rate of African Americans in Miami *rose* by 6.3 percentage points.[34]

---

[31] Jennifer Hunt, "The Impact of the 1962 Repatriates from Algeria on the French Labor Market," *Industrial and Labor Relations Review* 45 (April 1992): 556–572.

[32] William J. Carrington and Pedro de Lima, "The Impact of 1970s Repatriates from Africa on the Portuguese Labor Market," *Industrial and Labor Relations Review* 49 (January 1996): 330–347. For other international evidence, see Jörn-Steffen Pischke and Johannes Velling, "Employment Effects of Immigration to Germany: An Analysis Based on Local Labor Markets," *Review of Economics and Statistics* 79 (November 1997): 594–604; Rachel M. Friedberg, "The Impact of Mass Migration on the Israeli Labor Market," *Quarterly Journal of Economics* 116 (November 2001): 1373–1408; Joshua D. Angrist and Adriana D. Kugler, "Protective or Counter-Productive? European Labor Market Institutions and the Effect of Immigrants on EU Natives," *Economic Journal* 113 (June 2003): F302–F331; and Brath Erling, Bernt Bratsberg, and Oddbjorn Raaum, "Local Unemployment and the Earnings Assimilation of Immigrants in Norway," *Review of Economics and Statistics* 88 (May 2006): 243–263.

[33] Joshua D. Angrist and Alan B. Krueger, "Empirical Strategies in Labor Economics," in Orley C. Ashenfelter and David Card, editors, *Handbook of Labor Economics,* vol. 3A, Amsterdam: Elsevier, 1999, pp. 1277–1366.

[34] Moreover, it turns out that the margin of error around this quantity is sufficiently small that the estimate is statistically significantly different from zero.

FIGURE 4-13   The Short-Run Labor Demand Curve Implied by Different Natural Experiments

(*a*) The analysis of data resulting from the Mariel natural experiment implies that increased immigration does not affect the wage, so that the short-run labor demand curve is perfectly elastic. (*b*) The analysis of data resulting from the NJ-Pennsylvania minimum wage natural experiment implies that an increase in the minimum wage does not affect employment, so that the short-run labor demand curve is perfectly inelastic.

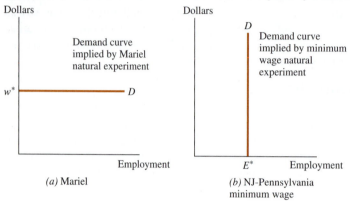

If one interprets this finding in the traditional way, it would seem to suggest that a phantom immigrant flow greatly harmed the economic opportunities of black workers. This evidence obviously raises some questions about whether one should interpret the evidence for the Mariel boatlift that *did* happen as indicating that immigration had little impact on Miami's labor market.

In addition to these interpretation difficulties, the natural experiment approach sometimes leads to contradictory evidence—contradictions that cannot be easily resolved. For example, suppose we take the results from the original Mariel study at face value, so that we infer that immigration had little impact on the wage of native workers—even in the short run. Figure 4-13*a* illustrates the short-run labor demand curve implied by the Mariel study. It is a perfectly elastic curve, indicating that wages are constant regardless of the level of labor supply.

In Chapter 3, we discussed an equally famous natural experiment study that attempted to measure the impact of the minimum wage on employment in the fast-food industry.[35] This empirical exercise compared employment in New Jersey and Pennsylvania prior to and after the imposition of a state minimum wage in New Jersey. Since the minimum wage increased only in New Jersey, one would have expected that fast-food employment in New Jersey would have declined relative to fast-food employment in Pennsylvania. In fact, the data resulting from this natural experiment showed that no such employment decline occurred in New Jersey as a result of the increase in the minimum wage—relative to the Pennsylvania control group.

---

[35] David Card and Alan B. Krueger, "Minimum Wages and Employment: A Case Study of the Fast-Food Industry in New Jersey and Pennsylvania," *American Economic Review* 84 (September 1994): 772–793.

Suppose again we take the results from the New Jersey–Pennsylvania minimum wage natural experiment at face value. We can then infer that minimum wages have little impact on employment. Figure 4-13*b* illustrates the short-run labor demand curve implied by this natural experiment. It is a perfectly inelastic curve, indicating that employment is essentially constant regardless of the level of the wage.

Needless to say, at least one of these two demand curves must be wrong. The short-run labor demand curve cannot be both perfectly elastic and perfectly inelastic at the same time. One could perhaps argue that the data are the data—and that in a particular time and in a particular context that is what the labor demand curve looked like. Unfortunately, this approach makes the inferences from experimental evidence completely useless—as the evidence cannot then be used to predict what would happen as a result of policy shifts at other times and in other contexts.

Even more disturbing is the fact that there is an intimate connection in the type of data analysis carried out by the two specific natural experiments in question. In particular, let Δw be the change in the wage before and after the "shock" and ΔE be the corresponding change in employment. In the Mariel context, for instance, the research strategy is to essentially estimate a regression model of the following type:

$$\Delta w = \alpha \Delta E + \text{Other variables} \qquad \textbf{(4-6)}$$

In other words, the strategy is to use data from different regions to estimate the relationship between the change in the wage over a particular time period and the corresponding immigration-induced change in supply. The key result of the Mariel study is that, essentially, there is zero correlation between the dependent and independent variables, so that the coefficient α is nearly zero. This zero correlation leads to the inference that immigration-induced changes in supply have little impact on wages.

Consider now the regression model estimated in the New Jersey–Pennsylvania minimum wage experiment:

$$\Delta E = \beta \Delta w + \text{Other variables} \qquad \textbf{(4-7)}$$

In other words, the research strategy is to relate changes in employment to changes in the wage across regions. The key result of the minimum wage natural experiment is that there is a zero correlation between employment and (minimum-wage-induced) wage changes across regions, so that the coefficient β is essentially zero. This result is then used to infer that an increase in the minimum wage has little effect on employment.

The core empirical finding in these two natural experiments is that there is little correlation between wage changes and employment changes across different geographic areas. In one experiment (i.e., the Mariel case), this zero correlation is interpreted as indicating that immigration has no effect on wages, while in the other experiment, this same zero correlation is interpreted as indicating that minimum wages have no effect on employment. As Figure 4-13 shows, however, these two interpretations contradict each other.

In short, the evidence from "natural experiments" should be interpreted with a great deal of caution. Not only does the interpretation of the evidence depend on the importance of properly defining the "treatment" and "control" groups, but it is also important to determine whether such results are internally consistent with any underlying theoretical framework.

Do Natives Respond to Immigration?

The fact that most cross-city studies find little evidence of a sizable adverse impact of immigration on native earnings raises two important questions: Why is the evidence so different from the typical presumption in the debate over immigration policy? And why does the evidence seem to be so inconsistent with the implications of the simplest supply-demand equilibrium model? Huge shifts in supply, like those observed in the Mariel flow or those observed when nearly 10 million immigrants entered the United States during a single decade (as happened in the 1990s), *should* affect the wage level in the labor market. And it is unlikely that the "long run" arrived in Miami after only a couple of years.

An important problem with the conceptual approach that underlies the interpretation of the spatial correlations (that is, Figure 4-10 in the case of perfect substitutes and Figure 4-11 in the case of complements) is that it ignores other responses that might occur in the labor market—even abstracting from the adjustments to the aggregate capital stock. The entry of immigrants into the local labor market may well lower the wage of competing workers and increase the wage of complementary workers initially. Over time, however, natives will likely respond to immigration. After all, it is not in the best interest of native workers to sit idly by and watch immigrants change economic opportunities. All natives now have incentives to change their behavior in ways that take advantage of the altered economic landscape.

Figure 4-14 illustrates the labor markets in two different localities, Los Angeles and Pittsburgh. Initially, the native wage w_0 is the same in both cities, with equilibrium occurring at the intersection of supply curve S_0 and the demand curve in each of the cities (at points P_{LA} and P_{PT}, respectively). Los Angeles then receives an influx of immigrants. Assuming that immigrants and natives are perfect substitutes in production, the supply curve shifts in the Los Angeles market to S_1 and the wage declines to w_{LA}.

The decline in the equilibrium wage in the Los Angeles labor market is likely to induce some natives to move to Pittsburgh, a city that did not receive an immigrant flow.[36] As a result, the supply curve of native workers shifts in both cities. As natives move out of Los Angeles, shifting the supply curve to the left (S_2), the native wage rises slightly to w^*. As the natives move to Pittsburgh, shifting the supply curve in that market to the right (S_3), the wage of natives declines to w^*. If migration between the two cities is costless, natives will migrate until wages are again the same in the two cities. Native migration decisions, therefore, lead to an equilibrium where natives in cities with many immigrants are no worse off than natives in cities with few immigrants. This conclusion, however, disguises the fact that *all* natives, regardless of where they live, are now worse off as a result of immigration.[37]

---

[36] For simplicity, the argument assumes that immigrants arrive in Los Angeles and remain there.

[37] The forces that tend to equalize economic opportunities across labor markets are reinforced by the fact that native-owned firms also will respond. For example, employers see that cities flooded by less-skilled immigrants tend to pay lower wages to less-skilled workers. Employers who demand this type of labor will want to relocate to those cities, and entrepreneurs thinking about starting up new firms will find it more profitable to open them in immigrant areas. In other words, immigration increases the returns to capitalists in the affected cities, and capital will naturally flow to the areas where the returns are the highest. The flow of jobs to the immigrant-hit areas helps cushion the adverse effect of immigration on the wage of competing workers in these localities.

FIGURE 4-14 **The Native Labor Market's Response to Immigration**

Initially, the two local labor markets are in equilibrium at wage w_0. The entry of immigrants into Los Angeles shifts the supply curve from S_0 to S_1 and lowers the wage to w_{LA}. The lower wage induces some LA natives to move to Pittsburgh, shifting the supply curve back from S_1 to S_2 and shifting the supply curve in Pittsburgh to S_3. The markets reestablish equilibrium at wage w^*. All natives earn less as a result of immigration, regardless of where they live.

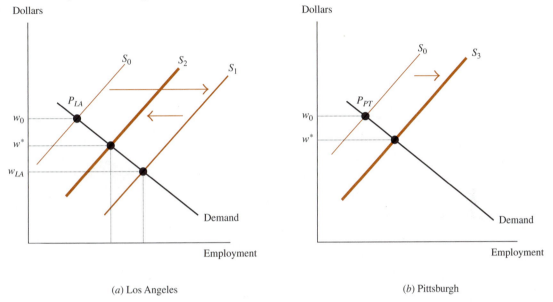

(*a*) Los Angeles (*b*) Pittsburgh

These intercity flows of labor create difficult problems if one wants to measure the labor market impact of immigration by comparing the economic opportunities of native workers in different cities. Using spatial correlations to measure the impact of immigration will not be very revealing because the flows of native-born workers effectively diffuse the impact of immigration throughout the national economy. In the end, all workers who compete with immigrants, regardless of where they live, are worse off because there are now many more such workers. Therefore, as long as natives respond to the entry of immigrants by "voting with their feet," there is little reason to expect *any* correlation between the earnings of native workers in particular cities and the presence of immigrants. In short, the comparison of local labor markets may be hiding the "macro" impact of immigration.

The evidence on whether native migration patterns are affected by the presence of immigrants is mixed.[38] Figure 4-15 presents what is perhaps the most suggestive evidence of a

[38] Randall Filer, "The Effect of Immigrant Arrivals on Migratory Patterns of Native Workers," in George J. Borjas and Richard B. Freeman, editors, *Immigration, Trade, and the Labor Market: Economic Consequences for the United States and Source Areas,* Chicago: University of Chicago Press, 1992, pp. 245–269. Conflicting evidence is presented in the recent studies of David Card, "Immigrant Inflows, Native Outflows, and the Local Labor Market Impacts of Higher Immigration," *Journal of Labor Economics* (January 2001): 22–64; and George J. Borjas, "Native Internal Migration and the Labor Market Impact of Immigration," *Journal of Human Resources* 41 (Spring 2006): 221–258.

FIGURE 4-15   **Trends in California's population, 1950–1990 (Percent of U.S. Population Living in California)**

Source: George J. Borjas, Richard B. Freeman, and Lawrence F. Katz, "How Much Do Immigration and Trade Affect Labor Market Outcomes?" *Brookings Papers on Economic Activity* 1 (1997): 27. The data refer to persons aged 18–64 who are not living in group quarters.

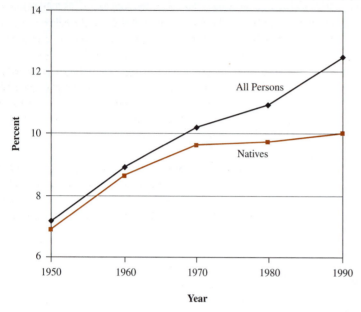

potential relation between immigration and native migration decisions. The resurgence of immigration in the United States began after 1968, when policy changes enacted in 1965 became effective. It seems natural, therefore, to contrast pre-1970 changes in the residential location of the native population with post-1970 changes to assess the effects of immigration on native location decisions.[39]

Not surprisingly, the share of natives who lived in California, the major immigrant-receiving state, was rising rapidly prior to 1970. What is surprising, however, is that the share of natives living in California barely budged between 1970 and 1990. Nevertheless, California's share of the *total* population kept rising continuously until 1990, from 7 percent in 1950, to 10 percent in 1970, to 12 percent in 1990. Put differently, an extrapolation of the population growth that existed before 1970—*before the resurgence of immigration*—would have accurately predicted the state's 1990 share of the population. But whereas natives pouring into the state fueled California's population growth before 1970, immigrants alone fueled the post-1970 growth.

How should one interpret this fact? One interpretation is that around 1970, for reasons unknown, Americans simply stopped moving to California. In other words, if it were not for immigration, California's rapid population growth would have stalled in the 1970s and 1980s. An alternative—and more controversial—interpretation is that immigration into

[39] George J. Borjas, Richard B. Freeman, and Lawrence F. Katz, "How Much Do Immigration and Trade Affect Labor Market Outcomes?" *Brookings Papers on Economic Activity* 1 (1997): 1–67.

California essentially "displaced" the population growth that *would have occurred* in the immigrants' absence, and this displacement effectively diffused the economic impact of immigration from California to the rest of the country.[40]

Immigration and the Wage Structure

The possibility that comparisons of local labor markets do not provide valuable information about the economic impact of immigration has motivated some researchers to search for this impact by looking at the evolution of the national wage structure. A recent study analyzes the wage growth experienced by native workers belonging to groups classified in terms of educational attainment and years of work experience, and attempts to see if the wage growth experienced by these skill groups is related to the growth in the number of immigrants in the various groups.[41] Put differently, the empirical exercise includes fixed effects for each skill group so that the impact of immigration on wages is being measured by "differencing" the data within each skill group.

Figure 4-16 summarizes the evidence. Each point in the scatter diagram relates the wage growth experienced by a skill group of native working men over a particular decade between 1960 and 2000 to the change in the percent of the number of workers in the group that are foreign born. There is an obvious negative correlation between the two variables. At the national level, therefore, wages grew fastest for those skill groups least affected by immigration. In fact, the data suggest that wages fall by 3 to 4 percent if immigration increases the number of workers in a skill group by 10 percent.

The national-level approach has been expanded to estimate a full-blown model that specifies the aggregate production functions linking output, capital, and the various skill groups. The structural approach typically uses the immigrant supply shock as the instrument that shifts the supply curve and that identifies the labor demand function. One benefit from this structural approach—as opposed to the simple estimation of correlations implied by the regression line in Figure 4-16—is that it allows us to estimate how the wages of a particular skill group of native workers (e.g., native college graduates) are affected by the immigration of, say, those who are high school dropouts. One can then use the own-elasticities and the cross-elasticities to simulate the impact of a particular immigrant influx on the U.S. wage structure.

[40] Recent evidence suggests that internal migration by "natives" also helped to equilibrate the labor market during the Great Depression. In the aftermath of the economic upheaval, some geographic areas began to receive a large number of in-migrants. It turns out that for every 10 new arrivals, two pre-existing residents moved out, two were unable to find a relief job, and two moved from full-time to part-time work; See Leah Platt Boustan, Price V. Fishback, and Shawn Kantor, "The Effect of Internal Migration on Local Labor Markets: American Cities during the Great Depression," *Journal of Labor Economics* 28 (October 2010): 719–746. A related study of how internal migration equilibrates wages in the UK context is given by Timothy J. Hatton and Massimiliano Tani, "Immigration and Inter-regional Mobility in the UK, 1982–2000," *Economic Journal* 115 (November 2005): F342–F358. A recent study by Nicole Fortin, "Higher Education Policies and the College Wage Premium: Cross-State Evidence from the 1990s," *American Economic Review* 96 (September 2006): 959–987, notes that interstate migration attenuates the measured impact of state-specific changes in the size of the high-skill population on the wage gap between college and less-educated workers in the state.

[41] George J. Borjas, "The Labor Demand Curve *Is* Downward Sloping: Reexamining the Impact of Immigration in the Labor Market," *Quarterly Journal of Economics* 118 (November 2003): 1335–1374.

FIGURE 4-16   Scatter Diagram Relating Wages and Immigration for Native Skill Groups Defined by Educational Attainment and Work Experience, 1960–2000

Source: George J. Borjas, "The Labor Demand Curve *Is* Downward Sloping: Reexamining the Impact of Immigration in the Labor Market," *Quarterly Journal of Economics* 118 (November 2003): 1335–1374. Each point in the scatter represents the decadal change in the log weekly wage and the immigrant share (that is, the percent of immigrants in the workforce) for a native group of working men defined by years of education and work experience. The slope of the regression line is –.450, with a standard error of .172.

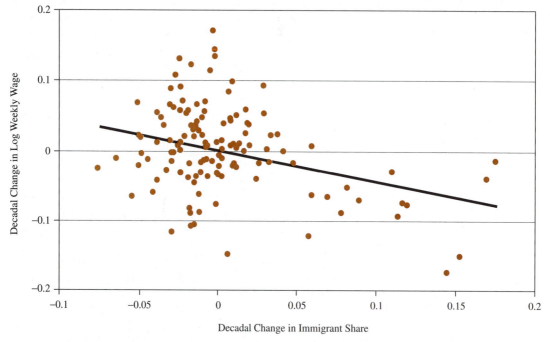

Table 4-3 summarizes the results from an influential study that uses this structural approach. Even after accounting for all the cross-effects of supply shifts on the wages of the various skill groups, the 1980–2000 immigrant influx lowered the wage of the typical worker in the United States by 3.4 percent in the short run. As implied by our theoretical analysis of long-run impacts, the predicted long-run impact must be 0.0 percent, since the typical worker in the economy is unaffected by immigration once all the capital adjustments take place. Note, however, that immigration has distributional effects even in the long run, with

TABLE 4-3   The Wage Impact of the 1980–2000 Immigrant Influx

Source: George J. Borjas and Lawrence F. Katz, "The Evolution of the Mexican-Born Workforce in the U.S. Labor Market," in George J. Borjas, editor, *Mexican Immigration to the United States,* Chicago: University of Chicago Press, 2007.

	Short Run	Long Run
All native workers	−3.4%	0.0%
High school dropouts	−8.2	−4.8
High school graduates	−2.2	1.2
Some college	−2.7	0.7
College graduates	−3.9	−0.5

the average wage of high school dropouts falling by about 5 percent and the average wage of workers in the middle of the education distribution increasing slightly.[42]

The national labor market approach also has been used to examine the link between migration and the wage structure of other countries. One particularly interesting case study examines the link between *emigration* and wages in Mexico.[43] Emigration (almost entirely to the United States) has quickly drained the Mexican labor market of about 10 percent of its workforce. The laws of supply and demand suggest that these labor outflows should increase wages in Mexico. As predicted by the theory, there is indeed a strong *positive* correlation between the number of emigrants in a particular skill group (again defined by education and labor market experience) and the wage growth experienced by that group. An outflow that reduces the number of workers in a skill group by 10 percent raises the wage of the workers who remained in Mexico by about 3 percent.

4-6   The Economic Benefits from Immigration

We have seen that immigrants may have an adverse impact on the job opportunities of the native workers whose skills resemble those of the immigrants. Immigrants also can make an important contribution to the receiving country. To assess the net economic impact of immigration, we must calculate the magnitude of these contributions. It turns out that there is an intimate link between the elasticity that measures the wage impact of immigration on the native workforce and the magnitude of the gains that accrue to receiving countries.

Consider the short-run supply-demand analysis presented in Figure 4-17. The supply curve of labor is given by S and the demand curve for labor is given by D. For simplicity, we assume that the labor supply curve is inelastic, so that there are N native-born workers. Competitive market equilibrium implies that the N native workers are employed at a wage of w_0.

Recall that the labor demand curve is given by the value of marginal product schedule, so that each point on the demand curve tells us the contribution of the last worker hired. As a

---

[42] Research has estimated this type of structural model by allowing for the possibility that immigrants and natives within narrowly defined skill groups are complements in production. In other words, the entry of immigrants who are, say, high school dropouts and are around 30 years old may raise the productivity of native workers who are high school dropouts and are also around 30 years old. Gianmarco Ottaviano and Giovanni Peri, "Rethinking the Effects of Immigration on Wages," NBER Working Paper No. 12497, August 2006, reports the existence of such complementarities, implying that it is possible for immigrants to raise the average wage of natives even in the long run. However, the replication study by George J. Borjas, Jeffrey Grogger, and Gordon Hanson, "Imperfect Substitution between Immigrants and Natives: A Reappraisal," NBER Working Paper No. 13887, March 2008, shows that the Ottaviano-Peri evidence is determined by their classification of currently enrolled high school students (mostly juniors and seniors) as "high school dropouts." Once these high school students are excluded from the analysis, the evidence supporting the existence of complementarities between comparably skilled immigrants and natives disappears. Recent research also explores how skill groups should be defined in the context of immigration. It turns out that if high school dropouts and high school graduates were perfect substitutes, the labor market impact of immigration on the wage structure is much smaller. See Borjas, Freeman, and Katz, "How Much Do Immigration and Trade Affect Labor Market Outcomes?"; and David Card, "Immigration and Inequality," *American Economic Review* 99 (May 2009): 1–21.

[43] Prachi Mishra, "Emigration and Wages in Source Countries: Evidence from Mexico," *Journal of Development Economics* 82 (January 2007): 180–199. See also Abdurrahman Aydemir and George J. Borjas, "A Comparative Analysis of the Labor Market Impact of Immigration: Canada, Mexico, and the United States," *Journal of the European Economic Association* 5 (June 2007): 663–708.

The economic forces that lead to wage equalization across countries as workers leave one market and enter another apply equally well to internal migration flows within a country. Presumably, workers leave low-wage areas and move to high-wage areas, and these flows should help to equilibrate the labor market.

One particularly interesting application of the national labor market approach used to measure the wage impacts of immigration is a recent study that estimates the economic impact of the large black migration from southern to northern states in the middle of the twentieth century. Between 1940 and 1970, over 4 million blacks left the rural South and moved to the industrialized North. In 1940, more than three-quarters of blacks lived in the South. By 1970, only half of blacks lived in the South. This historic "diaspora" of southern blacks altered the course of American history and fundamentally changed race relations in the United States.

The Great Black Migration had inevitable and predictable economic effects. As a result of this labor flow, the size of the typical skill group of workers in the North (defined by education and labor market experience) increased by 5 percent between 1940 and 1960. This 5 percent increase in labor supply reduced the annual earnings of northern black men (relative to those of whites) by about 3 percent. The sizable influx of black workers to the North, in effect, improved the economic well-being of the migrants at a cost: a delay in the rate of earnings convergence between black and white workers in the North.

Sources: Leah Platt Boustan, "Competition in the Promised Land: Blacks, Migration, and Northern Labor Markets, 1940–1970," *Journal of Economic History* 69 (September 2009): 755–782. A good account of this historic migration is given by Nicholas Lemann, *The Promised Land: The Great Black Migration and How It Changed America*, New York: Vintage Books, 1991.

result, the area under the demand curve gives the total product of all workers hired. Hence, the area in the trapezoid $ABN0$ measures the value of national income prior to immigration.

What happens to national income when immigrants enter the country? If we assume that immigrants and natives are perfect substitutes in production, the supply curve shifts to S' and the market wage falls to w_1. National income is now given by the area in the trapezoid $ACM0$. The figure shows that the total wage bill paid to immigrants is given by the area in the rectangle $FCMN$, so that the increase in national income accruing to natives is given by the area in the triangle BCF. This triangle is the **immigration surplus** and measures the increase in national income that occurs as a result of immigration and that accrues to natives.

Why does an immigration surplus arise? Because the market wage equals the productivity of the *last* immigrant hired. As a result, immigrants increase national income by more than what it costs to employ them. Put differently, all the immigrants hired except for the last one contribute more to the economy than they get paid.

The analysis in Figure 4-17 implies that if the demand curve is perfectly elastic (so that immigrants had no impact on the native wage rate), immigrants would be paid their entire value of marginal product and natives would gain nothing from immigration. Therefore, the immigration surplus exists *only* if native wage rates fall when immigrants enter the country. Therefore, immigration redistributes income from labor to capital. In terms of Figure 4-17, native workers lose the area in the rectangle w_0BFw_1, and this quantity plus the immigration surplus accrue to employers. Although native workers get a lower wage, these losses are more than offset by the increase in income accruing to native-owned firms.

FIGURE 4-17 The Immigration Surplus

Prior to immigration, there are N native workers in the economy and national income is given by the trapezoid $ABN0$. Immigration increases the labor supply to M workers and national income is given by the trapezoid $ACM0$. Immigrants are paid a total of $FCMN$ dollars as salary. The immigration surplus gives the increase in national income that accrues to natives and is given by the area in the triangle BCF.

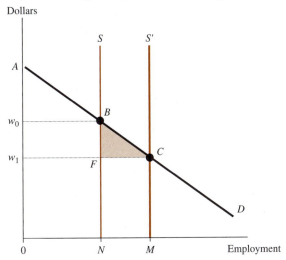

Calculating the Immigration Surplus

Recall that the formula for the area of the triangle is one-half times the base times the height. Figure 4-17 then implies that the dollar value of the immigration surplus is given by

$$\text{Immigration surplus} = \tfrac{1}{2} \times (w_0 - w_1) \times (M - N) \qquad \textbf{(4-8)}$$

This formula can be rewritten so as to obtain the immigration surplus as a fraction of national income. After rearranging the terms in the equation, we get[44]

$$\frac{\text{Immigration surplus}}{\text{National income}} = \tfrac{1}{2} \times (\% \text{ change in native wage rate})$$

$$\times (\% \text{ change in employment})$$

$$\times (\text{labor's share of national income}) \quad \textbf{(4-9)}$$

where labor's share of national income is the fraction of national income that accrues to workers.

Immigrants have increased labor supply by about 10 percent in the United States. Our discussion in the previous section indicated that a 10 percent immigrant-induced increase in supply lowers the wage by about 3 to 4 percent. Finally, it is well known that labor's

[44] In particular, we can rewrite the immigration surplus as

$$\frac{\text{Immigration surplus}}{\text{National income}} = \frac{1}{2} \times \frac{w_0 - w_1}{w_1} \times \frac{M - N}{M} \times \frac{w_1 M}{\text{National income}}$$

share of national income is on the order of 0.7. This implies that immigration increases the real income of natives by only about 0.13 percent (or $0.5 \times 0.035 \times 0.10 \times 0.7$). The gross domestic product (GDP) of the United States is around $14 trillion, so the economic gains from immigration are relatively small, about $18 billion per year.[45]

It is worth reemphasizing that this estimate of the immigration surplus is a short-run estimate. In the long run, neither the rate of return to capital nor the wage is affected by immigration. As a result, the long-run immigration surplus must be equal to zero. Immigrants increase GDP in the long run, but the entire increase in national income is paid to immigrants for their services. Ironically, in a constant-returns-to-scale economy, the economic benefits from immigration can only arise when workers in the receiving country are hurt by immigration. Equally important, *the larger the adverse wage effects, the greater the economic benefits.*

4-7 Policy Application: Hurricanes and the Labor Market

Hurricanes can be very destructive, in terms of both casualties and property damage.[46] Hurricanes develop over warm water, where the ocean's temperature exceeds 80 degrees Fahrenheit. As a result, hurricane season runs from June through November. Due to the high temperatures required to fuel the storm, most hurricanes that strike the United States first touch land in the states that surround the Gulf of Mexico or the Southeastern states, particularly Florida. In fact, all 67 counties of the state of Florida experienced some type of hurricane damage between 1988 and 2005. The hurricane threat during those years was remarkable because five of the six most damaging Atlantic hurricanes of all time hit Florida in this period.

On average, the state of Florida is typically hit by one to two hurricanes each year. Table 4-4 lists the 19 hurricanes that hit Florida between 1988 and 2005 and reports some of the key characteristics of the various hurricanes. There is clearly a lot of variation in the extent of damage unleashed by the storms. Hurricanes are categorized according to the Saffir-Simpson Scale based on their wind speed and are given a number ranging from 1 to 5. Category 1 hurricanes have wind speeds ranging from 74 to 95 miles per hour at the time of landfall. Category 2 hurricanes have wind speeds from 96 to 110 miles per hour; category 3 hurricanes have wind speeds between 111 and 130 miles per hour; and category 4 hurricanes have wind speeds between 131 and 155 miles per hour. Andrew, a category 5 hurricane, had wind speeds above 180 miles per hour when it first hit land.

Although we can predict with confidence that the hurricane season will generate some hurricanes and that Florida will likely be hit by some of these hurricanes during the course

---

[45] George J. Borjas, "The Economic Benefits from Immigration," *Journal of Economic Perspectives* 9 (Spring 1995): 3–22; and George E. Johnson, "Estimation of the Impact of Immigration on the Distribution of Income among Minorities and Others," in Daniel S. Hamermesh and Frank D. Bean, editors, *Help or Hindrance? The Economic Implications of Immigration for African-Americans,* New York: Russell Sage Press, 1998, pp. 17–50.

[46] The discussion in this section is based on Ariel R. Belasen and Solomon W. Polachek, "How Disasters Affect Local Labor Markets: The Effects of Hurricanes in Florida," *Journal of Human Resources* 44 (Winter 2009): 251–276.

TABLE 4-4   Hurricanes Hitting Florida between 1988 and 2005

Source: Ariel R. Belasen and Solomon W. Polachek, "How Disasters Affect Local Labor Markets: The Effects of Hurricanes in Florida," *Journal of Human Resources* 44 (Winter 2009), Table 1.

Hurricane	Category	Monetary Damage to Florida (millions)	Number of Deaths in Florida	Windspeed at Landfall (mph)	Rainfall (inches)
Florence (1988)	1	$0.6	0	75	5–10
Andrew (1992)	5	$43,000	44	175	5–7
Allison (1995)	1	$1.2	0	75	4–6
Erin (1995)	1	$0.5	6	87	5–12
Opal (1995)	3	$4,400	1	115	5–10
Danny (1997)	1	$100 (total to U.S.)	0	80	2–7
Earl (1998)	1	$64.5	2	92	6–16
Georges (1998)	2	$392	0	103	8–25
Irene (1999)	1	$1,100	8	75	10–20
Gordon (2000)	1	$11.9	1	75	3–5
Charley (2004)	4	$15,100	29	150	5–8
Frances (2004)	2	$8,900	37	105	10–20
Ivan (2004)	2	$8,100	19	130	7–15
Jeanne (2004)	3	$6,900 (total to U.S.)	3	121	8–13
Dennis (2005)	3	$2,200	14	120	10–15
Katrina (2005)	1	$115,000 (total to U.S.)	14	81	5–15
Ophelia (2005)	1	$70 (total to U.S.)	1	80	3–5
Rita (2005)	1	$10,000 (total to U.S.)	2	80	2–4
Wilma (2005)	3	$12,200	35	120	7–12

of a decade, the exact timing and path of the hurricanes cannot be forecast. As a result, each of these hurricanes generates exogenous economic shocks to the Florida counties that are directly hit. The randomness of the path and intensity of the hurricane, therefore, provide a "natural experiment" that can be used to analyze how the economic shocks set off by such deadly storms alter labor market conditions. Because so many hurricanes have hit Florida in the past two decades, we can use the available data to estimate difference-in-differences models that examine the economic impact on the affected Florida counties relative to the economic events unfolding in the unaffected counties.

We can use the basic tools of supply and demand to easily describe what one would expect to happen when a hurricane hits a specific Florida county randomly. When a hurricane strikes the county, some people will flee—causing at least a temporary decline in the number of workers available. Of course, the duration of this cut in supply will depend on how deadly the hurricane is expected to be and how extensive the damage, in fact, was. The hurricane-induced shift in the supply curve to the left suggests that wages would rise and employment would fall in the counties directly affected by the hurricane. Many of these "refugees" would be expected to move to neighboring counties at least in the short run. This implies that the supply of labor would increase in these neighboring counties, and that the wage may actually fall (and employment increase) in these neighboring counties.

TABLE 4-5 **Changes in Employment and Wages in Florida Counties hit by Hurricanes (relative to the change observed in the average Florida county)**

Source: Ariel R. Belasen and Solomon W. Polachek, "How Disasters Affect Local Labor Markets: The Effects of Hurricanes in Florida," *Journal of Human Resources* 44 (Winter 2009), Table 4.

	Percent Change in Employment	Percent Change in Earnings
1. Effect of category 1–3 hurricane on county directly hit	−1.5	+1.3
2. Effect of category 4–5 hurricane on county directly hit	−4.5	+4.4
3. Effect of category 1–3 hurricane on neighboring county	+0.2	−4.5
4. Effect of category 4–5 hurricane in neighboring county	+0.8	−3.3

The hurricane shock also may affect the county's labor demand curve, but it is harder to ascertain how this curve would shift. On the one hand, some firms might leave town alongside the workers, so that there would be a cutback in labor demand. On the other hand, if the hurricane destroyed a lot of the infrastructure, physical capital, and property, the reconstruction would likely shift the labor demand outwards, as firms expanded to speed up the rebuilding process.

In short, the effect of hurricanes on the labor market will depend on the relative strengths of the shift in labor demand and labor supply. Table 4-5 summarizes the key results from a careful study of the economic consequences of the 19 hurricanes that hit Florida between 1988 and 2005. The evidence seems consistent with a simple story that labor supply induced by the hurricane led to corresponding employment and wage shifts both in the county directly hit by the hurricane, as well as in surrounding counties. The wage rises in those counties that are hit by the hurricane, with the rise being stronger in counties that are hit by stronger hurricanes—suggesting that the exodus of workers is larger when the hurricane is more destructive. In fact, the wage rises by about 4 percent when a county is hit by a category 4 or 5 hurricane (relative to the wage change observed in the average Florida county at the same time). At the same time, the wage falls by a numerically similar amount in the neighboring counties—as the "surplus" labor moving to those counties increases the number of workers available.

It is worth noting that this approach to the study of data generated by natural experiments differs markedly from our earlier discussion of the impact of the Mariel supply shock or the New Jersey minimum wage increase. In each of these earlier cases, there is but *one* natural experiment to be analyzed.[47] This would be akin to injecting a particular (randomly chosen) person in the population with an experimental medicine and then comparing this person's reaction to that of the typical noninjected person. Clearly, such a comparison may be largely driven by idiosyncratic factors—for example, the randomly chosen person just happens to be allergic to some of the chemicals in the medicine, or he had the beginnings of a cold when the injection took place. By analyzing the mean outcome of a large number of

---

[47] See Stephen G. Donald and Kevin Lang, "Inference with Differences-in-Differences and Other Panel Data," *Review of Economics and Statistics* 89 (May 2007): 221–233, for a statistical discussion of this issue.

natural experiments, these idiosyncratic factors get "washed out." As a result, the study of the average consequence of a large number of natural experiments may yield more credible estimates of the labor market consequences of particular shocks.

4-8   The Cobweb Model

Our analysis of labor market equilibrium assumes that markets adjust instantaneously to shifts in either supply or demand curves, so that wages and employment change swiftly from the old equilibrium levels to the new. Many labor markets, however, do not adjust so quickly to shifts in the underlying supply and demand curves. There is some evidence, in fact, that markets for highly skilled workers, such as engineers and other specialized professionals, exhibit systematic periods of booms and busts that dispute the notion that labor markets attain competitive equilibrium quickly and cheaply.

Consider, for example, the market for new engineering graduates. It has long been recognized that the market for newly minted engineers fluctuates regularly between periods of excess demand for labor and periods of excess supply. As a result, there is a cyclical trend in the entry wage of engineering graduates over time. In a series of studies, Richard Freeman proposed a model that showed how these trends in the entry wage could be generated.[48] Two key assumptions underlie the model: (1) It takes time to produce a new engineer and (2) persons decide whether or not to become engineers by looking at conditions in the engineering labor market *at the time they enter school.*

Figure 4-18 presents the supply and demand curves for new engineers. Initially, this entry-level labor market is in equilibrium where the supply curve S intersects the demand curve D, so that there are E_0 new engineering graduates and the entry wage is w_0. Suppose there is a sudden increase in the demand for newly trained engineers (perhaps as a result of the race to get a man on the moon in the 1960s, or because the United States realizes that it might need a sophisticated system of missile defense in the post-9/11 environment). The demand curve for engineers shifts to D', and engineering firms would like to hire E^* new engineers at a wage of w^*.

Firms will find it extremely difficult to hire this desired number of new engineers. New engineers do not come out of thin air simply because firms want to hire them. It takes time to train new engineers. Because engineering schools are only producing E_0 engineers annually, the *short-run* supply curve is perfectly inelastic at E_0 workers. The combination of this inelastic supply curve (that is, a vertical line going through E_0 workers) and the demand shift increases the entry wage of engineers to w_1.

While all this is happening in the engineering labor market, a new generation of high school and college students is deciding whether to enter the engineering profession. These students see a relatively high wage in the engineering market and, hence, have a large incentive to become engineers. In fact, at the current wage of w_1, a total of E_1 persons will want to enroll in engineering schools.

[48] Richard B. Freeman, "A Cobweb Model of the Supply and Starting Salary of New Engineers," *Industrial and Labor Relations Review* 29 (January 1976): 236–246; Richard B. Freeman, "Supply and Salary Adjustments to the Changing Science Manpower Market: Physics, 1948–1973," *American Economic Review* 65 (March 1975): 27–39; and Richard B. Freeman, *The Overeducated American*, New York: Academic Press, 1976.

FIGURE 4-18   The Cobweb Model in the Market for New Engineers

The initial equilibrium wage in the engineering market is w_0. The demand for engineers shifts to D', and the wage will eventually increase to w^*. Because new engineers are not produced instantaneously and because students might misforecast future opportunities in the market, a cobweb is created as the labor market adjusts to the increase in demand.

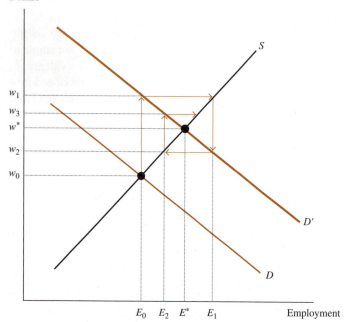

Dollars

After a few years, therefore, E_1 new engineers enter the marketplace. At the time in which this cohort of engineers enters the market, the short-run supply of new engineers is again perfectly inelastic at E_1 workers. Hence, the current market situation is summarized by this inelastic supply curve and the demand curve D' (assuming that demand conditions have not changed any further). Equilibrium occurs at a wage of w_2, which is substantially below the wage that the new engineers thought they were going to get. In effect, high school and college graduates presumed that they would get a wage of w_1 dollars; therefore, there was an oversupply of engineers.

But this is not the end of the story. Still another generation of high school and college students is trying to decide whether to become engineers. At the current low wage of w_2, the engineering profession does not look very attractive, and, hence, few persons will decide to attend engineering school. The supply curve in Figure 4-18 implies that at a wage of w_2 only E_2 persons become engineers. When these students graduate and enter the labor market, the entry wage rises to w_3 because there was an undersupply of engineers. This high wage induces the next generation of students to oversupply the marketplace, and so on.

The analysis illustrates the **cobweb** that is created around the equilibrium point as the engineering labor market adjusts to the initial demand shock. The entry wage exhibits a systematic pattern of booms and busts as the market slowly drifts toward its long-run equilibrium wage $w*$ and employment $E*$.[49]

The Underlying Assumptions of the Cobweb Model

The cobweb model makes two key assumptions. The first is reasonable: it does take time to produce new engineers, so the supply of engineers can be thought of as being perfectly inelastic in the short run. The second is more questionable. In essence, the model assumes that students are very myopic when they are considering whether to become engineers. Students choose an engineering career based entirely on the wage they currently observe in the engineering market and do not attempt to "look into the future" when comparing their various alternatives. Potential engineers have very strong incentives to be well informed about the trends in the wage of newly minted engineers. If they knew these trends, they could easily deduce what would happen to them when their cohort enters the market. In fact, even if many of these students did not bother collecting all the relevant information, *someone would!* The information could then be sold to students, who would be willing to pay for valuable information regarding their future wage prospects.

The cobwebs are generated, in effect, because the students are misinformed. They do not fully take into account the history of wages in the engineering labor market when choosing a career. Students who do take into account the entire history of wages are said to have **rational expectations.** If students had rational expectations, they would be much more hesitant to enter the engineering labor market when current wages are high and much more willing to enter when current wages are low. As a result, the cobweb might unravel.

The evidence provides strong support of cobwebs in many professional markets, so it seems as if students systematically misforecast future earnings opportunities.[50] It is worth noting, however, that students are not alone in misforecasting the future. There is some evidence that even professionals tend to have difficulty predicting future earnings opportunities.[51] The inherent uncertainty in forecasting the future might force students to place too heavy a weight on the wages they currently observe, and thus generate cobwebs in professional labor markets.

4-9 Noncompetitive Labor Markets: Monopsony

Up to this point, we have analyzed the characteristics of labor market equilibrium in competitive markets. Each firm in the industry faces the same competitive price p when trying to sell its output, regardless of how much output it sells. Moreover, each firm in the

---

[49] Although our analysis indicates that wages and employment in the engineering market drift toward their equilibrium levels over time, depending on the values of the elasticities of supply and demand, the cobweb model can generate booms and busts where wages and employment diverge *away* from equilibrium.

[50] Evidence on how students forecast the wages of their future professions is provided in Julian R. Betts, "What Do Students Know about Wages? Evidence from a Study of Undergraduates," *Journal of Human Resources* 31 (Winter 1996): 27–56; and Jeff Dominitz and Charles F. Manski, "Eliciting Student Expectations of the Returns to Schooling," *Journal of Human Resources* 31 (Winter 1996): 1–26.

[51] Jonathan Leonard, "Wage Expectations in the Labor Market: Survey Evidence on Rationality," *Review of Economics and Statistics* 64 (February 1982): 157–161.

industry pays a constant wage w to all workers, regardless of how many workers it hires. We now begin the study of the properties of labor market equilibrium under alternative market structures.

A **monopsony** is a firm that faces an upward-sloping supply curve of labor.[52] In contrast to a competitive firm that can hire as much labor as it wants at the going price, a monopsonist must pay higher wages in order to attract more workers. The one-company town (for example, a coal mine in a remote location) is the stereotypical example of a monopsony. The only way the firm can convince more townspeople to work is to raise the wage so as to meet the reservation wage of the nonworkers.

Although it is tempting to dismiss the relevance of the monopsony model because one-company towns are rare in a modern and mobile industrialized economy, it turns out that a particular firm may have an upward-sloping supply curve—the key feature of a monopsony—even when it faces a great deal of competition in the labor market. The circumstances that give rise to upward-sloping supply curves for seemingly competitive firms will be discussed in detail below.

Perfectly Discriminating Monopsonist

We consider two types of monopsonistic firms: a *perfectly discriminating* monopsony and a *nondiscriminating* monopsony. Consider first the case of a perfectly discriminating monopsony. Figure 4-19 illustrates the labor market conditions faced by this firm. As noted

FIGURE 4-19   **The Hiring Decision of a Perfectly Discriminating Monopsonist**

A perfectly discriminating monopsonist faces an upward-sloping supply curve and can hire different workers at different wages. The labor supply curve gives the marginal cost of hiring. Profit maximization occurs at point A. The monopsonist hires the same number of workers as a competitive market, but each worker gets paid his reservation wage.

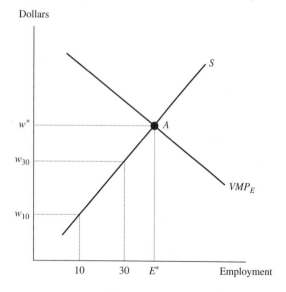

[52] A detailed conceptual and empirical examination of the monopsony model is given by Alan Manning, "A Generalised Model of Monopsony," *Economic Journal* 116 (January 2006): 84–100.

above, the monopsonist faces an upward-sloping labor supply curve. In addition, *a perfectly discriminating monopsonist can hire different workers at different wages.* In terms of the labor supply curve in the figure, this monopsonist need only pay a wage of w_{10} dollars to attract the 10th worker, and must pay a wage of w_{30} to attract the 30th worker. As a result, the supply curve of labor is identical to the marginal cost of hiring labor.

Because a monopsonist cannot influence prices in the output market, it can sell as much as it wants of the output at a constant price p. The revenue from hiring an extra worker equals the price times the marginal product of labor, or the value of marginal product. Hence, the labor demand curve for the monopsonist, as for a competitive firm, is given by the value of marginal product curve.

Regardless of whether firms operate in a competitive market or not, *a profit-maximizing firm should hire workers up to the point where the dollar value of the last worker hired equals the cost of hiring that last worker.* A perfectly discriminating monopsonist will then hire up to the point where the last worker's contribution to firm revenue (or VMP_E) equals the marginal cost of labor. Put differently, market equilibrium occurs at point A, where supply equals demand. The perfectly discriminating monopsonist hires E^* workers, exactly the same employment level that would have been observed if the labor market were competitive. The wage w^*, however, is *not* the competitive wage. Rather, it is the wage that the monopsonist must pay to attract the last worker hired. All other workers receive lower wages, with each worker receiving his or her reservation wage.

Nondiscriminating Monopsonist

A nondiscriminating monopsonist must pay all workers the same wage, regardless of the worker's reservation wage. Because the nondiscriminating monopsonist must raise the wage to all workers when he wishes to hire one more worker, the labor supply curve no longer gives the marginal cost of hiring. The numerical example in Table 4-6 illustrates this point. At a wage of $4, no one is willing to work. At a wage of $5, the firm attracts one worker, total labor costs equal $5, and the marginal cost of hiring that worker is $5. If the firm wishes to hire two workers, it must raise the wage to $6. Total labor costs then equal $12, and the marginal cost of hiring the second worker increases to $7. As the firm expands, therefore, it incurs an ever-higher marginal cost.

Figure 4-20 illustrates the relation between the labor supply curve and the marginal cost of labor curve for a nondiscriminating monopsonist. Because wages rise as the monopsonist tries to hire more workers, the marginal cost of labor curve (MC_E) is upward sloping, rises even faster than the wage, and lies above the supply curve. As we have seen, the marginal cost of hiring involves not only the wage paid to the additional worker but also

TABLE 4-6 Calculating the Marginal Cost of Hiring for a Non-discriminating Monopsonist	**Wage (w)**	**Number of Persons Willing to Work at That Wage (E)**	**$w \times E$**	**Marginal Cost of Labor**
	$4	0	$0	—
	5	1	5	$5
	6	2	12	7
	7	3	21	9
	8	4	32	11

FIGURE 4-20   **The Hiring Decision of a Nondiscriminating Monopsonist**

A nondiscriminating monopsonist pays the same wage to all workers. The marginal cost of hiring exceeds the wage, and the marginal cost curve lies above the supply curve. Profit maximization occurs at point A; the monopsonist hires E_M workers and pays them a wage of w_M.

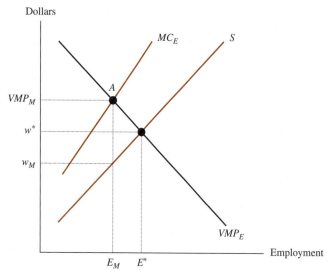

the fact that all workers previously hired must now be paid a higher wage.[53] The profit-maximizing monopsonist hires up to the point where the marginal cost of labor equals the value of marginal product, or point A in the figure. If the monopsonist hires fewer than E_M workers, the value of marginal product exceeds the marginal cost of labor, and the firm should hire additional workers. In contrast, if the monopsonist hires more than E_M workers, the marginal cost of labor exceeds the contribution of workers to the firm and the monopsonist should lay off some employees. Therefore, the profit-maximizing condition for a nondiscriminating monopsonist is given by

$$MC_E = VMP_E \qquad (4\text{-}10)$$

Note that the labor supply curve indicates that the monopsonist need only pay a wage of w_M to attract E_M workers to the firm.

The labor market equilibrium illustrated in Figure 4-20 has two important properties. First, a nondiscriminating monopsonist employs fewer workers than would be employed if the market were competitive. The competitive level of employment is given by the intersection of supply and demand, or E^* workers. As a result, there is underemployment

[53] Using calculus, it can be shown that the relationship between the wage and the marginal cost of hiring is given by $MC_E = w\left(1 + \dfrac{1}{\sigma}\right)$, where σ is the labor supply elasticity (that is, the percentage change in quantity supplied for a given percentage change in the wage). A competitive firm faces a perfectly elastic labor supply curve, so that the labor supply elasticity is infinite and the marginal cost of labor equals the wage. If the labor supply curve is upward sloping, the elasticity of labor supply will be positive and the marginal cost of labor exceeds the wage.

FIGURE 4-21   The Impact of the Minimum Wage on a Nondiscriminating Monopsonist

The minimum wage may increase both wages and employment when imposed on a monopsonist. A minimum wage set at $\overline{w}$ increases employment to $\overline{E}$.

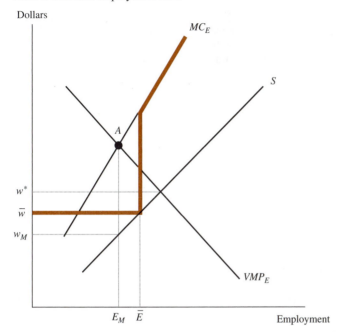

in a monopsony. Put differently, the allocation of resources in a nondiscriminating monopsony is not efficient.

Second, the monopsonistic wage w_M is less than the competitive wage, w^*, and also is less than the value of the worker's marginal product, VMP_M. In a monopsony, therefore, workers are paid less than their value of marginal product and are, in this sense, "exploited."

Monopsony and the Minimum Wage

The imposition of a minimum wage on a monopsonistic market can *increase* both wages and employment. In Figure 4-21, the nondiscriminating monopsonist is initially in equilibrium at point A, hiring E_M workers at a wage of w_M dollars. Suppose the government imposes a wage floor of $\overline{w}$. The firm can now hire up to $\overline{E}$ workers at the minimum wage (because these workers were willing to work for a wage at or below the minimum). In other words, the marginal cost of labor is equal to the minimum wage as long as the firm hires up to $\overline{E}$ workers. If the firm wants to hire more than $\overline{E}$ workers, the marginal cost of hiring reverts back to its old level (because the monopsonist must pay more than the minimum wage to all workers hired). The marginal cost of labor curve, therefore, is now given by the bold line in the figure: a perfectly elastic segment up to $\overline{E}$ workers and the upward-rising segment beyond that threshold.

A profit-maximizing monopsonist will still want to equate the marginal cost of hiring with the value of marginal product of labor. As drawn in Figure 4-21, the monopsonist hires $\overline{E}$ workers and pays them the minimum wage. Note that the minimum wage legislation increased both the employment level of the firm (from E_M to $\overline{E}$) and the wage received by workers (from w_M to $\overline{w}$). Moreover, there is no unemployment in the labor market. Everyone who is looking for work at a wage of $\overline{w}$ can find it.

In fact, Figure 4-21 suggests that the government can do even better. It could set the minimum wage at the competitive level w^* (where supply equals demand). The monopsonistic firm would then employ the same number of workers that would be employed if the market were competitive, workers would be paid the competitive wage, and there would be no unemployment. A well-designed minimum wage, therefore, can completely eliminate the market power of monopsonists and prevent the exploitation of workers.

In the last chapter, we noted the evidence that—at least in the fast-food industry—minimum wage increases do not seem to result in a reduction in the number of persons employed in that industry. In contrast, some of the evidence indicated that these fast-food establishments may have *increased* their employment after the minimum wage was imposed. It has been suggested that these positive employment effects of minimum wages occurred because the fast-food industry is a monopsony in terms of employing unskilled teenage workers. Because these youths have few other alternatives, some argue that fast-food restaurants could provide the "one-company" environment that can generate a monopsony.

Could a Competitive Firm Have an Upward-Sloping Labor Supply Curve?

The one-company town is the classic example of a firm that faces an upward-sloping labor supply curve. If this type of firm wishes to expand, it has to raise the wage to attract more persons into the workforce. This situation gives "monopsony power" to the single firm in the industry: the ability to pay its workers less than the value of marginal product, allowing the firm to make excess profits.

It turns out, however, that individual firms might have some degree of monopsony power even when there are many firms in the labor market competing for the same type of labor. We have argued that one channel through which a competitive equilibrium is eventually attained is worker mobility—workers moving across firms to take advantage of better job opportunities. When firms in one market pay relatively high wages, the mobility of workers across markets reduces the wage gap and eventually equilibrates wages throughout the economy. The "law of one price," in effect, depends crucially on the assumption that workers can costlessly move from one job to another.

It is probably the case, however, that workers incur substantial costs when they switch from one job to another. These costs are incurred as workers search for other jobs and as the workers move themselves and their families to unfamiliar economic and social environments. The presence of mobility costs implies that it does not make sense for a worker to accept every better-paying job offer that comes along. The mobility costs, after all, could well exceed the pay increase that the worker would get if he were to change jobs. As a result, mobility costs introduce a great deal of inertia into the labor market. A firm wishing to expand production and hire more workers will have to pay a wage premium that would induce workers already employed in other firms to quit those jobs, incur the mobility costs, and join the firm. In effect, mobility costs help generate an upward-sloping supply curve for a firm. A firm wishing to hire more and more workers will have to keep raising its wage to compensate workers for the costs incurred as they switch jobs.

A firm also may have an upward-sloping supply curve if the employer finds it harder to monitor its workers as employment rises. The larger the firm and the more workers it employs, the larger the possibilities for workers to "shirk" their responsibilities on the job and go undetected. It has been suggested that a possible solution to this monitoring problem is to offer the workers a higher wage. This high wage would make workers realize that they have much to lose if they are caught shirking and are fired from their jobs. According to this argument, therefore, workers who are highly paid would have much less incentive to shirk on the job. As the firm expands its employment and finds it more difficult to monitor its workers, the firm may want to pay a higher wage to keep the workers in line. In fact, there is a great deal of evidence suggesting that larger firms pay higher wages.[54]

The crucial insight to draw from this discussion is that upward-sloping supply curves for particular firms may arise even when there are many firms competing for the same workers. In short, many firms in competitive markets could have some degree of monopsony power.[55]

The realization that monopsony power need not be restricted to the extreme case of a one-company town has led to a resurgence of research that attempts to estimate the labor supply elasticity to a given firm.[56] A recent study, for instance, examines how the supply of registered nurses (RNs) to a particular hospital responds to changes in the RN wage.[57]

Before 1991, the U.S. Department of Veteran Affairs (VA) had a national pay scale that roughly determined RN wages in all of its facilities, regardless of whether those facilities were in high or low cost-of-living areas. This policy obviously affected the VA's ability to recruit nurses in high-wage regions, particularly during the 1980s when RN wages were rising rapidly. As an example, the starting RN hourly wage in Milwaukee in 1990 was $11.20 in non-VA hospitals and $11.65 in VA hospitals, so that the VA wage offer was quite competitive. In contrast, the starting RN hourly wage in San Francisco was $16.30, but the VA starting wage lagged far behind at $14.00.

The Nurse Pay Act of 1990 attempted to fix this problem by changing how the VA set wages in local facilities. In particular, the act tied the VA wage offer to the wages that prevailed in the local labor market. If the wage in VA hospitals were below the prevailing wage, the RN wage in the VA hospital would be raised immediately. However, if the wage in VA hospitals were above the prevailing wage, the VA wage would be held constant in nominal terms until the two wages reached parity. As a result, the law generated wage changes in VA hospitals that would presumably differentially change the supply of workers to each of these hospitals. In other words, the act would have mandated a rapid wage increase in the wage in VA hospitals in San Francisco, presumably attracting many new potential workers to those facilities, but little wage change in the VA hospitals in Milwaukee, where the supply of RNs would have remained relatively constant.

The difference-in-difference exercise reported in Table 4-7 illustrates how it is possible to use the enactment of the Nurse Pay Act of 1990 as an instrument to estimate the labor supply elasticity to VA hospitals. Between 1990 and 1992, the wage of RNs changed by

[54] Charles Brown, James Hamilton, and James Medoff, *Employers Large and Small,* Cambridge, MA: Harvard University Press, 1990.

[55] Note that the labor supply elasticity that is of interest in a study of monopsony—measuring the rate at which the firm must increase wages to attract more workers—differs conceptually from the labor supply elasticity that gives the relation between hours of work and wages for an individual worker. As a result, the empirical evidence on labor supply elasticities presented in Chapter 2 is of little use in attempting to measure the degree of monopsony power enjoyed by particular firms.

[56] See Alan Manning, *Monopsony in Motion.* Princeton, NJ: Princeton University Press, 2003, for an excellent summary of the models and estimation approaches.

[57] Douglas O. Staiger, Joanne Spetz, and Ciaran S. Phibbs, "Is There Monopsony in the Labor Market? Evidence from a Natural Experiment," *Journal of Labor Economics* 28 (April 2010): 211–236.

TABLE 4-7   **RN Wages and Employment, 1990–1992**

Source: Douglas O. Staiger, Joanne Spetz, and Ciaran S. Phibbs, "Is There Monopsony in the Labor Market? Evidence from a Natural Experiment," *Journal of Labor Economics* 28 (April 2010), p. 223.

	VA Hospitals	Non-VA Hospitals
Percent change in wage	12.5	9.9
Percent change in RN employment	8.3	5.6

12.5 percent in VA hospitals and by 9.9 percent in non-VA hospitals, or a difference of 2.6 percentage points. At the same time, these wage changes led to a sizable increase in 8.3 percent in the number of RNs working at VA hospitals but only to a 5.6 percent in the number of RNs working at non-VA hospitals, or a difference of 2.7 percentage points. Recall that the labor supply elasticity is defined as the ratio of the percent change in the number of workers employed to the percent change in the wage, or 2.7 ÷ 2.6, which is approximately equal to 1. In other words, a 1 percent increase in the wage that VA hospitals pay would attract 1 percent more nurses to those hospitals.

A number of recent studies use a similar methodology to estimate the labor supply elasticity to specific firms, and the findings tend to be remarkably similar.[58] For example, a study of the Norwegian teacher market documents that the labor supply elasticity of Norwegian teachers is about 1.4, while a study of schoolteachers in Missouri suggests that the elasticity is around 3.7. The crucial point about all of these estimates is that they are far below infinity, which would be the observed labor supply elasticity if the market were competitive—the firm would then face a constant wage regardless of the number of workers employed.

Some recent studies have also examined the long run behavior of the firm by observing the reaction of quit rates and recruitment rates changes in the firm's wage over time. Not surprisingly, there is an intimate relationship between a firm's monopsony power and the sensitivity of quite and recruitment rates to the firm's wage. The study of these types of responses also suggests that the elasticity of labor supply at the firm level is in the range of 2 to 4, again far below what one would expect if the firm had no monopsony power.[59]

4-10   Noncompetitive Labor Markets: Monopoly

A monopsonist's hiring decision influences the wage because the supply curve for labor is upward sloping. The more workers hired by a monopsony, the higher the wage that the firm will have to pay. We now consider hiring decisions in firms that influence the price of the output they sell. The simplest example of such a market structure is a **monopoly,** when there is only one seller in the market. As illustrated in Figure 4-22, the monopolist, unlike a competitive firm, faces a downward-sloping demand curve for his or her output.

[58] Torberg Falch, "The Elasticity of Labor Supply at the Establishment Level," *Journal of Labor Economics* 28 (April 2010): 237–266; and Michael Ransom and David P. Sims, "Estimating the Firm's Labor Supply Curve in a "New Monopsony" Framework: Schoolteachers in Missouri," *Journal of Labor Economics* 28 (April 2010): 331–355.

[59] Orley C. Ashenfelter, Henry Farber, and Michael R. Ransom, "Labor Market Monopsony," *Journal of Labor Economics* 28 (April 2010): 203–210, provides a survey of this literature and a very accessible summary of the dynamic approach.

FIGURE 4-22 The Output Decision of a Monopolist

A monopolist faces a downward-sloping demand curve for his output. The marginal revenue from selling an additional unit of output is less than the price of the product. Profit maximization occurs at point A; a monopolist produces q_M units of output and sells them at a price of p_M dollars.

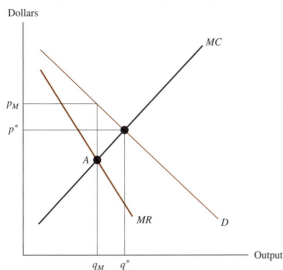

Because the price of the output falls as the monopolist expands production, the marginal revenue associated with selling an additional unit of output is not equal to the output price p. If the monopolist wants to sell an extra unit of output, he must lower the price not only for that customer but for all other customers who wish to purchase the good.[60] As a result, the marginal revenue is less than the price charged for that last unit and declines as the monopolist attempts to sell more output. Figure 4-22 shows that the marginal revenue curve (MR) for a monopolist is downward sloping and lies below the demand curve (D).[61]

A profit-maximizing monopolist produces up to the point where marginal revenue equals the marginal cost of production (or point A in the figure). The monopolist produces q_M units of output and charges a price of p_M dollars per unit because this is the point on the demand curve that indicates how much consumers are willing to pay to purchase q_M units. Finally, note that the monopolist produces less output than would have been produced if the industry had been competitive. In a competitive market, q^* units of output are exchanged at a price of p^* dollars. A monopolist, therefore, sells less output at a higher price.

We can now derive the implications of monopoly power in the output market for the firm's labor demand curve and hiring decision. A monopolist, like any other profit-maximizing

---

[60] This type of monopolist is called a *nondiscriminating monopolist* because the firm charges the same price to all customers. Monopolists who can charge different prices to different customers are called *perfectly discriminating monopolists*.

[61] Using calculus, it can be shown that the relationship between marginal revenue and price is given by $MR = p\left(1 + \dfrac{1}{\eta}\right)$ where η is the elasticity of demand for the output (that is, the percentage change in quantity demanded for a given percentage change in price). In a perfectly competitive market, the firm faces a perfectly elastic demand curve, so that the elasticity of output demand is infinite and, hence, $MR = p$. A monopolist faces a downward-sloping demand curve, so that η is negative and $MR < p$.

FIGURE 4-23   The Labor Demand Curve of a Monopolist

The marginal revenue product gives the worker's contribution to a monopolist's revenues (or the worker's marginal product times marginal revenue), and is less than the worker's value of marginal product. Profit maximization occurs at point A; the monopolist hires fewer workers (E_M) than would be hired in a competitive market.

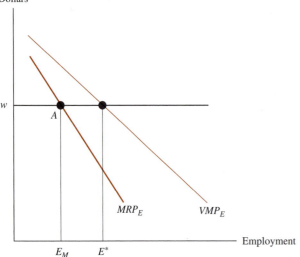

firm, hires up to the point where the contribution of the last worker hired equals the cost of hiring. For a monopolist, the additional revenue from hiring an extra person equals the worker's marginal product *times* the marginal revenue received from the last unit of output sold. This variable is called the **marginal revenue product** of labor (MRP_E) and equals

$$MRP_E = MR \times MP_E \qquad (4\text{-}11)$$

Note that the marginal revenue product of labor is less than the value of marginal product for a monopolist because the marginal revenue from selling the last unit of output (MR) is less than the price of the output.

Figure 4-23 illustrates the monopolist's hiring decision. Because the monopolist's actions can only influence prices in the market for the output, the monopolist can hire as much labor as it wants at the market wage w. A profit-maximizing monopolist hires E_M workers, where the wage equals the marginal revenue product of labor. If the firm hires fewer workers, an additional worker hired would generate more revenue than it would cost to hire him. Conversely, if the firm hires more than E_M workers, the last worker hired generates less revenue than it costs to employ him. The profit-maximizing condition for a monopolist is given by

$$MRP_E = w \qquad (4\text{-}12)$$

Note that a monopolist ends up hiring fewer workers (E_M) than would be hired if this industry were competitive. A competitive firm hires up to the point where the wage equals the value of marginal product, or E^* workers in Figure 4-23.

There is some evidence suggesting that monopolists (such as utility companies) and other firms that can influence price (such as firms in industries where production is highly concentrated in a small number of firms, or an **oligopoly**) pay higher wage rates than the competitive wage.[62] Workers employed in these highly concentrated industries earn about 10 percent more than comparable workers in competitive industries. Many regulated monopolists can pass on the costs of production to consumers. As a result, these firms have little incentive to hold down costs. The monopolists may then be willing to pay high wages to attract workers with attributes that they deem desirable (such as educational pedigrees, race, or looks).

Summary

- A competitive economy where a homogeneous group of workers and firms can freely enter and exit the market has a single equilibrium wage across all labor markets.
- There is no unemployment in a competitive labor market because all workers who wish to work can find a job at the going wage.
- A competitive equilibrium leads to an efficient allocation of resources. No other allocation of workers to firms generates higher gains from trade.
- A fraction of the payroll taxes imposed on firms is passed on to workers. The more inelastic the labor supply curve, the higher the fraction of payroll taxes that is shifted to workers.
- The payroll tax creates a deadweight loss.
- A payroll tax has the same impact on wages and employment regardless of whether it is imposed on workers or on firms.
- In the short run, immigration reduces the wage of workers who have skills similar to those of immigrants and increases the wages of workers who have skills that complement those of immigrants. In the long run, these wage effects are attenuated as the capital stock adjusts to the presence of immigrants.
- The evidence does not suggest that workers living in cities penetrated by immigrants earn much less than workers in cities where few immigrants reside. This result might arise because native workers respond to immigration by migrating from the immigrant cities to the nonimmigrant cities, thereby diffusing the impact of immigration over the national economy. Immigrants do seem to have an adverse impact on native wages at the national level.
- In the short run, immigration redistributes wealth from workers to employers, but the net income of natives increases.
- Markets for professional workers are sometimes characterized by systematic booms and busts, or cobwebs.
- A nondiscriminating monopsonist hires fewer workers than would be hired in a competitive labor market and pays them a lower wage.
- The imposition of a minimum wage on a monopsony can increase both the wage and the number of workers employed.
- A particular firm may have some monopsony power, even in labor markets that may seem competitive, when workers find it costly to move across firms.
- A monopolist hires fewer workers than would be hired in a competitive product market but pays the market wage.

[62] Ronald G. Ehrenberg, *The Regulatory Process and Labor Earnings,* New York: Academic Press, 1979; James Long and Albert Link, "The Impact of Market Structure on Wages, Fringe Benefits and Turnover," *Industrial and Labor Relations Review* 36 (January 1983): 239–250; and John S. Heywood, "Labor Quality and the Concentration-Earnings Hypothesis," *Review of Economics and Statistics* 68 (May 1986): 342–346.

Key Concepts

cobweb, *186*

deadweight loss, *157*

efficient allocation, *147*

gains from trade, *147*

immigration surplus, *180*

invisible hand theorem, *144*

mandated benefits, *161*

marginal revenue
    product, *196*

monopoly, *194*

monopsony, *188*

oligopoly, *196*

producer surplus, *146*

rational expectations, *187*

worker surplus, *147*

Review Questions

1. What is the producer surplus? What is the worker surplus? Show that a competitive market equilibrium maximizes the gains from trade.

2. Discuss the implications of equilibrium for a competitive economy containing many regional markets when labor and firms are free to enter and exit the various markets. Why is the resulting allocation of labor efficient?

3. Show what happens to producer surplus, worker surplus, and the gains from trade as workers migrate from a low-wage to a high-wage region.

4. Describe the impact of a payroll tax on wages and employment in a competitive industry. Why is part of the tax shifted to workers? What is the deadweight loss of the payroll tax?

5. Why does the payroll tax have the same impact on wages and employment regardless of whether it is imposed on workers or on firms?

6. How do mandated benefits affect labor market outcomes? Why do these outcomes differ from those resulting from a payroll tax? What is the deadweight loss arising from mandated benefits?

7. Do immigrants reduce the wage of native workers? Do immigrants "take jobs away" from native workers?

8. What is the immigration surplus?

9. Describe the trends in wages and employment implied by the cobweb model for the engineering market. What would happen to the cobwebs if an economics consulting firm sold information on the history of wages and employment in the engineering market?

10. Describe the hiring decision of a perfectly discriminating monopsonist and of a non-discriminating monopsonist. In what sense do monopsonists "exploit" workers?

11. Show how the imposition of a minimum wage on a monopsony can increase both wages and employment.

12. Describe the hiring decision of a monopolist.

Problems

4-1. Figure 4-9 discusses the changes to a labor market equilibrium when the government mandates an employee benefit for which the cost exceeds the worker's valuation (panel a) and for which the cost equals the worker's valuation (panel b).

   a. Provide a similar graph to those in Figure 4-9 when the cost of the benefit is less than the worker's valuation and discuss how the equilibrium level of employment and wages has changed. Is there deadweight loss associated with the mandated benefit?

b. Why is the situation in which a mandated benefit would cost less than the worker's valuation less important for public policy purposes than when the cost of the mandated benefit exceeds the worker's valuation?

4-2. In the United States, labor supply tends to be inelastic relative to labor demand, and according to law, payroll taxes are essentially assessed evenly between workers and firms. Given the above situation, are workers or firms more likely to bear the additional burden of an increased payroll tax in the United States? Could this burden be shifted to the firms by assessing the increase in payroll taxes on just firms rather than having firms and workers continue to be assessed payroll taxes equally?

4-3. Suppose the supply curve of physicists is given by $w = 10 + 5E$, while the demand curve is given by $w = 50 - 3E$. Calculate the equilibrium wage and employment level. Suppose now that the demand for physicists increases to $w = 70 - 3E$. Assume the market is subject to cobwebs. Calculate the wage and employment level in each round as the wage and employment levels adjust to the demand shock. (Recall that each round occurs on the demand curve—when the firm posts a wage and hires workers.) What are the new equilibrium wage and employment level?

4-4. The 1986 Immigration Reform and Control Act (IRCA) made it illegal for employers in the United States to knowingly hire illegal aliens. The legislation, however, has not reduced the flow of illegal aliens into the country. As a result, it has been proposed that the penalties against employers who break the law be substantially increased. Suppose that illegal aliens, who tend to be less-skilled workers, are complements with native workers. What will happen to the wage of native workers if the penalties for hiring illegal aliens increase?

4-5. a. What happens to wages and employment if the government imposes a payroll tax on a monopsonist? Compare the response in the monopsonistic market to the response that would have been observed in a competitive labor market.

b. Suppose a firm is a perfectly discriminating monopsonist. The government imposes a minimum wage on this market. What happens to wages and employment?

4-6. An economy consists of two regions, the North and the South. The short-run elasticity of labor demand in each region is -0.5. Labor supply is perfectly inelastic within both regions. The labor market is initially in an economywide equilibrium, with 600,000 people employed in the North and 400,000 in the South at a wage of $15 per hour. Suddenly, 20,000 people immigrate from abroad and initially settle in the South. They possess the same skills as the native residents and also supply their labor inelastically.

a. What will be the effect of this immigration on wages in each of the regions in the short run (before any migration between the North and the South occurs)?

b. Suppose 1,000 native-born persons per year migrate from the South to the North in response to every dollar differential in the hourly wage between the two regions. What will be the ratio of wages in the two regions after the first-year native labor responds to the entry of the immigrants?

c. What will be the effect of this immigration on wages and employment in each of the regions in the long run (after native workers respond by moving across regions to take advantage of whatever wage differentials may exist)? Assume labor demand does not change in either region.

4-7. A firm faces perfectly elastic demand for its output at a price of $6 per unit of output. The firm, however, faces an upward-sloped labor supply curve of

$$E = 20w - 120$$

where E is the number of workers hired each hour and w is the hourly wage rate. Thus, the firm faces an upward-sloped marginal cost of labor curve of

$$MC_E = 6 + 0.1E$$

Each hour of labor produces five units of output. How many workers should the firm hire each hour to maximize profits? What wage will the firm pay? What are the firm's hourly profits?

4-8. Polly's Pet Store has a local monopoly on the grooming of dogs. The daily inverse demand curve for pet grooming is

$$P = 20 - 0.1Q$$

where P is the price of each grooming and Q is the number of groomings given each day. This implies that Polly's marginal revenue is

$$MR = 20 - 0.2Q$$

Each worker Polly hires can groom 20 dogs each day. What is Polly's labor demand curve as a function of w, the daily wage that Polly takes as given?

4-9. The Key West Parrot Shop has a monopoly on the sale of parrot souvenir caps in Key West. The inverse demand curve for caps is

$$P = 30 - 0.4Q$$

where P is the price of a cap and Q is the number of caps sold per hour. Thus, the marginal revenue for the Parrot Shop is

$$MR = 30 - 0.8Q$$

The Parrot Shop is the only employer in town and faces an hourly supply of labor given by

$$w = 0.9E + 5$$

where w is the hourly wage rate and E is the number of workers hired each hour. The marginal cost associated with hiring E workers, therefore, is

$$MC_E = 1.8E + 5$$

Each worker produces two caps per hour. How many workers should the Parrot Shop hire each hour to maximize its profit? What wage will it pay? How much will it charge for each cap?

4-10. Ann owns a lawn-mowing company. She has 400 lawns she needs to cut each week. Her weekly revenue from these 400 lawns is $20,000. Given an 18-inch-deck push mower, a laborer can cut each lawn in two hours. Given a 60-inch-deck riding mower, a laborer can cut each lawn in 30 minutes. Labor is supplied inelastically at $5.00 per hour. Each laborer works eight hours a day and five days each week.

a. If Ann decides to have her workers use push mowers, how many push mowers will Ann rent and how many workers will she hire?

b. If she decides to have her workers use riding mowers, how many riding mowers will Ann rent and how many workers will she hire?

c. Suppose the weekly rental cost (including gas and maintenance) for each push mower is $250 and for each riding mower is $1,800. What equipment will Ann rent? How many workers will she employ? How much profit will she earn?

d. Suppose the government imposes a 20 percent payroll tax (paid by employers) on all labor and offers a 20 percent subsidy on the rental cost of capital. What equipment will Ann rent? How many workers will she employ? How much profit will she earn?

4-11. The immigration surplus, though seemingly small in the United States, redistributes wealth from workers to firms. Present a back-of-the-envelope calculation of the losses accruing to native workers and of the gains accruing to firms. Do these calculations help explain why some segments of society are emotional in their support of changes in immigration policy that would either increase or decrease the immigrant flow?

4-12. Labor demand for low-skilled workers in the United States is $w = 24 - 0.1E$ where E is the number of workers (in millions) and w is the hourly wage. There are 120 million domestic U.S. low-skilled workers who supply labor inelastically. If the United States opened its borders to immigration, 20 million low-skill immigrants would enter the United States and supply labor inelastically. What is the market-clearing wage if immigration is not allowed? What is the market-clearing wage with open borders? How much is the immigration surplus when the United States opens its borders? How much surplus is transferred from domestic workers to domestic firms?

4-13. Consider the policy application of hurricanes and the labor market that was presented in the text.

a. How do labor demand and labor supply typically shift following a natural disaster?

b. The data on changes in employment and wages in Table 4-5 suggest that the magnitude of relative shifts in labor demand and labor supply depend on the severity of the natural disaster. According to the data, does labor demand shift more relative to labor supply in mild or in extreme natural disasters. Provide intuition for this finding.

4-14. Suppose the Cobb-Douglas production function given in Equation 4-1 applies to a developing country. Instead of thinking of immigration from a developing to a developed country, suppose a developed country invests large amounts of capital (foreign direct investment, or FDI) in a developing country.

a. How does an increase in FDI affect labor productivity in the developing country? How will wages respond in the short-run?

b. What are the long-run implications of FDI, especially in terms of potential future immigration from the developing country?

4-15. A number of empirical studies suggest that labor demand is very elastic while labor supply is very inelastic. Assume too that payroll taxes are about 15 percent and legislated to be paid half by the employee and half by the employer.

    a. What would happen to worker wages if payroll taxes were eliminated?

    b. What would happen to employment costs paid by firms if payroll taxes were eliminated?

    c. What would happen to producer and worker surplus if payroll taxes were eliminated? Which measure is relatively more sensitive to payroll taxes? Why?

    d. Why might workers not want payroll taxes eliminated?

Selected Readings

Joshua D. Angrist, "Short-Run Demand for Palestinian Labor," *Journal of Labor Economics* 14 (July 1996): 425–453.

Orley C. Ashenfelter, Henry Farber, and Michael R. Ransom, "Labor Market Monopsony," *Journal of Labor Economics* 28 (April 2010): 203–210.

Ariel R. Belasen and Solomon W. Polachek, "How Disasters Affect Local Labor Markets: The Effects of Hurricanes in Florida," *Journal of Human Resources* 44 (Winter 2009): 251–276.

Olivier Jean Blanchard and Lawrence F. Katz, "Regional Evolutions," *Brookings Papers on Economic Activity* 1 (1992): 1–61.

George J. Borjas, "The Economic Benefits from Immigration," *Journal of Economic Perspectives* 9 (Spring 1995): 3–22.

George J. Borjas, "The Labor Demand Curve *Is* Downward Sloping: Reexamining the Impact of Immigration in the Labor Market," *Quarterly Journal of Economics* 118 (November 2003): 1335–1374.

David Card, "The Impact of the Mariel Boatlift on the Miami Labor Market," *Industrial and Labor Relations Review* 43 (January 1990): 245–257.

David Card, "Is the New Immigration Really So Bad?" *Economic Journal* 115 (November 2005): F300–F323.

Jonathan Gruber, "The Incidence of Payroll Taxation: Evidence from Chile," *Journal of Labor Economics* 15 (July 1997, Part 2): S102–S135.

Prachi Mishra, "Emigration and Wages in Source Countries: Evidence from Mexico," *Journal of Development Economics* 82 (January 2007): 180–199.

Douglas O. Staiger, Joanne Spetz, and Ciaran S. Phibbs, "Is There Monopsony in the Labor Market? Evidence from a Natural Experiment," *Journal of Labor Economics* 28 (April 2010): 211–236.

Web Links

The Web site of the Bureau of Citizenship and Immigration Services (BCIS) contains information on U.S. immigration policy: www.uscis.gov/graphics/index.htm.

The Department of Homeland Security reports detailed statistics on immigration to the United States: http://www.dhs.gov/ximgtn/statistics/.

Chapter 5

Compensating Wage Differentials

It's just a job. Grass grows, birds fly, waves pound the sand. I beat people up.

—*Muhammad Ali*

We have seen that as long as workers or firms can freely enter and exit a competitive labor market, there will be a single wage in the economy *if all jobs are alike and all workers are alike.*

The real-world labor market is not characterized by a single wage: workers are different and jobs are different. Workers differ in their skills. And jobs differ in the amenities they offer. Some jobs, for instance, are located in sunny California, and others are located in the tundras of Alaska; some jobs expose workers to dangerous chemicals, whereas others introduce workers to the wonders of delicious chocolates and gourmet meals.

Because workers care about whether they work in California or in the arctic and about whether they work amid toxic waste or in a luxurious French restaurant, we should think of a job offer not simply in terms of how much money the job pays, but in terms of the entire job package that includes both wages and working conditions. This chapter examines the impact of differences in job amenities on the determination of wages and employment.

The idea that job characteristics influence the nature of labor market equilibrium was first proposed by Adam Smith in 1776. In the first statement of what labor market equilibrium is about, Smith argued that **compensating wage differentials** arise to compensate workers for the nonwage characteristics of jobs. As Smith put it in a renowned passage of *The Wealth of Nations:*[1]

> The whole of the advantages and disadvantages of different employment of labour and stock must, in the same neighbourhood, be either perfectly equal or continually tending to equality. If in the same neighbourhood there was any employment either evidently more or less advantageous than the rest, so many people would crowd into it in the one case, and so many would

---

[1] Adam Smith, *The Wealth of Nations,* Chicago: University of Chicago Press, 1976 (1776), p. 111.

desert it in the other, that its advantages would soon return to the level of other employments. This at least would be the case in a society where things were left to follow their rational course, where there was perfect liberty and where everyman was perfectly free both to choose what occupation he thought proper, and to change it as often as he thought proper.

According to Smith, it is not the wage that is equated across jobs in a competitive market, but the "whole of the advantages and disadvantages" of the job. Firms that have unpleasant working conditions must offer some offsetting advantage (such as a higher wage) in order to attract workers; firms that offer pleasant working conditions can get away with paying lower wage rates (in effect, making workers pay for the enjoyable environment).

The nature of labor market equilibrium in the presence of compensating wage differentials differs radically from the equilibrium typified by the traditional supply-demand framework. In the traditional model, the wage guides the allocation of workers across firms so as to achieve an efficient allocation of resources. Workers and firms move to whichever market offers them the best opportunities, equating wages and the value of marginal product across markets in the process. In a real sense, workers and firms are anonymous and it does not matter who works where.

The introduction of compensating differentials breaks this anonymity. Workers differ in their preferences for job characteristics and firms differ in the working conditions they offer. The theory of compensating differentials essentially tells a story of how workers and firms "match and mate" in the labor market. Workers who are looking for a particular set of job amenities search out those firms that provide it. As a result, the allocation of labor to firms is not random and it matters who works where.

The theory of compensating wage differentials also provides a starting point for analyzing one of the central questions in economics: Why do different workers get paid differently? In this chapter, we focus on the role played by the characteristics of jobs in generating such wage differentials. In some of the remaining chapters, we focus on the role played by the characteristics of workers.

5-1   The Market for Risky Jobs

We begin by analyzing how compensating wage differentials arise in the context of a very simple (and policy-relevant) example.[2] Suppose there are only two types of jobs in the labor market. Some jobs offer a completely safe environment, and the probability of injury in these jobs is equal to zero. Other jobs offer an inherently risky environment, and the probability of injury in those jobs is equal to one.

We will assume that the worker has complete information about the risk level associated with every job. In other words, the worker knows whether she is employed in a safe job or in a risky job. This is an important assumption because some risks may not be detectable for many years. For instance, prior to the 1960s, asbestos products were regularly used to insulate buildings. Few persons knew that continuous exposure to asbestos (such as the exposure faced by many construction workers) had adverse effects on health. In fact, it took a long time for the scientific evidence on the relationship between asbestos

---

[2] Sherwin Rosen, "The Theory of Equalizing Differences," in Orley C. Ashenfelter and Richard Layard, editors, *Handbook of Labor Economics,* vol. 1, Amsterdam: Elsevier, 1986, pp. 641–692.

fibers and a host of health problems to become widely known. We will discuss below how our analysis is affected when the worker does not know that she is being exposed to particular risks.

Workers care about whether they work in a risky job or a safe job. And they also care about the wage (w) they earn on the job. We can then write the worker's utility function as

$$\text{Utility} = f(w, \text{risk of injury on the job}) \tag{5-1}$$

The marginal utility of income gives the change in utility resulting from a \$1 increase in the worker's income, holding constant the risk on the job. We assume that workers prefer higher wages, so that the marginal utility of income is positive. The marginal utility of risk gives the change in utility resulting from a one-unit change in the probability of injury, holding constant the worker's income. We assume initially that risk is a "bad" so that the marginal utility of risk is negative. Some workers may enjoy being exposed to the risk of injury (and the marginal utility of risk is positive for these workers). We will ignore the existence of these "risk lovers" until later in the discussion.

Suppose the "safe job" (that is, the job where workers do not get injured) offers a wage rate of w_0 dollars. Figure 5-1 illustrates the worker's indifference curve (U_0) that goes through the point summarizing the "employment package" offered by the safe job. At

FIGURE 5-1 **Indifference Curves Relating the Wage and the Probability of Injury on the Job**
The worker earns a wage of w_0 dollars and gets U_0 utils if she chooses the safe job. She would prefer the safe job if the risky job paid a wage of w_1' dollars, but would prefer the risky job if that job paid a wage of w_1'' dollars. The worker is indifferent between the two jobs if the risky job pays $\hat{w}_1$. The worker's reservation price is then given by $\Delta\hat{w} = \hat{w}_1 - w_0$.

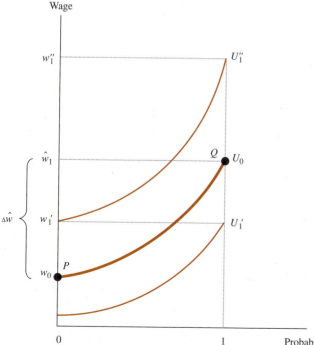

point P, the worker gets a wage of w_0 and has a zero probability of injury. The indifference curves that describe a worker's choices between income and risk of injury must be upward sloping because risk is a "bad." Suppose that the worker is currently at point P in the indifference curve. The only way to persuade the worker to move to the riskier job *and* hold her utility constant is by increasing her wage. She would obviously be worse off if she moved to a riskier job and her wage fell. The curvature of the indifference curve reflects the usual assumption that indifference curves are convex.

The Supply Curve to Risky Jobs

The indifference curve U_0 provides a great deal of information about how much this particular worker dislikes being injured. For example, she would obviously prefer working in the safe job to working in the risky job if the risky job paid only w_1'. Her utility in the safe job (U_0) would then exceed her utility in the risky job (U_1'). Similarly, the worker would prefer working in the risky job if that job paid w_1'. Her utility would then increase to U_1''. The worker, however, would be indifferent between the safe job and the risky job if the risky job paid a wage equal to $\hat{w}_1$. We define the worker's **reservation price** as the amount of money it would take to bribe her into accepting the risky job—or the difference $\Delta \hat{w} = \hat{w}_1 - w_0$. If the worker's income were to increase by $\Delta \hat{w}$ dollars as she switched from the safe job to the risky job, she would be indifferent about being exposed to the additional risk. The reservation price, therefore, is the worker's answer to the age-old question, "How much would it take for you to do something that you would rather not do?"

Different workers probably have very different attitudes toward risk. Depending on how we draw the indifference curves, the quantity $\Delta \hat{w}$ could be a small amount or a large amount. For instance, if the worker's indifference curves between income and risk were relatively flat, the reservation price $\Delta \hat{w}$ would be small, and if the indifference curves were very steep, the reservation price $\Delta \hat{w}$ would be high. The greater the worker's dislike for risk, the greater the bribe she demands for switching from the safe job to the risky job, and the greater the reservation price $\Delta \hat{w}$.

Figure 5-2 illustrates the supply curve to risky jobs in this labor market. This supply curve tells us how many workers are willing to offer their labor to the risky job as a function of the wage differential between the risky job and the safe job. Because we have assumed that all workers dislike risk, no worker would be willing to work at the risky job when the wage differential is zero. As the wage differential rises, there will come a point where the worker who dislikes risk the least is "bought off" and decides to work in the risky job. This threshold is illustrated by the reservation price $\Delta \hat{w}_{MIN}$ in Figure 5-2. As the wage differential between the risky job and the safe job keeps increasing, more and more workers are bribed into the risky occupation, and the number of workers who choose to work in risky jobs keeps rising. The market supply curve to the risky job, therefore, is upward sloping.

The Demand Curve for Risky Jobs

Just as workers decide whether to accept job offers from risky firms or from safe firms, a firm also must decide whether to provide a risky or a safe work environment to its workers. The firm's choice will depend on what is more profitable.

FIGURE 5-2   Determining the Market Compensating Differential

The supply curve slopes up because as the wage gap between the risky job and the safe job increases, more and more workers are willing to work in the risky job. The demand curve slopes down because fewer firms will offer risky working conditions if risky firms have to offer high wages to attract workers. The market compensation differential equates supply and demand and gives the bribe required to attract the last worker hired by risky firms.

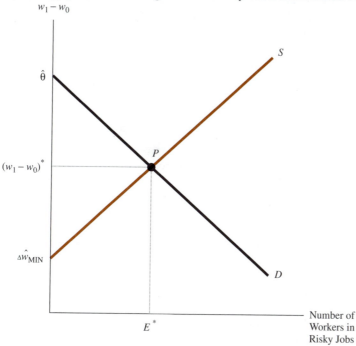

To easily show how the firm decides whether to offer a safe or a risky environment, suppose that the firm is going to hire E^* workers regardless of which environment it chooses. If the firm chooses to offer a safe work environment, the firm's production function is

$$q_0 = \alpha_0 E^* \qquad (5\text{-}2)$$

The parameter α_0 gives the change in output when a safe firm hires one more worker, so that α_0 is the marginal product of labor in a safe environment. If the price of the output equals p dollars, the value of marginal product of labor in a safe firm equals $p \times \alpha_0$.

If the firm offers a risky environment, the firm's production function is

$$q_1 = \alpha_1 E^* \qquad (5\text{-}3)$$

where α_1 is the marginal product of labor in a risky environment. The value of marginal product of labor in a risky firm then equals $p \times \alpha_1$.

At this point, we must address a crucial question: how does the marginal product of labor differ between safe and risky environments? Safety does not come for free. The firm has to allocate labor and capital to "produce" a safe environment—diverting these resources from the production of output. For example, it takes many resources to remove asbestos fibers from preexisting structures or to make a building earthquake-proof, and these resources could have been put to producing more output. This diversion of resources suggests that the marginal product of labor is higher in a risky environment, so that $\alpha_1 > \alpha_0$. Note that if the marginal product of labor were indeed higher in safe firms, we would never observe anyone working in a risky environment. After all, not only would workers be more productive in safe firms, but the firm could get away with paying them lower wages because workers value safety.

The firm's profits depend on whether it offers a safe or a risky environment. The profits under each of these two possibilities are given by

$$\pi_0 = p\,\alpha_0\,E^* - w_0\,E^* \qquad\qquad \text{(5-4)}$$
$$\pi_1 = p\,\alpha_1\,E^* - w_1\,E^* \qquad\qquad \text{(5-5)}$$

where π_0 is the profits that the firm can earn if it chooses to be a safe firm and π_1 is the firm's profits if it chooses to be a risky firm. The firm's profits equal the difference between the firm's revenues (the price of the output p times the output produced) and the firm's costs (the wage the firm has to pay times the number of workers it hires). Both the revenues and the costs are affected by the firm's decision of whether to offer a safe or a risky working environment. A risky firm has greater revenues (because more output is produced), but also incurs higher costs (because it must pay a higher wage to attract workers).

A profit-maximizing firm offers a risky environment if $\pi_1 > \pi_0$. Define the difference $\theta = p\alpha_1 - p\alpha_0$ as the dollar gain per worker when the firm switches from a safe environment to a risky environment. Simple algebraic manipulations of equations (5-4) and (5-5) indicate that the firm's decision rule is

$$\text{Offer a safe working environment if } w_1 - w_0 > \theta. \qquad \text{(5-6)}$$
$$\text{Offer a risky working environment if } w_1 - w_0 < \theta.$$

If the additional labor costs exceed the per-worker productivity gain (or $w_1 - w_0 > \theta$), the firm is better off by offering a safe environment. If the additional labor costs are less than the per-worker productivity gain (or $w_1 - w_0 < \theta$), the firm maximizes profits by offering a risky environment.

Different firms have different technologies for producing safety—implying that the parameter θ differs across firms. For example, universities do not have to allocate many resources to the production of safety in order to provide a safe environment for the staff, so that the per-worker gain θ is small. In contrast, coal mines find it much more difficult to produce safety. The productivity gains associated with offering a risky environment in coal mines are probably substantial and θ is very large.

The market labor demand curve for risky workers is derived by "adding up" the labor demand curve of risky firms. If the compensating wage differential is very high, no firm would choose to become a risky firm and the demand for risky workers is zero. As the wage differential falls, there will come a point where the firm that has the most to gain from becoming a risky firm decides that it is worth incurring the additional labor cost. This firm has a threshold value of θ equal to $\hat{\theta}$ in Figure 5-2. As the wage differential between the risky job and the safe job keeps falling, more and more firms will find it profitable to offer a risky environment and the quantity of labor demanded by risky firms rises. The labor demand curve for risky jobs, therefore, is downward sloping—as illustrated in Figure 5-2.

Equilibrium

The market-compensating wage differential and the number of workers employed in risky jobs are determined by the intersection of the market supply and demand curves, as illustrated by point P in Figure 5-2. The compensating wage differential received by workers in risky firms is $(w_1 - w_0)^*$, and E^* workers are employed in these jobs. If the wage differential exceeds this equilibrium level, more persons are willing to work in risky firms than are being demanded, so that the compensating wage differential would fall. Similarly, if the wage differential fell below the equilibrium level, there would be too few workers willing to work in risky jobs relative to the demand, and the compensating wage differential would rise.

A number of properties of the market wage differential $(w_1 - w_0)^*$ are worth noting. First, the compensating wage differential is positive. Risky jobs pay more than safe jobs. This result follows from our assumption that all workers dislike risk; if firms offering a risky environment wish to attract any workers, they will have to pay higher wages.

We are tempted to interpret the market wage differential $(w_1 - w_0)^*$ as a measure of the *average* dislike for risk among workers in the economy (that is, as a measure of the average reservation price). This interpretation, however, is not correct. The equilibrium compensating wage differential $(w_1 - w_0)^*$ is the wage differential that is required to attract the *marginal* worker (that is, the last worker hired) into the risky job. In other words, the equilibrium wage differential measures the reservation price of the last worker hired and has nothing to do with the average dislike for risk in the population.

As a result, all workers except for the marginal worker are *overcompensated* by the market. After all, every worker but the last worker hired was willing to work at the risky job at a lower wage. In other words, a competitive labor market with fully informed workers provides more than adequate compensation for the risks that workers encounter on the job.

Can the Compensating Wage Differential Go the "Wrong" Way?

Up to this point, we have assumed that all workers dislike risk. But it may be that some workers prefer to work in jobs where they face a high probability of injury. In other words, some persons (just like the motorcyclists who fly down the highway at 100 mph without a helmet) actually get utility from working in jobs where they can "test their courage." The reservation price for workers who like risk is negative because they are willing to pay for the right to be employed in risky jobs. The supply curve drawn in Figure 5-3 allows for the possibility that some workers have negative reservation prices and hence are willing to work in the risky job even though the risky job pays less than the safe job.

Suppose that the demand for workers in risky jobs is very small. There are, for example, an extremely limited number of job openings for test pilots and astronauts. The market demand curve, therefore, could then intersect the market supply curve at a point like P in the figure, which would imply a *negative* compensating wage differential for the E^* workers employed in risky jobs. Even though *almost everyone* in the population dislikes risk, the demand for labor in risky jobs is so small that firms offering a risky work environment need only hire those workers who are willing to pay to be in those jobs.

The equilibrium illustrated in Figure 5-3 reinforces our understanding of exactly what compensating wage differentials measure. Even though most of us would think it sensible that the theory should predict that workers employed in risky jobs should earn more than

FIGURE 5-3   Market Equilibrium When Some Workers Prefer to Work in Risky Jobs

If some workers like to work in risky jobs (they are willing to pay for the right to be injured) and if the demand for such workers is small, the market compensating differential is negative. At point P, where supply equals demand, workers employed in risky jobs earn less than workers employed in safe jobs.

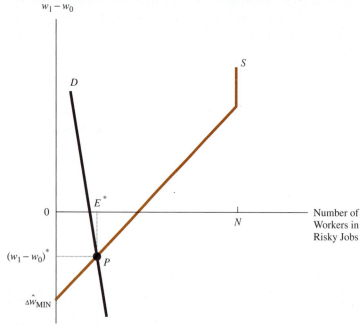

workers employed in safe jobs, it takes two to tango. If some workers are willing to pay for the right to be exposed to a high probability of injury, and if the demand for these types of workers is sufficiently small, the market differential will go in the opposite direction.

5-2   The Hedonic Wage Function

The simple model presented in the previous section illustrates the key insights of the compensating wage differential hypothesis in a labor market where there are only two types of jobs, a risky job and a safe job. Suppose that instead of having only two types of firms, there are now many types of firms. The probability of injury on the job, which we will denote by ρ, can take on any value between 0 and 1.

Indifference Curves of Different Workers

For convenience, we assume that workers dislike risk. Different workers, however, dislike risk differently. Figure 5-4 illustrates the indifference curves for three different workers, A, B, and C (with associated utilities U_A, U_B, and U_C). The slope of each indifference curve tells us how much the wage would have to increase if the particular worker were to voluntarily switch to a slightly riskier job. The slope of an indifference curve, therefore, is the reservation price that the worker attaches to moving to a slightly riskier job.

As drawn, worker A has the steepest indifference curve, and hence has the highest reservation price for risk. This worker, therefore, is very risk averse. At the other extreme,

FIGURE 5-4   Indifference Curves for Three Types of Workers

Different workers have different preferences for risk. Worker A is very risk-averse. Worker C does not mind risk as much.

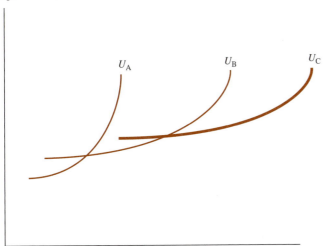

Probability of Injury

worker C has the flattest indifference curve and the lowest reservation price for risk. Although worker C does not like risk, she does not mind it that much.

Note that the indifference curves drawn in Figure 5-4 intersect. This would seem to contradict one of our basic tenets regarding the shape of indifference curves. The figure, however, illustrates the indifference curves of *different workers*. Even though the indifference curves of one worker cannot intersect, the indifference curves of workers who differ in their attitudes toward risk can certainly intersect.

The Isoprofit Curve

Profit-maximizing firms compete for these workers by offering different job packages, which contain both wage offers and particular types of work environment (as measured by the probability of injury on the job). To show how firms choose which type of environment to offer its workforce, we introduce a new concept, an **isoprofit curve.** As implied by its name, all points along an isoprofit curve yield the same level of profits, say π_0 dollars. A profit-maximizing employer, therefore, is indifferent among the various combinations of wages and risk that lie along a single isoprofit curve. Figure 5-5 illustrates the family of isoprofit curves for a particular employer. Isoprofit curves have a number of important properties.

1. *Isoprofit curves are upward sloping because it costs money to produce safety.* To see this, suppose the firm offers the wage-risk package at point P on the isoprofit curve that yields π_0 dollars of profit. What must happen to the wage if the firm wants to become a safer firm *and* hold profits constant? As we noted earlier, a firm must invest resources to improve the safety of the work environment. As a result, profits are held constant only if the firm investing in safety reduces the wage that it pays its workers (and moves toward

FIGURE 5-5   **Isoprofit Curves**

An isoprofit curve gives all the risk-wage combinations that yield the same profits. Because it is costly to produce safety, a firm offering risk level ρ* can make the workplace safer only if it reduces wages (while keeping profits constant), so that the isoprofit curve is upward sloping. Higher isoprofit curves yield lower profits.

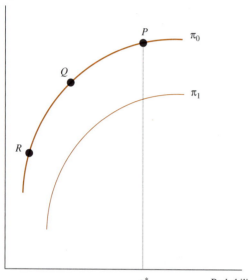

point Q). Hence, isoprofit curves slope up. If isoprofit curves were downward sloping, it would imply that the firm could "buy" safety, raise the wage, and have the same profits. This statement contradicts our assumption that it is costly to produce safety.

2. *Wage-risk combinations that lie on a higher isoprofit curve yield lower profits.* In particular, points on the isoprofit curve labeled π_0 are less profitable than points on the π_1 isoprofit curve. For any probability of injury (such as ρ* in the figure), a wage cut moves the firm to a lower isoprofit curve. This wage cut, however, increases profits.

3. *Isoprofit curves are concave.* The concavity of isoprofit curves arises because the law of diminishing returns applies to the production of safety. Consider initially a firm at point P in the π_0 isoprofit curve. The firm obviously offers a very risky work environment. There are many simple and relatively cheap things the firm can do in order to improve the safety of the workplace. For example, to prevent injury from earthquakes, the firm can nail the bookcases to the wall and tighten the screws on lighting fixtures. These activities would greatly reduce the risk of injury at a very low cost. As a result, the firm can reduce risk and hold profits constant by only slightly reducing the wage that it pays its workers. The isoprofit curve between points P and Q, therefore, is relatively flat. Suppose, however, that after reaching point Q the firm wishes to make the work environment even safer. All the cheap and simple things have already been done. To further reduce the risk of injury to point R, therefore, the firm will have to incur substantial expenditures. Additional protection from injury during an earthquake, for example, can be achieved only if the firm shores up weak points in the building's foundation or if the firm moves to another location. Further reductions in the risk of injury, therefore, can be very costly and

FIGURE 5-6   The Hedonic Wage Function

Different firms have different isoprofit curves and different workers have different indifference curves. The labor market marries workers who dislike risk (such as worker A) with firms that find it easy to provide a safe environment (like firm X); and workers who do not mind risk as much (worker C) with firms that find it difficult to provide a safe environment (firm Z). The observed relationship between wages and job characteristics is called a hedonic wage function.

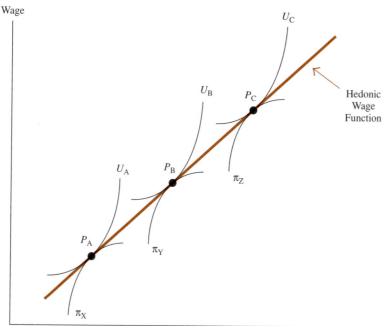

the firm has to greatly reduce the wage in order to hold profits constant. The segment of the isoprofit curve between points *Q* and *R*, therefore, may be quite steep.

We will assume that the firm operates in a competitive market with free entry and exit. When firms in the industry earn excess profits, many firms will enter the industry and depress profits. If profits were to become negative, firms would leave the industry, pushing up prices and increasing profits for the remaining firms. In the end, the only feasible wage-risk combinations are those that lie along the zero-profit isoprofit curve.

Equilibrium

The isoprofit curve gives the menu of wage-risk combinations available to a particular firm. As noted earlier, some firms will find it easy to offer a safe environment to their workers, whereas other firms will find it difficult. As a result, different firms will have different isoprofit curves. Figure 5-6 illustrates the zero-profit isoprofit curves for three firms: π_X for firm X, π_Y for firm Y, and π_Z for firm Z. As drawn, firm X (which might be producing computer software) can offer relatively low levels of risk, whereas firm Z (perhaps a firm building experimental fighter planes) finds it virtually impossible to provide a safe work environment.

A central implication of the theory of compensating differentials is that workers sort themselves across jobs. There is a rhyme and reason for the fact that, in the words of a well-known economist, "Musicians cannot be tone-deaf; footfall players tend to be large." Some jobs require particular skills, and some workers happen to have those specific skills—hence, the marriage that takes place in the labor market.

Much of the empirical evidence presented in the compensating differentials literature focuses on measuring the wage gaps that exist among different types of workers. For instance, those very rare people who have the narrow skill of being able to throw a ball accurately at 90 to 100 miles per hour over a 60.5-foot range are indeed compensated handsomely for that trait.

There is much less evidence, however, on the sorting that takes place between workers and firms. Do workers who happen to possess the skills that are valued by specific firms end up working in those types of jobs?

A recent study focuses on analyzes the job market sorting of workers who are "people" people. Some of us are gregarious. We enjoy interacting with friends, coworkers, and customers, and those interactions make our day. Other people, however, would much rather be left alone in their offices.

Some jobs obviously require frequent interaction with coworkers and customers and firms seeking to fill those jobs will likely search out for those workers who happen to like those types of interactions. It would not be savvy for firms to place workers who could care less about other people into positions where such interactions are crucial to the business's bottom line.

The results of the study are quite striking. The data were drawn from a survey that asked respondents about their level of gregariousness: "What would the people who know you say" about whether you enjoy being in company? It turns out that those persons who said that they enjoy being in company much more than average were also more likely to be in jobs where there were frequent interaction with coworkers. Moreover, the correlation is numerically large. A 10 percent increase in the fraction of nonworking time spent interacting with friends is associated with a 5 percent increase in the fraction of working time spent interacting with coworkers. Put differently, those people who have a "knack" for getting along well with others outside the work environment sort into jobs where interacting with coworkers is an important part of the working day.

Source: Alan B. Krueger and David Schkade, "Sorting in the Labor Market: Do Gregarious Workers Flock to Interactive Jobs?" *Journal of Human Resources* 43 (Fall 2008): 859–883.

Workers maximize utility by choosing the wage-risk offer that places them on the highest possible indifference curve. Worker A, who dislikes risk the most, maximizes utility at point P_A, and hence ends up working at firm X, which happens to be the firm that finds it easiest to provide a safe work environment. In contrast, worker C, who minds risk the least, maximizes utility at point P_C and ends up working at firm Z, the firm that finds it difficult to provide a safe work environment. There is, therefore, a nonrandom sorting of workers and firms. Safe firms are matched with safety-loving workers, and risky firms are matched with workers who are less risk-averse. In this type of equilibrium, workers self-select themselves across the spectrum of firms. Note that this sorting of workers to firms differs radically from the usual type of labor market equilibrium that we discussed in the last chapter. In the usual equilibrium, firms and workers are indistinguishable, and a random sorting of workers and firms is generated. In contrast, the compensating differential model "marries" workers and firms that have common interests.

The points P_A, P_B, and P_C in Figure 5-6 give the wage-risk combinations that will actually be observed in the labor market. If we connect these points, we generate what is called the **hedonic wage function**, which summarizes the relationship between the wage that workers get paid and job characteristics. Because workers dislike risk and because it is expensive to provide safety, the hedonic wage function is upward sloping. The slope of the hedonic wage function gives the wage increase offered by a slightly riskier job. At point P_A in Figure 5-6, the slope of the hedonic wage function equals the slope of worker A's indifference curve, so that the slope of the hedonic wage function gives worker A's reservation price. At point P_C, the hedonic wage function is tangent to worker C's indifference curve, and the slope of the hedonic wage function gives worker C's reservation price. As we shall see, this theoretical property of the hedonic wage function has had an important influence on public policy.

5-3   Policy Application: How Much Is a Life Worth?

Many studies estimate the hedonic function relating wages and the probability of injury on the job. These studies estimate the wage differences that exist across jobs that offer different probabilities of risk, after adjusting for other factors that might affect wage differentials such as the skills of the worker, the location of the job, and so on.[3]

As Table 5-1 shows, there is a great deal of variation in the injury rate (for both fatal and nonfatal injuries) among workers employed in different industries. The annual rate of fatal injuries per 100,000 workers was 29.0 in agriculture, 13.0 in transportation, and 0.6 in financial services.

Many empirical studies report a positive relation between wages and hazardous or unsafe work conditions, regardless of how the hazard or the unsafe nature of the work environment is defined.[4]

---

[3] The first and most influential study is that of Richard Thaler and Sherwin Rosen, "The Value of Saving a Life: Evidence from the Labor Market," in Nestor Terleckyj, editor, *Household Production and Consumption,* New York: Columbia University Press, 1976, pp. 265–298. The literature is surveyed by W. Kip Viscusi, "The Value of Risks to Life and Health," *Journal of Economic Literature* 31 (December 1993): 1912–46. The empirical studies typically estimate regressions of the form

$$w_i = a\,\rho_i + \text{Other variables}$$

where w_i gives the wage of worker i and ρ_i gives the probability of injury on the worker's job. The coefficient a then gives the wage change associated with a one-unit increase in the probability of injury.

[4] See Jeff Biddle and Gary Zarkin, "Worker Preferences and Market Compensation for Job Risks," *Review of Economics and Statistics* 70 (November 1988): 660–667; John Garen, "Compensating Wage Differentials and the Endogeneity of Job Riskiness," *Review of Economics and Statistics* 70 (February 1988): 9–16; Thomas Kniesner and John Leeth, "Compensating Wage Differentials for Fatal Injury Risk in Australia, Japan, and the United States," *Journal of Risk and Uncertainty* 4 (January 1991): 75–90; Daniel S. Hamermesh and John R. Wolfe, "Compensating Wage Differentials and the Duration of Wage Loss," *Journal of Labor Economics* 8 (January 1990 Supplement): S175–S197; and Morley Gunderson and Douglas Hyatt, "Workplace Risks and Wages: Canadian Evidence from Alternative Models," *Canadian Journal of Economics* 34 (May 2001): 377–395.

TABLE 5-1
**Injury Rates
in the United
States, by
Industry, 2008**

Notes: A disabling
injury is one that
results in death or
some degree of
physical impairment
or renders the person
unable to perform
regular activities for
a full day beyond the
day of the injury.

Source: U.S.
Department of
Commerce, *Statistical
Abstract of the
United States, 2011,*
Washington, DC:
Government Printing
Office, 2011, Table
656.

Industry Group	Deaths (per 100,000 Workers)	Number of Disabling Injuries (in 1000s)
Total	2.9	3,200
Agriculture	29.0	60
Mining	21.1	10
Construction	8.9	260
Manufacturing	2.3	390
Wholesale trade	3.8	80
Retail trade	0.9	380
Transportation and warehousing	13.0	160
Utilities	4.0	20
Information	1.0	30
Financial activities	0.6	70
Professional and business services	2.2	150
Educational and health services	0.5	510
Leisure and hospitality	0.9	270
Other services	1.8	110
Government	1.8	700

Perhaps the most interesting empirical results pertain to the relationship between wages and the probability of fatal injuries on the job. Workers who are exposed to high probabilities of fatal injuries earn more. Although there is a great deal of variation in the size of the estimated effect, a recent survey of the evidence concludes that a .001-point increase in the probability of fatal injury (so that, on average, an additional worker out of every thousand will die of job-related injuries in any given year) may increase annual earnings by about $7,600 (in 2007 dollars).[5]

Calculating the Value of Life

These correlations allow us to calculate the "value of life." To understand the mechanics of the calculation, let's compare two jobs. Workers employed in firm X have a probability of fatal injury equal to ρ_x and earn w_x dollars per year. Workers employed in firm Y have a probability of fatal injury that exceeds firm X's by 0.001 unit, and the evidence indicates that, on average, this riskier job pays about $7,600 more. We summarize these data as follows:

Firm	Probability of Fatal Injury	Annual Earnings
X	ρ_x	w_x
Y	$\rho_x + .001$	$w_x + \$7{,}600$

[5] Viscusi, "The Value of Risks to Life and Health"; see also Orley S. Ashenfelter, "Measuring the Value of a Statistical Life: Problems and Prospects," *Economic Journal* 116 (March 2006): C10–C23; and Per-Olov Johansson, "Is There a Meaningful Definition of the Value of a Statistical Life?" *Journal of Health Economics* 20 (January 2001): 131–139.

Suppose that firms X and Y each employs 1,000 workers. Because firm Y's probability of fatal injury exceeds that of X by .001 point, an additional worker is likely to die in firm Y during any given year. Workers in firm Y willingly accept this additional risk because *each* gets a compensating differential of $7,600.

Recall the theoretical property that the hedonic wage function is tangent to the workers' indifference curves. As a result, the change in the wage resulting from a .001-percentage-point increase in the probability of fatal injury is *exactly* what it takes to convince the marginal worker in firm Y to accept the slightly riskier job and hold her utility constant. In other words, it is the worker's reservation price. This interpretation of the data suggests that each of the workers in firm Y is willing to give up $7,600 per year to reduce the probability of fatal injury in their job by .001 unit. Put differently, the 1,000 workers employed in firm Y are willing to give up $7.6 million (or $7,600 × 1,000 workers) to save the life of the one worker who will almost surely die in any given year. The workers in firm Y, therefore, value a life at $7.6 million.

This is obviously not the answer we would get if the workers knew beforehand which one of the 1,000 was scheduled to suffer a fatal injury that year and we were to ask that unlucky person how much she would be willing to pay to avoid her fate. Our calculation instead gives the amount that workers are jointly willing to pay to reduce the likelihood that one of them will suffer a fatal injury in any given year. Put differently, it is the **value of a statistical life.**

It is important to note that there is a great deal of variation in the estimates of the correlation between wages and the probability of fatal injury on the job. As a result, there is much uncertainty about what the "true" value of a statistical life is. Part of the problem arises because the wage impact of a .001 increase in the probability of fatal injury depends on what types of workers we are analyzing. It matters if the data refer to workers who switch from a job with a .001 probability to a job with a .002 probability, or to workers who switch from a job with a .050 probability to a job with a .051 probability. The types of workers who end up in the "low-risk" jobs (that is, the jobs with a .001 or .002 probability) are obviously very different from the types of workers who end up in the "high-risk" jobs (the jobs with the .050 and .051 probabilities). As a result, the wage impact of a .001 increase in the probability of fatal injury depends greatly on what type of a .001 increase we have in mind.

Despite this methodological problem, the concept and estimates of the value of a statistical life have had a profound influence in evaluations of the costs and benefits of government regulation of safety hazards. For instance, when making construction decisions, highway departments typically compare the cost of a safer highway design with the dollar savings associated with fewer fatalities. In 2004, both the California Department of Transportation (Caltrans) and the U.S. Department of Transportation used a value of a statistical life of around $3 million to guide their decisions.[6] The Environmental Protection Agency (EPA) also makes frequent use of this concept when evaluating the cost of regulating environmental health and safety risks. For example, the agency wanted to limit the exposure of workers in glass manufacturing to arsenic poisoning. The cost of this regulation per statistical life saved would have been $142 million. It was not cost-effective, and the proposed regulation was rejected.[7]

[6] Ashenfelter, "Measuring the Value of a Statistical Life: Problems and Prospects."
[7] W. Kip Viscusi, *Fatal Tradeoffs: Public and Private Responsibilities for Risk,* New York: Oxford University Press, 1992.

In 1987, the federal government gave states the option to raise the speed limit on their rural interstate highways, from 55 mph to 65 mph. Some states adopted the higher limit despite the warning that such an increase would lead to more highway fatalities. Proponents of the legislation argued that increasing the speed limit would benefit travelers by reducing travel time. A report by the Indiana Department of Transportation makes the trade-off clear: "Speed limits represent trade-offs between risk and travel time . . . reflecting an appropriate balance between the societal goals of safety and mobility." Hence, the states that chose to increase the speed limit implicitly made a choice indicating that the value of time saved by driving faster was worth more than the value of the lives of the additional fatalities.

By the end of 1987, 38 states had raised the maximum speed limit on their rural interstates. The data clearly show that those states experienced an increase in their fatality rate on the affected highways. The increase in the speed limit raised the fatality rate (that is, the number of fatalities per 100 million vehicle-miles of travel) by around 35 percent, but reduced the time required to travel a mile by about 4 percent. Put differently, each fatality "saved" 125,000 hours of travel time. If we evaluate the dollar savings at the mean wage in the states that adopted the higher speed limit, states that increased the limit took actions that indicated their willingness to accept one additional fatality because it would save around $1.5 million (in 1997 dollars) in travel costs.

Source: Orley Ashenfelter and Michael Greenstone, "Using Mandated Speed Limits to Measure the Value of a Statistical Life," *Journal of Political Economy* 112 (February 2004): S226–S267.

5-4 Policy Application: Safety and Health Regulations

Since the enactment of the Occupational Safety and Health Act of 1970, the federal government in the United States has played a major role in setting safety standards at the workplace. The legislation created the Occupational Safety and Health Administration (OSHA), whose job is to protect the health and safety of the American labor force. In the past 20 years, OSHA has set workplace standards that mandate the maximum amount of cotton dust in the air in textile plants, the amount of asbestos in the air in work settings, and a host of other restrictions on the job environment.

These regulatory activities raise a number of important questions. Are workers better off as a result of these regulations? How do the safety standards alter the nature of the labor market equilibrium that generates compensating wage differentials? And, finally, do these government mandates actually reduce the probability of injury on the job?

For the most part, the regulatory mandates of OSHA set a ceiling of $\bar{\rho}$ on the permissible injury rate. Figure 5-7 illustrates the impact of this ceiling on the labor market. Prior to the regulation, the worker "purchased" the wage-risk package at point P, which offered a wage of w^* and exposed her to a probability of injury equal to ρ^*. The worker got U^* utils and the employer earned π^* dollars of profits.

The government regulation declares that this employment contract is illegal and forces the worker to accept a job at point Q on the hedonic wage function. The new job pays a lower wage of $\bar{w}$ and offers an injury rate of $\bar{\rho}$. The new employment contract *must* lower

FIGURE 5-7   **Impact of OSHA Regulation on Wage, Profits, and Utility**

A worker maximizes utility by choosing the job at point P, which pays a wage of w^* and offers a probability of injury of ρ^*. The government prohibits firms from offering a probability of injury higher than $\bar{\rho}$ shifting both the worker and the firm to point Q. As a result, the worker gets a lower wage and receives less utility (from U^* to $\bar{U}$), and the firm earns lower profits (from π^* to $\bar{\pi}$).

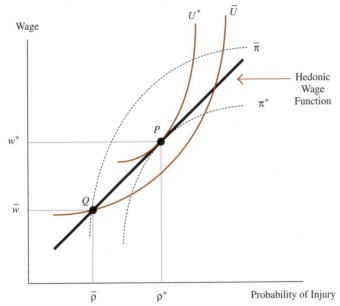

the utility of the worker to $\bar{U}$. After all, the worker was employed in the job that maximized her utility prior to the regulation. She obviously cannot be made better off when the government forces her to accept a job with different characteristics.

The OSHA regulations also affect the profitability of firms. The firm can no longer offer the wage-risk package of w^* and ρ^*. To comply with the injury rate ceiling, the firm also has to move to point Q on the hedonic wage function, placing the firm on a higher isoprofit curve $(\bar{\pi})$, hence reducing the firm's profits. If the new level of profits is very low (or negative), the firm may have to shut down as a result of the OSHA regulations.

Impact of Regulations When Workers Are Unaware of the Risks

We have seen that mandated safety standards reduce both the utility of affected workers and the profitability of affected firms. In view of this result, it is worth asking why governments bother to regulate safety standards at all. One argument used to justify the government mandates is that workers are unaware of the true risks associated with particular jobs. Construction workers in the 1950s and 1960s, for instance, did not know that continued exposure to asbestos fibers would eventually create serious health problems. It is worth pointing out, however, that neither firms nor government bureaucrats had that information, and, hence, it is doubtful that the problem could have been handled properly at the time.

FIGURE 5-8   Impact of OSHA Regulations When Workers Misperceive Risks on the Job

Workers earn a wage of w^* and incorrectly believe that their probability of injury is only ρ_0. In fact, their probability of injury is ρ^*. The government can mandate that firms do not offer a probability of injury higher than $\bar{\rho}$, making the uninformed workers better off (that is, increasing their actual utility from U^* to $\bar{U}$).

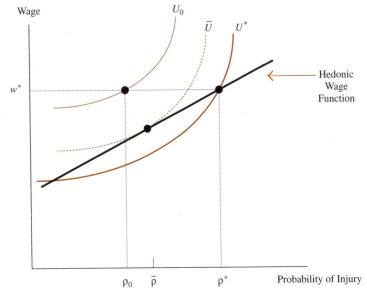

Nevertheless, suppose that employers know full well the risks associated with the job, and that workers systematically underestimate how much risk they are being exposed to. For instance, workers might be very optimistic about their own chances of escaping injury when they are employed as test pilots, even though a dispassionate and unblinking look at the data would suggest otherwise. Consider the hedonic wage function in Figure 5-8. The worker gets a wage of w^* dollars but believes that she is being exposed to a risk level of only ρ_0, rather than the true injury probability of ρ^*. Because of her misperception, the worker thinks she is getting U_0 utils, when in fact she is getting only U^* utils.

When workers misperceive their chances of getting injured, the government can step in and increase the worker's utility. In particular, the government can impose a ceiling on the injury rate anywhere between ρ_0 and ρ^*. This ceiling will increase the worker's *actual* utility. If the government sets the ceiling at $\bar{\rho}$, the worker's utility would be $\bar{U}$, which is lower than the worker's perceived utility, but that actually makes the worker better off. Safety standard regulations, therefore, can improve the workers' well being as long as workers consistently underestimate the true risk.[8]

It might seem redundant to ask if mandating employers to provide a safer work environment actually leads to a safer work environment. But it has been difficult to establish

---

[8] The extent to which workers misperceive risks is analyzed in W. Kip Viscusi and W. A. Magat, "An Investigation of the Rationality of Consumer Valuations of Multiple Health Risks," *Rand Journal of Economics* 18 (Winter 1987): 465–479; and W. Kip Viscusi, "Sources of Inconsistency in Societal Responses to Health Risks," *American Economic Review* 80 (May 1990): 257–261.

On March 11, 2011, a deadly earthquake measuring 9.0 on the Richter scale struck the east coast of Japan. Within minutes, tsunami waves more than 100 feet high struck the coast, and some of those waves traveled as much as six miles inland. The tsunami waves were extremely destructive, wiping out entire towns in a matter of minutes. Despite Japan's preparedness for such tragic events, there were at least 20,000 fatalities from the combined destruction of the earthquake and tsunami.

A number of cooling systems in some of the nuclear reactors that help provide electricity to Japan began to fail, and evacuations were required around the Fukushima nuclear plant, where thousands of tons of water were radioactive. The stabilization of the situation is obviously a dangerous task, requiring workers to be exposed to some radioactive material.

Because of the seriousness of the situation at the Fukushima reactor, the Tokyo Electric Power Company (TEPCO) needed workers, called "jumpers," who would dart into highly radioactive areas to conduct a particular task and leave as quickly as possible so as to minimize their exposure. TEPCO had a specific job requirement. It needed jumpers to help connect the equipment that

would help pump out the contaminated water. In the words of a TEPCO official: "The pump could be powered from an independent generator, and all that someone would have to do is bring one end of the pump to the water and dump it in, and then run out."

Despite the simplicity of the task, the excursion is obviously very dangerous. In the words of a news report, "The radiation might be so intense that jumpers can only make one such foray in their entire lives, or risk serious radiation poisoning." On average, a nuclear plant worker is exposed to 50 millisieverts of radiation over a five-year period. During the crisis, TEPCO reported that many employees had been exposed to 100 to 200 millisieverts in a single day.

TEPCO and its subcontractors began to recruit jumpers and offered eye-popping wages. The going pay for a jumper was around 200,000 yen, or roughly $2,400, for less than an hour's work. A worker's reaction summarizes the tragedy: "Ordinarily I'd consider that a dream job, but my wife was in tears and stopped me, so I declined."

Source: Terril Yue Jones, "'Jumpers' Offered Big Money to Brave Japan's Nuclear Plant," *Reuters*, April 1, 2011.

that OSHA regulations significantly improve safety in the workplace.[9] Recent studies find that OSHA has only slightly reduced the injury rates in firms and that the impact of the mandates has been declining over time.[10] By the 1990s, OSHA regulations had reduced the number of injuries by only about 1 percent.

5-5 Compensating Differentials and Job Amenities

Although we derived the hedonic wage function in terms of a single job characteristic—the probability of an on-the-job injury—the model clearly applies to many other job characteristics, such as whether the job involves repetitive and monotonous work, whether the job is located in an amenable physical setting (southern California versus northern Alaska),

[9] See, for example, Ann P. Bartel and L. G. Thomas, "Direct and Indirect Effects of OSHA Regulation," *Journal of Law and Economics* (April 1985): 1–26.

[10] John W. Ruser and Robert S. Smith, "Reestimating OSHA's Effects," *Journal of Human Resources* 26 (Spring 1991): 212–236; and Wayne B. Gray and John Mendeloff, "The Declining Effects of OSHA Inspections on Manufacturing Injuries: 1979 to 1998," *Industrial and Labor Relations Review* 58 (July 2005): 571–587.

whether the job involves strenuous physical work, and so on. The key implication of the theory is easily summarized: As long as *all* persons in the population agree on whether a particular job characteristic is a "good" or a "bad," good job characteristics are associated with low wage rates and bad job characteristics are associated with high wage rates.

The empirical studies in this literature typically estimate the hedonic wage function by correlating a worker's wage with various job characteristics—after adjusting for other factors, such as differences in skills that might generate wage differentials among workers. Despite the central role played by the theory of compensating differentials in our understanding of labor market equilibrium, the evidence does not provide a ringing endorsement of the theory. A careful survey of the evidence concluded that "tests of the theory of compensating wage differentials are inconclusive with respect to every job characteristic except the risk of death."[11]

For instance, jobs that demand physical strength are presumably more unpleasant than other jobs, and hence would be expected to pay higher wage rates. In fact, jobs requiring workers to have substantial physical strength often pay less, sometimes on the order of a 17 percent wage disadvantage.[12] Other studies, however, report correlations between wages and some job amenities that work in the expected direction. For instance, white teachers in schools that have a predominantly black student population receive a compensating differential (either because of the disutility associated with the location of the black school or because the white teachers do not enjoy teaching black students).[13]

Why Do Compensating Differentials Often Go the "Wrong" Way?

Our theoretical discussion suggests why many empirical tests of the theory of compensating differentials will inevitably contradict our expectations. Simply put, the "correct" direction of the wage differential typically reflects our own preferences and biases! We are obviously reasonable people, so jobs *we* find disagreeable should pay more. The theory, however, indicates that the market compensating wage differential measures what it took to get the marginal worker to accept that particular job. If the marginal worker happens

[11] Charles Brown, "Equalizing Differences in the Labor Market," *Quarterly Journal of Economics* 94 (February 1980): 113–134. Some of the studies include Randall Eberts and Joseph Stone, "Wages, Fringe Benefits, and Working Conditions: An Analysis of Compensating Differentials," *Southern Economic Journal* 52 (July 1985): 274–280; P. F. Kostiuk, "Compensating Differentials for Shift Work," *Journal of Political Economy* 98 (October 1990): 1054–1075; Stephen J. Trejo, "The Effects of Overtime Pay Regulation on Worker Compensation," *American Economic Review* 81 (September 1991): 719–740; and Edward Montgomery and Kathryn Shaw, "Pensions and Wage Premia," *Economic Inquiry* 35 (July 1997): 510–522.

[12] Robert E. B. Lucas, "The Distribution of Job Characteristics," *Review of Economics and Statistics* 56 (November 1974): 530–540; and Robert E. B. Lucas, "Hedonic Wage Equations and the Psychic Return to Schooling," *American Economic Review* 67 (September 1977): 549–558.

[13] Joseph Antos and Sherwin Rosen, "Discrimination in the Market for Public School Teachers," *Journal of Econometrics* 3 (May 1975): 123–150. Many studies also examine if regional wage differentials can be attributed to compensating differentials resulting from differences in regional amenities; see Jennifer Roback, "Wages, Rents, and the Quality of Life," *Journal of Political Economy* 90 (December 1982): 1257–1278; and Jennifer Roback, "Wages, Rents, and Amenities: Differences among Workers and Regions," *Economic Inquiry* 26 (January 1988): 23–41.

to like being employed in risky jobs or being told what to do on the job, the market wage differential will be in what seems to be the wrong direction.

In addition, the estimates of the compensating wage differentials associated with particular job characteristics are valid only if all the other factors that influence a worker's wages are held constant. Because more able workers are likely to earn higher wages, these workers will probably spend some of their additional income on job amenities. More able workers will then have higher wages *and* higher levels of "good" job amenities. This correlation will work against the compensating wage differential hypothesis. Because a worker's ability is seldom observed, the failure of the estimated correlations to show the right sign may be partly indicating that more able workers simply have more of everything—higher wages, better working conditions, and so on.

To rid the analysis of this type of **ability bias,** some studies argue that we must track the earnings of a particular worker over time as she changes jobs and purchases different packages of job amenities.[14] Put differently, the statistical models must control for individual-specific fixed effects. Because a worker's innate ability does not change from job to job, the correlation between the change in the wage and the change in the job amenity isolates the impact of compensating wage differentials. It turns out that the correlation between the change in a worker's wage and the change in her package of job amenities is much more consistent with the compensating differentials model.[15]

Compensating Differentials and Layoffs

A key justification for the unemployment insurance (UI) system is that workers need to be protected from the vagaries of the competitive labor market. In many countries, when workers become unemployed, the UI system pays a fraction of the worker's salary while the worker looks for alternative employment. Unemployment insurance thus stabilizes the flow of income (and consumption) for workers who are laid off from their jobs. In 2004, unemployed workers in the United States collected over $34 billion in unemployment compensation.[16]

The income-stabilization justification for the UI program, however, is much less appealing if the labor market, through compensating wage differentials, *already* compensates workers with high layoff probabilities. As Adam Smith first noted two centuries ago, the "constancy or inconstancy of employment" will generate compensating wage differentials. To illustrate the basic idea, suppose that a utility-maximizing worker has a job where she works h_0 hours per year at a wage rate of w_0 dollars. Using the neoclassical model of labor-leisure choice from Chapter 2, the situation is illustrated in Figure 5-9. Utility maximization occurs when the indifference curve is tangent to the budget line at point P, and, hence, the worker gets U_0 utils.

---

[14] Brown, "Equalizing Differences in the Labor Market."

[15] Greg Duncan and Bertil Holmlund, "Was Adam Smith Right after All? Another Test of the Theory of Compensating Differentials," *Journal of Labor Economics* 1 (October 1983): 366–379; see also Ernesto Villanueva, "Estimating Compensating Wage Differentials Using Voluntary Job Changes: Evidence from Germany," *Industrial and Labor Relations Review* 60 (July 2007): 544–561.

[16] U.S. Bureau of the Census, *Statistical Abstract of the United States, 2002,* Washington, DC: Government Printing Office, 2006, Table 549. For evidence on the extent to which unemployment insurance stabilizes a worker's consumption, see Jonathan Gruber, "The Consumption Smoothing Benefits of Unemployment Insurance," *American Economic Review* 87 (March 1997): 182–205.

FIGURE 5-9 Layoffs and Compensating Differentials

At point P, a person maximizes utility by working h_0 hours at a wage of w_0 dollars. An alternative job offers the worker a seasonal schedule, where she gets the same wage but works only h_1 hours. The worker is worse off in the seasonal job (her utility declines from U_0 to U' utils). If the seasonal job is to attract any workers, the job must raise the wage to w_1 so that workers will be indifferent between the two jobs.

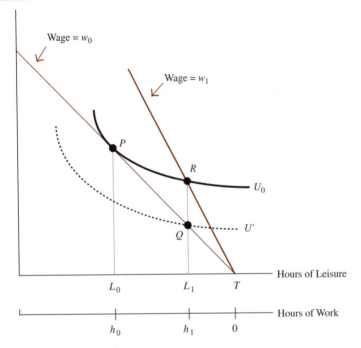

Suppose the worker receives an outside job offer. In this alternative job, the worker will continue to receive a wage rate of w_0 dollars, but she will not need to work as many hours. Because of *perfectly predictable* layoffs (perhaps due to seasonal factors like the retooling of an auto factory prior to the beginning of a new model year), the worker has to work only h_1 hours per year. The alternative job offer places the worker at point Q on the budget line, which moves the worker to a lower indifference curve (yielding U' utils).

The worker will not accept this job offer because it does not provide as much utility as her current job. In order to attract the worker, therefore, a job that offers only h_1 hours of work also must offer a higher wage. The new steeper budget line crosses the original indifference curve at point R, and the worker would be indifferent between a job package that offers h_0 hours of work at a wage of w_0 dollars and a job package that offers h_1 hours of work at a wage of w_1 dollars. When layoffs are perfectly predictable, therefore, a job with reduced work hours will have to compensate its workers by offering a higher wage.[17]

---

[17] Of course, the timing and duration of many layoffs are very hard to predict. It can be shown, however, that even if workers do not know if and when they will be laid off, the competitive market would still compensate workers who have a high probability of being laid off; see John Abowd and Orley Ashenfelter, "Anticipated Unemployment, Temporary Layoffs, and Compensating Wage Differentials," in Sherwin Rosen, editor, *Studies in Labor Markets,* Chicago: University of Chicago Press, 1981.

There is some evidence that the labor market indeed provides compensating differentials to workers at risk of layoff. For instance, wages are higher in industries that have higher layoff rates: An increase of 5 percentage points in the probability of layoff raises wages by about 1 percent.[18]

The extent to which the market compensates workers who face a high risk of unemployment is clearly determined by whether workers are covered by the unemployment insurance system. The available evidence suggests that if laid-off workers can receive unemployment insurance, an increase in the probability of unemployment has only a negligible effect on the wage. In other words, the UI system almost completely substitutes for compensating wage differentials. To a large extent, the unemployment insurance system seems to have replaced one insurance system (which was determined by the market) by another (which is taxpayer financed).[19]

Compensating Differentials and HIV

The rapid growth of Acquired Immunodeficiency Syndrome (AIDS) has created the most serious health crisis of the modern world. AIDS occurs when a person is infected with the human immunodeficiency virus (HIV), a virus that is transmitted by blood-to-blood or sexual contact. By 2009, around 33 million people were infected with HIV worldwide. The incidence of infection for adults varies widely across regions, from 0.5 percent in North America and Western Europe, to 1.6 percent in the Caribbean, and to 6.1 percent in sub-Saharan Africa. Even though the first case of AIDS was only diagnosed in 1981, a number of studies have already documented that the fear of HIV infection has created sizable compensating differentials in many labor markets.

Sonagachi is the red-light district of Calcutta. Workers in this district, conveniently located near Calcutta University, have been plying their trade for more than 150 years.[20] The price that the sex workers can charge, of course, depends on the characteristics associated with the transaction, including the physical attributes of the establishment (such as air conditioning and the amount of privacy) and the physical attributes of the sex worker (such as age and beauty).

In September 1992, the All India Institute of Public Health and Hygiene began to provide health care facilities to Sonagachi's sex workers and to educate them about HIV and AIDS. Prior to this education, the sex workers had practically no knowledge of the virus, of how it was transmitted, or how safe sex practices could reduce the risk of transmission. By November 1993, roughly half of the sex workers had received this valuable information.

---

[18] See also James Adams, "Permanent Differences in Unemployment and Permanent Wage Differentials," *Quarterly Journal of Economics* 100 (February 1985): 29–56; Elizabeth Li, "Compensating Differentials for Cyclical and Noncyclical Unemployment," *Journal of Labor Economics* 4 (April 1986): 277–300; Enrico Moretti, "Do Wages Compensate for Risk of Unemployment? Parametric and Semiparametric Evidence from Seasonal Jobs," *Journal of Risk and Uncertainty* 20 (January 2000): 45–66; and Susan Averett, Howard Bodenhorn, and Justas Staisiunas, "Unemployment Risk and Compensating Differentials in New Jersey Manufacturing," *Economic Inquiry* 43 (October 2005): 734–749.

[19] Robert H. Topel, "Equilibrium Earnings, Turnover, and Unemployment: New Evidence," *Journal of Labor Economics* 2 (October 1984): 500–522.

[20] The brief summary of the Calcutta sex market in the text is based on the much more detailed description provided by Vijayendra Rao, Indrani Gupta, Michael Lokshin, and Smarajit Jana, "Sex Workers and the Cost of Safe Sex: The Compensating Differential for Condom Use among Calcutta Prostitutes," *Journal of Development Economics* 71 (August 2003): 585–603.

As a result of this outreach, some of the female sex workers chose to practice safe sex and began to demand that customers use condoms. It is well known, however, that men have a strong preference against using condoms. This preference implies that the typical man is not willing to pay as much to a sex worker who demands the use of a condom as to one who will offer unprotected sex. Inevitably, compensating differentials arose in the Sonagachi marketplace. Sex workers engaged in unprotected sex would charge more to compensate for the additional risk, and they would attract male clients who were willing to pay to avoid using a condom. The compensating differential associated with condom use is quite large: sex workers who practice safe sex charge 70 percent less than sex workers who do not. The same type of compensating differential is also observed among sex workers in Mexico, where sex workers receive a 23 percent wage premium for unprotected sex and this premium jumps to almost 50 percent if the sex worker is considered attractive.[21]

Of course, the risk of HIV infection has repercussions even in labor markets that have little to do with the sex trade. Health care workers, for instance, risk contracting the virus from infected patients. By 2000, 195 health care workers in the United States, including 60 nurses, had acquired HIV even though they reported no risk factors but had a history of occupational exposure to blood.

The consequences of HIV infection are so severe that it would not be surprising if a compensating differential developed to compensate health care workers for their risky job environment. In fact, the evolution of the wage structure for nurses in the United States over the past 20 years reveals a link between the growth of the AIDS epidemic and nursing salaries. The risk of contracting HIV varies across metropolitan areas in the United States. The theory of compensating differentials would then suggest that nurses working in those areas with a higher risk of infection should get paid more than equally qualified nurses working in areas where the risk is lower. In fact, a 10 percent increase in the AIDS rate in a metropolitan area raises the wage of nurses in that area by around 1 percent.[22]

5-6 Policy Application: Health Insurance and the Labor Market

In the United States, employers provide health insurance coverage as a fringe benefit to a large fraction of the workforce. In 2001, 63 percent of the population was covered by an employer-provided health insurance program. A number of recent studies have applied the compensating differentials framework to evaluate the relation between wages and the availability of employer-provided insurance.

Suppose that all workers view the employer-provided program as a "good." The worker's indifference curve relating wages and health insurance would then have the usual downward-sloping convex shape, as illustrated in Figure 5-10. As drawn, worker A has the flat indifference curve U_A, implying that she does not attach much value to being covered

---

[21] Paul Gertler, Manisha Shah, and Stefano M. Bartozzi, "Risky Business: The Market for Unprotected Commercial Sex," *Journal of Political Economy* 113 (June 2005): 518–550.

[22] Jeff DeSimone and Edward J. Schumacher, "Compensating Wage Differentials and AIDS Risk," National Bureau of Economic Research Working Paper No. 10861, October 2004.

FIGURE 5-10 Health Benefits and Compensating Differentials

Workers A and B have the same earnings potential and face the same isoprofit curve giving the various compensation packages offered by firms. Worker A chooses a package with a high wage and no health insurance benefits. Worker B chooses a package with wage w_B and health benefits H_B. The observed data identify the trade-off between job benefits and wages. Workers B and B* have different earnings potential, so their job packages lie on different isoprofit curves. Their choices generate a positive correlation between wages and health benefits. The observed data do not identify the trade-off between wages and health benefits.

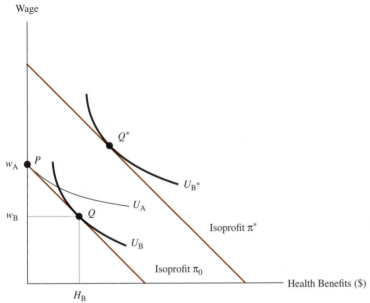

by health insurance. She is willing to give up health insurance benefits for a relatively small increase in her wage. Worker B's indifference curve U_B is steeper, implying that this worker attaches a high value to the employer-provided insurance.

In this context, the firm's isoprofit curve is also downward sloping. For a given level of profits, the firm can provide a package consisting of high wages and little health insurance coverage, or of low wages and a generous health insurance program. The isoprofit curve drawn in the figure, π_0, represents the zero-profit isoprofit curve for the group of persons that includes workers A and B. For simplicity, the isoprofit curve is drawn as a line.

If all workers faced the labor market opportunities lying along the isoprofit curve π_0, some workers (like A) would choose a corner solution at point P, indicating that they would rather work at a job that did not provide health insurance coverage at all, and they would receive a very high wage. In contrast, worker B would choose point Q, and she would split her total compensation between a wage of w_B dollars and a health insurance package worth H_B dollars. The data that we would observe in this labor market consists of the compensation packages of the two workers. These data trace out the isoprofit curve, and thus indicate the trade-off implied by the compensating differential model: the amount of earnings that worker B gives up in order to obtain her package of health insurance benefits.

Most studies that attempt to calculate this trade-off do not find a negative correlation between wages and the presence of employer-provided health insurance. Instead, they usually find a *positive* correlation.[23] To explain this apparent contradiction of the theory, it often has been argued that the positive correlation arises because the workers who have health insurance differ in important ways from the workers who do not.

Suppose, for example, that some workers have high levels of innate ability and have high earnings potential; other workers are less able and have lower earnings potential. The isoprofit curve π_0 applies to a group of workers who have equal productivity, say, the low-ability workers. A different (and higher) isoprofit curve would exist for workers who are more able; for a given level of health benefits, the firm can pay more productive workers a higher wage and still have zero profits.

The isoprofit curve labeled π^* in Figure 5-10 is the zero-profit isoprofit curve that summarizes the potential job offers available to high-ability worker B*. This worker chooses the compensation package at point Q*. Note that because of her high earnings potential, this worker can choose a compensation package that offers both high wages and generous health benefits. If we were to correlate the observed data on wages and health insurance benefits for workers B and B*, the correlation would be positive since high-wage workers also have more generous health benefits. One solution would be to control for the differences in ability among workers—effectively looking at workers who lie on the same isoprofit curve—but not all ability differences among workers can be observed by labor economists.

In recent years, the method of instrumental variables has been used to rid the data of the ability bias. In particular, researchers have searched for an instrument that places equally able workers along a single isoprofit curve so as to isolate the trade-off between wages and health insurance.

In one recent study, the instrument is suggested by the way in which employer-provided insurance contracts work in the United States. In the typical program, the employer-provided insurance covers not only the worker (say, the husband in the household), but also his wife and children. Put differently, only one of the two spouses needs to be covered by employer-provided insurance in order to obtain coverage for the entire family. As a result, a wife whose husband already has employer-provided insurance can be much more flexible in terms of her job choice; she can choose jobs that offer very little (or no!) health insurance without putting household members in jeopardy.[24]

Suppose we consider the relation between wages and health insurance coverage in a sample of married women. A variable indicating if the husband has health insurance coverage is a valid instrument if it affects the wife's choice of health insurance coverage (in other words, it affects the wife's choice of a particular compensation package along the isoprofit curve) *and* if it does not affect the wife's earnings potential (in other words, the wife's ability is not correlated with a variable indicating if the husband has health insurance).

Suppose that these conditions hold. The available evidence indicates that women whose husbands have employer-sponsored insurance are less likely to work in jobs that provide

[23] The evidence is summarized in Janet Currie and Brigitte C. Madrian, "Health, Health Insurance, and the Labor Market," in Orley C. Ashenfelter and David Card, editors, *Handbook of Labor Economics,* vol. 3C, Amsterdam: Elsevier, 1999, pp. 3309–3415.

[24] Craig A. Olson, "Do Workers Accept Lower Wages in Exchange for Health Benefits?" *Journal of Labor Economics* 20 (April 2002, part 2): S91–S114.

health insurance. In fact, the probability that a wife already covered by her husband's insurance obtains her own insurance is 15.5 percentage points lower than that of a wife whose husband does not have insurance. At the same time, the evidence indicates that women married to men who have health insurance earn 2.6 percent more than women married to men who do not have health insurance.

These statistics suggest that a 15.5-percentage-point drop in the probability of having own employer-provided insurance is associated with a wage increase of 2.6 percent. The method of instrumental variables then implies that the estimate of the trade-off is given by the ratio of $2.6 \div (-15.5) = -0.168$. In sum, women who choose jobs that offer employer-sponsored insurance earn 16.8 percent less than they would have earned had they chosen a job that did not offer health insurance benefits.

This estimate of the compensating differential is correct only if the variable indicating whether the husband has health insurance is a valid instrument. In other words, the husband's health insurance coverage affects the probability that the wife has her own employer-provided insurance but does not affect the wife's earnings potential. One can easily think of reasons as to why this set of assumptions may not be correct. For instance, high-wage men (who are more likely to have generous health insurance coverage) may be more likely to marry high-wage women (who also will end up in jobs that offer generous insurance coverage). A more complete study of the compensating differential, therefore, would have to take these considerations into account.

Summary

- The worker's reservation price gives the wage increase that will persuade the worker to accept a job with an unpleasant characteristic, such as the risk of injury.
- The worker will switch to a riskier job if the market-compensating wage differential exceeds the worker's reservation price.
- Firms choose whether to offer a risky environment or a safe environment to their workers. Firms that offer a risky environment must pay higher wages; firms that offer a safe environment must invest in safety. The firm offers whichever environment is more profitable.
- The market-compensating wage differential is the dollar amount required to convince the marginal worker (that is, the last worker hired) to move to the riskier job.
- If a few workers enjoy working in jobs that have a high probability of injury and if these types of jobs demand relatively few workers, the market wage differential will go the "wrong" way. In other words, risky jobs will pay lower wages than safe jobs.
- There is a "marriage" of workers and firms in the labor market. Workers who dislike particular job characteristics (such as the risk of injury) match with firms that do not offer those characteristics; workers who like the characteristics match with firms that provide them.
- The value of a statistical life can be calculated from the correlation between the worker's wage and the probability of fatal injury on the job.
- Workers with high earnings potential are likely to earn more and to have more generous job benefits. This positive correlation generates an ability bias that makes it difficult to find evidence that fringe benefits generate compensating wage differentials.

Key Concepts	ability bias, *223*	hedonic wage function, *215*	value of a statistical
	compensating wage	isoprofit curve, *211*	life, *217*
	differential, *203*	reservation price, *206*	

Review Questions

1. Suppose there are two types of jobs in the labor market: "safe" jobs and "risky" jobs. Describe how the worker decides whether to accept a safe job (where she cannot be injured) or a risky job (where she will certainly be injured).

2. Describe how the firm decides whether to offer a safe working environment or a risky environment.

3. How is the market-compensating wage differential between safe jobs and risky jobs determined? Which type of job will offer a higher wage?

4. Describe how workers and firms "marry" each other in the labor market when there are many types of jobs offering various levels of risk to their workers. What does the slope of the hedonic wage function measure?

5. How do we calculate the value of a statistical life?

6. What is the impact of health and safety regulations on the utility of workers and on the profits of firms?

7. Show that the competitive labor market compensates workers for the probability that they will be laid off.

8. Explain how the method of instrumental variables can be used to estimate the compensating differential associated with employer-provided health benefits.

Problems

5-1. Politicians who support the green movement often argue that it is profitable for firms to pursue a strategy that is "environmentally friendly" (for example, by building factories that do not pollute and are not noisy) because workers will be willing to work in environmentally friendly factories at a lower wage rate. Evaluate the validity of this claim.

5-2. Consider the demand for and supply of risky jobs.

 a. Derive the algebra that leads from equations (5-4) and (5-5) to equation (5-6).

 b. Describe why the supply curve in Figure 5-2 is upward sloping. How does your explanation incorporate θ? Why?

 c. Using a graph similar to Figure 5-2, demonstrate how the number of dirty jobs changes as technological advances allow the cost of making worsites cleaner to fall for all firms.

5-3. Suppose there are 100 workers in the economy in which all workers must choose to work a risky or a safe job. Worker 1's reservation price for accepting the risky job is $1; worker 2's reservation price is $2; and so on. Because of technological reasons, there are only 10 risky jobs.

 a. What is the equilibrium wage differential between safe and risky jobs? Which workers will be employed at the risky firm?

 b. Suppose now that an advertising campaign paid for by the employers who offer risky jobs stresses the excitement associated with "the thrill of injury," and this campaign changes the attitudes of the workforce toward being employed in a risky job.

Worker 1 now has a reservation price of $-\$10$ (that is, she is willing to pay $10 for the right to work in the risky job); worker 2's reservation price is $-\$9$; and so on. There are still only 10 risky jobs. What is the new equilibrium wage differential?

5-4. Suppose all workers have the same preferences represented by

$$U = \sqrt{w} - 2x$$

where w is the wage and x is the proportion of the firm's air that is composed of toxic pollutants. There are only two types of jobs in the economy: a clean job ($x = 0$) and a dirty job ($x = 1$). Let w_0 be the wage paid by the clean job and w_1 be the wage paid for doing the dirty job. If the clean job pays $16 per hour, what is the wage in dirty jobs? What is the compensating wage differential?

5-5. Suppose a drop in the compensating wage differential between risky jobs and safe jobs has been observed. Two explanations have been put forward:

- Engineering advances have made it less costly to create a safe working environment.

- The phenomenal success of a new reality show *Die on the Job!* has imbued millions of viewers with a romantic perception of work-related fatal risks.

Using supply and demand diagrams, show how each of the two developments can explain the drop in the compensating wage differential. Can information on the number of workers employed in the risky occupation help determine which explanation is more plausible?

5-6. Consider a competitive economy that has four different jobs that vary by their wage and risk level. The table below describes each of the four jobs.

Job	Risk (r)	Wage (w)
A	1/5	$3
B	1/4	$12
C	1/3	$23
D	1/2	$25

All workers are equally productive, but workers vary in their preferences. Consider a worker who values his wage and the risk level according to the following utility function:

$$u(w, r) = w + \frac{1}{r^2}$$

Where does the worker choose to work? Suppose the government regulated the workplace and required all jobs to have a risk factor of 1/5 (that is, all jobs must become A jobs). What wage would the worker now need to earn in the A job to be equally happy following the regulation?

5-7. Consider Table 5-1 and compare the fatality rate of workers in the mining, construction, manufacturing, and financial industries.

a. What would the distribution of wages look like across these four industries given the compensating differential they might have to pay to compensate workers for risk?

b. Now look at average hourly earnings in 2006 by industry as reported in Table 614 of the 2008 *U.S. Statistical Abstract.* Does the actual distribution of wages reinforce your answer to part (a)? If not, what else might enter the determination of median weekly earnings?

5-8. The Environmental Protection Agency (EPA) wants to investigate the value workers place on being able to work in "clean" mines over "dirty" mines. The EPA conducts a study and finds the average annual wage in clean mines to be $42,250 and the average annual wage in dirty mines to be $47,250.

a. According to the EPA, how much does the average worker value working in a clean mine?

b. Suppose the EPA could mandate that all dirty mines become clean mines and that all workers who were in a dirty mine must therefore accept a $5,000 pay decrease. Are these workers helped by the intervention, hurt by the intervention, or indifferent to the intervention?

5-9. There are two types of farming tractors on the market, the FT250 and the FT500. The only difference between the two is that the FT250 is more prone to accidents than the FT500. Over their lifetime, 1 in 10 FT250s is expected to result in an accident, as compared to 1 in 25 FT500s. Further, 1 in 1,000 FT250s is expected to result in a fatal accident, as compared to only 1 in 5,000 FT500s. The FT250 sells for $125,000 while the FT500 sells for $137,000. At these prices, 2,000 of each model are purchased each year. What is the statistical value farmers place on avoiding a tractor accident? What is the statistical value of a life of a farmer?

5-10. Consider the labor market for public school teachers. Teachers have preferences over their job characteristics and amenities.

a. One would reasonably expect that high-crime school districts pay higher wages than low-crime school districts. But the data consistently reveal that high-crime school districts pay lower wages than low-crime school districts. Why?

b. Does your discussion suggest anything about the relation between teacher salaries and school quality?

5-11. a. On a graph with the probability of injury on the x-axis and the wage level on the y-axis plot two indifference curves, labeled U_A and U_B, so that the person associated with U_A is less willing to take on risk relative to the person associated with U_B. Explain what it is about the indifference curves that reveals person A is less willing to take on risk relative to person B.

b. Consider a third person who doesn't care about the risk associated with the job. That is, he doesn't seek to limit risk or to expose himself to risk. On a new graph, draw several of this person's indifference curves. Include an arrow on the graph showing which direction is associated with higher levels of utility.

c. Consider a wage-risk equilibrium that is characterized by an upward-sloping hedonic wage function. Now suppose there is a government campaign that successfully alters people's perception of risk. In particular, each worker adjusts her preferences so that she now needs to be more highly compensated to take on risk.

Discuss, and show on a single graph, how the government's campaign affects indifference curves, isoprofit lines, the equilibrium hedonic wage function, and the distribution of workers to firms.

5-12. Suppose a firm must employ 20 workers in order to produce 2,000 units of output that the firm has contracted to supply to the government for $1.4 million. The firm must choose how much to invest in safety. The firm can choose any level of safety, S, from 0 to 100. The cost of safety is $C(S) = 50S^2$. Given the firm's choice of safety, the annual salary paid to workers is determined by

$$\text{Annual salary} = 60,000 - 300S$$

Thus, a firm that chooses $S = 30$ pays $45,000 for this level of safety and pays each worker $51,000. What level of safety will the firm choose, and how much does this cost? How much will each worker earn? How much profit will the firm earn?

5-13. Consider two identical jobs, but some jobs are located in Ashton while others are located in Benton. Everyone prefers working in Ashton, but the degree of this preference varies across people. In particular, the preference (or reservation price) is distributed uniformly from $0 to $5. Thus, if the Benton wage is $2 more than the Ashton wage, then 40 percent (or two-fifths) of the worker population will choose to work in Benton. Labor supply is perfectly inelastic, but firms compete for labor. There are a total of 25,000 workers to be distributed between the two cities. Demand for labor in both locations is described by the following inverse labor demand functions:

$$\text{Ashton: } w_A = 20 - 0.0024E_A.$$
$$\text{Benton: } w_B = 20 - 0.0004E_B.$$

Solve for the labor market equilibrium by finding the number of workers employed in both cities, the wage paid in both cities, and the equilibrium wage differential.

5-14. U.S. Trucking pays its drivers $40,000 per year, while American Trucking pays its drivers $38,000 per year. For both firms, truck drivers average 240,000 miles per year. Truck driving jobs are the same regardless of which firm one works for, except that U.S. Trucking gives each of its trucks a safety inspection every 50,000 miles, while American Trucking gives each of its trucks a safety inspection every 36,000 miles. This difference in safety inspection rates results in a different rate of fatal accidents between the two companies. In particular, one driver for U.S Trucking dies in an accident every 12 million miles while one driver for American Trucking dies in an accident every 15 million miles. What is the value of a trucker's life implied by the compensating differential between the two firms?

5-15. The hedonic wage function is the locus of points that illustrates the relationship between the wage that workers get paid and job characteristics. All else equal, the more pollutants miners breathe while working in a mine, the worse off the miners are. However, miners vary in their degree of dislike for breathing in pollutants. Given the current distribution of perfectly competitive firms (that is, mines) and technologies for cleaning up pollutants, a hedonic wage function comes about. Suppose the distribution of mines and technologies remains fixed, but, due to a public relations campaign by the American Cancer Society, all potential miners change their preferences so that they dislike breathing in pollutants even more.

a. What will happen to the hedonic wage function after the public relations campaign?

b. What will happen to where each individual miner locates on the hedonic wage function?

Selected Readings

John Abowd and Orley Ashenfelter, "Anticipated Unemployment, Temporary Layoffs, and Compensating Wage Differentials," in Sherwin Rosen, editor, *Studies in Labor Markets.* Chicago: University of Chicago Press, 1981.

Orley S. Ashenfelter, "Measuring the Value of a Statistical Life: Problems and Prospects," IZA Discussion Paper No. 1911, January 2006.

Orley Ashenfelter and Michael Greenstone, "Using Mandated Speed Limits to Measure the Value of a Statistical Life," *Journal of Political Economy* 112 (February 2004): S226–S267.

Charles Brown, "Equalizing Differences in the Labor Market," *Quarterly Journal of Economics* 94 (February 1980): 113–134.

Craig A. Olson, "Do Workers Accept Lower Wages in Exchange for Health Benefits?" *Journal of Labor Economics* 20 (April 2002, part 2): S91–S114.

Sherwin Rosen, "The Theory of Equalizing Differences," in Orley C. Ashenfelter and Richard Layard, editors, *Handbook of Labor Economics,* vol. 1. Amsterdam: Elsevier, 1986, pp. 641–692.

Richard Thaler and Sherwin Rosen, "The Value of Saving a Life: Evidence from the Labor Market," in Nestor Terleckyj, editor, *Household Production and Consumption.* New York: Columbia University Press, 1976, pp. 265–298.

W. Kip Viscusi, "The Value of Risks to Life and Health," *Journal of Economic Literature* 31 (December 1993): 1912–1946.

Web Links

The Web site of the Occupational Safety and Health Administration (OSHA) contains detailed information about job risks: www.osha.gov.

The workers' compensation program is administered at the state level. New York has a representative Web site containing relevant information on tax rates and benefits: www.wcb.state.ny.us.

The U.S. Bureau of the Census reports information on trends in health insurance coverage for various population subgroups: www.census.gov/hhes/www/hlthins.html.

The California Department of Transportation (Caltrans) describes how it uses calculations of the value of a statistical life: www.dot.ca.gov/hq/tpp/offices/ote/Benefit_Cost/benefits/accidents/value_estimates.html.

Chapter 6

Human Capital

If you think education's expensive, try ignorance!

—*Derek Bok*

The theory of compensating differentials suggests that wages will vary among workers because jobs are different. Wages also will vary because workers are different. We each bring into the labor market a unique set of abilities and acquired skills, or **human capital.** For instance, some persons train to be research biologists while other persons train to be musicians. This chapter discusses how we choose the particular set of skills that we offer to employers and how our choices affect the evolution of earnings over the working life.

We acquire most of our human capital in school and in formal and informal on-the-job training programs. The skills we acquire in school make up an increasingly important component of our stock of knowledge. In 1940, 75.5 percent of adults in the United States had not graduated from high school, and only 4.6 percent had a college degree. By 2010, only 11.6 percent of adults did not have a high school diploma, and 29.9 percent had at least a college degree.

This chapter analyzes why some workers obtain a lot of schooling and other workers drop out at an early age. Workers who invest in schooling are willing to give up earnings today in return for higher earnings in the future. For example, we earn a relatively low wage while we attend college or participate in a formal apprenticeship program. However, we expect to be rewarded by higher earnings later on as we collect the returns on our investment. The trade-off between lower earnings today and higher earnings later, as well as the financial and institutional constraints that limit access to education, determines the distribution of educational attainment in the population.

We also will discuss whether the money spent on education is a good investment. In particular, how does the rate of return to schooling compare with the rate of return on other investments? Putting aside our own personal interest in knowing whether we are getting a good deal out of our college education, the rate of return to schooling plays an important role in many policy discussions. It is often argued, for instance, that subsidizing investments to education and other learning activities is the surest way of improving the economic well-being of low-income and disadvantaged workers.

We do not typically stop accumulating skills and knowledge the day we finally leave school. Instead, we continue to add to our human capital stock throughout much of our working lives. As a result of the human capital acquired through training and vocational programs, college graduates in their fifties earn twice as much as college graduates in their twenties. This chapter also analyzes how workers choose a particular path for their post-school investments and investigates how these choices influence the evolution of earnings over the life cycle and determine the earnings distribution in the economy.

Our analysis will assume that the worker chooses the level of human capital investments that maximizes the present value of lifetime earnings. This approach to the study of the determinants of the earnings distribution differs fundamentally from alternative approaches that view a worker's wage as determined by luck and other random factors. These random events might include whether the worker happened to meet an aging billionaire on the way to work or whether the worker was having breakfast at a Hollywood diner when an influential agent walked in. The human capital approach does not deny that luck, looks, and being in the right place at the right time influence a worker's earnings. Rather, we stress the idea that our educational and training decisions play an important role in the determination of earnings.

6-1   Education in the Labor Market: Some Stylized Facts

Table 6-1 summarizes the distribution of education in the U.S. population. The table shows clearly that there are only slight differences in educational attainment between men and women, but that there are substantial differences among racial and ethnic groups. By 2010, only about 8 percent of white persons did not have a high school diploma, as opposed to 13 percent of African Americans and 34 percent of Hispanics. In contrast, more than 38 percent of whites had at least a college diploma, as compared to only 20 percent of African Americans and 14 percent of Hispanics.[1]

TABLE 6-1   Educational Attainment of U.S. Population, 2010 (Persons Aged 25 and Over)

Source: U.S. Bureau of Labor Statistics, *Annual Demographic Supplement of the Current Population Surveys*, March 2010.

Group	Highest Grade Completed (Percentage of Population in Education Category)					
	Less Than High School	High School Graduates	Some College	Associate Degree	Bachelor's Degree	Advanced Degree
All Persons	11.6%	32.5%	16.8%	9.1%	19.4%	10.5%
Gender:						
Male	11.3	31.7	17.1	10.2	18.4	10.2
Female	12.0	33.3	16.5	8.0	10.4	10.9
Race/ethnicity:						
White	8.1	32.5	17.5	9.7	26.4	11.9
Black	13.4	37.3	20.0	9.4	13.3	6.6
Hispanic	34.3	12.5	12.9	6.3	10.1	3.8

[1] A careful study of the differences in educational attainment among race/ethnic groups is given by Stephen V. Cameron and James J. Heckman, "The Dynamics of Educational Attainment for Black, Hispanic, and White Males," *Journal of Political Economy* 109 (June 2001): 455–499.

TABLE 6-2   **Labor Market Characteristics, by Education Group, 2010 (Persons Aged 25–64)**

Source: U.S. Bureau of Labor Statistics, *Annual Demographic Supplement of the Current Population Surveys*, March 2010.

		Less Than High School	High School Graduates	Some College	College Graduates
All workers:	Labor force participation rate	61.9	76.0	79.9	85.8
	Unemployment rate	16.9	12.2	8.7	4.7
	Annual earnings (in $1000)	22.1	33.1	40.5	69.8
Gender:					
Men	Labor force participation rate	74.0	83.1	85.6	91.6
	Unemployment rate	17.8	13.9	10.0	5.1
	Annual earnings (in $1000)	25.8	38.1	48.9	85.6
Women	Labor force participation rate	48.2	68.2	75.0	80.4
	Unemployment rate	15.4	9.9	7.5	4.3
	Annual earnings (in $1000)	17.2	26.5	32.6	53.8
Race/ethnicity:					
White	Labor force participation rate	56.3	76.4	80.4	86.1
	Unemployment rate	17.8	11.2	7.9	4.1
	Annual earnings (in $1000)	24.7	35.3	42.6	71.9
Black	Labor force participation rate	49.5	70.9	77.8	87.2
	Unemployment rate	23.3	17.7	12.6	7.9
	Annual earnings (in $1000)	19.5	29.0	33.5	56.1
Hispanic	Labor force participation rate	69.6	79.0	80.9	84.8
	Unemployment rate	15.3	12.3	9.7	5.6
	Annual earnings (in $1000)	21.1	28.2	36.3	57.9

The differences in educational attainment among workers are significant because, as Table 6-2 shows, education is strongly correlated with labor force participation rates, unemployment rates, and earnings. The labor force participation rate of persons who lack a high school diploma is only 62 percent, as compared to 86 percent for college graduates. Similarly, the unemployment rate of high school dropouts in the midst of a deep recession was 16.9 percent, but it was much lower (4.7 percent) for college graduates. Finally, high school dropouts earn just over $22,000 annually, but college graduates earn $70,000 three times as much.

The data also indicate that education has a substantial beneficial impact on the labor market experiences of women and minorities. For example, the unemployment rate of black high school dropouts is 23.3 percent, as compared to 17.7 percent for black high school graduates and 8 percent for black college graduates. Similarly, Hispanic high school dropouts earn only $21,000 as compared to nearly $58,000 for Hispanic college graduates.

Although there are sizable differences in labor market outcomes between men and women and across race and ethnic groups—and these differences will be discussed in detail in Chapter 9—this chapter investigates a different lesson that can be drawn from the data reported in Table 6-2: Education plays a crucial role in improving labor market outcomes for both men and women and for workers in all racial and ethnic groups.

6-2 Present Value

Any study of an investment decision—whether it is an investment in physical or in human capital—must contrast expenditures and receipts incurred at different time periods. In other words, an investor must be able to calculate the returns to the investment by comparing the current cost with the future returns. For reasons that will become obvious momentarily, however, the value of a dollar received today is not the same as the value of a dollar received tomorrow. The notion of **present value** allows us to compare dollar amounts spent and received in different time periods.

Suppose somebody gives you a choice between two monetary offers: You can have either $100 today or $100 next year. Which offer would you take? A little reflection should convince you that $100 today is better than $100 next year. After all, if you receive $100 today, you can invest it, and you will then have $100 \times (1 + 0.05)$ dollars next year (or $105), assuming that the rate of interest equals 5 percent. Note, moreover, that receiving $95.24 today (or $100 \div 1.05$) would be worth $100 next year. Hence, the present value (or the current dollar value) of receiving $100 tomorrow is only $95.24. In general, the present value of a payment of, say, y dollars next year is given by

$$PV = \frac{y}{1 + r} \qquad\qquad \textbf{(6-1)}$$

where r is the rate of interest, which is also called the **rate of discount.** The quantity PV tells us how much needs to be invested today in order to have y dollars next year. In effect, a future payment of y dollars is discounted so as to make it comparable to current dollars.

The discussion clearly suggests that receiving y dollars two years from now is not equivalent to receiving y dollars today or even to receiving y dollars next year. A payment of $100 today would be worth $100 \times (1 + 0.05) \times (1 + 0.05)$ two years from now. Hence, the present value of receiving y dollars two years from now is

$$PV = \frac{y}{(1 + r)^2} \qquad\qquad \textbf{(6-2)}$$

By arguing along similar lines, we can conclude that the present value of y dollars received t years from now equals

$$PV = \frac{y}{(1 + r)^t} \qquad\qquad \textbf{(6-3)}$$

These formulas are extremely useful when we study decisions that involve expenditures made or dollars received at different time periods because they allow us to state the value of these expenditures and receipts in terms of today's dollars.

6-3 The Schooling Model

Education is associated with lower unemployment rates and higher earnings. So why don't all workers get doctorates or professional degrees? In other words, what factors motivate some workers to get professional degrees while other workers drop out before they finish high school?

We begin our analysis of this important question by assuming that workers acquire the education level that maximizes the present value of lifetime earnings. Education and other forms of training, therefore, are valued only because they increase earnings. A college education obviously affects a person's utility in many other ways. It teaches the student how to read and appreciate Nietzsche and how to work out complex mathematical equations; it even reduces the cost of entering the "marriage market" by facilitating contact with a large number of potential mates. Important though they may be, we will ignore these side effects of human capital investments and concentrate exclusively on the monetary rewards of an education.[2]

Consider the situation faced by an 18-year-old man who has just received his high school diploma and who is contemplating whether to enter the labor market or attend college and delay labor market entry by an additional four years.[3] Suppose that there is no on-the-job training and that the skills learned in school do not depreciate over time. These assumptions imply that the worker's productivity does not change once he leaves school, so that real earnings (that is, earnings after adjusting for inflation) are constant over the life cycle.

Figure 6-1 illustrates the economic trade-off involved in the worker's decision. The figure shows the **age-earnings profile** (that is, the wage path over the life cycle) associated with each alternative. Upon entering the labor market, high school graduates earn w_{HS} dollars annually until retirement age, which occurs when the worker turns 65. If the person chooses to attend college, he gives up w_{HS} dollars in labor earnings and incurs "direct" costs of H dollars to cover tuition, books, and fees. After graduation, he earns w_{COL} dollars annually until retirement.

Figure 6-1 indicates that going to college involves two different types of costs. A year spent in college is a year spent out of the labor force (or at least a year spent working in a low-wage part-time job), so that a college education forces the worker to forgo some earnings. This is the **opportunity cost** of going to school—the cost of not pursuing the best alternative. The opportunity cost is w_{HS} dollars for each year the student goes to college. The student also has out-of-pocket expenses of H dollars for tuition, books, and a variety of other fees.

Because college has no intrinsic value to the student, employers who wish to attract a highly educated (and presumably more productive) worker will have to offer higher wages, so that $w_{COL} > w_{HS}$. In a sense, the high wage paid to workers with more schooling is a compensating differential that compensates workers for their training costs. If college graduates earned less than high school graduates, no one would bother to get a college education because we are assuming that workers do not get any other benefits from attending college.

[2] A more general approach would assume that workers choose to acquire the skill level that maximizes lifetime utility. Most of the key insights of the schooling model, however, are not affected by this generalization; see Robert T. Michael, "Education in Nonmarket Production," *Journal of Political Economy* 81 (March/April 1973): 306–327.

[3] The schooling model was first analyzed by Jacob Mincer, "Investment in Human Capital and Personal Income Distribution," *Journal of Political Economy* 66 (August 1958): 281–302. An even earlier study that anticipated many of the central concepts in the human capital literature is given by Milton Friedman and Simon Kuznets, *Income from Independent Professional Practice,* Princeton, NJ: Princeton University Press, 1954.

FIGURE 6-1 Potential Earnings Streams Faced by a High School Graduate

A person who quits school after getting his high school diploma can earn w_{HS} from age 18 until the age of retirement. If he decides to go to college, he forgoes these earnings and incurs a cost of H dollars for four years and then earns w_{COL} until retirement age.

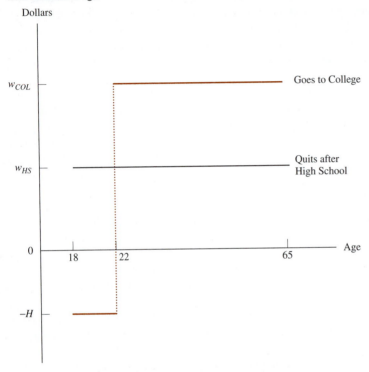

Present Value of Age-Earnings Profiles

The present value of the earnings stream if the worker gets only a high school education is

$$PV_{HS} = w_{HS} + \frac{w_{HS}}{(1 + r)} + \frac{w_{HS}}{(1 + r)^2} + \cdots + \frac{w_{HS}}{(1 + r)^{46}} \quad \text{(6-4)}$$

where r gives the worker's rate of discount. There are 47 terms in this sum, one term for each year that elapses between the ages of 18 and 64.

The present value of the earnings stream if the worker gets a college diploma is

$$PV_{COL} = \underbrace{-H - \frac{H}{(1 + r)} - \frac{H}{(1 + r)^2} - \frac{H}{(1 + r)^3}}_{\text{Direct Costs of Attending College}} + \underbrace{\frac{w_{COL}}{(1 + r)^4} + \frac{w_{COL}}{(1 + r)^5} + \cdots + \frac{w_{COL}}{(1 + r)^{46}}}_{\text{Post-college Earnings Stream}} \quad \text{(6-5)}$$

The first four terms in this sum give the present value of the direct costs of a college education, whereas the remaining 43 terms give the present value of lifetime earnings in the postcollege period.

A person's schooling decision maximizes the present value of lifetime earnings. Therefore, the worker attends college if the present value of lifetime earnings when he gets a college education exceeds the present value of lifetime earnings when he gets only a high school diploma, or

$$PV_{COL} > PV_{HS} \qquad \text{(6-6)}$$

Let's illustrate the worker's decision with a simple numerical example. Suppose a worker lives only two periods and chooses from two schooling options. He can choose not to attend school at all, in which case he would earn \$20,000 in each period. The present value of earnings is

$$PV_0 = 20{,}000 + \frac{20{,}000}{1+r} \qquad \text{(6-7)}$$

He also can choose to attend school in the first period, incur \$5,000 worth of direct schooling costs, and enter the labor market in the second period, earning \$47,500. The present value of this earnings stream is

$$PV_1 = -5{,}000 + \frac{47{,}500}{1+r} \qquad \text{(6-8)}$$

Suppose that the rate of discount is 5 percent. It is easy to calculate that $PV_0 = \$39{,}048$ and that $PV_1 = \$40{,}238$. The worker, therefore, chooses to attend school. Note, however, that if the rate of discount were 15 percent, $PV_0 = \$37{,}391$, $PV_1 = \$36{,}304$, and the worker would not go to school.

As this example shows, the rate of discount r plays a crucial role in determining whether a person goes to school or not. The worker goes to school if the rate of discount is 5 percent but does not if the rate of discount is 15 percent. The higher the rate of discount, therefore, the less likely a worker will invest in education. This conclusion should be easy to understand. A worker who has a high discount rate attaches a very low value to future earnings opportunities—in other words, he discounts the receipt of future income "too much." Because the returns to an investment in education are collected in the far-off future, persons with high discount rates acquire less schooling.

It is sometimes assumed that the person's rate of discount equals the market rate of interest, the rate at which funds deposited in financial institutions grow over time. After all, the discounting of future earnings in the present value calculations arises partly because a dollar received this year can be invested and is worth more than a dollar received next year.

The rate of discount, however, also depends on how we feel about giving up some of today's consumption in return for future rewards—or our "time preference." Casual observation (and a large number of psychological experiments) suggests that people differ in how they approach this trade-off. Some of us are "present oriented" and some of us are not. Persons who are present oriented have a high discount rate and are less likely to invest in schooling. Although there is some evidence suggesting that poorer families have a higher rate of discount than wealthier families, we know little about how a person's time preference is formed.[4]

[4] Emily C. Lawrance, "Poverty and the Rate of Time Preference: Evidence from Panel Data," *Journal of Political Economy* 99 (February 1991): 54–77. A theoretical analysis of the determinants of the rate of time preference is given by Gary S. Becker and Casey B. Mulligan, "The Endogenous Determination of Time Preference," *Quarterly Journal of Economics* 112 (August 1997): 729–758.

The Wage-Schooling Locus

The rule that a person should choose the level of schooling that maximizes the present value of earnings obviously generalizes to situations when there are more than two schooling options. The person would then calculate the present value associated with each schooling option (for example, one year of schooling, two years of schooling, and so on) and choose the amount of schooling that maximizes the present value of the earnings stream.

There is, however, a different way of formulating this problem that provides an intuitive "stopping rule."[5] This stopping rule tells the individual when it is optimal to quit school and enter the labor market. This alternative approach is useful because it also suggests a way for estimating the rate of return to education.

Figure 6-2 illustrates the **wage-schooling locus,** which gives the salary that employers are willing to pay *a particular worker* for every level of schooling. If the worker gets a high school diploma, his annual salary is $20,000; whereas if he gets 18 years of

FIGURE 6-2   **The Wage-Schooling Locus**

The wage-schooling locus gives the salary that a particular worker would earn if he completed a particular level of schooling. If the worker graduates from high school, he earns $20,000 annually. If he goes to college for one year, he earns $23,000.

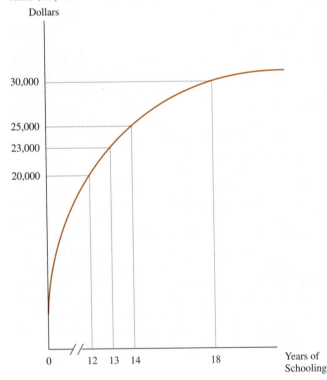

[5] Sherwin Rosen, "Human Capital: A Survey of Empirical Research," *Research in Labor Economics* 1 (1977): 3–39; and David Card, "The Causal Effect of Education on Earnings," in Orley Ashenfelter and David Card, editors, *Handbook of Labor Economics,* vol. 3A, Amsterdam: Elsevier, 1999, pp. 1801–1863.

schooling, his annual salary rises to $30,000. The wage-schooling locus is market determined. In other words, the salary for each level of schooling is determined by the intersection of the supply of workers with that particular schooling and the demand for those workers. From the worker's point of view, the salary associated with each level of schooling is a constant.

The wage-schooling locus shown in Figure 6-2 has three important properties:

1. *The wage-schooling locus is upward sloping.* Workers who have more education must earn more as long as educational decisions are motivated only by financial gains. To attract educated workers, employers must compensate those workers for the costs incurred in acquiring an education.

2. *The slope of the wage-schooling locus tells us by how much a worker's earnings would increase if he were to obtain one more year of schooling.* The slope of the wage-schooling locus, therefore, will be closely related to any empirical measure of "the rate of return" to school.

3. *The wage-schooling locus is concave.* The monetary gains from each additional year of schooling decline as more schooling is acquired. In other words, the law of diminishing returns also applies to human capital accumulation.[6] Each extra year of schooling generates less incremental knowledge and lower additional earnings than previous years.

The Marginal Rate of Return to Schooling

The slope of the wage-schooling locus (or $\Delta w / \Delta s$) tells us by how much earnings increase if the person stays in school one more year. In Figure 6-2, for example, the first year of college increases annual earnings in the postschool period by $3,000. The percentage change in earnings from getting this additional year of schooling is 15 percent (or $^{3,000}/_{20,000} \times 100$). In other words, the worker gets a 15 percent wage increase from staying in school and attending that first year of college. We refer to this *percentage* change in earnings resulting from one more year of school as the marginal **rate of return to schooling.**

The marginal rate of return to schooling gives the percentage increase in earnings per dollar spent in educational investments. To see why, suppose that the only costs incurred in going to college are forgone earnings. The high school graduate who delays his entry into the labor market by one year is then giving up $20,000. This investment outlay increases his future earnings by $3,000 annually, thus yielding an annual 15 percent rate of return for the first year of college.

Because the wage-schooling locus is concave, the marginal rate of return to schooling *must* decline as a person gets more schooling. For example, the marginal rate of return to the second year of college is only 8.7 percent (a $2,000 return on a $23,000 investment). Each additional year of schooling generates a smaller salary increase and it costs more to stay in school. In other words, the wage increase generated by each additional year of college gets smaller at the same time that the cost of staying in school keeps rising. The marginal rate of return schedule, therefore, is a declining function of the level of schooling, as

---

[6] See George Psacharapoulos, "Returns to Education: A Further International Update and Implications," *Journal of Human Resources* 20 (Fall 1985): 583–604, for evidence supporting the hypothesis that educational production functions exhibit diminishing marginal productivity.

FIGURE 6-3   The Schooling Decision

The *MRR* schedule gives the marginal rate of return to schooling, or the percentage increase in earnings resulting from an additional year of school. A worker maximizes the present value of lifetime earnings by going to school until the marginal rate of return to schooling equals the rate of discount. A worker with discount rate *r* goes to school for *s** years.

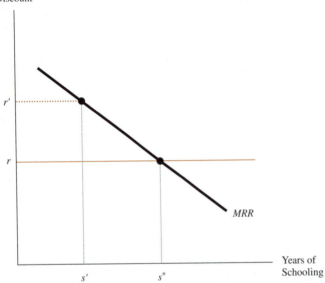

The Stopping Rule, or When Should I Quit School?

Suppose that the worker has a rate of discount *r* that is constant; that is, it is independent of how much schooling he gets. The rate of discount schedule, therefore, is perfectly elastic, as illustrated in Figure 6-3.

Which level of schooling should a person choose? It turns out that the intersection of the *MRR* curve and the horizontal rate of discount schedule determines the optimal level of schooling for the worker, or *s** years in the figure. In other words, the stopping rule that tells the worker when he should quit school is

Stop schooling when the marginal rate of return to schooling = *r*   (6-9)

This stopping rule maximizes the worker's present value of earnings over the life cycle. To see why, suppose that the worker's rate of discount equals the market rate of interest offered by financial institutions. Would it be optimal for the worker to quit school after completing only *s'* years in Figure 6-3? If the worker were to stay in school for an additional year, he would forgo, say, *w'* dollars in earnings, and the rate of return to this investment equals *r'*. His alternative would be to quit school, work, and deposit the *w'* dollars in a bank that offers a rate of return of only *r*. Because education yields a higher rate of return, the worker increases the present value of earnings by continuing in school.

Conversely, suppose that the worker gets more than s^* years of school. Figure 6-3 then shows that the marginal rate of return to this "excess" schooling is less than the market rate of interest, so that the extra years of schooling are not profitable.

Equation (6-9)—the stopping rule for schooling investments—describes a general property of optimal investment decisions. The wealth-maximizing student who must decide if he should quit school faces the same economic trade-off as the owner of a forest who must decide when to cut down a tree. The longer the tree is in the ground, the larger it gets and the more lumber and revenue it will eventually generate. But there are forgone profits (as well as maintenance costs) associated with keeping the tree in the ground. The tree should be cut down when the rate of return on investing in the tree equals the rate of return on alternative investments.

It is important to emphasize that the decision of whether to stay in school is influenced by many factors (such as chance encounters with influential teachers or "significant others"), not just the dollar value of the earnings stream. There is also a great deal of uncertainty in the rewards to particular types of education. The assumption that the student knows the shape of the wage-schooling locus—and the marginal rate of return provided by each level of schooling—is clearly false. Economic and social conditions change in unpredictable ways, and it is very difficult to forecast how these shocks shift the rewards to particular types of skills and careers. This uncertainty will surely play a role in our human capital decisions—just like the uncertainty in financial markets affects the type of financial portfolio that maximizes our wealth.[7]

6-4 Education and Earnings

The schooling model summarized by Figure 6-3 tells us how a particular worker decides how much schooling to acquire, and, as a result, also tells us where a worker places in the income distribution in the postschool period. Workers who get more schooling earn more (although they also give up more). The model isolates two key factors that lead different workers to obtain different levels of schooling and, hence, to have different earnings: Workers either have different rates of discount or face different marginal rate of return schedules.

Differences in the Rate of Discount

Consider a labor market with two workers who differ *only* in their discount rates, as illustrated in Figure 6-4a. Al's discount rate is r_{AL} and Bo's lower discount rate is r_{BO}. The figure shows that Al (who has a higher discount rate) drops out of high school and gets only 11 years of education; Bo gets a high school diploma. As we saw earlier, workers who discount future earnings heavily do not go to school because they are present oriented.

Figure 6-4b shows the implications of these choices for the observed earnings distribution in the postschool period. We have assumed that both workers face the same marginal rate of return schedule. Given our derivation of the marginal rate of return schedule, this assumption is equivalent to saying that both workers face the same wage-schooling locus.

[7] Joseph G. Altonji, "The Demand for and Return to Education When Outcomes Are Uncertain," *Journal of Labor Economics* 11 (January 1993): 48–83.

FIGURE 6-4   Schooling and Earnings When Workers Have Different Rates of Discount

Al has a higher rate of discount (r_{AL}) than Bo (r_{BO}), so that Bo graduates from high school but Al drops out. Al chooses point P_{AL} on the wage-schooling locus and Bo chooses point P_{BO}. The observed data on wages and schooling in the labor market trace out the common wage-schooling locus of the workers.

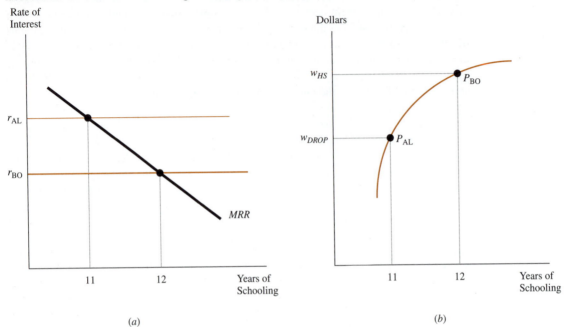

(a)   (b)

The different schooling decisions of the two workers, therefore, simply place them at different points of the common locus. Al ends up at point P_{AL}, where he goes to school 11 years and earns w_{DROP} dollars; Bo ends up at point P_{BO}, goes to school 12 years, and earns w_{HS} dollars. Note that by connecting points P_{AL} and P_{BO} we can trace out the common wage-schooling locus faced by all workers. Moreover, note also that the wage gap between Al and Bo lets us estimate the rate of return to the 12th grade, the percentage change in earnings that a worker would experience in going from the 11th to the 12th grade.

Estimates of the returns to schooling play a crucial role in many discussions of public policy. Consider, for example, the impact of a proposed law requiring all students to complete their high school education. By how much would this proposed policy increase the earnings of workers who are now high school dropouts?

In effect, this policy "injects" Al with one more year of schooling. The wage-schooling locus in Figure 6-4 shows that a high school graduate earns w_{HS} dollars. In other words, Al's earnings would increase to w_{HS} if the law went into effect. A compulsory high school diploma would move the worker along the *observed* wage-schooling locus.

As long as workers differ only in their discount rates, therefore, we can calculate the marginal rate of return to schooling from the wage differential between two workers who differ in their educational attainment. We can then correctly predict by how much earnings would increase if we pursued particular policies that injected targeted workers with more education.[8]

Differences in Ability

It is much more difficult to estimate the rate of return to schooling when all workers have the same rate of discount, but each worker faces a different wage-schooling locus—which, in turn, implies that each worker has a different marginal rate of return schedule. It is often assumed that higher ability levels shift the marginal rate of return schedule to the right, so that the earnings gain resulting from an additional year of schooling outweighs the increase in forgone earnings. In other words, more able persons get relatively more from an extra year of schooling. As illustrated in Figure 6-5a, Bob's *MRR* schedule lies to the right of Ace's. Because both Bob and Ace have the same rate of discount and because Bob gets more from an additional year of schooling, Bob gets more schooling (12 years versus 11 years).

Figure 6-5b illustrates the impact of this ability differential. Bob chooses point P_{BOB} on *his* wage-schooling locus; Bob gets 12 years of schooling and earns w_{HS} dollars. Ace chooses point P_{ACE} on *his* wage-schooling locus; Ace goes to school 11 years and earns w_{DROP} dollars. Note that Bob's wage-schooling locus lies above Ace's because Bob is more able.

The data at our disposal include the education and earnings of the two workers but *do not include* their ability levels. Innate ability, after all, is seldom observed. The observed data, therefore, connect the points P_{ACE} and P_{BOB} in the figure and trace out the line labeled Z. It is important to note that this line does *not* coincide with either Ace's or Bob's wage-schooling locus. As a result, the observed data on earnings and schooling do not allow us to estimate the rate of return to schooling.

Suppose that the government proposes a law requiring all persons to complete high school. To determine the economic impact of the proposed legislation, we wish to know by how much Ace's earnings would increase if he were injected with one more year of schooling. The available data tell us that a high school graduate earns w_{HS} and that a high school dropout earns w_{DROP}. Note, however, that the wage differential between Bob and Ace does *not* give the wage gain that Ace would get under the proposed legislation. Line Z in Figure 6-5b connects points on different wage-schooling curves and provides no information whatsoever about the wage increase that a particular worker would get if he or she were to obtain additional schooling. If the law goes into effect, Ace's earnings would

---

[8] Many studies examine how credit constraints, student aid, and other financial resources affect the education decision. The relaxation of financial constraints can be interpreted as a decrease in the rate of discount; the additional wealth may make students less present oriented or may allow students to borrow money (to finance their education) at a lower interest rate. The evidence often indicates that the relaxation of financial constraints typically leads to more schooling. See Thomas J. Kane, "College Entry by Blacks since 1970: The Role of College Costs, Family Background, and the Returns to Education," *Journal of Political Economy* 102 (October 1994): 878–911; and Susan M. Dynarski, "Does Aid Matter? Measuring the Effect of Student Aid on College Attendance and Completion," *American Economic Review* 93 (March 2003): 279–288. Contrary evidence is given by Stephen V. Cameron and Christopher Taber, "Estimation of Educational Borrowing Constraints Using Returns to Schooling," *Journal of Political Economy* 112 (February 2004): 132–182.

FIGURE 6-5   Schooling and Earnings When Workers Have Different Abilities

Ace and Bob have the same discount rate (r), but each worker faces a different wage-schooling locus. Ace drops out of high school and Bob gets a high school diploma. The wage differential between Bob and Ace (or $w_{HS} - w_{DROP}$) arises both because Bob goes to school for one more year and because Bob is more able. As a result, this wage differential does not tell us by how much Ace's earnings would increase if he were to complete high school (or $w_{ACE} - w_{DROP}$).

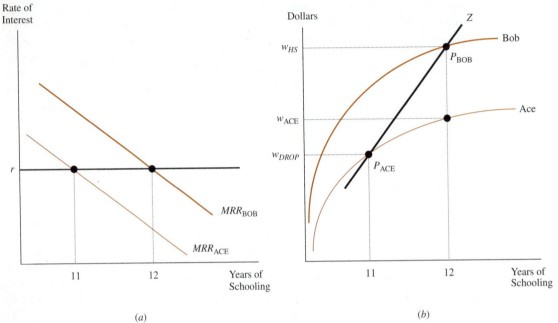

(a)   *(b)*

increase only from w_{DROP} to w_{ACE}, which is much less than what a high school graduate like Bob now earns (w_{HS}).

Put differently, the wage gap between Ace and Bob arises for two reasons. Bob has more schooling than Ace and, hence, is getting the returns to additional schooling. Bob, however, also earns more than Ace because Bob is more able (and his wage locus lies above Ace's). The wage differential between these two workers, therefore, incorporates the impact of both education and ability on earnings.

Ability Bias

The model provides an important lesson: If there are unobserved ability differences in the population, earnings differentials across workers do not estimate the returns to schooling. The correlation between schooling and earnings across workers is contaminated by ability differentials, and hence does not provide an answer to the question that initially motivated our analysis: By how much would the earnings of a particular worker increase if he were to obtain more schooling?

Why should one care about this type of ability bias? Suppose that a well-meaning government bureaucrat observes that high school graduates earn $15,000 more per year than high school dropouts. He uses these data to convince policymakers that funding programs that encourage students to complete high school would increase the average wage of high

Theory at Work
DESTINY AT AGE 6?

Between 1985 and 1989, 79 schools in Tennessee participated in an experiment that has greatly increased our understanding of what works (and what doesn't) in terms of improving children's outcomes in schools. Project STAR (which stands for the Student/Teacher Achievement Ratio) randomly assigned more than 11,000 students and their teachers to different classrooms within their schools in grades K–3. Some students, for instance, were assigned to small classes, while others were assigned to large classes.

The data collected from the STAR participants have become a gold mine for researchers—and not simply because we are now able to examine whether the random assignment to large and small classes improved the child's learning. In addition to these kinds of studies, it has become possible to "track" the children involved in the experiments over time and observe how they have done after they entered the labor market.

At the end of the school year, all of the kindergarten students in STAR were given a grade-appropriate Stanford Achievement Test to measure their performance in math and reading. Remarkably, these test scores are highly correlated with *adult* socioeconomic outcomes.

Suppose we divide the distribution of kindergarten test scores into 20 groups, representing 20 quantiles of the test score distribution. The available data allow us to calculate the mean earnings at ages 25–27 for each of these groups. The accompanying figure illustrates the relationship between mean earnings and the child's placement in the kindergarten score distribution.

There is a strong positive (and almost linear) correlation between these two variables.

Before one concludes that a person's life earnings are predetermined at age 6, it is important to note what this correlation does *not* show. Specifically, within each of the 20 quantiles of the kindergarten test score distribution, there is a huge amount of dispersion in socioeconomic outcomes. Some of the kids who scored poorly in kindergarten will do poorly as young adults in the labor market, but some of those kids will do quite well. The same kind of dispersion also exists for kids who had a high score in the kindergarten test. Even though there is a strong correlation between average earnings and placement in the test score distribution, there is a great deal of dispersion in the data that the "averaging" washes out. In fact, the dispersion in test scores among young children only explains about 5 percent of the earnings dispersion among young adults aged 25–27.

Nevertheless, it is remarkable that the scores from a standardized test given at the end of kindergarten plays even this relatively small role 20 years later. An interesting implication is that perhaps by allocating resources properly in the early grades, a young child's skills can be enhanced, and this improvement might pay substantial rewards decades later.

Source: Raj Chetty, John N. Friedman, Nathaniel Hilger, Emmanuel Saez, Diane Whitmore Schanzenbach, and Danny Yagan, "How Does Your Kindergarten Classroom Affect Your Earnings? Evidence from Project STAR," *Quarterly Journal of Economics*, forthcoming 2011.

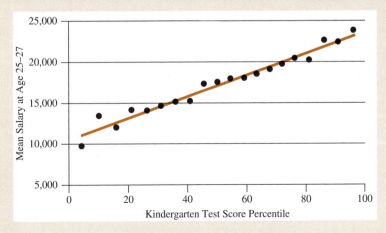

school dropouts by \$15,000. In the bureaucrat's calculations, this earnings gain implies that the program "funds itself" (presumably from higher tax revenues, lower expenditures on social assistance programs, and so forth).

We now know that the bureaucrat's argument is fatally flawed. He is assuming that high school graduates and high school dropouts have the same wage-schooling locus and that one can "fix" the earnings disadvantage of dropouts by injecting them with more schooling. It might be the case, however, that high school graduates have a higher wage-schooling locus. Encouraging high school dropouts to complete their high school education would not lead to a \$15,000 increase in their earnings upon graduation, and it might be much more difficult to argue that the program pays its way.

6-5   Estimating the Rate of Return to Schooling

As suggested by the discussion in the previous section, the typical method for estimating the rate of return to schooling uses data on the earnings and schooling of different workers and estimates the percentage wage differential associated with one more year of schooling—after adjusting the data for differences in other worker characteristics such as age, sex, and race. The "consensus" estimate of the rate of return to schooling in the United States was probably around 9 percent in the 1990s, so that schooling seems to be a good investment.[9]

The typical study estimates a regression of the form

$$\log w = bs + \text{Other variables} \qquad \textbf{(6-10)}$$

where w gives the worker's wage and s gives the number of years of schooling acquired by this worker. The coefficient b gives the percent wage differential between two workers who differ by one year of schooling (holding other variables constant) and is typically interpreted as the rate of return to schooling.

Although most of the empirical studies use this regression model to estimate the rate of return to schooling, one must not forget the central point made in the previous section. The percent wage differential between two workers who differ in their educational attainment estimates the rate of return to schooling only if the workers face the same wage-schooling locus so that there is no ability bias. Workers *do* differ in their abilities, however, and a lot of effort has been devoted to ensuring that the other variables included in the regression control for these ability differences. Some studies, for example, include measures of the

---

[9] Hundreds of studies estimate the rate of return to schooling in this fashion. The classic references include Gary S. Becker and Barry R. Chiswick, "Education and the Distribution of Earnings," *American Economic Review* 56 (May 1966): 358–369; Jacob Mincer, *Schooling, Experience, and Earnings,* New York: Columbia University, 1974; and Giora Hanoch, "An Economic Analysis of Earning and Schooling," *Journal of Human Resources* 2 (Summer 1967): 310–329. The "consensus" estimate of the rate of return to schooling rose between the 1970s and 1990s, from about 7 to 9 percent. Chapter 7 provides a detailed discussion of this rise in the returns to schooling. Recent international estimates of the rate of return to schooling are given by Philip Trostel, Ian Walker, and Paul Woolley, "Estimates of the Economic Return to Schooling for 28 Countries," *Labour Economics* 9 (February 2002): 1–16.

worker's IQ.[10] It is doubtful, however, that these test scores are good measures of a worker's innate productive capacity. After all, there is still an unsettled debate on what IQ measures, even in the context of scholastic achievement.

Using "Natural Experiments" to Compare Workers of the Same Ability

A number of studies have chosen a very clever way out of the fundamental problem raised by unobserved ability differences among workers. Our discussion suggests that the ability bias would disappear if we could compare the earnings of two workers who we know have the same ability but who have different levels of schooling. These two persons would necessarily face the same wage-schooling locus, and the wage gap between the two workers would provide a valid estimate of the rate of return to schooling. The comparison of the earnings of identical twins provides a natural experiment that seems to satisfy these restrictions.

Suppose that we have a sample of identical twins in which each twin reports both earnings and years of schooling. We can calculate the percentage wage differential per year of schooling for each pair of twins and average this number across the twin pairs. The average percentage wage differential is a valid estimate of the rate of return to schooling because ability differences have been completely controlled for.

Although the idea is intuitively appealing, the evidence is mixed. Some early studies reported that the rate of return to schooling in a sample of identical twins is roughly on the order of 3 percent, which is much lower than the rate of return typically estimated in studies that do not adjust for ability bias. These studies conclude that ability differences account for much of the earnings gap between highly educated and less educated workers.[11] More recent studies, however, find that using data on twins raises the rate of return to schooling to about 15 percent, far higher than conventional estimates.[12]

Even if the studies in the literature agreed on the direction of the ability bias, the study of identical twins raises an important question: *Why* do identical twins have different levels of schooling in the first place?

Our theoretical model of the schooling decision isolated two variables that determine how much schooling a person acquires: ability and the rate of discount. Since identical twins that differ in their schooling do not presumably differ in their innate ability, it must be the case that they had different discount rates. The identical twins, in other words, differ in important and unobserved ways. In short, the identical twins do not seem to be completely

---

[10] Excellent reviews of the econometric issues involved are given by Zvi Griliches, "Estimating the Returns to Schooling: Some Econometric Problems," *Econometrica* 45 (January 1977): 1–22; and Card, "The Causal Effect of Education on Earnings."

[11] Paul Taubman, "Earnings, Education, Genetics, and Environment," *Journal of Human Resources* 11 (Fall 1976): 447–461.

[12] Orley C. Ashenfelter and Alan B. Krueger, "Estimates of the Economic Return to Schooling from a New Sample of Twins," *American Economic Review* 84 (December 1994): 1157–1173; and Orley Ashenfelter and Cecilia Rouse, "Income, Schooling, and Ability: Evidence from a New Sample of Identical Twins," *Quarterly Journal of Economics* 113 (February 1998): 253–284.

identical. Unless we can understand how and why identical twins differ, therefore, it is not clear that we should interpret the earnings differential between identical twins as a measure of the "true" rate of return to schooling.

Examples of Instrumental Variables

Many government policies generate instruments that allow the comparison of earnings among equally able workers. One particularly famous example is the existence of compulsory schooling legislation. Some states, for instance, enact compulsory schooling laws that force workers to remain in school until they reach some predetermined age, such as 16 or 17.

In the United States, children typically are not allowed to enter the first grade unless they are six years old by January 1 of the academic year in which they enter school. That means that persons born early in the year "miss" the deadline and are older when they start school than persons who are born later in the year. A compulsory schooling age of 16 then implies that children born in the early months of the year attain the legal dropout age after having attended school for a shorter time than children born near the end of the year. This variation serves as an instrument that "nudges" some persons along a particular wage-schooling locus and that can be used to estimate the rate of return to schooling.[13]

To easily understand the nature of the empirical exercise, suppose there is a compulsory schooling age of 16 and compare two children: one born on December 31 and the other born a couple of days later, on January 2. The child born on December 31 qualifies to enter the first grade at an earlier chronological age than the child born in early January. In fact, in the 1960 census, children who are born in the first quarter of the year enter the first grade when they are 6.5 years old, as compared to an age of entry of 6.1 years for children born in the last quarter of the year. As a result, even though both children will turn 16 years old at almost the same time, the child born in December will have attended school for a longer period. The relationship between compulsory schooling and month of birth would be a valid instrument—that is, it would nudge persons along the same wage-schooling locus—if the ability of children born on December 31 is the same, on average, as that of children born on January 2.

Put differently, the biological "accident" of a birth just before January 1 means that the child will be required to be in school for a longer period than a comparable child born just after January 1. The wage gap between the two children, therefore, measures the true rate of return to schooling because there should be no ability differences between them. The only reason that earnings could differ is because those born in late December have slightly more schooling, on average, than those born in early January. If one controls for ability bias in this fashion, the estimated rate of return to schooling is on the order of 7.5 percent.

Another excellent (and very clever) example of how government policies create instrumental variables that allow us to estimate the rate of return to schooling arises from the

---

[13] Joshua Angrist and Alan B. Krueger, "Does Compulsory Schooling Affect Schooling and Earnings?" *Quarterly Journal of Economics* 106 (November 1991): 979–1014. A critical appraisal of this study is given by John Bound, David A. Jaeger, and Regina Baker, "Problems with Instrumental Variables Estimation When the Correlation between the Instruments and the Endogenous Explanatory Variable Is Weak," *Journal of the American Statistical Association* 90 (June 1995): 443–450. For an application of the basic framework to German and British data, see Jörn-Steffen Pischke and Till von Wachter, "Zero Returns to Compulsory Schooling in Germany: Evidence and Interpretation," *Review of Economics and Statistics,* forthcoming, 2008; and Philip Oreopoulos, "Estimating Average and Local Average Treatment Effects of Education When Compulsory Schooling Laws Really Matter," *American Economic Review* 96 (March 2006): 152–175.

1968 student riots that brought French society to a standstill and led to the dissolution of the French Parliament.[14] In May 1968, after months of simmering conflict between students and university administrators, the administrators decided to close the University of Nanterre in Paris on May 2. The resulting protests expanded to other university towns in France and eventually brought the workers out into the streets. Roughly 10 million workers (or two-thirds of the French workforce) joined the general strike in support of the students.

Because these events took place at the end of the school year, an important component of the negotiations between the students and the authorities involved questions on how to deal with the delay in the university exams that determine the academic future of French students. One particularly important exam is the *baccalauréat*, an exam that effectively signals the successful completion of a secondary education and opens the doors for higher education. Typically, the *baccalauréat* involves several days of written and oral exams. In 1968, however, French authorities acquiesced to a revised *baccalauréat* that only involved oral exams and took place in one day.

As a result of the less stringent requirements, a relatively large number of the affected age cohort obtained their *baccalauréat*. In particular, the number of persons obtaining this credential in 1968 was about 30 percent larger than in adjacent years. The higher pass rate, therefore, allowed a much large fraction of French students *in that age cohort* to continue their education. The 1968 riots, in effect, created a valid instrument. It is unlikely that the average ability of the 1968 cohort differs from that of adjacent cohorts. Nevertheless, that cohort was "nudged" along on the wage-schooling locus and they were able to get more schooling and presumably earn more.

There was indeed a sizable increase in the number of persons in the 1968 cohort who obtained a higher education credential: roughly about 20 percent of the cohort obtained higher degrees as compared to about 17 percent of the adjacent cohorts. In addition, the earnings of the cohorts affected by the 1968 riots were around 3 percent more than they would have earned otherwise. The implied rate of return to schooling is around 14 percent.[15]

6-6   Policy Application: School Construction in Indonesia

Many studies document that the wage gap between high-educated and low-educated workers in developing countries is even higher than the gap in industrialized economies.[16] It is tempting to infer from these findings that developing labor markets offer a high rate of return to schooling, and that these high rates of return justify sizable investments in the

---

[14] Eric Maurin and Sandra McNally, "Vive la Revolution! Long-Term Educational Returns of 1968 to the Angry Students," *Journal of Labor Economics* 26 (January 2008): 1–33.

[15] Another example of an instrument that has been used to estimate the rate of return to schooling is the GI bill that subsidized education expenditures for World War II veterans. See Marcus Stanley, "College Education and the Midcentury GI Bills," *Quarterly Journal of Economics* 118 (May 2003): 671–708; and John Bound and Sarah Turner, "Going to War and Going to College: Did World War II and the G.I. Bill Increase Educational Attainment for Returning Veterans?" *Journal of Labor Economics* 2002 (October 2002): 784–815.

[16] John Strauss and Duncan Thomas, "Human Resources: Empirical Modeling of Household and Family Decisions," in Jere Behrman and T. N. Srinivasan, editors, *Handbook of Development Economics,* Amsterdam: Elsevier, 1995, pp. 1885–2023.

education infrastructure. As we have seen, however, these wage gaps need not suggest that increasing schooling opportunities for a wide segment of the population would substantially improve the earnings of those workers.

In Indonesia, children typically go to school between the ages of 7 and 12. In 1973, the Indonesian government launched a major school construction program (INPRES) designed to increase the enrollment of children in disadvantaged areas.[17] By 1978–79, more than 61,000 new primary schools had been built, approximately two schools per 1,000 children. The typical school was designed for three teachers and 120 students. This construction program cost almost $700 million (2002 U.S. dollars), representing 1.5 percent of the Indonesian GDP as of 1973. As a way of grasping the scale of the construction, a similar commitment by the United States (in terms of GDP share) would require an expenditure of around $150 billion.

It has been reported that INPRES was the fastest primary school construction program in world history. The results were immediate: enrollment rates among children aged 7 to 12 rose from 69 percent in 1973 to 83 percent by 1978.

A recent study uses data drawn from the Indonesian labor market in 1995 (two decades after the school construction) to determine if the huge investment increased the educational attainment and earnings of the targeted Indonesians, and also to calculate the rate of return to schooling in Indonesia. As noted above, the program attempted to equalize education opportunities across the various regions of Indonesia, building more schools in those parts of Indonesia that had relatively low enrollment rates. Table 6-3 illustrates how education and earnings were affected for persons residing in two different parts of Indonesia—the "high-construction" area, where many new schools were built, and the "low-construction" area, where relatively few schools were built. In rough terms, about one more school per 1,000 children was built in the high-construction area than in the low-construction area.

The table examines the outcomes experienced by two different demographic groups: persons who were 2–6 years old and 12–17 years old as of 1974. The younger of these groups was clearly affected by the construction program. These boys and girls were about to enter school as the construction program began, and they form the treatment group. The older persons—the control group—were past the school-going age, and their educational attainment should not be affected by the presence of more schools.

TABLE 6-3   **The Impact of School Construction on Education and Wages in Indonesia**

Source: Duflo, "Schooling and Labor Market Consequences of School Construction in Indonesia."

	Years of Education			Log Wages		
	Persons Aged 12–17 in 1974	Persons Aged 2–6 in 1974	Difference	Persons Aged 12–17 in 1974	Persons Aged 2–6 in 1974	Difference
Low-construction area	9.40	9.76	0.36	7.02	6.73	−0.29
High-construction area	8.02	8.49	0.47	6.87	6.61	−0.26
Difference-in-differences	—	—	**0.11**	—	—	**0.03**

[17] The discussion in this section is based on the findings reported in Esther Duflo, "Schooling and Labor Market Consequences of School Construction in Indonesia," *American Economic Review* 91 (September 2001): 795–813.

Table 6-3 uses the difference-in-differences methodology to calculate the impact of the construction on the educational attainment of the targeted population. In the low-construction area, the educational attainment increased by 0.36 year between the older and younger cohorts, while in the high-construction area, the educational attainment rose by 0.47 year. The difference-in-differences approach thus suggests that the additional construction increased educational attainment by 0.11 year. By using a similar approach, the table also shows that the earnings of the younger cohort living in the high-construction area rose by an additional 3 percent.

We can now use the method of instrumental variables to calculate the rate of return to schooling in Indonesia. The instrument is school construction. This variable clearly "nudged" some students along the wage-schooling locus. The instrument is valid if students in the high-construction areas have the same ability as those in the low-construction areas and if the older cohort of students has the same innate ability as the younger cohort. Each additional 0.11 year of schooling increased earnings by 3 percent. This implies that each additional year of school increased earnings by 27 percent (or 0.03 ÷ 0.11). The rate of return to schooling in Indonesia, therefore, seems to be quite high, justifying the sizable expenditure made by the school construction program. In fact, a more thorough analysis of the data, which controls for many of the other factors that also affected trends in educational attainment and wages in Indonesia, suggests that the rate of return to schooling may be as high as 10 percent.

6-7 Policy Application: School Quality and Earnings

Conventional wisdom has it that today's high school graduates are not as good as yesterday's graduates. The media often report that a large fraction of high school graduates are "functionally" illiterate despite the fact that expenditures on primary and secondary education rose dramatically in the past two decades (per-student real expenditures in public schools increased from \$4,600 in 1980 to \$9,500 in 2008).[18] Does "throwing money" at the public school system raise the rate of return to schooling? Put differently, does school quality, as measured by teacher salaries or pupil/teacher ratios, matter?

Prior to 1992, the consensus was that high levels of school expenditures had little impact on educational or labor market outcomes. As an influential survey concluded, "There appears to be no strong or systematic relationship between school expenditures and student performance."[19] The 1992 publication of an influential study by David Card and Alan Krueger, showing that school quality is indeed positively correlated with the rate of return to schooling, sparked a heated debate over the economic importance of school quality.[20]

---

[18] U.S. Bureau of the Census, *Statistical Abstract of the United States, 2008,* Washington, DC: Government Printing Office, 2008, Table 209. A detailed survey of the trends in expenditures and "quality" of the public schools is given by Eric A. Hanushek, "The Economics of Schooling: Production and Efficiency in the Public Schools," *Journal of Economic Literature* 24 (September 1986): 1141–1177.

[19] Hanushek, "The Economics of Schooling: Production and Efficiency in Public Schools."

[20] David Card and Alan B. Krueger, "Does School Quality Matter? Returns to Education and the Characteristics of Public Schools in the United States," *Journal of Political Economy* 100 (February 1992): 1–40; see also David Card and Alan B. Krueger, "School Resources and Student Outcomes: An Overview of the Literature and New Evidence from North and South Carolina," *Journal of Economic Perspectives* 10 (Fall 1996): 31–50.

FIGURE 6-6
**School Quality
and the Rate
of Return to
Schooling**

Source: David Card
and Alan B. Krueger,
"Does School Qual-
ity Matter? Returns
to Education and the
Characteristics of
Public Schools in the
United States," *Journal
of Political Economy*
100 (February 1992),
Tables 1 and 2. The
data in the graphs refer
to the rate of return to
school and the school
quality variables for
the cohort of persons
born in 1920–1929.

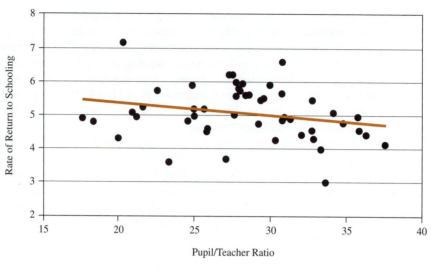

(*a*) Impact of Pupil-Teacher Ratio

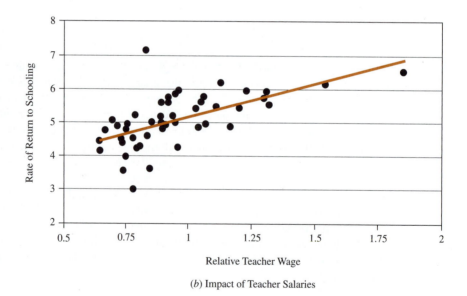

(*b*) Impact of Teacher Salaries

Card and Krueger used data on worker earnings from the 1980 census to calculate the
rates of return to schooling to cohorts of workers born in a particular state; for example,
workers born in Kansas between 1920 and 1929. The two panels of Figure 6-6 summarize the core of the Card-Krueger evidence. There is obviously a great deal of variation
in the rate of return to schooling for workers in this age cohort, depending on where they
were born. The range in the rate of return is from 3 percent (for workers born in Louisiana)
to slightly more than 7 percent (for those born in Wyoming). Figure 6-6*a* shows that the

rate of return to schooling is negatively correlated with the state's pupil/teacher ratio, while Figure 6-6*b* shows that the rate of return to schooling is positively correlated with the state's average teacher salary (relative to the average wage in the state). After analyzing these data as well as the rates of return to schooling of other birth cohorts, Card and Krueger concluded that children born in states that offered better schools had a substantially higher rate of return to schooling. Decreasing the pupil/teacher ratio by 10 students increased the rate of return by about 1 percentage point, whereas increasing the relative wage of teachers by 30 percent (which presumably attracts better teachers) increased the rate of return to schooling by 0.3 percentage point.

The striking findings in this article motivated a great deal of research in the past decade that attempts to determine the robustness of the correlations. Although many of the subsequent studies report evidence that contradict the Card-Krueger findings, it is difficult to understand why the evidence is so mixed.[21] After all, why do elementary schools incur the extra cost of breaking up 100 third-grade students into four sections with four teachers if the students would be just as well off herded together in one big section? Moreover, there is evidence documenting a strong positive relation between property values and school quality.[22] Why would parents pay more for housing in school districts that offer smaller classes and better teachers if these inputs do not matter?

To resolve some of the confusion, a number of recent studies have analyzed experimental data, observing the outcomes of students who are randomly assigned to classes of different sizes. As noted earlier, beginning in 1985, the Tennessee Student/Teacher Achievement Ratio (STAR) experiment randomly assigned kindergarten students *and* their teachers to small classes (with a pupil/teacher ratio of 13–17) or to larger classes (with a ratio of 22–25 students). After the initial assignment, students remained in the same class type for four years. Between 6,000 and 7,000 students were involved in this experiment each year. A careful evaluation of the data resulting from the STAR experiment indicates that students assigned to the small classes scored higher in achievement tests than students assigned to the larger classes.[23]

Other studies use the method of instrumental variables to estimate the impact of class size on scholastic achievement in nonexperimental settings. The problem, of course, is finding a variable that affects class size but does not affect other outcomes directly. One study used an instrument based on the interpretation of the Talmud by the twelfth-century

---

[21] See, for example, Julian R. Betts, "Does School Quality Matter? Evidence from the National Longitudinal Survey," *Review of Economics and Statistics* 77 (May 1995): 231–250; James J. Heckman, Anne S. Layne-Farrar, and Petra E. Todd, "Does Measured School Quality Really Matter," in Gary Burtless, editor, *Does Money Matter? The Effect of School Resources on Student Achievement and Adult Success,* Washington, DC: The Brookings Institution, 1996; Jeffrey Grogger, "Does School Quality Explain the Recent Black/White Wage Trend?" *Journal of Labor Economics* 14 (April 1996): 231–253; Carolyn M. Hoxby, "The Effects of Class Size on Student Achievement: New Evidence from Population Variation," *Quarterly Journal of Economics* 115 (November 2000): 1239–1285; and Eric A. Hanushek, "Some Simple Analytics of School Quality," National Bureau of Economic Research Working Paper No. 10229, January 2004.

[22] Sandra E. Black, "Do Better Schools Matter? Parental Valuation of Elementary Education," *Quarterly Journal of Economics* 114 (May 1999): 577–599.

[23] Alan B. Krueger, "Experimental Estimates of Education Production Functions," *Quarterly Journal of Economics* 114 (May 1999): 497–532.

The process through which attending school—listening to lectures, doing homework, and interacting with teachers and peers—translates into a larger human capital stock remains mysterious. A multitude of factors are likely to influence how the human capital accumulation occurs.

The recent deployment of a large number of American troops to Afghanistan and Iraq creates an interesting "natural experiment" through which to measure the importance of parental inputs in the educational production function. Between 2002 and 2004, nearly 1 million U.S. troops were deployed to these two countries, with more than a third of the soldiers serving two overseas tours within a span of three years.

It seems sensible to argue that the anxiety and uncertainty associated with these relocations likely affect a child's achievement in school. For instance, a mother recently remarked about her son: "it affected his grades last year when he knew his father was in Afghanistan—he worries more about daddy dying than just going away and coming back."

A recent study examined the academic achievement of Texas children with parents serving in the active duty army. To a large extent, the military's assignment of particular parents to a hostile zone was random. In other words, the two groups of children—those with parents who were deployed to a hostile zone and those with parents who were not deployed—have the same average ability. The deployment can then be viewed as an instrument that shifts the opportunity set available to the children.

The study found that deployment to a hostile zone indeed had an adverse impact on the academic achievement of these children. The typical child whose enlisted parent was deployed in a hostile zone for less than two months during the current school year scored 77.2 on the Texas Learning Index (TLI) math test, while the typical child whose parents had been deployed at least three months scored 75.9. There was a similar test gap in the children of officers—with the children of those officers who had been deployed in a hostile zone for longer periods scoring less well on the math test.

These results, of course, have implications well beyond the military. A stable family environment seems to be an important input in the educational production function.

Source: David S. Lyle, "Military Deployments and Job Assignments to Estimate the Effect of Parental Absences and Household Relocations on Children's Academic Achievement," *Journal of labor Economics* 24 (April 2006): 319–350.

rabbinic scholar Maimonides.[24] According to Maimonides's rule, "Twenty-five children may be put in charge of one teacher. If the number in the class exceed twenty-five but is not more than forty, he should have an assistant to help with the instruction. If there are more than forty, two teachers must be appointed."

The Israeli public school system uses Maimonides's rule to distribute students among various classes. The maximum class size is 40. According to Maimonides's rule, class size increases with enrollment until 40 pupils are enrolled. An extra student, however, implies that class size drops sharply to 20.5. Because there is little reason to suspect that the shift from a class size of 40 to one of 20.5 has anything to do with the underlying ability of the students, Maimonides's rule provides a valid instrument—it shifts class size without affecting any other variables. The analysis of the outcomes experienced by Israeli students consistently suggests a negative relation between class size and academic achievement.

[24] Joshua D. Angrist and Victor Lavy, "Using Maimonides' Rule to Estimate the Effect of Class Size on Scholastic Achievement," *Quarterly Journal of Economics* 114 (May 1999): 533–575.

There also have been detailed studies of how children perform in specific school systems, such as the Chicago public high schools.[25] A recent study, for example, analyzes data that identify specific teachers in that system. Not surprisingly, there seems to be a subset of "high-quality" teachers that consistently improve the test scores of those students lucky enough to be assigned to their classes. The improvement seems to be particularly large for lower-ability students.

Finally, a number of studies have investigated if attending an "elite" college or university, which presumably offers a higher quality of education, affects earnings. The problem with comparing the earnings of students who attend selective institutions with the earnings of students who do not is that there may be underlying ability differences between the two groups that will affect earnings. Any resulting wage gap may have little to do with the "value added" by the selective institution, and may simply reflect the preexisting ability gap between the two groups of students.

To avoid the problem of ability bias, a recent study compares the earnings of students who attend highly selective schools, as measured by the average SAT score of freshmen, with the earnings of students who were accepted by those institutions but decided to go to a less-selective college.[26] These two groups presumably have the same underlying ability— they were all accepted by the same selective institutions. Interestingly, this comparison reveals that selective schools provide no value-added: Students who graduate from selective schools earn no more than students who were accepted by those schools but decided to go elsewhere. In short, there seems to be little return to attending a selective college.

6-8   Do Workers Maximize Lifetime Earnings?

The schooling model provides the conceptual framework that allows us to estimate the rate of return to schooling. We have seen that—under certain conditions—percent wage differentials among workers who differ in their education can be interpreted as a rate of return to schooling. This calculation of the rate of return to schooling, however, does *not* test the theory. Rather, the calculations use the theory to interpret the earnings differences among workers in a particular way.

Therefore, we want to determine if the schooling model provides a useful "story" of how students actually go about the business of deciding whether to stay in school. The schooling model assumes that persons choose the level of schooling that maximizes the present value of lifetime earnings. If we could observe the age-earnings profile of a particular worker both if he were to go to college and if he were to stop after high school, it would be easy to test the key hypothesis of the schooling model. We could use these annual earnings

[25] Daniel Aaronson, Lisa Barrow, and William Sander, "Teachers and Student Achievement in the Chicago Public High Schools," *Journal of Labor Economics* 25 (January 2007): 95–135.

[26] Stacy Berg Dale and Alan B. Krueger, "Estimating the Payoff to Attending a More Selective College: An Application of Selection on Observables and Unobservables," *Quarterly Journal of Economics* 117 (November 2002): 1491–528. Conflicting evidence is provided by Dominic J. Brewer, Eric R. Eide, and Ronald G. Ehrenberg, "Does It Pay to Attend an Elite Private College? Cross-Cohort Evidence on the Effects of College Type on Earnings," *Journal of Human Resources* 34 (Winter 1999): 104–123. See also Dan A. Black and Jeffrey A. Smith, "Estimating the Returns to College Quality with Multiple Proxies for Quality," *Journal of Labor Economics* 24 (July 2006): 701–728.

to calculate the present value of each option, compare the two numbers, and check to see if the worker chose the one with the largest present value.

This simple test, however, can *never* be conducted. The reason is both trivial (because it is painfully obvious) and profound (because it raises a number of conceptual questions that have yet to be adequately resolved). *Once a worker makes a particular choice, we can only observe the earnings stream associated with that choice.* Consider the group of workers who go to college. For these college graduates, we can observe only their life cycle earnings after college graduation, and we will never observe what they would have earned had they not attended college. Similarly, consider the group of workers who quit after completing high school. For these high school graduates, we observe the earnings stream subsequent to their high school graduation, and we will never observe what they would have earned had they gone on to college.

It is tempting to work out a simple solution to this problem. Even though we will never observe how much a worker who quits after completing high school would have earned if he had attended college, we do observe the earnings of those workers who did attend college. We could then predict the high school graduate's earnings had he attended college by using the observed data on what college graduates actually make. Similarly, even though we do not observe how much college graduates would have earned had they stopped after high school, we do observe the earnings of high school graduates. We could then predict the college graduate's earnings (had he not attended college) from the salary data for high school graduates.

Our earlier discussion suggests that this exercise is valid only if college graduates and high school graduates lie on the same wage-schooling locus. This calculation is invalid if there are ability differences. The observed wage differential between college graduates and high school graduates reflects not only the returns to college, but also the returns to differences in ability between the two groups. Therefore, using the observed wage differential to determine if workers choose the "right" schooling option yields meaningless results.

A Numerical Example

To illustrate the importance of this problem, let's work through a simple numerical example with two workers, Willie and Wendy. Willie is particularly adept at "blue-collar" work, and this type of work requires no schooling. Wendy is particularly adept at "white-collar" work, and this type of work requires one year of schooling. Suppose also that there are two periods in the life cycle. If a person does not go to school, he works in the blue-collar job in both periods. If the person goes to school, the person would go to school in the first period and work in the white-collar job in the second period.

The wage-schooling locus for each worker is summarized by these data:

Worker	Earnings in Blue-Collar Job	Earnings in White-Collar Job
Willie	$20,000	$40,000
Wendy	$15,000	$41,000

Because Willie is better at doing blue-collar work, he earns more at the blue-collar job ($20,000) than Wendy would ($15,000). Similarly, because Wendy is better at white-collar work, she earns more in the white-collar job than Willie would.

Suppose that both Willie and Wendy have a discount rate of 10 percent. Each worker calculates the present value of lifetime earnings for each schooling option and chooses the one that has the highest present value. The present values of Willie's alternative earnings streams are

$$\text{Willie's present value if he does not go to school} = 20{,}000 + \frac{20{,}000}{1.1} = \$38{,}182 \quad \textbf{(6-11)}$$

$$\text{Willie's present value if he goes to school} = 0 + \frac{40{,}000}{1.1} = \$36{,}364 \quad \textbf{(6-12)}$$

Willie will decide that he should not go to school and will be a blue-collar worker.

The present values of Wendy's potential earnings streams are

$$\text{Wendy's present value if she does not go to school} = 15{,}000 + \frac{15{,}000}{1.1} = \$28{,}636 \quad \textbf{(6-13)}$$

$$\text{Wendy's present value if she goes to school} = 0 + \frac{41{,}000}{1.1} = \$37{,}273 \quad \textbf{(6-14)}$$

Wendy, therefore, goes to school in the first period and works in a white-collar job in the second.

What data do we observe in the labor market? We observe the earnings of persons who do not go to school and work in blue-collar jobs (like Willie). The present value of their earnings is $38,182. We also observe the earnings of persons who do go to school and work in white-collar jobs (like Wendy). The present value of their earnings stream is $37,273.

A comparison of the two numbers that can be observed would suggest that Wendy made a terrible mistake. In our numerical example, persons who go to school earn less over their lifetime than persons who do not go to school. Because workers sort themselves into particular occupations, however, this is an irrelevant comparison. Both Willie and Wendy made the right choice. The problem lies in comparing the earnings of the two types of workers. This comparison is akin to comparing apples and oranges and is contaminated by **selection bias,** the fact that workers self-select themselves into jobs for which they are best suited. In our numerical example, the selection bias leads to an incorrect rejection of the validity of the human capital model.

Selection Bias Corrections

In view of the significance of the issues associated with selection bias, it is not surprising that a great deal of study has been devoted to this problem. This research has developed statistical techniques, known as "selection bias corrections," that allow us to test correctly the hypothesis underlying the schooling model.[27] These techniques give a statistically valid methodology for predicting what a high school graduate would have earned had he attended college and what a college graduate would have earned had he quit school after getting a high school diploma.

[27] James J. Heckman, "Sample Selection Bias as a Specification Error," *Econometrica* 47 (January 1979): 153–162. See also James J. Heckman, "Varieties of Selection Bias," *American Economic Review* 80 (May 1990): 313–318; and Charles F. Manski, "Anatomy of the Selection Problem," *Journal of Human Resources* 24 (Summer 1989): 343–360.

A well-known study uses these selection bias corrections to estimate the life cycle earnings profiles associated with each of two alternatives (going to college or quitting after high school) for a large number of workers.[28] The empirical analysis confirms the basic hypothesis of the theory: On average, workers choose the schooling option that maximizes the present value of lifetime earnings. Moreover, the evidence indicates that when both a high school graduate and a college graduate are placed in the type of job that high school graduates typically fill, the high school graduate would be more productive. Conversely, if both high school graduates and college graduates were placed in jobs typically filled by college graduates, the college graduate would be more productive.

As implied by our numerical example, this empirical result suggests that the notion that there is only one type of ability that inevitably leads to higher earnings does not correctly describe how workers differ in the labor market. There exist various types of abilities, and each of us may be particularly adept at doing some things and quite inept at doing others. Some persons have a knack for doing work that is best learned in college, whereas other persons have a knack for doing blue-collar work. Put differently, some workers have a *comparative advantage* at doing skilled work; other workers have a comparative advantage at doing less-skilled work.

6-9   Schooling as a Signal

The schooling model is based on the idea that education increases a worker's productivity and that this increase in productivity raises wages. An alternative argument is that education need not increase the worker's productivity at all, but that "sheepskin" levels of educational attainment (such as a high school or college diploma) signal a worker's qualifications to potential employers.[29] In this view, education increases earnings not because it increases productivity, but because it certifies that the worker is cut out for "smart" work. Education can play this signaling role only when it is difficult for potential employers to observe the worker's ability directly. If the employer could determine cheaply whether the worker is qualified for the job, the firm would not have to rely on third-party certifications.

To illustrate how workers decide how much schooling to get when education plays only a signaling role, let's work through a simple numerical example. Suppose there are two types of workers in the labor market, low-productivity workers and high-productivity workers, and that the distribution of productivity in the population is given by

[28] Robert J. Willis and Sherwin Rosen, "Education and Self-Selection," *Journal of Political Economy* 87 (October 1979 Supplement): S7–S36. See also Lawrence W. Kenny, Lung-Fei Lee, G. S. Maddala, and R. P. Trost, "Returns to College Education: An Investigation of Self-Selection Bias Based on the Project Talent Data," *International Economic Review* 20 (October 1979): 775–789; and John Garen, "The Returns to Schooling: A Selectivity-Bias Approach with a Continuous Choice Variable," *Econometrica* 52 (September 1984): 1199–1218.

[29] A. Michael Spence, "Job Market Signaling," *Quarterly Journal of Economics* 87 (August 1973): 355–374. See also Kenneth J. Arrow, "Higher Education as a Filter," *Journal of Public Economics* 2 (July 1973): 193–216; and Joseph Stiglitz, "The Theory of Screening, Education, and the Distribution of Income," *American Economic Review* 65 (June 1975): 283–300. For evidence on sheepskin effects, see David A. Jaeger and Marianne E. Page, "Degrees Matter: New Evidence on Sheepskin Effects in the Returns to Education," *Review of Economics and Statistics* 78 (November 1996): 733–740.

Type of Worker	Proportion of Population	Present Value of Lifetime Productivity
Low-productivity	q	$200,000
High-productivity	$1 - q$	300,000

The productivity differences between the two types of workers exist since birth and have *nothing* to do with how much schooling a particular worker gets.

If an employer could determine easily if a job applicant is a high-productivity worker, he would pay the worker $300,000 over the life cycle. After all, if the employer's wage offer did not match the high-productivity applicant's true value, the job applicant would simply go elsewhere, where his high productivity was better appreciated. Similarly, if the employer could determine easily that the applicant is a low-productivity worker, he would pay the worker only $200,000.

But life is not quite this easy. Even though a particular worker knows which group he belongs to, it might take some years for the employer to learn that. Therefore, there is **asymmetric information** in the labor market, where one of the parties in the transaction knows more about the terms of the contract. Moreover, if an employer asks the job applicant if he is a low- or high-productivity worker, the applicant (who wants a high salary) will always reply that he is a high-productivity worker regardless of his true ability. When a job applicant shows up at the firm, therefore, there is a great deal of uncertainty about whether he is a low-productivity or a high-productivity worker.

Pooling Workers

Because low-productivity workers will always lie about their productivity, the firm will disregard what anyone says about their own qualifications. In the absence of any other information, therefore, the employer simply pools all job applicants and treats them identically. The average productivity and salary of the workers hired by the firm is then given by

$$\text{Average salary} = (200,000 \times q) + [300,000 \times (1 - q)]$$

$$= 300,000 - 100,000q \qquad \textbf{(6-15)}$$

The average salary is simply a weighted average of the workers' productivities, where the weights are the proportions in the population that belong to each productivity group.

Because the proportion q is between 0 and 1, the average salary in this "pooled equilibrium" is between $200,000 and $300,000. Low-productivity workers prefer a pooled equilibrium because they are being pooled with more productive workers, who push up their salary. Neither employers nor high-productivity workers like the pooled equilibrium. Employers find that they are mismatching workers and jobs. Some high-productivity workers are being assigned to menial jobs, and low-productivity workers are placed in jobs that they are not qualified to perform. This mismatching reduces the firm's efficiency and output. Similarly, the earnings of high-productivity workers are dragged down by the low-productivity workers, and, hence, the high-productivity workers would like to find a way of demonstrating to the employer that they truly are more productive.

A Signal Helps Distinguish the Workers

High-productivity workers have an incentive to provide *and* firms have an incentive to take into account credible information that can be used to allocate the worker into either productivity group. This type of information is called a **signal.** It turns out that an educational diploma or certificate can perform this signaling job and that it can perform the task with absolute precision. *No mismatches occur.*

Suppose a firm chooses the following rule of thumb for allocating workers to the two types of jobs. If a worker has at least $\bar{y}$ years of college, the firm assumes that the worker is a high-productivity worker, allocates him to a job that requires a high level of skills, and pays him a (lifetime) salary of $300,000. If a worker has fewer than $\bar{y}$ years of college, the firm assumes that the worker is a low-productivity worker, allocates him to an unskilled job, and pays him a salary of $200,000.

Because employers are willing to pay more to workers who get at least $\bar{y}$ years of college, all workers will want to get the required college credits. Obtaining these credits, however, is expensive. We assume that obtaining credits is more expensive for less-able workers; in particular, a year's worth of college credits costs $20,000 for a high-productivity worker, but $25,001 for a low-productivity worker. Obviously, tuition and fees do not differ according to ability, but the *real* cost of a college credit is higher for a low-productivity worker. To attain a particular level of achievement, a low-productivity worker will have to devote more time to studying and may have to pay for tutors, study guides, and special classes. This assumption that low-productivity workers find it more costly to obtain the signal is the fundamental assumption of the signaling model—and, in fact, is what makes the model work.

Given the firm's wage offer, workers must now decide how many years of college to get. A "separating equilibrium" occurs when low-productivity workers choose not to get $\bar{y}$ years of schooling and voluntarily signal their low productivity, and high-productivity workers choose to get at least $\bar{y}$ years of schooling and separate themselves from the pack.

Figure 6-7a illustrates the firm's wage offer and the cost function facing a low-productivity worker. The wage offer is such that if the worker has fewer than $\bar{y}$ years of college, he earns $200,000, and if he has $\bar{y}$ or more years, he earns $300,000. The cost function is upward sloping and has a slope of $25,001 because each additional year of college costs $25,001 for a low-productivity worker.

In our numerical example, a worker will decide either not to go to college at all or to go to college for $\bar{y}$ years. After all, a worker's earnings do not increase if he goes to college for more than $\bar{y}$ years, yet it costs the worker $25,001 to get an additional year's worth of college credits. Similarly, because the worker's lifetime salary equals $200,000 for *any* level of education between 0 and $\bar{y}$ years of college, there is no point to getting "just a few" credits.

A separating equilibrium requires that low-productivity workers do not go to college at all. This will occur whenever the net return from getting zero years of college exceeds the net return from getting $\bar{y}$ years. Figure 6-7a indicates that when a low-productivity worker does not go to college, he "takes home" $200,000 (because he does not incur any college attendance costs). If he goes to college $\bar{y}$ years, his net salary is the vertical difference between the $300,000 wage offer and the cost of going to college for $\bar{y}$ years (which equals $25,000 \times \bar{y}$). Therefore, the low-productivity worker will not attend college if

$$\$200,000 > \$300,000 - (\$25,001 \times \bar{y}) \qquad \text{(6-16)}$$

FIGURE 6-7   **Education as a Signal**

Workers get paid $200,000 if they get less than $\bar{y}$ years of college, and $300,000 if they get at least $\bar{y}$ years. Low-productivity workers find it expensive to invest in college, and will not get $\bar{y}$ years. High-productivity workers do obtain $\bar{y}$ years. As a result, the worker's education signals if he is a low-productivity or a high-productivity worker.

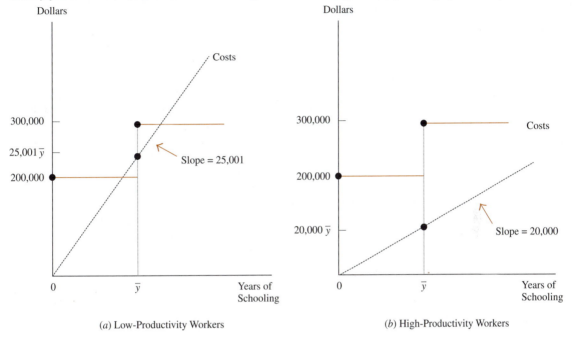

(*a*) Low-Productivity Workers   (*b*) High-Productivity Workers

Solving for $\bar{y}$ implies that

$$\bar{y} > 3.999 \qquad\qquad \textbf{(6-17)}$$

In other words, if the firm chooses a rule of thumb where only workers who get more than 3.999 years of college will be considered high-productivity workers, *no* low-productivity worker will bother going to college—it is just too expensive. By choosing not to attend college, low-productivity workers "voluntarily" signal their low productivity and separate themselves out.

A separating equilibrium also requires that high-productivity workers *do* get $\bar{y}$ years of college. Figure 6-7*b* illustrates their decision. The net salary of a high-productivity worker who does not go to college is $200,000. The net salary of a high-productivity worker who goes to college for $\bar{y}$ years is the vertical difference between the $300,000 wage offer and the cost of going to college (which equals $20,000 \times \bar{y}$). Therefore, high-productivity workers get $\bar{y}$ years of college whenever

$$\$200{,}000 < \$300{,}000 - (\$20{,}000 \times \bar{y}) \qquad\qquad \textbf{(6-18)}$$

Solving for $\bar{y}$ yields

$$\bar{y} < 5 \qquad\qquad \textbf{(6-19)}$$

In other words, as long as the firm does not demand "too many" years of higher education (such as a master's degree or Ph.D.), high-productivity workers go to college and voluntarily signal that they are highly productive.

Putting together both conditions implies that low-productivity workers do not go to college and that high-productivity workers do whenever

$$3.999 < \bar{y} < 5 \qquad\qquad \textbf{(6-20)}$$

A firm can choose any hiring standard in this range and generate a separating equilibrium. The firm can say, for instance, that workers who obtain more than 4.5 years of college will be considered high-productivity workers, and the two types of workers will sort themselves out accordingly. There seem to be an infinite number of valid thresholds that the firm can use (4 years of college, 4.5 years, 4.666 years, 4.999 years, and so on). Not all of these solutions, however, can survive the competitive pressures of the marketplace. Suppose, for instance, that some firms require 4.333 years of college to allocate high-productivity workers into skilled jobs, whereas other firms require only 4.000 years. High-productivity workers prefer the firm with the 4.000 hiring threshold because both firms pay the same competitive salary (of $300,000) and high-productivity workers have nothing to gain from getting more education than the minimum required. The competitive solution, therefore, is the smallest possible threshold, so that using a college diploma (four years of college) to separate out job applicants generates a separating equilibrium.

The signaling model shows that education can play the role of signaling the worker's innate ability without increasing the worker's productivity. It has been extremely difficult, however, to establish empirically if education plays a productivity-enhancing role, a signaling role, or a combination of the two.[30] Regardless of which model is correct, an outsider looking at a particular labor market will observe that more-educated workers earn higher wages. Because both the schooling model and the signaling model predict that more education leads to higher earnings, the positive correlation between earnings and education cannot be used to disentangle which of the two mechanisms is more important in the labor market. As a result, there is no widely accepted calculation that decomposes the wage differential between highly educated and less-educated workers into its productivity and signaling components.

There are reasons to believe, however, that the signaling role of education may be less important than is commonly assumed. It costs over $150,000 for the typical student to go to college (including both forgone earnings and direct costs). If college provided only an impressive-looking piece of paper, firms that specialize in printing equally impressive pieces of paper at lower prices would appear in the marketplace. The fact that we do not see a large industry of firms that sell credentials certifying a person's innate productivity

---

[30] See, for example, Kevin Lang and David Kropp, "Human Capital versus Sorting: The Effects of Compulsory Schooling Laws," *Quarterly Journal of Economics* 101 (August 1986): 609–624; Eugene A. Kroch and Kriss Sjoblom, "Schooling as Human Capital or a Signal: Some Evidence," *Journal of Human Resources* 29 (Winter 1994): 156–180; Joseph G. Altonji and Charles R. Pierret, "Employer Learning and the Signaling Value of Education," in Isao Ohashi and Toshiaki Tachibanaki, editors, *Internal Labour Markets, Incentives, and Employment,* Macmillan: New York, 1998, pp. 159–195; and Kelly Bedard, "Human Capital versus Signaling Models: University Access and High School Dropouts," *Journal of Political Economy* (August 2001): 749–775.

There has been a substantial increase in the number of persons who obtain their high school diplomas by passing an equivalency test rather than by going through the normal route of spending 12 years in a classroom and then graduating from high school. In 1968, only 5 percent of high school graduates obtained their diplomas by taking the GED test (which stands for General Equivalency Diploma). By 1987, 14 percent of persons receiving a high school diploma received GED certificates.

A comparison of the earnings of traditional high school graduates with the earnings of workers who get their high school diplomas via the GED can help determine if the schooling process actually matters. In other words, does passing the GED provide the same skills as attending school for 12 years?

A recent study reports that the labor market characteristics of GED graduates and high school *dropouts* are virtually indistinguishable. In particular, the wages of GED graduates are no higher than the wages of high school dropouts. It seems, therefore, that simply certifying someone who passes a standardized test to be a high school graduate is no substitute for the learning that takes place when persons actually go to school. As the authors of the study conclude, "there is no cheap substitute for schooling."

Sources: Stephen V. Cameron and James J. Heckman, "The Nonequivalence of High School Equivalents," *Journal of Labor Economics* 11 (January 1993, Part 1): 1–47; and James J. Heckman and Paul A. LaFontaine, "Bias-Corrected Estimates of GED Returns," *Journal of Labor Economics* 24 (July 2006): 661–700. Contrary evidence is provided by John H. Tyler, Richard J. Murnane, and John B. Willett, "Estimating the Labor Market Signaling Value of the GED," *Quarterly Journal of Economics* 115 (May 2000): 431–468.

must imply that education does more than just signal a worker's productivity; it also must alter the human capital stock.

Although this is a sensible argument, it would be preferable to document empirically the relative importance of the signaling and productivity-enhancing roles of education. Separating out the two effects is important because the human capital framework and the signaling hypothesis have very different implications for many policy questions. The human capital model, for example, suggests that human capital investments, such as education, provide a way out of low incomes and poverty. Indeed, the rationale behind government programs that subsidize on-the-job training and tuition expenses is that these programs increase the human capital stock of the targeted groups. The signaling model says that education does not really increase a worker's innate productivity. Low-productivity workers remain low-productivity workers regardless of the billions of dollars spent on these government programs.

Private and Social Rates of Return

The different policy recommendations made by the two approaches suggest that the **private rate of return to schooling,** as measured by the increase in a worker's earnings resulting from an additional year of schooling, may differ substantially from the **social rate of return to schooling,** as measured by the increase in national income resulting from the same year of education. Suppose the signaling model is correct and education does not increase productivity. From a worker's point of view, education still has a positive private rate of return. The highly productive worker gains from signaling that he is highly productive. From a social point of view, however, educational expenditures are wasteful. National income is not increased because the worker's productivity is the same both before and after the investment in education. The social rate of return is zero.

These conclusions, however, ignore the fact that—even in the context of the signaling model—education serves the very useful role of sorting workers into the right jobs. The employer can use the education signal to allocate highly productive workers to so-called skilled jobs and to allocate the less-productive workers into other types of jobs. The mismatching of workers and jobs in the labor market—for instance, assigning a low-productivity worker to run a nuclear power plant—would surely have a detrimental effect on national income. As a result, education could have a positive social rate of return even if it does not increase a particular worker's human capital. We know very little about the magnitude of the misallocation costs that would arise if education did not help sort workers among jobs so that many of the questions concerning the "true" magnitude of the social rate of return to education have not been answered.

Some recent studies have argued that the definition of the "social" rate of return to schooling should be expanded to include the impact of education on civic engagement and attitudes in a democracy, or the impact of an educated workforce on the rate of economic growth. In fact, additional schooling raises voter participation rates and support for free speech and leads to a better-informed electorate (as measured by the frequency of newspaper readership). Similarly, the evidence suggests that a more educated workforce may promote faster growth.[31]

6-10   Postschool Human Capital Investments

The evolution of wages over the life cycle is illustrated by the age-earnings profiles presented in Figure 6-8, which report the average weekly earnings of U.S. workers in a particular schooling group at different ages. The figure reveals three important properties of age-earnings profiles:

1. *Highly educated workers earn more than less-educated workers.* We have seen that education increases earnings either because education increases productivity or because education serves as a signal of a worker's innate ability.

2. *Earnings rise over time, but at a decreasing rate.* The wage increase observed over the life cycle suggests that a worker's productivity rises even after leaving school, perhaps as a result of on-the-job or off-the-job training programs.[32] The rate of wage growth, however, slows down as workers get older. Younger workers seem to add more to their human capital than older workers.

3. *The age-earnings profiles of different education groups diverge over time.* Put differently, earnings increase faster for more educated workers. The steeper slope of age-earnings

---

[31] Mark Bils and Peter J. Klenow, "Does Schooling Cause Growth?" *American Economic Review* 90 (December 2000): 1160–1183; Eric A. Hanushek and Dennis D. Kimko, "Schooling, Labor-Force Quality, and the Growth of Nations," *American Economic Review* 90 (December 2000): 1184–1208; and Thomas S. Dee, "Are There Civic Returns to Education?" *Journal of Public Economics* 88 (August 2004): 1697–1720.

[32] This interpretation of upward-sloping age-earnings profiles assumes that the worker's productivity rises throughout the life cycle. As we will see in Chapter 11, other models of the labor market imply an upward-sloping age-earnings profile even if the worker's productivity is constant over time.

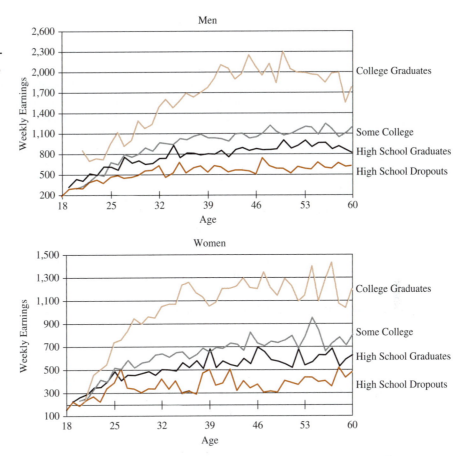

FIGURE 6-8

Age-Earnings Profiles of Full-Time Workers, 2010

Source: U.S. Bureau of Labor Statistics, *Annual Demographic Supplement of the Current Population Surveys,* 2010.

profiles for more-educated workers suggests a complementarity between investments in education and investments in on-the-job training. In other words, workers who are highly educated experience the fastest wage growth because they also invest the most during the postschool period. This complementarity between pre- and postschool investments might arise if some workers have a "knack" for acquiring all types of human capital.[33]

6-11   On-the-Job Training

Until now, we have focused on one particular aspect of human capital investments—the schooling decision. Most workers augment their human capital stock after completing their education, particularly through on-the-job training (OJT) programs. The diversity of OJT investments is striking: Secretaries learn word processing skills, lawyers get courtroom

---

[33] A detailed study of the link between schooling and earnings changes over the life cycle is given by Henry S. Farber and Robert Gibbons, "Learning and Wage Dynamics," *Quarterly Journal of Economics* 111 (November 1996): 1007–1047.

experience, investment bankers concoct new financial instruments, and politicians learn from failed policies. Evidently, OJT is an important component of a worker's human capital stock, making up at least half of a worker's human capital.[34]

There are two types of OJT: **general training** and **specific training**.[35] General training is the type of training that, once acquired, enhances productivity equally in all firms. These general skills, which include such things as typing, learning how to drive, and learning how to use a calculator, are found frequently in the labor market. Specific training is the type of training that enhances productivity only in the firm where it is acquired and the productivity gains are lost once the worker leaves the firm. Examples of specific training also abound in the labor market: learning how to drive a tank in the army or memorizing the hierarchical nature of a particular organization. In reality, much OJT is a mixture of general and specific training, but the conceptual separation into purely general and purely specific training is extremely useful.

Consider a simple framework where the employment relationship between a competitive firm and the worker lasts two periods. Suppose that in the first period (when the worker is hired), the *total* labor costs equal TC_1 dollars, and in the second period, the costs equal TC_2 dollars. Similarly, the values of marginal product in each of the two periods are VMP_1 and VMP_2, respectively. Finally, let r be the rate of discount. The profit-maximizing condition giving the optimal level of employment for the firm over the two periods is

$$TC_1 + \frac{TC_2}{1+r} = VMP_1 + \frac{VMP_2}{1+r} \qquad (6\text{-}21)$$

The left-hand side of the equation gives the present value of the costs associated with hiring a worker over the two-period life cycle. The right-hand side gives the present value of the worker's contribution to the firm. It is easy to see that this equation generalizes the condition that the wage equals the value of marginal product. In a multiperiod framework, the analogous condition is that the present value of employment costs equals the present value of the value of marginal product.

Suppose OJT takes place only in the first period. It costs the firm H dollars to put a worker through the training. These costs include teacher salaries and the purchase of training equipment. The total cost of hiring a worker during the first period can be written as the sum of training costs H and the wage paid to the worker during the training period, or w_1. This implies that $TC_1 = w_1 + H$. Because no training occurs in the second period, the total cost of hiring the worker in the second period simply equals the wage. We can then rewrite equation (6-21) as

$$w_1 + H + \frac{w_2}{1+r} = VMP_1 + \frac{VMP_2}{1+r} \qquad (6\text{-}22)$$

[34] Jacob Mincer, "On-the-Job Training: Costs, Returns, and Some Implications," *Journal of Political Economy* 70 (October 1962, Part 2): 50–79.

[35] The concepts of general and specific training are due to Gary S. Becker, *Human Capital,* 3rd ed., Chicago: University of Chicago Press, 1993. Becker's framework continues to be the cornerstone of the human capital literature and is an essential component in the toolkit of modern labor economics.

Who Pays for General Training?

Consider the case where all training is general. In the posttraining period, the worker's value of marginal product increases to VMP_2 in *all* firms. As a result, many firms are willing to pay the worker a wage equal to VMP_2. The firm that provided the training must either follow suit and increase the wage to VMP_2 or lose the worker. Therefore, the second period wage, w_2, will equal VMP_2. As a result, equation (6-22) simplifies to

$$w_1 = VMP_1 - H \qquad \text{(6-23)}$$

Therefore, the first-period wage equals the value of the worker's initial marginal product minus training costs. In other words, workers pay for general training by accepting a lower "trainee wage" during the training period. In the second period, workers get the returns from the training by receiving a wage that equals the value of their posttraining marginal product. *Competitive firms provide general training only if they do not pay any of the costs.*

There are many examples of workers paying for general training through lower wages. It is common for trainees in formal apprenticeship programs to receive low wages during the training period and to receive higher wages after the training is completed. Similarly, medical interns (even though they already have a medical degree) earn low wages and work long hours during their residency, but their investment is well rewarded once they complete their training.

If a firm were to pay for general training, as some firms claim to do when they pay for the tuition of workers who enroll in an MBA program, the firm would surely attract a large number of job applicants. After all, many workers would quickly realize that this firm was offering free general training. Because the firm cannot legally enslave its employees after they receive their degree, the workers would take advantage of the free training opportunities and then run to a firm that offers them a wage commensurate with their newly acquired skills. Therefore, a firm that paid for general training and did not raise the posttraining wage would get an oversupply of trainees and the workers would quit in the posttraining period. This firm faces the worst of all possible outcomes: It pays for the training and gets none of the benefits. A profit-maximizing firm would quickly learn that it can lower the wage because there is an oversupply of trainees, passing on the training costs to the workers.[36]

Who Pays for Specific Training?

The productivity gains resulting from specific training vanish once the worker leaves the firm. As a result, the worker's alternative wage (that is, the wage that other firms are willing

---

[36] Studies have shown that noncompetitive firms may be willing to pay for general training under some circumstances; see Daron Acemoglu and Jörn-Steffen Pischke, "The Structure of Wages and Investment in General Training," *Journal of Political Economy* 107 (June 1999): 539–572. Empirical studies of who pays for training are given by John M. Barron, Mark C. Berger, and Dan A. Black, "Do Workers Pay for On-the-Job Training?" *Journal of Human Resources* 34 (Spring 1999): 235–252; and David H. Autor, "Why Do Temporary Help Firms Provide Free General Skills Training?" *Quarterly Journal of Economics* 116 (November 2001): 1409–1448.

to pay) is *independent* of the training and equals his pretraining productivity. Who then pays for specific training and who collects the returns?[37]

Consider what would happen if the firm paid for specific training. The firm could incur the cost and collect the returns by not changing the wage in the posttraining period, even though the worker's value of marginal product in this firm has increased. Because VMP_2 would then exceed w_2, there are gains to providing the training. If the worker were to quit in the second period, however, the firm would suffer a capital loss. The firm, therefore, would hesitate paying for specific training unless it has some assurance that the trained worker will not quit.

Suppose instead that the worker pays for the specific training. Workers would then receive a low wage during the training period and higher wages in the posttraining period. The worker, however, does not have an ironclad assurance that the firm will employ him in the second period. If the worker were to get laid off, he would lose his investment because specific training is not portable. The worker, therefore, is not willing to invest in specific training unless he is very confident that he will not be laid off.

Both the firm and the worker, therefore, are reluctant to invest in specific training. The problem arises because there does not exist a legally binding contract that ties together workers and firms "until death do them part." Neither party wishes to take the initiative and pay for the training.

The way out of this dilemma is to note that fine-tuning the posttraining wage can reduce the probabilities of *both* quits and layoffs. Consider a labor contract in which the worker's posttraining wage, w_2, is set such that

$$\overline{w} < w_2 < VMP_2 \qquad\qquad (6\text{-}24)$$

where $\overline{w}$ is the alternative wage. This contract implies that the worker and the firm share the returns from specific training. The worker's posttraining wage w_2 is higher than his productivity elsewhere, but less than his productivity at the current firm. Note that because the worker is better off in this firm than elsewhere, he has no incentive to quit. Similarly, because the firm is better off by employing the worker than by laying him off (that is, the worker gets paid less than his value of marginal product), the firm does not want to let the worker go. If *both* the firm and the worker share the returns of the specific training, therefore, the possibility of job separation in the posttraining period is eliminated.

If firms and workers do share the returns of specific training, they also will have to share the costs. After all, if firms paid all the costs of providing specific training and got only part of the returns, they would attract an oversupply of trainees. Therefore, if firms pay, say, 30 percent of the costs of specific training, they also will get 30 percent of the returns. Otherwise, the firm would attract either too few or too many job applicants.

---

[37] A more detailed discussion of these issues is given by Masanori Hashimoto, "Firm-Specific Human Capital as a Shared Investment," *American Economic Review* 71 (June 1981): 475–482. For an alternative approach to modeling specific training, see Edward P. Lazear, "Firm-Specific Human Capital: A Skill-Weights Approach," *Journal of Political Economy* 117 (October 2009): 914–940. There has been a flurry of recent work examining what it is about a worker's skills that is specific to certain jobs, occupations, or industries. See, for example, Maxim Poletaev and Chris Robinson, "Human Capital Specificity: Evidence from the Dictionary of Occupational Titles and Displaced Worker Surveys, 1984–2000," *Journal of Labor Economics* 26 (July 2008): 387–420.

Some Implications of Specific Training

It is important to note that specific training breaks the link between the worker's wage and the value of marginal product throughout the worker's life cycle. During the training period, workers get paid less than their value of marginal product because they are paying part of the training costs. In the posttraining period, workers get paid less than their value of marginal product in the firm that provided the training, but get paid more than their marginal product in other firms (that is, they get paid more than the alternative wage).

As a result of this contract, workers who have specific training are effectively granted a type of tenure or lifetime contract in the firm. Neither workers nor firms that have invested in specific training want to terminate the employment contract. It might seem surprising to argue that lifetime contracts might be common in labor markets where workers and firms are evidently very mobile, such as in the United States. Nevertheless, the evidence indicates that jobs lasting more than 20 years are the rule rather than the exception even in the United States.[38]

The concept of specific training has many other implications for labor markets. It provides a simple explanation of the "last hired, first fired" rule that typically determines who gets laid off during an economic downturn. Workers who have been with a firm for many years probably have more specific training than newly hired workers. When the demand for the firm's output falls, the price of the output and the value of the worker's marginal product decline. Workers with seniority have a buffer between their value of marginal product and their wage, so that the drop in the value of the worker's contribution to the firm protects these senior workers from layoffs. Put differently, because specifically trained workers produce more than they get paid, the firm need not lay off many of these workers when it experiences a sudden drop in the demand for its product. Profit-maximizing employers who want to cut the size of the workforce, therefore, will lay off newly hired workers.

Moreover, if a specifically trained worker does get laid off, he will have little incentive to find alternative employment. After all, these workers will suffer a capital loss if they change employers. Specifically trained workers, therefore, will prefer to "wait out" the unemployment spell until they are recalled by their former employers. There is, in fact, a very high incidence of **temporary layoffs** in many labor markets. At least 60 percent of the layoffs in the United States end when their former employers recall laid-off workers.[39]

Because specific training "marries" firms and workers, the probability of job separation for a given worker (either through a quit or a layoff) declines with job seniority. Newly hired workers will have high turnover rates, whereas more senior workers will have low turnover rates. This negative correlation between job turnover propensities and job seniority would not arise if all training were general. General training is portable and can be carried to any firm at any time. As a result, there would be no reason to expect the worker's economic opportunities

[38] Robert E. Hall, "The Importance of Lifetime Jobs in the U.S. Economy," *American Economic Review* 72 (September 1982): 716–724; see also Manuelita Ureta, "The Importance of Lifetime Jobs in the U.S. Economy, Revisited," *American Economic Review* 82 (March 1992): 322–335.

[39] Martin S. Feldstein, "Temporary Layoffs in the Theory of Unemployment," *Journal of Political Economy* 84 (October 1976): 937–957.

in the current firm (relative to other firms) to improve over time. The important relationship between specific training and job turnover is discussed in more detail in Chapter 8.[40]

6-12   On-the-Job Training and the Age-Earnings Profile

The shape of the age-earnings profile depends on the timing of human capital investments over the working life.[41] At every age, we will want to invest in human capital up to the point where the marginal revenue of the investment equals the marginal cost of the investment. To describe the timing of human capital acquisitions, therefore, we must describe what happens to the marginal revenue and the marginal cost of human capital investments as workers get older.

For convenience, let's measure the human capital stock in **efficiency units.** Efficiency units are standardized units of human capital. The total human capital stock of the worker equals the total number of efficiency units embodied in him or her. If David has 100 efficiency units and Mac has only 50 units, David is equivalent to two Macs—at least in terms of his labor market productivity.

An efficiency unit of human capital can be rented out in the labor market, and the rental rate per efficiency unit is R dollars. The market for efficiency units is competitive, so the per-unit rental price is R dollars regardless of how many efficiency units a worker has. Finally, to keep things simple, let's assume that all training is general and that there is no depreciation of the human capital stock over time. Therefore, an efficiency unit of human capital generates R dollars per year from the date when it is acquired until retirement, which occurs at age 65.

Suppose that the worker enters the labor market at age 20 and plans to retire at age 65. The marginal revenue of acquiring one efficiency unit of human capital at age 20 is

$$MR_{20} = R + \frac{R}{1+r} + \frac{R}{(1+r)^2} + \frac{R}{(1+r)^3} + \cdots + \frac{R}{(1+r)^{45}} \quad \text{(6-25)}$$

where r is the discount rate. The intuition behind equation (6-25) is easy to understand. If a worker acquires one efficiency unit at age 20, this investment yields a return of R dollars during that first year in the labor market. In the second year, the present value of the return to that same efficiency unit is $R/(1+r)$ dollars; in the third year, the return equals $R/(1+r)^2$ dollars; and so on. Equation (6-25) simply adds the discounted returns to the efficiency unit over the entire working life.

The curve MR_{20} in Figure 6-9 illustrates the relationship between the marginal revenue of an efficiency unit acquired at age 20 and the number of efficiency units that

[40] Although the discussion assumes that the specific capital embodied in the worker is specific to the firm, it may well be the case that some of the specific capital is specific to the industry where the worker is employed; see Daniel Parent, "Industry-Specific Capital and the Wage Profile: Evidence from the National Longitudinal Survey of Youth and the Panel Study of Income Dynamics," *Journal of Labor Economics* 18 (April 2000): 306–323.

[41] Yoram Ben-Porath, "The Production of Human Capital and the Life Cycle of Earnings," *Journal of Political Economy* 75 (August 1967): 352–365; and James J. Heckman, "A Life-Cycle Model of Earnings, Learning, and Consumption," *Journal of Political Economy* 84 (August 1976 Supplement): S11–S46.

FIGURE 6-9   **The Acquisition of Human Capital over the Life Cycle**

The marginal revenue of an efficiency unit of human capital declines as the worker ages (so that MR_{20}, the marginal revenue of a unit acquired at age 20, lies above MR_{30}). At each age, the worker equates the marginal revenue with the marginal cost, so that more units are acquired when the worker is younger.

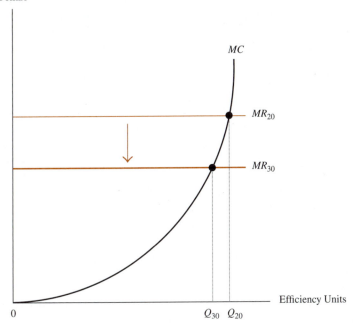

the worker acquires. Because we assumed that the rental rate R is the same regardless of how much human capital the worker acquires, the marginal revenue curve MR_{20} is horizontal.

Suppose the worker looks into the future and wants to know how many efficiency units of human capital he would have acquired if he were 30 years old. The marginal revenue of an efficiency unit acquired at age 30 is given by

$$MR_{30} = R + \frac{R}{1+r} + \frac{R}{(1+r)^2} + \frac{R}{(1+r)^3} + \cdots + \frac{R}{(1+r)^{35}} \quad \text{(6-26)}$$

Equation (6-26) indicates that the marginal revenue of acquiring an efficiency unit at age 30 is the discounted sum of the returns collected at age 30, at age 31, and so on. Note that the worker is now 10 years closer to retirement, so the sum in equation (6-26) has 10 fewer terms than the sum in equation (6-25).

By comparing the marginal revenue of acquiring an efficiency unit at ages 20 and 30, we can see that the marginal revenue of investing at age 20 exceeds the marginal revenue of investing at age 30. This fact is illustrated in Figure 6-9, which shows that the MR_{30} curve lies below the MR_{20} curve. The marginal revenue of human capital investment falls as the worker ages for a simple reason: We do not live forever. Human capital acquired when young can be rented out for a long period of time, whereas investments undertaken at older ages can be rented out only for shorter periods. As a result, human capital investments are more profitable the earlier they are undertaken.

As noted earlier, the actual number of efficiency units acquired at any age is determined by equating the marginal revenue with the marginal cost of human capital investments. The marginal cost curve (MC), also illustrated in Figure 6-9, has the usual shape: Marginal costs rise as more efficiency units are acquired. The shape of the marginal cost curve is determined by the underlying production function for human capital. The assumption of diminishing returns in the production of efficiency units guarantees that marginal costs increase at an increasing rate as the worker attempts to acquire more and more human capital.

The intersection of MR_{20} and the marginal cost curve in Figure 6-9 implies that the worker will acquire Q_{20} efficiency units at age 20. Because the marginal revenue of human capital investments declines over time, the optimal investment level at age 30 falls to Q_{30}. In other words, the worker acquires fewer efficiency units as he gets older. This result helps us understand why workers typically go to school when young, why this period of complete specialization in human capital investments is followed by a period of considerable on-the-job training, and why on-the-job training activities taper off as the worker ages. This timing of investments over the life cycle maximizes the present value of lifetime earnings.[42]

Because the worker acquires more human capital when he is young, the worker's age-earnings profile is upward sloping, as illustrated in Figure 6-10. As we have seen, workers pay for on-the-job training through reduced wages. Older workers, therefore, earn more than younger workers because older workers acquire fewer efficiency units of human capital and, hence, have lower forgone earnings. Older workers also earn more because they are collecting the returns made on prior investments.

The optimal timing of investments over the working life also implies that the age-earnings profile is concave so that earnings increase over time but at a decreasing rate. Year-to-year wage growth depends partly on how many additional efficiency units the worker acquires. Because fewer units are acquired as the worker ages, the rate of wage growth declines over time.

The Mincer Earnings Function

The implications of the human capital model for the age-earnings profile have been the subject of extensive empirical analysis. This line of research culminated in the development

---

[42] Our discussion assumes that the marginal cost curve is constant over time (that is, it does not shift as the worker ages). It may be that older workers are more efficient at producing human capital, and, hence, the marginal cost curve would shift down. The forgone earnings incurred in producing human capital, however, are higher for older workers so that the marginal cost curve shifts up with age. It is sometimes assumed that these two opposing effects exactly outweigh each other (this assumption is called the "neutrality assumption"). As a result, the marginal cost curve does not shift over time. For a discussion of these issues, see Yoram Ben-Porath, "The Production of Human Capital over Time," in W. Lee Hansen, editor, *Education, Income, and Human Capital*, New York: Columbia University Press, 1970.

FIGURE 6-10   **The Age-Earnings Profile Implied by Human Capital Theory**
The age-earnings profile is upward-sloping and concave. Older workers earn more because they invest less in human capital and because they are collecting the returns from earlier investments. The rate of growth of earnings slows down over time because workers accumulate less human capital as they get older.

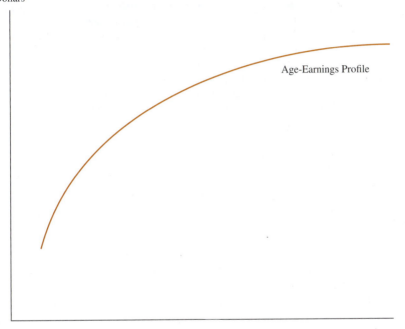

of Jacob Mincer's human capital earnings function.[43] In particular, Mincer showed that the human capital model generates an age-earnings profile of the form

$$\log w = as + bt - ct^2 + \text{Other variables} \qquad \text{(6-27)}$$

where w is the worker's wage rate, s is the number of years of schooling, t gives the number of years of labor market experience, and t^2 is a quadratic on experience that captures the concavity of the age-earnings profile.

In the **Mincer earnings function,** as this widely used equation has come to be known, the coefficient on schooling a estimates the percent increase in earnings resulting from one additional year of schooling and is typically interpreted as the rate of return

[43] Jacob Mincer, *Schooling, Experience, and Earnings,* New York: Columbia University Press, 1974. This literature is surveyed by Robert J. Willis, "Wage Determinants: A Survey and Reinterpretation of Human Capital Earnings Functions," in Orley C. Ashenfelter and Richard Layard, editors, *Handbook of Labor Economics,* vol. 1, Amsterdam: Elsevier, 1986, pp. 525–602; and James J. Heckman, Lance J. Lochner, and Petra E. Todd, "Earnings Functions, Rates of Return and Treatment Effects: The Mincer Equation and Beyond," in Eric Hanushek and Finis Welch, editors, *Handbook of Education Economics,* Amsterdam: Elsevier, 2006.

Most of the examples that dominate discussions of the economic impact of human capital deal with investments that have a beneficial impact on the worker's productivity, such as schooling and on-the-job training. Many workers, however, also undertake activities that presumably have an adverse impact on the value of their human capital stock, such as alcoholism and drug use.

Alcoholism is a major social and economic problem in many countries. In the United States, this disorder afflicts about 5 percent of the population at any point in time, and nearly 10 percent of the population at some point in their lives. There is strong evidence that alcoholics pay a heavy price not only in terms of their health and the well-being of their families, but also in the labor market. Among workers aged 30 to 59, alcoholics are 15 percentage points less likely to work and earn 17 percent less than nonalcoholics, even if we look at alcoholics whose health has not yet been impaired.

Drug use is an equally important problem. By the time workers reach the age of 30, nearly 30 percent have used cocaine and about 3 percent have used it in the past month. Surprisingly, the evidence does not suggest that cocaine users have systematically lower wages or employment rates.

It is important to stress that these correlations between substance abuse and labor market characteristics do not necessarily prove that alcoholism "causes" lower wages or that cocaine use "does not reduce" productivity. The population of substance abusers is self-selected. Perhaps alcoholism does not reduce earnings, but those workers who are less successful in the labor market have a greater chance of becoming alcoholics. Similarly, it may be that only those workers who can handle the adverse consequences of cocaine use—or who can afford to buy cocaine—become habitual users.

The range of activities that may have adverse labor market consequences will likely increase as employers increasingly use Internet searches to gain information on the personal life of job applicants, often by searching through personal Web pages published by the applicants themselves. There are widespread reports that some employers now engage in this type of systematic search as a routine part of the hiring process, and that various forms of personal behavior are seen as "deal breakers" in the process.

Sources: Thomas S. Dee and William N. Evans, "Teen Drinking and Educational Attainment: Evidence from Two-Sample Instrumental Variables Estimates," *Journal of Labor Economics* 21 (January 2003): 178–209; John Muhally and Jody L. Sindelar, "Alcoholism, Work, and Income," *Journal of Labor Economics* 11 (July 1993): 494–520; and Robert Kaestner, "New Estimates of the Effect of Marijuana and Cocaine Use on Wages," *Industrial and Labor Relations Review* 47 (April 1994): 454–470.

to schooling. We have seen that this interpretation is correct only when workers do not differ in their unobserved ability. The coefficients on experience and experience squared estimate the rate of growth in earnings resulting from one additional year of labor market experience and are typically interpreted as measuring the impact of on-the-job training on earnings. If the worker did not invest in OJT, the coefficients of the experience variables would be zero because there would be no reason for real earnings to increase with labor market experience.

Hundreds of studies have found that the Mincer earnings function provides a reasonably accurate description of age-earnings profiles not only in the United States, but also in the labor markets of many other countries (even in countries with very different labor market institutions). As we saw earlier in this chapter, actual age-earnings profiles in the United States are concave and are higher for more-educated workers. The evidence also suggests that differences in education and labor market experience among workers account for about a third of the variation in wage rates in the population. The human capital model, therefore, goes a long way toward providing a useful story of how the earnings distribution arises.[44]

6-13 Policy Application: Evaluating Government Training Programs

Perhaps the most important policy implication of the human capital model is that the provision of training to low-skill workers may substantially improve their economic well-being. Since the declaration of the War on Poverty in the mid-1960s, a large number of government programs have indeed attempted to provide training to disadvantaged workers. These programs include the Manpower Development and Training Act of 1962 (MDTA), the Comprehensive Employment and Training Act of 1973 (CETA), and the Job Training Partnership Act of 1982 (JTPA).

Each of these programs spent a lot of money trying to "expose" minority and other low-income groups to formal training programs. Federal expenditures on job training programs now exceed over $4 billion per year. In view of the large cost of setting up, maintaining, and operating these programs, it is not surprising that a large number of studies attempt to determine if these programs do what they are supposed to do—namely, increase the human capital and earnings of the trainees.[45]

The program evaluations have raised a number of still-unresolved conceptual issues. It would seem that by comparing the earnings of trainees before and after the "treatment," we could measure the effectiveness of the program (at least in terms of the program's impact on earnings capacity). A number of studies have made this type of before-and-after comparison and have found that there are some earnings gains associated with the training programs. Typically, trainees earn about $300 to $1,500 more per year after the program than before the program.[46]

Unfortunately, this calculation may not be very meaningful. As in many other contexts in labor economics, the problem of self-selection mars the analysis. In particular, only those workers who have the most to gain from the program and are most committed to "self-improvement" are likely to enroll and subject themselves to the treatment. The earnings gain achieved by this nonrandom sample of workers, therefore, tells us something about how the training programs affect motivated workers but may say nothing about

---

[44] For contrary evidence on the importance of OJT as a determinant of earnings growth in the post-school period, see Burkhanettin Burusku, "Training and Lifetime Income," *American Economic Review* 96 (June 2006): 832–846.

[45] This literature is surveyed in James J. Heckman, Robert J. LaLonde, and Jeffrey A. Smith, "The Economics and Econometrics of Active Labor Market Programs," in Orley C. Ashenfelter and David Card, editors, *Handbook of Labor Economics,* vol. 3A, Amsterdam: Elsevier, 1999, pp. 1865–2097.

[46] See, for example, Orley C. Ashenfelter, "Estimating the Effect of Training Programs on Earnings," *Review of Economics and Statistics* 60 (February 1978): 47–57; Orley C. Ashenfelter and David Card, "Using the Longitudinal Structure of Earnings to Estimate the Effect of Training Programs," *Review of Economics and Statistics* 67 (November 1985): 648–660; and Burt Barnow, "The Impact of CETA Programs on Earnings: A Review of the Literature," *Journal of Human Resources* 22 (Spring 1987): 157–193.

how the program would affect a randomly chosen person in the disadvantaged population. From a policy point of view, therefore, the before-and-after calculation is useless because it cannot be used to predict how the earnings of targeted workers (such as persons currently receiving public assistance) would respond to the treatment.

Social Experiments

To avoid these pitfalls, there has been a revolutionary shift in the methodology used in program evaluation in recent years. The newer evaluations use randomized experiments, akin to the experimental methods used in the physical sciences, to estimate the impact of the program on trainee earnings. In these experiments, potential trainees are randomly assigned to participate in the training program. Every other applicant, for instance, is allocated to the "treatment" group (that is, they are exposed to the training program), whereas the remaining applicants form the control group and are administered a placebo (that is, they are not put through the training program).

The National Supported Work Demonstration (NSW) provides a good example of such a randomization scheme.[47] The key objective of the NSW was to ease the transition of disadvantaged workers into the labor market by exposing them to a work environment where experience and counseling could be provided. In this experiment, eligible applicants were assigned randomly to one of two tracks. The lucky workers who were treated by the program received all the benefits provided by the NSW, whereas those assigned to the control group received none of the benefits and were left on their own. The NSW guaranteed persons in the treatment group a job for 9 to 18 months, at which time they had to find regular employment. The program cost about $12,500 per participant (in 1998 dollars).

It is easy to estimate the impact of the program on the worker's earnings capacity in the context of this experimental scheme. Table 6-4 summarizes the evidence from an influential evaluation of the NSW program. The typical worker who was treated by the program earned

TABLE 6-4   **The Impact of the NSW Program on the Earnings of Trainees (in 1998 dollars)**

Source: Robert J. LaLonde, "Evaluating the Econometric Evaluations of Training Programs with Experimental Data," *American Economic Review* 76 (September 1986): 604–620, Table 2.

Group	Pretraining Annual Earnings (1975)	Posttraining Annual Earnings (1979)	Difference
Treatment group	1,512	7,888	6,376
Control group	1,481	6,450	4,969
Difference-in-differences	—	—	**1,407**

[47] Robert J. LaLonde, "Evaluating the Econometric Evaluations of Training Programs with Experimental Data," *American Economic Review* 76 (September 1986): 604–620. Other studies of experimental data include Stephen H. Bell and Larry L. Orr, "Is Subsidized Employment Cost Effective for Welfare Recipients? Experimental Evidence from Seven State Demonstrations," *Journal of Human Resources* 29 (Winter 1994): 42–61; and Alberto Abadie, Joshua D. Angrist, and Guido W. Imbens, "Instrumental Variables Estimates of the Effects of Training on the Quantiles of Trainee Earnings," *Econometrica* 70 (January 2002): 91–117. Some international evidence on the impact of training programs is given by Laura Abramovsky, Erich Battistin, Emla Fitzsimons, Alissa Goodman, and Helen Simpson, "Providing Employers with Incentives to Train Low-Skilled Workers: Evidence from the UK Employer Training Pilots," *Journal of Labor Economics* 29 (January 2011): 153–193.

$1,512 annually in the pretraining period and $7,888 after the training. The typical trainee, therefore, experienced a wage gain of almost $6,400.

This wage gain, however, does *not* estimate the impact of the training program because the earnings of trainees could have changed between 1975 and 1979 for other reasons, such as aging and changes in aggregate economic conditions. To isolate the true impact of the NSW program, therefore, we must net out the impact of these extraneous events on earnings. It turns out that workers in the control group—those who were *not* exposed to the training activities provided by the program—earned $1,481 annually before the training and $6,450 after the training, so they experienced an earnings gain of almost $5,000. Since earnings would have increased by $5,000 regardless of whether the worker was injected with the training, the true impact of the training program is the difference-in-differences, or about $1,400.

As noted above, the NSW program cost about $12,500 per participant. Therefore, it would take longer than a decade (if future earnings gains are discounted) for the program to reach the "breakeven" point, the point at which the per-worker training costs equal the present value of the benefits accrued by the worker. Nevertheless, the rate of return to the investment is on the order of 10 percent.

Although the experimental approach is rapidly becoming the standard way of evaluating the impact of worker training programs, the methodology has its detractors.[48] These detractors argue that it is incorrect to assume that the $1,400 increase in earnings is the net gain that would be observed if the program were made available to the entire disadvantaged population, and a randomly chosen person in that population were admitted into the program. The criticism is valid because the treatment and control groups do not truly represent a natural experiment. Only persons who are interested in receiving the training in the first place bother to go to the training center and fill out an application. As a result, there is already self-selection in the sample of persons who end up in the treatment group. Moreover, some persons allocated to the treatment group may not show up for the training, whereas persons allocated to the control group may find a way of qualifying for some type of training program (perhaps by trying out at other training sites). Experimental methods, therefore, may not entirely get rid of the selection bias that is at the heart of the evaluation problem.

Summary

- A dollar received today does not have the same value as a dollar received tomorrow. The present value of a future income receipt gives the value of that amount in terms of today's dollars.
- The wage-schooling locus gives the salary that a worker earns if he or she completes a particular level of schooling.
- Workers choose the point on the wage-schooling locus that maximizes the present value of lifetime earnings. In particular, workers quit school when the marginal rate of return to schooling equals the rate of discount.

[48] See James J. Heckman and V. Joseph Hotz, "Choosing among Alternative Nonexperimental Methods for Estimating the Impact of Social Programs: The Case of Manpower Training," *Journal of the American Statistical Association* 84 (December 1989): 862–874; and James J. Heckman and Jeffrey A. Smith, "Assessing the Case for Social Experiments," *Journal of Economic Perspectives* 9 (Spring 1995): 85–110.

- When workers differ only in their discount rates, the rate of return to schooling can be estimated by comparing the earnings of different workers. When workers differ in their innate abilities, the wage differential among workers does not measure the rate of return to schooling because the wage gap also depends on the unobserved ability differential.

- Workers sort themselves into those occupations for which they are best suited. This self-selection implies that we cannot test the hypothesis that workers choose the schooling level that maximizes the present value of lifetime earnings by comparing the earnings of different workers.

- In the United States, the rate of return to schooling was around 9 percent in the 1990s.

- Schooling can play a signaling role in the labor market, indicating to employers that the worker carrying the certificate or diploma is a highly productive worker. The signaling value of education can help firms differentiate highly productive workers from less productive workers.

- If education plays only a signaling role, workers with more schooling earn more not because education increases productivity, but because education signals a worker's innate ability.

- The observed age-earnings profile is upward sloping and concave. Earnings increase over the life cycle, but at a decreasing rate.

- General training is valuable in all firms. Specific training is valuable only in the firm that provides the training. Workers pay for and collect the returns from general training. Workers and firms share both the costs and the returns of specific training.

- The optimal timing of human capital investments over the life cycle implies that the age-earnings profile is upward sloping and concave.

Key Concepts

age-earnings profile, *239*
asymmetric information, *263*
efficiency units, *274*
general training, *270*
human capital, *235*
Mincer earnings function, *277*

opportunity cost, *239*
present value, *238*
private rate of return to schooling, *267*
rate of discount, *238*
rate of return to schooling, *243*
selection bias, *261*

signal, *264*
social rate of return to schooling, *267*
specific training, *270*
temporary layoffs, *273*
wage-schooling locus, *242*

Review Questions

1. Discuss how the present value of a future income payment is calculated.
2. Discuss how the wage-schooling locus is determined in the labor market, and why it is upward sloping and concave.
3. Derive the stopping rule for investments in education.
4. Why does the percentage gain in earnings observed when a worker gets one more year of schooling measure the marginal rate of return to education?
5. Discuss how differences in discount rates or in ability across workers lead to differences in earnings and schooling. Under what conditions can the rate of return to schooling be estimated?

6. Discuss the relationship between ability bias in the estimation of the rate of return to schooling and selection bias in tests of the hypothesis that workers choose the level of schooling that maximizes the present value of earnings.

7. Discuss how empirical studies estimate the rate of return to schooling and the methods used to avoid the problem of ability bias.

8. Show how education can signal the worker's innate ability in the labor market. What is a pooled equilibrium? What is a perfectly separating signaling equilibrium?

9. How can we differentiate between the hypothesis that education increases productivity and the hypothesis that education is a signal for the worker's innate ability?

10. Discuss the difference between general training and specific training. Who pays for and collects the returns from each type of training?

11. Discuss the implications of general and specific training for the worker's age-earnings profile.

12. Why are experimental methods now commonly used to evaluate the impact of training programs? Discuss how and under what conditions we can use the results of an experiment to estimate the rate of return to the program.

Problems

6-1. Debbie is about to choose a career path. She has narrowed her options to two alternatives. She can become either a marine biologist or a concert pianist. Debbie lives two periods. In the first, she gets an education. In the second, she works in the labor market. If Debbie becomes a marine biologist, she will spend $15,000 on education in the first period and earn $472,000 in the second period. If she becomes a concert pianist, she will spend $40,000 on education in the first period and then earn $500,000 in the second period.

a. Suppose Debbie can lend and borrow money at a 5 percent rate of interest between the two periods. Which career will she pursue? What if she can lend and borrow money at a 15 percent rate of interest? Will she choose a different option? Why?

b. Suppose musical conservatories raise their tuition so that it now costs Debbie $60,000 to become a concert pianist. What career will Debbie pursue if the interest rate is 5 percent?

6-2. Peter lives for three periods. He is currently considering three alternative education-work options. He can start working immediately, earning $100,000 in period 1, $110,000 in period 2 (as his work experience leads to higher productivity), and $90,000 in period 3 (as his skills become obsolete and his physical abilities deteriorate). Alternatively, he can spend $50,000 to attend college in period 1 and then earn $180,000 in periods 2 and 3. Finally, he can receive a doctorate degree in period 2 after completing his college education in period 1. This last option will cost him nothing when he is attending graduate school in the second period as his expenses on tuition and books will be covered by a research assistantship. After receiving his doctorate, he will become a professor in a business school and earn $400,000 in period 3. Peter's discount rate is 20 percent per period. What education path maximizes Peter's net present value of his lifetime earnings?

6-3. Jane has three years of college, Pam has two, and Mary has one. Jane earns $21 per hour, Pam earns $19, and Mary earns $16. The difference in educational attainment is due completely to different discount rates. How much can the available information reveal about each woman's discount rate?

6-4. Suppose the skills acquired in school depreciate over time, perhaps because technological change makes the things learned in school obsolete. What happens to a worker's optimal amount of schooling if the rate of depreciation increases?

6-5. a. Describe the basic self-selection issue involved whenever discussing the returns to education.

b. Does the fact that some high school or college dropouts go on to earn vast amounts of money (e.g., Bill Gates dropped out of Harvard without ever graduating) contradict the self-selection story?

c. Most government-provided job training programs are optional to the worker. Describe how the self-selection issue might be used to call into question empirical results suggesting there are large economic benefits to be gained by requiring all workers to receive government-provided job training.

6-6. Suppose Carl's wage-schooling locus is given by

Years of Schooling	Earnings
9	$18,500
10	$20,350
11	$22,000
12	$23,100
13	$23,900
14	$24,000

Derive the marginal rate of return schedule. When will Carl quit school if his discount rate is 4 percent? What if the discount rate is 9 percent?

6-7. Table 217 of the 2006 *U.S. Statistical Abstract* shows that, among all 25–34 year olds, the average annual earnings of a high school graduate with no further education was $26,073 while the average annual earnings of a college graduate with no further education was $43,794 in 2003.

a. Assuming college requires five years, show that the annual return to each year of college education averages 10.9 percent.

b. It is typically thought that this type of calculation of the returns to schooling is biased because it doesn't take into account innate ability (i.e., ability in the workplace not due to college) or innate motivation. If this criticism is true, is the actual return to each year of a college education more than or less than 10.9 percent?

6-8. Suppose there are two types of persons: high-ability and low-ability. A particular diploma costs a high-ability person $8,000 and costs a low-ability person $20,000. Firms wish to use education as a screening device where they intend to pay $25,000 to workers without a diploma and K to those with a diploma. In what range must K be to make this an effective screening device?

6-9. Some economists maintain that the returns to additional years of education is actually quite small but that there is a substantial "sheepskin" effect whereby one receives a higher salary with the successful completion of degrees or the earning of diplomas (i.e., sheepskins).

    a. Explain how the sheepskin effect is analogous to a signaling model.

    b. Typically in the United States, a high school diploma is earned after 12 years of schooling while a college degree is earned after 16 years of school. Graduate degrees are earned with between 2 and 6 years of postcollege schooling. Redraw Figure 6-2 under the assumption that there are no returns to years of schooling but there are significant returns to receiving diplomas.

    c. Devise a difference-in-differences estimator (i.e., what data would you need and what would you do with the data) that would allow one to get at whether completing each year of school or completing degrees matters more when determining wages.

6-10. Jill is planning the timing of her on-the-job training investments over the life cycle. What happens to Jill's OJT investments at every age if

    a. The market-determined rental rate to an efficiency unit falls?

    b. Jill's discount rate increases?

    c. The government passes legislation delaying the retirement age until age 70?

    d. Technological progress is such that much of the OJT acquired at any given age becomes obsolete within the next 10 years?

6-11. Suppose 3 million high school graduates start college each year. Those who earn a college degree will do so in four years. However, some students will drop out along the way. The first-year attrition rate is 20 percent, while the second- and third-year attrition rates are 10 and 2.5 percent, respectively.

    a. What is the distribution of college students by year in college? How many students graduate from college each year?

    b. Believing that education is the key to the future, a presidential candidate proposes that the federal government pay the first $3,000 of college expenses each year for everyone attending a four-year college. It is expected that this proposal will encourage 1 million more high school graduates to enroll in a four-year college each year. Of these 1 million new college students, the first-, second-, and third-year attrition rates are 40, 20, and 5 percent. Why is it likely that attrition rates will be higher among these groups of students?

    c. What is the yearly projected cost of the program in part (b)? What is the average cost of each new four-year college graduate?

6-12. In 1970, men aged 18 to 25 were subject to the military draft to serve in the Vietnam War. A man could qualify for a student deferment, however, if he was enrolled in college and made satisfactory progress on obtaining a degree. By 1975, the draft was no longer in existence. The draft did not pertain to women. Using the data in Table 269 of the 2008 edition of the *U.S. Statistical Abstract,* use women as the control group to estimate (using the difference-in-differences methodology) the effect abolishing the draft had on male college enrollment.

6-13. a. Draw the wage-schooling locus for someone for whom the returns to schooling decrease through college but increase after college. (Assume college is completed after 16 years of schooling and that one can receive at most 6 years of postcollege schooling.)

b. On a new graph, plot the marginal rate of return to schooling implied by the wage-schooling locus described in part a.

c. What can be said about a college graduate who faces the wage-schooling locus described in part a?

6-14. A high school graduate has to decide between working and going to college. If he works, he will work for the next 50 years of his life. If he goes to college, he will be in college for 5 years, and then work for 45 years. In this model, the rate of discount that equates the lifetime present value of not going to college and going to college is 8.24 percent when the cost of each year of college is $15,000, each year of noncollege work pays $35,000, and each year of postcollege work pays $60,000. For each of the parts below, discuss how the rate of discount that equalizes the two options would change and who would make a different schooling decision based on the change. (Extra credit: Use Excel to show that the rate of return to schooling is 8.24 percent in the above case and solve for the rates of discount associated with each of the parts below.)

a. Each year of college still costs $15,000 and each year of postcollege work still pays $60,000, but each year of noncollege work now pays $40,000.

b. Each year of college still costs $15,000 and each year of noncollege work still pays $35,000, but each year of postcollege work now pays $80,000.

c. Each year of noncollege work and postcollege work still pays $35,000 and $60,000 respectively, but now each year of college costs $35,000.

d. Each year of college still costs $15,000. The first year of noncollege work pays $35,000 but then increases by 3 percent each year thereafter. The first year of postcollege work pays $60,000 but then increases by 5 percent each year thereafter.

6-15. Suppose the decision to acquire schooling depends on three factors–preferences (joy of learning), costs (monetary and psychic), and individual-specific returns to education.

a. Explain how each of these factors affects one's optimal amount of schooling.

b. Using these three factors, explain why someone who faces a very steep wage-schooling locus may still opt to obtain very little schooling.

c. Consider two groups of people—Alphas and Betas. The cost of schooling is the same for each. The average level of schooling and salary for Alpha types is 15 years and $120,000, while the average level of schooling and salary for Beta types is 13 years and $100,000. Why is it that 10 percent, which is calculated as ($120,000 – $100,000)/(15 – 13), is not a good estimate of the annual return to an additional year of education?

d. Suppose you know that the actual annual rate of return on a year of education is 5 percent for both types. Given the numbers in part (c), which type (Alphas or Betas) most likely receives more pure enjoyment from education?

Selected Readings

Joshua Angrist and Alan B. Krueger, "Does Compulsory Schooling Affect Schooling and Earnings?" *Quarterly Journal of Economics* 106 (November 1991): 979–1014.

Orley C. Ashenfelter and Alan B. Krueger, "Estimates of the Economic Return to Schooling from a New Sample of Twins," *American Economic Review* 84 (December 1994): 1157–1173.

Yoram Ben-Porath, "The Production of Human Capital and the Life Cycle of Earnings," *Journal of Political Economy* 75 (August 1967): 352–365.

Raj Chetty, John N. Friedman, Nathaniel Hilger, Emmanuel Saez, Diane Whitmore Schanzenbach, and Danny Yagan, "How Does Your Kindergarten Classroom Affect Your Earnings? Evidence from Project STAR," *Quarterly Journal of Economics*, forthcoming 2011.

Eric Maurin and Sandra McNally, "Vive la Revolution! Long-Term Educational Returns of 1968 to the Angry Students," *Journal of Labor Economics* 26 (January 2008): 1–33.

David Card and Alan B. Krueger, "Does School Quality Matter? Returns to Education and the Characteristics of Public Schools in the United States," *Journal of Political Economy* 100 (February 1992): 1–40.

A. Michael Spence, "Job Market Signaling," *Quarterly Journal of Economics* 87 (August 1973): 355–374.

Robert J. Willis and Sherwin Rosen, "Education and Self-Selection," *Journal of Political Economy* 87 (October 1979 Supplement): S7–S36.

Web Links

The U.S. Department of Education's Web site provides an essential introduction to many of the education programs in the United States: www.ed.gov/index.jsp.

The American Council on Education gives useful information to prospective takers of the General Education Development (GED) exam: www.acenet.edu/calec/ged.

Chapter 7

The Wage Structure

What makes equality such a difficult business is that we only want it with our superiors.

—Henry Becque

The laws of supply and demand determine the structure of wages in the labor market. There is bound to be some inequality in the allocation of rewards among workers. Some workers will typically command much higher earnings than others. In the end, the observed wage dispersion reflects two "fundamentals" of the labor market. First, there exist productivity differences among workers. The greater these productivity differences, the more unequal the wage distribution will be. Second, the rate of return to skills will vary across labor markets and over time, responding to changes in the supply and demand for skills. The greater the rewards for skills, the greater the wage gap between skilled and unskilled workers, and the more unequal the distribution of income.[1]

This chapter examines the factors that determine the shape of the wage distribution. In all industrialized labor markets, the wage distribution exhibits a long tail at the top end of the distribution. In other words, a few workers get a very large share of the rewards distributed by the labor market.

The shape of the wage distribution in the United States changed in historic ways during the 1980s. There was a sizable increase in inequality as the wage gap between high-skill and low-skill workers, as well as the wage dispersion within a particular skill group, rose rapidly. Although the fact that income inequality rose in the United States is indisputable, we have not yet reached a consensus on *why* this happened. A great deal of research has established that no single culprit can explain the changes in the wage structure. Instead, changes in labor market institutions and in economic conditions seem to have worked jointly to create a historic shift in how the U.S. labor market allocates its rewards among workers.

This chapter concludes by showing how wage differentials among workers can persist from generation to generation. Because parents care about the well-being of their children, many parents will make substantial investments in their children's human capital.

---

[1] For convenience, this chapter uses the terms *income distribution, earnings distribution,* and *wage distribution* interchangeably.

These investments induce a positive correlation between the earnings of parents and the earnings of children, ensuring that part of the wage dispersion observed in the current generation will be preserved into the next.

7-1   The Earnings Distribution

Figure 7-1 illustrates the distribution of full-time weekly earnings for working men in the United States in 2010. The mean weekly wage was $928 and the median was $760. The wage distribution exhibits two important properties. First, there is a lot of wage dispersion. Second, the wage distribution is not symmetrical with similar-looking tails on both sides of the distribution. Instead, the wage distribution is positively skewed—it has a long right tail. A **positively skewed wage distribution** implies that the bulk of workers earn relatively low wages and that a small number of workers in the upper tail of the distribution receive a disproportionately large share of the rewards.[2]

As Table 7-1 shows, there are sizable differences in the shape of the income distribution across countries. The top 10 percent of U.S. households get 30 percent of the total income. The respective statistic for Belgium is 28 percent; for Germany, 22 percent, and for Mexico, 41 percent. Similarly, the bottom 10 percent of the households receive only

FIGURE 7-1   **The Wage Distribution in the United States, 2010**

Source: U.S. Bureau of Labor Statistics, *Current Population Survey, Outgoing Rotation Group*, 2010.

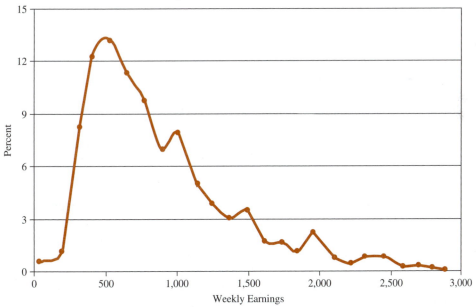

[2] A good description of the characteristics of the U.S. income distribution is given by Frank Levy, *The New Dollars and Dreams: American Incomes and Economic Change*, New York: Russell Sage, 1999.

TABLE 7-1   International Differences in the Income Distribution

Source: World Bank, *World Development Indicators,* CD-ROM, 2010. The statistics report the shape of the income distribution as of 2000 for most countries.

Country	Percentage of Total Income Received by Bottom 10% of Households	Percentage of Total Income Received by Top 10% of Households
Australia	2%	25%
Austria	3	23
Belgium	3	28
Canada	3	25
Chile	2	42
Dominican Republic	2	38
France	3	25
Germany	3	22
Guatemala	1	43
Hungary	4	24
India	4	31
Israel	2	29
Italy	2	27
Mexico	1	41
Norway	4	23
Sweden	4	22
United Kingdom	2	29
United States	2	30

2 percent of the income in the United States. The poorest households receive 3 percent of the income in Canada, but they only receive 1 percent in Guatemala.

Most studies of the shape of the wage distribution use the human capital model as a point of departure. This approach has proved popular because it helps us understand many of the key characteristics of the wage distributions that are typically observed in modern labor markets. In the human capital framework, wage differentials exist not only because some workers accumulate more human capital than others, but also because young workers are still accumulating skills (and are forgoing earnings), whereas older workers are collecting the returns from prior investments.

The human capital model also provides an interesting explanation for the positive skewness in the wage distribution. Recall that a worker invests in human capital up to the point where the marginal rate of return to the investment equals the rate of discount. This stopping rule generates a positively skewed wage distribution *even if the distribution of ability in the population is symmetric.* To illustrate, suppose that a third of the workforce is composed of low-ability workers, a third is composed of medium-ability workers, and the remaining third is composed of high-ability workers. Furthermore, suppose all workers have the same rate of discount.

Figure 7-2 illustrates the investment decision for workers in each of the ability groups. The curve MRR_L gives the marginal rate of return schedule for low-ability workers. This

FIGURE 7-2   **Income Distribution When Workers Differ in Ability**

Low-ability workers face the marginal rate of return schedule MRR_L and acquire H_L units of human capital. High-ability workers face the MRR_H schedule and acquire H_H units of human capital. High-ability workers earn more than low-ability workers both because they have more ability and because they acquire more human capital. The positive correlation between ability and acquired human capital "stretches out" the wage distribution, creating positive skewness.

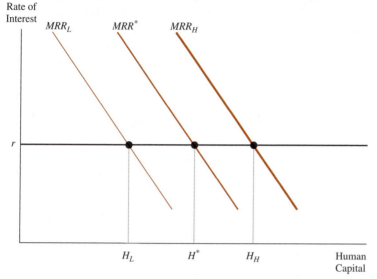

group will acquire H_L efficiency units of human capital. Similarly, the curve MRR^* gives the schedule for medium-ability workers, who acquire H^* units; and the curve MRR_H gives the schedule for high-ability workers, who acquire H_H units. High-ability workers, therefore, have higher wages than low-ability workers for two distinct reasons. First, high-ability workers would earn more than low-ability workers even if both groups acquired the same amount of human capital. After all, ability is itself a characteristic that increases productivity and earnings. High-ability workers also earn more because they acquire more human capital than less able workers. Put differently, the positive correlation between ability and human capital investments "stretches out" wages in the population, generating a positively skewed distribution.

7-2   Measuring Inequality

There are several ways of measuring the extent of inequality in an income distribution.[3] Many of the measures are based on calculations of how much income goes to particular segments of the distribution. To illustrate, consider an extreme example. Suppose we rank

[3] A large literature addresses the important question of how income inequality is best measured. A good summary is given by Daniel J. Slottje, *The Structure of Earnings and the Measurement of Income Inequality in the U.S.* Amsterdam: Elsevier, 1989.

all households according to their income level, from lowest to highest. Let's now break the population of households into five groups of equal size. The first quintile contains the 20 percent of the households with the lowest incomes and the fifth quintile contains the 20 percent of the households with the highest incomes.

We can now calculate how much income accrues to households in each quintile. If every household in this example earned the same income—so that there were perfect income equality—it would be the case that 20 percent of the income accrues to the first quintile, 20 percent of the income accrues to the second quintile, 20 percent of the income accrues to the third quintile, and so on. We can summarize these data graphically by relating the *cumulative* share of income accruing to the various groups. In the case of perfect equality, the result would be the straight line *AB* in Figure 7-3. This line indicates that 20 percent of the income accrues to the bottom 20 percent of the households; 40 percent of the income accrues to the bottom 40 percent of the households; 60 percent of the income accrues to the bottom 60 percent of the households. The line *AB* is called a **Lorenz curve;** it reports the cumulative share of the income accruing to the various quintiles of households. The "perfect-equality" Lorenz curve must be a straight line with a 45° angle.

Table 7-2 reports the actual distribution of household income in the United States as of 2006. The bottom 20 percent of the households received 3.4 percent of all income and the next quintile received 8.6 percent. The cumulative share received by the bottom two quintiles must then be 12.0 percent. Obviously, the cumulative share received by all quintiles must equal 1.0.

FIGURE 7-3 **The Lorenz Curve and the Gini Coefficient**

The "perfect-equality" Lorenz curve is given by the line *AB,* indicating that each quintile of households gets 20 percent of aggregate income, while the Lorenz curve describing the actual income distribution lies below it. The ratio of the shaded area to the area in the triangle *ABC* gives the Gini coefficient.

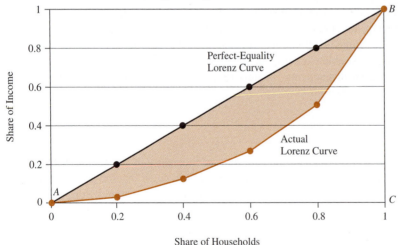

TABLE 7-2 **Household Shares of Aggregate Income, by Fifths of the Income Distribution, 2010**

Source: U.S. Bureau of the Census, *Income, Poverty, and Health Insurance Coverage in the United States: 2010,* Table 3; http://www.census.gov/prod/2010pubs/p60-238.pdf.

Quintile	Share of Income	Cumulative Share of Income
First	0.034	0.034
Second	0.086	0.120
Third	0.147	0.267
Fourth	0.233	0.500
Fifth	0.500	1.000

Figure 7-3 also illustrates the Lorenz curve derived from the actual distribution of household income. This Lorenz curve lies below the perfect-equality Lorenz curve. In fact, the construction of the Lorenz curve suggests that the more inequality in an income distribution, the further away the actual Lorenz curve will be from the 45° line. To illustrate, consider a world in which all income accrues to the fifth quintile, the top fifth of the households. In this world of "perfect inequality," the Lorenz curve would look like a mirror image of the letter L; it would lie flat along the horizontal axis, so that 0 percent of the income accrues to 80 percent of the households, and then shoot up so that 100 percent of the income accrues to 100 percent of the households.[4]

The intuition behind the construction of the Lorenz curve suggests that the area between the perfect-equality Lorenz curve and the actual Lorenz curve can be used to measure inequality. The **Gini coefficient** is defined as

$$\text{Gini coefficient} = \frac{\text{Area between perfect-equality Lorenz curve and actual Lorenz curve}}{\text{Area under perfect-equality Lorenz curve}} \quad \textbf{(7-1)}$$

In terms of Figure 7-3, the Gini coefficient is given by the ratio of the shaded area to the triangle given by *ABC*.[5] This definition implies that the Gini coefficient would be 0 when the actual distribution of income exhibits perfect equality and would equal 1 when the distribution of income exhibits perfect inequality (that is, when all income goes to the highest quintile). By repeatedly calculating the areas of various triangles and rectangles in Figure 7-3 and then applying equation (7-1), it is easy to show that the Gini coefficient for household income in the United States is 0.43.

Although an increase in the Gini coefficient represents an increase in income inequality, there are subtleties that are being overlooked by summarizing the entire shape of the income distribution into a single number. Consider, for example, the impact of a shift in income from the bottom quintile to the top quintile. This shift obviously increases the Gini

[4] It is possible for two "real-world" Lorenz curves to intersect. It would then be difficult to ascertain which of the two distributions is more unequal.

[5] Note that the area of the triangle *ABC* must equal 0.5.

coefficient. It turns out that we can obtain a similar numerical increase in the Gini coefficient by transferring some amount of income from, say, the second and third quintiles to the top quintile. Although the numerical increase in the Gini coefficient is the same, the two redistributions are not identical.

Because of this ambiguity, many studies use additional measures of inequality. Two commonly used measures are the **90-10 wage gap** and the **50-10 wage gap.** The 90-10 wage gap gives the percent wage differential between the worker at the 90th percentile of the income distribution and the worker at the 10th percentile. The 90-10 wage gap thus provides a measure of the range of the income distribution. The 50-10 wage gap gives the percent wage differential between the worker at the 50th percentile and the worker at the 10th percentile. The 50-10 wage gap thus provides a measure of inequality between the "middle class" and low-income workers.

7-3 The Wage Structure: Basic Facts

Many studies have attempted to document the historic changes in the U.S. wage distribution that occurred during the 1980s and 1990s.[6] The dispersion in the wage distribution increased substantially in this period. In particular:

- The wage gap between those at the top of the wage distribution and those at the bottom widened dramatically.

- Wage differentials widened among education groups, among experience groups, and among age groups.

- Wage differentials widened within demographic and skill groups. In other words, the wages of workers of the same education, age, sex, occupation, and industry were much more dispersed in the mid-1990s than they were in the late 1970s.

This section briefly documents some of these changes in the U.S. wage structure. Figure 7-4a begins the descriptive analysis by showing the trend in the Gini coefficient. The Gini coefficient declined steadily from the 1930s through 1950. It was then relatively stable until about 1970, when it began a dramatic rise. Note also that most of the increase in the Gini coefficient in the past 30 years is due to the widening of the 80-50 wage gap, suggesting that it is the "stretching" of income at the upper end of the distribution that is mostly responsible for the rise in inequality.

---

[6] The key studies include Kevin M. Murphy and Finis Welch, "The Structure of Wages," *Quarterly Journal of Economics* 107 (February 1992): 285–326; Lawrence F. Katz and Kevin M. Murphy, "Changes in Relative Wages, 1963–1987: Supply and Demand Factors," *Quarterly Journal of Economics* 107 (February 1992): 35–78; and Chinhui Juhn, Kevin M. Murphy, and Brooks Pierce, "Wage Inequality and the Rise in Returns to Skills," *Journal of Political Economy* 101 (June 1993): 410–442. An excellent review of the literature is given by Lawrence F. Katz and David H. Autor, "Changes in Wage Structure and Earnings Inequality," in Orley Ashenfelter and David Card, editors, *Handbook of Labor Economics,* vol. 3A, Amsterdam: Elsevier, 1999, pp. 1463–1555.

FIGURE 7-4   Earnings Inequality, 1937–2005

Wojciech Kopczuk, Emmanuel Saez, and Jae Song, "Earnings Inequality and Mobility in the United States from Social Security Data Since 1937," *Quarterly Journal of Economics* 125 (February 2010): 91–128.

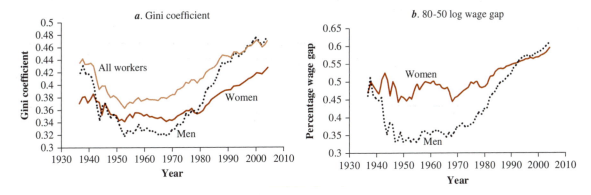

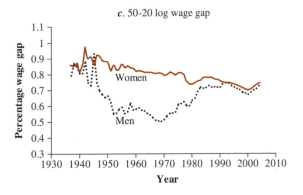

Figure 7-5 shows that some of the increase in wage inequality can be directly attributed to a sizable increase in the returns to schooling. In particular, the figure illustrates the 1963–2005 trend in the percent wage differential between college graduates and high school graduates. This wage gap rose slightly throughout the 1960s until about 1971. It then began to decline until about 1979, when it made "a great U-turn" and began a very rapid rise. In 1979, college graduates earned 47 percent more than high school graduates. By 2001, college graduates earned 90 percent more than high school graduates. If we interpret the wage gap across education groups as a measure of the rate of return to skills, the data illustrated in Figure 7-5 suggest that the structural changes in the U.S. labor market led to a historic increase in the rewards for skills. It is important to emphasize that there was a concurrent rise in the wage gap between experienced workers and new labor market entrants. In other words, the returns to skill, whether in terms of schooling or experience, rose dramatically in the past two decades.

There is also a great deal of evidence suggesting that wage inequality increased not only across schooling groups or across experience groups, but also *within* narrowly defined skill groups. Figure 7-6 shows the trend in the average 90-10 wage gap within a group of workers who have the same age, education, gender, and race. This measure of "residual"

FIGURE 7-5   **Wage Differential between College Graduates and High School Graduates, 1963–2005**

Source: David H. Autor, Lawrence F. Katz, and Melissa S. Kearney, "Trends in U.S. Wage Inequality: Revising the Revisionists," *Review of Economics and Statistics* 90 (May 2008): 300–323. The percent wage differentials give the differences in weekly earnings for full-time, full-year workers who are 18 to 65 years old.

FIGURE 7-6   **Trend in the "Residual" 90-10 Wage Gap, 1963–2006**

Source: David H. Autor, Lawrence F. Katz, and Melissa S. Kearney, "Trends in U.S. Wage Inequality: Revising the Revisionists," *Review of Economics and Statistics* 90 (May 2008): 300–323. The wage differentials give the differences in weekly earnings for full-time, full-year workers who are 18 to 65 years old and have similar socioeconomic characteristics, including education, age, and race.

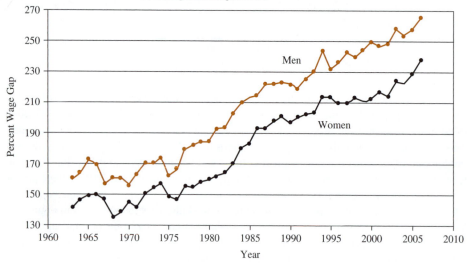

wage inequality shows a striking upward trend from the late 1970s to the late 1990s.[7] In other words, wage dispersion increased even within groups of workers who offer relatively similar characteristics to employers.

---

[7] There is also evidence indicating that income inequality increased even within narrowly defined occupation and industry groups.

The evidence summarized in this section leads to an unambiguous and striking conclusion. Between 1980 and 2006, the U.S. labor market witnessed a sizable increase in wage inequality—both across and within skill groups. This fact ranks among the most important economic events of the last half of the twentieth century, and its social, economic, and political consequences are sure to be felt for many decades.

7-4 Policy Application: Why Did Wage Inequality Increase?

Although the increase in wage inequality in the 1980s and 1990s is well documented, there is still a lot of disagreement over *why* this increase in inequality took place. Many researchers have searched for the smoking gun that would explain the historic change in the wage structure. The search, however, has not been successful. No single factor seems to be able to explain all—or even most—of the changes in the wage structure. Instead, the increase in inequality seems to have been caused by concurrent changes in economic "fundamentals" and labor market institutions.

For the most part, the studies that attempt to explain why inequality increased in the United States use a simple framework that illustrates how shifts in the labor supply and labor demand curves could have caused such a sizable increase in wage inequality.[8] Suppose there are two types of workers in the labor market: skilled and unskilled. Let r be the wage ratio between skilled and unskilled workers and let p be the ratio of the number of skilled workers to the number of unskilled workers.

Figure 7-7 illustrates the basic model. The downward-sloping demand curve gives the demand for skilled workers *relative* to the demand for unskilled workers. It is downward sloping because the greater the wage gap between skilled and unskilled workers (that is, the greater r), the lower the fraction of skilled workers that employers would like to hire (the lower p). For simplicity, suppose that the relative supply of skilled workers is perfectly inelastic. The assumption that p is constant means that a certain fraction of the workforce is skilled regardless of the wage gap between skilled and unskilled workers. In the long run, of course, this assumption is false because an increase in the rewards for skills would likely induce many more workers to stay in school and acquire more human capital.

Initially, the relative supply and demand curves are given by S_0 and D_0, respectively. The competitive labor market then attains equilibrium at point A in Figure 7-7. In equilibrium, a fraction p_0 of the workforce is skilled and the relative wage of skilled workers is given by r_0. In the context of this simple model, there are only two ways in which changes in the underlying economic conditions could have increased the wage gap between skilled and unskilled workers. The first would be for the supply curve to shift to the left, indicating a reduction in the relative number of skilled workers, and, hence, driving up their relative wage. The second would be for the demand curve to shift to the right, indicating a relative increase in the demand for skilled workers, and, again, driving up their relative wage.

As we will see shortly, there has been a sizable *increase* in the relative number of skilled workers in the United States in recent decades, shifting the relative supply curve outwards to S_1. In the absence of any other changes in the labor market, this supply shift

[8] See Murphy and Welch, "The Structure of Wages"; Katz and Murphy, "Changes in Relative Wages, 1963–1987: Supply and Demand Factors"; and David Card and Thomas Lemieux, "Can Falling Supply Explain the Rising Return to College for Younger Men," *Quarterly Journal of Economics* 116 (May 2001): 705–746.

FIGURE 7-7 **Changes in the Wage Structure Resulting from Shifts in Supply and Demand**

The downward-sloping demand curve implies that employers wish to hire relatively fewer skilled workers when the relative wage of skilled workers is high. The perfectly inelastic supply curve indicates that the relative number of skilled workers is fixed. Initially, the labor market is in equilibrium at point A. Suppose the relative supply of skilled workers increased to S_1. The rising relative wage of skilled workers can then be explained only if there was a sizable outward shift in the relative demand curve (ending up at point C).

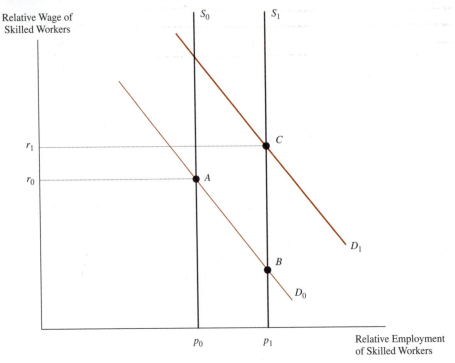

should have moved the labor market to equilibrium point B, *reducing* the relative wage of skilled workers. The type of supply shift that seems to have actually occurred in the United States, therefore, cannot explain why there was a rapid rise in the relative wage of skilled workers. In terms of the simple model in Figure 7-7, it must have been the case that the relative demand curve for skilled workers also shifted to the right, to D_1. If this demand shift is sufficiently large, the final equilibrium at point C is characterized by an increase in the fraction of skilled workers in the labor market *and* by a larger wage gap between skilled and unskilled workers.

The supply-demand framework clearly shows that any attempt to understand the rise in the relative wage of skilled workers must identify factors that increased the relative demand for skilled labor. Moreover, this rightward shift in the demand curve must have been sufficiently large to outweigh the impact of the increase in the relative supply of skilled workers. In a sense, the relative supply and demand curves for skilled workers were in a race in recent years—both curves were shifting to the right. The observed trend in wage inequality suggests that the demand curve "won" the race in the sense that the relative demand for skilled workers was rising at a faster rate than the relative supply of skilled workers.

TABLE 7-3   **Educational Composition of the Workforce (Percent Distribution of Workers by Education)**

Source: David H. Autor, Lawrence F. Katz, and Alan B. Krueger, "Computing Inequality: How Computers Changed the Labor Market," *Quarterly Journal of Economics* 113 (November 1998): 1169–1213, Table 1.

Year	High School Dropouts	High School Graduates	Some College	College Graduates
1960	49.5%	27.7%	12.2%	10.6%
1970	35.9	34.7	15.6	13.8
1980	19.1	38.0	22.0	20.9
1990	12.7	36.2	25.1	26.1
1996	9.4	33.4	28.9	28.3

Although there has been a lot of debate over which factors best explain these shifts in the labor market, the existing research has isolated a few key variables that have become the "usual suspects" in any analysis of the changes in the wage structure.

Supply Shifts

As noted above, there was a sizable increase in the relative number of skilled workers in the 1980s and 1990s. Table 7-3 shows how the educational composition of employment shifted between 1960 and 1996. In 1960, almost half the workforce lacked a high school diploma and only 11 percent were college graduates. By 1996, fewer than 10 percent of workers lacked a high school diploma and 28 percent were college graduates. These supply shifts toward a more skilled workforce clearly indicate that changes in the relative supply of skilled workers alone cannot explain the post-1979 rise in wage inequality. Such an increase in the relative supply of skilled workers should have narrowed, rather than widened, the wage gap between skilled and unskilled workers.

Nevertheless, some of the changes in wage inequality can be attributed to supply shifts.[9] As Table 7-3 shows, there was only a relatively slight change in the supply of educated workers in the 1960s, but there was a substantial change in the 1970s, with the growth slowing down somewhat after that. It is suspected that the labor market entry of the baby boom cohort in the 1970s shifted out the supply curve of college graduates at the time, thus depressing the payoff to a college education throughout much of that decade. In fact, there was a decline in the relative wage of skilled workers between 1970 and 1979 (see Figure 7-5). Similarly, there is evidence that the changing rewards for similarly educated workers who differ in their experience may be due to "cohort effects," changes in the number of workers in particular age groups that reflect long-run demographic shifts.[10]

One particular supply shift that has received some attention is the increase in the number of immigrants in the U.S. labor market. Nearly 25 million legal immigrants were admitted between 1966 and 2000, and an additional 8 million foreign-born persons lived in the United States illegally in 2000.

[9] Richard B. Freeman, *The Overeducated American,* New York: Academic Press, 1976; Finis Welch, "Effects of Cohort Size on Earnings: The Baby Boom Babies' Financial Bust," *Journal of Political Economy* 87 (October 1979, Part 2): S65–S97; and Katz and Murphy, "Changes in Relative Wages, 1963–1987: Supply and Demand Factors."

[10] David Card and Thomas Lemieux, "Can Falling Supply Explain the Rising Return to College for Younger Men? A Cohort-Based Analysis," *Quarterly Journal of Economics* 116 (May 2001): 705–746.

This supply shift would not affect the relative wage of skilled and unskilled workers if the immigrant flow were "balanced" in the sense that it had the same skill composition as the native-born workforce. A balanced immigrant flow would not change relative supply—the number of skilled workers per unskilled worker would remain the same. It turns out, however, that the actual immigration that occurred between 1979 and 1995 increased the supply of high school dropouts by 20.7 percent but increased the supply of workers with at least a high school education by only 4.1 percent.[11] In other words, the supply shift attributable to immigration greatly increased the relative number of workers at the very bottom of the skill distribution.

The wage of high school dropouts relative to that of high school graduates fell by 14.9 percent during the 1979–1995 period. Some studies have attempted to determine if the large increase in the relative number of high school dropouts attributable to immigration can account for the large decline in relative wages experienced by the least-educated native workers. The available data suggest that perhaps a third of the decline in the relative wages of high school dropouts between 1980 and 1995 can be directly traced to immigration.[12]

It seems, therefore, that shifts in the relative supply curve—such as the labor market entry of the relatively well-educated baby boom cohort in the 1970s, or the increase in the number of unskilled immigrants in the 1980s—can account for some of the changes in the wage structure. It is important to emphasize, however, that supply shifts alone cannot explain the basic fact of the overall increase in wage inequality. After all, the number of college graduates relative to the number of high school graduates continued to rise in the 1980s—at the same time that the relative wage of college graduates was rising. Similarly, the rise in wage inequality *within* skill groups probably has little to do with immigration. In short, it is impossible to explain the increase in the wage gap between college and high school graduates in the 1980s and 1990s without resorting to a story where shifts in the relative demand curve play the dominant role.

International Trade

Some researchers attribute part of the increase in the relative demand for skilled workers to the internationalization of the U.S. economy.[13] In 1970, the ratio of exports and imports to GDP stood at 8 percent; by 1996, this ratio had risen to about 19 percent. And much of this increase can be attributed to trade with less-developed countries. By 1996, nearly 40 percent of all imports came from these countries.

---

[11] George J. Borjas, Richard B. Freeman, and Lawrence F. Katz, "How Much Do Immigration and Trade Affect Labor Market Outcomes?" *Brookings Papers on Economic Activity* (1997): 1–67.

[12] George J. Borjas, "The Labor Demand Curve *Is* Downward Sloping: Reexamining the Impact of Immigration on the Labor Market," *Quarterly Journal of Economics* 118 (November 2003): 1335–1374; and George J. Borjas and Lawrence F. Katz, "The Evolution of the Mexican-Born Workforce in the U.S. Labor Market," in George J. Borjas, editor, *Mexican Immigration to the United States,* Chicago: University of Chicago Press, 2007.

[13] Kevin M. Murphy and Finis Welch, "The Role of International Trade in Wage Differentials," in Marvin Kosters, editor, *Workers and Their Wages,* Washington, DC: AEI Press, 1991, pp. 39–69; and Robert C. Feenstra and Gordon H. Hanson, "The Impact of Outsourcing and High-Technology Capital on Wages: Estimates for the United States, 1979–1990," *Quarterly Journal of Economics* 114 (August 1999): 907–940. For some contradictory evidence, see Robert Z. Lawrence and Matthew J. Slaughter, "International Trade and American Wages in the 1980s: Giant Sucking Sound or Small Hiccup," *Brookings Papers on Economic Activity* (1993): 161–226.

Not surprisingly, the United States tends to export different types of goods than it imports.[14] The workers employed in the importing industries tend to be less educated, and the workers employed in the exporting industries tend to be well educated. Put simply, imports hurt the less skilled, whereas exports help the skilled.

The internationalization of the U.S. economy—with rising exports and even more rapidly rising imports—would then have a beneficial impact on the demand for skilled workers and an adverse impact on the demand for unskilled workers. As foreign consumers increased their demand for the types of goods produced by American skilled workers, the labor demand for these skilled workers rose. As American consumers increased their demand for foreign goods produced by unskilled workers, domestic firms hired fewer unskilled workers because the goods that they used to produce are now produced abroad at lower costs. In short, the increase in foreign trade increased the demand for skilled labor at the same time that it reduced the demand for unskilled labor. The globalization of the U.S. economy, therefore, can be graphically represented as an outward shift in the relative labor demand curve in Figure 7-7.

It is also worth noting that many of the U.S. industries hardest hit by imports (such as automobiles and steel) were industries that were highly concentrated and unionized and paid relatively high wages.[15] The high degree of concentration in these industries suggests that these industries can be quite profitable. In fact, it is these excess profits that attract foreign imports. Because these industries tend to be unionized, the unions ensure that the excess profits are shared between the stockholders and the workers. As foreign competition enters the market, part of the "excess" wage paid to American workers in these industries is, in effect, transferred to workers in the exporting countries. Moreover, as the targeted industries cut employment, many of the less-skilled workers will have to move to the nonunion, competitive sectors of the labor market, pushing down the competitive wage.

Many researchers have attempted to measure the contribution of foreign trade to the changes in the wage structure. Although there is heated disagreement over the methodology used to measure the impact of trade on relative wages, it seems that increased foreign trade contributed modestly to the rise in wage inequality, probably accounting for less than 20 percent of the increase.

Skill-Biased Technological Change

The demand for skilled workers may have increased by more than the demand for unskilled workers because of **skill-biased technological change.** If the technological advances that are being introduced constantly into the labor market are good substitutes for unskilled workers and complement the skills of highly educated workers, this type of technological change would lower the demand for unskilled labor and increase the demand for skilled labor. For instance, the rapid introduction of the personal computer into the workplace may have had an important impact on the wage structure. Workers who use computers earn more than workers who do not, and workers who use computers tend to be more

[14] Borjas, Freeman, and Katz, "How Much Do Immigration and Trade Affect Labor Market Outcomes?" Table 4.

[15] George J. Borjas and Valerie A. Ramey, "Foreign Competition, Market Power, and Wage Inequality," *Quarterly Journal of Economics* 110 (November 1996): 1075–1110.

highly educated. Skill-biased technological change could then generate the outward shift in the relative labor demand curve illustrated in Figure 7-7.[16]

It should not be too surprising that the introduction of high-tech capital into the labor market is particularly beneficial to highly skilled workers. As we saw in Chapter 3, there is some evidence suggesting that capital and skills are complements—increases in the capital stock help increase the productivity of skilled workers.

Some researchers have argued that skill-biased technological change explains most of the increase in wage inequality in the United States.[17] Although there is some consensus that this type of technological change has probably been an important contributor to increased inequality, there is some debate over whether the existing evidence warrants such a strong conclusion. The debate revolves around the fact that there is no widely accepted measure of skill-biased technological change that one can correlate with the changes in the wage structure.[18] As a result, some studies use a "residual" methodology to measure the impact of technological change on the wage structure. In other words, a typical study will account for the impact of supply shifts, immigration, trade, and so on—and attribute whatever is left unexplained to skill-biased technological change. This methodology is not completely satisfactory because it is attributing the effects of variables that we have not yet thought of or that are hard to measure to skill-biased technological change.

Moreover, a number of studies point out that the timing of the increase in wage inequality cannot be reconciled with the skill-biased technological change hypothesis.[19] These studies argue that much of the increase in wage inequality occurred during the 1980s, and that the information revolution continued (if not accelerated) during the 1990s. There is also strong evidence that data problems with the wage inequality time series tend to

---

[16] Skill-biased technological change also could occur if the technological shift increased the demand for skilled workers at a faster rate than the increase in demand for unskilled workers.

[17] John Bound and George Johnson, "Changes in the Structure of Wages in the 1980s: An Evaluation of Alternative Explanations," *American Economic Review* 82 (June 1992): 371–392; see also Steven J. Davis and John Haltiwanger, "Wage Dispersion between and within U.S. Manufacturing Plants, 1963–1986," *Brookings Paper on Economic Activity: Microeconomics* (1991): 115–180; and Eli Berman, John Bound, and Zvi Griliches, "Changes in the Demand for Skilled Labor within U.S. Manufacturing Industries: Evidence from the Annual Survey of Manufacturing," *Quarterly Journal of Economics* 109 (May 1994): 367–398.

[18] Studies of the link between technological change and wages include Ann P. Bartel and Nachum Sicherman, "Technological Change and Wages: An Interindustry Analysis," *Journal of Political Economy* 107 (April 1999): 285–325; Timothy F. Bresnahan, Erik Brynjolfsson, and Lorin M. Hitt, "Information Technology, Workplace Organization and the Demand for Skilled Workers: Firm-Level Evidence," *Quarterly Journal of Economics* 117 (February 2002): 339–376; Stephen Machin and John Van Reenen, "Technology and Changes in Skill Structure: Evidence from Seven OECD Countries," *Quarterly Journal of Economics* 113 (November 1998): 1215–1244; and Mark Doms, Timothy Dunne, and Kenneth Troske, "Workers, Wages, and Technology," *Quarterly Journal of Economics* 112 (February 1997): 217–252. A review of the literature is given by Daron Acemoglu, "Technical Change, Inequality, and the Labor Market," *Journal of Economic Literature* 40 (March 2002): 7–72.

[19] David Card and John E. DiNardo, "Skill-Biased Technological Change and Rising Wage Inequality: Some Problems and Puzzles," *Journal of Labor Economics* 20 (October 2002): 733–783; and Thomas Lemieux, "Increasing Residual Wage Inequality: Composition Effects, Noisy Data, or Rising Demand for Skill?" *American Economic Review* 96 (June 2006): 461–498.

overstate the increase in inequality during the 1990s. Accounting for these data issues seems to suggest that inequality within skill groups may have *declined* slightly during the 1990s. It would be very difficult to explain this decline in terms of the technological change story unless one is willing to believe that technological change was biased in favor of skilled workers in the 1980s and then biased against them in the 1990s. In short, even though the skill-biased technological change hypothesis has been (and probably remains) a favored explanation for the changing wage structure, research poses a number of questions about its validity that have yet to be resolved satisfactorily.

Institutional Changes in the U.S. Labor Market

There has been a steady decline in the importance of unions in the U.S. labor market. In 1973, 24 percent of the workforce was unionized. By 2006, the proportion of workers who were unionized had fallen to 12 percent.

In the United States, unions have traditionally been considered effective institutions that, on balance, raise the wages of less-skilled workers. A relatively large number of the workers employed in unions do not have college diplomas. And unions have traditionally propped up the wages of these workers, guaranteeing them a wage premium. In fact, as we will see in Chapter 10, many studies suggest that union workers get paid around 15 percent more than nonunion workers—even after adjusting for differences in the skills of those employed in the two sectors.

The weakening bargaining power of unions can be interpreted as an outward shift in the relative demand curve for skilled labor in Figure 7-7. Suppose unions provide a "safety net" for less-skilled workers—guaranteeing that employers demand a certain number of less-skilled workers at a given wage. As union power weakens, employers would be willing to hire the same relative number of less-skilled workers only if less-skilled workers are paid a lower wage—effectively shifting the relative demand up. The decline of unions in the U.S. labor market, therefore, can be an important "shifter" in the relative demand curve for skilled workers. Some studies, in fact, claim that about 10 percent of the increasing wage gap between college graduates and high school graduates can be attributable to the decline in unions.[20]

An additional institutional factor that has traditionally propped up the wage of low-skill workers in the United States is the minimum wage. The *nominal* minimum wage remained constant at $3.35 an hour between 1981 and 1989. In constant 1995 dollars, however, the minimum wage declined from $5.62 an hour in 1981 to $4.12 an hour in 1990. If many of the low-skill workers happen to work at minimum-wage jobs, the decline in the real minimum wage would increase the wage gap between skilled and unskilled workers.

A number of studies have attempted to estimate the impact of the minimum wage on the wage structure.[21] These studies, in a sense, create a "counterfactual" wage distribution where the real minimum wage was constant throughout the 1980s and assume that the higher level of the minimum wage would not have generated any additional unemployment—so that the sample of workers remained roughly constant over time. The studies typically find that there is a substantial impact of the minimum wage on wages at the very bottom of the distribution. Because so few educated workers get paid the minimum wage, however, the minimum wage hypothesis cannot provide a credible explanation of the increase in the wage differential between college graduates and high school graduates or of why wage inequality rose within the group of educated workers.

Problems with the Existing Explanations

As the discussion suggests, each of the usual suspects (that is, changes in labor supply, the de-unionization of the labor market, minimum wages, international trade, immigration, and skill-biased technological change) seems to be able to explain some part of the change in the U.S. wage structure. The main lesson provided by the literature is that no single "story" can explain the bulk of the changes that occurred in the U.S. wage structure. Some of the

[20] John DiNardo, Nicole Fortin, and Thomas Lemieux, "Labor Market Institutions and the Distribution of Wages, 1973–1992: A Semi-Parametric Approach," *Econometrica* 64 (September 1996): 1001–1044; Richard B. Freeman, "How Much Has De-Unionization Contributed to the Rise in Male Earnings Inequality?" in Sheldon Danziger and Peter Gottschalk, editors, *Uneven Tides,* New York: Russell Sage, 1993, pp. 133–163; David Card, "The Effects of Unions on the Structure of Wages: A Longitudinal Analysis," *Econometrica* 64 (July 1996): 957–979; and David Card, Thomas Lemieux, and Craig W. Riddell, "Unions and Wage Inequality," *Journal of Labor Research* 25 (2004): 519–562.

[21] DiNardo, Fortin, and Lemieux, "Labor Market Institutions and the Distribution of Wages"; David Lee, "Wage Inequality in the United States during the 1980s: Rising Dispersion or Falling Minimum Wage," *Quarterly Journal of Economics* 114 (August 1999): 977–1023; and Coen Teulings, "The Contribution of Minimum Wages to Increasing Wage Inequality," *Economic Journal* 113 (October 2003): 801–833.

TABLE 7-4
International Trends in Wage Inequality for Male Workers (90-10 Percent Wage Gap)

Source: OECD, *Employment Outlook,* July 1996, Paris: OECD, Table 3.1.

Country	1984	1994
Australia	174.6	194.5
Canada	301.5	278.1
Finland	150.9	153.5
France	232.0	242.1
Germany	138.7	124.8
Italy	129.3	163.8
Japan	177.3	177.3
Netherlands	150.9	158.6
New Zealand	171.8	215.8
Norway	105.4	97.4
Sweden	103.4	120.3
United Kingdom	177.3	222.2
United States	266.9	326.3

variables (for example, immigration or trade) can explain the increasing wage gap between skilled and unskilled workers but fail to explain why inequality increased within skill groups. Similarly, the stability of the minimum wage may explain why the real wage of low-skill workers fell but cannot explain why the real wage of workers at the top of the skill distribution rose rapidly. And the leading explanation—skill-biased technological change—does not seem to be consistent with the timing of the changes in the wage structure.

In the end, any truly complete accounting of what happened to the U.S. wage structure will have to explain both the timing of the changes in inequality as well as the structure of these changes throughout the entire labor market. As a result, labor economists have found it very difficult to reach a consensus on these issues. It is fair to conclude that we still do not have a good sense of why wage inequality increased so rapidly in the past quarter century.

Moreover, any story that we eventually develop must confront an additional empirical puzzle. As Table 7-4 shows, the wage structure of different developed countries did not evolve in similar ways over the past two decades. For example, in the United Kingdom, the percentage wage gap between the 90th percentile and the 10th percentile worker rose from 177 to 222 percent between 1984 and 1994, whereas in Germany it fell from 139 to 125 percent. Presumably, the skill-biased technological change induced by the Information Revolution occurred simultaneously in most of these advanced economies. One might then expect that the wage structure of these countries would have changed in roughly similar ways. Many researchers have noted that these countries have very different labor market institutions—particularly with regards to the safety nets designed to protect the well-being of low-skill workers.[22] It is also well known that the various countries have experienced

---

[22] See the studies in Richard B. Freeman and Lawrence F. Katz, editors, *Differences and Changes in Wage Structures,* Chicago: University of Chicago Press, 1995. See also Francine D. Blau and Lawrence M. Kahn, "International Differences in Male Wages Inequality: Institutions versus Market Forces," *Journal of Political Economy* 104 (August 1996): 791–837; and David Card, Francis Kramarz, and Thomas Lemieux, "Changes in the Relative Structure of Wages and Employment: A Comparison of the United States, Canada, and France," *Canadian Journal of Economics* 32 (August 1999): 843–877; and Christian Dustmann, Johannes Lundsteck, and Uta Schönberg, "Revisiting the German Wage Structure," *Quarterly Journal of Economics* 124 (May 2009): 843–881.

very different trends in the unemployment rate. The unemployment rate in the United States declined throughout much of the 1990s—at the same time that the unemployment rate in many western European countries rose rapidly.

It has been suggested that the changes in wage inequality and the changes in unemployment experienced by these countries are reverse sides of the same coin.[23] The same factors that led to widening wage inequality in the United States—where the institutional framework of the labor market permits such wage dispersion to grow and persist—manifested itself as higher unemployment rates in those countries where the safety net mechanisms did not allow for wages to change.[24]

In short, the labor market in some countries responded to the increase in the relative demand for skilled workers by changing quantities (that is, employment). In other countries, the market responded by changing prices (that is, wages). Although this hypothesis is quite provocative and has generated much interest, we do not yet know if the explanations of the rise in U.S. wage inequality also can explain the trends in labor market conditions experienced by other developed countries.

7-5   The Earnings of Superstars

In the last section, we analyzed some of the factors responsible for a widening of the wage distribution. This analysis is useful in helping us understand trends in wage differences between broadly defined skilled and unskilled groups. We now turn to an analysis of how economic rewards are determined at the very top of the wage distribution.

It is a widespread characteristic of wage distributions in advanced economies that a very small number of workers in some professions get a very large share of the rewards. Table 7-5, for example, reports the income of the top 15 "superstars" in the entertainment industry. Even though most aspiring actors and singers are reportedly waiting on tables or driving cabs at any point in time, a few established entertainers commanded salaries exceeding $50 million annually. Similarly, most of us do not get paid when we play baseball with our friends and the typical rookie in the minor leagues earns only $1100 per month during the season. Nevertheless, Alex Rodriguez (of the New York Yankees), the highest-paid person in the history of baseball, earns $32.0 million annually.[25] The fact that a few persons in some professions earn astronomically high salaries and seem to dominate the field has come to be known as the **superstar phenomenon.**

Interestingly, the superstar phenomenon does not occur in every occupation. For example, the most talented professors in research universities (such as recent Nobel Prize winners) might earn three or four times the entering salary of a newly minted Ph.D. The entry salary of an assistant professor of economics was around $100,000 in 2010. Few

---

[23] Adrian Wood, "How Trade Hurt Unskilled Workers," *Journal of Economic Perspectives* 9 (Summer 1995): 57–80.

[24] There is some debate as to whether the *relative* unemployment rate of less-skilled workers rose in some of the European countries. See, for example, Stephen Nickell and Brian Bell, "Changes in the Distribution of Wages and Unemployment in OECD Countries," *American Economic Review* 86 (May 1996): 302–308; and Card, Kramarz, and Lemieux, "Changes in the Relative Structure of Wages and Employment: A Comparison of the United States, Canada, and France."

[25] Detailed salary data for major league baseball is online at http://asp.usatoday.com/sports/baseball/salaries/default.aspx.

TABLE 7-5

The Income of Superstars in the Entertainment Industry

Source: Reported income is from entertainment sources. *Forbes, Magazine:* http://www.forbes.com/lists/2010/53/celeb-100-10_The-Celebrity-100.html.

Rank	Name	2010 Income (in millions of dollars)
1	Oprah Winfrey	315
2	James Cameron	210
3	U2	130
4	Tyler Perry	125
5	Michael Bay	120
6	AC/DC	114
7	Tiger Woods	105
8	Steven Spielberg	100
8	Jerry Bruckheimer	100
10	George Lucas	95
11	Beyonce Knowles	87
12	Simon Cowell	80
12	Dr. Phil McGraw	80
14	Johnny Depp	75
14	Jerry Seinfeld	75

academic economists, regardless of their stellar standing in the profession, earn more than $300,000 per year from their university jobs. Similarly, it is doubtful that even the most talented grocery clerks earn more than two or three times the salary of the typical grocery clerk. The upper tail of the earnings distribution, therefore, "stretches" for persons who have a slightly more powerful stage presence or are better baseball players, yet does not stretch very much for college professors or grocery clerks.

To understand why the very talented earn much more in some occupations and not in others, let's begin by noting the obvious: The various sellers of a particular service are not perfect substitutes.[26] We can all hit a ball with a bat. But even if we were to make 1,000 trips to the plate, the excitement and "output" generated by our pathetic attempts would not compare with the excitement and output generated by a single trip to the plate by great hitters like Babe Ruth or Hank Aaron. Similarly, the best song chosen from the lifetime work of a randomly selected rock group pales when compared to the artistry and craftsmanship of the typical Beatles song. Different people have different abilities even when they attempt to perform the same type of job.

We, as consumers, prefer seeing a great baseball player and hearing the beautiful melodies and songs of Mozart and the Beatles rather than seeing mediocre baseball players fail miserably or listening to the latest (and instantly forgettable) dribble emanating from the radio. In other words, we will prefer to attend a single Major League Baseball game where a legendary pitcher or hitter is scheduled to play rather than attend five other randomly chosen games, and to purchase the Beatles' *Revolver* rather than purchase five albums by second-tier groups. Because only a few sellers have the exceptional ability to produce the quality goods that we demand, we will be willing to pay a very high premium for talent. Suppose, for instance, that the patients of an extremely able heart surgeon have a survival rate that is 20 percentage points higher than that of other heart surgeons. We would obviously be willing to pay much more than a 20 percent wage premium to this talented heart

[26] Sherwin Rosen, "The Economics of Superstars," *American Economic Review* 71 (December 1981): 845–858.

Theory at Work
ROCK SUPERSTARS

Despite its pretentious aspirations, rock music is a business. And, like everyone else, rock stars want to make a buck. Paul McCartney knows the game well: "Somebody said to me, 'But the Beatles were antimaterialistic.' That's a huge myth. John and I literally used to sit down and say, 'Now, let's write a swimming pool.'" Not all aspiring rock artists, however, can sit down for an hour or two and come up with the "*Penny Lane*" or "*All You Need Is Love*" that will allow them to buy a nice beachfront property.

But some rock artists have the ability and talent to separate themselves from the crowd. And it is these rock artists that become the superstars in a very crowded field. In the 1960s and 1970s, rock superstars would routinely sell millions of copies of their latest album release, giving many of them (for example, the Beatles) the financial freedom to tour infrequently or not at all.

The changing technology of the music business has changed all that. The latest release of any rock superstar is now available at minimal (ahem!, even zero) cost with just a click of a mouse. Inevitably, concert revenues make up an increasing fraction of the earnings of rock artists. And rock concerts have become ever-more elaborate affairs, designed to bring in ticket-paying fans who will buy all the artist-related paraphernalia.

The superstar phenomenon is evident in concert ticket pricing. In particular, there is a significant positive correlation between the "star quality" of a rock artist (as measured by the amount of space devoted to them in *The Rolling Stone Encyclopedia of Rock & Roll*) and the price of a concert ticket. Each additional five inches of attention by the editors of the *Rolling Stone Encyclopedia* allowed the artist to raise concert ticket prices by 3 percent in the early 1980s. The concert-related rewards for being a superstar have increased over time: By the late 1990s, those extra five inches of attention translated into a 7 percent increase in ticket prices.

The increasing returns to superstardom in the rock concert business probably reflect the changing technology of music. In a world inundated with iPods and MP3s, rock superstars can now only control access to their output in one specific place: the concert arena. It is only in this arena that they can use the price system to attract fans that are willing to pay. In 2010, the typical ticket for a Paul McCartney concert was $288. Former London School of Economics student Mick Jagger understands the business lessons well: "You can't always get what you want, but if you try sometimes, you get what you need."

Source: Alan B. Krueger, "The Economics of Real Superstars: The Market for Rock Concerts in the Material World," *Journal of Labor Economics* 23 (January 2005): 1–30.

surgeon. In short, because skills are not perfect substitutes and because we demand the best, those workers who are lucky enough to have exceptional abilities will command relatively high salaries.

This argument, of course, implies that the most talented in *every* profession will earn more than the less talented. The superstar phenomenon, however, arises only in some occupations. The superstar phenomenon requires that sellers are not perfect substitutes *and* that the technology of mass production allows the very talented to reach very large markets. Madonna, for example, need only sing a particular song a few times in a studio until a perfect take is recorded. Modern technology translates this performance into digital code and permits the pristine recording to be heard in millions of homes around the world. The fact that Madonna can come "live" in a very large number of homes expands the size of her market and rewards her with an astronomically high salary (as long as Internet swapping of her songs does not overwhelm the market and substantially cut her record sales!). In contrast, a talented heart surgeon must have personal contact with each of her patients, thus constraining the size of the market for her services.

In some occupations, therefore, the cost of distributing the product to the consumers does not increase in proportion to the size of the market. The superstar phenomenon thus arises in occupations that allow extraordinarily talented persons to reach very large markets at a very low price.

A study of television ratings for games in the National Basketball Association shows that more fans watch the games when certain players—the superstars—play. This larger television audience increases revenues from advertisers and raises the value of particular players to the NBA teams. In the mid-1990s, it was estimated that the value of "owning the rights" to Michael Jordan, the Chicago Bulls player who many consider to be the finest basketball player in history, was worth at least $50 million.[27]

7-6   Inequality across Generations

Up to this point, we have analyzed how human capital investments can generate a great deal of income inequality within a particular population and how changes in the structure of the economy can change the wage distribution in significant ways within a very short time period.

We now address the question of whether wage inequality in a particular generation is transmitted to the next generation. The link between the skills of parents and children—or, more generally, the rate of **social mobility**—is at the heart of many of the most hotly discussed policy questions. Consider, for instance, the debate over whether the lack of social mobility in particular segments of society contributes to the creation of an "underclass"; or the debate over whether government policies help strengthen the link in poverty and welfare dependency across generations.

Throughout our discussion, we have assumed that workers invest in their own human capital. In fact, a large part of our human capital was chosen and funded by our parents, so it is useful to think of the human capital accumulation process in an intergenerational context. Parents care both about their own well-being and about the well-being of their children. As a result, parents will invest in their children's human capital.

The investments that parents make in their children's human capital help create the link between the skills of parents and the skills of their children. High-income parents will typically invest more in their children, creating a positive correlation between the socioeconomic outcomes experienced by the parents and the outcomes experienced by the children.

Many empirical studies have attempted to estimate the relationship between the income of the children and the income of the parents. Figure 7-8 illustrates various possibilities for the regression line that connects the earnings of fathers and children. The slope of this line is often called an **intergenerational correlation.** An intergenerational correlation equal to 1 (as in line *A* in the figure) implies that if the earnings gap between any two parents is $1,000, their children's income also will differ by $1,000. If the correlation were equal to 0.5, a $1,000 earnings gap between the two parents translates to a $500 earnings gap between their children. Most empirical studies find that the intergenerational correlation is less than 1 so that earnings differences among any two parental households will typically exceed the expected earnings differences found among the children of these two households.

[27] Jerry A. Hausman and Gregory K. Leonard, "Superstars in the National Basketball Association: Economic Value and Policy," *Journal of Labor Economics* 15 (October 1997): 586–624.

FIGURE 7-8 The Intergenerational Link in Skills

The slope of the regression line linking the earnings of the children and the earnings of the parents is called an intergenerational correlation. If the slope is equal to 1, the wage gap between any two parents persists entirely into the next generation and there is no regression toward the mean. If the slope is equal to 0, the wage of the children is independent of the wage of the parents and there is complete regression toward the mean.

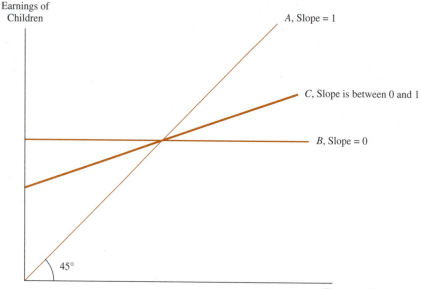

The possible attenuation of the differences in skills or incomes across generations is known as **regression toward the mean**—a tendency for income differences across families to get smaller and smaller over time as the various families move toward the mean income in the population. The phenomenon of regression toward the mean may arise because parents do not devote their entire wealth to investing in their children's human capital—but rather consume some of it themselves. Regression toward the mean also may occur if the parents encounter diminishing returns when they try to invest in their children's human capital—the marginal cost of education would then rise very rapidly as parents try to "inject" more schooling in their children. Finally, regression toward the mean in income also may arise because there is probably some regression toward the mean in ability—it is unlikely that the children of exceptionally bright parents will be even brighter. Note that the closer the intergenerational correlation gets to 0, the faster the regression toward the mean across generations. In fact, if the intergenerational correlation were equal to zero (as in line B in Figure 7-8), there would be complete regression toward the mean because none of the differences in parental skills are transmitted to their children.

Until recently, it was generally believed that the intergenerational correlation between the earnings of fathers and children was in the order of 0.2.[28] Put differently,

[28] A survey of the evidence is given by Gary S. Becker and Nigel Tomes, "Human Capital and the Rise and Fall of Families," *Journal of Labor Economics* 4 (July 1986 Supplement): S1–S39.

if the wage differential between any two parents is in the order of 30 percent, the wage differential between their children would be expected to be in the order of only 6 percent (or 30 percent $\times$ 0.2). If the rate of regression toward the mean were constant over time, the wage differential among the grandchildren would then be only 1.2 percent (or 30 percent $\times$ 0.2 $\times$ 0.2). An intergenerational correlation of 0.2, therefore, implies that there is a great deal of social mobility in the population because the economic status of workers in the parental generation would not be a good predictor of the economic status of the grandchildren.

A number of studies, however, raise serious doubts about the validity of this conclusion.[29] These studies argue convincingly that the intergenerational correlation is probably much higher, perhaps in the order of 0.3 to 0.4. The problem with the earlier results is that there is a great deal of error in observed measures of parental skills. When workers are asked about the socioeconomic status of their parents, the responses regarding parental education and earnings are probably not very precise. This measurement error weakens the estimated correlation between the skills of parents and children. It turns out that if we net out the impact of measurement error in the estimation of the intergenerational correlation, the estimated correlation often doubles. If the intergenerational correlation were indeed around 0.4, it would imply that a 30 percent wage gap between two parents translates into a 12 percent wage gap between the children and a 5 percent wage gap between the grandchildren. Skill and income differentials among workers, therefore, would be more persistent across generations.

These intergenerational correlations, typically estimated in a sample of workers who represent the entire population, seem to also describe the social mobility experienced by disadvantaged groups. For example, a study examines the economic performance of the grandchildren of slaves in the United States.[30] Surprisingly, this study concludes that the grandchildren of slaves experienced the same rate of social mobility as the grandchildren of free blacks. For instance, having a slave mother reduced the probability that black children were in school in 1880 by 36 percent. By 1920, however, having a slave grandmother reduced the probability that black children were in school by only 8.8 percent. It took approximately two generations, therefore, for the descendants of slaves to "catch up" with the descendants of free blacks. Note, however, that this finding does not have any implications about the rate of catch-up between the black and white populations. As we will see in Chapter 9, there remains a sizable gap in economic outcomes between African Americans and whites in the United States.

[29] Gary R. Solon, "Intergenerational Income Mobility in the United States," *American Economic Review* 82 (June 1992): 393–408; David J. Zimmerman, "Regression toward Mediocrity in Economic Stature," *American Economic Review* 82 (June 1992): 409–429; Joseph G. Altonji and Thomas A. Dunn, "Relationship among the Family Incomes and Labor Market Outcomes of Relatives," *Research in Labor Economics* 12 (1991): 269–310; and Kenneth A. Couch and Tomas A. Dunn, "Intergenerational Correlations in Labor Market Status," *Journal of Human Resources* 32 (Winter 1997): 210–232. A good summary of the literature is given by Gary Solon, "Intergenerational Mobility in the Labor Market," in Orley Ashenfelter and David Card, editors, *Handbook of Labor Economics,* vol. 3A, Amsterdam: Elsevier, 1999, pp. 1761–1800.

[30] Bruce Sacerdote, "Slavery and the Intergenerational Transmission of Human Capital," *Review of Economics and Statistics* 87 (May 2005): 217–234.

Theory at Work
NATURE VERSUS NURTURE

The estimates of intergenerational correlations between parents and children can be used to get some insight into the nature versus nurture debate—that is, how much of the transmission of skills between parents and children is due to prebirth factors versus postbirth factors.

One study uses Swedish data that seem particularly well suited to advance this very contentious debate. In particular, these data report the skills of *both* biological and adoptive parents for children who were adopted at an early age. The impact of the biological parents on the labor market outcomes of the children would reflect the influence of prebirth factors, while the impact of the adoptive parents would reflect the influence of postbirth factors.

It turns out that both sets of parental influences matter, but the characteristics of the biological parents matter somewhat more in these data. For this set of adoptive children, the total intergenerational correlation in educational attainment was around 0.3, with about two-thirds of it due to the influence of the biological parents. In short, nature matters.

Harry and Beltha Holt made their fortune in lumber and farming. The plight of Korean war orphans induced them to lobby Congress for a special act that would allow them to adopt Korean children. They ended up adopting eight of them. Through the agency that grew out of the Holt's initial concern, Holt International Children Services, American families have adopted over 100,000 Korean children in the last half-century.

The process of adopting a Korean child takes between 12 and 18 months. Adoptive parents must meet certain criteria, including having a minimum family income and having been married for at least three years. The adoptive parents also must satisfy criteria set out in Korean law—for example, the parents must be between 25 and 45 years old and there can be no more than four children in the family.

Korean children are then matched to the American adopting parents on a first-come, first-served basis. In other words, it is the timing of the application—rather than any matching of characteristics between parents and children—that determines the type of household where the Korean child will end up in the United States.

Another study exploits this random assignment of Korean children to American families to determine if the characteristics of American parents affect the socioeconomic outcomes of the adopted children. Because of the random assignment, there's little reason to suspect that adopted children who end up in families with highly educated parents are innately different from those adopted children who end up in less-educated households.

It turns out that if a Korean child is assigned to a high-education, small family, the adopted child ends up with about one year more schooling and is 16 percent more likely to complete college than an adopted child assigned to a low-educated, large family. Nurture also matters.

Sources: Anders Bjorklund, Mikael Lindahl, and Erik Plug, "The Origins of Intergenerational Associations: Lessons from Swedish Adoption Data," *Quarterly Journal of Economics* 121 (August 2006): 999–1028; and Bruce Sacerdote, "How Large Are the Effects from Changes in Family Environment? A Study of Korean American Adoptees," *Quarterly Journal of Economics* 122 (February 2007): 119–157.

Summary

- The positive correlation between human capital investments and ability implies that the wage distribution is positively skewed so that workers in the upper tail of the wage distribution get a disproportionately large share of national income.
- The Gini coefficient measures the amount of inequality in an income distribution.
- Wage inequality rose rapidly in the 1980s and 1990s. Wage dispersion increased between education and experience groups, as well as within narrowly defined skill groups.

- Some of the changes in the wage structure can be explained in terms of shifts in supply (such as immigration), the increasing globalization of the U.S. economy, institutional changes in the labor market (including the de-unionization of the labor force and the decline in the real minimum wage in the 1980s), and skill-biased technological change. No single variable, however, is the "smoking gun" that explains the bulk of the changes in the wage structure.
- Superstars receive a large share of the rewards in some occupations. The output produced by very talented workers is not perfectly substitutable with the output produced by less-talented workers. Superstars arise when the highly talented can reach very large markets at a very low price.
- Wage dispersion among workers is transmitted from one generation to the next because parents care about the well-being of their children and invest in their children's human capital. The typical intergenerational correlation exhibits some regression toward the mean, with the wage gap between any two families narrowing across generations.

Key Concepts

50-10 wage gap, *294*
90-10 wage gap, *294*
Gini coefficient, *293*
intergenerational
   correlation, *309*

Lorenz curve, *292*
positively skewed wage
   distribution, *289*
regression toward the
   mean, *310*

skill-biased technological
   change, *301*
social mobility, *309*
superstar phenomenon, *306*

Review Questions

1. Why is the wage distribution positively skewed?
2. Describe how to calculate a Gini coefficient.
3. Describe the key changes that occurred in the U.S. wage distribution during the 1980s and 1990s.
4. Why did the U.S. wage distribution change so much after 1980?
5. What is the superstar phenomenon? What factors create superstars in certain occupations and not in others?
6. What factors determine how much parents invest in their children's human capital?
7. Discuss why there is regression toward the mean in the correlation between the earnings of parents and children.
8. Discuss the implications of regression toward the mean for the changing shape of the wage distribution across generations.

Problems

7-1. Evaluate the validity of the following claim: The increasing wage gap between highly educated and less-educated workers will itself generate shifts in the U.S. labor market over the next decade. As a result of these responses, much of the "excess" gain currently accruing to highly educated workers will soon disappear.
7-2. What effect will each of the following proposed changes have on wage inequality?
   a. Indexing the minimum wage to inflation.
   b. Increasing the benefit level paid to welfare recipients.

c. Increasing wage subsidies paid to firms that hire low-skill workers.

d. An increase in border enforcement, reducing the number of illegal immigrants entering the country.

7-3. From 1970 to 2000, the supply of college graduates to the labor market increased dramatically, while the supply of high school (no college) graduates shrank. At the same time, the average real wage of college graduates stayed relatively stable, while the average real wage of high school graduates fell. How can these wage patterns be explained?

7-4. a. Is the presence of an underground economy likely to result in a Gini coefficient that overstates or understates poverty?

b. Consider a simple economy where 90 percent of citizens report an annual income of $10,000 while the remaining 10 percent report an annual income of $110,000. What is the Gini coefficient associated with this economy?

c. Suppose the poorest 90 percent of citizens actually have an income of $15,000 because each receives $5,000 of unreported income from the underground economy. What is the Gini coefficient now?

7-5. Use the two wage ratios for each country in Table 7-4 to calculate the percent increase in the 90-10 wage ratio from 1984 to 1994. Which countries experienced a compression in the wage distribution over this time? Which three countries experienced the greatest percent increase in wage dispersion over this time?

7-6. Consider an economy with the following income distribution: each person in the bottom quartile of the income distribution earns $15,000; each person in the middle two quartiles earns $40,000; and each person in the top quartile of the income distribution earns $100,000.

a. What is the Gini coefficient associated with this income distribution?

b. Suppose the bottom quartile pays no taxes, the middle two quartiles pay 10 percent of its income in taxes, and the top quartile pays 28 percent of its income in taxes. Two-thirds of all tax money is redistributed equally to all citizens in the form of military defense, government pensions (social security), roads/highways, and so on. The remaining one-third of tax money is distributed entirely to the poorest quartile. What is the Gini coefficient associated with this redistribution plan? Would you consider this tax and redistribution plan to be a particularly aggressive income redistribution policy?

7-7. The two points for the international income distributions reported in Table 7-1 can be used to make a rough calculation of the Gini coefficient. Use a spreadsheet to estimate the Gini coefficient for each country. Which three countries have the most equal income distribution? Which three countries have the most unequal income distribution?

7-8. Consider the following (highly) simplified description of the U.S. wage distribution and income and payroll tax schedule. Suppose 50 percent of households earn $40,000, 30 percent earn $70,000, 15 percent earn $120,000, and 5 percent earn $500,000. Marginal income tax rates are 0 percent up to $30,000, 15 percent on income earned from $30,001 to $60,000, 25 percent on income earned from $60,001 to $150,000, and 35 percent on income earned in excess of $150,000. There is also a 7.5 percent payroll tax on all income up to $80,000.

a. What are the marginal tax rate and average tax rate for each of the four types of households? What are the average household income, payroll, and total tax bill? What percent of the total income tax is paid by each of the four types of households? What percent of the total payroll tax bill is paid by each of the four types of households?

b. What is the Gini coefficient for the economy when comparing after-tax incomes across households? (Hint: Assume there are 1,000 households in the economy.) What happens to the Gini coefficient if all taxes were replaced by a single 20 percent flat tax on all incomes?

c. A presidential candidate wants to remove the cap on payroll taxes so that every household would pay payroll taxes on all of its income. To what level could the payroll tax rate be reduced under the proposal while keeping the total amount of payroll tax collected the same?

7-9. Suppose Hinterland has been a closed economy (meaning there is no immigration from foreign countries and no international trade). The current labor force has 4 million skilled workers and 8 million unskilled workers. Both types of labor have perfectly inelastic supply curves, and the current skilled-unskilled wage ratio is 2.5. The elasticity of demand of skilled labor is -0.4, while the elasticity of demand of unskilled labor is -0.1. Suppose Hinterland allows a brief period of immigration, during which time 50,000 skilled workers and 200,000 unskilled workers migrate to Hinterland. Suppose there are no other changes to the economy. Approximately what is the new skilled-unskilled wage ratio? (Hint: The percent change in the wage ratio is approximately equal to the percent change in the skilled wage minus the percent change in the unskilled wage.)

7-10. Ms. Aura is a psychic. The demand for her services is given by $Q = 2,000 - 10P$, where Q is the number of one-hour sessions per year and P is the price of each session. Her marginal revenue is $MR = 200 - 0.2Q$. Ms. Aura's operation has no fixed costs, but she incurs a cost of $150 per session (going to the client's house).

a. What is Ms. Aura's yearly profit?

b. Suppose Ms. Aura becomes famous after appearing on the Psychic Network. The new demand for her services is $Q = 2,500 - 5P$. Her new marginal revenue is $MR = 500 - 0.4Q$. What is her profit now?

c. Advances in telecommunications and information technology revolutionize the way Ms. Aura does business. She begins to use the Internet to find all relevant information about clients and meets many clients through teleconferencing. The new technology introduces an annual fixed cost of $1,000, but the marginal cost is only $20 per session. What is Ms. Aura's profit? Assume the demand curve is still given by $Q = 2,500 - 5P$.

d. Summarize the lesson of this problem for the superstar phenomenon.

7-11. Suppose two households earn $40,000 and $56,000 respectively. What is the expected percent difference in wages between the children, grandchildren, and great-grandchildren of the two households if the intergenerational correlation of earnings is 0.2, 0.4, or 0.6?

7-12. Suppose the bottom 50 percent of a population (in terms of earnings) all receive an equal share of p percent of the nation's income, where $0 \leq p \leq 50$. The top 50 percent of the population all receive an equal share of $1 - p$ percent of the nation's income.

a. For any such p, what is the Gini coefficient for the country?

b. For any such p, what is the 90-10 wage gap?

7-13. Consider two developing countries. Country A, though quite poor, uses government resources and international aid to provide public access to quality education. Country B, though also quite poor, is unable to provide quality education for institutional reasons. The distribution of innate ability is identical in the two countries.

a. Which country is likely to have a more positively skewed income distribution? Why? Plot the hypothetical income distributions for both countries on the same graph.

b. Which country is more likely to develop faster? Why? Plot the hypothetical income distributions in 20 years for both countries on the same graph.

7-14. File-sharing software threatens the music industry in part because artists will not be fully compensated for their recordings of songs. Suppose that the government decides that file-sharing software products are legal anyway.

a. The almost immediate result will be that artists start earning very little money for their recordings, but they continue to earn money for live performances. How will income change for the music industry? How does your answer relate to the superstar phenomenon?

b. Although one would expect lower prices to benefit the music-listening public if the government decides that file-sharing software products are legal, in what way(s) could the music-listening public also be hurt from the policy?

7-15. Explain why the intergenerational correlation of earnings would likely be higher or lower than average for the following groups or as a consequence of policy changes in the United States:

a. Improved educational outcomes for all populations (e.g., minority, low-income, rural) as hoped for by No Child Left Behind.

b. The elimination of legacy admits to colleges and universities.

c. The implementation of a federal inheritance tax.

d. The economic elite.

Selected Readings

David H. Autor, Lawrence F. Katz, and Melissa S. Kearney, "Trends in U.S. Wage Inequality: Revising the Revisionists," *Review of Economics and Statistics* 90 (May 2008): 300–323.

John DiNardo, Nicole Fortin, and Thomas Lemieux, "Labor Market Institutions and the Distribution of Wages, 1973–1992: A Semi-Parametric Approach," *Econometrica* 64 (September 1996): 1001–1044.

Lawrence F. Katz and Kevin M. Murphy, "Changes in Relative Wages, 1963–1987: Supply and Demand Factors," *Quarterly Journal of Economics* 107 (February 1992): 35–78.

Wojciech Kopczuk, Emmanuel Saez, and Jae Song, "Earnings Inequality and Mobility in the United States from Social Security Data Since 1937," *Quarterly Journal of Economics* 125 (February 2010): 91–128.

Alan B. Krueger, "The Economics of Real Superstars: The Market for Rock Concerts in the Material World," *Journal of Labor Economics* 23 (January 2005): 1–30.

David Lee, "Wage Inequality in the United States during the 1980s: Rising Dispersion or Falling Minimum Wage," *Quarterly Journal of Economics* 114 (August 1999): 977–1023.

Thomas Lemieux, "Increasing Residual Wage Inequality: Composition Effects, Noisy Data, or Rising Demand for Skill?" *American Economic Review* 96 (June 2006): 461–498.

Sherwin Rosen, "The Economics of Superstars," *American Economic Review* 71 (December 1981): 845–858.

Bruce Sacerdote, "How Large Are the Effects from Changes in Family Environment? A Study of Korean American Adoptees," *Quarterly Journal of Economics* 122 (February 2007): 119–157.

Gary Solon, "Intergenerational Mobility in the Labor Market," in Orley Ashenfelter and David Card, editors, *Handbook of Labor Economics,* vol. 3A. Amsterdam: Elsevier, 1999, pp. 1761–1800.

Web Links

The United Nations Development Programme maintains an extensive database describing income inequality in many countries: www.undp.org/poverty/initiatives/wider/wiid.htm.

The International Trade Administration publishes detailed information on trade patterns and regulations: www.ita.doc.gov.

Forbes magazine regularly publishes lists of superstar salaries in various fields: www.forbes.com/lists.

Chapter 8

Labor Mobility

Immigration is the sincerest form of flattery.

—Jack Paar

The allocation of workers to firms implied by a competitive labor market equilibrium maximizes the total value of labor's product. Workers are continually searching for higher-paying jobs and firms are searching for cheaper workers. As a result of these search activities, the value of marginal product of labor is equated across firms and across labor markets (for workers of given skills). The equilibrium allocation of workers and firms, therefore, is efficient. No other allocation can increase the value of labor's contribution to national income.

Needless to say, actual labor markets are not quite so neat. Workers often do not know their own skills and abilities and are ill informed about the opportunities available in other jobs or in other labor markets. Firms do not know the true productivity of the workers they hire. As in a marriage, information about the value of the match between the worker and the firm is revealed slowly as both parties learn about each other. Therefore, the existing allocation of workers and firms is not efficient and other allocations are possible that would increase national income.

This chapter studies the determinants of **labor mobility,** the mechanism that labor markets use to improve the allocation of workers to firms. There is a great deal of mobility in the labor market. In fact, it seems as if the U.S. labor market is in constant flux: Nearly 4 percent of workers in their early twenties switch jobs in any given month, 3 percent of the population moves across state lines in a year, and nearly 1.4 million legal and illegal immigrants enter the country annually. This chapter argues that all these "flavors" of labor mobility are driven by the same fundamental factors: Workers want to improve their economic situation and firms want to hire more productive workers.

The analysis of labor mobility helps us address a number of key questions in labor economics: What are the determinants of migration? How do the migrants differ from the persons who choose to stay? What factors determine how migrants are self-selected? What are the consequences of migration, both for the migrants themselves and for the localities that they move to? Do the migrants gain substantially from their decision? And how large are the efficiency gains from migration?

8-1   Geographic Migration as a Human Capital Investment

In 1932, Nobel Laureate John Hicks proposed that "differences in net economic advantages, chiefly differences in wages, are the main causes of migration."[1] Practically all modern analysis of migration decisions uses this hypothesis as the point of departure and views the migration of workers as a form of human capital investment. Workers calculate the value of the employment opportunities available in each of the alternative labor markets, net out the costs of making the potential move, and choose whichever option maximizes the net present value of lifetime earnings.

The study of the migration decision, therefore, is a simple application of the human capital framework set out in Chapter 6. Suppose there are two specific labor markets where the worker can be employed. These labor markets might be in different cities, in different states, or perhaps even in different countries. Suppose that the worker is currently employed in New York and is considering the possibility of moving to California. The worker, who is 20 years old, now earns w_{20}^{NY} dollars. If he were to move, he would earn w_{20}^{CA} dollars. It costs M dollars to move to California. These migration costs include the actual expenditures incurred in transporting the worker and his family (such as airfare and the costs of moving household goods), as well as the dollar value of the "psychic cost"—the pain and suffering that inevitably occurs when one moves away from family, friends, and social networks.

Like all other human capital investments, migration decisions are guided by the comparison of the present value of lifetime earnings in the alternative employment opportunities. Let PV^{NY} be the present value of the earnings stream if the person stays in New York. This quantity is given by

$$PV^{NY} = w_{20}^{NY} + \frac{w_{21}^{NY}}{(1 + r)} + \frac{w_{22}^{NY}}{(1 + r)^2} + \cdots \qquad (8\text{-}1)$$

where r is the discount rate and the sum in equation (8-1) continues until the worker reaches retirement age. Similarly, the present value of the earning stream if the person moves to California is given by

$$PV^{CA} = w_{20}^{CA} + \frac{w_{21}^{CA}}{(1 + r)} + \frac{w_{22}^{CA}}{(1 + r)^2} + \cdots \qquad (8\text{-}2)$$

The net gain to migration is then given by

$$\text{Net gain to migration} = PV^{CA} - PV^{NY} - M \qquad (8\text{-}3)$$

The worker moves if the net gain is positive.

A number of empirically testable propositions follow immediately from this framework:

1. An improvement in the economic opportunities available in the destination increases the net gains to migration and raises the likelihood that the worker moves.

---

[1] John R. Hicks, *The Theory of Wages,* London: Macmillan, 1932, p. 76; see also Larry A. Sjaastad, "The Costs and Returns of Human Migration," *Journal of Political Economy* 70 (October 1962): 80–93.

2. An improvement in the economic opportunities at the current region of residence decreases the net gains to migration and lowers the probability that the worker moves.

3. An increase in migration costs lowers the net gains to migration and reduces the likelihood of a move.

All these implications deliver the same basic message: Migration occurs when there is a good chance that the worker will recoup his investment.[2]

8-2 Internal Migration in the United States

Americans are very mobile. Between 2008 and 2009, 2.1 percent of the population moved across counties within the same state, and another 1.9 percent moved across states or out of the country.[3] Many studies have attempted to determine if the size and direction of these migration flows (or "internal migration") are consistent with the notion that workers migrate in search of better employment opportunities.[4] These empirical studies often relate the rate of migration between any two regions to variables describing differences in economic conditions in the regions (such as wages and unemployment rates) and to a measure of migration costs (typically the distance involved in the move).

The Impact of Region-Specific Variables on Migration

The evidence indicates that the probability of migration is sensitive to the income differential between the destination and the origin. A 10-percentage-point increase in the wage differential between the states of destination and origin increases the probability of migration by about 7 percentage points.[5] There is also a positive correlation between employment conditions and the probability of migration. A 10-percentage-point increase in the rate of employment growth in the state of origin reduces the probability of migration by about 2 percent. Finally, many empirical studies report a negative correlation between the probability of migration and distance, where distance is often interpreted as a measure of migration costs.[6] A doubling of the distance between destination and origin reduces the migration rate by about 50 percent. Therefore, the evidence is consistent with the hypothesis that workers move to those regions that maximize the present value of lifetime earnings.

[2] Although our discussion focuses on a worker's choice between two regions, the same insights can be derived if the worker were choosing a location from many alternative regions, such as the 50 states of the United States. The worker would then calculate the present value of earnings in each of the 50 states and would choose the one that maximized the present value of lifetime earnings net of migration costs.

[3] U.S. Bureau of the Census, "Table 1. General Mobility, by Race and Hispanic Origin, Region, Sex, Age, Relationship to Householder, Educational Attainment, Marital Status, Nativity, Tenure, and Poverty Status: 2008 to 2009," www.census.gov/population/www/socdemo/migrate.html.

[4] Michael Greenwood, "Internal Migration in Developed Countries," in Mark R. Rosenzweig and Oded Stark, editors, *Handbook of Population and Family Economics,* vol. 1B, Amsterdam: Elsevier, 1997, pp. 647–720, surveys the literature.

[5] Robert A. Naskoteen and Michael Zimmer, "Migration and Income: The Question of Self-Selection," *Southern Economic Journal* 46 (January 1980): 840–851.

[6] Aba Schwarz, "Interpreting the Effect of Distance on Migration," *Journal of Political Economy* 81 (September/October 1973): 1153–1169.

These correlations help us understand the direction of some of the major internal migration waves in the United States. Between 1900 and 1960, for example, there was a sizable and steady flow of African-American workers from the rural South to the industrialized cities of the North.[7] In 1900, 90 percent of the African-American population lived in the South; by 1950, the fraction of African Americans living in the South had declined to 68 percent and, by 1960, to 60 percent. The size and direction of this migration should not be too surprising. The availability of better employment opportunities in the booming manufacturing sector of northern cities (as well as the possibility of encountering less racial discrimination in both the labor market and the public school system) obviously persuaded many blacks to move north.[8]

Similarly, during much of the postwar period, California's booming economy attracted many workers from other states. Partly as a consequence of the downsizing of the defense industry, California's employment declined by 750,000 jobs between 1990 and 1993, and California's unemployment rate soared to 9.1 percent (as compared to a national unemployment rate of 7.0 percent).[9] As a result, the direction of the migration flow between California and the rest of the country took a U-turn in the early 1990s, and California became a source of, rather than a destination for, internal migrants.

The Impact of Worker Characteristics on Migration

We have seen that region-specific variables (such as mean incomes in the origin and destination states) play a major role in migration decisions. Many studies also indicate that demographic characteristics of workers such as age and education also play an important role. Migration is most common among younger and more-educated workers.

Figure 8-1 illustrates the relationship between age and the probability that a worker will migrate across state lines in any given year. This probability declines systematically over the working life. About 4 percent of college graduates in their twenties move across state lines, but the probability declines to 1 percent for college graduates in their fifties.

Older workers are less likely to move because migration is a human capital investment. As a result, older workers have a shorter period over which they can collect the returns to the migration investment. The shorter payoff period decreases the net gains to migration and hence lowers the probability of migration.

There is also a positive correlation between a worker's educational attainment and the probability of migration. As Figure 8-1 also shows, college graduates move across state lines at a substantially higher rate than high school graduates. The positive impact of education on migration rates might arise because highly educated workers may be more efficient at learning about employment opportunities in alternative labor markets, thus reducing migration costs. It is also possible that the geographic region that makes up the relevant

[7] Nicholas Lemann, *The Promised Land: The Great Black Migration and How It Changed America,* New York: Knopf, 1991.

[8] For a study of this migration, see Leah Platt Boustan, "Competition in the Promised Land: Black Migration and Racial Wage Convergence in the North, 1940–1970," *Journal of Economic History* 69 (September 2009): 755–782. There is also evidence that the migration of blacks from the rural South to northern cities was partly responsible for "white flight" into the suburbs; see Leah Platt Boustan, "Was Postwar Suburbanization "White Flight"? Evidence from the Black Migration," *Quarterly Journal of Economics* 125 (February 2010): 417–443.

[9] See "California in the Rearview Mirror," *Newsweek,* July 19, 1993, pp. 24–25.

FIGURE 8-1
**Probability
of Migrating
across State
Lines in 2005
to 2006, by
Age and
Educational
Attainment**

Source: U.S. Bureau
of the Census, "Table 6.
General Mobility of
Persons 25 Years
and Over, by Region,
Age, and Educational
Attainment," www.
census.gov/population/
www/socdemo/migrate/
cps2006.html.

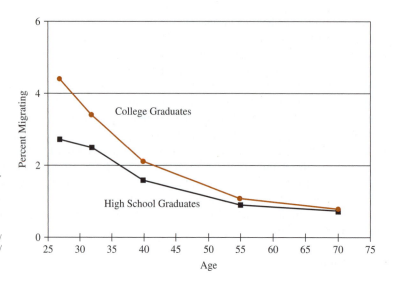

labor market for highly educated workers is larger than the geographic region that makes up the labor market for the less educated. Consider, for instance, the labor market faced by college professors. Not only are there few "firms" in any given city, but also professors' skills are very portable across colleges and universities. In effect, college professors sell their skills in a national (and often even an international) labor market.

As noted earlier, geographic migration helps improve the quality of the match between workers and firms. The data suggest that workers gain substantially from the migration, getting a wage increase of over 10 percent.[10] Because workers move to areas that offer better employment opportunities, internal migration also reduces wage differentials across regions and improves labor market efficiency. As we saw in Chapter 4, there is evidence that wages across states in the United States are converging, and some of this convergence is caused by internal migration flows.

Return and Repeat Migration

Workers who have just migrated are extremely likely to move back to their original locations (generating **return migration** flows) and are also extremely likely to move onward to still other locations (generating **repeat migration** flows). The probability of a migrant returning to the state of origin within a year is about 13 percent, and the probability of a migrant moving on to yet another location is 15 percent.[11]

---

[10] Anthony M. J. Yezer and Lawrence Thurston, "Migration Patterns and Income Change: Implications for the Human Capital Approach to Migration," *Southern Economic Journal* 42 (April 1976): 693–702; and Kenneth E. Grant and John Vanderkamp, "The Effects of Migration on Income: A Micro Study with Canadian Data," *Canadian Journal of Economics* 13 (August 1980): 381–406.

[11] Julie DaVanzo, "Repeat Migration in the United States: Who Moves Back and Who Moves On?" *Review of Economics and Statistics* 65 (November 1983): 552–559; see also Christian Dustmann, "Return Migration, Wage Differentials, and the Optimal Migration Duration," *European Economic Review* 47 (April 2003): 353–367.

Unless economic conditions in the various states change drastically soon after the migration takes place, the high propensity of migrants to move again is *not* consistent with the income-maximization model we developed earlier. Prior to the initial migration, the worker's cost-benefit calculation indicated that a move from, say, Illinois to Florida maximized his present value of lifetime earnings (net of migration costs). How can a similar calculation made just a few weeks after the move indicate that returning to Illinois or perhaps moving on to Texas maximizes the worker's income?

Two factors can generate return and repeat migration flows. Some of these flows arise because the worker has learned that the initial migration decision was a mistake. After all, a worker contemplating the move from Illinois to Florida faces a great deal of uncertainty about economic conditions in Florida. Once he arrives in Florida, he might discover that the available employment opportunities—or local amenities—are far worse than expected. Return and repeat migration flows arise as workers attempt to correct these errors.

Return or repeat migration also might be the career path that maximizes the present value of lifetime earnings in some occupations, even in the absence of any uncertainty about job opportunities. For instance, lawyers who specialize in tax law quickly realize that a brief stint at the Department of the Treasury, the Department of Justice, or the Internal Revenue Service in Washington, DC, provides them with valuable human capital. This human capital includes intricate knowledge of the tax code as well as personal connections with policymakers and other government officials. After their government service, the lawyers can return to their home states or can move to other areas of the country where their newly acquired skills will be highly rewarded. In effect, the temporary stay of the lawyers in the District of Columbia is but one rung in the career ladder that maximizes lifetime earnings.[12]

There is evidence supporting the view that return and repeat migration flows are generated both by mistakes in the initial migration decision and by stepping-stone career paths.[13] For instance, workers who move to a distant location are more likely to return to their origin. Persons who move far away probably have less precise information about the true economic conditions at the destination, increasing the probability that the original move was a mistake and making repeat or return migration more likely. It is also the case that highly educated persons are more likely to engage in repeat migration. This finding is consistent with the hypothesis that skills acquired in one particular location can be profitably marketed in another.

Why Is There So Little Migration?

Even though Americans are very mobile, the volume of internal migration is not sufficient to completely equalize wages across regions. Only about half of the wage gap between

[12] A theory of human capital investments and occupational choice based on this stepping-stone hypothesis is presented in Sherwin Rosen, "Learning and Experience in the Labor Market," *Journal of Human Resources* 7 (Summer 1972): 326–342.

[13] DaVanzo, "Repeat Migration in the United States"; Julie DaVanzo and Peter A. Morrison, "Return and Other Sequences of Migration in the United States," *Demography* 18 (February 1981): 85–101. A study of return migration in the Canadian context is given by Jennifer Hunt, "Are Migrants More Skilled Than Non-migrants? Repeat, Return, and Same-Employer Migrants," *Canadian Journal of Economics* 37 (November 2004): 830–849.

any two regions disappears after 30 years.[14] The persistence of regional wage differentials raises an important question: Why do more people *not* take advantage of the higher wage in some regions?

The human capital model suggests an answer: Migration costs must be very high. In fact, one can easily apply the model to get a rough idea of the magnitude of these costs. In 2003, average annual compensation per worker was approximately $22,000 in Puerto Rico and $51,000 in the United States.[15] Because Puerto Ricans are U.S. citizens by birth, there are no legal restrictions limiting their entry into the United States. In fact, the large income gap has induced over a quarter of the Puerto Rican population to migrate to the United States in the past 50 years.[16] But, just as important, 75 percent of Puerto Ricans chose not to move.

Let w_{PR} be the wage the worker can earn in Puerto Rico and let w_{US} be the wage he can earn in the United States. For simplicity, let's assume these wages are constant over the life cycle. It turns out that if the sums in equations (8-1) and (8-2) have many terms—so that the worker lives on practically forever—we can write the discounted present values as[17]

$$PV_{PR} = \frac{(1 + r)w_{PR}}{r} \quad \text{and} \quad PV_{US} = \frac{(1 + r)w_{US}}{r} \qquad \textbf{(8-4)}$$

The human capital framework indicates that a worker is indifferent between moving and staying if the discounted gains from moving are exactly equal to migration costs:

$$\frac{(1 + r)(w_{US} - w_{PR})}{r} = M \qquad \textbf{(8-5)}$$

To get an idea of how large M must be in order to make a worker indifferent, consider the following algebraic rearrangement of equation (8-5): Divide both sides by w_{PR} and define $\pi = M/w_{PR}$. The variable π gives the fraction of a worker's salary in Puerto Rico that is spent on migration costs. We can then rewrite the equation as

$$\frac{(1 + r)}{r} \frac{(w_{US} - w_{PR})}{w_{PR}} = \pi \qquad \textbf{(8-6)}$$

The ratio $(w_{US} - w_{PR})/w_{PR}$ is around 1.2, indicating that a worker can increase his income by 120 percent by migrating to the United States. If the rate of discount is 5 percent, the

[14] Robert J. Barro and Xavier Sala-i-Martin, "Convergence across States and Regions," *Brookings Papers on Economic Activity* (1991): 107–158; and Olivier Jean Blanchard and Lawrence F. Katz, "Regional Evolutions," *Brookings Papers on Economic Activity* 1 (1992): 1–61.

[15] U.S. Department of Commerce, *Statistical Abstract of the United States, 2006,* Washington, DC: Government Printing Office, 2002, Tables 627, 1302; see www.census.gov/compendia/statab/. These differences remain large even if income is adjusted for differences in purchasing power. In 2005, per capita GDP (in PPP dollars) was $18,600 in Puerto Rico and $41,800 in the United States; see U.S. Central Intelligence Agency, *The World Factbook, 2006,* Washington, DC: Government Printing Office, 2006, available at www.cia.gov/cia/publications/factbook/index.html.

[16] George J. Borjas, "Labor Outflows and Labor Inflows in Puerto Rico," *Journal of Human Capital* 2 (Spring 2008): 32–68.

[17] Let $S = 1 + 1/(1 + r) + 1/(1 + r)^2$ and so on. This implies that $(1 + r)S = (1 + r) + 1 + 1/(1 + r) + 1/(1 + r)^2$ and so on. After canceling out many terms, the difference $(1 + r)S - S = 1 + r$, so $S = (1 + r)/r$.

Theory at Work
MIGRATION AND EU EXPANSION

The freedom of movement of persons—together with the freedom of movement of capital, goods, and services—is a general right within the European Union. In theory, the creation of a single market should create many additional employment and earnings opportunities for the workers in the member states of the EU. The unimpeded flows of labor, capital, goods, and service also should greatly reduce intercountry wage differentials within the community.

In 1998, the European Union began to negotiate entry conditions for several central and eastern European countries, including the Czech Republic, Estonia, Hungary, and Poland. An important concern was the possibility that migration flows into the richer member states from the acceding countries would cause downward pressures on wages in the richer states and further aggravate the serious unemployment problem that already exists in many EU countries.

In the past, these concerns had encouraged EU negotiators to propose a "transition period" during which citizens from the acceding countries would face some restrictions if they wished to migrate within the EU. In fact, this transition period was part of the agreement that enabled the entry of Greece, Portugal, and Spain into the community. Although there was fear that the accession of these countries would generate substantial population flows, these migration flows never materialized. In 1993, 17 million foreigners lived in the various EU countries, but only about 5 million of these foreigners originated in other EU countries. These "EU internal immigrants" accounted for only 1.3 percent of the EU population.

Media reports and politicians in the EU now claim that perhaps 40 million eastern Europeans will take advantage of the open borders and migrate west. But this scenario is unlikely to occur. The combination of large migration costs—particularly across countries that differ in language and culture—and relatively small (and narrowing) wage gaps suggests that the migration gains are not sufficiently large to generate large population flows. A careful analysis of the available data concludes that perhaps 3 percent of the population of the acceding countries (or around 3 million people) will migrate west within the next 15 years. These immigrants would increase the population of the current European Union by less than 1 percent.

Source: Thomas K. Bauer and Klaus F. Zimmermann, *Assessment of Possible Migration Pressure and Its Labour Market Impact Following EU Enlargement to Central and Eastern Europe,* Bonn: IZA Research Report No. 3, July 1999.

---

left-hand side of equation (8-6) takes on the value of 25. In other words, migration costs for a worker who is indifferent between migrating to the United States and staying in Puerto Rico are 25 times his salary. If this worker earns the average income in Puerto Rico (or $22,000), migration costs are around $550,000![18]

What exactly is the nature of these costs? This quantity obviously does not represent the cost of transporting the family and household goods to a new location in the United States. Instead, the marginal Puerto Rican probably attaches a very high utility to the social and cultural amenities associated with remaining in his birthplace. Needless to say, migration costs are likely to be even larger in other contexts—such as international migration, where there are legal restrictions and much greater differences in language and culture. In short,

---

[18] A more sophisticated analysis of the migration decision that also provides estimates of migration costs is given by John Kennan and James R. Walker, "The Effect of Expected Incomes on Individual Migration Decisions," *Econometrica*, forthcoming 2011. See also Philip McCann, Jacques Poot, and Lynda Sanderson, "Migration, Relationship Capital, and International Travel: Theory and Evidence," *Journal of Economic Geography* 10 (May 2010): 361–387.

although internal migration increases labor market efficiency, the gains are limited by the fact that regional wage differentials are likely to persist because the flow of migrants is not sufficiently large.

8-3 Family Migration

Thus far, our discussion of geographic migration focuses on the choices made by a single worker as he or she compares employment opportunities across regions and chooses the one location that maximizes the present value of lifetime earnings. However, most migration decisions are not made by single workers, but by families. The migration decision, therefore, should not be based on whether a particular member of the household is better off at the destination than at the origin, but on whether the family *as a whole* is better off.[19]

The impact of the family on the migration decision can be easily described. Suppose that the household is composed of two persons, a husband and a wife. Let's denote by ΔPV_H the change in the present value of the husband's earnings stream if he were to move geographically (say from New York to California). And let ΔPV_W be the change in the present value of the wife's earnings stream if she were to make the same move. Note that ΔPV_H also can be interpreted as the husband's gains to migration if he were single and were making the migration decision completely on his own. These gains are called the husband's "private" gains to migration. If the husband were not tied down by his family responsibilities, he would migrate if the private gains ΔPV_H were positive. Similarly, the quantity ΔPV_W gives the wife's private gains to migration. If she were single, she would move if ΔPV_W were positive.

The family unit (that is, the husband and the wife) will move if the *family's* net gains are positive:

$$\Delta PV_H + \Delta PV_W > 0 \qquad \text{(8-7)}$$

In other words, the family migrates if the sum of the private gains to the husband and to the wife is positive.

Figure 8-2 illustrates the basic ideas. The vertical axis in the figure measures the husband's private gains to migration, and the horizontal axis measures the wife's private gains. As noted above, if the husband were making the migration decision completely on his own, he would migrate whenever ΔPV_H was positive, which is given by the outcomes that lie above the horizontal axis (or the combination of areas *A, B,* and *C*). Similarly, if the wife were making the migration decision on her own, she would migrate whenever ΔPV_W was positive, which is given by the outcomes to the right of the vertical axis (or areas *C, D,* and *E*).

Let's now examine the family's migration decision. The 45° downward-sloping line that goes through the origin connects the points where the net gains to the family are zero, or $\Delta PV_H + \Delta PV_W = 0$. The family might have zero gains from migration in a number of

[19] Jacob Mincer, "Family Migration Decisions," *Journal of Political Economy* 86 (October 1978): 749–773.

FIGURE 8-2 Tied Movers and Tied Stayers

If the husband were single, he would migrate whenever $\Delta PV_H > 0$ (or areas *A, B,* and *C*). If the wife were single, she would migrate whenever $\Delta PV_W > 0$ (or areas *C, D,* and *E*). The family migrates when the sum of the private gains is positive (or areas *B, C,* and *D*). In area *D,* the husband would not move if he were single but moves as part of the family, making him a tied mover. In area *E,* the wife would move if she were single but does not move as part of the family, making her a tied stayer.

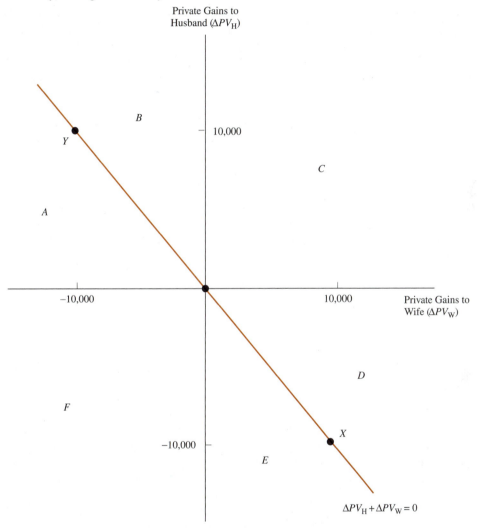

ways. For instance, at point *X,* the wife gains $10,000 if she were to move, but the husband loses $10,000. At point *Y,* the husband gains $10,000, but the wife loses $10,000.

The family moves if the sum of the private gains $\Delta PV_H + \Delta PV_W$ is positive. The family's decision to maximize the *family's* lifetime earnings implies that the family will move whenever the gains lie above the 45° line, or the combination of areas *B, C,* and *D.*

The area in which the family wants to move, therefore, does not coincide with the areas indicating what each person in the family would do if he or she were single. In other words, the *optimal decision for the family is not necessarily the same as the optimal choice for a single person.*

Tied Stayers and Tied Movers

To see why the family's incentives to migrate differ from the private incentives of each family member, consider any point in area E. In this area, the wife would move on her own if she were single, for there are private gains to her move (that is, $\Delta PV_W > 0$). Note, however, that the husband's loss exceeds her gain (so that $\Delta PV_H + \Delta PV_W < 0$), and hence, it is not optimal for the family to move. The wife is, in effect, a **tied stayer.** She sacrifices the better employment opportunities available elsewhere because her husband is much better off in their current region of residence.

Similarly, consider any point in area D. In this area, the husband experiences an income loss if he moves on his own (that is, $\Delta PV_H < 0$). Nevertheless, when he moves as part of a family unit, the wife's gain exceeds the husband's loss, so that $\Delta PV_H + \Delta PV_W > 0$. The family moves and the husband is a **tied mover.** He follows the wife even though his employment outlook is better at their current residence.

The analysis of family migration decisions shows that all persons in the family need not have positive private gains from migration. A comparison of the premigration and postmigration earnings of tied movers would indicate that they "lost" from the migration. In fact, the evidence suggests that the postmigration earnings of women are often lower than their premigration earnings.[20]

We have seen, however, that the premigration and postmigration comparison of wives' earnings does not necessarily imply that migration is a bad investment. The family as a whole gained, so that both parties in the household are potentially better off.

The rapid rise in the female labor force participation rate implies that *both* husbands and wives increasingly find themselves in situations in which their private incentives to migrate do not coincide with the family's incentives. Because both spouses are often looking for work in the same city and sometimes even in the same narrowly defined profession, the chances of finding adequate jobs for the two parties are slim, reducing the likelihood that the family will move.

The increase in the number of two-worker households has given rise to creative labor market arrangements. Employers interested in hiring one of the spouses facilitate the job search process for the other and sometimes even hire both. There also has been an increase in the number of married couples who maintain separate households in different cities, so as to minimize the financial losses of being tied movers or tied stayers. Finally, the conflict between the migration decision that is best for a single person and the migration decision that is best for the family makes the household unit more unstable. We do not know, however, to what extent divorce rates are driven by the refusal of tied movers and tied stayers to go along with the family's migration decision.

---

[20] Sandell, "Women and the Economics of Family Migration"; see also Paul J. Boyle et al., "A Cross-National Comparison of the Impact of Family Migration on Women's Employment Status," *Demography* 38 (May 2001): 201–213.

There are an increasing number of "power couples" in the United States, couples in which both spouses are college graduates. The proportion of power couples rose from 2 percent in 1940, to 9 percent in 1970, and to 15 percent in 1990. Because highly educated women are more likely to participate in the labor force, power couples are predominantly dual-career couples. In 1940, the probability that the wife in a power couple worked was 20.1 percent; this statistic rose to 73.3 percent by 1990.

Because both spouses in a power couple tend to work, it may be difficult for both spouses to obtain their "optimal" jobs in the same geographic labor market. As a result, power couples may have to split and reside in different cities, or one of the spouses in a power couple will have to accept the fact that he or she is a tied stayer (or a tied mover) and work at a job that does not provide the best employment opportunities.

Power couples can minimize these problems by settling in those parts of the country that are likely to provide many employment opportunities for high-skill workers, such as large metropolitan areas. The diversified labor markets in these large cities have the potential to provide satisfactory job matches for both spouses. It turns out that this is precisely what power couples have done in the past few decades. Table 8-1 summarizes the evidence.

The proportion of power couples settling in a large metropolitan area rose from 14.6 to 34.8 percent between 1970 and 1990. In contrast, the similar proportion for couples in which neither spouse is a college graduate (or a "low-power couple") rose only from 8.3 to 20.0 percent. If we treat the locational choice made by the low-power couples as the choice of a control group, the difference-in-differences approach implies that being in a power couple increases the probability of residing in a large metropolitan area by 8.5 percentage points. Many power couples, therefore, chose to reduce the cost associated with being a power couple by moving to different parts of the country.

Source: Dora L. Costa and Matthew E. Kahn, "Power Couples: Changes in the Locational Choice of the College Educated, 1940–1990," *Quarterly Journal of Economics* 115 (November 2000): 1287–314; see also Janice Compton and Robert A. Pollak, "Why Are Power Couples Increasingly Concentrated in Large Metropolitan Areas," *Journal of Labor Economics* 25 (July 2007): 475–512.

TABLE 8-1   **Percent of Couples with Working Wives That Reside in a Large Metropolitan Area**

	1970	1990	Difference
Power couples	14.6	34.8	20.2
Low-power couples	8.3	20.0	11.7
Difference-in-differences	—	—	**8.5**

8-4   Immigration in the United States

There has been a resurgence of large-scale immigration in the United States and in many other developed countries. The United Nations estimates that 214 million people, or slightly over 3 percent of the world's population, now reside in a country where they were not born.[21]

[21] United Nations, Department of Economic and Social Affairs. Trends in International Migrant Stock: The 2008 Revision, http://esa.un.org/migration/p2k0data.asp

FIGURE 8-3   Legal Immigration to the United States by Decade, 1820–2010

Source: U.S. Immigration and Naturalization Service, *Statistical Yearbook of the Immigration and Naturalization Service, 2010,* Washington, DC: Government Printing Office, 2010; www.dhs.gov/files/statistics/publications/LPR10.shtm, Table 1.

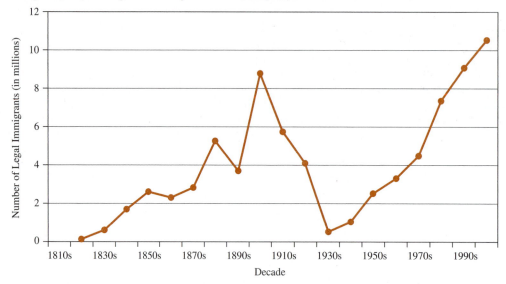

We begin our study of this important population flow by providing a brief history of immigration in the country that receives the largest immigrant flow—the United States.[22] As Figure 8-3 shows, the size of the immigrant flow reaching the United States has fluctuated dramatically in the past century. Reacting to the large number of immigrants who entered the country at the beginning of the twentieth century, Congress closed the floodgates in the 1920s by enacting the national-origins quota system, which limited the number of immigrants as well as granted most of the available visas to persons born in northwestern European countries.

During the entire 1930s, only 500,000 immigrants entered the United States. Since then, the number of legal immigrants has increased substantially and is now at historic levels. In 2010, slightly more than 1 million persons were admitted legally. There also has been a steady increase in the number of illegal immigrants. It is estimated that around 10.8 million persons were present illegally in the United States in January 2010 and that the *net* flow of illegal immigrants is at least 500,000 persons per year.[23]

The huge increase in immigration in recent decades can be attributed partly to changes in U.S. immigration policy. The 1965 amendments to the Immigration and Nationality Act (and subsequent revisions) repealed the national-origins quota system, increased the number of available visas, and made family ties to U.S. residents the key factor that determines

[22] For a more detailed discussion, see George J. Borjas, *Heaven's Door: Immigration Policy and the American Economy,* Princeton, NJ: Princeton University Press, 1999.

[23] U.S. Immigration and Naturalization Service, "Estimates of the Unauthorized Immigrant Population Residing in the United States, January 2010," February 2011, www.dhs.gov/xlibrary/assets/statistics/publications/ois_ill_pe_2010.pdf.

whether an applicant is admitted into the country. As a consequence of both the 1965 amendments and major changes in economic and political conditions in the source countries, the national-origin mix of the immigrant flow has changed substantially in the past few decades. More than two-thirds of the legal immigrants admitted during the 1950s originated in Europe or Canada, 25 percent originated in Latin America, and only 6 percent originated in Asia. By the 1990s, only 17 percent of the immigrants originated in Europe or Canada, 47 percent originated in Latin America, and an additional 31 percent originated in Asia.

An important factor that motivates these migration flows is the sizable income difference that exists between the United States and the source countries. A study of Mexican illegal immigration shows that the flow of illegal immigrants is extremely responsive to changes in economic conditions in the two countries.[24] In a typical month between 1968 and 1996, the Border Patrol apprehended 42,890 persons at the Mexican border attempting to enter the country illegally. The elasticity of the number of apprehensions with respect to the wage in the Mexican labor market is around -0.8; a 10 percent reduction in the Mexican wage increases the number of apprehensions by around 8 percent. Similarly, the elasticity of border apprehensions with respect to the wage in the U.S. labor market is around $+1$; a 10 percent increase in the U.S. wage increases the number of apprehensions by 10 percent. Moreover, the number of apprehensions responds almost immediately—within one month—to a change in the Mexican wage or the U.S. wage. Put differently, there seems to be a large pool of potential illegal immigrants in Mexico who are ready to almost instantaneously pack up and move at the slightest change in economic conditions.

8-5   Immigrant Performance in the U.S. Labor Market

How do immigrants do in the U.S. labor market? This question plays a crucial role in the debate over immigration policy, not only in the United States but in other receiving countries as well. Immigrants who can adapt well and are relatively successful in their new jobs can make a significant contribution to economic growth. Moreover, natives need not be concerned about the possibility that these immigrants will enroll in public assistance programs and become a tax burden. In short, the economic impact of immigration will depend on the skill composition of the immigrant population.

The Age-Earnings Profiles of Immigrants and Natives in the Cross Section

To assess the relationship between immigrant economic performance and the process of assimilation, many early studies used *cross-section* data sets (that is, data sets that give a snapshot of the population at a point in time, such as a particular U.S. census) to trace out the age-earnings profiles of immigrants and natives.[25] A cross-section data set lets us

---

[24] Gordon Hanson and Antonio Spilimbergo, "Illegal Immigration, Border Enforcement, and Relative Wages," *American Economic Review* 89 (December 1999): 1337–1357. For a more general analysis of the migration flow from Mexico to the United States, see Gordon H. Hanson and Craig McIntosh, "The Great Mexican Emigration," *Review of Economics and Statistics* 92 (November 2010): 798–810.

[25] Barry R. Chiswick, "The Effect of Americanization on the Earnings of Foreign-Born Men," *Journal of Political Economy* 86 (October 1978): 897–921.

FIGURE 8-4
**The Age-
Earnings
Profiles of
Immigrant and
Native Men
in the Cross
Section**

Source: Barry
R. Chiswick, "The
Effect of American-
ization on the Earn-
ings of Foreign-Born
Men," *Journal of
Political Economy*
86 (October 1978):
Table 2, Column 3.

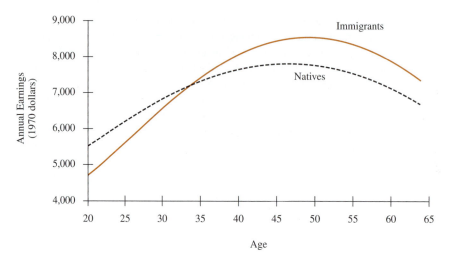

compare the *current* (that is, as of the time the snapshot is taken) earnings of newly arrived immigrants with the *current* earnings of immigrants who migrated years ago. Figure 8-4 uses data from the 1970 census to illustrate the typical age-earnings profiles for immigrants and natives. At the time of entry into the United States (at age 20 in the figure), the wages of immigrant men are about 15 percent lower than the wages of comparable native men. The age-earnings profile of immigrants, however, is much steeper. In fact, after 14 years in the United States, the earnings of immigrants seem to "overtake" the earnings of native-born workers. The typical immigrant who has been in the United States for 30 years earns about 10 percent more than comparable natives. The cross-section data thus suggest that upward mobility is an important aspect of the immigrant experience because immigrants who arrived many years ago earn much more than newly arrived immigrants.

There are three distinct results in Figure 8-4 that are worth discussing in detail. First, note that immigrant earnings are initially below the earnings of natives. This finding is typically interpreted as follows: When immigrants first arrive in the United States, they lack many of the skills that are valued by American employers. These "U.S.-specific" skills include language, educational credentials, and information on what the best-paying jobs are and where they are located.

The second result is that the immigrant age-earnings profile is steeper than the native age-earnings profile. As we saw in Chapter 6, the human capital model implies that greater volumes of human capital investment steepen the age-earnings profile. As immigrants learn English and learn about the U.S. labor market, the immigrants' human capital stock grows relative to that of natives, and economic assimilation occurs in the sense that immigrant earnings begin to converge to the earnings of natives.

The human capital model thus provides a reasonable story of why immigrant earnings start out below and grow faster than the earnings of natives. This story, however, cannot account for the third finding in the figure: After 14 years in the United States, immigrants seem to earn more than natives. After all, why should immigrants end up accumulating more human capital than natives?

To explain why immigrants eventually earn more than natives, some researchers resort to a selection argument: Some workers in the source countries choose to migrate and others choose to stay, and immigrants are not randomly selected from the population of the countries of origin. It seems plausible to argue that only the persons who have exceptional ability, or a lot of drive and motivation, would pack up everything they own, leave family and friends behind, and move to a foreign country to start life anew. If immigrants are indeed selected from the population in this manner, it would not be surprising to find that immigrants are more productive than natives (and earn more) once they acquire the necessary U.S.-specific skills.

Assimilation and Cohort Effects

The bottom line of the cross-section data summarized in Figure 8-4 is that immigrants who migrated many years ago earn more than newly arrived immigrants. The "assimilationist" interpretation of this result would say that those who migrated many years ago have acquired U.S.-specific skills. In time, the new arrivals will also acquire these skills and will be just as successful as the older waves of immigrants.

The basic problem with this interpretation of the cross-sectional evidence is that we are drawing inferences about how the earnings of immigrant workers evolve over time from a single snapshot of the immigrant population. It might be the case, for example, that newly arrived immigrants are inherently different from those who migrated 20 years ago. Hence, it is invalid to use the economic experience of those who migrated 20 years ago to forecast the future labor market performance of current immigrants. Figure 8-5 illustrates the logic behind this alternative hypothesis.[26]

To simplify, let's consider a hypothetical situation where there are three separate immigrant waves, and these waves have distinct productivities. One wave arrived in 1960, the second arrived in 1980, and the last arrived in 2000. Suppose also that all immigrants enter the United States at age 20.

Let's also assume that the earliest cohort has the highest productivity level of any group in the population, including U.S.-born workers. If we could observe their earnings in every year after they arrive in the United States, their age-earnings profile would be given by the line *PP* in Figure 8-5. For the sake of argument, let's assume that the last wave of immigrants (that is, the 2000 arrivals) is the least productive of any group in the population, including natives. If we could observe their earnings throughout their working lives, their age-earnings profile would be given by the line *RR* in the figure. Finally, suppose that the immigrants who arrived in 1980 have the same skills as natives. If we could observe their earnings at every age in their working lives, the age-earnings profiles of this cohort and of natives would be given by the line *QQ*. Note that the age-earnings profiles of each of the immigrant cohorts is parallel to the age-earnings profile of the native population. There is *no* wage convergence between immigrants and natives in our hypothetical example.

Suppose we now have access to data drawn from the 2000 decennial census. This cross-section data set, which provides a snapshot of the U.S. population as of April 1, 2000, provides information on each worker's wage rate, age, whether native or foreign born, and the year the worker arrived in the United States. As a result, we can observe the wage of

---

[26] George J. Borjas, "Assimilation, Changes in Cohort Quality, and the Earnings of Immigrants," *Journal of Labor Economics* 3 (October 1985): 463–489.

FIGURE 8-5   Cohort Effects and the Immigrant Age-Earnings Profile

The typical person migrating in 1960 is skilled and has age-earnings profile *PP;* the 2000 immigrant is unskilled and has age-earnings profile *RR;* the 1980 immigrant has the same skills as the typical native and has age-earnings profile *QQ.* Suppose all immigrants arrive at age 20. The 2000 census cross section reports the wages of immigrants who have just arrived (point *R**); the wage of immigrants who arrived in 1980 when they are 40 years old (point *Q**); and the wage of immigrants who arrived in 1960 when they are 60 years old (point *P**). The cross-sectional age-earnings profile erroneously suggests that immigrant earnings grow faster than those of natives.

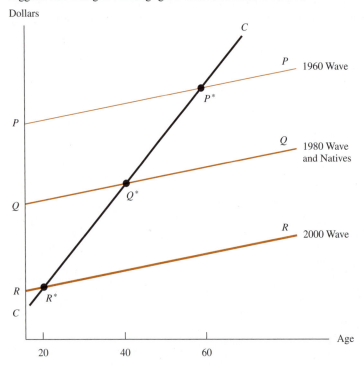

immigrants who have just arrived as part of the 2000 cohort when they are 20 years old (see point *R** in the figure). We also can observe the wage of immigrants who arrived in 1980 when they are 40 years old (point *Q**), and we observe the wage of immigrants who arrived in 1960 when they are 60 years old (point *P**). A cross-section data set, therefore, allows us to observe only one point on each of the immigrant age-earnings profiles.

If we connect points *P**, *Q**, and *R**, we trace out the immigrant age-earnings profile that is generated by the cross-sectional data, or line *CC* in Figure 8-5. This cross-section line has two important properties. First, it is substantially steeper than the native age-earnings profile. The tracing out of the age-earnings profile of immigrants using cross-section data makes it seem as if there is wage convergence between immigrants and natives, when in fact there is none. Second, the cross-section line *CC* crosses the native line at age 40. This gives the appearance that immigrant earnings overtake those of natives after they have been in the United States for 20 years. In fact, no immigrant group experienced such an overtaking.

Figure 8-5 illustrates how the cross-sectional age-earnings profile can yield an errone-ous perception about the adaptation process experienced by immigrants if there are intrinsic differences in productivity across immigrant cohorts. These differences in skills across cohorts are called **cohort effects.**

The hypothetical example illustrated in the figure assumed that more recent immigrant cohorts are less skilled than earlier cohorts. This type of cohort effect can arise if changes in U.S. immigration policy deemphasize skills as a condition of admission. The cohort effects also can arise because of nonrandom return migration by immigrants. Perhaps one-third of all immigrants eventually leave the United States, presumably to return to their countries of origin.[27] Suppose that immigrants who have relatively low earnings in the United States are the ones who make the return trip. In any given cross section, earlier immigrant waves have been filtered out and the survivors have high earnings, whereas more recent waves have yet to be filtered and their average earnings are dragged down by the presence of future emigrants. This process of return migration generates a positive correlation between earnings and years since migration in the cross section, but this correlation says nothing about economic assimilation.

Evidence on Cohort Effects and Immigrant Assimilation

The data suggest that there are skill differentials across immigrant cohorts and that these cohort effects are quite large.[28] Figure 8-6 illustrates the trend in the entry wage gap between immigrants and natives across successive immigrant waves between 1960 and 2000. Newly arrived immigrants in 1960 earned about 11 percent less than natives. By 1990, the newest immigrant arrivals earned about 37 percent less than natives. Interestingly, there was a slight turnaround in the 1990s, and by 2000, newly arrived immigrants earned about 31 percent less than natives.[29]

To determine if the earnings of a specific immigrant cohort reach parity with those of natives, a number of studies "track" the earnings of the cohort across censuses. For instance, the 1980 census reports the average wage of persons who migrated in 1980 when

[27] Robert Warren and Jennifer Marks Peck, "Foreign-Born Emigration from the United States: 1960 to 1970," *Demography* 17 (February 1980): 71–84; and George J. Borjas and Bernt Bratsberg, "Who Leaves? The Outmigration of the Foreign-Born," *Review of Economics and Statistics* 78 (February 1996): 165–176.

[28] The evidence is surveyed by George J. Borjas, "The Economic Analysis of Immigration," in Orley C. Ashenfelter and David Card, editors, *Handbook of Labor Economics,* vol. 3A, Amsterdam: Elsevier, 1999, pp. 1697–1760. The tracking of immigrant cohorts across cross sections also is affected by the existence of "period effects," the impact of macroeconomic changes on the wage structure (due either to inflation or to cyclical fluctuations). These period effects might have a different impact on native and on immigrant wages; see George J. Borjas, "Assimilation and Changes in Cohort Quality Revisited: What Happened to Immigrant Earnings in the 1980s?" *Journal of Labor Economics* 13 (April 1995): 201–245; and Darren Lubotsky, "Chutes or Ladders: A Longitudinal Analysis of Immigrant Earnings," *Journal of Political Economy* 115 (October 2007): 820–867; and Darren Lubotsky, "The Effect of Changes in the U.S. Wage Structure on Recent Immigrants' Earnings," *Review of Economics and Statistics* 93 (February 2011): 59–71.

[29] The earnings turnaround of the 1990s was partly due to changes in immigration policy, including the very large increase in the number of high-tech workers admitted as part of the H1-B visa program; see George J. Borjas and Rachel Friedberg, "The Immigrant Earnings Turnaround of the 1990s," Working Paper, Harvard University and Brown University, July 2006; see also Linnea Polgreen and Nicole B. Simpson, "Recent Trends in the Skill Composition of Legal U.S. Immigrants," *Southern Economic Journal* 72 (April 2006): 938–957.

FIGURE 8-6

**The Wage
Differential
between
Immigrant and
Native Men at
Time of Entry**

Source: George J.
Borjas and Rachel
Friedberg, "The Immi-
grant Earnings Turn-
around of the 1990s,"
Working Paper,
Harvard University
and Brown University,
July 2006.

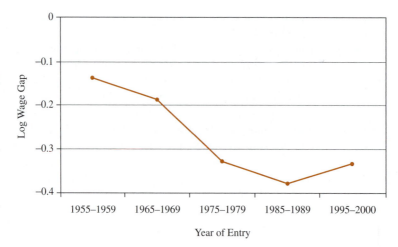

they are 25 years old; the 1990 census reports the average wage of the same immigrants when they are 35 years old; and the 2000 census reports the average wage for the same persons when they are 45 years old. The tracking of specific immigrant cohorts across censuses, therefore, traces out the age-earnings profile for each of the cohorts.

Figure 8-7 illustrates the evidence provided by this type of tracking analysis. The immigrant waves that arrived before 1970 started with a slight wage disadvantage and either caught up with or surpassed the earnings of native workers within one or two decades.

FIGURE 8-7   **Evolution of Wages for Specific Immigrant Cohorts over the Life Cycle (Relative to Wages of Comparably Aged Native Men)**

Source: George J. Borjas and Rachel Friedberg, "The Immigrant Earnings Turnaround of the 1990s," Working Paper, Harvard University and Brown University, July 2006.

Relative Wage of Immigrants Who Arrived
When They Were 25–34 Years Old

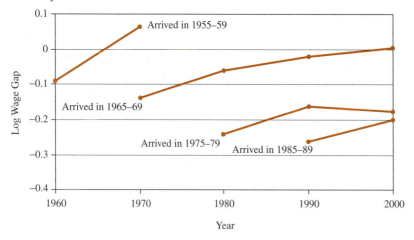

The cohorts that arrived in the 1970s or 1980s, however, start out at a much greater disadvantage, making it unlikely that they will catch up with comparably aged native workers during their working lives.[30]

8-6 The Decision to Immigrate

A number of studies have tried to identify the factors responsible for the decline in relative skills across immigrant waves.[31] Some of the studies have pointed to a single culprit: the changing national-origin mix of the immigrant flow. As noted earlier, post-1965 immigrants are much more likely to originate in Latin American and Asian countries. Table 8-2 documents a lot of variation in the relative wage of immigrants across national-origin groups. Immigrants from the United Kingdom earn 37 percent more than natives, whereas those from Mexico earn 40 percent less.

Two factors account for the dispersion in relative wages across national-origin groups. First, skills acquired in advanced, industrialized economies are more easily transferable to the American labor market. After all, the industrial structure of advanced economies and

TABLE 8-2

Wages of Immigrant Men in 1990, by Country of Birth

Source: George J. Borjas, "The Economics of Immigration," *Journal of Economic Literature* 32 (December 1994): 1686.

Country of Birth	Percent Wage Differential between Immigrants and Natives
Europe	
Germany	24.5
Portugal	−3.1
United Kingdom	37.2
Asia	
India	17.6
Korea	−12.0
Vietnam	−18.9
Americas	
Canada	24.0
Dominican Republic	−29.2
Mexico	−39.5
Africa	
Egypt	12.2
Ethiopia	−21.0
Nigeria	−18.9

[30] An interesting study of the factors that contribute to immigrant assimilation in the Swedish context is given by Per-Anders Edin, Peter Fredriksson, and Olof Aslund, "Settlement Policies and the Economic Success of Immigrants," *Journal of Population Economics* 17 (February 2004): 133–155.

[31] George J. Borjas, "Self-Selection and the Earnings of Immigrants," *American Economic Review* 77 (September 1987): 531–553; and LaLonde and Topel, "The Assimilation of Immigrants in the U.S. Economy."

the types of skills rewarded by firms in those labor markets greatly resemble the industrial structure of the United States and the types of skills rewarded by American employers. In contrast, the industrial structure of less-developed countries probably rewards skills that are less useful in the American labor market. The human capital embodied in residents of those countries is, to some extent, specific to those countries and cannot be easily transferred to the United States.

There is, in fact, a strong positive correlation between the earnings of an immigrant group in the United States and per capita GDP in the country of origin; a doubling of the source country's per capita GDP may increase the U.S. earnings of an immigrant group by as much as 4 percent.[32] Because more recent immigrant waves tend to originate in low-income countries, they will be somewhat less successful in the U.S. labor market.

The Roy Model

There also will be dispersion in skills among national-origin groups in the United States because different types of immigrants come from different countries. Which subset of workers in a given source country finds it worthwhile to migrate to the United States: the most skilled or the least skilled?

Consider workers residing in a country that offers a low rate of return to a worker's human capital so that the skilled do not earn much more than the unskilled. This is typical in countries such as Sweden that have relatively egalitarian income distributions and almost confiscatory income tax systems. Relative to the United States, these countries tax able workers and insure the unskilled against poor labor market outcomes. This situation generates incentives for the skilled to migrate to the United States because they have the most to gain by moving. Put differently, the United States is the recipient of a "brain drain."

Consider instead workers originating in source countries that offer a high rate of return to human capital. This is typical in countries with substantial income inequality, as in many less-developed countries. In this situation, it is the United States that taxes the skilled and subsidizes the unskilled (relative to the source country). The United States thus becomes a magnet for workers with relatively low earnings capacities.

The economic intuition underlying these arguments is based on the influential **Roy model,** which describes how workers sort themselves among employment opportunities.[33] The key insights of the Roy model can be derived easily. Suppose that persons currently residing in the source country are trying to decide if they should migrate to the United States. We assume that earnings in both the source country and the United States depend on a single factor—skills—that is completely transferable across countries. Let the

---

[32] Guillermina Jasso and Mark R. Rosenzweig, "What's in a Name? Country-of-Origin Influences on the Earnings of Immigrants in the United States," *Research in Human Capital and Development* 4 (1986): 75–106.

[33] Andrew D. Roy, "Some Thoughts on the Distribution of Earnings," *Oxford Economic Papers* 3 (June 1951): 135–146. The model was applied to the migration decision by Borjas, "Self-Selection and the Earnings of Immigrants." Recent research also examines how international migrants are sorted across the potential countries of destination; see Gordon H. Hanson and Jeffrey T. Grogger, "Income Maximization and the Selection and Sorting of International Migrants," *Journal of Development Economics*, forthcoming 2011.

FIGURE 8-8 **The Distribution of Skills in the Source Country**

The distribution of skills in the source country gives the frequency of workers in each skill level. If immigrants have above-average skills, the immigrant flow is positively selected. If immigrants have below-average skills, the immigrant flow is negatively selected.

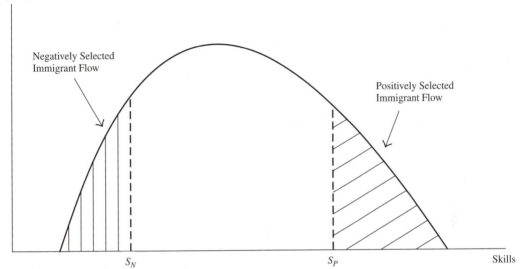

variable s denote the number of efficiency units embodied in the worker. The frequency distribution of skills in the source country's population is illustrated in Figure 8-8. We wish to determine which subset of workers chooses to migrate to the United States.

Each worker makes his or her migration decision by comparing earnings in the source country and in the United States. Figure 8-9 illustrates the relation between wages and skills for each of the countries. The slope of these wage-skill lines gives the dollar payoff to an additional efficiency unit in the United States or in the source country. In Figure 8-9*a,* the wage-skills line is steeper in the United States, so the payoff to an efficiency unit of human capital is higher in the United States than in the source country. In Figure 8-9*b,* the wage-skill line is steeper in the source country, so the payoff to skills is higher in the source country. To easily illustrate how the migration decision is reached, let's assume initially that workers do not incur any costs when they move to the United States. The decision rule that determines immigration is then quite simple: A worker migrates to the United States whenever U.S. earnings exceed earnings in the source country.[34]

Consider first the sorting that occurs in Figure 8-9*a.* Workers with fewer than s_P efficiency units earn more if they stay in the source country than if they migrate to the United States. Workers with more than s_P efficiency units, however, earn more in the United States than in the source country. Hence, workers with relatively high skill levels migrate to the United States.

---

[34] Note that the model is also implicitly assuming that immigration policy does not restrict the entry of any immigrants who find it worthwhile to move to the United States.

FIGURE 8-9   The Self-Selection of the Immigrant Flow

(a) If the rate of return to skills is higher in the United States than in the source country (so that the wage-skills line is steeper in the United States), the immigrant flow is positively selected. Workers with more than s_P efficiency units find it profitable to migrate to the United States. (b) If the rate of return to skills is lower in the United States, the immigrant flow is negatively selected. Workers with fewer than s_N efficiency units emigrate.

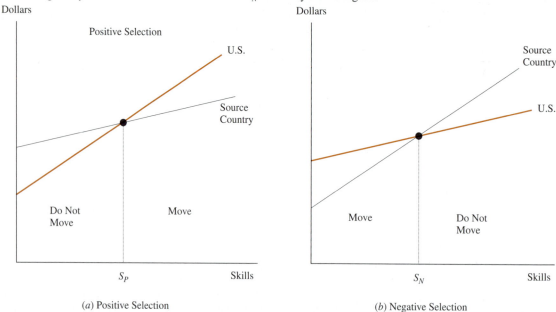

(a) Positive Selection   (b) Negative Selection

As long as the payoff for skills in the United States exceeds the payoff for skills in the source country, all persons who have a skill level exceeding the threshold s_P are better off in the United States. Therefore, the migration flow is composed of workers in the upper tail of the skill distribution illustrated in Figure 8-8. This type of self-selection is called **positive selection.** Immigrants, on average, are very skilled and do quite well in the United States.

Consider now Figure 8-9b, where the payoff for skills in the source country exceeds the payoff in the United States. Workers with fewer than s_N efficiency units earn more in the United States and will want to move. In contrast, workers who have more than s_N efficiency units have higher earnings in the source country and will not emigrate. When the payoff for skills in the United States is relatively low, therefore, the immigrant flow will be composed of the least-skilled workers in the source country. This type of self-selection is called **negative selection.** Immigrants, on average, are unskilled and perform poorly in the United States.

The key implication of the Roy model is clear: *The relative payoff for skills across countries determines the skill composition of the immigrant flow.* If an efficiency unit of human capital is highly valued in the United States, immigrants will originate in the upper tail of the skill distribution and will have higher-than-average skills. In contrast, if the source country offers a higher payoff, the immigrant flow contains workers from the lower tail of the skill distribution, who will have lower-than-average skills. Workers "selling" their skills behave just like firms selling their products. Both workers and goods flow to those markets where they can get the highest price.

Theory at Work

HITLER'S IMPACT ON THE PRODUCTION OF THEOREMS

Immediately after seizing power in 1933, the National Socialist Party enacted legislation known as the *Law for the Restoration of the Professional Civil Service*. This Orwellian-named statute, in fact, led to the dismissal of all Jewish professors (as well as professors with unacceptable political orientations) from German universities.

As a result, a remarkable 18 percent of German mathematics professors were dismissed between 1932 and 1934. The dismissals included some of the most famous mathematicians of the time, including John von Neumann, Richard Courant, and Richard von Mises. Many of the dismissed mathematicians eventually managed to migrate to other countries, mainly the United States. Von Neumann, for instance, moved to Princeton University where, after teaming with an economist, Oskar Morgenstern, he wrote his landmark text, *The Theory of Games and Economic Behavior*, in 1944. Most of the small number of Jewish mathematicians who remained in Germany, however, died in concentration camps.

The Jewish mathematicians had not been randomly employed across German universities prior to 1933, so some university departments barely noticed the departure of the luminaries, while other departments lost more than 50 percent of the faculty. The most affected departments included some of the (at the time) best mathematics departments in the country, including Göttingen and Berlin. A remarkable exchange between David Hilbert, one of the most famous mathematicians of the twentieth century, and the Nazi Minister of Education summarizes the impact:

Minister: How is mathematics in Göttingen now that it has been freed of Jewish influence?

Hilbert: Mathematics in Göttingen? There is really none any more.

A recent study exploits the differential impact of the dismissals on the various German universities to document how the exodus affected the productivity of the doctoral students left behind. If highly skilled mathematicians have beneficial effects on the productivity of those students with whom they interact, one would expect that the doctoral students in the most affected departments in Nazi Germany would experience worse outcomes than other cohorts of graduate students. In fact, those doctoral students stranded in the most affected departments had a much harder time in the "mathematics market" after completing their dissertations. They were far less likely to publish their dissertations, and those publications received far fewer citations.

The emigration of a positively selected group of workers, therefore, may have significant effects not only on labor market outcomes in the sending and receiving countries, but may also have particular detrimental effects on the productivity of those left behind.

Source: Fabian Waldinger, "Quality Matters: The Expulsion of Professors and the Consequences for PhD Student Outcomes in Nazi Germany," *Journal of Political Economy* 118 (August 2010): 787–831.

The Roy model implies that immigrants who originate in countries that offer a low rate of return to human capital will earn more than immigrants who originate in countries that offer a higher rate of return. The available evidence indeed indicates that there may be a negative correlation between measures of the source country's income inequality (which proxies for the rate of return to skills) and the earnings of immigrants in the United States.[35] The income distribution in Mexico, for instance, has about three times more dispersion than the income distribution in the United Kingdom. As a result, part of the sizable wage differential between a Mexican and a British immigrant arises because different types of persons choose to emigrate from these two countries.

[35] Borjas, "Self-Selection and the Earnings of Immigrants"; and Deborah Cobb-Clark, "Immigrant Selectivity and Wages: The Evidence for Women," *American Economic Review* 83 (September 1993): 986–993.

FIGURE 8-10   The Impact of a Decline in U.S. Incomes

If incomes in the United States fall (or if there is an increase in migration costs), the wage-skills line for the United States shifts down and fewer workers migrate. The decline in U.S. incomes, however, does not change the type of selection that characterizes the immigrant flow.

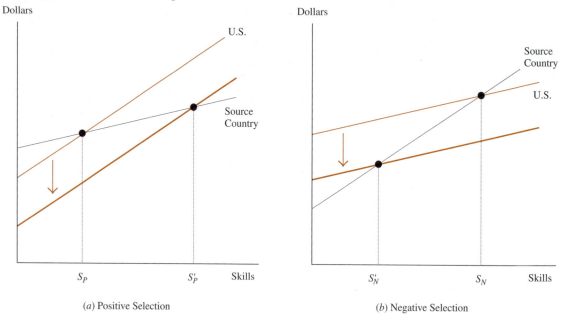

(a) Positive Selection   (b) Negative Selection

Changes in Income Levels and Migration Costs

A surprising implication of the Roy model is that the "base level" of income in the source country or in the United States (as measured by the height of the wage-skills lines in Figure 8-9) do not determine the type of selection that generates the immigrant flow. Changes in these base income levels, however, do affect the *size* of the flow.

Suppose, for instance, that income levels in the United States fall because of a severe recession. The recession pushes down the wage-skills line in the United States, as illustrated in Figure 8-10. If the payoff for skills in the United States exceeds the payoff in the source country, as in Figure 8-10a, the threshold level s_P increases to s_P'. This implies that fewer workers now find it optimal to migrate to the United States. It is still the case, however, that workers who are above the new threshold s_P' are the ones who find it optimal to migrate, and hence the immigrant flow is positively selected.

If the payoff for skills is higher in the source country, as illustrated in Figure 8-10b, the threshold level s_N falls to s_N'. Because only workers who have skill levels below the threshold level want to move, the drop in U.S. incomes again reduces the number of immigrants. The immigrant flow is still negatively selected because immigrants originate in the lower tail of the skill distribution.

We have derived our main conclusions using the simplifying assumption that the worker does not incur any costs when migrating to the United States. We can now easily introduce migration costs into our framework. To simplify, suppose that it costs, say, $5,000 to migrate to the United States, *regardless* of the worker's skill level. Migration costs obviously reduce the net income the worker can expect to receive in the United

States. Therefore, migration costs shift down the wage-skills line in the United States and are *equivalent* to the reduction in the U.S. income level that we illustrated in Figure 8-10. If migration costs are constant in the population, therefore, an increase in migration costs reduces the number of immigrants, but does not alter the type of selection that generates the immigrant flow.[36]

8-7 Policy Application: Labor Flows in Puerto Rico

Puerto Rico became a possession of the United States after the Spanish-American war in 1898.[37] The Jones Act of 1917 granted U.S. citizenship to all Puerto Ricans, implying that Puerto Ricans could move freely to the United States without the legal restrictions facing immigrants from foreign countries.

Despite the absence of legal restrictions, there was relatively little out-migration until after World War II. High unemployment in postwar Puerto Rico and the introduction of low-cost air travel (the six-hour flight from San Juan to New York City cost less than $50) sparked the initial out-migration. In 1940, only 59 thousand Puerto Ricans lived in the United States; by 1960, there were 627 thousand.

Figure 8-11 illustrates the trend in the out-migration rate between 1940 and 2000. The out-migration rate gives the fraction of the Puerto Rican–born population that moved to the United States. In 1940, the out-migration rate was 3.1 percent. By 1960, it had risen to 21.1 percent. This remarkable exodus inspired Stephen Sondheim to have one of the key characters in the 1961 movie version of *West Side Story* predict that the island would soon empty out:

> BERNARDO: I think I'll go back to San Juan.
> ANITA: I know a boat you can get on.
> BERNARDO: Everyone there will give big cheer.
> ANITA: Everyone there will have moved here.

Anita was wrong, however. The outflow of Puerto Ricans to the United States slowed down in the 1960s.

The Puerto Rican case study is interesting for several reasons. First, the outflow involved a large fraction of the island's population and it happened at a remarkable speed. Second, U.S. immigration policy did not restrict the number and skill composition of the

---

[36] The predictions of the model are somewhat different if migration costs vary across workers who differ in their skills; see Daniel Chiquiar and Gordon Hanson, "International Migration, Self-Selection, and the Distribution of Wages: Evidence from Mexico and the United States," *Journal of Political Economy* 113 (April 2005): 239–281. Chiquiar and Hanson find that the probability of emigration to the United States is highest for Mexican workers in the middle of the Mexican skill distribution. More recent work, however, suggests that the undercount of illegal immigrants in the U.S. Census can seriously bias any analysis of the selection of Mexican emigrants and that a correction of this problem suggests that Mexican immigrants in the United States tended to do relatively poorly in Mexico prior to their migration; see Jesús Fernández-Huertas Moraga, "New Evidence on Emigrant Selection," *Review of Economics and Statistics* 93 (February 2011): 72–96.

[37] The discussion presented in this section is based on the findings reported in George J. Borjas, "Labor Outflows and Labor Inflows in Puerto Rico," *Journal of Human Capital* 2 (Spring 2008): 32–68. See also Fernando Ramos, "Out-Migration and Return Migration of Puerto Ricans," in George J. Borjas and Richard B. Freeman, editors, *Immigration and the Work Force: Economic Consequences for the United States and Source Areas,* Chicago: University of Chicago Press, 1992; and Maria E. Enchautegui, "Selectivity Patterns in Puerto Rican Migration," Working Paper, University of Puerto Rico, 2005.

FIGURE 8-11   **Trends in Out-migration Rates and In-migration Rates in Puerto Rico**

Source: George J. Borjas, "Labor Outflows and Labor Inflows in Puerto Rico," *Journal of Human Capital* 2 (Spring 2008): 32–68.

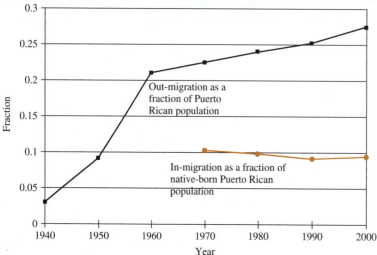

Puerto Rican out-migration—so the observed flows can be used to test the implications of income-maximizing models of labor flows. Finally, the Puerto Rican context is quite rare because the island was both a source and a destination region: Puerto Rico was losing a sizable fraction of its people *at the same time* that it was the recipient of large inflows of persons born outside the island. The in-migration rate also illustrated in Figure 8-11 gives the number of in-migrants as a share of the Puerto Rican population. Between 1970 and 2000, approximately 10 percent of the Puerto Rican population was born outside Puerto Rico. Put differently, Puerto Rico had an immigrant influx that was proportionately similar to that entering the United States.

It turns out that about 80 or 90 percent of the in-migrants entering Puerto Rico in the 1990s were born in the United States and have Puerto Rican ancestry. These in-migrants are *not* return migrants; that is, they are not Puerto Ricans who had left the island at an earlier point and had subsequently decided to return. Because the in-migrants are predominantly U.S.-born persons with Puerto Rican ancestry, the in-migrants are mostly the descendants of earlier generations of Puerto Ricans who moved to the United States.

The simultaneous presence of the two opposing flows creates obvious problems for the income-maximizing model of migration, since labor should presumably flow only in the direction of the highest-paying area. It is easy to reconcile two-way flows, however, if different regions offer differential rewards for different types of human capital, and if the opposing labor flows are composed of different types of people.

The rate of return to skills is much higher in Puerto Rico than in the United States. In 1990, for instance, the age-adjusted wage gap between college graduates and high school graduates was 125 percent in Puerto Rico and 86 percent in the United States. The Roy model would then predict that a relatively higher fraction of the least-educated Puerto Ricans would leave the island.

TABLE 8-3   Labor Flows in and out of Puerto Rico in 2000 (in the sample of working-aged men)

Source: George J. Borjas, "Labor Outflows and Labor Inflows in Puerto Rico," *Journal of Human Capital* 2 (Spring 2008): 32–68.

Years of Education	Fraction of Puerto Ricans That Moved to the United States	Fraction of U.S.-Born Persons with Puerto Rican Ancestry That Moved to Puerto Rico
Less than 12 years	0.447	0.069
12 years	0.401	0.086
13–15 years	0.364	0.121
At least 16 years	0.304	0.189

The differences in out-migration rates across education groups illustrated in the first column of Table 8-3 are consistent with this prediction. Nearly 45 percent of Puerto Rican–born working-age men who lacked a high school diploma had moved to the United States as of 2000. In contrast, only 30 percent of working-age men with at least a college education had moved to the United States.

The selection that characterizes the reverse migration of U.S.-born workers who move to Puerto Rico also can be understood in terms of the Roy model. The second column of Table 8-3 reports the fraction of U.S.-born men with Puerto Rican ancestry who have moved to Puerto Rico. The skill composition of this population is a mirror image of that of Puerto Ricans choosing to move to the United States. Because Puerto Rico offers relatively higher returns to skills, it should not be surprising that the out-migration rates of U.S.-born Puerto Ricans are largest for college-educated workers. In 2000, the out-migration rate of college graduates was 18.9 percent, as compared to 6.9 percent for workers who had not finished high school.

The Puerto Rican case study confirms an important insight of the Roy model: skills flow to where they receive their highest return.

8-8   Policy Application: Intergenerational Mobility of Immigrants

It is widely believed that, on average, the socioeconomic performance of the children of immigrants far surpasses that of their parents.[38] This perception originated in early empirical studies that compared the earnings of various generations of workers in the United States at a particular point in time, such as the 1970 decennial census.[39] Table 8-4 summarizes the available evidence for three such cross-sections: 1940, 1970, and 2000.

Each of these cross-section data files allows the precise identification of two generations of Americans: the immigrant generation (i.e., persons born abroad) and the second generation (i.e., persons born in the United States who have at least one parent born abroad). The generation of the remaining persons in the sample (i.e., of persons who have American-born parents and were themselves born in the United States) cannot be determined exactly, but they are typically referred to as "third-generation" Americans. It should

[38] The discussion in this section is based on George J. Borjas, "Making It in America: The Immigrant Experience," *The Future of Children* 16 (Fall 2006): 57–71.

[39] Barry R. Chiswick, "Sons of Immigrants: Are They at an Earnings Disadvantage?" *American Economic Review* 67, no. 1 (1977): 376–380.

TABLE 8-4   Relative Wages of Men across Generations

Source: George J. Borjas, "Making It in America: The Immigrant Experience," *The Future of Children* 16 (Fall 2006).

	1940	1970	2000
Age-adjusted log weekly wage, relative to 3rd generation			
1st generation	0.058	0.014	−0.197
2nd generation	0.178	0.146	0.063

be noted, however, that this residual group contains persons who are grandchildren of immigrants as well as descendants of the Mayflower Pilgrims.

For each of the available cross-sections, Table 8-4 reports the (age-adjusted) log weekly wage of first- and second-generation male workers relative to that of the baseline third generation. In 1970, for example, immigrant men earned about 1.4 percent more than men in the third generation, while second-generation working men earned 14.6 percent more than the baseline workforce. In short, second-generation workers in 1970 earned more than both the immigrants and the subsequent generations.

In fact, Table 8-4 reveals the same empirical pattern for every single cross section of data. In 1940, second-generation working men earned 17.8 percent more than the baseline third generation, while immigrants earned only 5.8 percent more. In 2000, second-generation working men earned 6.3 percent more than the baseline third generation, while immigrants earned 19.7 percent less.

The wage superiority of the second generation in each cross-section snapshot seems to imply that second-generation Americans earn more than both their parents and their children. A common story used to explain this inference is that the children of immigrants are "hungry" and have the drive and ambition that ensures economic success in the U.S. labor market—and that this hunger is lost once the immigrant household becomes fully Americanized by the third generation. If this interpretation were correct, the policy concern over the relatively low skill level of the immigrants who have migrated to the United States in the past three decades may be misplaced. If historical patterns were to hold in the future, the children of these immigrants will outperform not only their parents but the rest of the workforce as well in only a few decades.

However, the evidence summarized in Table 8-4 does not necessarily justify this inference. After all, the family ties among the three generations identifiable in any cross section of data are very tenuous. It is *biologically impossible* for most second-generation workers enumerated in a particular cross section to be the direct descendants of the immigrants enumerated at the same time. For instance, working-age immigrants enumerated in 2000 (most of whom arrived in the 1980s and 1990s) typically cannot have American-born children who are also of working age. Second-generation Americans of working age can only be the descendants of immigrants who have been in the country for at least two or three decades. Put differently, most of the second-generation workers enumerated in 2000 are unlikely to be the children of the immigrant workers enumerated at the same time.

As a result, the fact that second-generation workers earn more than other workers at a point in time does not necessarily imply that second-generation workers earn more than either their parents or their children. To calculate the improvement in economic status between the first and second generations, one must link the economic performance of parents and children, rather than compare the economic performance of workers belonging to different generations in a cross section.

It is possible to approximate the correct intergenerational comparison by tracking the immigrant population over time.[40] For instance, the 1970 census provides information on the economic performance of the immigrants present in the United States at that time. Many of these immigrants are, in fact, the parents of the second-generation workers enumerated in the 2000 cross section. Similarly, the 1940 census provides information on the economic performance of immigrants in 1940. These immigrants, in turn, are probably the parents of the second-generation workers enumerated by the 1970 census. It is only by comparing the economic performance of immigrant workers in 1940 with the economic performance of second-generation workers in 1970—or the economic performance of immigrant workers in 1970 with that of the second generation in 2000—that one can correctly determine the economic progress experienced by the children of immigrants.

Consider again the wage information summarized in Table 8-4. If we (incorrectly) used only the information provided by the 2000 cross section, we would conclude that since second-generation workers earn 6.3 percent more than the baseline third generation and first-generation workers earn 19.7 percent less than the baseline, second-generation workers earn 26.0 percent more than first-generation workers. A correct calculation of the second-generation improvement, however, reveals much less intergenerational improvement. After all, the typical immigrant in 1970 earned 1.4 percent more than the typical third-generation worker. And the typical second-generation worker in 2000 (who is presumably the descendant of the immigrants enumerated in 1970) earns 6.3 percent more than the baseline. In short, the true intergenerational growth in relative wages was only on the order of 5 percent—rather than the 26 percent implied by the wage differentials observed in 2000.

The data presented in Section 8-6 documented that there was a lot of variation in socioeconomic status among national origin groups in the first generation. Some immigrant groups do quite well in the U.S. labor market, while other groups fare much worse. To determine how much of the ethnic differences in economic status that exist among immigrants persist into the second generation, some studies estimate statistical models that relate the relative wage of a second-generation national origin group to the relative wage of their first-generation counterpart.[41] The statistical analysis, of course, accounts for the fact that first- and second-generation workers observed in a single cross section of data have little biological connection with each other, so the statistical models link the relative earnings of second-generation workers at a particular point in time (e.g., the 2000 cross section) to the earnings of first-generation workers a few decades past (e.g., the 1970 census).

---

[40] George J. Borjas, "The Intergenerational Mobility of Immigrants," *Journal of Labor Economics* 11 (January 1993): 113–135.

[41] Borjas, "The Intergenerational Mobility of Immigrants"; George J. Borjas, "Long-Run Convergence of Ethnic Skill Differentials: The Children and Grandchildren of the Great Migration," *Industrial and Labor Relations Review* 47 (July 1994): 553–573; and David Card, John DiNardo, and Eugena Estes, "The More Things Change: Immigrants and the Children of Immigrants in the 1940s, the 1970s, and the 1990s," in George J. Borjas, editor, *Issues in the Economics of Immigration,* Chicago: University of Chicago Press, 2000, pp. 227–270. See also Hoyt Bleakley and Aimee Chin, "What Holds Back the Second Generation? The Intergenerational Transmission of Language Human Capital among Immigrants," *Journal of Human Resources* 43 (Spring 2008): 267–298.

FIGURE 8-12   **Earnings Mobility between First and Second Generations of Americans, 1970–2000**

Source: George J. Borjas, "Making It in America: The Immigrant Experience," *The Future of Children* 16 (Fall 2006).

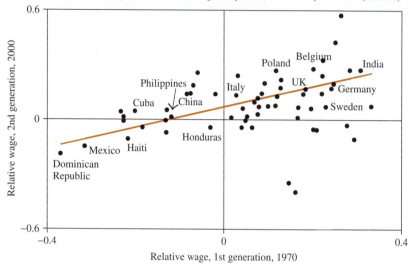

Figure 8-12 shows the intergenerational link for male workers belonging to a large number of national origin groups in the 1970–2000 period. The horizontal axis gives the age-adjusted relative wage of working men in the immigrant generation. These data are obtained from the 1970 census. The vertical axis gives the age-adjusted relative wage of the working men in the second generation, and these data are obtained from the 2000 cross section. There is a strong positive correlation between the average skills of workers in the two generations; the national origin groups that fared economically well in the first generation also fared well in the second.

The upward-sloping regression line illustrated in Figure 8-12 summarizes the statistical link between the relative wages of particular national origin groups across the two generations. If the regression line were relatively flat, it would indicate that there is little connection between the average skills of the ethnic groups in the second generation and the average skills of the immigrant groups. Put differently, all second-generation groups would have relatively similar wages regardless of the economic performance of their parents. In this case, the intergenerational correlation would be near zero, and there would be complete regression toward the mean. If the regression line were relatively steep, there would then be a substantial link between relative wages in the first and second generations. The intergenerational correlation implied by the regression line in the figure is 0.56.

This estimated intergenerational correlation suggests that about half of the wage differential between any two national origin groups in the first generation persists into the second generation. If the average wage of two ethnic groups is 30 percentage points apart in the first generation, the average wage of the two groups is expected to be about 15 percentage points apart in the second. There is some intergenerational mobility, therefore, but ethnicity remains an important determinant of earnings in the second generation.

Human Capital Externalities

Some researchers argue that **social capital**—the set of variables that characterizes the "quality" of the environment where a person grows up or lives—also helps determine the worker's human capital.[42] For a given level of parental skills, children exposed to "role models" and "peer groups" that are highly educated, have steady employment, and are economically successful will turn out differently from children exposed to role models who are predominantly unemployed or receive public assistance. In effect, the quality of the environment where the child grows up acts as a **human capital externality** in the production of the children's human capital. In other words, the environment is an external factor—beyond the control of the parents—that affects the human capital accumulation process.

Human capital externalities attenuate the regression toward the mean across generations. The children's human capital will depend both on parental skills and on the social capital to which the children are exposed. Children raised in disadvantaged environments will be "pulled down" by the human capital externality, whereas children raised in high-skill neighborhoods will be "pushed up" by the externality. In effect, the human capital externality acts as a double-sided magnet—preventing the children of the particular demographic group from deviating too far from the group mean.

Human capital externalities also can help explain why racial and ethnic differences in labor market outcomes seem to persist across generations. Some racial or ethnic groups do particularly well generation after generation, whereas other ethnic groups do poorly for a very long time. As we have seen, the evidence suggests that 50 percent of the gap in the average wage between any two ethnic groups persists from one generation to the next. Part of this may be attributable to the fact that children who are raised in disadvantaged ethnic environments will tend to have less human capital, even after adjusting for differences in the human capital of the parents.[43]

Of course, race and ethnicity are not the only environmental factors that influence the human capital accumulation process. There is evidence that such variables as the overall quality of the neighborhood, membership in religious organizations, and the socioeconomic background of a child's classmates influence a child's human capital.[44] For instance, residing in a neighborhood that has relatively high levels of criminal activity greatly increases the probability that an individual will enter that profession, even holding parental background constant. Many studies also document "neighborhood effects" in the accumulation of skills, welfare dependency, substance abuse, and teenage pregnancy.

---

[42] Glenn C. Loury, "A Dynamic Theory of Racial Income Differences," in Phyllis A. Wallace and A. LaMond, editors, *Women, Minorities, and Employment Discrimination,* Lexington, MA: Lexington Books, 1977; Shelly Lundberg and Richard Startz, "On the Persistence of Racial Inequality," *Journal of Labor Economics* 16 (April 1998): 292–323; and George J. Borjas, "Ethnic Capital and Intergenerational Mobility," *Quarterly Journal of Economics* 107 (February 1992): 123–150.

[43] Borjas, "Ethnic Capital and Intergenerational Mobility."

[44] Mary Corcoran, Robert Gordon, Deborah Laren, and Gary Solon, "The Association between Men's Economic Status and Their Family and Community Origins," *Journal of Human Resources* 27 (Fall 1992): 575–601; William N. Evans, Wallace E. Oates, and Robert M. Schwab, "Measuring Peer Group Effects," *Journal of Political Economy* 100 (October 1992): 966–991; and Joshua D. Angrist and Kevin Lang, "Does School Integration Generate Peer Effects? Evidence from Boston's Metco Program," *American Economic Review* 94 (December 2004): 1613–1634.

8-9   Job Turnover: Facts

We now turn to one particular type of mobility that occurs frequently in many labor markets: job turnover. As Figure 8-13 shows, the frequency of job turnover among newly hired young workers in the United States is remarkable. The probability that newly hired young workers (who are in their twenties) will leave their jobs within the next 24 months is nearly 75 percent. In contrast, workers who have a lot of seniority rarely leave their jobs: The probability that a job that has already lasted 10 years will terminate in the next 24 months is less than 5 percent. There is also a strong negative correlation between the probability of job separation and a worker's age. Workers in their twenties are much more likely to move than workers in their forties and fifties.

It is interesting to note that both the probability of a quit (that is, an employee-initiated job separation) and the probability of a layoff (an employer-initiated job separation) decline with job seniority and with age. Newly hired workers probably have the highest quit *and* layoff rates because both workers and firms are "testing the waters." Young workers are probably shopping around and trying out employment opportunities in different types of firms, in different industries, and perhaps even in different occupations. Over time, workers find their niche in the firm so that both types of separations occur less frequently. The decline in the quit rate over the life cycle is also implied by the hypothesis that labor turnover is a human capital investment. Older workers have a smaller payoff period over

FIGURE 8-13 **Probability of Job Turnover over a Two-Year Period for Young and Older Workers**

Source: Jacob Mincer and Boyan Jovanovic, "Labor Mobility and Wages," in Sherwin Rosen, editor, *Studies in Labor Markets,* Chicago: University of Chicago Press, 1981, p. 25.

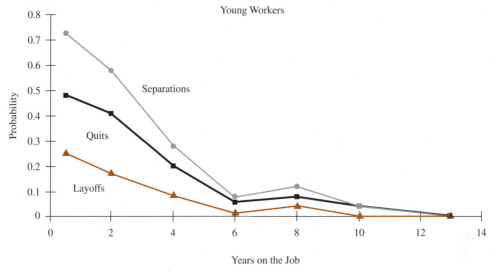

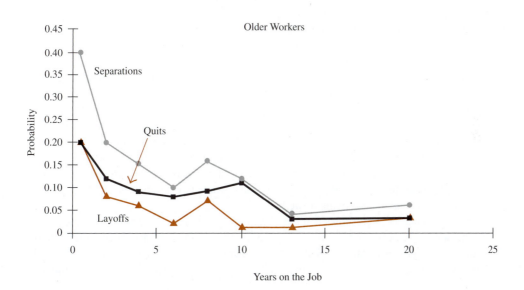

which they can recoup the costs associated with job search, and hence they are less likely to move.

Despite the high probabilities of job turnover among some workers, these statistics disguise an important feature of the U.S. labor market: Long jobs have been the norm rather than the exception. As Figure 8-14 shows, a large (though declining) fraction of men over

FIGURE 8-14 Incidence of Long-Term Employment Relationships, 1979–1996 (percent of workers aged 35–64 in jobs lasting at least 20 years)

Source: Henry S. Farber, "Mobility and Stability: The Dynamics of Job Change in Labor Markets," in Orley C. Ashenfelter and David Card, editors, *Handbook of Labor Economics,* vol. 3B, Amsterdam: Elsevier, 1999, p. 2449.

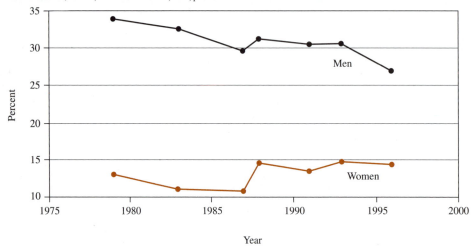

the age of 35 are in jobs that last at least 20 years.[45] The period of "job shopping" and frequent turnover observed among young workers seems to end by the time the workers are in their thirties. This result might seem surprising because U.S. employers do not have an explicit "lifetime employment" clause in employment contracts. Nevertheless, many workers in the United States end up in so-called lifetime jobs.

Even though the probabilities of quits and layoffs exhibit the same declining trend within a job and over the life cycle, the evidence indicates that quitters usually move on to higher-paying jobs, whereas workers who are laid off move on to lower-paying jobs. On average, young men who quit get at least a 5 percent wage increase (relative to the wage gain of stayers), whereas young men who are laid off suffer a 3 percent wage decline.[46] There are also important differences in the postseparation employment histories of workers who quit and who are laid off. Most workers who quit find employment without any intervening unemployment spell in between jobs, whereas workers who are laid off typically experience an unemployment spell.

In fact, recent research shows that the adverse consequences of losing a job involuntarily can be substantial, even outside the U.S. labor market. A study of displaced workers in the United Kingdom, for instance, finds that the subsequent wage of workers who lost their jobs because of a mass layoff is about 15 to 25 percent lower than the pre-layoff wage. Similarly,

[45] Robert E. Hall, "The Importance of Lifetime Jobs in the U.S. Economy," *American Economic Review* 72 (September 1982): 716–724; and Manuelita Ureta, "The Importance of Lifetime Jobs in the U.S. Economy, Revisited," *American Economic Review* 82 (March 1992): 322–335.

[46] Ann P. Bartel and George J. Borjas, "Wage Growth and Job Turnover: An Empirical Analysis," in Sherwin Rosen, editor, *Studies in Labor Markets,* Chicago: University of Chicago Press, 1981, pp. 65–90; see also Jacob Mincer, "Wage Changes and Job Changes," *Research in Labor Economics* 8 (1986, Part A): 171–197.

FIGURE 8-15 **The Rate of Job Loss in the United States, 1981–2001 (percent of workers losing their jobs in a three-year period)**

Source: Henry S. Farber, "Job Loss in the United States, 1981–2001," *Research in Labor Economics* 23 (2004): 69–117.

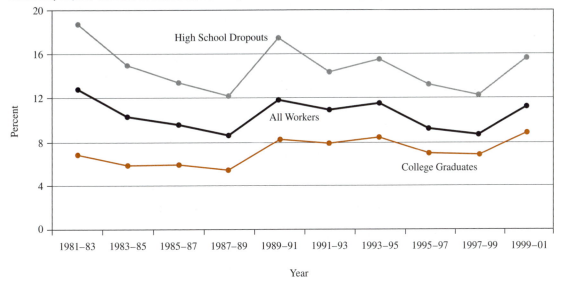

there is evidence that job loss in Sweden can have significantly harmful health effects, even leading to higher mortality rates. The mortality rate of Swedish men whose firm has shut down rises by about 44 percent during the first five years after the plant closing.[47]

As we saw in the last chapter, there was a substantial increase in wage inequality in the United States in the 1980s and 1990s. This change in the wage structure seems to have been accompanied by an increase in job instability.[48] A larger number of workers report that they have lost their jobs because of slack work, because the plant closed, or because their positions were abolished. In fact, the rate of job loss—that is, the fraction of workers who claim to have lost their jobs for these reasons—remained high in the 1990s, despite the fact that the economy was booming during this period. Figure 8-15 illustrates the trend in the rate of job loss over the 1981–2001 period. Between 1981 and 1983, about 12.8 percent of workers had lost a job. This three-year job loss rate declined to about 9 percent in the late 1980s and then increased to almost 12 percent in the mid-1990s.

---

[47] See Alexander Hijzen, Richard Upward, and Peter W. Wright, "The Income Losses of Displaced Workers," *Journal of Human Resources* 45 (Winter 2010): 243–269; and Marcus Eliason and Donald Storrie, "Does Job Loss Shorten Life?" *Journal of Human Resources* 44 (Spring 2009): 277–302.

[48] Henry S. Farber, "The Changing Face of Job Loss in the United States, 1981–1995," *Brookings Papers on Economic Activity, Microeconomics* (1997): 55–142. See also Francis X. Diebold, David Neumark, and Daniel Polsky, "Job Stability in the United States," *Journal of Labor Economics* 15 (April 1997): 206–233; Daniel Jaeger and Ann Huff Stevens, "Is Job Stability in the U.S. Falling? Reconciling Trends in the Current Population Survey and Panel Study of Income Dynamics," *Journal of Labor Economics* 17 (October 1999, Part 2): S1–S28; and Henry S. Farber, "What Do We Know about Job Loss in the United States? Evidence from the Displaced Workers Survey, 1984–2004," *Federal Reserve Bank of Chicago Economic Perspectives* 29 (2nd Quarter 2005): 13–28.

Not surprisingly, the rate of job loss is highest among the least-educated workers. About 16 percent of high school dropouts lost their jobs between 1999 and 2001. It turns out, however, that there was also increased job instability among highly educated workers. Although the rate of job loss for college graduates hovered around 6 or 7 percent throughout much of the 1980s, it increased to over 9 percent by the end of the 1990s. It seems, therefore, that the increase in job instability in the U.S. labor market has even affected skill groups that would probably have been relatively immune in earlier years.

8-10   The Job Match

In the simple supply-demand model of competitive labor market equilibrium, the interaction of workers looking for the best job opportunities and employers attempting to maximize profits equalizes the value of marginal product of labor across firms. The equilibrium allocation of workers to firms maximizes the value of labor's contribution to national income. A worker's value of marginal product would not increase if he or she were to switch to another firm, so there is no incentive for *any* type of job separation to occur.

Nevertheless, quits and layoffs are commonly and persistently observed in competitive labor markets. Job turnover arises partly because workers differ in their abilities and because firms offer different working conditions. Moreover, workers lack information about which firm provides the best opportunities, and firms lack information about the workers' true productivity.[49]

Suppose, for instance, that different firms offer different work environments. At Joe's Newsstand, Joe is well organized, plans the worker's schedule well in advance, and gives the worker a reasonable amount of time in which to complete an assigned task (such as creating a computerized inventory of the store's newspaper and magazine holdings). At Microsoft, the supervisor waits until the last minute to inform the worker of an upcoming task (such as writing new code for the latest update of a spreadsheet program) and then imposes a tight deadline. If a particular worker does not perform well under such stressful conditions, the value of the match between this worker and Joe may be higher than the value of the match at Microsoft. Other workers, however, might find that their productive juices flow when faced with tight deadlines, and, for those workers, the value of the match at Microsoft would be higher.

The notion that each **job match** (that is, each particular pairing of a firm and a worker) has its own unique value implies that both workers and firms can improve their situations by shopping around.[50] In other words, it matters if a particular computer programmer is employed at Microsoft or at Joe's Newsstand. A worker has an incentive to search for a work environment that "fits." This search would increase the worker's productivity and wage. The firm also wants to search for workers who are well suited to the firm's environment. This search would increase the firm's profits.

---

[49] Boyan Jovanovic, "Job Matching and the Theory of Turnover," *Journal of Political Economy* 87 (October 1979): 972–990; see also Derek Neal, "The Complexity of Job Mobility among Young Men," *Journal of Labor Economics* 17 (April 1999): 237–261.

[50] An interesting study of the link between the expectation of job loss and subsequent job turnover is given by Melvin Stephens Jr., "Job Loss Expectations, Realizations, and Household Consumption Behavior," *Review of Economics and Statistics* 86 (February 2004): 253–269.

The efficient turnover hypothesis suggests that the optimal allocation of workers to firms results when workers move to those jobs where they are most productive. A number of factors, however, may block workers from moving to "better" jobs and hence prevent the economy from attaining an efficient allocation of labor.

For example, a worker's employer-provided health insurance is generally not portable across jobs in the United States. Moreover, many health insurance programs refuse to cover a new worker's preexisting medical conditions (sometimes for up to two years). As a result, workers who have a health problem may not want to move to a job where they are more productive because of the potential costs associated with losing health insurance coverage. In fact, 30 percent of the respondents in a CBS/*New York Times* Poll reported that they had stayed in a job they wanted to leave mainly because they did not want to lose their health coverage. The employer-based health insurance system, therefore,

induces a form of "job-lock," where workers are locked into their jobs even though this allocation of workers to firms might not be efficient.

Studies suggest that this type of job-lock may be a significant problem in the U.S. labor market. For instance, families in which a wife is pregnant (a form of preexisting medical condition) show increased mobility among workers who have no health insurance, but reduced mobility among workers who have employer-provided health insurance. Overall, it has been estimated that job-lock reduces the voluntary turnover rate of workers with employer-provided health insurance by as much as 25 percent per year.

Sources: Brigitte C. Madrian, "Employment-Based Health Insurance and Job Mobility: Is There Evidence of Job-Lock?" *Quarterly Journal of Economics* 109 (February 1994): 27–54; and Mark C. Berger, Dan A. Black, and Frank A. Scott, "Is There Job Lock? Evidence from the Pre-HIPAA Era," *Southern Economic Journal* 70 (April 2004): 953–976.

If workers and firms knew exactly which particular match had the highest value, workers would look for the best firm, firms would look for the best worker, and there would be no need for turnover after the initial "marriage" was consummated. The sorting of workers and firms would be the optimal sorting, the one that maximizes the total value of labor's product.

Both firms and workers, however, are ill-informed about the true value of the match at the time the job begins. Over time, both the worker and the firm may realize that they incorrectly predicted the value of the match. Moreover, firms and workers know that there are other workers and firms out there that would provide a better match. Job turnover, therefore, is the mechanism that labor markets use to correct matching errors and leads to a better and more efficient allocation of resources. This type of turnover is called **efficient turnover,** for it increases the total value of labor's product in a competitive labor market.

8-11   Specific Training and Job Turnover

As we saw earlier, workers who have been employed on the job for only a short time have a very high probability of both quitting and being laid off, whereas workers who have more seniority are unlikely to experience either type of job separation. A simple explanation of this relationship uses the concept of firm-specific training introduced in

FIGURE 8-16   **Specific Training and the Probability of Job Separation for a Given Worker**

If a worker acquires specific training as he accumulates more seniority, the probability that the worker will separate from the job declines over time.

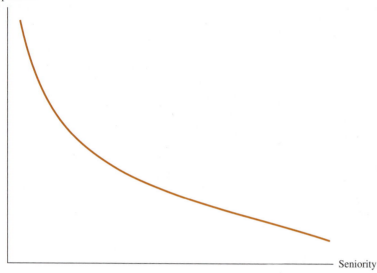

Chapter 6.[51] At the beginning of an employment relationship, the worker and firm have not yet invested in skills that are specific to that job, and hence no "bond" between the two parties exists. Once firm-specific skills are acquired, the worker's productivity in this firm exceeds his wage (lowering the probability of layoff) and the worker's wage in this firm exceeds the wage he could get elsewhere (lowering the probability of a quit). Therefore, specific training implies that there should be a negative relationship between the probability of job separation and job seniority *for a given worker*, as illustrated in Figure 8-16.[52]

As we saw earlier, the available evidence clearly indicates that workers with seniority are less likely to change jobs than newly hired workers. It is tempting to conclude from this cross-sectional correlation that labor turnover rates indeed decline as a particular worker acquires more experience on the job. To document this correlation correctly, however, we have to show that as a *given* worker ages on the job, *his* probability of job separation declines. The comparison of different workers at different points of their tenure on the job may say nothing about whether the probability of separation declines for a particular worker.

---

[51] An excellent survey of this literature is given by Henry S. Farber, "Mobility and Stability: The Dynamics of Job Change in Labor Markets," in Orley Ashenfelter and David Card, editors, *Handbook of Labor Economics*, vol. 3B, Amsterdam: Elsevier, 1999, pp. 2440–2483. An empirical study is given by Lalith Munasinghe, "Specific Training Sometimes Cuts Wages and Always Cuts Turnover," *Journal of Labor Economics* 23 (April 2005): 213–233.

[52] When a worker's probability of job separation declines the longer he has been employed on a particular job, we say that the probability of job separation exhibits "negative state dependence." In other words, the probability of turnover depends negatively on the length of time that the individual has spent in a particular employment state (that is, on a particular job).

To see why, consider a labor market where there are two types of workers: "movers" and "stayers." Movers perennially believe that the grass is greener elsewhere and incur the necessary costs to try out alternative opportunities. In contrast, stayers doubt that things will improve if they move elsewhere and are not willing to incur the costs associated with job turnover. Movers, therefore, have a high probability of job separation; stayers have a low probability.

The key implication of the stayer-mover distinction for the analysis of turnover probabilities is easy to grasp. Because movers are footloose and have a high propensity for turnover, it is unlikely that many movers have acquired a lot of seniority. Most movers, therefore, will have short job tenures and very high turnover propensities. At the same time, because stayers exhibit a lot of inertia, they will tend to have higher job tenure. The correlation between the probability that a worker might quit his job in the next year with the level of job tenure would be negative. But this correlation does not arise because the probability of separation declines for a particular worker—after all, the movers are always movers and the stayers are always stayers—but because workers with low job tenures are likely to be movers. Therefore, it is incorrect to conclude that specific training is important simply because the data indicate that more senior workers are less likely to change jobs than newly hired workers.

A few studies have attempted to determine if the probability of separation declines for a single worker as he or she acquires more job experience. This research typically analyzes the histories of labor mobility for a large number of individual workers over a large span of their working lives. These studies generally find some evidence of the mover-stayer phenomenon in the labor market. There is, for instance, a very strong correlation between a worker's probability of changing jobs today and the same worker's probability of changing jobs in the near future. Put differently, there seems to be something like the "mover" phenomenon in the population.[53]

At the same time, there is evidence suggesting that separation rates *do* decline within the job for a particular worker. Even after controlling for differences in turnover probabilities among workers, the probability that a new job terminates in the first year is 0.5, the probability that the job terminates in the second year is 0.3, in the third year 0.25, and in the fourth year 0.2. After 10 years on the job, the probability of separation is less than 3 percent.[54] The evidence thus suggests that specific training may play an important role in cementing the employment relationship between the firm and the worker.

8-12   Job Turnover and the Age-Earnings Profile

Job turnover changes the shape of the worker's age-earnings profile. As noted earlier, young men who quit their jobs experience substantial increases in their wages, whereas workers who are laid off often experience wage cuts. Job turnover, therefore, causes an immediate shift on the *level* of the mover's age-earnings profile, as illustrated in Figure 8-17. As drawn, the wage level increases substantially at ages t_1 and t_3, when the worker quits his job, and declines at age t_2 when he is laid off.

[53] Henry S. Farber, "The Analysis of Interfirm Worker Mobility," *Journal of Labor Economics* 12 (October 1994): 554–593; and Jacob Mincer and Boyan Jovanovic, "Labor Mobility and Wages," in Sherwin Rosen, editor, *Studies in Labor Markets,* Chicago: University of Chicago Press, 1981, pp. 21–63.

[54] Farber, "The Analysis of Interfirm Worker Mobility."

FIGURE 8-17   Impact of Job Mobility on Age-Earnings Profile

The age-earnings profile of movers is discontinuous, shifting up when they quit and shifting down when they are laid off. Long jobs encourage firms and workers to invest in specific training and steepen the age-earnings profile. As a result, stayers will have a steeper age-earnings profile within any given job.

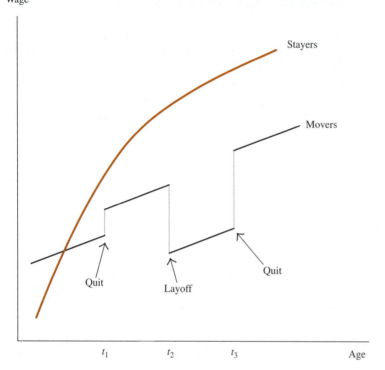

However, the impact of labor turnover on the age-earnings profile is not restricted to the level of the postseparation wage.[55] Figure 8-17 also shows the potential impact of labor turnover on the *slope* of the age-earnings profile by contrasting the age-earnings profiles of two workers, a mover and a stayer. The stayer has a continuous profile that is quite steep, so that the rate of wage growth *within the job* is substantial. The mover switches jobs several times and experiences a change in the wage level at each job change. Within a given job, however, the age-earnings profile of the mover is relatively flat.

The existence of firm-specific training, in fact, implies this type of relationship between job turnover and the slope of the age-earnings profile within a job. Workers and firms engaged in a long-term employment relationship have incentives to invest in specific skills. Because workers pay for part of the costs and collect part of the returns to the investment, wage growth is steeper in those jobs that have relatively large specific capital investments, namely, longer jobs. A worker's earnings, therefore, depend not only

---

[55] A careful study of the evolution of earnings with experience is given by Henry S. Farber and Robert Gibbons, "Learning and Wage Dynamics," *Quarterly Journal of Economics* 111 (November 1996): 1007–1047.

on total labor market experience but also on his job history and on his seniority on the current job.

Many studies document that workers who have been on the job for a long time earn more than newly hired workers, even after controlling for differences in the worker's age. The wage gap between two similarly aged workers who differ only in that one of the workers has one more year of seniority is on the order of 2 to 3 percent.[56] Although this evidence seems to be consistent with the specific training hypothesis, there has been a heated debate over whether job tenure truly has an independent impact on earnings.

The source of the problem is that the positive correlation between earnings and job tenure *across workers* can be interpreted in a very different way. Suppose that some workers got lucky and found high-paying jobs. These workers are in good matches and earn w_H per year as long as they remain in their jobs. Note that the earnings of a well-matched worker do not grow over time. Other workers have not been as lucky; they are badly matched and have low earnings. These workers earn w_L per year as long as they remain in their bad jobs. Note that the earnings of a poorly matched worker also do not grow over time. In this hypothetical example, therefore, job tenure has no impact on earnings. Put differently, specific training plays no role in determining wages.

The lucky workers who earn w_H are satisfied with their current economic situation and feel little need to "test the waters" and look for alternative employment. Workers in good matches, therefore, will have low probabilities of job separation, and these workers will tend to have a lot of seniority. In contrast, the workers who are not well matched are dissatisfied with their current employment situation. These workers will have high probabilities of job turnover and little seniority.

The correlation between earnings and job tenure across workers will be positive, implying that wages grow with job tenure for a given worker when no such thing is actually observed in this simple market. For a given worker, wages do not grow with tenure. Across workers, however, seniority is associated with higher wages because workers with a lot of job seniority are likely to be in good matches, and workers with little seniority are in bad matches. It would be incorrect, therefore, to conclude that the cross-sectional correlation says anything about the importance of specific training in the labor market.

To isolate the impact of seniority on a given worker's wage, we need to track a worker's earnings over time both as he gets older and as he accumulates firm-specific experience. Many studies attempt to track the worker's employment history over a large span of the working life. The evidence on the relationship between wages and seniority is mixed. In fact, a flurry of studies conducted in the late 1980s concluded that job tenure had *no* impact on earnings above and beyond the effect of total labor market experience.[57] In other words, there was no evidence that earnings actually grew on the job after controlling for the quality of the match between the worker and the firm.

[56] Michael R. Ransom, "Seniority and Monopsony in the Academic Labor Market," *American Economic Review* 83 (March 1993): 221–233.

[57] Katherine G. Abraham and Henry S. Farber, "Job Duration, Seniority, and Earnings," *American Economic Review* 77 (June 1987): 278–297; Joseph G. Altonji and Robert A. Shakotko, "Do Wages Rise with Job Seniority?" *Review of Economic Studies* 54 (July 1987): 437–459; Robert H. Topel, "Job Mobility, Search, and Earnings Growth," *Research in Labor Economics* 8 (1986, Part A): 199–233; and Robert C. Marshall and Gary A. Zarkin, "The Effect of Job Tenure on Wage Offers," *Journal of Labor Economics* 5 (July 1987): 301–324.

If correct, the finding that wages are unaffected by seniority has important policy implications and would fundamentally alter the way we think about and interpret many labor market outcomes. For example, the unimportance of seniority would suggest that skills in the labor market are mainly general. This portability of skills across firms implies that the costs of worker displacement and unemployment are relatively small (because the worker's human capital stock is not adversely affected by involuntary job separations).

Other work reexamines the evidence and concludes that wages do indeed increase with tenure, although there is still some disagreement over the magnitude of the correlation.[58] The first 10 years of job seniority may increase a worker's earnings by about 10 percent more than he could earn elsewhere. Put differently, each year of seniority may expand the worker's earnings opportunities by about 1 percent.

Summary

- The probability of moving across geographic regions depends on economic conditions in both the destination and origin states, and on migration costs. The probability of migration rises when incomes are low in the state of origin or when incomes are high in the state of destination. The probability of migration also rises if migration costs are low.

- If mobility decisions are made jointly by all household members, the migration flow includes a number of tied movers. Tied movers suffer a private loss from the migration, but the loss is more than outweighed by the gains of other family members.

- If there are cohort effects in the skill composition of the immigrant flow, the fact that earlier immigrants earn more than newly arrived immigrants in a cross section need not indicate that immigrants experience significant assimilation as they accumulate "U.S.-specific" labor market experience. There seem to be sizable cohort effects in the immigrant flow entering the United States, with more recent waves being relatively less skilled than earlier waves.

- Immigrants are not randomly chosen from the population of a source country. If the rate of return to skills in the receiving country exceeds the rate of return to skills in the country of origin, the immigrant flow is positively selected and immigrants have above-average skills. If the rate of return to skills in the receiving country is lower than the rate of return to skills in the country of origin, the immigrant flow is negatively selected and immigrants have below-average skills.

- Efficient turnover improves the quality of the job match between worker and firm and increases labor's contribution to national income.

- Workers who have been on the job for a long time are less likely to move than younger workers. This correlation arises because workers differ in their turnover propensities and because specific training reduces the probability of turnover as workers age on the job.

[58] Robert H. Topel, "Specific Capital, Mobility, and Wages: Wages Rise with Job Seniority," *Journal of Political Economy* 99 (February 1991): 145–176; Joseph G. Altonji and Nicolas Williams, "The Effects of Labor Market Experience, Job Seniority, and Mobility on Wage Growth," *Research in Labor Economics* 17 (1998): 233–276; and Margaret Stevens, "Earnings Functions, Specific Human Capital, and Job Matching: Tenure Bias Is Negative," *Journal of Labor Economics* 21 (October 2003): 783–806.

- Workers who have been on the job for a long time earn more than newly hired workers. This correlation arises because workers in good matches tend to stay on the job longer and because the accumulation of specific training increases the worker's productivity.

Key Concepts

cohort effects, *335*	labor mobility, *318*	Roy model, *338*
efficient turnover, *355*	negative selection, *340*	social capital, *349*
human capital	positive selection, *340*	tied mover, *328*
externality, *349*	repeat migration, *322*	tied stayer, *328*
job match, *354*	return migration, *322*	

Review Questions

1. Show how workers who wish to maximize the present value of lifetime earnings calculate the net gains to migration, and discuss how this net gain depends on incomes in the states of origin and destination and on migration costs.

2. Show how one can use the human capital framework to obtain an estimate of migration costs.

3. Why is there a difference between the private gains to migration and the family's gains to migration? Discuss how this difference generates tied stayers and tied movers. Can both the husband and the wife be tied movers?

4. Show how cohort effects in the immigrant flow affect the interpretation of the cross-sectional age-earnings profiles of immigrants.

5. Describe how the immigrant flow is chosen from the population of the country of origin. Why are some immigrant flows positively selected and other immigrant flows negatively selected?

6. How do quits and layoffs help improve labor market efficiency?

7. How should one interpret the fact that—all other things equal—workers with a lot of seniority are less likely to separate from their jobs than newly hired workers?

8. How should one interpret the fact that—all other things equal—workers with a lot of seniority earn more than newly hired workers?

Problems

8-1. Suppose a worker with an annual discount rate of 10 percent currently resides in Pennsylvania and is deciding whether to remain there or to move to Illinois. There are three work periods left in the life cycle. If the worker remains in Pennsylvania, he will earn $20,000 per year in each of the three periods. If the worker moves to Illinois, he will earn $22,000 in each of the three periods. What is the highest cost of migration that a worker is willing to incur and still make the move?

8-2. Suppose high-wage workers are more likely than low-wage workers to move to a new state for a better job.

   a. Explain how this migration pattern can be due solely to differences in the distribution of wages.

   b. Explain how this migration pattern can take place even if the cost to move is greater for high-wage workers.

8-3. Mickey and Minnie live in Orlando. Mickey's net present value of lifetime earnings in Orlando is $125,000, while Minnie's is $500,000. The cost of moving to Atlanta is $25,000 *per person.* In Atlanta, Mickey's net present value of lifetime earnings would be $155,000, while Minnie's would be $510,000. If Mickey and Minnie choose where to live based on their joint well-being, will they move to Atlanta? Is Mickey a tied mover or a tied stayer or neither? Is Minnie a tied mover or a tied stayer or neither?

8-4. Suppose a worker's skill is captured by his efficiency units of labor. The distribution of efficiency units in the population is such that worker 1 has one efficiency unit, worker 2 has two efficiency units, and so on. There are 100 workers in the population. In deciding whether to migrate to the United States, these workers compare their weekly earnings at home (w_0) with their potential earnings in the United States (w_1). The wage-skills relationship in each of the two countries is given by

$$w_0 = 700 + 0.5s$$

and

$$w_1 = 670 + s$$

where s is the number of efficiency units the worker possesses.

a. Assume there are no migration costs. What is the average number of efficiency units among immigrants? Is the immigrant flow positively or negatively selected?

b. Suppose it costs $10 to migrate to the United States. What is the average number of efficiency units among immigrants? Is the immigrant flow positively or negatively selected?

8-5. Suppose the United States enacts legislation granting all workers, including newly arrived immigrants, a minimum income floor of $\bar{y}$ dollars. (Assume there is positive selection of migrants from the home country to the United States.)

a. Generalize the Roy model to show how this type of welfare program influences the incentive to migrate to the United States. Ignore any issues regarding how the welfare program is funded.

b. Does this welfare program change the selection of the immigrant flow? In particular, are immigrants more likely to be negatively selected than in the absence of a welfare program?

c. Which types of workers, the highly skilled or the less skilled, are most likely to be attracted by the welfare program?

8-6. In the absence of any legal barriers on immigration from Neolandia to the United States, the economic conditions in the two countries generate an immigrant flow that is negatively selected. In response, the United States enacts an immigration policy that restricts entry to Neolandians who are in the top 10 percent of Neolandia's skill distribution. What type of Neolandian would now migrate to the United States?

8-7. A country has two regions, the North and the South, which are identical in all respects except the hourly wage and the number of workers. The demand for labor in each region is

$$w_N = 20 - .5E_N \qquad \text{and} \qquad w_S = 20 - .5E_S$$

where E_N and E_S are millions of workers. Currently there are 6 million workers in the North and 18 million workers in the South.

a. What is the wage in each region?

b. If there are no shocks to the economy, migration over time will result in an equalization of wages and employment. What would be the long-run wage and employment level in each region?

c. Return to the original setup where there are 6 million workers in the North and 18 million workers in the South. As a policymaker, you decide not only to allow 2 million immigrants of working age to enter the country, but you have the authority to resettle the immigrants wherever you want. How should you distribute immigrants across the regions to maximize the country's immigration surplus? Besides maximizing the immigration surplus in the short-run, in what other ways does your distribution of immigrants help the economy?

8-8. Phil has two periods of work remaining prior to retirement. He is currently employed in a firm that pays him the value of his marginal product, $50,000 per period. There are many other firms that Phil could potentially work for. There is a 50 percent chance of Phil being a good match for any particular firm and a 50 percent chance of him being a bad match. If he is in a good match, the value of his marginal product is $56,000 per period. If he is in a bad match, the value of his marginal product is $40,000 per period. If Phil quits his job, he can immediately find employment with any of the alternative firms. It takes one period to discover whether Phil is a good or a bad match with a particular firm. In that first period, while Phil's value to the firm is uncertain, he is offered a wage of $48,000. After the value of the match is determined, Phil is offered a wage equal to the value of his marginal product in that firm. When offered that wage, Phil is free to (a) accept, (b) reject and try some other firm, or (c) return to his original firm and his original wage. Phil maximizes the present value of his expected lifetime earnings, and his discount rate is 10 percent. What should Phil do?

8-9. Under 2001 tax legislation enacted in the United States, all income tax filers became eligible to deduct from their total income half of the expenses incurred when moving more than 50 miles to accept a new job. Prior to the change, only tax filers who itemized their deductions were allowed to deduct their moving expenses. (Typically, homeowners itemize their deductions and renters do not itemize.) How would this change in tax policy likely affect the mobility of homeowners and renters?

8-10. Suppose the immigrant flow from Lowland to Highland is positively selected. In order to mitigate the "brain drain" Lowland experiences as a result of this migration, public officials of Lowland successfully convince all Lowlanders who migrate to Highland to remit 10 percent of their wages to family members.

a. What effect will this policy have on the immigrant flow?

b. Provide a graph that details the extent to which this policy will limit the brain drain.

8-11. a. According to standard migration theory, how will skill selection (positive versus negative) change on average as the distance between the source country and the destination country increases?

b. Does Table 8-2 lend empirical support for the idea that skill selection is a monotonic function of the distance between countries?

8-12. a. Explain how a universal health care system would likely cause a greater amount of efficient turnover.

b. Defined-benefit retirement plans promise a fixed amount of retirement income to workers, but in order to receive benefits workers must be vested in the plan that usually requires working at the firm for 10 or 15 years. In contrast, a defined-contribution retirement plan specifies a fixed amount of money the firm contributes each pay period to a worker's retirement fund, which the worker then largely controls and can access even if she changes jobs. Do defined-benefit or defined-contribution retirement plans allow for more efficient turnover? How is the social security system in the United States like a defined-benefit plan? How is it like a defined-contribution plan?

c. When federal workers in Washington, D.C., move jobs from one federal agency to another, the worker keeps her same health insurance and retirement benefits. In order to quantify the degree to which ease of transfer of benefits affects turnover, two groups of new economist Ph.D.s who accept a job in Washington, D.C., are observed. The first group contains U.S. citizens. The second group contains non-U.S. residents who eventually received permanent resident status after three years of work experience. By law, several government agencies cannot hire nonresidents. Among the group of US citizens, 42 percent changed jobs within the first three years of work while 33 percent changed jobs during their fourth to sixth years of work. Among the group of non-U.S. residents, 17 percent changed jobs in the three years before becoming a resident while 29 percent changed jobs in the three years after becoming a U.S. resident. Provide a difference-in-differences estimator of the effect of being a U.S. resident/citizen in Washington, D.C., for Ph.D. economists.

8-13. The Immigration Reform Act of 2006 provided fewer work visas than were available in previous years for college graduates to remain in the United States. The exception is that work visas remained plentiful for college graduates who majored in technical areas such as math, computer programming, and physics.

a. How will this policy likely affect the skill distribution of immigrants to the United States and the age-earnings profile of immigrants in the United States?

b. In the future a demographer uses the 2010 U.S. census to study immigrant wages and concludes that the U.S. policy actually had the unintended consequence of attracting immigrants with lower levels of productivity as shown by a flatter age-earnings profile. Using a graph similar to Figure 8-5, show why the demographer's conclusions are sensitive to cohort effects.

8-14. KAPC, a pharmaceutical company located in rural Kansas, is finding it difficult to retain its employees, who frequently leave after just six months of working at KAPC for jobs at pharmaceutical companies paying higher wages in Chicago. To address its problem with labor turnover, human resource officers at KAPC decide to run an experiment. Of their next 100 newly hired employees, 25 will randomly be selected to receive a housing voucher worth up to $4,000 per year to offset property taxes. To take advantage of this program, the employee must not only be randomly selected into the program but she must also purchase a home. Of the 25 employees selected into the housing voucher program, 7 leave KAPC within 12 months of starting. Of the 75 employees not selected into the program, 37 leave KAPC within 12 months of starting.

    a. Provide an estimate of the effect the housing voucher program has on retention at KAPC.

    b. Suppose KAPC spends $10,000 in hiring costs each time a position is vacated. Would you endorse expanding the housing voucher program to all new employees? Justify your decision.

8-15. Consider the Roy model of potential immigrant flows as discussed in the chapter.

    a. Why is it that a source country can experience both an outflow of low-skill workers and an outflow of high-skill workers at the same time?

    b. Provide a graph of the returns to skills in the destination and source countries that would suggest both behaviors occur simultaneously.

    c. How do the social and economic (that is, tax) policies of the United States encourage both types of flows?

Selected Readings

George J. Borjas, "Assimilation, Changes in Cohort Quality, and the Earnings of Immigrants," *Journal of Labor Economics* 3 (October 1985): 463–489.

George J. Borjas, "Self-Selection and the Earnings of Immigrants," *American Economic Review* 77 (September 1987): 531–553.

Leah Platt Boustan, "Was Postwar Suburbanization "White Flight"? Evidence from the Black Migration," *Quarterly Journal of Economics* 125 (February 2010): 417–443.

Barry R. Chiswick, "The Effect of Americanization on the Earnings of Foreign-Born Men," *Journal of Political Economy* 86 (October 1978): 897–921.

Dora L. Costa and Matthew E. Kahn, "Power Couples: Changes in the Locational Choice of the College Educated, 1940–1990," *Quarterly Journal of Economics* 115 (November 2000): 1287–1314.

Henry S. Farber, "The Changing Face of Job Loss in the United States, 1981–1995," *Brookings Papers on Economic Activity, Microeconomics* (1997): 55–142.

Brigitte C. Madrian, "Employment-Based Health Insurance and Job Mobility: Is There Evidence of Job-Lock?" *Quarterly Journal of Economics* 109 (February 1994): 27–54.

Lalith Munasinghe, "Specific Training Sometimes Cuts Wages and Always Cuts Turnover," *Journal of Labor Economics* 23 (April 2005): 213–233.

Robert H. Topel, "Specific Capital, Mobility, and Wages: Wages Rise with Job Seniority," *Journal of Political Economy* 99 (February 1991): 145–176.

Fabian Waldinger, "Quality Matters: The Expulsion of Professors and the Consequences for Ph.D. Student Outcomes in Nazi Germany," *Journal of Political Economy* 118 (August 2010): 787–831.

Web Links

The U.S. Census Bureau maintains up-to-date information on mobility patterns within the United States: www.census.gov/population/www/socdemo/migrate.html.

The Web site of Citizen and Immigration Canada has the "test" that allows a potential applicant to determine if he or she qualifies for a visa: www.cic.gc.ca/english/skilled/assess/index.html.

The Web site of Australia's Department of Immigration and Multicultural and Indigenous Affairs has the similar test required by Australian authorities: www.immi.gov.au/allforms/skill_points.htm.

Chapter 9

Labor Market Discrimination

God, what gorgeous staff I have. I just can't understand those who have ugly people working for them, I really can't. Just call me a pathetic aesthetic.

—*Jade Jagger (Mick's daughter)*

In previous chapters, we analyzed how differences in the characteristics of jobs or the skills of workers generate wage dispersion in competitive labor markets. We will now demonstrate that differences in earnings and employment opportunities may arise even among equally skilled workers employed in the same job simply because of the workers' race, gender, national origin, sexual orientation, or other seemingly irrelevant characteristics.

These differences are often attributed to labor market discrimination. Discrimination occurs when participants in the marketplace take into account such factors as race and sex when making economic exchanges. For instance, employers might care about the gender of the workers they hire; employees might be concerned about the race of their coworkers; and customers might take into account the race and gender of the seller. Although economists have little to say about the psychological roots of prejudice, we can easily reinterpret this type of behavior in terms of the language of economics: The costs and benefits of an economic exchange depend on the color and gender of the persons involved in the exchange.

It turns out that racial and gender differences in labor market outcomes may arise even if market participants are not prejudiced. We often "read" a person's socioeconomic background to learn more about that person's productivity and skills. For instance, we all know that teenagers are more likely to engage in reckless driving. Surely this information is useful to a stranded motorist who has been offered a ride by a teenage driver. Similarly, employers, workers, and customers will use race, gender, and any other relevant traits to fill in information gaps about participants in the marketplace.

Finally, the chapter illustrates how economists typically measure discrimination in the labor market and discusses the long-run trends in the black-white and male-female wage differentials. The study of these long-run trends provides important insights into the impact of controversial government policies, such as affirmative action, on the relative economic well-being of minorities and women.

9-1   Race and Gender in the Labor Market

Table 9-1 reports various measures of human capital and labor market outcomes in the U.S. labor market, by race and gender. Perhaps most striking are the gaps in annual earnings. Men earn more than women, and whites earn more than nonwhites. In particular, white men have the highest annual earnings of any of the groups ($55,800). In contrast, white women earn only $37,000, black men earn $41,200, and Hispanic women earn $28,100.

The data also indicate, however, that these differences in annual earnings arise partly because of labor supply differentials among the various groups. For example, the typical white man earns about 51 percent more than the typical white woman ($55,800 versus $37,000). The typical white man employed full-time, however, earns "only" 40 percent more than the typical white woman employed full-time (or $65,900 versus $47,000).

Part of the wage differential among the groups also arises because of differences in educational attainment. Only about 13 percent of white men do not have a high school diploma, as compared to 16 percent of black men and almost 40 percent of Hispanic men. Similarly, 31 percent of white men are college graduates, as compared to 29 percent of white women, 18 percent of black men, and 13 percent of Hispanic men. If the rate of return to schooling is between 7 and 9 percent, as the evidence discussed in Chapter 6 suggests, the differences in educational attainment between whites and minorities would clearly generate substantial wage differentials. As we shall see below, differences in observed human capital do account for a sizable part of the wage differential between blacks and whites (as well as between Hispanics and whites).

TABLE 9-1   **Gender and Racial Differences in Skills and Labor Market Outcomes, 2009–2010**

Sources: The data on educational attainment refer to persons aged 25 and over and are drawn from *U.S. Statistical Abstract 2011*, Table 226, "Educational Attainment by Race, Hispanic Origin, and Sex: 1970 to 2009." The data on labor force participation and unemployment rates refer to persons aged 20 and over and are available online at www.bls.gov/cps/cpsatabs.htm. The data for Asians refer to persons aged 16 and over. The data on earnings refers to workers aged 25 and over and are drawn from "Table PINC-03, Educational Attainment—People 25 Years Old and Over, by Total Money Earnings in 2009, Work Experience in 2009, Age, Race, Hispanic Origin and Sex," www.census.gov/hhes/www/income/dinctabs.html.

	White		Black		Hispanic		Asian	
	Male	Female	Male	Female	Male	Female	Male	Female
Percent high school graduate or more	86.5	87.7	84.0	81.1	60.6	63.3	90.4	86.2
Percent bachelor's degree or more	30.6	29.3	17.8	20.6	12.5	14.0	55.7	49.3
Labor force participation rate	74.6	59.9	69.5	63.2	82.6	59.5	73.2	57.0
Unemployment rate	8.9	7.2	17.3	12.8	11.7	11.4	7.8	7.1
Annual earnings (in $1,000)	55.8	37.0	41.2	32.5	35.2	28.1	66.6	45.9
Annual earnings (among workers employed full-time, year-round) (in $1,000)	65.9	47.0	48.4	39.5	42.8	35.3	76.1	55.2

FIGURE 9-1

International Differences in Female-Male Wage Ratios and Employment Rates

Source: Claudia Olivetti and Barbara Petrongolo, "Unequal Pay or Unequal Employment? A Cross-Country Analysis of Genger Gaps," *Journal of Labor Economics* 26 (October 2008): 621–654.

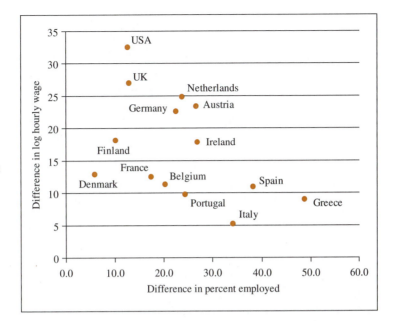

It is important to stress that race and gender matter not only in the U.S. labor market but also in other countries. In Malaysia, for example, the Malay/Chinese wage ratio is around 0.57 and the Indian/Chinese wage ratio is 0.81. Similarly, black men in Canada earn 18 percent less than Canadian whites; nonwhite immigrants in Britain earn 10 to 20 percent less than similarly skilled white immigrants; Jews of Oriental-Sephardic background in Israel earn less than Jews of Ashkenazic (that is, European) background; and there are substantial wage differentials among the various castes that make up Indian society.[1] Finally, as shown in Figure 9-1, there is a sizable wage gap between men and women in most developed countries. In fact, the figure shows not only large international differences in the size of the gender wage gap, but an equally sizable dispersion in employment rates. Moreover, there is a marked negative correlation between these two variables. In other words, the gender wage gap is higher in countries where the employment gap between men and women is smaller. As we will note later, this negative correlation has important implications for the interpretation of the gender wage differential.

[1] William Darity Jr. and Jessica Gordon Nembhard, "Racial and Ethnic Economic Inequality: The International Record," *American Economic Review* 90 (May 2000): 308–311; Juliet Howland and Christos Sakellariou, "Wage Discrimination, Occupational Segregation and Visible Minorities in Canada," *Applied Economics* 25 (November 1993): 1413–1422; Mark Stewart, "Racial Discrimination and Occupational Attainment in Britain," *Economic Journal* 93 (September 1983): 521–543; and Biswajit Banerjee and J. B. Knight, "Caste Discrimination in the Indian Labour Market," *Journal of Development Economics* 17 (April 1985): 277–307.

9-2   The Discrimination Coefficient

The birth of the modern economic analysis of discrimination can be traced back to the 1957 publication of Nobel Laureate Gary Becker's doctoral dissertation entitled *The Economics of Discrimination.*[2] Much of the subsequent literature on discrimination is motivated and guided by the analytical framework set out in that influential study.

Becker's theory of labor market discrimination is based on the concept of **taste discrimination.** This concept essentially translates the notion of racial prejudice into the language of economics. Suppose there are two types of workers in the labor market: white workers and black workers. A competitive employer faces constant prices for these inputs; w_W is the wage rate for a white worker and w_B is the wage rate for a black worker. If the employer is prejudiced against blacks, the employer gets disutility from hiring black workers. In other words, even though it costs only w_B dollars to hire one person-hour of black labor, the employer will *act as if* it costs $w_B(1 + d)$ dollars, where d is a positive number and is called the **discrimination coefficient.**

In effect, racial prejudice blinds the employer to the true monetary cost of the transaction; the employer's perceived cost of hiring blacks exceeds the actual cost. Suppose that $w_B = \$10$ per hour and that $d = 0.5$. The employer will then act as if hiring a black worker costs $15 per hour, a 50 percent increase in cost. The discrimination coefficient d, therefore, gives the percentage "markup" in the cost of hiring a black worker attributable to the employer's prejudice. The greater the prejudice, the greater is the disutility from hiring blacks, and the greater is the discrimination coefficient d.

Some employers (perhaps black-owned firms) might have a different type of prejudice; they *prefer* to hire blacks. This type of behavior, which we call **nepotism,** implies that an employer's utility-adjusted cost of hiring a favored worker equals $w_B(1 - n)$ dollars, where the "nepotism coefficient" n is a positive number. If these black employers prefer to hire black workers, they will act as if hiring a black worker is cheaper than it actually is.

It is easy to apply Becker's definition of taste discrimination to other types of economic interactions. White workers, for instance, might dislike working alongside black workers, and white customers might dislike purchasing goods and services from black sellers. If a prejudiced white worker's wage equals w_W, she will act as if her wage equals $w_W(1 - d)$ if she has to work alongside a black worker (where d is a positive number). The white worker then perceives her take-home pay to be less than it actually is. Similarly, if a prejudiced white customer purchases a good from a black seller, he acts as if the price of the good is not equal to p dollars, but instead equals $p(1 + d)$. The discrimination coefficient, therefore, "monetizes" prejudice, regardless of whether the source of the prejudice is the employer (leading to **employer discrimination**), the employee (leading to **employee discrimination**), or the customer (leading to **customer discrimination**).

[2] Gary S. Becker, *The Economics of Discrimination,* 2d ed., Chicago: University of Chicago Press, 1971 (1957). This literature is surveyed by Joseph G. Altonji and Rebecca M. Blank, "Race and Gender in the Labor Market," in Orley Ashenfelter and David Card, editors, *Handbook of Labor Economics,* vol. 3C, Amsterdam: Elsevier, 1999, pp. 3143–1259. A recent paper provides the best attempt to empirically test Becker's theory of discrimination; see Kerwin Kofi Charles and Jonathan Guryan, "Prejudice and Wages: An Empirical Assessment of Becker's The Economics of Discrimination," *Journal of Political Economy* 116 (October 2008): 773–809.

One can interpret Becker's definition of taste discrimination in terms of the theory of compensating differentials that we developed in Chapter 5. The theory of compensating differentials is based on the idea that persons consider "the whole of the advantages and disadvantages" of an economic exchange. A prejudiced person incorporates the race, national origin, and gender of market participants in the long list of advantages and disadvantages that influence the value of the exchange. The labor market, therefore, will have to generate compensating differentials to compensate prejudiced persons for their utility loss or gain.

9-3   Employer Discrimination

Suppose there are two types of workers in the labor market: white and black workers.[3] Consider a competitive firm that is deciding how much of these inputs to hire. We assume that black and white workers are perfect substitutes in production, so that the production function can be written as

$$q = f(E_W + E_B) \tag{9-1}$$

where q is the firm's output, E_W gives the number of white workers hired, and E_B gives the number of black workers hired. Note that the firm's output depends on the *total* number of workers hired, regardless of their race. In other words, the firm gets the same output if it hires 50 white workers and 50 black workers, or if it hires 100 white workers and no black workers, or if it hires 100 black workers and no white workers. As a result, the output produced by hiring one more worker, or the marginal product of labor (MP_E), is the same regardless of whether the firm hires a black or a white worker. Because black and white workers are equally productive, any differences that arise in the economic status of the two groups cannot be attributed to skill differentials, but must arise from the discriminatory behavior of market participants. For simplicity, we ignore the role of capital in the production process.

Before introducing the employer's prejudice into the analysis, we first review the hiring decision of a firm that does not discriminate. This color-blind firm faces constant input prices of w_W and w_B dollars for white and black labor, respectively. Because both groups of workers have the same value of marginal product, a nondiscriminatory firm will hire whichever group is cheaper. If the market wage for black workers were below the market wage for white workers, the firm would hire only black workers. The opposite would happen if the black wage exceeded the white wage.

Let's suppose that the market-determined wage of black labor is less than the market-determined wage of white labor, or $w_B < w_W$. A firm that does not discriminate will hire black workers up to the point where the black wage equals the value of their marginal product, or

$$w_B = VMP_E \tag{9-2}$$

Figure 9-2 illustrates this profit-maximizing condition. A color-blind firm, therefore, hires E_B^* black workers.

[3] Modern versions of Becker's theory of employer discrimination are given by Kenneth J. Arrow, "The Theory of Discrimination," in Orley Ashenfelter and Albert Rees, editors, *Discrimination in Labor Markets,* Princeton, NJ: Princeton University Press, 1973; and Matthew S. Goldberg, "Discrimination, Nepotism, and Long-Run Wage Differentials," *Quarterly Journal of Economics* 97 (May 1982): 307–319. The discussion in the text is based on Goldberg's exposition.

FIGURE 9-2   The Employment Decision of a Firm That Does Not Discriminate

If the market-determined black wage is less than the white wage, a firm that does not discriminate will hire only blacks. It hires black workers up to the point where the black wage equals the value of marginal product of labor, or E_B^*.

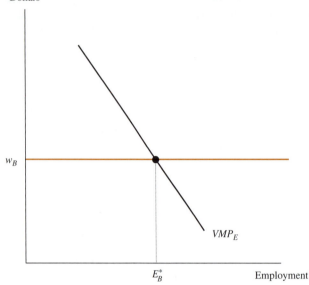

Employment in a Discriminatory Firm

Let's now describe the hiring decision of a firm that discriminates. The employer acts as if the black wage is not w_B, but is instead equal to $w_B(1 + d)$, where d is the discrimination coefficient. The employer's hiring decision, therefore, is not based on a comparison of w_W and w_B, but on a comparison of w_W and $w_B(1 + d)$. The employer will then hire whichever input has a lower utility-adjusted price. As a result, the decision rule for an employer that discriminates against blacks is

$$\text{Hire only blacks if } w_B(1 + d) < w_W$$

$$\text{Hire only whites if } w_B(1 + d) > w_W \qquad \text{(9-3)}$$

Equation (9-3) highlights a key implication of the Becker model of employer discrimination: *As long as black and white workers are perfect substitutes, firms have a segregated workforce.*[4]

There are, therefore, two types of firms: those that hire an all-white workforce, which for convenience we will call "white firms," and those that hire an all-black workforce, or

---

[4] An empirical study of the racial composition of a firm's workforce is given by William J. Carrington and Kenneth R. Troske, "Interfirm Segregation and the Black/White Wage Gap," *Journal of Labor Economics* 16 (April 1998): 231–260. This study finds little evidence that blacks and whites tend to be employed by different firms. See also Kimberly Bayard, Judith K. Hellerstein, David Neumark, and Kenneth Troske, "Ethnicity, Language, and Workplace Segregation: Evidence from a New Matched Employer-Employee Data Set," *Journal of Labor Economics* 21 (October 2003): 877–922.

FIGURE 9-3   The Employment Decision of a Prejudiced Firm

Firms that discriminate can be either white firms (if the discrimination coefficient is very high) or black firms (if the discrimination coefficient is relatively low). A white firm hires white workers up to the point where the white wage equals the value of marginal product. A black firm hires black workers up to the point where the utility-adjusted black wage equals the value of marginal product. Firms that discriminate hire fewer workers than firms that do not discriminate.

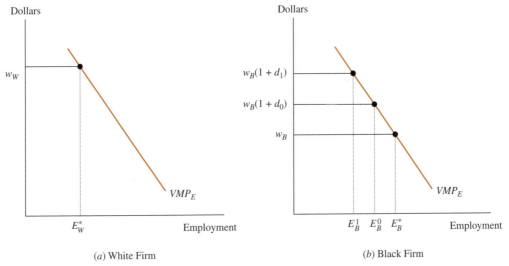

(a) White Firm   (b) Black Firm

"black firms." The race of the firm's workforce depends on the magnitude of the employer's discrimination coefficient. Employers who have little prejudice, and small discrimination coefficients, will hire only blacks; employers who are very prejudiced, with large discrimination coefficients, will hire only whites. Figure 9-3a illustrates the employment decision of white firms, while Figure 9-3b illustrates the employment decision of black firms.

The white firm hires workers up to the point where the wage of white workers equals the value of marginal product, or $w_W = VMP_E$. We are assuming that the white wage exceeds the black wage. The white firm, therefore, is paying an excessively high price for its workers and hires relatively few workers (or E_W^* in the figure). Employers who dislike black workers sufficiently, therefore, not only hire an all-white workforce but also hire relatively few white workers because white labor is expensive.

Figure 9-3b shows that even black firms will tend to hire too few workers. Recall that a color-blind firm hires E_B^* black workers, where the *actual* black wage equals the value of marginal product. A firm with discrimination coefficient d_0, however, acts as if the price of black labor is $w_B(1 + d_0)$. This discrimination coefficient is small enough that the firm will still want to hire an all-black workforce. The firm hires black workers up to the point where the utility-adjusted price of a black worker equals the value of marginal product, or $w_B(1 + d_0) = VMP_E$. As shown in Figure 9-3b, this firm hires only E_B^0 workers. A firm with a larger discrimination coefficient d_1 hires even fewer workers (or E_B^1), and so on. The number of black workers hired, therefore, is smaller for firms that have larger discrimination coefficients. Because employers do not like hiring black workers, they minimize their discomfort by hiring fewer blacks.

FIGURE 9-4   Profits and the Discrimination Coefficient

Discrimination reduces profits in two ways. Even if the discriminatory firm hires only black workers, it hires too few workers. If the discriminatory firm hires only white workers, it hires too few workers at a very high wage.

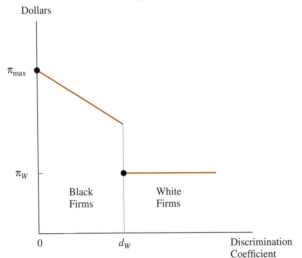

Discrimination and Profits

Figure 9-3 yields a fundamental implication of Becker's theory: *Discrimination does not pay.* To see why, consider first the profitability of white firms. These firms are hiring E_W^* workers. This hiring decision is unprofitable in two distinct ways. First, the prejudiced employer could have hired the same number of black workers at a lower wage. In other words, because black and white workers are perfect substitutes, white firms could have produced the same output at a lower cost. In addition, white firms are hiring the *wrong* number of workers; a color-blind firm would hire many more workers, or E_B^*. By not hiring the right number of workers, white firms further reduce their profits. This argument also implies that even black firms that discriminate are giving up profits. Because discriminatory black firms are hiring too few workers (such as E_B^0 or E_B^I), they too are giving up profits in order to minimize contact with black workers.

Figure 9-4 illustrates the relation between the firm's profits and the discrimination coefficient. The most profitable firm is the firm that has a zero discrimination coefficient. This color-blind firm hires an all-black workforce containing E_B^* workers and has profits equal to π_{max} dollars. Firms with slightly positive discrimination coefficients still have an all-black workforce but employ fewer black workers and earn lower profits. At some threshold level of prejudice, given by the discrimination coefficient d_W, the utility loss of hiring blacks is too large and the firm hires only whites. As a result, profits take a dramatic plunge (to π_W dollars) because the firm is paying a much higher wage than it needs to. Because all-white firms hire the same number of white workers (or E_W^*) regardless of their discrimination coefficient, all all-white firms earn the same profits.

The Becker model of employer taste discrimination, therefore, predicts that discrimination is unprofitable. Firms that discriminate lose on two counts: They are hiring the "wrong color" of workers and/or they are hiring the "wrong number" of workers. Both of these hiring decisions move the firm away from the profit-maximizing level of employment, or E_B^* workers.

The implications of this conclusion are far-reaching. If the source of racial prejudice in competitive markets is the employer, competition is a minority group's best friend. Because free entry and exit of firms ensure that firms in the market are not earning excess profits, employers must pay for the right to discriminate out of their own pocket. A color-blind firm, therefore, should eventually be able to buy out all the other firms in the industry. As a result, employer discrimination will "wither away" in competitive markets.[5]

Labor Market Equilibrium

The comparison of the utility-adjusted price with the actual price of labor summarized in equation (9-3) tells us if a particular firm becomes a black firm or a white firm. Firms with small discrimination coefficients will tend to become black firms and firms with large discrimination coefficients will tend to become white firms. We can use this insight to derive the demand curve for black workers in the labor market. Let's initially suppose that *all* employers discriminate against blacks, so every firm has a positive discrimination coefficient.

When the black wage exceeds the white wage so that the black-white wage ratio (w_B/w_W) is above 1, no employer, not even the employer who minds blacks the least (and hence has the smallest discrimination coefficient), wants to hire black workers. After all, when the actual price of blacks is above the price of whites, the utility-adjusted price of blacks will be even higher. As illustrated in Figure 9-5, there is no demand for black workers. In fact, even if the black wage were slightly less than the white wage, the utility-adjusted black wage will probably exceed the white wage for all firms, and no employers will want to hire any black workers.

Consider what happens as the relative black wage decreases further. At some point, the firm with the least prejudice crosses a threshold (given by point R in the figure), and this firm becomes a black firm because blacks are relatively cheaper than whites—even after adjusting for the disutility that blacks cause the employer. As the black wage keeps on falling, more firms decide to become black firms because the lower black wage compensates them for their prejudice. Moreover, those firms that were already hiring blacks take advantage of the lower black wage by hiring even more black workers. As the relative wage of blacks falls further and further, therefore, the quantity demanded of black workers increases. If the black wage is very low relative to the white wage, even firms with a very large discrimination coefficient have been "bought off" and will hire blacks. The market demand curve for black labor (or D in Figure 9-5), therefore, is downward sloping.

Of course, the equilibrium black-white wage ratio depends not just on the demand for black workers but also on the supply of black workers. For convenience, Figure 9-5 assumes that the supply curve of black workers is perfectly inelastic, so that there are N black persons in the labor market regardless of the relative black wage. The equilibrium black-white wage ratio, or $(w_B/w_W)^*$, equates the supply and demand for black workers. If the relative black wage is above the equilibrium level, there are too many blacks looking

---

[5] This argument assumes that all firms face the same production function. If discriminatory firms are more efficient and can produce output at lower costs, they can persist in their discriminatory behavior.

FIGURE 9-5   **Determination of Black/White Wage Ratio in the Labor Market**

If the black-white wage ratio is very high, no firm in the labor market will want to hire blacks. As the black-white wage ratio falls, more and more firms are compensated for their disutility and the demand for black workers rises. The equilibrium black-white wage ratio is given by the intersection of supply and demand, and equals $(w_B/w_W)^*$. If some firms prefer to hire blacks, they would be willing to hire blacks even if the black-white wage ratio exceeds 1, shifting the demand curve up to D'. If the supply of blacks is sufficiently small, it is then possible for the black-white wage ratio to exceed 1.

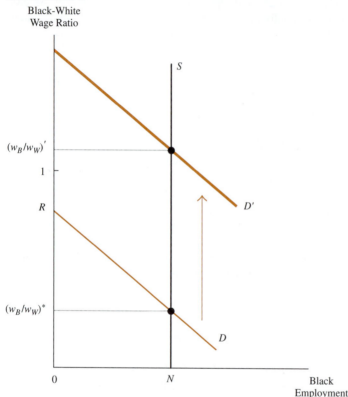

for work relative to the demand for black workers, and hence there is downward pressure on the relative black wage. Conversely, if the relative black wage is below equilibrium, there are too few black workers looking for work, and the black wage would rise as employers compete for these workers.

The Equilibrium Black-White Wage Differential

Several properties of the equilibrium illustrated in Figure 9-5 are worth noting. Most important, the intersection of the supply and demand curves occurs below the point where the black-white wage ratio equals 1, so employer discrimination generates a wage gap between equally skilled black and white workers. The employer cares about working conditions, particularly the color of the workforce. Because all employers dislike hiring blacks, a compensating differential arises to compensate employers for hiring these workers. In effect, black workers must "compensate" employers so as to soften employer resistance to hiring blacks.

Note that the allocation of black workers to firms is not random. Black workers are hired by the firms that choose to become black firms. Employers who have the smallest discrimination coefficients run these black firms. Black workers, therefore, are matched with the employers who have the least prejudice, whereas white workers are matched with employers who dislike blacks the most.

We have assumed that all firms discriminate against blacks. Some firms, however, might prefer to hire blacks. Because nepotistic firms get utility from hiring blacks, many of these firms would hire blacks even if the black wage were higher than the white wage. As a result, the demand curve for black labor shifts up, as illustrated by the demand curve D' in Figure 9-5. If there are relatively few blacks in this labor market, the equilibrium black-white wage ratio could be above 1, *even if most firms in the labor market dislike hiring blacks.* Because the labor market matches black workers with employers who prefer to hire blacks and matches white workers with employers who prefer to hire whites, blacks may be able to sell their services to those firms that are willing to pay for the right to hire them.

This conclusion has interesting implications for the creation and economic impact of racial or ethnic "enclave economies." Many minority groups tend to cluster in a small number of geographic areas, or enclaves. The typical black, for instance, lives in a neighborhood that is 57 percent black.[6] This geographic clustering opens up sizable opportunities for minority employers to hire minority workers. As a result, enclave economies may allow blacks and other minorities to escape the adverse impact of discrimination in the labor market that lies outside the enclave.

9-4 Employee Discrimination

The source of discrimination in the labor market need not be the employer, but might instead be fellow workers. Suppose that whites dislike working alongside blacks and that blacks are indifferent about the race of their coworkers. As we have seen, white workers who receive a wage of w_W dollars will act as if their wage rate is only $w_W(1 - d)$, where d is the white worker's discrimination coefficient. Because black workers do not care about the race of their fellow employees, both their actual and utility-adjusted wage rates are given by w_B. We continue to assume that black and white workers are perfect substitutes in production.

Suppose a white worker who dislikes working alongside blacks has two job offers. Both employers offer the same wage of, say, $15 per hour, but working conditions vary in the two firms. In particular, one firm has a completely white workforce, and the other firm has an integrated workforce, consisting of black and white workers. Because the worker dislikes blacks, the two firms are not offering equivalent utility-adjusted wages. In the worker's view, the integrated firm offers a lower wage. Therefore, integrated firms will have to offer more than $15 per hour if they wish to attract white workers.

However, a color-blind profit-maximizing employer would never choose to have an integrated workplace. The employer would not hire both black and white workers because white workers have to be paid a compensating wage differential, yet they have the same value of marginal product as blacks. Hence, the employer will hire only whites if the white wage is below the black wage and will hire only blacks if the black wage is below the white wage. Because it does not pay to "mix," black and white workers are employed by different firms. Employee discrimination (like employer discrimination) implies a completely segregated workforce.

Unlike employer discrimination, however, employee discrimination does *not* generate a wage differential between equally skilled black and white workers. Color-blind employers hire whichever labor is cheaper. If blacks are cheaper, employers increase their demand for black labor and decrease their demand for white labor. If whites are cheaper, employers increase their demand for white labor and decrease their demand for black labor. In the end, competition for the cheapest workers equalizes the wage of the two groups of workers. If blacks and whites were perfect substitutes, therefore, a model of employee discrimination could not explain why equally skilled blacks might earn less than equally skilled whites.

[6] David M. Cutler and Edward L. Glaeser, "Are Ghettos Good or Bad?" *Quarterly Journal of Economics* 112 (August 1997): 827–872; Robert W. Fairlie, "The Absence of the African-American Owned Business: An Analysis of the Dynamics of Self-Employment," *Journal of Labor Economics* 17 (January 1999): 80–108; and Kaivan Munshi, "Networks in the Modern Economy: Mexican Migrants in the U.S. Labor Market," *Quarterly Journal of Economics* 118 (May 2003): 549–597.

Finally, note that employee discrimination does not affect the profitability of firms. Because all firms pay the same price for an hour of labor, and because black and white workers are perfect substitutes, there is no advantage to being either a black or a white firm. There are no market forces, therefore, that will tend to diminish the importance of employee discrimination over time.[7]

9-5 Customer Discrimination

If customers have a taste for discrimination, their purchasing decisions are not based on the actual price of the good, p, but on the utility-adjusted price, or $p(1 + d)$, where d is the discrimination coefficient. If whites dislike purchasing from black sellers, customer discrimination reduces the demand for goods and services sold by minorities.

As long as a firm can allocate a particular worker to one of many different positions within the firm, customer discrimination may not matter much. The firm can place its black workers in jobs that require little customer contact (such as jobs in the manufacturing division of the firm), and place many of its white workers in the service division (where they may be more visible). In effect, the employer segregates the workforce so that white workers fill "sensitive" sales positions and black workers remain hidden from outside view. If black workers were cheaper than white workers, firms looking to fill the manufacturing positions would compete for black workers and, in the end, equally skilled black and white workers would receive the same wage. Moreover, catering to customer tastes does not reduce the firm's profits.[8]

Customer discrimination can have an adverse impact on black wages when the firm cannot easily hide its black workers from public view. A firm employing a black worker in a sales position will have to lower the price of the product so as to compensate white buyers for their disutility. The wage of black workers would then fall because black workers have to compensate the employer for the loss in profits.

A survey of employers conducted in four metropolitan areas (Atlanta, Boston, Detroit, and Los Angeles) shows how the interaction between the customers' racial background and the extent of the contact between the workers and the customers alters the hiring decisions of firms. Suppose we classify the firms in this survey into two types: "contact" firms, where the workers talk "face-to-face" with the customers and clients, and "noncontact" firms. Table 9-2 shows that 58 percent of newly hired workers are black in contact firms where most customers are black. This contrasts strikingly with the fact that only 9 percent of newly hired workers are black in contact firms where most customers are white. The difference between these two statistics would seem to suggest that customer discrimination reduces the fraction of blacks among newly hired workers by 49.0 percentage points.

---

[7] A comparison of the theories of employer and employee discrimination is given by Barry R. Chiswick, "Racial Discrimination in the Labor Market: A Test of Alternative Hypotheses," *Journal of Political Economy* 81 (November 1973): 1330–1352.

[8] A more detailed discussion of the implications of customer discrimination is given by Lawrence M. Kahn, "Customer Discrimination and Affirmative Action," *Economic Inquiry* 24 (July 1991): 555–571; see also George J. Borjas and Stephen G. Bronars, "Consumer Discrimination and Self-Selection into Self-Employment," *Journal of Political Economy* 97 (June 1989): 581–605.

TABLE 9-2   Relation between Customer Discrimination and Percentage of Newly Hired Workers Who Are Black

Source: Harry J. Holzer and Keith R. Ihlanfeldt, "Customer Discrimination and Employment Outcomes for Minority Workers," *Quarterly Journal of Economics* 113 (August 1998): 846.

Type of Firm	More Than Half of Firm's Customers Are Black	More Than 75% of Firm's Customers Are White	Difference
Contact between customers and workers	58.0%	9.0%	49.0%
No contact between customers and workers	46.6	12.2	34.4
Difference-in-differences	—	—	**14.6**

Before reaching this conclusion, however, it is important to note that the black employment gap between these two types of firms may be attributable to other factors. It is likely, for instance, that contact firms with a mainly black customer base are located in black areas of the city. These firms would likely attract a relatively larger number of black job applicants, and the racial composition of the applicant pool would likely affect the racial composition of the firm's workforce.

To measure the impact of customer discrimination, therefore, one needs a "control group." The firms in the survey where workers do not have any contact with customers give one possible control group. As Table 9-2 shows, the fraction of newly hired workers who are black falls from 46.6 percent to 12.2 percent as the customer base shifts from being mainly black to mainly white, a reduction of 34.4 percentage points. It would be difficult to blame customer discrimination for this decline in black employment because the customers in these firms do not have any contact with the workers. Instead, the 34.4-point difference estimates what one might expect to happen to black employment—*even in the absence of customer discrimination*—when a firm caters mainly to black customers, perhaps because this shift requires that the firms open up shop in black neighborhoods and hence attract many black job applicants.

The difference-in-differences estimate of the impact of customer discrimination would then be given by 14.6 percent. In other words, face-to-face contact between black workers and white customers substantially lowers the probability that the firm hires black workers.

Perhaps the most interesting evidence of customer discrimination has been uncovered in the market for baseball memorabilia. Collecting baseball cards is not a children's pastime. A 1909 Honus Wagner baseball card sold for $630,500 in 1996.[9] Remarkably, it turns out that the market price of baseball cards depends not only on the most obvious factors—such as the number of career home runs and at-bats for a hitter and the number of wins and strikeouts for a pitcher—but also on the race of the player. In other words, the player's race seems to affect the entertainment value of owning the card. Even after controlling for the position played and for the "stats" of the playing career, the cards of white players cost about 10 to 13 percent more than the cards of black players.[10]

---

[9] Bill Hutchinson, "Ball Sale Figure Is Much Ado over $2.7 Million," *New York Daily News,* January 14, 1999.

[10] Clark Nardinelli and Curtis Simon, "Customer Racial Discrimination in the Market for Memorabilia: The Case of Baseball," *Quarterly Journal of Economics* 105 (August 1990): 575–596; and Torben Andersen and Sumner LaCroix, "Customer Racial Discrimination in Major League Baseball," *Economic Inquiry* 29 (October 1991): 665–677.

9-6   Statistical Discrimination

The concept of taste discrimination helps us understand how differences between equally skilled blacks and whites (or men and women) can arise in the labor market. Racial and gender differences may arise *even in the absence of prejudice* when membership in a particular group (for example, being a black woman) carries information about a person's skills and productivity.[11]

The economic incentives that generate statistical discrimination are easy to describe. Suppose that a color-blind, gender-blind, profit-maximizing employer has a job opening. The employer wants to add a worker to a finely tuned team that will develop a revolutionary word processing program in the next few years. The employer is looking for a worker who, in addition to the usual requisites of intelligence and ambition, can be counted on to be a team member over the long haul.

Two persons apply for the job. The résumés of the two job applicants are identical; both just graduated from the same college, majored in the same field, enrolled in the same courses, and had similar class rankings. Moreover, both applicants passed the interview with flying colors. The employer found them to be bright, motivated, knowledgeable, and articulate. It just happens, however, that one of the applicants is a man and the other is a woman.

During the interview, the employer specifically asked the applicants if they viewed the prospective job as one where they could grow and develop over the next few years. Both applicants replied that they saw the job as a terrific opportunity and that it was hard to foresee how any other employment or nonmarket opportunities could conceivably compete. Based on the "paper trail" (that is, the résumé, the information gathered during the interview, and any other screening tests), the employer will find it difficult to choose between the two applicants. The employer knows, however, that because both applicants need a job, the assertion that they intend to stay at the firm for the next few years may not be sincere.

To make an informed decision (rather than just toss a coin), the employer will evaluate the employment histories of similarly situated men and women that this firm—or other firms—hired in the past. Suppose that this review of the statistical record reveals that many women leave the firm when they reach their late twenties (perhaps to engage in child-rearing). The employer has no way of knowing if the female job applicant under consideration intends to leave the labor force eventually. Nevertheless, the employer infers from the statistical data that the woman has a higher probability of quitting her job prior to the completion of the software program.[12] Because a quit would disrupt the team's work and substantially increase the costs of development, the profit-maximizing employer offers the job to the man.

---

[11] Edmund S. Phelps, "The Statistical Theory of Racism and Sexism," *American Economic Review* 62 (September 1972): 659–661; Dennis J. Aigner and Glen G. Cain, "Statistical Theories of Discrimination in Labor Markets," *Industrial and Labor Relations Review* 30 (January 1977): 175–187; and Shelly J. Lundberg and Richard Startz, "Private Discrimination and Social Intervention in Competitive Labor Markets," *American Economic Review* 73 (June 1983): 340–347.

[12] It is important to point out that, despite the premise made in this example for illustrative purposes, much of the evidence does *not* suggest that women have higher quit rates than men; see Francine D. Blau and Lawrence M. Kahn, "Race and Sex Differences in Quits by Young Workers," *Industrial and Labor Relations Review* 34 (July 1981): 563–577; and W. Kip Viscusi, "Sex Differences in Worker Quitting," *Review of Economics and Statistics* 62 (August 1980): 388–398. Contradictory evidence is given by Nachum Sicherman, "Gender Differences in Departures from a Large Firm," *Industrial and Labor Relations Review* 49 (April 1996): 484–505.

The National Basketball Association (NBA) has approximately 60 referees. Each game is officiated by three referees, and this assignment is essentially random. A typical referee will officiate about 75 games per year, and no referee can officiate more than nine games per team. Refereeing an NBA game, of course, involves a series of quick, often subjective decisions. Not surprisingly, NBA officials intensively review the referees' performance, and the internal ranking of referees determines which referees are assigned to playoff games (which can lead to a substantial increase in a referee's salary).

for white players is 4.90, while the average foul rate for black players is 4.32, or a 0.58 difference in the foul rate. The difference-in-difference estimate of the impact of having an all white referee team for white players is −0.25. In other words, an all-white referee team leads to 0.25 fewer fouls for white players.

By looking at the underlying data reported in the table, it seems as if the number of fouls received by black players is essentially constant regardless of the racial composition of the refereeing team. In contrast,

	White Players	Black Players	Difference	Difference-in-Difference of Comparing 3 White Referees to 0 White Referees
0 white referees	5.25	4.42	0.83	
1 white referees	4.99	4.32	0.67	
2 white referees	4.99	4.34	0.65	
3 white referees	4.90	4.32	0.58	−0.25

Despite the high degree of accountability involved in refereeing an NBA game, a recent study shows that the race of the referees can have an important outcome on the typical game. About 3 percent of all games played during a season have zero white referees, 21 percent have one white referee, 47 percent have two white referees, and 29 percent have an exclusively white referee team. The table below shows the number of fouls called against black and white players during the typical game.

If all three referees are black, the average foul rate for white players is 5.25, while the average foul rate for black players is 4.42, or a 0.83 difference in the foul rate. However, if all referees are white, the average foul rate

the number of average fouls received by white players is lower when the refereeing team is "whiter." Therefore, it seems as if the underlying type of discrimination in the refereeing process is one of nepotism—where the white referees tend to "go easier" on white players.

It turns out that this type of discrimination may play a decisive role in close games. In rough terms, the nepotistic behavior of referees leads to about 4 or 5 percent fewer fouls for players that have the same race as the referees, and this translates into roughly to 2 or 3 percent more points per game.

Source: Joseph Price and Justin Wolfers, "Racial Discrimination among NBA Referees," *Quarterly Journal of Economics* 125 (November 2010): 1859–1887.

As this example illustrates, statistical discrimination arises because the information gathered from the résumé and the interview does not predict perfectly the applicant's true productivity. The underlying uncertainty encourages the employer to use statistics about the average performance of the group (hence the name **statistical discrimination**) to predict a particular applicant's productivity. As a result, applicants from high-productivity groups benefit from their membership in those groups, whereas applicants from low-productivity groups do not.[13]

It is important to stress that statistical discrimination arises not only in the labor market, but in many other markets as well. Insurance companies, for instance, constantly practice statistical discrimination when setting premiums. Women tend to live longer than men. Suppose that a man and a woman who were born on the same day and who have the same overall physical condition apply to buy life insurance. The insurance company has no way of knowing who will live longer, but its prior experience indicates that the man will probably have a shorter life. As a result, the cost of life insurance will be lower for the woman than for the man. Similarly, teenagers tend to have more accidents than older drivers. Again, if a teenager and a 40-year-old apply on the same day to buy auto insurance, the insurance company will typically charge a higher premium to the teenager—even though both drivers may have "clean" driving records. In short, competitive firms commonly use statistical discrimination to fill in the information gaps that arise when the firm cannot perfectly predict the risks or rewards associated with particular economic transactions.

The Impact of Statistical Discrimination on Wages

Let's gather all the information contained in the applicant's résumé, the interview, and any other screening tests and give it a score, say, T. Suppose that this test score was perfectly correlated with productivity so that a test score of 15 indicated that the true value of marginal product of the applicant was $15, a test score of 30 indicated a true value of marginal product of $30, and so on. The job applicant would then be offered a wage that equaled the test score. Of course, the assumption that the test score predicts productivity perfectly is very unrealistic. Some low-scoring applicants will turn out to be quite productive, whereas some high-scoring applicants will be spectacular failures. Therefore, employers may want to link the applicant's wage offer not only to the applicant's own score T, but also to the average test score of the applicant's group $\overline{T}$.

Under some conditions, it turns out that the applicant's expected productivity will be a weighted average of the applicant's own test score and of the average test score of the group:[14]

$$w = \alpha T + (1 - \alpha)\overline{T} \qquad \qquad (9\text{-}4)$$

If the parameter α is equal to one, then the applicant's wage depends only on the applicant's test score. Because the employer ignores the group average when setting the worker's wage, this is the extreme case where the screening test predicts the applicant's productivity perfectly. The other extreme is the case where the parameter α is equal to zero. Equation (9-4) then indicates that the worker's own test score is meaningless and plays no role in the wage-setting process. Put differently, the data gathered from the résumé and interview provide no

[13] There is an important difference between statistical discrimination and the signaling model presented in Chapter 6. In the signaling model, workers invest in education to separate themselves from the pack. In the statistical discrimination model, the traits that employers use to predict productivity—such as race, sex, or national origin—are immutable (at least for most of us).

[14] Lundberg and Startz, "Private Discrimination and Social Intervention in Competitive Labor Markets." The key assumption used in deriving equation (9-4) is that the frequency distribution of the unobserved component of an applicant's productivity follows a normal distribution.

FIGURE 9-6   The Impact of Statistical Discrimination on Wages

The worker's wage depends not only on his own test score, but also on the mean test score of workers in his racial group. (*a*) If black workers, on average, score lower than white workers, a white worker who gets *T** points earns more than a black worker with the same score. (*b*) If the test is a better predictor of productivity for white workers, high-scoring whites earn more than high-scoring blacks, and low-scoring whites earn less than low-scoring blacks.

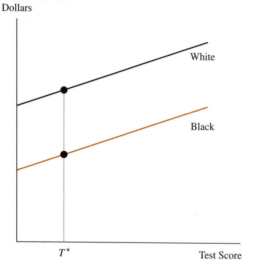

(*a*) Whites have a higher average score

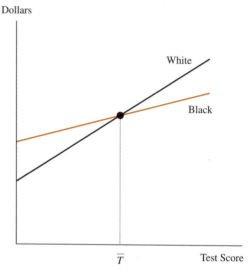

(*b*) Test is better predictor for white workers

information whatsoever about the applicant, and the employer will rely entirely on the group average to determine the worker's wage. The parameter α, therefore, measures the correlation between the test score and true productivity. The higher the predictive power of the test, the higher the value of α.

Equation (9-4) isolates two distinct ways in which statistical discrimination influences the wages of minorities and women. The first is illustrated in Figure 9-6a, which shows the relation between wages and test scores for blacks and whites. Statistical discrimination affects both the intercept and the slope of the curves relating wages and test scores. Suppose the average test score that blacks obtain on the screening test, $\overline{T}_B$, is lower than the average test score of whites, $\overline{T}_W$, but the correlation between test scores and productivity (α) is the same for the two groups. Equation (9-4) then implies that the white line lies above the black line because whites, on average, do better on the screening test, and both lines have the same slope. If a black and a white worker get the same test score (T^* in Figure 9-6a), the white worker is offered a higher wage because—for any given test score—employers expect the typical white applicant to be more productive than the typical black applicant.

It is also possible that the two groups have the same mean test score (say $\overline{T}$), but the test is more informative for whites than for blacks. In fact, it often has been argued that some tests predict the true productivity of blacks and other groups imprecisely because of "cultural bias." Standardized tests tend to be constructed by white male academics and reflect a set of upper-middle-class values and experiences that may be unfamiliar to persons raised in different environments. As a result, the value of the parameter α may differ between blacks and whites as well as between men and women. For instance, if the test is a very bad predictor of productivity for black workers, then α_B will be smaller than α_W.

Figure 9-6*b* shows the impact of this type of cultural bias on the wages of blacks and whites. If the test were a very bad predictor of the productivity of a particular black worker, this type of cultural bias implies that the line relating the wages and test scores of black workers would be relatively flat. Because the test is a very imperfect predictor of productivity for blacks, employers would treat most black workers as having relatively similar productivities and hence would pay them relatively similar wages. Put differently, the black worker's wage is mostly set on the basis of the group average, whereas the white worker's wage is mostly set on the basis of her own qualifications. Low-scoring blacks benefit relative to high-scoring blacks because the employer does not trust the worker's test score. As a result, statistical discrimination implies that low-scoring blacks will earn more than low-scoring whites, but that the opposite will be true for high-scoring workers.[15]

Should the Employer Use Group Averages?

The fact that profit-maximizing employers want to use statistics describing group performance in their hiring decisions raises a number of important policy questions. Perhaps the most important is whether employers *should* use the average performance of a particular group to predict productivity for members of that group. This policy debate, of course, is related to the question of whether there should be "race norming" or "gender norming" of scores in hiring tests. This type of grading would, in principle, construct a test score that would assign the same mean grade to all groups.

The allocation of workers into particular positions within the firm is more efficient the more information the employer uses in making the sorting decision (as long as the information is a valid predictor of productivity). Although using information on "group stereotypes" might improve labor market efficiency, it also creates racial and gender gaps in earnings and employment opportunities. Note, however, that even if profit-maximizing employers are forced to race norm or gender norm test scores, they will still want to use as much information as possible in the wage-setting process. Mandatory race and gender norming will reduce the predictive power of screening tests for *all* workers, so that profit-maximizing employers will simply search out other methods of predicting a worker's productivity. If these alternative signals are correlated with race or gender, statistical discrimination will remain a fixture of labor markets.

---

[15] An analysis of the statistical discrimination hypothesis, which pursues some of the more subtle empirical implications of the theory, is given by Joseph G. Altonji and Charles R. Pierret, "Employer Learning and Statistical Discrimination," *Quarterly Journal of Economics* 116 (February 2001): 313–350. See also David H. Autor and David Scarborough, "Does Job Testing Harm Minority Workers? Evidence from Retail Establishments," *Quarterly Journal of Economics* 123 (February 2008): 219–277.

9-7 Experimental Evidence on Discrimination

It is very difficult to measure a particular employer's discrimination coefficient against blacks or other minorities, or to determine if a particular employer is engaging in statistical discrimination. After all, it is illegal to discriminate on the basis of race, gender, and national origin, so employers will not willingly reveal their prejudicial behavior.

A number of studies have attempted to bypass this measurement problem by conducting labor market experiments. In these experiments, the researchers typically contact a number of employers at random. The experiments are cleverly designed to induce employers to reveal their preferences about hiring women and minorities. For example, a study shows that something as seemingly innocuous as a person's name—and the inference that most people would make regarding that person's race—can have a sizable impact on the employment opportunities of a job applicant.[16]

In this particular experiment, researchers sent out about 5,000 fake résumés in response to about 1,300 job ads that actually appeared in Boston and Chicago newspapers. The résumé did not specify the applicant's race. But the researchers gave employers a *hint* of the applicant's race by giving the fake applicant a name that was either "white-sounding" or "black-sounding." Among the white-sounding names were Emily Walsh and Greg Baker, while the black-sounding names included Lakisha Washington and Jamal Jones.[17] In addition, the researchers varied the résumés slightly in terms of the applicant's marketable skills. Some résumés stated that the applicant had many years of experience, or that the applicant had completed some type of certification degree, or that the applicant knew a foreign language.

After mailing out the fake résumés, the researchers sat back and waited for employers to call back the fake applicants for interviews. Remarkably, holding the skills in the applicant's résumé constant, the applicants with white-sounding names got about one callback for every 10 résumés sent. In contrast, the applicants with black-sounding names got only one callback for every 15 résumés sent. A black applicant would need eight more years of work experience to even out the gap!

The experimental approach has been extended beyond the simple act of mailing out fake résumés. Some researchers have actually sent out "experimental" human beings in actual job interviews to see how employers would react to the characteristics of these applicants. In these "hiring audits," two matched job applicants are similar in all respects, except that they differ in their race or gender. The hiring audit is conducted at a number

---

[16] Marianne Bertrand and Sendhil Mullanaithan, "Are Emily and Greg More Employable than Lakisha and Jamal? A Field Experiment on Labor Market Discrimination," *American Economic Review* 94 (September 2004): 991–1013.

[17] There is a growing divergence in the naming conventions used by black and white parents. A study of the names given to every single child born in California between 1961 and 2000 discovered that 40 percent of the black girls born in California in that period were given a name that not a single white girl born in those years was given; see Roland Fryer and Steven Levitt, "The Causes and Consequences of Distinctive Black Names," *Quarterly Journal of Economics* 119 (August 2004): 767–805. Recent work has examined the role played by *changes* in surnames in Sweden. It turns out that there is a significant increase in earnings when immigrants from Asian, African, or Slavic countries change their names to something that is more Swedish-sounding. See Mahmood Arai and Peter Skogman Thoursie, "Renouncing Personal Names: An Empirical Examination of Surname Change and Earnings," *Journal of Labor Economics* 27 (January 2009): 127–147.

of firms and the data are then examined to determine if the outcome of the job application differs between whites and blacks, or between men and women.

In the summer of 1989, for example, a hiring audit was conducted of employers in the Chicago and San Diego areas.[18] The employers, who were trying to fill entry-level jobs requiring few skills, were chosen at random from the classified ads in the Sunday edition of the *Chicago Tribune* and the *San Diego Union*. The average job applicant participating in the audit was a neatly dressed 22-year-old man who had a high school diploma, did not have a criminal record, had some college credits, and had some work experience as a stockperson or waiter. The only notable difference between the matched pair of job applicants sent to a particular firm was that one was Hispanic, with a slight Spanish accent, dark hair, and light brown skin, and the other was a non-Hispanic white who did not have an accent and had brown, blonde, or red hair.

The job applicants audited 360 firms and discovered systematic differences in the way that employers responded. After applying for the job, the white job applicant was 33 percent more likely to be interviewed and 52 percent more likely to receive a job offer.

A study of the hiring practices of low-priced and high-priced restaurants also indicated that employers value men and women differently.[19] Young men and women carrying identical (and fictitious) résumés were sent out to apply for jobs at Philadelphia restaurants. A waiter can typically do much better—in terms of wages and tips—at a high-priced restaurant. Even though the applicants looked alike on paper, 8 of the 10 job offers made by low-priced restaurants were made to women, whereas 11 of the 13 job offers made by high-priced restaurants were made to men.

9-8   Measuring Discrimination

Before discussing the evidence on the magnitude and persistence of racial and gender wage differentials, we describe how economists measure discrimination in the labor market. Suppose that we have two groups of workers: male and female. The average male wage is given by $\overline{w}_M$ and the average female wage is given by $\overline{w}_F$. One possible definition of discrimination is given by the difference in mean wages, or

$$\Delta\overline{w} = \overline{w}_M - \overline{w}_F \qquad \text{(9-5)}$$

This definition is unappealing because it is comparing apples and oranges. Many factors, other than discrimination, generate wage differentials between men and women. Men, for instance, are more likely to have professional degrees than women. We would not want to claim that employers discriminate against women if men earn more than women simply because men are more likely to have professional degrees. A more appropriate definition of labor market discrimination compares the wages of equally skilled workers.

[18] Harry Cross, *Employer Hiring Practices: Differential Treatment of Hispanic and Anglo Job Seekers,* Urban Institute Report 90-4, Washington, DC: The Urban Institute Press, 1990.

[19] David Neumark, Roy J. Bank, and Kyle D. Van Nort, "Sex Discrimination in Restaurant Hiring: An Audit Study," *Quarterly Journal of Economics* 111 (August 1996): 915–941. Some recent nonexperimental evidence on how the manager's race affects the race of the workers they hire is given by Laura Giuliano, David I. Levine, and Jonathan Leonard, "Manager Race and the Race of New Hires," *Journal of Labor Economics* 589 (October 2009): 589–631.

Therefore, we would like to adjust the "raw" wage differential given by $\Delta\overline{w}$ for differences in the skills between men and women. This adjustment is typically conducted by estimating regressions that relate the earnings of men or women to a wide array of socioeconomic and skill characteristics. To simplify the exposition, suppose that only one variable, schooling (which we denote by s), affects earnings. The earnings functions for each of the two groups can then be written as

$$\text{Male earnings function: } w_M = \alpha_M + \beta_M s_M$$

$$\text{Female earnings function: } w_F = \alpha_F + \beta_F s_F \qquad (9\text{-}6)$$

The coefficient β_M tells us by how much a man's wage increases if he gets one more year of schooling, while the coefficient β_F gives the same statistic for a woman. If employers value the education acquired by women as much as they value the education acquired by men, these two coefficients would be equal (so that $\beta_M = \beta_F$). Similarly, the intercepts α_M and α_F give the intercept of the earnings profile for each of the two groups. If employers valued the skills of men and women who have zero years of schooling equally, the two intercepts would be the same (or $\alpha_M = \alpha_F$).

The regression model implies that the raw wage differential can be written as

$$\Delta\overline{w} = \overline{w}_M - \overline{w}_F = \alpha_M + \beta_M \overline{s}_M - \alpha_F - \beta_F \overline{s}_F \qquad (9\text{-}7)$$

where $\overline{s}_M$ gives the mean schooling of men and $\overline{s}_F$ gives the mean schooling of women.

The Oaxaca Decomposition

We can now decompose the raw wage differential $\Delta\overline{w}$ into a portion that arises because men and women, on average, have different skills and a portion attributable to labor market discrimination. To conduct this decomposition, which has come to be known as the **Oaxaca decomposition** (after Ronald Oaxaca, who first introduced it into the economics literature).[20] Let's play a harmless algebraic trick. Let's add and subtract the term $(\beta_M \times \overline{s}_F)$ to the right-hand side of equation (9-7). The various terms in the equation can then be rearranged so that we can rewrite the raw wage differential as

$$\Delta\overline{w} = \underbrace{(\alpha_M - \alpha_F) + (\beta_M - \beta_F)\overline{s}_F}_{\substack{\text{Differential Due to} \\ \text{Discrimination}}} + \underbrace{\beta_M(\overline{s}_M - \overline{s}_F)}_{\substack{\text{Differential Due to} \\ \text{Differences in Skills}}} \qquad (9\text{-}8)$$

Equation (9-8) shows that the raw wage differential consists of two parts. It is useful to begin by discussing the second term in the equation. This term is zero if men and women have the same average schooling (or $\overline{s}_M - \overline{s}_F = 0$). Part of the raw wage differential between men and women, therefore, arises because the two groups differ in their skills.

---

[20] Ronald L. Oaxaca, "Male-Female Wage Differentials in Urban Labor Markets," *International Economic Review* 14 (October 1973): 693–709; see also Ronald L. Oaxaca and Michael R. Ransom, "On Discrimination and the Decomposition of Wage Differentials," *Journal of Econometrics* 61 (March 1994): 5–21; and David Card and Thomas Lemieux, "Wage Dispersion, Returns to Skills, and Black-White Wage Differentials," *Journal of Econometrics* 74 (October 1996): 319–361.

FIGURE 9-7 Measuring the Impact of Discrimination on the Wage

The average woman has $\bar{s}_F$ years of schooling and earns $\bar{w}_F$ dollars. The average man has $\bar{s}_M$ years of schooling and earns $\bar{w}_M$ dollars. Part of the wage differential arises because men have more schooling than women. If the average woman was paid as if she were a man, she would earn w_F^* dollars. A measure of discrimination is then given by $(w_F^* - \bar{w}_F)$.

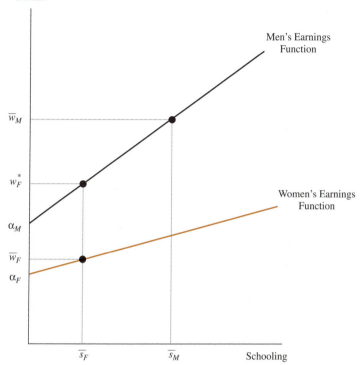

The first term in the equation will be positive if either employers value a man's schooling more than they value a woman's schooling ($\beta_M > \beta_F$) or if employers just pay men more than women for any level of schooling so that the intercept of the earnings function is higher for men than for women ($\alpha_M > \alpha_F$). The wage gap that arises because of this differential treatment of men and women is typically defined as discrimination.

Figure 9-7 illustrates the intuition behind the Oaxaca decomposition. As drawn, the relationship between earnings and schooling has a higher intercept and a steeper slope for men than for women. In other words, men start off with an advantage (they get paid more than women even if the two groups have zero years of schooling), and then get a bigger payoff from each additional year of schooling. Suppose also that men have more schooling than women on average. The raw wage differential between men and women is then given by the vertical difference $\bar{w}_M - \bar{w}_F$. The average woman with $\bar{s}_F$ years of schooling would earn w_F^* if she were "treated like a man." Therefore, the difference $(w_F^* - \bar{w}_F)$ can be attributed to discrimination. Part of the raw differential, however, also arises because men have more schooling than women. The difference $(\bar{w}_M - w_F^*)$ is the part of the differential that is attributable to skill differentials between men and women.

To keep the exposition simple, we derived the Oaxaca decomposition in a model where there is only one explanatory variable in the earnings function (that is, schooling). The decomposition can be extended easily to a model where there are many such variables (such as age, labor market experience, marital status, and region of the country where the worker lives). The basic insight is the same: The raw wage differential can be decomposed into a portion that is due to differences in characteristics between the two groups and a portion that remains unexplained and that we call discrimination.

Does the Oaxaca Decomposition Really Measure Discrimination?

The validity of the measure of discrimination obtained from the Oaxaca decomposition depends largely on whether we have controlled for *all* the dimensions in which the skills of the two groups differ. If there are some skill characteristics that affect earnings but are left out of the regression model, we will have an incorrect measure of labor market discrimination.

In fact, we seldom observe all the variables that make up a worker's human capital stock. Most data sets, for instance, provide little information on the quality of education that a particular worker received (as opposed to the number of years the worker attended school). If men and women or blacks and whites systematically attend institutions that vary in quality, the Oaxaca decomposition generates a biased measure of discrimination. For example, suppose that blacks attend lower-quality schools. There will then be a wage gap between black and white workers who have the same level of schooling. It would be incorrect, therefore, to label wage differences between workers with the same schooling as discrimination because, in fact, the workers are not equally skilled.

As a result, anyone who doubts that discrimination plays an important role in the labor market can always point out that a variable was left out of the model used to calculate the Oaxaca decomposition. Even if we try to include in the model every single measure of skills that we can think of *and* that we can observe, someone can still assert that we have omitted such variables as ability, effort, motivation, and drive and that these variables differ between the groups.

On the other hand, one could argue that defining discrimination as the wage differential between observationally equivalent men and women or blacks and whites underestimates the impact of discrimination in the economy. It is no coincidence that blacks have less schooling and attend lower-quality schools than whites or that women become grammar school teachers but do not become plumbers and electricians. Cultural discrimination as well as differential funding of black and white schools influenced the human capital accumulation of the various groups prior to their entry into the labor market. Even though employers are not responsible for these skill differentials, *somebody is.* A more complete accounting of the economic impact of discrimination, therefore, would not net out the differences in skills among groups and would focus much more on the raw wage differential.

Despite these problems of interpretation, the Oaxaca decomposition has a life of its own in the courtroom. Typically, class-action suits accusing an employer of discriminatory behavior are resolved by highly paid experts who argue over estimates of discrimination based on the statistical analysis summarized in equation (9-8). Experts hired by the plaintiff will argue that much of the raw wage differential cannot be explained in terms of skill differences between the groups, and hence is rightly called discrimination. Experts hired by the defendants will argue that most of the raw wage differential can be explained by differences in the skills between the two groups.

In view of the very large sums of money involved in these lawsuits (as well as the high consulting fees for the economists who do the statistical analysis), there is potential for the abuse and misuse of the Oaxaca measure of discrimination. If nothing else, the discussion should make us a bit skeptical of the facts that are carelessly thrown around in the debate over the measurement of discrimination.

9-9   Policy Application: Determinants of the Black-White Wage Ratio

In 1995, black workers earned about 21 percent less than white workers. Table 9-3 reports the results obtained from two alternative Oaxaca decompositions. The first adjusts for differences in educational attainment, age, sex, and region of residence between the two groups. The second controls for all of these factors as well as for differences in the occupation and industry of employment of the groups. The extent of measured discrimination clearly depends on the list of controls used. In the first decomposition, racial differences in educational attainment, age, and region of residence generated an 8.2 percent wage differential between the two groups so that labor market discrimination accounts for the residual, or a 13.4 percent wage gap. However, if the analysis also adjusts for differences in occupation and industry of employment, there is an 11.4 percent wage gap attributable to observable differences in socioeconomic variables and "only" a 9.8 percent wage gap can be attributed to labor market discrimination.

This type of exercise raises an important conceptual question that we alluded to earlier: What is the right set of controls to use in the Oaxaca decomposition? In particular, should one calculate the wage differences among similarly skilled blacks and whites employed in the same occupation and industry before we decide whether there is labor market discrimination? Or is it possible that part of the differences in the occupation and industry of employment between blacks and whites is due to employment barriers that prevent blacks from moving into certain types of jobs? The right choice of controls for the Oaxaca decomposition will typically depend on the context in which the discrimination is being measured. The key lesson of Table 9-3 is that one should look carefully at the "fine print" behind any Oaxaca decomposition before one concludes that discrimination either plays a small role or plays a substantial role in the labor market.

TABLE 9-3   **The Oaxaca Decomposition of the Black-White Wage Differential, 1995**

Source: Joseph G. Altonji and Rebecca M. Blank, "Race and Gender in the Labor Market," in Orley Ashenfelter and David Card, editors, *Handbook of Labor Economics,* vol. 3C, Amsterdam: Elsevier, 1999, Table 5. The log wage differential between any two groups can be interpreted as being approximately equal to the percentage wage differential between the groups.

	Controls for Differences in Education, Age, Sex, and Region of Residence	Controls for Differences in Education, Age, Sex, Region of Residence, *and* Occupation and Industry
Raw log wage differential	−0.211	−0.211
Due to differences in skills	−0.082	−0.114
Due to discrimination	−0.134	−0.098

FIGURE 9-8   Trend in Black-White Earnings Ratio, 1967–2009

Sources: U.S. Bureau of the Census, "Historical Income Tables—People," Table 38. "Full-Time Year-Round Black and White Workers by Median Earnings and Sex," www.census.gov/hhes/www/income/histinc/incpertoc.html. The earnings refer to the median earnings of full-time, full-year workers aged 15 or above.

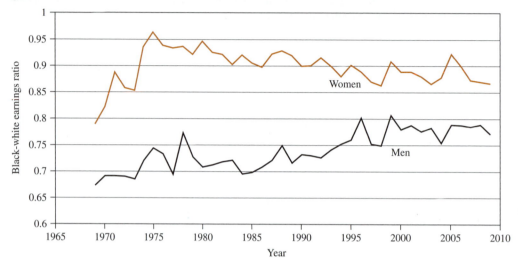

The Trend in the Black-White Wage Ratio

As Figure 9-8 illustrates, the wage ratio between black and white men rose dramatically in the past 40 years. In 1967, the ratio stood at about 0.65; by 1980, it had risen to 0.71; and by 2009, it stood at 0.77. This improvement in the relative economic status of black men is a continuation of long-run trends; the ratio was about 0.4 around 1940. Figure 9-8 also shows that the wage ratio between black and white women rose very rapidly between 1967 and 1975 but had a slow downward drift in the 1980s and 1990s. Between 1967 and 1975, this ratio rose from 0.75 to 0.96; it now stands at around 0.90. Overall, the long-run trends are clear: the relative wage of both black men and women is substantially higher today than it was in the late 1960s.

A number of hypotheses have been proposed to explain the improving economic status of African Americans.[21] The first is that the increasing level of human capital in the black population, particularly in terms of the quantity and quality of education, can explain much of the rise in the black wage. In 1940 the typical 30-year-old white man had 9.9 years of schooling, as compared to 6.0 years for a comparable black man. By 1980, the typical 30-year-old white man had 13.6 years of schooling and the comparable black man had 12.2 years, a difference of only 1.4 years.

---

[21] The data summarized in this discussion are drawn from James P. Smith and Finis R. Welch, "Black Economic Progress after Myrdal," *Journal of Economic Literature* 27 (June 1989): 519–564; and David Card and Alan B. Krueger, "School Quality and Black-White Relative Earnings: A Direct Assessment," *Quarterly Journal of Economics* 107 (February 1992): 151–200. The human capital hypothesis is also explored by Steven G. Rivkin, "School Desegregation, Academic Attainment, and Earnings," *Journal of Human Resources* 35 (Spring 2000): 333–346.

The disparity in school quality between the schools attended by black and white students also decreased dramatically. In the 1920s, pupil-teacher ratios in southern states were about 50 percent higher in black schools than in white schools. By the late 1950s, this quality differential had essentially disappeared. As a result, the racial gap in the rate of return to school also vanished. The rate of return to school for white workers who entered the labor market around 1940 was 9.8 percent, whereas for black workers it was only 4.7 percent. For the cohorts that entered in the late 1970s, blacks actually had a higher rate of return to school (9.6 percent versus 8.5 percent for whites).

The increasing quantity *and* quality of black schooling contributed to the narrowing of the black-white wage gap. It has been estimated that at least half the increase in the black-white wage ratio in recent decades can be attributed to the increase in black human capital.

The Impact of Affirmative Action

Part of the increase in the relative wage of black workers also can be attributed to the impact of government programs, particularly the enactment of the 1964 Civil Rights Act.[22] This landmark legislation prohibits employment discrimination on the basis of race and sex. Title VII of the act established the Equal Employment Opportunity Commission (EEOC) to monitor compliance with the legislation. It is under this provision of the legislation that costly class action suits can be initiated to force employers to discontinue discriminatory hiring practices, as well as compensate the affected workers for past discrimination.

The federal civil rights program was further strengthened in the 1960s by Executive Order No. 11246 and No. 11375, which prohibited discrimination by race and sex among government contractors. Under Executive Order No. 11246, federal contractors agree "not to discriminate against any employee or applicant for employment because of race, color, religion, sex, national origin, and to take affirmative action to ensure that applicants and employees are treated during employment without regard to their race, color, sex, or national origin."

It is worth stressing that these executive orders compel federal contractors to (1) not discriminate and (2) take *affirmative action* to ensure that they do not. As a result, federal contractors are now required to construct detailed affirmative action plans, which include employment goals for affected groups as well as timetables for meeting these goals. Although there has been an emotional debate over whether these plans force employers to set hiring quotas, there is little operational difference between establishing employment "goals" and "quotas" that require that x percent of new workers belong to a particular group.

---

[22] Richard B. Freeman, "Black Economic Progress after 1964: Who Has Gained and Why?" in Sherwin Rosen, editor, *Studies in Labor Markets,* Chicago: University of Chicago Press, 1981, pp. 247–294; John J. Donohue and James J. Heckman, "Continuous versus Episodic Change: The Impact of Civil Rights Policy on the Economic Status of Blacks," *Journal of Economic Literature* 29 (December 1991): 1603–1643; and Kenneth Y. Chay, "The Impact of Federal Civil Rights Policy on Black Economic Progress: Evidence from the Equal Employment Opportunity Act of 1972," *Industrial and Labor Relations Review* 51 (July 1998): 608–632. See Harry Holzer and David Neumark, "Assessing Affirmative Action," *Journal of Economic Literature* 38 (September 2000): 483–568, for an exhaustive review of the consequences of affirmative action programs.

Theory at Work

"DISPARATE IMPACT" AND BLACK EMPLOYMENT IN POLICE DEPARTMENTS

The most aggressive affirmative action programs in the United States have been the court-ordered racial hiring quotas imposed on local police departments. For instance, both Boston and Cambridge, Massachusetts, remain subject to hiring quotas that were first imposed in 1973.

The initial imposition of these quotas arose from the racial disparity in the passing rates in the police department entrance examinations. Black applicants (both then and now) simply do not do as well. In the late 1960s, for example, the Detroit entrance exam had a passing rate of 44 percent for blacks and 81 percent for whites. It was argued that the exams tested for aptitudes that had little to do with the day-to-day work of a police officer. Detroit, for instance, simply used a three-hour IQ test, while the District of Columbia used a civil service examination that had been designed for jobs in the federal government. As an example, consider this question in the DC exam:

"Crisp" means most nearly (A) broken (B) frosty (C) brittle (D) burnt (E) dry.

Efforts to improve the relevance of the questions were not entirely successful in terms of the passing rate of black applicants. Many of the questions in the 1970 New York City exam had applicants evaluate a hypothetical situation that presumably occurred in the day-to-day experience of a police officer. Yet this exam still had a passing rate of 55 percent for blacks and 82 percent for whites.

In the 1970s, the federal courts concluded that use of these exams in police hiring was discriminatory. The courts relied on the notion of *disparate impact,* a legal theory developed in the 1960s. This theory holds that "an employment practice with no apparent racial motivation may nonetheless be interpreted as tentative evidence of discrimination if the employment practice disproportionately harms a group protected under civil rights law, such as African Americans or women." The Supreme Court approved this theory in the 1971 *Griggs v. Duke Power Company* case: "If an employment practice which operates to exclude Negroes cannot be shown to be related to job performance, the practice is prohibited."

As a result of the judicial history, there exists a great deal of data on the racial composition of police departments in many localities. Some of these data are summarized in the table below:

The Share of African-American Employment in Police Departments

Year	Litigated	Unlitigated
1970	0.07	0.05
1980	0.12	0.08
1990	0.18	0.11
2000	0.23	0.13

Source: Justin McCrary, "The Effect of Court-Ordered Hiring Quotas on the Composition and Quality of Police," *American Economic Review* 97 (March 2007), Table 1.

There is a notable relation between the existence of litigation and the relative number of black police. The two sets of cities were roughly similar in 1970—with blacks making up 5 to 7 percent of the police force. By 2000, however, the black share in police employment had risen to 23 percent in the litigated cities but only to 13 percent in the unlitigated cities.

It has been estimated that the 25-year gain in the black share due to the involvement of the federal judiciary was around a 10-percentage point gain. Equally important, this change in the racial composition of the city's police force was accomplished without any corresponding change in the city's crime rate.

Source: Justin McCrary, "The Effect of Court-Ordered Hiring Quotas on the Composition and Quality of Police," *American Economic Review* 97 (March 2007): 318–353.

The enforcement effort to ensure compliance has been substantial. For instance, federal contractors who have at least $50,000 worth of contracts and 50 employees must fill out an annual form on which they report their total employment by occupation, race, and sex. These data can trigger "compliance reviews" that audit the contractor's employment practices and may lead to costly negotiations or litigation designed to influence the employer's hiring behavior. In view of these regulations, it is not surprising that affirmative action programs have influenced employment decisions. In 1966, black men were 10 percent less likely than white men to work in firms that were federal contractors (that is, in firms covered by the provisions of the executive orders); by 1980, they were 25 percent more likely to work in covered firms.[23]

A clear example of the impact of affirmative action is provided by employment trends among manufacturing firms in South Carolina.[24] There was little change in the share of black employment in the textile industry (the main manufacturing employer in that state) between 1910 and 1964. The fraction of black employment in the industry stood at roughly 4 to 5 percent throughout the period. The South Carolina textile industry, however, sold 5 percent of its output to the U.S. government, so it was clearly covered by the executive orders. By 1970, nearly 20 percent of the workers in the industry were black.

The impact of affirmative action on black employment is well documented, but its impact on the relative black wage has been harder to detect. In fact, there is no consensus on whether these programs have increased the black wage at all. Although some studies have interpreted the rising wage of blacks in the post-1964 period as the result of affirmative action programs, it is worth noting that the black relative wage was rising even prior to the 1960s.[25] Some evidence, however, suggests a "back-door" way by which affirmative action may have increased black wages. The executive orders requiring federal contractors to establish affirmative action programs affect mainly large firms, and large firms tend to pay higher wages. The number of blacks employed by large firms increased substantially in the 1970s, raising the average black wage. It is estimated that the increasing representation of blacks in the workforce of large firms accounts for about 15 percent of the increase in the black-white wage ratio over the period.[26]

The Decline in Black Labor Force Participation

Despite the increase in the black wage in recent decades, the labor force participation rate of black men fell precipitously. Figure 9-9 illustrates this important trend. In the mid-1950s, 85 percent of both black and white men were in the labor force. By 2009, the gap between the black and white participation rates was over 7 percentage points.

---

[23] See Jonathan S. Leonard, "The Impact of Affirmative Action on Employment," *Journal of Labor Economics* 2 (October 1984): 439–463; and Jonathan S. Leonard, "The Impact of Affirmative Action and Equal Employment Law on Black Employment," *Journal of Economic Perspectives* 4 (Fall 1990): 47–63.

[24] James J. Heckman and Brook S. Payner, "Determining the Impact of Federal Antidiscrimination Policy on the Economic Status of Blacks: A Study of South Carolina," *American Economic Review* 79 (March 1989): 138–177.

[25] Richard B. Freeman, "Changes in the Labor Market for Black Americans," *Brookings Papers on Economic Activity* 20 (1973): 67–120; Joan Gustafson Haworth, James Gwartney, and Charles Haworth, "Earnings, Productivity, and Changes in Employment Discrimination during the 1960s," *American Economic Review* 65 (March 1975): 158–168; and Harry Holzer and David Neumark, "Are Affirmative Action Hires Less Qualified? Evidence from Employer-Employee Data on New Hires," *Journal of Labor Economics* 17 (July 1999): 534–569.

[26] William J. Carrington, Kristin McCue, and Brooks Pierce, "Using Establishment Size to Measure the Impact of Title VII and Affirmative Action," *Journal of Human Resources* 35 (Summer 2000): 503–523.

FIGURE 9-9   Male Labor Force Participation Rates, by Race, 1955–2009

Sources: U.S. Bureau of the Census, *Historical Statistics of the United States, Colonial Times to 1970,* Washington, DC: Government Printing Office, 1975; U.S. Bureau of the Census, *Statistical Abstract of the United States,* Washington, DC: Government Printing Office, various issues.

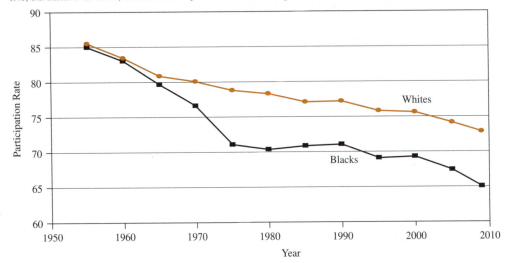

Suppose that black workers who drop out of the labor market are relatively low-skill. This would imply that the average wage of *working* blacks would rise over time, simply because blacks at the lower tail of the wage distribution are no longer included in the cal-culations.[27] In other words, the observed increase in the black wage need not indicate an improvement in the employment opportunities of black workers, but might simply indicate that the least-skilled blacks are no longer working.

The intuition underlying this hypothesis is illustrated in Figure 9-10, which shows the wage distribution for blacks. Recall from our analysis of the labor supply decision in Chapter 2 that persons decide whether to work by comparing the reservation wage with the market wage. Suppose that the reservation wage of black workers is initially given by $\tilde{w}_1$, meaning that all blacks who can earn more than $\tilde{w}_1$ work. The mean wage observed in the sample of labor market participants is then given by $\overline{w}_1$.

Suppose that for some reason—such as the introduction of large-scale public assistance programs in the 1960s—the reservation wage of black workers increased. The increase in the reservation wage (to $\tilde{w}_2$) lowers the labor force participation rate of black workers and increases the average wage of black persons who are actually in the labor market to $\overline{w}_2$ in the figure. Therefore, the upward drift in the relative wage of black men may be an illusion created by sample selection bias.

There is a lot of disagreement over whether this type of selection has contributed sig-nificantly to the increase in the relative black wage. Some studies conclude that only about a third of the improvement in the relative black wage between 1969 and 1989 can

---

[27] This argument was first advanced by Richard J. Butler and James J. Heckman, "The Government's Impact on the Labor Market Status of Black Americans: A Critical Review," in Leonard J. Hausman, edi-tor, *Equal Rights and Industrial Relations,* Madison, WI: Industrial Relations Research Association, 1977.

FIGURE 9-10   **The Decline in the Labor Force Participation of Blacks and the Average Black Wage**

If blacks have reservation wage $\tilde{w}_1$, the mean wage observed among workers is $\overline{w}_1$. If the reservation wage rises to $\tilde{w}_2$, the black labor force participation rate falls, and the mean wage observed among workers rises to $\overline{w}_2$. The increase in the black wage is an "illusion" caused by the declining labor force participation rate of blacks.

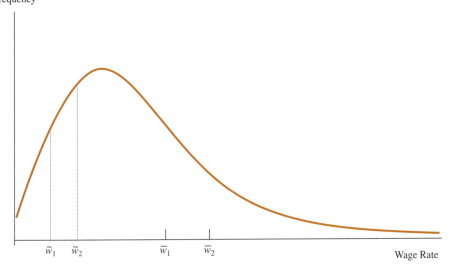

be attributed to the declining labor force participation of the black population, while other studies claim that much of the perceived improvement is due to the selection bias.[28]

Unobserved Skill Differences and the Black-White Wage Differential

The empirical measure of discrimination based on the Oaxaca decomposition effectively measures the wage gap between black and white workers who are "statistically similar" in the sense that they have the same number of years of schooling, have the same amount of labor market experience, live in the same region, work in the same industry and occupation, and so on. As we noted earlier, there may well be other skill differences between the two groups that are not observed, and that may account for part of the wage differential that the Oaxaca decomposition labels "discrimination."

Some studies have begun to investigate whether such unobserved skill differences exist. These studies often use a particular measure of skills: the test score in the Armed Forces Qualification Test (AFQT). As the name implies, this standard test is given to all recruits in the U.S. military. The test also was administered to a randomly chosen sample of American young men and women in the 1980s (regardless of whether they planned to be in the military).

[28] Chinhui Juhn, "Labor Market Dropouts and Trends in Black and White Wages," *Industrial and Labor Relations Review* 56 (July 2003): 643–662; Amitabh Chandra, "Is the Convergence in the Racial Wage Gap Illusory?" National Bureau of Economic Research Working Paper No. 9476, January 2003; and Derek Neal, "The Measured Black-White Wage Gap among Women Is Too Small," *Journal of Political Economy* 112 (February 2004): S1–S28.

Theory at Work
SHADES OF BLACK

There is a great deal of variation in skin tone in the African-American population. Remarkably, research documents that there are substantial differences in economic outcomes within the black population that depend on skin tone. Typically, African Americans with a lighter skin tone have more education and earn more than African Americans with darker tones.

In one survey, for example, the average white man earned $15.94 an hour. Black respondents were asked to classify their skin tone in one of three categories: light black, medium black, or dark black. African Americans who indicated that they had a light skin tone earned $14.42, those indicating a medium tone earned $13.23, and those indicating a dark tone earned $11.72. Moreover, these wage differences remain even after controlling for observed differences in socioeconomic characteristics, including education and age. The typical light-skin black earned roughly the same as a comparably skilled white man, while dark-skin blacks earned about 10 percent less.

There are many potential explanations for the link between skin tone and socioeconomic outcomes. For instance, it may well be that African Americans with lighter skin tones are considered more attractive, and we know that "beauty" leads to better labor market outcomes. Alternatively, a lighter skin color may help to break down some of the racial segregation barriers and improves access to better schools and jobs. Although we do not yet know why the labor market rewards some skin tones more than others, the study of these differences can perhaps increase our understanding of why racial wage differentials persist in the United States.

In fact, recent work has also shown that it is not only the visual aspects of "blackness" that matter. There is strong evidence that speech that can be distinctly identified as belonging to a black speaker is penalized in the labor market. Blacks whose speech cannot be differentiated from "white speech" earn essentially the same as comparably skilled whites, while blacks whose speech can be distinctly identified earn about 12 percent less.

Although we do not yet know why the labor market rewards some skin tones or some types of speech more than others, the study of these differences can perhaps increase our understanding of why racial wage differentials persist in the United States.

Sources: Arthur H. Goldsmith, Darrick Hamilton, and William Darity Jr., "Shades of Discrimination: Skin Tone and Wages," *American Economic Review* 96 (May 2006): 242–245; and Joni Hersch, "Skin-Tone Effects among African Americans: Perceptions and Reality," *American Economic Review* 96 (May 2006): 251–255; and Jeffrey Grogger, "Speech Patterns and Racial Wage Inequality," *Journal of Human Resources* 46 (Winter 2011): 1–25.

There are substantial racial differences in the AFQT score; blacks tend to have lower scores than whites. More important, however, is the fact that these racial differences in the AFQT score account for practically the entire wage differential between young black and white workers. Even though the *actual* black-white wage ratio is about 0.8 for these young workers, the *adjusted* black-white wage ratio jumps to about 0.95 once we control for differences in AFQT scores between the groups.[29] Put differently, even though the typical young black worker earns about 20 percent less than the typical young white worker, the typical young black worker earns only 5 percent less than a young white worker who has the same AFQT score. In short, much of the wage differential between young black and white workers disappears once the wage data are adjusted for the racial differences in AFQT scores.

[29] O'Neill, "The Role of Human Capital in Earnings Differences between Black and White Men"; Nan Maxwell, "The Effect on Black-White Wage Differences of Differences in the Quantity and Quality of Schooling," *Industrial and Labor Relations Review* 47 (January 1994): 249–264; Derek A. Neal and William R. Johnson, "The Role of Premarket Factors in Black-White Wage Differences," *Journal of Political Economy* 104 (October 1996): 869–895.

Although there is little doubt about the validity of the evidence, the interpretation is not clear. What exactly is the AFQT score measuring?[30] There is convincing evidence that the AFQT score is not a straightforward measure of innate ability. Persons who have more schooling or go to better schools have higher AFQT scores. The score in this particular test, therefore, partly measures skills that were acquired prior to a person entering the labor market. As a result, the studies can be interpreted as indicating that much of the wage gap between young black and white workers in the 1990s can be attributed to skill differentials between the groups—and that these skills were acquired *prior* to the entry of the workers into the labor market. This interpretation, in turn, suggests that the importance of labor market discrimination in the U.S. labor market may have diminished substantially in recent decades.

9-10 Discrimination against Other Groups

The resurgence of large-scale immigration in the past few decades greatly altered the racial and ethnic mix of the U.S. population and sparked interest in documenting the wage determination process for other racial and ethnic groups.

The growth of the Hispanic population in the United States is astounding.[31] In 1980, Hispanics made up only 6.4 percent of the population, as compared to 11.7 percent for blacks. By 2002, Hispanics had become the largest minority group in the population, comprising 13.4 percent of the population, but the proportion of blacks had risen by only one percentage point, to 12.7 percent.[32]

Figure 9-11 illustrates the trend in the Hispanic-white wage ratio. This ratio declined between 1980 and 2009 for both Hispanic men and Hispanic women. Because the number of Hispanic immigrants grew substantially during this period, however, the decline in the observed wage ratio between Hispanics and non-Hispanics may reflect the changing composition of the Hispanic population, rather than a growing disadvantage to a fixed group of workers.

It is also worth noting that the Hispanic population is not a single monolith, but is composed of many subgroups, including Mexicans, Puerto Ricans, Cubans, Nicaraguans, and Colombians. As reported in Table 9-4, there are sizable differences in educational attainment and earnings not only between Hispanics and non-Hispanics, but also among the groups that make up the Hispanic population. In 2008, 44.8 percent of Mexican men were high school dropouts and only 9.1 percent were college graduates. In contrast, only 23.6 percent of Puerto Ricans were high school dropouts and 15.5 percent were college graduates. To put these numbers in perspective, note that only 8.5 percent of non-Hispanic whites were high school dropouts and almost a third were college graduates.

---

[30] A well-known study that claims that AFQT scores provide a good measure of innate ability is Richard Herrnstein and Charles Murray, *The Bell Curve: Intelligence and Class Structure in American Life,* New York: Free Press, 1994.

[31] A comprehensive analysis of Hispanic economic status is given by Gregory DeFreitas, *Inequality at Work: Hispanics in the U.S. Labor Market,* New York: Oxford University Press, 1991.

[32] The latest estimates of the size of the U.S. population by race and ethnicity are posted online at http://eire.census.gov/popest/estimates.php.

FIGURE 9-11   Trend in Earnings Ratio of Hispanics and Asians, 1974–2009

Sources: U.S. Bureau of the Census, "Historical Income Tables—People," Table P-38, "Full-Time Year-Round Asian and Hispanic Workers by Median Earnings and Sex," www.census.gov/hhes/www/income/histinc/incpertoc.html. The earnings refer to the median earnings of full-time, full-year workers aged 15 or above. The denominator in the ratios gives the earnings of white men or women, respectively.

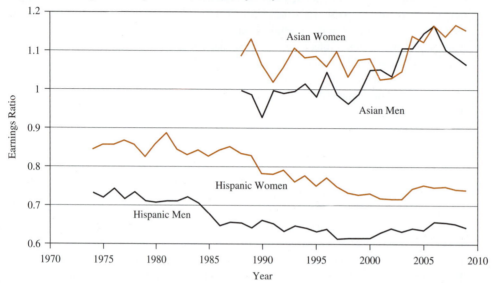

TABLE 9-4   Educational Attainment and Earnings of Hispanics, 2008

Source: U.S. Department of Labor, Bureau of Labor Statistics, "Hispanic Population in the United States, 2004 March CPS," www.census.gov/population/www/socdemo/hispanic.html. The data on educational attainment refer to the population aged 25 or over; the data on earnings give the median earnings of full-time, year-round workers aged 15 and over.

	Educational Attainment	
	Percent High School Dropouts	Percent College Graduates
All Hispanics	37.7%	13.3%
Mexicans	44.8	9.1
Puerto Ricans	23.6	15.5
Cubans	20.0	28.1
Central American origin	44.5	11.7
Non-Hispanic whites	8.5	32.6

A careful study of the wage differential between men of Mexican origin and non-Hispanic whites concludes that over three-quarters of the substantial wage gap between the two groups can be attributed to differences in observable skill measures.[33] In other words,

---

[33] Stephen J. Trejo, "Why Do Mexican Americans Earn Low Wages?" *Journal of Political Economy* 105 (December 1997): 1235–1268.

A large German-speaking population resided in the United States at the onset of World War I. That conflict encouraged many states to enact statutes specifically aimed at this population. For instance, the *Harvard Encyclopedia of American Ethnic Groups* reports that "by summer 1918 about half of the [U.S.] states had restricted or eliminated German-language instruction, and several had curtailed freedom to speak German in public . . . The total number of German language publications declined from 554 in 1910 to 234 in 1920."

The post-9/11 reaction against the Arab and Muslim population living in the United States was not as severe—and the reaction was certainly not part of a concerted effort by governmental units to enact specific regulations. Nevertheless, the emotions unleashed by the terrorist attack likely led to an increase in prejudice against this population, and this increased prejudice seems to have affected the labor market outcomes of the target groups.

The increase in prejudice has been well documented. There were reports of increased hate crime activities against Arabs and Muslims in the aftermath of 9/11. Both FBI statistics and local crime data report an increased number of crimes against these groups soon after the attack. This emotional reaction spilled over into the labor market. Arabs and Muslims reported increased discrimination at work and by early 2002 the U.S. Equal Employment Opportunity Commission had received 488 complaints of 9/11-related employment discrimination, including 301 firings.

A careful study found that the weekly earnings of Arab and Muslim men fell by about 10 percent subsequent to 9/11. The reduction in earnings, however, does not seem to have been long-lasting. The wage reduction was significantly smaller by 2005. It is also interesting that the wage impact of the 9/11 attack affected practically all Arab and Muslim men—regardless of their education, their immigration status, and their country of origin. It is also notable that the earnings reduction was larger in those areas of the country that reported a larger increase in hate crimes related to religious, ethnic, or country-of-origin bias.

Sources: Kathleen M. Conzen, "Germans," in Stephen Thernstrom, editor, *Harvard Encyclopedia of American Ethnic Groups,* Cambridge, MA: Harvard University Press, 1980, p. 423; and Neeraj Kaushal, Robert Kaestner, and Cordelia Reimers, "Labor Market Effects of September 11th on Arab and Muslim Residents of the United States," *Journal of Human Resources* 42 (Spring 2007): 275–308.

the largest group of Hispanic Americans earn less not because of their "Hispanicness," but because they are less skilled.

The Asian population also has grown rapidly in the past three decades. In 1980, only 1.5 percent of the population was of Asian ancestry. By 2002, the Asian share of the population had almost tripled, to 4.1 percent. Figure 9-11 also shows the available trend in the data for the Asian-white wage ratio. These ratios hover between 1.0 and 1.2 for both men and women. In other words, it seems that the typical person of Asian background in the United States has a slight wage advantage over white workers. Much of this advantage can be attributed to the fact that many Asian workers have relatively high skill levels.[34]

[34] Barry R. Chiswick, "An Analysis of the Earnings and Employment of Asian-American Men," *Journal of Labor Economics* 1 (April 1983): 197–214.

9-11   Policy Application: Determinants of the Female-Male Wage Ratio

The oldest documented wage differential between men and women dates back to the days of the Old Testament:

> The Lord spoke to Moses and said, Speak to the Israelites in these words. When a man makes a special vow to the Lord which requires your valuation of living persons, a male between twenty and fifty years old shall be valued at fifty silver shekels, that is shekels by the sacred standard. If it is a female, she shall be valued at thirty shekels. (Leviticus 27:1–4)

By 1999, the Biblical female-male wage ratio of 0.6 had increased to 0.78 in the Netherlands, 0.76 in the United Kingdom, and 0.72 in the United States.[35] The literature on male-female wage differentials focuses on a simple question: What factors explain the existence and persistence of this huge wage gap?[36]

The Female-Male Wage Gap and Labor Market Experience

There is an ongoing debate over how much of the wage differential between men and women remains after we control for differences in socioeconomic characteristics between the two groups. As Table 9-5 shows, women earned about 28.6 percent less than men in 1995. Differences in education, age, and region of residence generate only a trivial wage gap between men and women, about 0.8 percent. Even after adjusting for occupation and industry, differences in observable socioeconomic characteristics between the two groups generate only a 7.6 percent wage gap. It should not be too surprising that gender differences in such variables as educational attainment, region of residence, and age fail to explain much of the gender wage gap. After all, the typical man and woman have roughly the same level of schooling, are about the same age, and live in the same place. As a result,

TABLE 9-5   **The Oaxaca Decomposition of the Female-Male Wage Differential, 1995**

Source: Joseph G. Altonji and Rebecca M. Blank, "Race and Gender in the Labor Market," in Orley Ashenfelter and David Card, editors, *Handbook of Labor Economics*, vol. 3C, Amsterdam: Elsevier, 1999, Table 5. The log wage differential between any two groups can be interpreted as being approximately equal to the percentage wage differential between the groups.

	Controls for Differences in Education, Age, Sex, and Region of Residence	Controls for Differences in Education, Age, Sex, Region of Residence, *and* Occupation and Industry
Raw log wage differential	−0.286	−0.286
Due to differences in skills	−0.008	−0.076
Due to discrimination	−0.279	−0.211

[35] Claudia Olivetti and Barbara Petrongolo, "Unequal Pay or Unequal Employment? A Cross-Country Analysis of Gender Gaps," *Journal of Labor Economics* 26 (October 2008): 621–654.

[36] A good survey of the literature that examines the trends in socioeconomic outcomes experienced by women in the United States is given by Francine D. Blau, "Trends in the Well-Being of American Women, 1970–1995," *Journal of Economic Literature* 36 (March 1998): 112–165.

discrimination—in the Oaxaca sense—accounts for the bulk of the wage gap between men and women.

The Oaxaca decompositions reported in Table 9-5, however, ignore a key determinant of female earnings. Even though the decompositions control for age differences between working men and women, they ignore the fact that similarly aged men and women have very different labor market histories.[37] It is not uncommon for many married women to drop out of the labor market during their child-raising years. In the late 1960s, for instance, the typical woman's career path consisted of a three- to four-year spell of employment after she completed school, followed by a seven-year spell in the household sector, and then a permanent return to the labor market. This "typical" career path is changing rapidly in the United States. Nevertheless, even by the late 1980s, the typical woman worked only about 71 percent of her potential years of labor market experience. In contrast, the typical man worked about 93 percent of his potential years of labor market experience.[38]

It has been argued that the discontinuity in women's labor market attachment may help explain a substantial part of the gender wage gap.[39] The argument can be easily stated. Human capital is more profitable the longer the payoff period over which the returns on the investment can be collected. Consider the payoffs to human capital investments made by new labor market entrants. Because the vast majority of men expect to participate in the labor market throughout their entire lives, the human capital acquired by men has a long payoff period. In contrast, some women expect to devote time to the household sector, shortening the payoff period and reducing the returns on the investment. It would not be surprising if women, on average, acquired less human capital.

Moreover, the human capital that a woman acquires will depreciate somewhat during the years when she is engaged in household production. After all, skills that are not used or kept up-to-date either are forgotten or become obsolete. The value of the woman's human capital stock, therefore, is reduced by her intermittent labor market attachment.

This hypothesis thus suggests that the discontinuity in female labor supply over the life cycle generates a gender wage gap for two distinct reasons. First, it creates a wage differential because men tend to acquire more human capital. Second, the child-raising years increase the wage gap because women's skills tend to depreciate during that period.

---

[37] The decompositions reported in the table actually adjust for differences in "potential labor market experience," defined as age minus years of schooling minus 5. Since the decompositions also control for differences in education, the only variation in potential labor market experience between the groups must arise because of differences in the mean age of men and women.

[38] Francine D. Blau and Lawrence F. Kahn, "Swimming Upstream: Trends in the Gender Wage Differential in the 1980s," *Journal of Labor Economics* 15 (January 1997): 1–42; June O'Neill and Solomon Polachek, "Why the Gender Gap in Wages Narrowed in the 1980s," *Journal of Labor Economics* 11 (January 1993, Part 1): 205–228; Anne M. Hill and June E. O'Neill, "Intercohort Change in Women's Labor Market Status," *Research in Labor Economics* 13 (1992): 215–286; and Shirley Smith, "Revised Worklife Tables Reflect 1979–80 Experience," *Monthly Labor Review* 108 (August 1985): 23–30.

[39] Jacob Mincer and Solomon W. Polachek, "Family Investments in Human Capital: Earnings of Women," *Journal of Political Economy* 82 (March 1974 Supplement): S76–S108.

Overall, the evidence supports the hypothesis, although there is disagreement about how much of the wage gap between men and women can be explained by the difference in labor market histories.[40] A clear example of the impact of labor market experience on the gender wage gap is provided by a study of the postgraduation experiences of the University of Michigan law school classes of 1973 to 1975.[41] Fifteen years after graduation, male attorneys earned $141,000 annually as compared to only $86,000 for female attorneys. It turns out, however, that about two-thirds of this wage gap can be explained by differences in the work histories of male and female attorneys. For instance, if a female attorney decided to work part-time for three years in order to care for her children, as many women did, her earnings were *permanently* reduced by 17 percent! This wage reduction might occur because a full-time attachment to the profession enlarges the attorney's client base and increases opportunities for career advancement.

Obviously, this study does not end the debate over this important issue. Nevertheless, although there is disagreement over the extent to which the human capital story can account for the gender wage gap, it is now widely accepted that differences in human capital accumulation between men and women do matter.[42]

Despite its influence, the human capital model faces an important conceptual obstacle. The human capital explanation of gender wage differentials states that because women have shorter payoff periods, they invest less in on-the-job training and other forms of human capital, and hence have lower wages. Low-wage persons, however, also have less incentive to work. In effect, we have a "Which came first, the chicken or the egg?" problem.[43] Did a woman's weaker work attachment lead to lower wage rates (through reduced

[40] Steven H. Sandell and David Shapiro, "The Theory of Human Capital and the Earnings of Women: A Reexamination of the Evidence," *Journal of Human Resources* 13 (Winter 1978): 103–117; Mary Corcoran and Greg J. Duncan, "Work History, Labor Force Attachment, and Earnings Differences between Races and Sexes," *Journal of Human Resources* 14 (Winter 1979): 3–20; and Donald Cox, "Panel Estimates of the Effects of Career Interruptions on the Earnings of Women," *Economic Inquiry* 22 (July 1984): 386–403. A study of Swedish data concluded that each year of nonemployment is equal to moving down the skill distribution by 5 percentiles; see Per-Anders Edin and Magnus Gustavsson, "Time Out of Work and Skill Depreciation," *Industrial and Labor Relations Review* 61 (January 2008): 163–180.

[41] Robert G. Wood, Mary E. Corcoran, and Paul N. Courant, "Pay Differences among the Highly Paid: The Male-Female Earnings Gap in Lawyers' Salaries," *Journal of Labor Economics* 11 (July 1993): 417–441.

[42] Since 1993, the Family and Medical Leave Act (FMLA) in the United States has mandated that large employers (with over 50 workers) grant unpaid leave of up to 12 weeks to employees who must care for a newborn or for an ill family member. This legislation, in effect, guarantees women the right to be reinstated in their jobs after a short time off from work while they take care of a newborn child. The available evidence suggests that women covered by the FMLA lose much less as a result of their maternity leave. See Jane Waldfogel, "The Family Gap for Young Women in the United States and Britain: Can Maternity Leave Make a Difference?" *Journal of Labor Economics* 16 (July 1998): 505–545; Christopher J. Ruhm, "The Economic Consequences of Parental Leave Mandates: Lessons from Europe," *Quarterly Journal of Economics* 113 (February 1998): 285–317; and Jane Waldfogel, "Family and Medical Leave: Evidence from the 2000 Surveys," *Monthly Labor Review* 124 (September 2001): 17–23.

[43] Reuben Gronau, "Sex-Related Wage Differentials and Women's Interrupted Labor Careers—The Chicken or the Egg," *Journal of Labor Economics* 6 (July 1988): 277–301; and David Neumark, "Sex Discrimination and Women's Labor Market Outcomes," *Journal of Human Resources* 30 (Fall 1995): 713–740.

human capital investments)? Or did the lower wage rates (perhaps arising from discrimination) lead to weaker work attachment? The statistical problems introduced by these feedback effects are difficult to resolve and are the subject of current research.

Occupational Crowding

There is a lot of occupational segregation between men and women in the labor market. As Table 9-6 shows, fewer than 5 percent of aircraft engine mechanics are women, but over 95 percent of kindergarten teachers and receptionists are women.[44] A discrimination-based explanation of this difference, known as the **occupational crowding** hypothesis, argues that women are intentionally segregated into particular occupations.[45] This crowding need not be the outcome of discrimination by male employers, but may simply be the result of a social climate in which young women are taught that some occupations "are not for girls" and, thus, are channeled into "appropriate" jobs. The crowding of women into a relatively small number of occupations inevitably reduces the wage of so-called female jobs and generates a gender wage gap.

[44] Studies of occupational segregation include Andrea H. Beller, "Trends in Occupational Segregation by Sex and Race: 1960–1981," in Barbara F. Reskin, editor, *Sex Segregation in the Workplace: Trends, Explanations, and Remedies,* Washington, DC: National Academy Press, 1984; Deborah Anderson, Francine D. Blau, and Patricia Simpson, "Continuing Progress? Trends in Occupational Segregation over the 1970s and 1980s," *Feminist Economics* 4 (Fall 1998): 29–71; and Michael Baker and Nicole Fortin, "Occupational Gender Composition and Wages in Canada: 1987–1988," *Canadian Journal of Economics* 34 (May 2001): 345–376.

[45] Barbara F. Bergmann, "The Effect on White Incomes of Discrimination in Employment," *Journal of Political Economy* 79 (March/April 1971): 294–313; and Elaine Sorensen, "The Crowding Hypothesis and Comparable Worth," *Journal of Human Resources* 25 (Winter 1990): 55–89.

TABLE 9-6

Female Employment in 2009, by Occupation

Sources: U.S. Department of Commerce, *Statistical Abstract of the United States, 2011*, Washington, DC: Government Printing Office, 2011, Table 615; U.S. Department of Labor, Bureau of Labor Statistics, Occupational Earnings Data, Table 39. Median weekly earnings of full-time wage and salary workers by detailed occupation and sex, 2009, see www.bls.gov/emp/ep_sources_earnings.htm..

Occupation	Percent Female	Median Weekly Earnings
Carpenters	1.6%	$623
Aircraft mechanics	3.8	980
Truck drivers	5.2	686
Police and sheriff's patrol officers	15.5	961
Chemical engineers	18.4	1,505
Architects	25.3	1,209
Lawyers	32.4	1,757
Physicians	32.2	1,975
Security guards	21.9	507
Cooks	41.5	393
Postal clerks	49.6	915
Financial managers	54.7	830
Real estate sales	54.6	820
Teachers: secondary school	54.9	987
Teachers: elementary school	81.9	946
Maids and housemen	89.8	387
Tellers	87.0	487
Child care workers	95.0	400
Receptionists	91.5	530
Teachers: kindergarten	97.8	621

A number of studies investigate the relation between the wage in a particular occupation and the relative employment of women in that occupation. These studies typically find that "female jobs" pay lower wages—even after holding constant the worker's human capital and other socioeconomic characteristics. One study, for instance, finds that a woman working in an occupation where at least 75 percent of the coworkers are women earns about 14 percent less than a comparable woman working in an occupation where more than 75 percent of the coworkers are men. The study also reports that a *man* working in an occupation that is predominantly female also earns 14 percent less than a man working in an occupation that is predominantly male.[46] In short, it is the "femaleness" of the job that leads to lower wages, regardless of whether the worker employed in that job is a man or a woman.

A blatant example of occupational crowding is given by the so-called marriage bars that restricted the employment of married women in some sectors of the U.S. labor market from the late 1800s until about 1950.[47] The marriage bars prohibited married women from working, primarily in teaching and clerical jobs. Married women looking for work in these occupations would not be hired, and single women working in these jobs were often

[46] David A. Macpherson and Barry T. Hirsch, "Wages and Gender Composition: Why Do Women's Jobs Pay Less?" *Journal of Labor Economics* 13 (July 1995): 426–471, Table 4; see also Paula England, George Farkas, Barbara Stanek Kilbourne, and Thomas Dou, "Explaining Occupational Sex Segregation and Wages: Findings from a Model with Fixed Effects," *American Sociological Review* 53 (August 1998): 544–558.

[47] Claudia Goldin, *Understanding the Gender Gap: An Economic History of American Women,* New York: Oxford University Press, 1990, pp. 159–179.

fired once they married. Marriage bars, however, did not affect the employment status of women employed as waitresses, as domestic servants, or in manufacturing jobs. The marriage bars, therefore, can be interpreted as a device that drove well-educated women out of the labor market or crowded them into lower-paying jobs.

Although many of the sexist influences that result in occupational segregation might still be operating, the human capital model provides an alternative, "supply-side" explanation of why women rationally *choose* certain occupations and avoid others. Some occupations (for example, kindergarten teachers or child care workers) require skills that do not have to be updated frequently, whereas other occupations (such as concert pianists or nuclear physicists) require skills that must be updated constantly. Women who wish to maximize the present value of lifetime earnings will not enter occupations where their skills will depreciate rapidly during the years they spend in the household sector.

There is some evidence indicating that women tend to choose the occupations that maximize lifetime earnings.[48] For instance, women work in occupations where their skills are less likely to depreciate, so that they have a higher wage upon reentry from the household sector. Moreover, a woman's choice of college major (which obviously opens doors to particular jobs) is partly determined by her innate abilities, so women are not being intentionally "channeled" into particular majors. For instance, women who score well in standardized tests of mathematical abilities tend to enter more technical fields.[49]

The Trend in the Female-Male Wage Ratio

The historical trend in the female-male wage ratio in the U.S. labor market is illustrated in Figure 9-12. Among persons who worked full-time year-round, the female-male wage ratio hovered around 0.6 between 1960 and 1980. Beginning in the early 1980s, however, the female-male wage ratio increased rapidly, and stood at 0.77 by 2009.

The fact that the wage ratio was roughly constant in the 1960s and 1970s does *not* necessarily imply that the economic status of women did not improve during those decades. The labor force participation rate of women was increasing rapidly at the same time, so the average female wage in 1960 and in 1980 is calculated in very different samples of working women. Suppose, for example, that the newer labor market entrants had lower wages than women already working. Adding the lower-wage persons to the sample of female workers would mask any improvement in female wages over time. It turns out that the data indicate substantial improvement in female wages even prior to 1980 once we control for

[48] Solomon W. Polachek, "Occupational Self-Selection: A Human Capital Approach to Sex Differences in Occupational Structure," *Review of Economics and Statistics* 63 (February 1981): 60–69. For a critical appraisal of the evidence, see Paula England, "The Failure of Human Capital Theory to Explain Occupational Sex Segregation," *Journal of Human Resources* 17 (Summer 1982): 358–370.

[49] Morton Paglin and Anthony Rufolo, "Heterogeneous Human Capital, Occupational Choice, and Male-Female Earnings Differences," *Journal of Labor Economics* 8 (January 1990): 123–144; and Arthur E. Blakemore and Stuart A. Low, "Sex Difference in Occupational Selection: The Case of College Majors," *Review of Economics and Statistics* 86 (February 1984): 157–163. Recent research shows that a woman's human capital accumulation may be influenced by the gender of her mentors. See Florian Hoffmann and Philip Oreopoulos, "A Professor Like Me: The Influence of Instructor Gender on College Achievement," *Journal of Human Resources* 44 (Spring 2009): 479–494; and Scott E. Carrell, Marianne E. Page, and James E. West, "Sex and Science: How Professor Gender Perpetuates the Gender Gap," *Quarterly Journal of Economics* 125 (August 2010): 1101–1144.

FIGURE 9-12   **Trend in Female-Male Earnings Ratio, 1960–2009**

Sources: U.S. Bureau of the Census, "Historical Income Tables—People," Table P-40, "Women's Earnings as a Percentage of Men's Earnings by Race and Hispanic Origin," www.census.gov/hhes/www/income/histinc/p40.html. The earnings refer to the median earnings of full-time, full-year workers aged 15 or above.

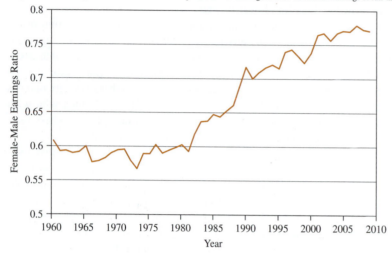

these cohort effects. In fact, the growth rate of the female wage was 20 percent higher than the growth rate of male wages prior to 1980.[50]

This approach also helps us understand the negative correlation between the gender wage gap and the gap in employment rates across countries illustrated in Figure 9-1. Those countries where women have the largest employment rates (so the employment gap between men and women is smallest) are also the countries where women tend to have the largest wage gap. As more women enter the labor market, the sample composition of working women is changing, and the "marginal" woman is likely to have lower potential earnings, hence contributing to a larger gender wage gap.[51]

As we have seen, wage inequality increased—even within skill groups—in the 1980s and 1990s. This increase in wage inequality might have been expected to further widen the wage gap between men and women. As Figure 9-12 reveals, however, women's economic status improved rapidly in the 1980s and 1990s. A careful study of this trend concludes that the relative improvement in women's wages can be attributed mainly to an increase in the labor market experience of women. Perhaps as much as 50 percent of the increase in the female-male wage ratio is attributable to the increasing work attachment of American women.[52]

[50] James P. Smith and Michael Ward, "Women in the Labor Market and in the Family," *Journal of Economic Perspectives* 3 (Winter 1989): 9–23; and June O'Neill, "The Trend in the Male-Female Wage Gap in the United States," *Journal of Labor Economics* 3 (January 1985): 91–116.

[51] Claudia Olivetti and Barbara Petrongolo, "Unequal Pay or Unequal Employment? A Cross-Country Analysis of Gender Gaps," *Journal of Labor Economics* 26 (October 2008): 621–654. See also Casey B. Mulligan and Yona Rubinstein, "Selection, Investment, and Women's Relative Wages over Time," *Quarterly Journal of Economics* 123 (August 2008): 1061–1110.

[52] Blau and Kahn, "Swimming Upstream: Trends in the Gender Wage Differential in the 1980s"; June O'Neill and Solomon Polachek, "Why the Gender Gap in Wages Narrowed in the 1980s," *Journal of Labor Economics* 11 (January 1993, Part 1): 205–228.

There also seems to have been a decline in the extent to which women and men are treated differentially by the labor market—in the sense that the gap in the rate of return to skills between men and women narrowed during the period.

Although it would seem that the widespread adoption of affirmative action programs might be responsible for the rise in the female-male wage ratio, there is little evidence to back up this assertion. The data suggest that affirmative action had a very weak impact on the employment prospects of white women, but did have a sizable impact on black women. For example, federal contractors employed 28 percent of all working white women in 1970, but only 30 percent in 1980. In contrast, federal contractors employed 35 percent of black women in 1970, but almost half of all black women by 1980. Affirmative action thus induced a huge increase in the demand for black women by these firms. Black women were the main beneficiaries because they effectively "allow firms to fill two quotas for the price of one."[53]

Comparable Worth

The weak impact of affirmative action programs on the economic well-being of white women has led some observers to propose that employers adopt **comparable worth** programs.[54] The typical comparable worth program brings in outside consultants to study the jobs at a particular firm. The jobs are evaluated in terms of the skills and effort required to conduct a particular task, the level of responsibility associated with the job, working conditions, and so on. Points are assigned to each of these attributes and a "job score" is calculated. Jobs that have equal scores should have equal wages.

By their very nature, *comparable worth programs break the link between the wage and labor market conditions.* When comparable worth programs are implemented, the supply and demand for workers in particular occupations do not affect earnings as long as the jobs have equal scores. Because the job evaluations typically yield roughly equal scores for "men's jobs" (such as mechanics) and "women's jobs" (such as receptionists), the implementation of comparable worth programs can have a huge impact on the female-male wage ratio. The gain in women's wages, however, must come at a substantial cost in economic efficiency. After all, workers no longer have any incentive to train in occupations or move to those jobs where they have the largest value of marginal product. They will now seek out jobs that happen to have the highest point scores.

The available evidence indicates that when comparable worth programs are strictly implemented, they can greatly reduce the gender wage gap. A careful study of the impact of comparable worth on the wage of public employees in Minnesota and in San Jose, California, found that the gender wage gap was reduced by 6 to 10 percentage points. Similarly, when Australia imposed a comparable worth policy, the female-male wage ratio rose significantly.[55] One

---

[53] Smith and Ward, "Women in the Labor Market and in the Family."

[54] Detailed discussions of the economic impact of comparable worth are given by Mark R. Killingsworth, *The Economics of Comparable Worth,* Kalamazoo, MI: W. E. Upjohn Institute for Employment Research, 1990; and Elaine Sorenson, *Comparable Worth: Is It a Worth Policy?* Princeton, NJ: Princeton University Press, 1994.

[55] Robert Gregory, R. Anstie, Anne Daly, and V. Ho, "Women's Pay in Australia, Great Britain and the United States: The Role of Laws, Regulations, and Human Capital," in Robert Michael, Heidi I. Hartmann, and Brigid O'Farrell, editors, *Pay Equity: Empirical Inquiries,* Washington, DC: National Academy Press, 1989; and Mark Wooden, "Gender Pay Equity and Comparable Worth in Australia: A Reassessment," *Australian Economic Review* 32 (June 1999): 157–171.

might suspect that employers respond to the imposition of comparable worth programs by reducing the demand for workers employed in jobs that are now "overpaid" relative to the market. However, the evidence on the disemployment effects of comparable worth is mixed. Some studies find that the labor demand response reduced the female-male *employment* ratio significantly, but other studies do not find any decrease in female employment.[56]

Summary

- Taste discrimination affects the employer's hiring decision because prejudice blinds the employer to the true monetary costs associated with hiring a particular worker. An employer who discriminates will act as if the cost of hiring a black or female worker exceeds the actual cost.

- If black and white workers are perfect substitutes in the production process, employer discrimination leads to the segregation of black and white workers in the labor market and to unequal pay for equal work. The firm's discriminatory behavior also reduces profits.

- Employee discrimination leads to segregation of black and white workers but does not create a wage differential between the two groups. Customer discrimination might create a wage differential between black and white workers if employers cannot "hide" blacks in positions where they have little contact with customers.

- Wage differentials by race, ethnicity, and gender can arise even if employers are not prejudiced. When firms do not have complete information on a particular worker's productivity, they might use aggregate characteristics of the group as an indicator of the worker's productivity. Statistical discrimination leads to differential treatment of equally skilled workers belonging to different groups.

- The impact of discrimination on the wage structure is measured by comparing the wages of workers who have the same observable skills, such as educational attainment and labor market experience, but who belong to different racial or gender groups. If this comparison does not control for all the dimensions in which skills might differ across workers, our measure of discrimination does not isolate the impact of prejudice or statistical discrimination on the wage of minorities and women.

- The wage ratio between black and white workers in the United States has risen significantly in the past few decades. In 1995, whites earned about 24 percent more than blacks, and about half of this wage gap could be attributed to differences in observable skills.

- The wage ratio between female and male workers in the United States rose significantly in the 1980s and 1990s. In 1995, men earned about 33 percent more than women. It may be the case, however, that a sizable fraction of this wage gap can be attributed to the fact that women, on average, have less labor market experience than men.

---

[56] George Johnson and Gary Solon, "Estimates of the Direct Effects of Comparable Worth Policy," *American Economic Review* 76 (December 1986): 1117–1125; and Sorenson, *Comparable Worth: Is It a Worth Policy?*

Key Concepts

comparable worth, *409*
customer discrimination, *370*
discrimination
   coefficient, *370*
employee discrimination, *370*

employer discrimination, *370*
nepotism, *370*
Oaxaca decomposition, *388*
occupational
   crowding, *405*

statistical discrimination, *382*
taste discrimination, *370*

Review Questions

1. What is the discrimination coefficient?

2. Discuss the implications of employer discrimination for the employment decisions of the firm, for the profitability of the firm, and for the black-white wage ratio in the labor market.

3. Can employer discrimination against blacks lead to a situation where the equilibrium black wage exceeds the equilibrium white wage?

4. Derive the implications of employee discrimination for the employment decisions of firms and for the black-white wage differential.

5. Discuss the implications of customer discrimination for the employment decisions of firms and for the black-white wage differential.

6. What is statistical discrimination? Why do employers use group membership as an indicator of a worker's productivity? What is the impact of statistical discrimination on the wage of the affected workers? Must statistical discrimination reduce the average wage of blacks or women?

7. Derive the Oaxaca measure of discrimination. Does this statistic truly measure the impact of discrimination on the relative wage of the affected groups?

8. Discuss the factors that might explain why the black-white wage ratio rose significantly in the past few decades.

9. Discuss why a sizable part of the female-male wage differential might be attributable to "supply-side" factors, such as a woman's decision to work and acquire human capital.

Problems

9-1. Feeling that local firms follow discriminatory hiring practices, a nonprofit firm conducts the following experiment. It has 200 white individuals and 200 black individuals, all of whom are similar in age, experience, and education, apply for local retail jobs. Each individual applies to two jobs, one in a predominantly black part of town and one in a predominantly white part of town. Of the white applicants, 120 are offered jobs in the white part of town while only 80 are offered jobs in the black part of town. Meanwhile, 90 of the black applicants are offered jobs in the black part of town while only 50 are offered jobs in the white part of town. Using a difference-in-differences estimator, do you find evidence of discriminatory hiring practices? If there is discrimination, is it most likely employer-based, employee-based, customer-based, or statistical?

9-2. Suppose black and white workers are complements in that the marginal product of whites increases when more blacks are hired. Suppose also that white workers do not like working alongside black workers. Will discrimination by white employees lead to the firm choosing to completely segregate its workplace? Does it create a wage differential between black and white workers?

9-3. a. Suppose a restaurant hires only women to wait on tables, and only men to cook the food and clean the dishes. Is this most likely to be indicative of employer, employee, consumer, or statistical discrimination?

b. The dropout rate of minority and international students at U.S. colleges and universities is higher than it is for white American students. Suppose you strongly believe this is due to discrimination. Is the empirical pattern most likely indicative of employer (college administrations), employee (college faculty and staff), consumer (students), or statistical discrimination?

9-4. In 1960, the proportion of blacks in southern states was higher than the proportion of blacks in northern states. The black-white wage ratio in southern states was also much lower than in northern states. Does the difference in the relative black-white wage ratios across regions indicate that southern employers discriminated more than northern employers?

9-5. Suppose years of schooling, s, is the only variable that affects earnings. The equations for the weekly salaries of male and female workers are given by

$$w_m = 500 + 100s$$

and

$$w_f = 300 + 75s$$

On average, men have 14 years of schooling and women have 12 years of schooling.

a. What is the male-female wage differential in the labor market?

b. Using the Oaxaca decomposition, calculate how much of this wage differential is due to discrimination?

c. Can you think of an alternative Oaxaca decomposition that would lead to a different measure of discrimination? Which measure is better?

9-6. Suppose the firm's production function is given by

$$q = 10\sqrt{E_w + E_b}$$

where E_w and E_b are the number of whites and blacks employed by the firm respectively. It can be shown that the marginal product of labor is then

$$MP_E = \frac{5}{\sqrt{E_w + E_b}}$$

Suppose the market wage for black workers is $10, the market wage for whites is $20, and the price of each unit of output is $100.

a. How many workers would a firm hire if it does not discriminate? How much profit does this nondiscriminatory firm earn if there are no other costs?

b. Consider a firm that discriminates against blacks with a discrimination coefficient of 0.25. How many workers does this firm hire? How much profit does it earn?

c. Finally, consider a firm that has a discrimination coefficient equal to 1.25. How many workers does this firm hire? How much profit does it earn?

9-7. Suppose that an additional year of schooling raised wages by 7 percent in 1970, regardless of the worker's race or ethnicity. Suppose also that the wage differential between the average white and the average Hispanic was 36 percent. Finally, assume education is the only factor that affects productivity, and the average white worker had 12 years of schooling in 1970, while the average Hispanic worker had 9 years. By 1980, the average white worker had 13 years of education, while the average Hispanic worker had 11 years. A year of schooling still increased earnings by 7 percent, regardless of the worker's ethnic background, and the wage differential between the average white worker and the average Hispanic worker fell to 24 percent. Was there a decrease in wage discrimination during the decade? Was there a decrease in the share of the wage differential between whites and Hispanics that can be attributed to discrimination?

9-8. Use Table 220 of the 2008 *U.S. Statistical Abstract* to do the following. Conditioned on educational attainment (not a high school graduate, high school graduate, bachelor's degree, master's degree, and doctorate degree), how much did the average female worker earn for every one dollar earned by the average male in 2005? Repeat for the average black worker compared to the average white worker, and repeat again for the average Hispanic worker compared to the average white worker.

9-9. Each employer faces competitive weekly wages of $2,000 for whites and $1,400 for blacks. Suppose employers undervalue the efforts/skills of blacks in the production process. In particular, every firm is associated with a discrimination coefficient, d $(0 \leq d \leq 1)$. In particular, although a firm's actual production function is $Q = 10(E_W + E_B)$, the firm manager acts as if its production function is $Q = 10E_W + 10(1 - d)E_B$. Every firm sells its output at a constant price of $240 per unit up to a weekly total of 150 units of output. No firm can sell more than 150 units of output without reducing its price to $0.

   a. What is the value of the marginal product of each white worker?

   b. What is the value of the marginal product of each black worker?

   c. Describe the employment decision made by firms for which $d = 0.2$ and $d = 0.8$ respectively.

   d. For what value(s) of d is a firm willing to hire blacks and whites?

9-10. After controlling for age and education, it is found that the average woman earns $0.80 for every $1.00 earned by the average man. After controlling for occupation to control for compensating differentials (i.e., maybe men accept riskier or more stressful jobs than women, and therefore are paid more), the average woman earns $0.92 for every $1.00 earned by the average man. The conclusion is made that occupational choice reduces the wage gap 12 cents and discrimination is left to explain the remaining 8 cents.

   a. Explain why discrimination may explain more than 8 cents of the 20-cent differential (and occupational choice may explain less than 12 cents of the differential).

   b. Explain why discrimination may explain less than 8 cents of the 20-cent differential.

9-11. Consider a town with a population that is 10 percent black (and the remainder is white). Because blacks are more likely to work the night shifts, 20 percent of all cars driven at night are driven by blacks. One out of every 20 people driving at night is drunk, regardless of race. Persons who are not drunk never swerve their car, but 10 percent of all drunk drivers, regardless of race, swerve their cars. On a typical night, 5,000 cars are observed by the police force.

a. What percent of blacks driving at night are driving drunk? What percent of whites driving at night are driving drunk?

b. Of the 5,000 cars observed, how many are driven by blacks? How many of these cars are driven by a drunk? Of the 5,000 cars observed at night, how many are driven by whites? How many of these cars are driven by a drunk? What percent of nighttime drunk drivers are black?

c. The police chief believes the drunk-driving problem is mainly due to black drunk drivers. He orders his policemen to pull over all swerving cars *and* one in every two nonswerving cars that is driven by a black person. The driver of a nonswerving car is then given a breathalyzer test that is 100 percent accurate in diagnosing drunk driving. Under this enforcement scheme, what percent of people arrested for drunk driving will be black?

9-12. Suppose 100 men and 100 women graduate from high school. After high school, each can work in a low-skill job and earn $200,000 over his or her lifetime, or each can pay $50,000 and go to college. College graduates are given a test. If someone passes the test, he or she is hired for a high-skill job paying lifetime earnings of $300,000. Any college graduate who fails the test, however, is relegated to a low-skill job. Academic performance in high school gives each person some idea of how he or she will do on the test if he or she goes to college. In particular, each person's GPA, call it x, is an "ability score" ranging from 0.01 to 1.00. With probability x, the person will pass the test if he or she attends college. Upon graduating high school, there is one man with $x = 0.01$, one with $x = 0.02$, and so on up to $x = 1.00$. Likewise, there is one woman with $x = 0.01$, one with $x = 0.02$, and so on up to $x = 1.00$.

a. Persons attend college only if the expected lifetime payoff from attending college is higher than that of not attending college. Which men and which women will attend college? What is the expected pass rate of men who take the test? What is the expected pass rate of women who take the test?

b. Suppose policymakers feel not enough women are attending college, so they take actions that reduce the cost of college for women to $10,000. Which women will now attend college? What is the expected pass rate of women who take the test?

9-13. Suppose the discrimination coefficient increases as the firm employs more black workers. In particular, suppose the discrimination coefficient is $d = 0.01E_B$ where E_B is the number of blacks hired by the firm so that each employer facing competitive wages of w_W for whites and w_B for blacks acts as if she faces competitive wages of w_W for whites and $w_B(1 + d)$ for blacks. As usual, assume the labor market is competitive so that the firm faces wages of w_B and w_W. Lastly, assume that the firm must employ 200 workers. Define the wage ratio to be w_W / w_B and do the following:

a. Solve for the number of blacks hired as a function of the wage ratio. Graph the number of blacks hired against the wage ratio.

b. Solve for the number of whites hired as a function of the wage ratio. Graph the number of whites hired (*x*-axis) against the wage ratio (*y*-axis).

9-14. Consider a data set with the following descriptive statistics.

	Men			Women		
	Mean	**Min**	**Max**	**Mean**	**Min**	**Max**
Ln(wages)	3.562	1.389	5.013	3.198	1.213	4.875
Black	0.231	0	1	0.191	0	1
Age	42.2	19	68	39.2	19	63.
Work experience	18.1	0	42	16.1	0	35
Schooling	13.9	9	21	14.1	9	21
Percent female in occupation	0.182	0.023	.954	0.623	0.067	.985

Wage is the worker's hourly wage; Black takes on a value of 1 if the worker is black and a value of 0 otherwise; work experience is actual years of work experience; schooling is measured in years; and percent female in occupation is the percent of all employees in the worker's occupation who are female. The following table reports the regression results from a log-wage regression.

	Men	Women
Constant	2.314	2.556
Black	−0.198	−0.154
Age	0.054	0.037
Years of work experience	0.042	0.059
Years of schooling	0.085	0.083
Percent female in occupation	−0.121	0.002
Number of observations	442	278
R-squared	0.231	0.254

Decompose the raw difference in average wages using the Oaxaca decomposition. Specifically, decompose the raw difference into the portion due to differences in personal characteristics (schooling, race, age, and experience), the portion due to occupation, and the portion left unexplained possibly due to gender discrimination.

9-15. In 2006, Evo Morales assumed the presidency in Bolivia, a South American country in which official commerce is done in Spanish. Morales is the first Bolivian president of indigenous decent. As president, he quickly instituted reforms that were designed to reduce discrimination against indigenous populations with the aim of eventually reducing inequality. Suppose discrimination before Morales took two forms–discrimination in education by not providing state funds to educate all children (and particularly not educating indigenous children in their native language or in Spanish) and discrimination in the job market by firms not willingly hiring indigenous workers.

    a. In terms of education, which policy would be better at combating discrimination and inequality: (1) providing state funds to educate all people in their native languages or (2) providing state funds for a public education system that requires all people to learn Spanish and a second, indigenous language? Why?

    b. In terms of the job market, which policy would be best at combating discrimination and inequality: (1) increasing the minimum wage, (2) requiring all firms with at least 50 workers to hire some indigenous workers, or (3) improving the legal system to protect economic rights and activities? Why?

Selected Readings

Marianne Bertrand and Sendhil Mullanaithan, "Are Emily and Greg More Employable Than Lakisha and Jamal? A Field Experiment on Labor Market Discrimination," *American Economic Review* 94 (September 2004): 991–1013.

Francine D. Blau, "Trends in the Well-Being of American Women, 1970–1995," *Journal of Economic Literature* 36 (March 1998): 112–165.

Kerwin Kofi Charles and Jonathan Guryan, "Prejudice and Wages: An Empirical Assessment of Becker's The Economics of Discrimination," *Journal of Political Economy* 116 (October 2008): 773–809.

Matthew S. Goldberg, "Discrimination, Nepotism, and Long-Run Wage Differentials," *Quarterly Journal of Economics* 97 (May 1982): 307–319.

Daniel S. Hamermesh and Jeff E. Biddle, "Beauty and the Labor Market," *American Economic Review* 84 (December 1994): 1174–1194.

James J. Heckman and Brook S. Payner, "Determining the Impact of Federal Antidiscrimination Policy on the Economic Status of Blacks: A Study of South Carolina," *American Economic Review* 79 (March 1989): 138–177.

Harry Holzer and David Neumark, "Assessing Affirmative Action," *Journal of Economic Literature* 38 (September 2000): 483–568.

Shelly J. Lundberg and Richard Startz, "Private Discrimination and Social Intervention in Competitive Labor Markets," *American Economic Review* 73 (June 1983): 340–347.

Jacob Mincer and Solomon W. Polachek, "Family Investments in Human Capital: Earnings of Women," *Journal of Political Economy* 82 (March 1974 Supplement): S76–S108.

Joseph Price and Justin Wolfers, "Racial Discrimination Among NBA Referees," *Quarterly Journal of Economics* 125 (November 2010): 1859–1887.

Web Links

The U.S. Equal Employment Opportunity Commission enforces the legislation prohibiting racial and gender employment discrimination in the United States: www.eeoc.gov.

The U.S. Census Bureau reports historical data on incomes by race and gender: www.census.gov/hhes/www/income/histinc/incpertoc.html.

Chapter 10

Labor Unions

Union gives strength.

— *Aesop*

Up to this point, we have ignored the institution of labor unions. The omission of labor unions may seem surprising. After all, supporters of the union movement often argue that labor unions, as the sole institution representing workers' interests in the labor market, are mainly responsible for the improvement in working conditions witnessed in many developed countries. Moreover, even though union membership in the United States has declined rapidly in recent decades, unions *still* represent 12 percent of workers.

This chapter argues that unions, like workers attempting to maximize utility and firms attempting to maximize profits, choose among various options in order to maximize the well-being of their members. As a result, the labor market impact of unions depends not only on the political and institutional environment that regulates the employer-union relationship, but also on the factors that motivate unions to pursue certain strategies (such as making wage demands that may lead to a strike) and to ignore others.

It has long been recognized that unions can arise and prosper only under certain conditions. Because the free entry and exit of firms into the marketplace reduce profits to a normal return on investment (that is, zero excess profits), unions can flourish only when firms earn above-normal profits, or what economists call "rents." In effect, unions provide an institutional mechanism through which employers share the rents with workers.

This chapter investigates how unions influence the terms of the employment relationship between workers and firms. We will find that unions influence practically every aspect of the employment contract, including hours of work, wages, fringe benefits, labor turnover, job satisfaction, worker productivity, and the firm's profitability.[1]

---

[1] Good summaries of the evidence include Richard B. Freeman and James L. Medoff, *What Do Unions Do?* New York: Basic Books, 1984; Barry T. Hirsch and John T. Addison, *The Economic Analysis of Unions: New Approaches and Evidence,* Boston: Allen & Unwin, 1986; and John H. Pencavel, *Labor Markets under Trade Unionism: Employment, Wages, and Hours,* Cambridge, MA: Basil Blackwell, 1991.

10-1 Unions: Background and Facts

Figure 10-1 illustrates the trend in union membership in the United States. In 1930, fewer than 10 percent of civilian workers were union members. During the 1930s, mainly as a result of important policy changes described below, union membership began to rise rapidly. By the early 1950s, over a quarter of the civilian workforce was unionized. Unionization rates remained roughly at that level until the mid-1960s, when a steady decline in union membership began, with the decline accelerating in the 1980s. By 2010, only 11.9 percent of civilian workers were unionized. The phenomenon of the "vanishing" union is even more evident if we look at the fraction of unionized workers in the private sector: only 6.9 percent of workers in the private sector are now unionized.

Table 10-1 shows that the U.S. experience is not unique. Other developed countries also experienced a decline in unionization over the 1970–2003 period. For example, the fraction of Irish workers who are unionized declined from 53 to 35 percent between 1970 and 2003, while the French unionization rate dropped from 22 to 8 percent. In other countries, however, the decline was much less pronounced or the unionization rate even increased. In Italy, for instance, the unionization rate declined from 37 to 34 percent, while in Sweden it rose from 68 to 78 percent.

The variation in the proportion of workers who are unionized across countries is influenced by differences in the political effectiveness of the various union movements, which obviously influences the legislation that regulates all interactions between employers and unions. In Great Britain, for example, the Labor Party was traditionally the political arm of the union movement.[2] Historically, U.S. unions had not been overly attached to any

FIGURE 10-1   Union Membership in the United States, 1900–2010 (Percent of Civilian Workforce Unionized)

Sources: Barry T. Hirsch and John T. Addison, *The Economic Analysis of Unions: New Approaches and Evidence,* Boston, MA: Allen & Unwin, 1986, pp. 46–47; and Barry T. Hirsch and David A. Macpherson, *Union Membership and Earnings Data Book: Compilations from the Current Population Survey (2011 Edition),* Washington, DC: Bureau of National Affairs, 2011.

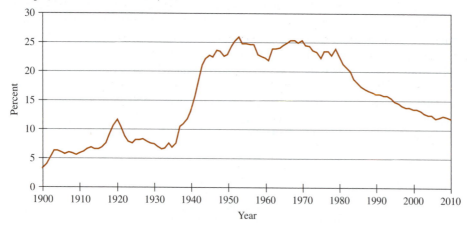

[2] An interesting study of recent trends in the British union movement is given by John Pencavel, "The Surprising Retreat of Union Britain," in David Card, Richard Blundell, and Richard B. Freeman, editors, *Seeking a Premier Economy: The Economic Effects of British Economic Reforms, 1980–2000,* Chicago: University of Chicago Press, 2004. Much of the decline in the British unionization rate seems to be explained by a weakening in the government's support for collective bargaining.

TABLE 10-1

Trends in Union Membership in Industrialized Economies, 1970–2003 (percent of workers unionized)

Source: Jelle Visser, "Union Membership Statistics in 24 Countries," *Monthly Labor Review* (January 2006): 38–49.

Country	1970	1979	2003
Australia	50	41	23
Austria	63	47	35
Canada	32	33	28
France	22	10	8
Germany	32	31	23
Ireland	53	51	35
Italy	37	39	34
Japan	35	25	20
Netherlands	37	24	22
Norway	57	59	53
Sweden	68	81	78
Switzerland	29	24	18
United Kingdom	45	39	29
United States	24	16	12

political party, and had pursued a tradition of **business unionism,** where the main goal of the union movement was to improve the wages and working conditions of its members, mainly through collective bargaining, rather than to push a particular social agenda through legislative and political action. This approach, however, seems to have changed dramatically in the past two decades as the union movement has forged ever closer political and financial ties with the Democratic Party.

A Brief History of American Unions

Prior to the Great Depression, social attitudes and the political climate toward labor unions in the United States were quite unfavorable.[3] A number of legal restrictions and employer practices kept union membership in check. For instance, in the *Loewe v. Lawlor* decision of 1908, the Supreme Court upheld a judgment against the Hatters' Union because the union had organized a consumer boycott against a nonunion producer in Danbury, Connecticut. The Supreme Court decision was based on the view that the union's actions reduced the flow of goods in interstate commerce and was a "restraint of trade" prohibited by the Sherman Antitrust Act. In subsequent decisions, the Court used the antitrust analogy to outlaw strikes that affected interstate commerce. This interpretation of the antitrust legislation was not reversed until 1940.

In addition, employers made frequent use of **yellow-dog contracts.** These contracts stipulated that as a condition of employment, the worker would not join a union. When unions attempted to organize workers who had signed these contracts, the unions were found guilty of inducing a breach of contract. In 1917, the Supreme Court upheld the constitutionality of yellow-dog contracts.

As part of the legislative program associated with the New Deal, the legal environment regulating the relationship between unions and private-sector firms changed substantially

---

[3] A more detailed history of the union movement is given by Albert Rees, *The Economics of Trade Unions,* 2nd ed, Chicago: University of Chicago Press, 1977, Chapter 1.

in the 1930s. Four major pieces of federal legislation lay out the ground rules for the new relationship:

- *The Norris-LaGuardia Act of 1932.* This was the first major federal regulation of the union-employer relationship. It attempted to "even out" the game by restricting the employer's use of court orders and injunctions to hamper union organizing drives, as well as by making yellow-dog contracts unenforceable in federal courts.

- *The National Labor Relations Act of 1935* (also known as the *Wagner Act*). This legislation further increased the power of unions by defining a set of **unfair labor practices** for employers. It requires that employers bargain "in faith" with unions and that employers do not interfere with the workers' right to organize. Among the specific unfair labor practices prohibited by the Wagner Act are the firing of workers involved in union activities and discrimination against workers who support the union. The Wagner Act also established the National Labor Relations Board (NLRB) to enforce the provisions of the legislation. The NLRB can investigate unfair labor practices and can order that such practices be stopped. The NLRB also runs the elections where workers decide if a particular union is to represent them in collective bargaining. These elections are called **certification elections.**

- *The Labor-Management Relations Act of 1947* (also known as the *Taft-Hartley Act*). This legislation curbed union power by permitting states to pass **right-to-work laws.** These laws prohibit unions from requiring that workers become union members as a condition of employment in unionized firms. By 2011, 22 states had enacted right-to-work laws. The Taft-Hartley Act also permits workers to hold elections that would decertify a union from representing them in collective bargaining (or **decertification elections**).

- *The Labor-Management Reporting and Disclosure Act of 1959* (also known as the *Landrum-Griffin Act*). This legislation, passed in reaction to the increasing evidence of corruption among union leaders, requires the complete disclosure of union finances. The Landrum-Griffin Act also makes the union leadership more accountable by requiring unions to hold regularly scheduled elections.

Up to this point, our discussion has focused on the laws that regulate the employer-union relationship in the private sector. Prior to the 1960s, public-sector workers were specifically prohibited from forming unions. In 1962, President John Kennedy, through Executive Order No. 10988, gave federal workers the right to organize. The Civil Service Reform Act of 1978, which superseded President Kennedy's executive order, now regulates unions in the federal sector. Most important, this legislation prohibits strikes and protects the right of federal workers to either join or not join unions. A number of state laws also have extended the right to organize to state and local workers in many jurisdictions. As a result, there was a remarkable rise in public-sector unionization rates *at the same time* that union membership in the private sector was collapsing. As shown in Figure 10-2, only about 20 percent of public-sector workers were unionized in the 1960s. By 2010, this fraction had risen to around 36 percent.

FIGURE 10-2   **Union Membership in the Public Sector, 1962–2010**

Sources: Richard B. Freeman, Casey Ichniowski, and Jeffrey Zax, "Appendix A: Collective Organization of Labor in the Public Sector," in Richard B. Freeman and Casey Ichniowski, editors, *When Public Sector Workers Unionize,* Chicago: University of Chicago Press, 1988, pp. 374–375; and Barry T. Hirsch and David A. Macpherson, *Union Membership and Earnings Data Book: Compilations from the Current Population Survey (2011 Edition),* Washington, DC: Bureau of National Affairs, 2011.

The Structure of American Unions

It is useful to think of the union movement in the United States today as a pyramid. At the top of the pyramid is the AFL-CIO (which stands for American Federation of Labor and Congress of Industrial Organizations). The AFL-CIO is a federation of unions. The diverse set of unions affiliated with the AFL-CIO, which includes the American Federation of Teachers, the United Mine Workers, and the Actors' Equity Association, account for about 80 percent of all union members in the United States. Most of the unions affiliated with the AFL-CIO are national unions, representing workers throughout the country (and sometimes even representing workers outside the United States). In turn, these national unions are composed of "locals," or unions established at the city level or even the plant level. These locals are at the bottom of the pyramid. The main objective of the AFL-CIO is to provide a single, national voice for the diverse unions under its umbrella, to engage in political lobbying, and to support political candidates who are sympathetic to labor's social and economic agenda.

Union members in the United States typically belong to a local. The local in a craft union may represent all members of that craft who reside in a particular geographic area, usually a city or a metropolitan area. For example, Local 4321 of the American Postal Workers Union represents postal workers employed in Salisbury, Maryland, and surrounding areas.

Each tier in the union pyramid plays a different role in collective bargaining. The AFL-CIO does not engage in any direct collective bargaining with employers. Instead, it represents the interests of the labor movement before other forums. The roles played by the local union and the national union depend on the market served by the unionized firm. If the unionized firm provides goods and services mostly to a local economy—such as construction workers—the local union tends to play the key role in collective bargaining. The national union may provide expertise during the negotiations, but local officials make the decisions. If the unionized firm serves a market that extends nationally or internationally, the national union then plays the lead role in the collective bargaining process.

The AFL-CIO and national unions also engage in political lobbying. The AFL-CIO Committee on Political Education is an important source of union political activity in the United States, promoting advertising campaigns on issues of concern to the labor movement and funding candidates that are friendly to labor issues. National unions often play a major role in the political debate over social policy issues that are of particular concern to their members. In 2007–2008, the various political action committees of the labor movement spent $265.0 million, including $62.7 million in direct contributions to candidates.[4]

The organization structure of unions varies a great deal across unions. For example, the AFL-CIO holds a convention every two years. Delegates to this convention, who represent the affiliated national unions, elect a president to a four-year term. Richard Trumka was elected as president of the AFL-CIO in 2009. The UAW, which mainly organizes autoworkers and aerospace workers, holds a constitutional convention every three years. Delegates to this convention are elected by secret ballot at the local union, and any UAW member in good standing is eligible to run for the position of delegate. The delegates elect the president, secretary-treasurer, and other officials for three-year terms.

Unions typically assess fees on their members. Union dues average about 1 percent of a worker's annual income. Members of the UAW pay 1.15 percent of their monthly incomes—equivalent to two hours' pay. Unions use these fees for a variety of purposes. The UAW allocates 38 percent of the dues to the local union, 32 percent to the national union's general fund, and 30 percent to the strike insurance fund.[5]

Unions provide many other services to their workers, with the nature of the services varying greatly among unions. The Amalgamated Transit Union, which covers many transit workers, assists members in obtaining commercial driver's licenses and has a scholarship program for its members and their dependents. Many unions also offer low-cost credit cards and subsidized mortgage loans to their members.

10-2   Determinants of Union Membership

Workers choose whether to join a union. A worker joins if the union offers him a wage-employment package that provides more utility than the wage-employment package offered by a nonunion employer.[6] To see the worker's trade-off in this decision, consider the familiar

---

[4] U.S. Department of Commerce, *U.S. Statistical Abstract, 2011,* Washington, DC: Government Printing Office, 2011, Table 421.

[5] More details are available at the UAW's Web site: www.uaw.org.

[6] Although the worker's utility depends on many aspects of the job (such as fringes and working conditions), we focus on a simpler model where the characteristics of the job include only wages and employment. For a detailed discussion of the worker's decision to join a union, see Henry S. Farber and Daniel H. Saks, "Why Workers Want Unions: The Role of Relative Wages and Job Characteristics," *Journal of Political Economy* 88 (April 1980): 349–369; and Henry S. Farber, "The Determination of the Union Status of Workers," *Econometrica* 51 (September 1983): 1417–1437.

FIGURE 10-3   The Decision to Join a Union

The budget line is given by AT, and the worker maximizes utility at point P by working h^* hours. The proposed union wage increase (from w^* to w_U) shifts the budget line to BT. If the employer cuts back hours of work to h_0, the worker is worse off (utility falls from U to U_0 units). If the employer cuts back hours to h_1, the worker is better off.

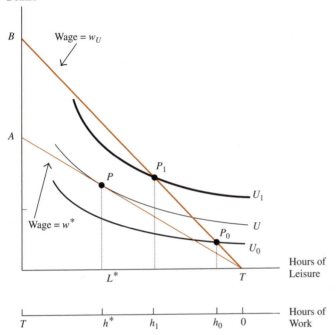

model of labor-leisure choice illustrated in Figure 10-3. Suppose that the person is initially working at a nonunion firm offering the competitive wage w^*. At this wage rate, the worker's budget line is given by AT. A worker maximizes utility by choosing the consumption-leisure bundle where the indifference curve U is tangent to the budget line (or point P). The nonunion worker consumes L^* hours of leisure and works h^* ($h^* = T - L^*$) hours.

The firm is targeted by union organizers, and these organizers promise a new and improved employment contract. In particular, the union promises a wage increase to w_U dollars. The worker's budget line, therefore, shifts to BT.

The worker knows that there is no free lunch. The wage increase comes at a cost, and the cost may be a cutback in employment. Suppose that the firm's demand curve for labor is downward sloping and elastic. If the firm responds to the union wage increase by moving up the labor demand curve, the union-mandated wage increase reduces the worker's workweek to, say, h_0 hours, placing him at point P_0 on the BT budget line. If the union organizes the firm's workforce, therefore, the worker would be worse off (he moves to a lower indifference curve U_0). This worker, therefore, opposes the union in the certification election.

If the firm's demand curve for labor is inelastic, the employment reduction is small and the union offers the wage-employment combination at point P_1 (where the workweek lasts h_1 hours). The union shifts the worker to a higher indifference curve (given by U_1) and the worker supports the union in the certification election.

The Demand for and Supply of Union Jobs

In general, workers are more likely to support unionization when the union organizer can promise a high wage and a small employment loss. Moreover, because there are additional costs to joining a union (such as union dues), the worker will be more likely to support unions when these costs are small. These factors generate the "demand" for union jobs.

The demand for union jobs is not the sole determinant of the extent of unionization in the labor market. The ability of union organizers to deliver union jobs depends on the costs of organizing the workforce, on the legal environment that permits certain types of union activities and prohibits others, on the resistance of management to the introduction of collective bargaining, and on whether the firm is making excess rents that can be captured by the union membership. These forces, in effect, determine the "supply" of union jobs.

The extent of unionization observed in the labor market is determined by the interaction of these two forces. As a result, the unionization rate will be higher the more workers have to gain by becoming unionized and will be lower the harder it is to convert jobs from nonunion to union status. This "cost-benefit" approach helps us understand differences in unionization rates across demographic groups, across industries, and over time. Table 10-2 summarizes some of the key differences in the U.S. labor market. There are sizable differences in unionization rates by gender, race, industry, and occupation.

Men have significantly higher unionization rates than women. In 2010, 12.6 percent of working men were unionized, but only 11.1 percent of women. The gender differential in unionization rates arises partly because women are more likely to be employed in part-time jobs or in jobs that offer flexible work schedules. These types of jobs tend not to be unionized. In contrast, blacks have higher unionization rates than whites. In 2010, the unionization rate of black workers was 13.4 percent, as compared to about 12 percent for whites and 11 percent for Hispanics. It is not surprising that blacks are more likely to support unions because, as we will see below, unions compress wages within the firm, greatly reducing the impact of labor market discrimination on the black wage. The somewhat lower participation rate of Hispanics might be due to the predominance of immigrant

TABLE 10-2 Union Membership by Selected Characteristics, 2010 (percent of workers who are union members)

Source: Barry T. Hirsch and David A. Macpherson, *Union Membership and Earnings Data Book: Compilations from the Current Population Survey (2008 Edition)*, Washington, DC: Bureau of National Affairs, 2011, Tables 3a and 7a.

Gender:		Industry:	
Men	12.6	Private workforce	6.9
Women	11.1	Agriculture	2.3
		Mining	8.0
Race:		Construction	14.6
White	11.7	Manufacturing	10.9
Black	13.4	Transportation	28.8
Hispanic	11.0	Wholesale trade	5.2
Asian	10.9	Retail trade	4.8
		Finance	1.6
		Government	36.2

workers in the Hispanic population; many of these workers might be on the "fringes" of the labor market, and it is unlikely that those types of jobs are unionized.

There are also sizable differences in unionization rates across private-sector industries, with workers in construction, manufacturing, and transportation being the ones most likely to be unionized, and workers in agriculture and finance being the least likely. The available evidence, in fact, suggests that workers employed in concentrated industries, where most of the output is produced by a few firms, are more likely to be unionized.[7] This result is consistent with our cost-benefit approach to understanding differences in unionization rates. After all, firms in concentrated industries earn excess profits because of their monopoly power, so unions have a good chance of extracting some of the rents for the workers. Moreover, the goods produced by highly concentrated industries tend to have relatively few substitutes, implying that the elasticity of demand for the output is small. As we saw in Chapter 3, low elasticities of output demand imply relatively inelastic labor demand curves. These two forces suggest that unions can offer workers in these industries large wage gains without a corresponding loss in employment.

The unionization rate also responds to the macroeconomic environment. There is, for example, a positive relation between unionization rates and both the unemployment rate and the rate of inflation.[8] It seems that the demand for unionization increases when economic conditions worsen, either because of the job insecurity implied by high unemployment rates or because of the decline in real wages implied by high rates of inflation.

Finally, the legal environment regulating the employer-union relationship has a large impact on the success of union organizing drives. States with right-to-work laws have much lower unionization rates than other states. In 2009, for instance, the five states with the lowest unionization rates (Arkansas, Georgia, North Carolina, South Carolina, and Virginia) were also states with right-to-work laws. In these states, the unionization rate ranges from 3.1 to 4.7 percent.[9]

We must be careful, however, when interpreting the negative correlation between unionization rates and right-to-work laws as "proof" that right-to-work laws reduce the unionization rate. Part of the correlation might arise because right-to-work laws are politically feasible only in states where workers have little demand for unions in the first place. There is some evidence, however, that right-to-work laws do have a direct impact on unionization rates. In particular, states that enacted right-to-work laws experienced reduced union organizing activity *after* the passage of the law, but did not experience such a reduction in organizing activities *prior* to the enactment of the legislation.[10]

[7] Barry T. Hirsch and Mark C. Berger, "Union Membership Determination and Industry Characteristics," *Southern Economic Journal* 50 (January 1984): 665–679.

[8] Orley C. Ashenfelter and John H. Pencavel, "American Trade Union Growth: 1900–1960," *Quarterly Journal of Economics* 83 (August 1969): 434–448.

[9] U.S. Bureau of the Census, *Statistical Abstract of the United States, 2008,* Washington, DC: Government Printing Office, 2008, Table 644.

[10] David Ellwood and Glenn Fine, "The Impact of Right-to-Work Laws on Union Organizing," *Journal of Political Economy* 95 (April 1987): 250–273. See also Joe C. Davis and John H. Huston, "Right-to-Work Laws and Free Riding," *Economic Inquiry* 31 (January 1993): 52–58; and Steven E. Abraham and Paula B. Voos, "Right-to-Work Laws: New Evidence from the Stock Market," *Southern Economic Journal* 67 (October 2000): 345–362.

Are American Unions Obsolete?

The most noticeable feature of the American union movement today is the steady decline in unionization rates since 1970.[11] There have been major changes in the structure of the U.S. economy during this period. In 1960, 31 percent of workers were employed in manufacturing, where union organizing drives have typically been successful. By 2001, the proportion of workers in manufacturing had fallen to 14 percent. The location of jobs also shifted. In the 1950s, only 42 percent of the jobs were located in southern and western states (which tend to have less favorable environments for union organizing, such as right-to-work laws). By 2001, 57 percent of the jobs were located in these states. There is, in fact, strong evidence suggesting that manufacturing activity is substantially higher in right-to-work states.[12] Finally, there was a marked increase in the labor force participation rate of women. This trend has a depressing effect on unionization rates because women are less likely to join unions.

It turns out, however, that these structural factors can explain at most a third of the drop in unionization rates.[13] After all, there also have been drastic drops in unionization rates even within industries and occupations, within states, and within demographic groups.

In addition to the structural shifts in the economy, therefore, it seems as if workers' demand for unionization declined. In fact, there have been marked changes in the voting patterns of workers in union certification elections. The NLRB holds an election to certify a union as a collective bargaining agent after 30 percent of the workers petition for such an election. The union can represent the workers if a simple majority of the workers who will make up the bargaining unit vote for union representation. There has been a significant drop in the proportion of certification elections won by the union. In 1955, unions won more than 66 percent of representation elections. By the early 1990s, unions won fewer than half the elections.[14] Moreover, the probability that unions are decertified as collective bargaining agents has tripled since 1950, although the decertification rate is still tiny (only 0.2 percent of unionized workers voted for decertification in 1990).

[11] Henry S. Farber and Bruce Western, "Accounting for the Decline of Unions in the Private Sector, 1973–1998," *Journal of Labor Research* 22 (Summer 2001): 459–486; and Henry S. Farber, "Union Membership in the United States: The Divergence between the Public and Private Sectors," Working Paper, Princeton University, September 2005.

[12] Thomas J. Holmes, "The Effect of State Policies on the Location of Manufacturing: Evidence from State Borders," *Journal of Political Economy* 106 (August 1998): 667–705.

[13] Henry S. Farber, "The Decline of Unionization in the United States: What Can Be Learned from Recent Experience," *Journal of Labor Economics* 8 (January 1990): 75–105; and Richard B. Freeman, "Contraction and Expansion: The Divergence of Private Sector and Public Sector Unionism in the United States," *Journal of Economic Perspectives* 2 (Spring 1988): 63–88.

[14] Bruce C. Fallick and Kevin A. Hassett, "Investment and Union Certification," *Journal of Labor Economics* 17 (July 1999): 570–582, show that the certification of a union leads to a substantial decline in investment activity for the firm; see also John DiNardo and David S. Lee, "The Impact of Unionization on Establishment Closure: A Regression Discontinuity Analysis of Representation Elections," National Bureau of Economic Research Working Papers, No. 8993, June 2002.

Theory at Work

THE RISE AND FALL OF PATCO

The Professional Air Traffic Controllers Organization (PATCO) was the union that represented air controllers in collective bargaining negotiations with their employer, the Federal Aviation Administration (FAA). The union's brief (and militant) 13-year history ended when they called a strike in 1981. Because controllers are federal civil servants, their salaries are set by Congress and their right to strike is specifically prohibited by law. Nevertheless, much of PATCO's history was marked by the union's demands that they should be able to bargain directly over wages and that they had a right to strike.

PATCO began as an organization of New York City controllers in January 1968. By July 1968, under the leadership of attorney F. Lee Bailey—a future member of the "dream team" that defended O. J. Simpson at his murder trial—PATCO had already sponsored a work slowdown that seriously disrupted commercial air travel.

In 1980, air controllers earned high wages and had extraordinarily liberal retirement and disability programs. They were among the highest-paid government employees, averaging $82,000 annually (in 2011 dollars), and could retire at age 50 after 20 years of service. In contrast, most other federal employees needed 30 years of service if they wished to retire at age 55.

Despite the high salary and generous benefits, the PATCO leadership decided that 1981 would be a crucial year for the union and prepared to aggressively demand even higher earnings and better benefits. Most important, the leadership decided that the way to persuade Congress to agree was through a strike. PATCO made unreasonable demands in the initial rounds of the negotiation: An immediate $20,000 salary increase, a 32-hour workweek, and more generous pension and disability benefits. The Reagan administration countered with an immediate pay raise of $4,000, overtime pay after 36 hours per week (rather than 40), and various other benefits. If PATCO had accepted the administration's offer (and Congress had consented), controllers would have gotten pay increases exceeding 11 percent, more than twice what other federal employees got.

But PATCO wanted much more, and the rest is history. PATCO's strike began at 7 a.m. on August 3, 1981. The FAA was prepared and moved quickly to staff the control towers with military personnel, retirees, supervisors, and controllers who refused to strike.

Four hours after the strike began, President Reagan personally announced that the law would be enforced and that any striker not on the job within 48 hours would be fired and could not be reemployed by any other federal agency. About one-fourth of the 16,395 controllers did not go on strike and another 875 returned to work before the deadline. The 48 hours passed and 11,301 controllers were fired. It soon became obvious that the system was overstaffed. The system eventually reached full capacity, with about 20 percent fewer controllers.

The militancy of the PATCO leadership—combined with President Reagan's resolve to enforce the law—created a political and cultural environment that likely influences labor relations in the government and private sector to this day.

Source: Herbert R. Northrup, "The Rise and Demise of PATCO," *Industrial and Labor Relations Review* 37 (January 1984): 167–184.

The worsening performance of unions in certification and decertification elections is partly due to an increase in aggressive antiunion tactics by management.[15] Management activities can reduce the success of union organizing drives in many ways, including filing petitions to delay the certification election, firing workers for union activities, and hiring

[15] Richard B. Freeman and Morris Kleiner, "Employer Behavior in the Face of Union Organizing Drives," *Industrial and Labor Relations Review* 43 (April 1990): 351–365; see also William T. Dickens, "The Effect of Company Campaigns on Certification Elections: *Law and Reality* Once Again," *Industrial and Labor Relations Review* 36 (July 1983): 560–575; and Stephen G. Bronars and Donald R. Deere, "Union Organizing Activity, Firm Growth, and the Business Cycle," *American Economic Review* 83 (March 1993): 203–220.

consultants to handle the management campaign. A survey conducted in 1982 indicates that 70 percent of firms facing a union organizing drive hired lawyers or consultants, 56 percent of the firms were accused of unfair labor practices, 91 percent sent out letters to workers, and 91 percent gave so-called captive-audience antiunion speeches in the workplace. Not surprisingly, these activities reduced the probability of union representation.

The increasing antiunion activities of management are attributable partly to the rise in foreign competition as well as to the deregulation of certain unionized industries (such as trucking, airlines, and railroads).[16] The tide of foreign goods into the United States captured part of the excess rents that were previously shared between firms and workers in these affected industries. Similarly, deregulation of unionized industries introduced competitive forces into the marketplace and again dissipated the excess rents. As a result, firms became much more resistant to union wage demands and to the introduction of union work rules.

10-3 Monopoly Unions

Samuel Gompers, founder of the American Federation of Labor, was once asked what unions wanted. His reply was simple and memorable: "More." Economists keep this response in mind when they construct models of union behavior.[17] It is typically assumed that the union's utility depends on wages w and employment E—and that unions want more of both. The union's indifference curves then have the usual shape and are illustrated in Figure 10-4 (see the curves U and U').[18]

We will assume that the union wishes to maximize its utility. The union's demands, however, are constrained by the firm's behavior. We assume that the union is dealing with a profit-maximizing competitive firm so that the firm cannot influence the price of the output. This firm has a downward-sloping labor demand curve that specifies how many workers it is willing to hire at any wage. In a sense, the firm's labor demand curve can be viewed as a constraint on union behavior. If firms cannot be induced to move off the

---

[16] John M. Abowd and Thomas Lemieux, "The Effects of International Competition on Collective Bargaining Outcomes: A Comparison of the United States and Canada," in John M. Abowd and Richard B. Freeman, editors, *Immigration, Trade, and the Labor Market,* Chicago: University of Chicago Press, 1991; and David Macpherson and James Stewart, "The Effect of International Competition on Union and Nonunion Wages," *Industrial and Labor Relations Review* 43 (April 1990): 435–446.

[17] A good survey of models of union behavior is given by Henry S. Farber, "The Analysis of Union Behavior," in Orley Ashenfelter and Richard Layard, editors, *Handbook of Labor Economics,* vol. 2, Amsterdam: Elsevier, 1986, pp. 1039–1089.

[18] There is one serious conceptual problem with this approach to modeling the behavior of unions. What exactly does it mean to say that the union gets utility from having higher wages and more employment? After all, the union is not a person but is composed of many workers. If all workers had the same preferences over wages and employment, and if the leadership were elected democratically so that it bargains for what workers want, the union's preferences would be identical to that of the typical worker. It is doubtful, however, that all workers have the same preferences. Young workers, for example, will probably be less concerned with the details of the pension program than older workers. See Henry S. Farber, "Individual Preferences and Union Wage Determination," *Journal of Political Economy* 86 (October 1978): 923–942, for a detailed discussion of how the union's utility function can be derived.

FIGURE 10-4 **The Behavior of Monopoly Unions**

A monopoly union maximizes utility by choosing the point on the demand curve D that is tangent to the union's indifference curve. The union demands a wage of w_M dollars and the employer cuts back employment to E_M (from the competitive level E^*). If the demand curve were inelastic (as in D'), the union could demand a higher wage and get more utility.

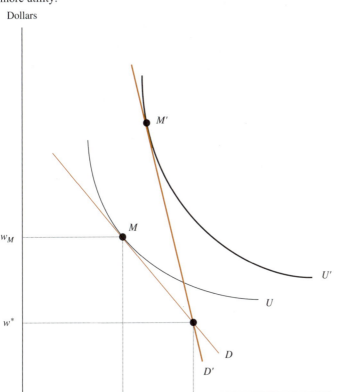

demand curve, the maximization of union utility occurs at a point like M in Figure 10-4, where the labor demand curve D is tangent to the union's indifference curve U.

The competitive wage is given by w^*. In the absence of a union, the firm would hire E^* workers. The union, however, demands a wage of w_M and the firm responds by cutting employment to E_M. This solution has a number of interesting properties. Most important, note that the union chooses the wage and the firm then moves along the demand curve to set the profit-maximizing level of employment. The model of union behavior summarized in Figure 10-4 is called a model of **monopoly unionism.** The union has an effective monopoly on the sale of labor to the firm. The union sets the price of its product (that is, the union sets the wage) and firms look at the demand curve and determine how many workers to hire.

The model of monopoly unions implies that some workers will lose their jobs as a result of the union's wage demand. It is not surprising, therefore, that unions get more utility when the demand curve for labor is inelastic. Figure 10-4 shows that if the demand curve were given by D' (which is more inelastic than D), the union can demand a higher wage (at point M') and jump to a higher indifference curve because employment does not fall very much.

As we noted in our discussion of Marshall's rules of derived demand in Chapter 3, unions will want to manipulate the labor demand elasticity by making it difficult for firms to substitute between union and nonunion labor and for consumers to substitute between goods produced by union and nonunion firms. Because workers choose whether to join unions, union organizing drives will be more successful in firms that have relatively inelastic labor demand curves. In fact, the evidence suggests that the elasticity of labor demand in union firms is about 20 percent smaller than in nonunion firms.[19]

10-4   Policy Application: Unions and Resource Allocation

It is important to note that the wage-employment solution implied by the model of monopoly unionism is inefficient because unions reduce the total value of labor's contribution to national income. If employers move along the demand curve as a result of union-mandated wage increases, unions reduce employment in union firms and increase employment in nonunion firms (as long as the displaced workers move to nonunion jobs). Because the wage (and the value of marginal product of labor) differs between the two sectors, unionism introduces an allocative inefficiency into the economy. The last worker hired by nonunion firms would have a greater productivity if he or she had been hired in the union sector, and hence the value of labor's contribution to national income would increase if some workers were reallocated across sectors.[20]

What is the cost of this misallocation of labor? Figure 10-5 illustrates the efficiency losses associated with unions (assuming that union wage-employment combinations are on the demand curve). There are two sectors in the economy: sector 1 and sector 2. Sector 1's demand curve for labor is given by D_1 and sector 2's demand curve is given by D_2. For convenience, both demand curves are drawn in the same graph. The demand curve for sector 1 is drawn in the typical fashion, whereas the demand curve for sector 2 goes from right to left. Finally, we assume that there is an inelastic labor supply curve to the economy, so that a total of $\overline{H}$ workers will be employed in one of the two sectors.

The competitive wage must equal w^*. At this wage, all workers are employed in one of the two sectors. Prior to the introduction of unionism, therefore, sector 1 employs E_1 workers and sector 2 employs E_2 workers (or $\overline{H} - E_1$). Because the labor demand curve gives the value of marginal product of labor, the area under the demand curve measures the value of total product. Prior to the imposition of a union, therefore, the value of output in

---

[19] Richard B. Freeman and James L. Medoff, "Substitution between Production Labor and Other Inputs in Unionized and Nonunionized Manufacturing," *Review of Economics and Statistics* 64 (May 1982): 220–233.

[20] Albert Rees, "The Effects of Unions on Resource Allocation," *Journal of Law and Economics* 6 (October 1963): 69–78; and Robert DeFina, "Unions, Relative Wages, and Economic Efficiency," *Journal of Labor Economics* 1 (October 1983): 408–429.

FIGURE 10-5 Unions and Labor Market Efficiency

In the absence of unions, the competitive wage is w^* and national income is given by the sum of the areas $ABCD$ and $A'BCD'$. Unions increase the wage in sector 1 to w_U. The displaced workers move to sector 2, lowering the nonunion wage to w_N. National income is now given by the sum of areas $AEGD$ and $A'FGD'$. The misallocation of labor reduces national income by the area of the triangle EBF.

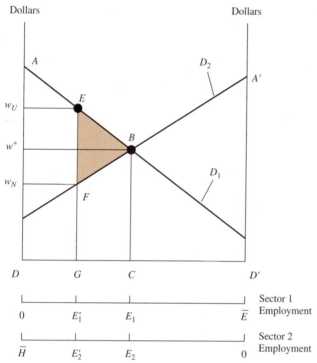

sector 1 equals the area of the trapezoid $ABCD$ and the value of output in sector 2 equals the area of the trapezoid $A'BCD'$. The sum of these two areas equals national income.

Suppose a union covers the workers in sector 1 and mandates a wage increase to w_U. Employment in the union sector falls to E_1'. In the nonunion sector, employment increases to E_2' and the wage falls to w_N. The value of output in the union sector is now given by the area of the trapezoid $AEGD$ and the value of output in the nonunion sector increases to the area of the trapezoid $A'FGD'$. Note that the sum of these two areas is smaller than national income in the absence of a union, the gap being the area of the shaded triangle EBF. This triangle is the deadweight loss that arises because the union sector is hiring too few workers and the nonunion sector is hiring too many workers.

The analysis in Figure 10-5 suggests a simple way for calculating the deadweight loss resulting from unionization in the U.S. economy. The area of the shaded triangle EBF in the figure is given by

$$\text{Efficiency loss} = \tfrac{1}{2} \times (w_U - w_N) \times (E_1 - E_1') \qquad \textbf{(10-1)}$$

After rearranging the terms in this equation, it can be shown that the efficiency loss as a fraction of national income is given by[21]

$$\frac{\text{Efficiency loss}}{\text{National income}} = {}^1\!/_2 \times (\text{Percent union-nonunion wage gap})$$

$$\times (\text{Percentage decline in employment in union sector})$$

$$\times (\text{Fraction of labor force that is unionized})$$

$$\times (\text{Labor's share of national income}) \qquad \textbf{(10-2)}$$

Suppose that unions increase wages by around 15 percent. Further, let's assume that the demand curve for union workers is unit elastic so that employment in the union sector also falls by 15 percent. Finally, about 12 percent of workers were unionized in 2010, and labor's share of national income is around 0.7. Plugging these values into equation (10-2) implies that the efficiency loss as a fraction of national income is on the order of 0.1 percent (or ${}^1\!/_2 \times 0.15 \times 0.15 \times 0.12 \times 0.7$). Since national income in the United States is around $15 trillion (as of April 2011), the losses attributable to the misallocation of labor equal $15 billion, a relatively small amount.

10-5   Efficient Bargaining

As we have seen, the wage-employment solution implied by monopoly unionism is inefficient because unions reduce the value of labor's contribution to national income. This fact suggests that perhaps the firm and the union could find—and agree on—an employment contract that does not lie on the demand curve and that would make at least one of the parties better off, without making the other party worse off.

The Firm's Isoprofit Curves

Before showing how both the union and the firm can benefit by moving off the demand curve, we first derive the firm's isoprofit curves. An isoprofit curve gives the various wage-employment combinations that yield the same level of profits. A profit-maximizing firm is indifferent among the various wage-employment combinations that lie on a single isoprofit curve.

Suppose the wage is set at w_0 dollars. A profit-maximizing firm would then choose point P on the labor demand curve in Figure 10-6, hiring 100 workers. This wage-employment combination yields a particular level of profits, say, $100,000. It turns out that there are other wage-employment combinations that yield the same level of profits. Suppose, for instance, that the firm did not hire 100 workers, but hired fewer workers instead, say, 50. If the wage remained constant at w_0, the firm would earn more profits by hiring 100 workers than by hiring 50 workers. After all, 100 workers is the *right* (that is, profit-maximizing)

---

[21] In particular, note that equation (10-1) can be rewritten as

$$\frac{\text{Efficiency loss}}{\text{National income}} = \frac{1}{2} \times \frac{w_U - w_N}{w_N} \times \frac{E_1 - E_1'}{E_1} \times \frac{E_1}{H} \times \frac{w_N \bar{H}}{\text{National income}}$$

FIGURE 10-6   The Demand Curve and the Firm's Isoprofit Curves

If the wage is w_0, the firm maximizes profits (and earns $100,000) by hiring 100 workers. If the employer wants to hire 50 workers and maintain profits constant, it must reduce the wage. Similarly, if the employer wants to hire 150 workers and maintain profits constant, it also must reduce the wage. The isoprofit curve, therefore, has an inverse-U shape. Lower isoprofit curves yield more profits.

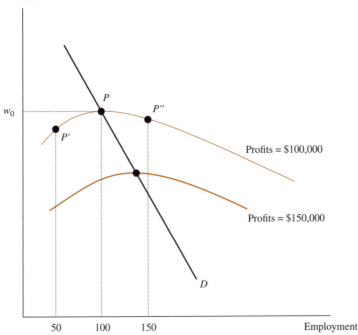

number of workers at wage w_0. The firm can hire 50 workers and maintain constant profits, therefore, only if it pays them a lower wage, as illustrated by point P' in the figure.

Suppose instead that the firm hired "too many" workers, say, 150. Again, at wage w_0 the firm earns higher profits by hiring 100 workers than by hiring 150 workers. The only way profits could remain constant if the firm hired 150 workers would be to pay a lower wage, as at point P'' in Figure 10-6. The firm's isoprofit curve, therefore, has an inverted-U shape and reaches a peak where it intersects the demand curve for labor.

We can derive an entire family of isoprofit curves, one curve for each level of profits. Note, however, that lower isoprofit curves are associated with *higher* profits. In Figure 10-6, for example, a firm hiring 100 workers would be better off if it located itself on a lower isoprofit curve (such as the one yielding $150,000); the firm would then be paying the workers a lower wage.

The Contract Curve

Figure 10-7 shows why both firms and unions have an incentive to move off the demand curve. The competitive wage is w^*. At that wage, the firm employs E^* workers (as given

FIGURE 10-7   Efficient Contracts and the Contract Curve

At the competitive wage w^*, the employer hires E^* workers. A monopoly union moves the firm to point M, demanding a wage of w_M. Both the union and the firm are better off by moving off the demand curve. At point R, the union is better off and the firm is no worse off than at point M. At point Q, the employer is better off, but the union is no worse off. If all bargaining opportunities between the two parties are exhausted, the union and the firm agree to a wage-employment combination on the contract curve PZ.

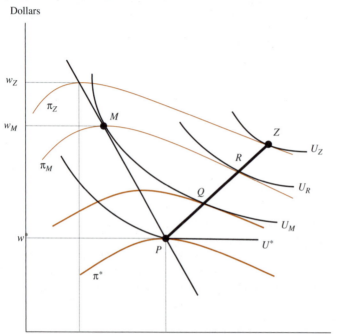

by point P) and earns π^* dollars in profits. If the union workers were to accept the wage-employment offer at point P, the union would get U^* units of utility.[22]

If the union were a monopoly union, it would pick point M on the demand curve (and get U_M utils). Note, however, that the firm could try to talk the union into moving to point Q. The union would be indifferent between the wage-employment combinations given by points M and Q (both points lie on the same indifference curve), but the firm would be better off because Q lies on a lower isoprofit curve. By moving *off* the demand curve to point Q, therefore, the firm would be better off and the union would be no worse off. Similarly, the union could try to talk the firm into moving to point R. At this point, the firm would earn the same level of profits as at point M, but the union would be better off because it could jump to the indifference curve U_R. If the union and the firm could agree to move off the demand curve to any point between point Q and point R, then *both* the union and the firm would be better off than at the monopoly union solution (point M on the demand curve).

---

[22] The indifference curve U^* is drawn so that the union would not accept a wage level below the competitive wage. This ensures that the competitive solution (point P) lies on the contract curve that we are about to derive.

Suppose that the highest wage the firm can pay without incurring a loss is given by w_Z. At that wage, the firm hires E_Z workers. The isoprofit curve going through this particular wage-employment combination is given by π_Z and gives all the wage-employment combinations that generate zero profits. This isoprofit curve provides an upper bound to the wage-employment combinations that the firm is willing to offer. If the firm chooses any point above the zero-profit isoprofit curve, it would incur a loss and go out of business.

Therefore, there are many off-the-demand-curve wage-employment combinations that are beneficial to both the union and the firm. The curve PZ gives all the points where the union's indifference curves are tangent to the firm's isoprofit curves. These wage-employment combinations are **Pareto optimal,** because once a deal is struck anywhere on this curve, deviations from that particular deal can improve the welfare of one of the parties only at the expense of the other. The curve PZ is called the **contract curve.** If the union and the firm agree to a wage-employment combination on the contract curve, the resulting contract is called an **efficient contract.**[23]

Note that the two extreme points on the contract curve bound the range of possible outcomes of the collective bargaining process. At point $P,$ the union workers get paid the competitive wage and the firm gets to keep all the rents. At point $Z,$ all the rents are transferred to the workers and the firm makes zero profits. The contract curve, therefore, provides the basis for negotiations between the union and the firm.

It is important to note that the contract curve lies to the right of the demand curve. For any given wage, therefore, an efficient contract leads to more employment than would be observed with monopoly unionism. Put differently, an efficient contract suggests that the employer-union relationship is not characterized by the union demanding a higher wage and by the firm responding by moving up the demand curve. Rather, efficient contracts imply that unions and firms bargain over both wages *and* employment.

Featherbedding

As illustrated in Figure 10-7, the contract curve is upward sloping. As long as the contract curve is upward sloping, the unionized firm hires *too many* workers; that is, it hires more workers than the competitive level E^*. If the union contract makes the firm hire more workers than the "right" amount it would have hired at the competitive wage, the firm is, in a sense, overstaffed. For instance, even though airlines need only two pilots to fly a particular type of aircraft, they hire three. The firm and the union will then have to negotiate "make-work" or **featherbedding practices** to share the available tasks among the many workers.[24]

An extreme example of featherbedding is a worker who is added to the payroll but never even shows up for work. Make-work rules, however, need not be that extreme. Instead, the union might force the firm to employ a certain number of workers to conduct a particular task, or to maintain a particular capital/labor ratio regardless of changes in the underlying

[23] The efficient contract model has its origins in Wassily Leontief, "The Pure Theory of the Guaranteed Annual Wage Contract," *Journal of Political Economy* 54 (February 1946): 76–79; and Ian McDonald and Robert Solow, "Wage Bargaining and Employment," *American Economic Review* 71 (December 1981): 896–908. A good discussion of how bargaining power affects the final location of the settlement along the contract curve is given by Jan Svejnar, "Bargaining Power, Fear of Disagreement, and Wage Settlements: Theory and Evidence," *Econometrica* 54 (September 1986): 1055–1078.

[24] A detailed discussion of how featherbedding practices arise in union contracts is given by George E. Johnson, "Work Rules, Featherbedding, and Pareto-Optimal Union-Management Bargaining," *Journal of Labor Economics* 8 (January 1990, Part 2): S237–S259.

technology. For instance, over half the contracts in the construction industry require that a foreman be hired to supervise as few as three workers.[25] Many union contracts also limit the firm's use of prefabricated tools and equipment: 70 percent of the contracts in the plumbers' union restrict the use of prefabricated materials and 83 percent of the contracts in the painters' union have rules regarding the maximum brush size.

Similarly, many communities in Massachusetts require private companies to hire police officers to guide traffic around construction sites, such as when utilities are installing a gas pipe or fixing an electric line. The earnings from these traffic details often make police officers the highest-paid public employees in many communities. Past efforts to limit this perk, such as not requiring the presence of a police officer at a construction site in a dead-end street, have been strongly opposed by police unions.

Strongly Efficient Contracts

An interesting possible shape for the contract curve is illustrated in Figure 10-8, where the shape of the union's indifference curves generates a *vertical* contract curve *PZ*. The firm,

FIGURE 10-8   **Strongly Efficient Contracts: A Vertical Contract Curve**

If the contract curve *PZ* is vertical, the firm hires the same number of workers that it would have hired in the absence of a union. The union and the firm are then splitting a fixed-size pie as they move up and down the contract curve. At point *P*, the employer keeps all the rents; at point *Z*, the union gets all the rents. A contract on a vertical contract curve is called a strongly efficient contract.

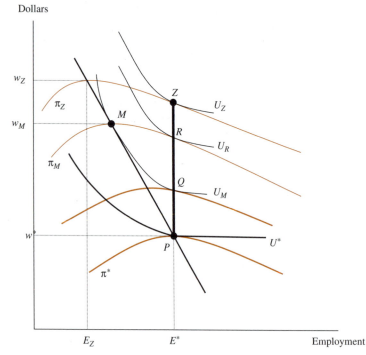

therefore, hires the same number of workers, E^*, regardless of whether it is unionized or not. If the contract curve is vertical, the deal struck between the union and the worker is called a **strongly efficient contract** because the unionized firm is hiring the competitive level of employment.

Because employment is the same regardless of which deal is struck on the vertical contract curve, the firm's output and revenue are also constant. As a result, a vertical contract curve essentially describes the many ways in which a fixed-size pie can be divided between the union and the worker. The firm's profits clearly depend on which particular point is chosen along the vertical line *PZ.* At point *P,* the firm keeps all the excess profits. As the firm and the union move up the contract curve, the union keeps more and more of the rents. The choice of a point along the vertical contract curve, therefore, is equivalent to a particular way of slicing the *same* pie.

It is unfortunate that the term *efficient contracts* is now commonly applied to all contracts that lie on the contract curve regardless of whether the contract curve is vertical or not. *Wage-employment combinations on an upward-sloping contract curve are efficient only in the sense that they exhaust all bargaining opportunities between the employer and the union.* In other words, any other wage-employment combinations can improve the welfare of one of the parties only at the expense of the other. These wage-employment combinations, however, are *not* efficient in an allocative sense because these contracts do not yield an optimal allocation of labor within the firm and between the union and nonunion sectors. Unionized firms are not hiring the number of workers they would have hired in the absence of a union.

Wage-employment combinations that lie on a vertical contract curve, however, are efficient in two distinct ways. First, they exhaust all bargaining opportunities between the employer and the union. Second, firms hire the "right" number of workers so that the union does not distort the allocation of labor, and there is no deadweight loss to the national economy.

Evidence on Efficient Contracts

The contract curve defines the range over which unions and firms can bargain over wages and employment. The process of collective bargaining narrows down the possibilities to a single point on the contract curve. The point that is chosen depends on the bargaining power of the two parties involved, which in turn is influenced by such factors as the economic conditions facing the firm and the workers, the ability of unions to provide financial support to its members in the case of a prolonged strike, and the legal environment regulating the actions that firms and unions can take to "convince" the other party to accept a particular offer. There is no widely accepted model of the collective bargaining process showing how a particular point on the contract curve is chosen.

Regardless of how the bargaining process ends, our analysis of efficient contracts suggests that both firms and unions will want to move off the demand curve. This theoretical implication has motivated a lot of empirical research to determine if unions and firms indeed reach an efficient contract. Many of the studies in this literature estimate regressions that relate the employment in union firms to the union wage and to the competitive wage in the industry. If unions behaved like monopoly unions, the level of employment in union firms would depend only on the union wage and would not depend on the competitive wage in the industry. In contrast, if union contracts were strongly efficient, the level of employment in the union firm should be unrelated to the union wage, but would depend instead on the level of the competitive wage.

The available studies seem to indicate that wage-employment outcomes in unionized firms do *not* lie on the labor demand curve.[26] For instance, detailed analysis of the wage and employment policies of the International Typographical Union (ITU), where the data on union wages and employment date back to 1946, suggests that union employment depends on the competitive wage in the labor market, as implied by the efficient contracts model. There is, however, some disagreement over whether the contract curve is vertical. Some studies find that union employment is also sensitive to the union wage, contradicting the hypothesis that the firm hires the competitive level of employment regardless of the union wage.

The strongest evidence in favor of a vertical contract curve is given by a study of the relationship between the timing of union contracts and the value of the firm in the stock market.[27] This analysis indicates that a $1 unexpected increase in the share of rents going to union workers reduces the value of the firm (that is, the shareholders' wealth) by exactly $1. This result is precisely what we would expect to find if the contract curve were vertical because a fixed-size pie is being shared, and there would be a dollar-for-dollar trade-off in rents between workers and firms.[28]

10-6 Strikes

Economists have had a very difficult time explaining why strikes occur. The problem can be easily described.[29] Suppose there are $100 worth of rents to be shared between the union and the firm. The downward-sloping line shown in Figure 10-9 illustrates the many ways in which these rents can be shared. The firm offers the division of rents indicated by point R_F, where the firm keeps $75 and the union gets $25. The union makes the counteroffer at R_U, where the union keeps $75 and the firm gets $25. Neither party wants to give in to the other, so a strike occurs.

[26] Thomas E. MaCurdy and John H. Pencavel, "Testing between Competing Models of Wage and Employment Determination in Unionized Markets," *Journal of Political Economy* 94 (June 1986): S3–S39; and James N. Brown and Orley Ashenfelter, "Testing the Efficiency of Employment Contracts," *Journal of Political Economy* 94 (June 1986): S40–S87. See also Randall W. Eberts and Joe A. Stone, "On the Contract Curve: A Test of Alternative Models of Collective Bargaining," *Journal of Labor Economics* 4 (January 1986): 66–81.

[27] John M. Abowd, "The Effect of Wage Bargains on the Stock Market Value of the Firm," *American Economic Review* 79 (September 1989): 774–800.

[28] Several studies have tried to estimate the sharing ratio, the fraction of rents distributed to union workers. However, the estimates range from 0.1 to 0.7. See Jan Svejnar, "Bargaining Power, Fear of Disagreement and Wage Settlements: Theory and Evidence from U.S. Industry," *Econometrica* 54 (September 1986): 1055–1078; John M. Abowd and Thomas Lemieux, "The Effects of Product Market Competition on Collective Bargaining Agreements: The Case of Foreign Competition in Canada," *Quarterly Journal of Economics* 108 (November 1993): 983–1014; and Louis N. Christofides and Andrew J. Oswald, "Real Wage Determination and Rent-Sharing in Collective Bargaining Agreements," *Quarterly Journal of Economics* 107 (August 1992): 985–1002.

[29] The discussion in this section is based on John Kennan, "The Economics of Strikes," in Orley C. Ashenfelter and Richard Layard, editors, *Handbook of Labor Economics,* vol. 2, Amsterdam: Elsevier, 1986, pp. 1091–1137.

FIGURE 10-9   The Hicks Paradox: Strikes Are Not Pareto Optimal

The firm makes the offer at point R_F, keeping $75 and giving the union $25. The union wants point R_U, getting $75 for its members and giving the firm $25. The parties do not come to an agreement and a strike occurs. The strike is costly, and the poststrike settlement occurs at point S; each party keeps $40. Both parties could have agreed to a prestrike settlement at point R^*, and both parties would have been better off.

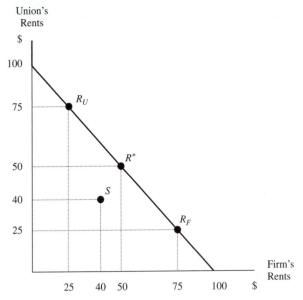

Strikes are costly to both parties. The firm's profits decline; it may lose customers permanently; and a highly publicized strike may diminish the long-run value of the brand name. Workers lose income and perhaps even their jobs. As a result of these costs, the size of the available pie shrinks and the two parties finally come to terms at point S, where each party gets $40. As a result of the strike, the firm kept a bigger share of the pie than the union wanted to give (that is, $40 versus $25), so the firm can claim that it "won." Similarly, the union gets a bigger share of the pie than the firm was willing to grant (again, $40 versus $25), and the union also can claim that it "won."

Both sides, however, achieved a hollow victory. After all, if both parties could have foreseen the end result, they could have agreed to other sharing solutions (such as point R^*, where each side keeps $50) which would have made both parties better off relative to the poststrike outcome. In other words, strikes are not Pareto optimal. When the parties have reasonably good information about the costs and the likely outcome of the strike, it is irrational to strike. The firm and the union can agree to the strike outcome in advance, save the cost associated with the strike and share the savings between them, and both parties will be better off. The irrationality of strikes has come to be known as the **Hicks paradox.**[30]

---

[30] The irrationality of strikes was first stressed by John R. Hicks, *The Theory of Wages,* London: Macmillan, 1932.

Strikes and Asymmetric Information

Many ingenious models have been proposed to escape the Hicks paradox. The most influential models tend to stress that strikes occur because workers are not well informed about the firm's financial status and may have unreasonably optimistic expectations about the size of the pie and how much of it the firm is willing to give away. In effect, there is **asymmetric information** at the bargaining table. The firm knows more about the size of the pie than does the union or the workers.[31]

Because workers do not know the firm's true financial conditions, the strike "teaches a lesson" to the workers. Figure 10-10 illustrates the **union resistance curve** summarizing the lesson that is learned. Based on their incomplete information about the size of the pie prior to the strike, the union makes a perhaps unrealistic initial wage demand of w_0. The occurrence and duration of a strike signal to the union that perhaps the firm is not as profitable as the union thought it was and encourages the union to moderate its demands. Moreover, the union rank and file may find it difficult to pay their bills during a long strike, further moderating union wage demands. The longer the strike, therefore, the lower the wage the union demands. Eventually, union demands fall to w_{min}, the lowest wage the union is willing to accept.

It is worth noting that the unrealistically high initial wage demand w_0 may be the union's optimal response to asymmetric information. After all, asymmetric information

FIGURE 10-10   The Optimal Duration of a Strike

Unions will moderate their wage demands the longer the strike lasts, generating a downward-sloping union resistance curve. The employer chooses the point on the union resistance curve that puts him on the lowest isoprofit curve (thus maximizing profits). This occurs at point P; the strike lasts t periods and the poststrike settlement wage is w_t.

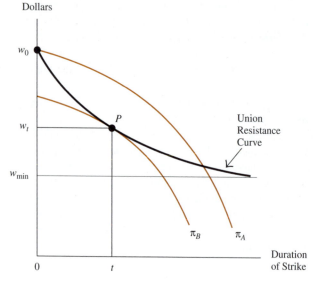

[31] This approach was introduced by Orley C. Ashenfelter and George E. Johnson, "Bargaining Theory, Trade Unions, and Industrial Strike Activity," *American Economic Review* 74 (March 1969): 35–49.

In August 2000, Firestone and Ford recalled 14.4 million size P235/75R15 tires. At the time of the recall, more than 6 million of these tires were still on the road, mostly on Ford Explorers. The National Highway Traffic Safety Administration (NHTSA) reported that the tire models being recalled were associated with tire failures that had led to 271 fatalities and more than 800 injuries. The most common source of failure was tread separation, a defect that causes the tire to blow out when the rubber tread detaches from the steel belts.

Workers in three of Firestone's 11 North American plants, including a plant in Decatur, Illinois, went on a bitter strike in July 1994. After Bridgestone/Firestone insisted on moving workers from an 8-hour to a 12-hour shift and on cutting pay for new hires by 30 percent, 4,200 workers went on strike. The company hired replacement workers. By May 1995, the Decatur plant employed 1,048 replacement workers and 371 permanent workers who had crossed the picket line. The Decatur plant is significant because it manufactured nearly a third of the tires in question, and its tires had the highest rate of defects. In May 1995, almost a year after the strike began, the union offered to return to work without a contract, but Bridgestone/Firestone announced that it would permanently retain the replacement workers. A final agreement, which included provisions to recall all workers, was not reached until December 1996.

The working conditions for the recalled workers were difficult. A document produced by the United Steel Workers of America claims that "the strikers were assigned to the hardest jobs on the worst machines, rather than the jobs they had held for 10, 20, and even 30 years. The company supervisors had a field day harassing, intimidating, and firing union members for the smallest infractions." The bitterness was equally strong on the union side. The union imposed a $4,500 fine on workers who crossed the picket line if they wanted to rejoin the union.

Tire manufacturing is a complex, labor-intensive task. The production line at the Decatur plant was not automated, so workers had some discretion in determining how much effort to put into wrapping the steel belts. A recent study finds that "one of every 400 tires produced in the Decatur, IL, plant in 1995 was returned under warranty because of a tread separation by 2000." In fact, the tires manufactured at Decatur during the labor dispute had higher failure rates than tires produced at that facility before or after the dispute, and higher than tires produced at other plants.

Source: Alan B. Krueger and Alexandre Mas, "Strikes, Scabs and Tread Separations: Labor Strife and the Production of Defective Bridgestone/Firestone Tires," *Journal of Political Economy* 112 (April 2004): 253–289.

encourages the firm to lie about its financial condition.[32] If unions do not threaten to strike and impose a substantial cost on the firm, the firm will always claim that the available pie is very small. Unions, therefore, may be better off demanding high wages initially because there is a chance that the firm *is* earning excess rents and that the firm *will* accept the union's wage demands to avoid the cost of a strike.

The firm knows that the union will moderate its demands over time. Even though the firm would obviously have a lower payroll if it waited out the strike (because of a lower wage settlement), strikes are costly. Therefore, the firm will want to compare the present value of profits if it gives in to the union's initial wage demands with the present value of profits if the strike lasts one period, or if the strike lasts two periods, and so on. *The firm*

[32] Beth Hayes, "Unions and Strikes with Asymmetric Information," *Journal of Labor Economics* 2 (January 1984): 57–83; and John Schnell and Cynthia Gramm, "Learning by Striking: Estimates of the Teetotaler Effect," *Journal of Labor Economics* 5 (April 1987): 221–241.

then chooses the strike duration that maximizes the present value of profits. This choice is determined by a simple trade-off: If the firm gives in too quickly, the increased payroll costs eat away at profits; if the firm waits too long to settle, the costs of the strike can be substantial.

Figure 10-10 illustrates how the "optimal" length of the strike is determined. The firm's profit opportunities can be summarized in terms of isoprofit curves. The isoprofit curve labeled π_A gives the various combinations of wage settlements and strike durations that generate A dollars' worth of profits. The isoprofit curve must be downward sloping because the firm is indifferent between long and short strikes only if the long strikes lead to a lower settlement wage. Moreover, a lower isoprofit curve yields a higher level of profits because, for any given strike duration, the firm is paying a lower wage. Hence, the isoprofit curve labeled π_B in the figure indicates a higher level of profits than the isoprofit curve π_A.

As drawn, the isoprofit curve π_A gives the firm's profits if the firm accepts the union's initial wage demands. We have assumed, however, that the firm knows the shape of the union's wage resistance curve. The firm will then choose the point along that curve that maximizes profits. The firm, therefore, moves to the lowest possible isoprofit curve and maximizes the present value of profits by choosing the point of tangency between the isoprofit curve and the union resistance curve, or point P in Figure 10-10. The "optimal" strike—that is, the strike that maximizes the firm's profits for a given union resistance curve—lasts t periods, and the settlement wage will equal w_t dollars.

Empirical Determinants of Strike Activity

The asymmetric information model has a number of interesting empirical implications. For instance, strikes are more likely to occur and last longer the higher the initial level of union wage demands (w_0). If the union's initial offer is unreasonable, the firm will find it worthwhile to wait until the union members learn "the facts of life." Similarly, a strike will be more likely to occur if unions are willing to settle for a low wage eventually (that is, when $w_{\min}$ is low).

Figure 10-11 summarizes the pattern of strike activity in the United States since 1967. Despite the importance that strikes play in media discussions of the impact of unions, strikes are relatively rare and do not involve a large fraction of the workforce. In 2009, only 13,000 workers were involved in a strike that lasted more than one day. The fraction of work time lost to strike activity was less than a hundredth of 1 percent!

The main problem with testing the implications of the asymmetric information model is that the variables that determine strike activity (such as the initial wage demand w_0 and the "bottom-line" wage $w_{\min}$) are seldom observed. Nevertheless, a number of empirical proxies seem to successfully explain the variation in strike activity over time and across industries.[33] For instance, the model suggests that unions will not make excessive wage demands in

---

[33] See Henry S. Farber, "Bargaining Theory, Wage Outcomes, and the Occurrence of Strikes: An Econometric Analysis," *American Economic Review* 68 (June 1978): 262–271; and Susan B. Vroman, "A Longitudinal Analysis of Strike Activity in U.S. Manufacturing: 1957–1984," *American Economic Review* 79 (September 1989): 816–826. See also David Card, "Longitudinal Analysis of Strike Activity," *Journal of Labor Economics* 6 (April 1988): 147–176; and Peter C. Cramton and Joseph S. Tracy, "Strikes and Holdouts in Wage Bargaining: Theory and Data," *American Economic Review* 82 (March 1992): 100–121.

FIGURE 10-11   **Strike Activity in the United States, 1967–2011**

Source: U.S. Bureau of the Census, *Statistical Abstract of the United States,* Washington, DC: Government Printing Office, various issues. The statistics refer to strikes lasting more than one day and involving more than 1,000 workers.

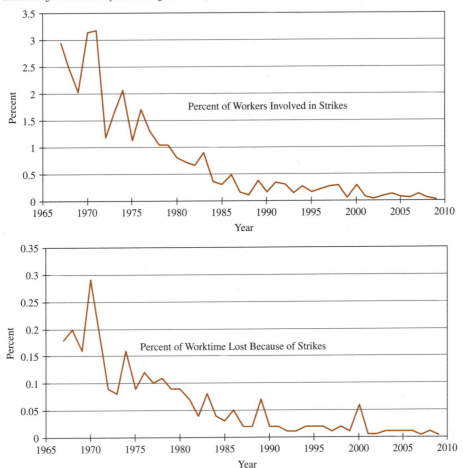

periods of high unemployment. In fact, a 1 percentage point increase in the unemployment rate decreases the probability of a strike by about 1 percentage point. Several studies have estimated the union resistance curve by relating the union wage settlement to the length of the strike. The evidence suggests that the settlement wage falls by about 2 percent after a 50-day strike and by about 4 percent after a 100-day strike.[34]

As noted earlier, a key assumption of the model is that the firm knows more about its financial conditions than the workers do. Recent studies have indeed shown that strikes are more likely to occur when unions are uncertain about the firm's financial condition.

[34] Sheena McConnell, "Strikes, Wages, and Private Information," *American Economic Review* 79 (September 1989): 801–815; and David Card, "Strikes and Wages: A Test of an Asymmetric Information Model," *Quarterly Journal of Economics* 105 (August 1990): 625–659.

For instance, the likelihood of a strike increases if the firm has a volatile stock value.[35] Volatility in the stock market reflects the investors' (and, therefore, the workers') uncertainty about the firm's financial condition.

The costs of a strike, in terms of forgone output and revenues, are an important deterrent to strike activity. For the typical firm, the costs associated with a strike are substantial and are quickly reflected in the market value of the firm. A strike reduces the value of shareholders' wealth by about 3 percent.[36]

It is important to stress the difference between the "private" costs of a strike, which are borne by the firm and the affected union workers, and the "social" costs of the strike, which include the forgone output in the economy, adverse spillover effects on other industries, and a reduction in national income. The perception that the social costs may be substantial was responsible for the enactment of the "cooling-off provision" in the Taft-Hartley Act of 1947. This provision gives the president the power to declare an 80-day cooling-off period during which the union and firm can continue to negotiate and reach agreement. The cooling-off provision has been invoked only 35 times. The most famous example occurred in 1959, when President Eisenhower invoked it to end a 116-day steel strike. Most recently, President George W. Bush invoked it in October 2002 when he ordered the Pacific Maritime Association to end its lockout of 10,500 dockworkers at 29 West Coast ports.

Despite the political concerns over the magnitude of the social costs of strikes, the available evidence suggests that these costs are not very important. Because of the hoarding of inventories as well as because other firms in the industry typically "fill in" during the strike, the social costs of strikes are only on the order of 0.2 percent of national income.

10-7   Union Wage Effects

By how much do unions increase the wages of their members?[37] We begin our analysis of this important question by defining precisely what we mean by a "union wage effect." Suppose a particular worker i earns w_N^i if he works at a nonunion job but would earn w_U^i if the firm became unionized. The percentage wage gain *for this worker* is defined as

$$\Delta_i = \text{Union wage gain for a particular worker} = \frac{w_U^i - w_N^i}{w_N^i} \quad (10\text{-}3)$$

[35] Joseph S. Tracy, "An Empirical Test of an Asymmetric Information Model of Strikes," *Journal of Labor Economics* 5 (April 1987): 149–173.

[36] Melvin W. Reder and George R. Neumann, "Output and Strike Activity in U.S. Manufacturing: How Large Are the Losses," *Industrial and Labor Relations Review* 37 (January 1984): 197–211; Brian Becker and Craig Olson, "The Impact of Strikes on Shareholder Equity," *Industrial and Labor Relations Review* 39 (April 1986): 425–438; and John DiNardo and Kevin F. Hallock, "When Unions' Mattered': Assessing the Impact of Strikes on Financial Markets," *Industrial and Labor Relations Review* 55 (January 2002): 219–33. For an interesting study of how strikes affect consumer demand, see Martin B. Schmidt and David J. Berri, "The Impact of Labor Strikes on Consumer Demand: An Application to Professional Sports," *American Economic Review* 94 (March 2004): 344–357.

[37] A comprehensive summary of the large literature that addresses this question is given by H. Gregg Lewis, *Union Relative Wage Effects: A Survey*, Chicago: University of Chicago Press, 1986.

Suppose there are k workers in the labor market. We could then calculate how much each of the workers would gain if the workers became unionized and define the **union wage gain** as

$$\text{Union wage gain} = \frac{\sum_{i=1}^{k} \Delta_i}{k} \qquad (10\text{-}4)$$

The union wage gain thus measures what the average worker in the economy would gain (in percentage terms) if he or she suddenly became a union member.

Although we are interested in knowing the size of the union wage gain, this statistic is very difficult to calculate. After all, we need to know how much the worker would earn if he were employed in a nonunion job and how much he would earn if the job suddenly became unionized. Typically, we observe only one of these two wages (that is, either the job is unionized or it is not). As a result, we instead calculate a very different sort of union-nonunion wage differential. In particular, suppose that the average wage in union jobs is given by $\overline{w}_U$ and the average wage in nonunion jobs is given by $\overline{w}_N$. The **union wage gap** is then defined by

$$D = \frac{\overline{w}_U - \overline{w}_N}{\overline{w}_N} \qquad (10\text{-}5)$$

which is the percent wage differential between union jobs and nonunion jobs. Estimates of the union wage gap typically adjust for differences in socioeconomic characteristics (such as education, age, industry, and region of employment) between workers who are in union jobs and workers who are in nonunion jobs. These adjustments are similar to those used in the Oaxaca decomposition of Chapter 9, which estimated the wage differential between comparable blacks and whites or comparable men and women. Although the union wage gap gives the wage differential between workers who are in union jobs and comparably skilled workers who are in nonunion jobs, we will see below that the union wage gap may have little to do with the union wage gain.

Estimates of the Union Wage Gap

Figure 10-12 illustrates the trend in the union wage gap between 1920 and 2010. The wage differential between union and nonunion workers is large in some time periods, but narrows substantially in others. During the early 1930s, union members earned about 39 percent more than nonunion members. Since the 1970s, however, the union wage gap has hovered in the 15 to 20 percent range. In 2010, the union wage gap stood at 15 percent.[38] There is

---

[38] This statistic gives the percentage wage gap between workers in union and nonunion firms, holding constant the worker's education, age, gender, region of residence, metropolitan status, industry of employment, and occupation. Recent studies of the union wage gap include John W. Budd and In-Gang Na, "The Union Membership Wage Premium for Employees Covered by Collective Bargaining Agreements," *Journal of Labor Economics* 18 (October 2000): 783–806; and David G. Blanchflower and Alex Bryson, "What Effect Do Unions Have on Wages Now and Would Freeman and Medoff Be Surprised?" *Journal of Labor Research* 25 (Summer 2004): 383–414; and John DiNardo and David S. Lee, "Economic Impacts of New Unionization on Private Sector Employers: 1984–2001," *Quarterly Journal of Economics* 119 (November 2004): 1383–1441. The DiNardo-Lee study is noteworthy because it presents a novel way for estimating the wage impact of unions. In particular, the study compares the wage evolution in firms where the union barely won the representation election with the wage evolution in firms where the union barely lost the election. This approach suggests that the wage impact of unions is very small—wages grew by roughly the same amount in both types of firms. We do not yet understand, however, why this approach leads to such divergent results.

FIGURE 10-12   Wage Gap between Union and Nonunion Workers, 1920–2010

Source: The pre-1970 data are drawn from John Pencavel and Catherine E. Hartsog, "A Reconsideration of the Effects of Unionism on Relative Wages and Employment in the United States, 1920–1980," *Journal of Labor Economics* 2 (April 1984): 193–232. The post-1970 data are drawn from Barry T. Hirsch and David A. Macpherson, *Union Membership and Earnings Data Book: Compilations from the Current Population Survey (2011 Edition),* Washington, DC: Bureau of National Affairs, 2011, Table 2a.

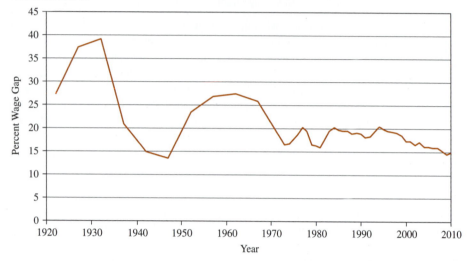

some evidence that the union wage gap is slightly countercyclical; it widens in periods of high unemployment and narrows during economic expansions.[39]

Does the Union Wage Gap Measure the Union Wage Gain?

The union wage gap is informative because it measures the wage differential between similarly skilled workers in the union and nonunion sectors. Can this wage gap be interpreted as a measure of the union wage gain? In other words, does the fact that the typical union worker earns about 15 percent more than the typical nonunion worker imply that if *we* became unionized, we also would earn 15 percent more? The answer is no!

Suppose that a union contract forces the firm to pay its workers 15 percent more than the competitive wage. Typically, the collective bargaining agreement also makes it difficult for the firm to fire or lay off workers. Because of the high cost of labor and because the firm is stuck with the workers it hires, the unionized firm may want to screen job applicants very carefully. Moreover, the 15 percent wage premium encourages many workers to apply for jobs at the unionized firm. As a result, the firm can choose only the most productive workers from the applicant pool. Over time, therefore, the firm's workforce will be composed mostly of workers who are relatively more productive than workers in nonunion firms.[40]

---

[39] John Pencavel and Catherine E. Hartsog, "A Reconsideration of the Effects of Unionism on Relative Wages and Employment in the United States, 1920–1980," *Journal of Labor Economics* 2 (April 1984): 193–232.

[40] For an alternative model suggesting that unions hire lower-quality workers, see Walter J. Wessels, "Do Unionized Firms Hire Better Workers?" *Economic Inquiry* 32 (October 1994): 616–629.

The union wage gap is typically estimated by comparing workers in union and non-union jobs who have the same socioeconomic background. Because these observable measures of skills do not completely account for skill differentials among workers, the typical worker in a union job will be more productive than a seemingly comparable worker in a nonunion job. The union wage gap, therefore, overestimates the union wage gain. As a result, estimates of the union wage gap cannot be used to predict how much a randomly chosen worker would gain if his or her firm suddenly became unionized.

Our discussion suggests that we have to be very careful in specifying what we mean by a union wage effect and in how we go about calculating it. Because different types of workers end up in union and nonunion jobs, many studies attempt to net out the impact of the skill differentials between the two sectors when calculating the union wage gap. Two solutions have been proposed. The first applies sophisticated econometric techniques to estimate "selectivity-corrected" estimates of the union wage gain.[41] In principle, this methodology allows us to predict what a union worker would earn if he were to work in a nonunion job and what a nonunion worker would earn if he were to join a union. The evidence provided by these studies, however, is mixed, with some studies suggesting that the union wage gain is improbably high (greater than 50 percent) or ridiculously low (sometimes even suggesting that unions decrease wages).

An alternative approach estimates the union wage gain to a given worker from longitudinal data. These data track workers over time so that particular workers can be observed either entering or leaving union jobs. The union wage gain is then given by the average wage increase or decrease experienced by the workers as they enter or leave a unionized job. These studies typically report that the union wage gain is smaller than the union wage gap (10 percent versus 15 percent).[42] It seems, therefore, that selection bias has an important effect on the calculation of the union wage effect.

The longitudinal studies, however, view the worker's move between the union and non-union sectors as if it were a natural experiment, with a person being assigned randomly to the various jobs. We know, however, that workers are picky when they decide which job offers to accept and which job offers to reject. A worker who trades a highly paid union job for a lower-wage nonunion job is providing very relevant information about other job characteristics (such as amenities of the work environment). Therefore, it is unlikely that the tracking of workers over time estimates the "true" value of the union wage gain.

Threat and Spillover Effects

Up to this point, our calculation of the union wage effect assumed that the existence of the union sector had no influence on the nonunion wage. Unions, however, have an impact not only on the wage of union workers, but also on the wage of nonunion workers. As a result,

[41] Greg Duncan and Duane Leigh, "Wage Determination in the Union and Nonunion Sectors: A Sample Selectivity Approach," *Industrial and Labor Relations Review* 34 (October 1980): 24–34; and Chris Robinson and Nigel Tomes, "Union Wage Differentials in the Public and Private Sectors: A Simultaneous Equations Specification," *Journal of Labor Economics* 2 (January 1984): 106–127. A critical appraisal of these studies is given by H. Gregg Lewis, *Union Relative Wage Effects: A Survey*, Chicago: University of Chicago Press, 1986, Chapter 4.

[42] See Richard B. Freeman, "Longitudinal Analysis of the Effects of Trade Unions," *Journal of Labor Economics* 2 (January 1984): 1–26; and George Jakubson, "Estimation and Testing of the Union Wage Effect Using Panel Data," *Review of Economic Studies* 58 (October 1991): 971–992.

calculating the wage differential between union jobs and nonunion jobs does not truly measure the union wage gain (even in the absence of selection biases).

One way in which unions influence wage setting in the nonunion sector is through **threat effects.** Profit-maximizing employers in the industry have an incentive to keep the union out and might be willing to share some of the excess rents in the hope that the workers will not unionize.[43] Threat effects, therefore, imply that unions have a positive impact on nonunion wages. As a result, union wage effects based on the wage differential between union and nonunion jobs underestimate the true impact of the union on the wage.

Unions also might have **spillover effects** on the nonunion sector. As workers lose their jobs in union firms (perhaps because firms move up along the demand curve in response to the union-mandated wage increase), the supply of workers in the nonunion sector increases and the competitive wage falls. A comparison of wages between union and nonunion jobs would overestimate the impact of the union on the wage of unionized workers.

The evidence on threat and spillover effects is based typically on the sign of the correlation between the nonunion wage in a labor market and the rate of unionization in that market.[44] If this correlation is negative, indicating that nonunion wages are lower in labor markets with high unionization rates, spillover effects are important; if the correlation is positive, the evidence would suggest that threat effects dominate. Many studies suggest that unions have both threat and spillover effects on the nonunion wage. For example, the wage of nonunion workers is lower in cities that have high unionization rates, indicating the existence of spillover effects. At the same time, however, the wage of nonunion police is higher in metropolitan areas where a powerful police union exists, indicating the existence of threat effects.

An extreme example of how the union affects the wages of nonunion workers is given by the provision in the Davis-Bacon Act of 1931 requiring that workers employed in federally subsidized construction projects be paid a "prevailing wage." The U.S. Department of Labor has typically interpreted the prevailing wage to be the union wage. It has been estimated that the prevailing wage provision increases the cost of construction projects by perhaps as much as 25 percent.[45] Further, its appeal would increase construction employment by at least 40,000 jobs, with most of those jobs going to minorities.[46]

Unions and Wage Dispersion

The wage distribution of unionized workers has less dispersion than that of nonunion workers. The evidence suggests that wage dispersion in union firms is about 25 percent

[43] Sherwin Rosen, "Trade Union Power, Threat Effects, and the Extent of Organization," *Review of Economic Studies* 36 (April 1969): 185–196.

[44] Richard B. Freeman and James L. Medoff, "The Impact of the Percentage Organized on Union and Nonunion Wages," *Review of Economics and Statistics* 63 (November 1981): 561–572; Casey Ichniowski, Richard Freeman, and Harrison Lauer, "Collective Bargaining Laws, Threat Effects and the Determinants of Police Compensation," *Journal of Labor Economics* 7 (April 1989): 191–209; and Henry Farber, "Nonunion Wage Rates and the Threat of Unionization," *Industrial and Labor Relations Review* 58 (April 2005): 335–352.

[45] Martha Fraundorf, John Farrell, and Robert Mason, "The Effect of the Davis-Bacon Act on Construction Costs in Rural Areas," *Review of Economics and Statistics* 66 (February 1984): 142–146; see also Steven Allen, "Much Ado about Davis-Bacon: A Critical Review and New Evidence," *Journal of Law and Economics* 6 (October 1983): 707–736.

[46] Farrell Bloch, "Minority Employment in the Construction Trades," *Journal of Labor Research* 24 (Spring 2003): 271–291.

Theory at Work

OCCUPATIONAL LICENSING

The precipitous decline in the fraction of workers who are unionized in the United States does not necessarily imply that American workers are less protected against the vicissitudes of labor market competition. At the same time that the private union sector was collapsing, there was a substantial increase in the number of workers who were required by either the federal, the state, or the local government to obtain a license to do their work. Examples of jobs that require a license include such varied occupations as teachers and barbers, and accountants and cosmetologists.

In *Capitalism and Freedom,* Milton Friedman proposed an influential theory of licensing in the labor market. Friedman emphasized that the incumbents in a particular occupation have an incentive to create a formal set of standards that limit entry into the occupation, and to lobby legislatures to enact such barriers. The licensing agency, in effect, is "captured" by the incumbents in the occupation. As a result, the agency will take actions that restrict entry and that raise the occupation's wage.

Fewer than 5 percent of the workers in the United States were required to be licensed in the early 1950s. Remarkably, almost 30 percent of the workers are now required to have a license to perform their jobs. The best available estimates suggest that the entry barriers created by licensing raise the wage of the protected incumbents by around 15 percent even after adjusting for differences in skills between licensed and unlicened workers. It is worth noting that the wage effect resulting from licensing is identical to the wage effect resulting from unionization.

Sources: Morris M. Kleiner and Alan B. Krueger,"The Prevalence and Effects of Occupational Licensing," *British Journal of Industrial Relations* 48 (December 2010): 1–12; Morris M. Kleiner "Occupational Licensing," *Journal of Economic Perspectives* 14 (Fall 2000): 189–202; and Milton Friedman, *Capitalism and Freedom,* Chicago: University of Chicago Press, 1962.

lower than in nonunion firms. The evidence also suggests that unionization reduces wage dispersion in the aggregate economy by as much as 10 percent.[47]

The "compression" of the wage distribution in the union sector arises partly because union workers are a more homogeneous group (in terms of education and other observable skill measures) than nonunion workers. Unionized firms, however, also offer their workers a lower payoff for skills than nonunion firms.[48] The rate of return to education among nonunion workers is perhaps twice as high as the rate of return among union workers. The lower payoff to skills found in union firms might occur because unions stress pay equity considerations in collective bargaining negotiations. These considerations prohibit employers from making wage-setting decisions that reward very productive workers and penalize less-productive workers.

There is also evidence that unions flatten the age-earnings profile, partly because there seem to be fewer training opportunities in the union sector. Union workers spend about 4.2 hours per week on job-training activities, as compared to 6.1 hours per week for comparable

[47] Richard B. Freeman, "Unionism and the Dispersion of Wages," *Industrial and Labor Relations Review* 34 (October 1980): 3–23; Richard B. Freeman, "Union Wage Practices and Wage Dispersion within Establishments," *Industrial and Labor Relations Review* 36 (October 1982): 3–21; and David Card, "The Effect of Unions on the Structure of Wages: A Longitudinal Analysis," *Econometrica* 64 (July 1996): 957–979.

[48] Farrell E. Bloch and Mark S. Kuskin, "Wage Determination in the Union and Nonunion Sectors," *Industrial and Labor Relations Review* 31 (January 1978): 183–192.

nonunion workers.[49] It has been argued that union workers receive less-formal on-the-job training than nonunion workers because the rigid union rules specifying how and when workers might be used in the production process reduce the profitability of training.

Unions and Fringe Benefits

Unions also affect the value of the fringe benefit package offered by firms. These fringe benefits include health and life insurance, vacation and sick days, pensions, and bonuses. The ratio of the value of fringe benefits to the wage is 20 percent in unionized firms and only 15 percent in nonunion firms.[50] Because union wages are higher than nonunion wages, the package of fringe benefits received by union workers is worth more than the package received by nonunion workers. As a result, the union effect on *total* compensation (that is, the wage plus the dollar value of fringe benefits) exceeds the union wage effects we have discussed in this chapter. The evidence suggests that the "union compensation gap" (that is, the percent difference in total compensation between workers in union and nonunion jobs) may be about 2 to 3 percentage points higher than the union wage gap.

10-8   Nonwage Effects of Unions

Although much of the literature focuses on the impact unions have on the wage structure, unions influence many other aspects of the employment relationship, including the worker's productivity, labor turnover, and job satisfaction. One important channel through which unions extend their influence is known as the **exit-voice hypothesis**.[51] In the absence of unions, workers do not have an established mechanism for informing employers of grievances regarding working conditions, wages, or other aspects of the employment relationship. If a single worker were to complain, the employer might respond by demoting or firing the worker. The only way that nonunion workers can typically register their dissatisfaction is through "exit"—they vote with their feet and leave the firm.

Unions give workers a formal channel for airing their grievances. The union, in effect, acts as an agent for the workers and provides the workers with a "voice." Workers who are dissatisfied with the job can let the union pass on the information to the employer without fear of employer reprisals.

The voice model has many interesting implications for the employment relationship in unionized firms. For example, because workers need no longer vote with their feet, labor turnover should be lower in unionized firms. In fact, the probability of job separation over a two-year period in nonunion firms is 14 percent, whereas in union firms it is only 7 percent.

---

[49] Greg Duncan and Frank P. Stafford, "Do Union Members Receive Compensating Wage Differentials?" *American Economic Review* 70 (June 1980): 355–371; see also Jacob Mincer, "Union Effects: Wages, Turnover, and Job Training," *Research in Labor Economics* (1983, Supplement 2): 217–252; and John M. Barron, Scott Fuess, and Mark Loewenstein, "Further Analysis of the Effect of Unions on Training," *Journal of Political Economy* 95 (June 1987): 632–640.

[50] Richard B. Freeman, "The Effect of Unionism on Fringe Benefits," *Industrial and Labor Relations Review* 34 (July 1981): 489–509; and Thomas C. Buchmueller, John DiNardo and Robert G. Valletta, "Union Effects on Health Insurance Provision and Coverage," *Industrial and Labor Relations Review* 55 (July 2002): 610–627.

[51] Freeman and Medoff, *What Do Unions Do?*

Part of the lower quit rate in unionized firms is due to the fact that union workers earn high wages and would have little incentive to quit even in the absence of a voice mechanism. It turns out, however, that even after carefully controlling for differences in the value of union and nonunion compensation packages (including wages and fringe benefits), union workers are still much less likely to quit.[52]

The exit-voice mechanism influences the job satisfaction of union members. Surprisingly, many studies have shown that union members report being *less* satisfied with their jobs than nonunion members.[53] This finding might seem to contradict the exit-voice hypothesis. After all, the effective voice provided by unions should remedy many of the workers' grievances. In order for unions to be effective, however, the workers' voices must be heard "loud and clear." A by-product of unionization, therefore, might well be the politicization of the workforce. Union members would then be expected to express less job satisfaction than nonunion members. Note, however, that the dissatisfaction is not genuine because it does not lead to more quits. Instead, it is a device through which the unions can tell the firm that its workers are unhappy and want more.

Unions, Productivity, and Profits

The greater stability of employment in unionized firms provides a channel through which unions can have a favorable impact on the firm's productivity. Labor turnover, after all, is quite costly. It disrupts the production process, requires substantial expenditures in headhunting activities, and increases the cost of training the workforce. The exit-voice hypothesis, therefore, implies that the union could increase the productivity of unionized firms.

This controversial implication has received a great deal of attention. Overall, the evidence seems to indicate that workers in unionized firms are indeed more productive. A careful study of productivity in the concrete industry, for instance, reports that the productivity of workers in unionized firms (measured as the tonnage of concrete per worker) is about 9 percent higher than the productivity of workers in nonunion firms.[54]

In one sense, we should not be too surprised to find that unionized firms are more productive. After all, if firms move up the demand curve as a result of the union wage increase, employment falls and the value of marginal product of labor rises. Moreover, the union wage increase may "shock" the firm into more diligent hiring practices. Because unions often impose restrictive rules on the dismissal of their members, unionized firms will be much more selective in their hiring decisions, and a better-screened workforce will typically be more productive.

---

[52] Richard B. Freeman, "The Exit-Voice Trade-off in the Labor Market: Unionism, Job Tenure, Quits, and Separations," *Quarterly Journal of Economics* 94 (June 1980): 643–674.

[53] George J. Borjas, "Job Satisfaction, Wages, and Unions," *Journal of Human Resources* 14 (Winter 1979): 21–40; and Joni Hersch and Joe Stone, "Is Union Job Dissatisfaction Real?" *Journal of Human Resources* 25 (Fall 1990): 736–751.

[54] Steven G. Allen, "Unionized Construction Workers Are More Productive," *Quarterly Journal of Economics* 99 (May 1984): 251–274; see also Charles Brown and James Medoff, "Trade Unions in the Production Process," *Journal of Political Economy* 86 (June 1978): 355–378. A critical assessment of these studies is given by Walter J. Wessels, "The Effects of Unions on Employment and Productivity: An Unresolved Contradiction," *Journal of Labor Economics* 3 (January 1985): 101–108; see also Barry T. Hirsch, "What Do Unions Do for Economic Performance?" *Journal of Labor Research* 25 (Summer 2004): 415–455.

FIGURE 10-13   Stock Market Returns before and after the 1999 Representation Election at National Linen
Service Corporation

Source: David S. Lee and Alexandre Mas, "Long-Run Impacts of Unions on Firms: New Evidence from Financial Markets, 1961–1999," Quarterly Journal of
Economics, forthcoming 2011, Figure I.

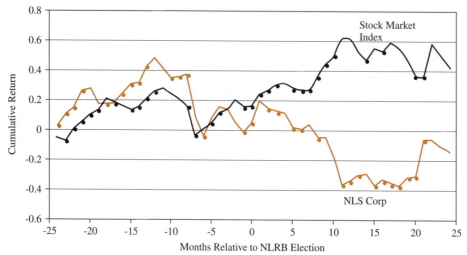

The favorable impact of unions on productivity, however, is not sufficiently large to
compensate the firm for its larger payroll costs. As a result, unionized firms have lower
profits. A careful study of profits in union and nonunion firms indicates that unions reduce
the rate of return to the firm's capital by 19 percent.[55]

As we noted earlier, there is evidence that the market value of a firm (that is, the wealth
of its shareholders) decreases on a dollar-for-dollar basis as the rents are redistributed to
union workers. A recent study examined the stock market value of the National Linen
Service Corp. (NLS), a large linen supplier.[56] Workers at NLS voted overwhelmingly to
organize themselves into a local chapter of the Union of Needletrades, Industrial, and Textile Employees. Figure 10-13 illustrates the stock market's reaction. The figure shows the
cumulative return to NLS stock during the period beginning 25 months prior to the election (which is labeled as time 0 in the figure) and ending 25 months after the election. Prior
to the election, the trend in the return to NLS stock was roughly similar to the trend in the
overall stock market. Soon after the election, however, the returns to NLS stock began to

---

[55] Kim B. Clark, "Unionization and Firm Performance: The Impact on Profits, Growth, and Productiv-
ity," *American Economic Review* 74 (December 1984): 893–919. See also Richard Ruback and Martin
B. Zimmerman, "Unionization and Profitability: Evidence from the Capital Market," *Journal of Political
Economy* 92 (December 1984): 1134–1157; Barry T. Hirsch, John T. Addison, and Robert A. Connolly,
"Do Unions Capture Monopoly Profits," *Industrial and Labor Relations Review* 41 (October 1987):
136–138; and Paula Voos and Lawrence R. Mishel, "The Union Impact on Profits: Evidence from
Industry Price-Cost Margin Data," *Journal of Labor Economics* 4 (January 1986): 105–133.

[56] David S. Lee and Alexandre Mas, "Long-Run Impacts of Unions on Firms: New Evidence from
Financial Markets, 1961–1999," Princeton Industrial Relations Section Working Paper, January 2008.

fall behind. After two years, the price of NLS shares had fallen by about 25 percent, while the broad market index had risen by 50 percent.

In view of the negative impact that unions have on profits and shareholder wealth, it is not surprising that a firm's management often makes ingenious attempts to keep the unions out. A recent study suggests that firms will incur large amounts of debt to reduce the threat of impending unionization.[57] The issuance of debt ties down the firm's future wealth. These obligations reduce the excess rents that are currently available to union workers, diminish the gain to unionization, and lower the probability that unions will want to target the firm. The available evidence indicates that a nonunion firm will increase its debt level by roughly $1 million for every additional percentage point increase in the industry's unionization rate.

10-9   Policy Application: Public-Sector Unions

There has been a rapid increase in the proportion of public-sector workers in the United States who are unionized. Much of the research on the economic impact of public-sector unions is motivated by the fact that labor demand curves for many essential public-sector workers—such as police officers, firefighters, and teachers—tend to be inelastic. If public-sector unions behaved like monopoly unions (so that wage-employment outcomes lie on the labor demand curve), Marshall's rules of derived demand imply that public-sector unions could "extort" very high wages from the taxpayers. Moreover, because public-sector workers are often a potent political force, some politicians might be willing to grant high wage increases to public-sector unions in exchange for votes.

The evidence, however, does not suggest that the union wage effect in the public sector is very large.[58] Most studies, in fact, report that the union wage gap in the public sector (that is, the percentage wage differential between comparable union and nonunion public-sector workers) is on the order of 5 to 10 percent.

Public-sector unions might not generate very high wage increases because state and local governments *do* face constraints. A wage increase for public-sector workers has to be funded by taxpayers, and higher taxes will encourage the outmigration of jobs and workers from the locality. In effect, governmental units compete with each other to attract residents and business opportunities, and this competition keeps down the costs of public services.

It is important to stress, however, that much of the existing research on how public-sector unions affect the labor market is quite dated, done mainly in the 1980s and 1990s. Since then, there has been a lively (and contentious) public debate on the level of pay and benefits that public-sector workers receive, especially in the context of increasingly severe economic constraints faced by state and local governments. We do not yet know, however, whether the coming wave of studies of public-sector unions will confirm the early findings.

---

[57] Stephen G. Bronars and Donald R. Deere, "The Threat of Unionization, the Use of Debt, and the Preservation of Shareholder Wealth," *Quarterly Journal of Economics* 106 (February 1991): 231–254.

[58] Robert G. Valletta, "Union Effects on Municipal Employment and Wages: A Longitudinal Approach," *Journal of Labor Economics* 11 (July 1993): 545–574; and Janet Currie and Sheena McConnell, "Collective Bargaining in the Public Sector: The Effect of Legal Structure on Dispute Costs and Wages," *American Economic Review* 81 (September 1991): 693–718. See Richard B. Freeman, "Unionism Comes to the Public Sector," *Journal of Economic Literature* 24 (March 1986), pp. 41–86, for a survey of the literature.

Few social policy issues are as controversial as the proper role of public sector unions and whether state and local governments need to take action to curtail their power. Much of the debate focuses on whether public sector unions are benefiting disproportionately by demanding (and obtaining) high salaries and very generous benefits with little to show in terms of increased productivity.

An important target in these policy debates has been the teachers' unions. Depending on one's perspective, teachers' unions either help provide quality education to millions of students or funnel millions of dollars of contributions to politicians who just happen to back the union objectives after they get elected—and, in particular, support collective bargaining agreements that keep teachers' pay and benefits much more generous than they would otherwise be.

Teachers' unions are a relatively recent phenomenon in U.S. labor markets. Although teachers' organizations have long existed (93 percent of school districts in 1963 reported having such an organization), most of these groups acted only in an advisory capacity, and only 1 percent of the districts had a collective bargaining agreement. Moreover, the few school school districts bound by collective bargaining agreements were located mostly in Michigan, Massachusetts, and Rhode Island. By 1992, however, more than a third of school districts had collective bargaining agreements, and at least half of the teachers were members of the organization.

This growth was the result of statutory changes in the laws regulating collective bargaining of public-sector workers. Many states explicitly prohibited collective bargaining by teachers in 1960. Between 1960 and 1990, many states extended collective bargaining rights to teachers. However, there was a great deal of difference in the timing of the liberalizing legislation, with some states

(such as California and New York) granting collective bargaining rights to teachers before 1970, while other states (such as Connecticut and Illinois) granting such rights only after 1980.

The differences in the enactment and timing of these laws provide an instrument that can help us determine how teachers' unions affect a variety of outcomes in the education system. Not surprisingly, it has been found that the creation of a teachers' union affects a wide array of outcomes. For instance, per-pupil spending increases by about 12 percent. Some of this increase, of course, results in an increase in teacher salaries of about 5 percent. Some of the increase also results in the school district hiring more teachers, so the student-teacher ratio falls. Despite the fact that there are more teachers and that these teachers are paid more, there is no evidence that students' academic achievement improves. In fact, there is an *increase* in the dropout rate, of around 2 percentage points. In general, the available data tend to reveal that inputs—such as more teachers or higher per-pupil spending—simply are not as effective in unionized schools as they are in nonunionized schools.

Needless to say, these results are controversial and are hotly debated. Nevertheless, the increasing constraints on government resources in many states and localities guarantees that the debate over whether there should be limits on the collective bargaining rights of public-sector employees will continue unabated.

Sources: Caroline Minter Hoxby, "How Teachers' Unions Affect Education Production," *Quarterly Journal of Economics* 111 (August 1996): 671–718. Some conflicting evidence is presented in Michael F. Lovenheim, "The Effect of Teachers' Union on Education Production: Evidence from Union Election Certifications in Three Midwestern States," *Journal of Labor Economics* 27 (October 2009): 525–587.

Arbitration

The power of public-sector unions is also constrained because most states prohibit strikes by public-sector workers. As a result, public-sector unions often choose (or are mandated to choose) *binding arbitration* as a way of resolving collective bargaining disputes. Two types of arbitration procedures are in widespread use. Under **conventional arbitration,** both parties to the dispute present their offers to an objective arbitrator. The arbitrator, who is effectively the judge in the case, compares the two offers. After studying the facts, he comes up with a solution that both sides are bound to accept. The arbitrator's solution might lie anywhere in between the two offers, and might even lie outside this range. In **final-offer arbitration,** both sides again present their offers to the arbitrator, but the arbitrator must choose from one of the two offers. Again, both sides are bound to accept the arbitrator's decision.

Because wage settlements in the public sector depend so heavily on the arbitrator's judgment, it is of interest to examine how arbitrators reach decisions and how employers and unions strategically make offers designed to influence the arbitrator's behavior.[59] In the typical model of conventional arbitration, both employers and unions have expectations about what the arbitrator considers to be a reasonable outcome. Both parties believe that if they present an outlandish offer to the arbitrator (too high a wage demand in the case of the union or too low a wage offer in the case of the employer), the arbitrator will disregard their position and the arbitrator's decision will be greatly influenced by the other party's offer. Both parties obviously want to influence the arbitrator, so they tend to position themselves around what they believe to be the arbitrator's desired outcome. The arbitrator, in effect, only needs to "split the difference" between the offers. Note that arbitrators do *not* follow a "blind" rule of thumb that tells them to split the difference. Rather, arbitrators do this because the two parties strategically place themselves around the arbitrator's preferred position.

Final-offer arbitration introduces a somewhat different set of incentives for the parties. After studying the facts of the case, the arbitrator again has a notion of what constitutes a fair settlement. The arbitrator will then choose whichever of the two offers comes closest to his or her assessment. Obviously both the employer and the union will avoid making offers that deviate greatly from the arbitrator's preferred outcome. After all, arbitrators will completely ignore outlandish offers. Parties who are risk-averse and are not willing to take a chance with the arbitrator, therefore, will make offers that are very close to the arbitrator's preferred position and will "win" a higher fraction of final-offer awards. As a result, evidence that one party, say, the union, wins most of the cases need not indicate a systematic bias on the part of the arbitrator. It might just indicate that unions are more risk-averse than firms.

A number of studies have analyzed how arbitration affects the wages of police personnel in New Jersey.[60] Under that state's law, parties who cannot resolve the conflict on their own submit their dispute to conventional arbitration if *both* parties agree. Otherwise, the dispute is resolved through final-offer arbitration. If the dispute reached mandated

---

[59] Henry S. Farber and Harry C. Katz, "Interest Arbitration, Outcomes, and Incentives to Bargain," *Industrial and Labor Relations Review* 33 (October 1979): 55–63; Henry S. Farber, "Splitting-the-Difference in Interest Arbitration," *Industrial and Labor Relations Review* 35 (October 1981): 70–77; and Vincent P. Crawford, "On Compulsory-Arbitration Schemes," *Journal of Political Economy* 87 (February 1979): 131–160.

[60] Orley C. Ashenfelter and David E. Bloom, "Models of Arbitrator Behavior: Theory and Evidence," *American Economic Review* 74 (March 1984): 111–124; and Janet Currie, "Arbitrator Behavior and the Variances of Arbitrated and Negotiated Wage Settlements," *Journal of Labor Economics* 12 (January 1994): 29–39.

Theory at Work
LAWYERS AND ARBITRATION

Suppose Laura and Myra are charged with participating in the same crime and are held incommunicado. The police do not have evidence to convict either one unless one of them confesses. If only one confesses, the police will set the informer free as a reward for turning state's evidence. The prisoner who held out is then convicted and given a stiffer sentence than if she had also confessed. If neither prisoner confesses, they both go free.

In this situation, each prisoner will want to squeal regardless of what the other party does. For example, if Laura does not confess, Myra will want to confess and go free. If Laura confesses, Myra also will want to confess and get a lighter sentence. Therefore, it is in the *private* interest of each prisoner to confess, and both prisoners end up going to jail. It is in the *collective* interest of the two prisoners, however, to hold out, because both would eventually go free. This well-known problem in strategic behavior is known as the "prisoner's dilemma."

Consider now a union and an employer who are having their disputes settled by final arbitration. Each party makes an offer to the arbitrator and the arbitrator will pick whichever offer is closer to the arbitrator's notion of a just award. Each party believes that hiring a lawyer "helps" because it moves the arbitrator's perception of a just settlement closer to the party's position. If the gain from hiring a lawyer (in terms of a larger monetary award) exceeds the lawyer's fees, each party will have private incentives to hire an attorney. Because both parties will want to hire an attorney, however, the lawyers counterbalance each other and neither party gains an edge, yet each party must pay legal fees. It is, therefore, in the collective interest of the two parties *not* to hire a lawyer.

A recent study of arbitrator decisions in disputes involving public safety workers in New Jersey shows the prisoner's dilemma at work. The fraction of awards won by the employer depending on which party hired a lawyer is given by

		Union uses:	
		No Lawyer	Lawyer
Employer uses:	No Lawyer	41%	19%
	Lawyer	71%	45%

If only one party hires a lawyer, the arbitrator's decision is biased toward that party. This fact gives both parties private incentives to hire lawyers. If both parties hire lawyers, however, the two lawyers neutralize each other's effectiveness, and the share of cases won by the employer is roughly the same as if neither party had hired a lawyer. The prisoner's dilemma thus leads each party to take an action that makes both parties worse off in the end and that only serves to redistribute income toward the law firm.

Source: Orley Ashenfelter and Gordon Dahl, "Lawyers as Agents of the Devil in a Prisoner's Dilemma Game," Princeton University, August 2002.

final-offer arbitration, the typical employer offered only a 5.7 percent increase in compensation, whereas the typical union wanted an 8.5 percent wage increase, and the union "won" about two-thirds of the time. It is useful, however, to compare this track record with settlements reached in comparable disputes under conventional arbitration. In these disputes, the arbitrator typically awarded the union an 8.3-percentage-point increase in compensation. There is little difference, therefore, in the average award made under conventional and final-offer arbitration. If we interpret the conventional arbitration award as a measure of the "preferred" settlement, it is evident that the union was more risk-averse than the firm and hence made more reasonable offers to the arbitrator (if the dispute had to be settled through final arbitration).

Summary

- There has been a precipitous decline in private-sector union membership in the United States since the mid-1960s. This decline is attributable partly to structural changes in the U.S. economy, including the shrinking of the manufacturing sector and the movement of the population to southern and western states. At the same time, union membership in the public sector rose rapidly.

- Monopoly unions choose a wage, and firms respond to the wage demand by moving along the labor demand curve.

- The wage-employment outcome in the model of monopoly unions is inefficient in two distinct ways. First, unions distort the allocation of labor in the economy. The deadweight loss created by this distortion in the allocation of resources is small, perhaps on the order of $13 billion annually. A second type of inefficiency arises because both firms and workers can be made better off by moving off the demand curve.

- The contract curve summarizes the wage-employment combinations that are off the demand curve and that exhaust the gains from bargaining. Once a deal is struck on the contract curve, deviations from this point improve the welfare of one of the parties only at the expense of the other.

- If contract curves are not vertical, unionized firms will still distort the allocation of labor in the economy. If contract curves are vertical, unionized firms hire the "right" number of workers and the only impact of unions is to transfer part of the firms' rents to workers.

- Strikes are irrational if both parties have reasonably good information about the costs and the likely outcome of the strike. Strikes might nevertheless occur if one of the parties is better informed about the financial conditions of the firm.

- The union wage gain gives the percentage wage increase if a randomly chosen worker in the economy were to join a union. The union wage gap gives the percentage wage differential between workers in union firms and workers in nonunion firms. The union wage gap may not provide a good estimate of the union wage gain.

- The union wage gap is around 15 percent.

Key Concepts

asymmetric information, *440*
business unionism, *419*
certification elections, *420*
contract curve, *435*
conventional arbitration, *454*
decertification elections, *420*
efficient contract, *435*
exit-voice hypothesis, *450*

featherbedding practices, *435*
final-offer arbitration, *455*
Hicks paradox, *439*
monopoly unionism, *429*
Pareto optimal, *435*
right-to-work laws, *420*
spillover effects, *448*

strongly efficient contract, *437*
threat effects, *448*
unfair labor practices, *420*
union resistance curve, *440*
union wage gain, *445*
union wage gap, *445*
yellow-dog contracts, *419*

Review Questions

1. What factors account for the decline in private-sector unionism in the United States since the mid-1960s? What factors account for the rapid increase in public-sector unionism during the same period?

2. What does it mean to say that a union has a utility function? How exactly is this utility function derived from the preferences of the workers?

3. Describe the wage-employment outcome in a model of monopoly unionism. Explain why (and in what sense) this wage-employment outcome is inefficient.

4. Describe how we calculate the percentage decline in national income resulting from the misallocation of labor in a model of monopoly unionism. What is the dollar value of this allocative inefficiency if unions and firms reach efficient contracts and the contract curve is vertical?

5. Discuss how both unions and firms can be better off if they move off the demand curve. Derive the contract curve.

6. Discuss the difference between efficient contracts and strongly efficient contracts.

7. What is the Hicks paradox?

8. Describe how employers "choose" the optimal length of a strike in a model where there is asymmetric information.

9. Define the union wage gain and the union wage gap. Why should we care about the magnitude of the union wage gain? Why should we care about the magnitude of the union wage gap? Under what conditions will the union wage gap provide a reasonable estimate of the union wage gain?

10. What are threat and spillover effects? How do they bias our estimates of the union wage effect?

11. What is the exit-voice hypothesis? What is the implication of this hypothesis for the observed productivity of workers in unionized firms?

12. What is conventional arbitration? What is final-offer arbitration? How do the union and firm take into account the arbitrator's behavior when deciding which wage offers to put on the table?

Problems

10-1. Suppose the firm's labor demand curve is given by

$$w = 20 - 0.01E$$

where w is the hourly wage and E is the level of employment. Suppose also that the union's utility function is given by

$$U = w \times E$$

It is easy to show that the marginal utility of the wage for the union is E and the marginal utility of employment is w. What wage would a monopoly union demand? How many workers will be employed under the union contract?

10-2. Suppose the union in problem 10-1 has a different utility function. In particular, its utility function is given by

$$U = (w - w^*) \times E$$

where w^* is the competitive wage. The marginal utility of a wage increase is still E, but the marginal utility of employment is now $w - w^*$. Suppose the competitive wage is $8 per hour. What wage would a monopoly union demand? How many workers will be employed under the union contract? Contrast your answers to those in problem 10-1. Can you explain why they are different?

10-3. Figure 10-3 demonstrates some of the trade-offs involved when deciding to join a union.

    a. Provide a graph that shows how the presence of union dues affects the decision to join a union. (Assume all workers pay a flat rate for dues.) Show on your graph how the presence of union dues may lead the worker to be less inclined to join the union.

    b. Suppose in addition to higher wages the union negotiates a 10 percent employer contribution to a defined contribution pension plan. Provide a graph that incorporates this retirement benefit into the decision of whether to join a union. Show on your graph how additional fringe benefits such as a retirement plan may cause the worker to be more inclined to join the union.

10-4. A bank has $5 million in capital that it can invest at a 5 percent annual interest rate. A group of 50 workers comes to the bank wishing to borrow the $5 million. Each worker in the group has an outside job available to him or her paying $50,000 per year. If the group of workers borrows the $5 million from the bank, however, they can set up a business (in place of working their outside jobs) that returns $3 million in addition to maintaining the original investment.

    a. If the bank has all of the bargaining power (that is, the bank can make a take-it-or-leave-it offer), what annual interest rate will be associated with the repayment of the loan? What will be each worker's income for the year?

    b. If the workers have all of the bargaining power (that is, the workers can make a take-it-or-leave-it offer), what annual interest rate will be associated with the repayment of the loan? What will be each worker's income for the year?

10-5. Consider a firm that faces a constant per unit price of $1,200 for its output. The firm hires workers, E, from a union at a daily wage of w, to produce output, q, where

$$q = 2E^{1/2}$$

Given the production function, the marginal product of labor is $1/E^{1/2}$. There are 225 workers in the union. Any union worker who does not work for the firm can find a nonunion job paying $96 per day.

    a. What is the firm's labor demand function?

    b. If the firm is allowed to specify w and the union is then allowed to provide as many workers as it wants (up to 225) at the daily wage of w, what wage will the firm set? How many workers will the union provide? How much output will be produced? How much profit will the firm earn? What is the total income of the 225 union workers?

10-6. Consider the same setup as in problem 10-5, but now the union is allowed to specify any wage, w, and the firm is then allowed to hire as many workers as it wants (up to 225) at the daily wage of w. What wage will the union set in order to maximize the total income of all 225 workers? How many workers will the firm hire? How much output will be produced? How much profit will the firm earn? What is the total income of the 225 union workers?

10-7. Suppose the union's resistance curve is summarized by the following data. The union's initial wage demand is $10 per hour. If a strike occurs, the wage demands change as follows:

Length of Strike:	Hourly Wage Demanded
1 month	$9
2 months	8
3 months	7
4 months	6
5 or more months	5

Consider the following changes to the union resistance curve and state whether the proposed change makes a strike more likely to occur, and whether, if a strike occurs, it is a longer strike.

a. The drop in the wage demand from $10 to $5 per hour occurs within the span of two months, as opposed to five months.

b. The union is willing to moderate its wage demands further after the strike has lasted for six months. In particular, the wage demand keeps dropping to $4 in the sixth month, $3 in the seventh month, and so on.

c. The union's initial wage demand is $20 per hour, which then drops to $9 after the strike lasts one month, $8 after two months, and so on.

10-8. At the competitive wage of $20 per hour, firms A and B both hire 5,000 workers (each working 2,000 hours per year). The elasticity of demand is −2.5 and −0.75 at firms A and B respectively. Workers at both firms then unionize and negotiate a 12 percent wage increase.

a. What is the employment effect at firm A? How has total worker income changed?

b. What is the employment effect at firm B? How has total worker income changed?

c. How much would the workers at each firm be willing to pay in annual union dues to achieve the 12 percent gain in wages?

10-9. Suppose the value of marginal product of labor in the steel industry (in dollars per year) is given by $VMP_E = 100,000 - E$, where E is the number of steel workers. The competitive wage for the workers with the skills needed in steel production is $30,000 a year, but the industry is unionized so that steel workers earn $35,000 a year. The steelworkers' union is a monopoly union. What is the efficiency cost of the union contract in this industry?

10-10. Suppose the economy consists of a union and a nonunion sector. The labor demand curve in each sector is given by $L = 1,000,000 - 20w$. The total (economywide) supply of labor is 1,000,000, and it does not depend upon the wage. All workers are equally skilled and equally suited for work in either sector. A monopoly union sets the wage at $30,000 in the union sector. What is the union wage gap? What is the effect of the union on the wage in the nonunion sector?

10-11. In Figure 10-7, the contract curve is *PZ*.

    a. Does point *P* represent the firm or the workers having all of the bargaining power? Does point *Z* represent the firm or the workers having all of the bargaining power? Explain.

    b. Suppose the union has the power to be a monopoly union in setting wages if it chooses, but it doesn't have the power to force a wage and an employment level on the firm. On what portion of the contract curve *PZ* would you expect the bargained wage-employment contract to occur?

10-12. Consider Table 632 in the 2008 *U.S. Statistical Abstract*.

    a. Calculate the union wage effect. Calculate the union effect on total benefits. Calculate the union effect on total compensation.

    b. Note that for nonunion workers, retirement and savings increase total compensation by 75 cents per hour, with 60 percent of this expense coming in defined contribution retirement plans. In contrast, retirement and savings add $2.57 to the hourly compensation of union workers, and over three-fourths of this comes in the form of defined benefit pension plans, not defined contribution plans. What is the difference between defined benefit and defined contribution plans? Why might a union prefer (and be able to negotiate) more compensation in defined benefit plans than defined contribution plans?

10-13. Use a graph to demonstrate the likely bargaining outcomes of three industries, all with identical union resistance curves.

    a. Firm A has been losing money recently as wages and fringe benefits have risen from 63 to 89 percent of all costs in just the last three years.

    b. Most of firm B's revenues come from supplying a product to three customers who use the product in their manufacturing of computers using a just-in-time inventory system.

    c. Firm C is a local government that finds itself negotiating with its unionized employees. Government officials are pleased with the employees' productivity, but they also face local pressure to keep taxes low.

10-14. Major League Baseball players are not eligible for arbitration or free-agency until they have been in the league for several years. During these "restricted" years, a player can only negotiate with his current team. Consider a small-market team that happens to own the rights to last year's Rookie-of-the-Year. This player is currently under contract for $500,000 for the next three years. Because his current team is in a small market, the player's marginal revenue product for his current team is $6 million per year (now and in the future). When the player becomes eligible for free-agency, he will likely command $10 million per year for seven years in free-agency from competing large-market teams. In the questions below, assume the player wants to maximize his lifetime earnings.

    a. What is the worst 10-year contract extension from the player's point of view that the player would accept from his current team?

    b. What is the best 10-year contract extension from the player's point of view that his current team would offer him?

    c. Would you expect this player to sign a contract extension or to play out his contract and enter free-agency three years from now?

10-15. Soon after the football season ended in 2011, the National Football League Players Association (NFLPA), which is the union for the players in the National Football League (NFL), and the team owners (the NFL) experienced a labor impasse in the form of a lockout. For the record, each year about 150 players (called rookies) enter the NFL and 150 exit the league (via retirement or not making a team roster). While renegotiating the labor settlement, the union took several stances. Explain why a union of players would advocate against:

a. Expanding the number of games played.

b. Expanding the size of team rosters.

c. A team salary cap.

d. A rookie salary cap.

Selected Readings

John M. Abowd, "The Effect of Wage Bargains on the Stock Market Value of the Firm," *American Economic Review* 79 (September 1989): 774–800.

Orley C. Ashenfelter and George E. Johnson, "Bargaining Theory, Trade Unions, and Industrial Strike Activity," *American Economic Review* 74 (March 1969): 35–49.

Henry S. Farber, "The Determination of the Union Status of Workers," *Econometrica* 51 (September 1983): 1417–1437.

Henry S. Farber, "The Decline of Unionization in the United States: What Can Be Learned from Recent Experience," *Journal of Labor Economics* 8 (January 1990): 75–105.

Richard B. Freeman, "The Exit-Voice Trade-off in the Labor Market: Unionism, Job Tenure, Quits, and Separations," *Quarterly Journal of Economics* 94 (June 1980): 643–674.

Richard B. Freeman, "Contraction and Expansion: The Divergence of Private Sector and Public Sector Unionism in the United States," *Journal of Economic Perspectives* 2 (Spring 1988): 63–88.

Caroline Minter Hoxby, "How Teachers' Unions Affect Education Production," *Quarterly Journal of Economics* 111 (August 1996): 671–718.

Alan B. Krueger and Alexandre Mas, "Strikes, Scabs and Tread Separations: Labor Strife and the Production of Defective Bridgestone/Firestone Tires," *Journal of Political Economy* 112 (April 2004): 253–289.

Thomas E. MaCurdy and John H. Pencavel, "Testing between Competing Models of Wage and Employment Determination in Unionized Markets," *Journal of Political Economy* 94 (June 1986): S3–S39.

Web Links

The Web site of the AFL-CIO provides a lot of information on the union movement and on current political issues that concern labor: www.aflcio.org.

The National Labor Relations Board (NLRB) administers the National Labor Relations Act: www.nlrb.gov.

Chapter 11

Incentive Pay

I like work; it fascinates me. I can sit and look at it for hours.

—*Jerome K. Jerome*

Throughout much of this book, we have studied the nature of the employment contract in what are called **spot labor markets.** In each period, firms decide how many workers to hire at given wages; workers decide how many hours to work; and the interaction of workers and firms determines the equilibrium wage and employment. Once the market "shouts out" the equilibrium wage, workers and firms make the relevant labor supply and labor demand decisions. In these spot labor markets, the wage equals the worker's value of marginal product.

This chapter analyzes in more detail the nature of the employment contract between the worker and the firm. The problem with the simple story of how spot labor markets operate is that the nature of the labor market contract affects both the productivity of the workforce and the profits of the firm. The type of labor market contract matters because employers often do not know the workers' true productivity and workers would like to get paid a high salary while putting in as little effort as possible.

Some firms, for instance, might choose to offer workers a piece rate for their efforts, whereas other firms offer workers an hourly wage rate. Because the piece-rate worker's salary depends strictly on how much output is produced, he or she "works hard for the money." The time-rate worker's salary, however, is essentially independent of current effort, so the worker will want to shirk on the job. If it is difficult for the employer to monitor a worker's activities, the time-rate worker can get away with daydreaming, Web surfing, making personal phone calls, and reading the gossip in the tabloids during work hours.

Labor markets, in fact, use a wide menu of compensation systems, with piece rates and time rates being only the tip of the iceberg.[1] The employer will naturally view **incentive pay,** a compensation package designed to elicit particular levels of effort from the worker, as yet another tool it can use to increase its profits. This chapter analyzes the various forms

---

[1] A good survey of the compensation issues discussed in this chapter is given by Edward P. Lazear, "Compensation, Productivity, and the New Economics of Personnel," in David Lewin, Olivia S. Mitchell, and Peter D. Sherer, editors, *Research Frontiers in Industrial Relations and Human Resources,* Madison, WI: Industrial Relations and Research Association, 1992, pp. 341–380.

of incentive pay that arise in labor markets and shows how the nature of the compensation package alters both the worker's productivity and the firm's profits.

11-1   Piece Rates and Time Rates

The simplest way of showing the link between the method of compensation and the work incentives of workers is to compare two widely used pay systems: **piece rates** and **time rates.** A piece-rate system compensates the worker according to some measure of the worker's output. For example, garment workers might be paid on the basis of how many pairs of pants they produce; salespersons are often paid a commission based on the volume of sales; and California strawberry pickers are paid according to how many boxes of strawberries they fill. In 1987, "Junk Bond King" Michael Milken's salary at Drexel Burnham Lambert totaled $550 million (more than $1 billion in inflation-adjusted 2011 dollars). Most of this salary was the result of a 35 percent commission rate (or a piece rate) on the profits generated by his junk bond group.[2] In contrast, the compensation of time-rate workers depends only on the number of hours the worker allocates to the job and has nothing to do with the number of units the worker produces, at least in the short run. Over the long run, of course, the firm will make decisions on retention and promotion based on the worker's performance record. For simplicity, we assume that the weekly earnings of time-rate workers depend only on hours worked, and do not depend on the worker's performance.

There is a great deal of variation across U.S. manufacturing industries in their use of these two alternative pay systems.[3] More than 90 percent of workers employed in the candy, industrial chemicals, and fabricated structural steel industries are paid time rates. In contrast, more than 75 percent of workers producing footwear, men's shirts, or basic iron and steel are paid piece rates.

Should a Firm Offer Piece Rates or Time Rates?

Workers differ in their productivity, either because there are ability differentials across workers or because some workers put in a lot of effort on the job and other workers do not.

Consider a firm deciding whether to offer piece rates or time rates.[4] If the firm offers a piece rate, the worker's wage should equal exactly her value of marginal product. If the firm offers the piece-rate worker a wage lower than her value of marginal product, the worker will find another firm that is willing to pay a higher wage and move there.

However, although the worker may know precisely how much she has produced, the firm may be much less certain about the worker's productivity. In other words, the firm may not be able to measure the worker's productivity *and* cannot expect the worker to

---

[2] Connie Bruck, *The Predators' Ball,* New York: Penguin Books, 1989, pp. 31–32.

[3] Eric Seiler, "Piece Rate vs. Time Rate: The Effect of Incentives on Earnings," *Review of Economics and Statistics* 66 (August 1984): 363–376; see also Daniel Parent, "Methods of Pay and Earnings: A Longitudinal Analysis," *Industrial and Labor Relations Review* 53 (October 1999): 71–86.

[4] The exposition in the text follows that of Charles Brown, "Firms' Choice of Method of Pay," *Industrial and Labor Relations Review* 43 (February 1990, Special Issue): 165S–182S. See also Edward P. Lazear, "Salaries and Piece Rates," *Journal of Business* 59 (July 1986): 405–431; Robert Gibbons, "Piece-Rate Incentive Schemes," *Journal of Labor Economics* 5 (October 1987): 413–429; and Eugene F. Fama, "Time, Salary, and Incentive Payoffs in Labor Contracts," *Journal of Labor Economics* 9 (January 1991): 25–44.

report her productivity truthfully. If the firm wishes to pay the worker by the piece, therefore, the firm will have to monitor the worker constantly. These resources could have been used by the firm in other ways, such as leasing additional capital for the production line. As a result, the firm that monitors workers incurs "monitoring costs." These costs will typically vary from firm to firm, depending on how easy or how hard it is to monitor workers in a particular environment, and could be substantial for some firms. Alternatively, the firm can choose a time-rate system and pay the worker a fixed salary of, say, $500 per week. At least in the short run, a firm that chooses a time-rate system does not have to monitor the worker's performance.

Competitive firms choose whichever system is most profitable.[5] Regardless of whether the monitoring costs, in the end, are borne by the firm or by the worker (through a lower piece rate), firms that have very high monitoring costs will not be able to offer piece-rate systems because few workers would want to receive such low take-home salaries. Firms facing very high monitoring costs, therefore, opt for time rates, and firms facing low monitoring costs choose piece rates. Therefore, it is not surprising that piece rates are often paid to workers whose output can be observed easily (the number of pants produced, the number of boxes of strawberries picked, the dollar volume of sales made in the last period), whereas time rates are offered to workers whose output is more difficult to measure (such as college professors or workers on a software production team).

How Much Effort Do Workers Allocate to Their Jobs?

A piece-rate worker chooses how much output to produce at the firm. We assume that the worker chooses the level of effort (or output) that maximizes her utility. The more output she produces, the greater her take-home salary and, hence, the greater her utility. At the same time, however, it takes a lot of effort to work hard, and working hard causes disutility or "pain." The worker would rather be surfing the Web, socializing, and making personal phone calls than writing endless strings of computer code.

Figure 11-1 illustrates the worker's effort decision when she is paid a piece rate. The piece-rate worker is paid a constant r dollars per unit produced.[6] Put differently, the marginal revenue from producing one more unit of output is r dollars. The marginal revenue of effort curve (*MR* in the figure) is horizontal. Each additional unit of output produced, however, causes pain, and this pain rises as the worker allocates more effort to the job. As a result, the marginal cost of effort curve (or *MC*) is upward sloping. A worker who wants to maximize her utility produces up to the point where the marginal revenue equals the marginal cost, or q^* in the figure.

Workers differ in their innate ability, so different workers behave differently. Suppose that more-able workers find it easier to produce output. In other words, more-able workers face a lower marginal cost of effort curve (such as MC_{able} in Figure 11-1). More-able workers, therefore, produce more output than less-able workers.

The analysis, therefore, indicates that piece-rate workers allocate effort so that the marginal revenue of an additional unit of effort equals the marginal cost of the effort. Because

[5] An interesting illustration of the link between profitability and method of pay is given by Richard B. Freeman and Morris M. Kleiner, "The Last American Shoe: Manufacturers Changing the Method of Pay to Survive Foreign Competition," National Bureau of Economic Research Working Paper No. 6750, October 1998.

[6] The piece rate r is net of the monitoring costs that the worker might have to incur.

FIGURE 11-1   The Allocation of Work Effort by Piece-Rate Workers

The piece rate is r dollars, so the marginal revenue of an additional unit of output equals r. The worker gets disutility from producing output, as indicated by the upward-sloping marginal cost of effort curve. The level of effort chosen by a piece-rate worker equates marginal revenue to marginal cost, or q^* units. If it is easier for more able workers to allocate effort to their jobs, they face lower marginal cost curves and produce more output.

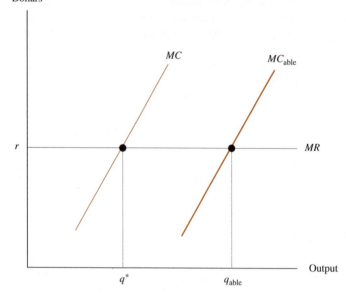

more-able workers find it easier to produce, more-able workers will allocate more effort to piece-rate jobs.

How much effort do time-rate workers allocate to their jobs? Suppose there is a minimum level of output, call it $\bar{q}$, that can be easily monitored by the firm. In other words, the firm knows if the worker shows up for work and sits at her desk or takes her spot on the assembly line. If the worker does not achieve this minimum level of effort, she is fired. A time-rate worker will then produce $\bar{q}$ units of output, *and no more.* After all, it is painful to produce output, and the time-rate worker can get away with producing this minimum amount. Of course, firms know that if they offer a time-rate pay system, the worker produces $\bar{q}$ units of output, and time-rate workers will be paid a salary of $r \times \bar{q}$. If we assume that there is no "pain" associated with simply showing up at the workplace and doing the very minimum that is expected, the utility of a time-rate worker is given by $r \times \bar{q}$.

The Sorting of Workers across Firms

Figure 11-2 illustrates the relation between a worker's utility and her ability. In the time-rate job, the worker's utility equals her income in that job (or $r \times \bar{q}$ dollars). Note that all workers, *regardless of their abilities,* get the same level of utility from time-rate jobs (because all workers allocate the same minimal level of effort to time-rate jobs). If the worker is paid by the piece, her utility depends on her ability. As we have seen, less-able workers find it difficult to produce many units of output and hence, have relatively low incomes and utility. High-ability workers produce much more output, have higher incomes, and have higher utilities.

FIGURE 11-2   **Effort and Ability of Workers in Piece-Rate and Time-Rate Jobs**

All workers, regardless of their abilities, allocate the same minimal level of effort to time-rate jobs. Because more-able workers find it easier to allocate effort, they will allocate more effort to piece-rate jobs and will have higher earnings and utility. Workers with more than x^* units of ability sort themselves into piece-rate jobs, and less-able workers choose time-rate jobs.

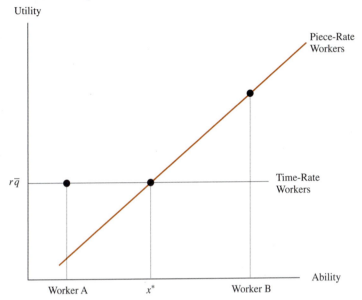

Workers are not indifferent between these two types of employment contracts and will sort themselves across firms according to what is best for them. Consider the choice of a less-able worker, such as worker A in Figure 11-2. This worker is better off accepting a job offer from a time-rate firm. In contrast, a very-able worker (such as worker B) is better off working for a firm offering piece rates. The figure indicates that all workers with fewer than x^* units of ability choose to work for time-rate firms and workers with more than x^* units work for piece-rate firms.

Therefore, workers sort themselves according to their abilities. More-productive workers want to separate themselves out of the pack and choose firms that offer piece-rate systems. Less-productive workers choose time-rate firms, where their low productivity is less easily discernible. Moreover, high-ability workers in piece-rate firms allocate a lot of effort to their jobs. As a result, piece-rate workers have higher weekly earnings than time-rate workers.

The evidence tends to support the implications of this model. In particular, piece-rate workers are more productive and earn more than time-rate workers.[7] In the footwear industry, for example, piece-rate workers earn 13 percent more per hour than time-rate workers;

[7] Seiler, "Piece Rate vs. Time Rate." See also John H. Pencavel, "Work Effort, On-the-Job Screening, and Alternative Methods of Remuneration," *Research in Labor Economics* 1 (1977): 225–258; Harry J. Paarsch and Bruce S. Shearer, "The Response of Worker Effort to Piece Rates: Evidence from the British Columbia Tree-Planting Industry," *Journal of Human Resources* 34 (Fall 1999): 643–667; and Jean-Marie Baland, Jean Dreze, and Luc Leruth, "Daily Wages and Piece Rates in Agrarian Economies," *Journal of Development Economics* 59 (August 1999): 445–461.

The Safelite Glass Corporation is the largest installer of automobile glass in the United States. Until January 1994, glass installers were paid an hourly wage rate that was unrelated to the number of windows they installed. In 1994 and 1995, the company shifted its pay structure to a piece-rate plan. On average, installers were paid about $20 per window installed.

The company adopted an incentive pay system because it believed that the piece rate would increase worker productivity. Moreover, it was easy to monitor the actual production of each installer. A computerized system kept track of how many units a worker installed in any given week. In fact, the very detailed records means that we have information on the number of windows *a particular worker* installed both under the old hourly wage rate system and under the new piece-rate system.

A careful analysis of these data indicates that the number of windows installed by a particular worker increased by around 20 percent when the piece-rate system went into effect. In other words, a key prediction of the theory—that piece rates elicit more effort from a worker—is strongly confirmed by Safelite's experience.

The data also reveal that there are strong sorting effects among new workers hired. The piece-rate system will tend to attract high-productivity workers because these are the workers who have the most to gain from being paid their actual marginal product. Workers hired by Safelite after the piece-rate system went into effect are about 20 percent more productive than workers hired under the old pay regime.

Finally, not only were workers more productive and had higher earnings, but the firm's profits also increased.

Source: Edward P. Lazear, "Performance Pay and Productivity," *American Economic Review* 90 (December 2000): 1346–1361.

among garment workers producing men's and boys' suits and coats, piece-rate workers earn 15 percent more; and among workers in auto repair shops, piece-rate workers earn at least 20 percent more. As we have seen, piece-rate workers earn more than time-rate workers both because of differences in ability and because piece-rate workers work harder. Because a worker's innate ability is unobserved, it is often difficult to determine if the wage gap is due to ability differences or to the incentive effects of a piece-rate system.

Disadvantages of Using a Piece-Rate Compensation System

Our discussion suggests that there are advantages to piece-rate incentive pay. A piece rate attracts the most-able workers, elicits high levels of effort from the workforce, ties pay directly to performance, minimizes the role of discrimination and nepotism, and increases the firm's productivity.

In view of these benefits, why are piece rates not used more often in the labor market? Perhaps the most obvious reason is that the work incentives introduced by piece rates are of little use when the firm's production depends on team effort as opposed to individual effort. Offering piece rates to one of the workers along an automobile production line would have little impact on her productivity since the speed at which the line moves also depends on the productivity of all the other workers on the line. Although it might be possible to structure compensation so as to offer a piece rate to the entire team based on the team's output, there is always the possibility that some members of the team will "free ride" on the effort of other members. Piece-rate systems, therefore, work best when the worker's own pay can be tied directly to her own productivity.

A piece-rate compensation system also overemphasizes the *quantity* of output produced. In the typical piece-rate system, the worker will want to trade off quality for quantity. This problem could be reduced if the worker's earnings depend on the number of units produced that meet a well-defined quality standard. Incorporating both quality and quantity as variables in the pay-setting formula, however, would probably increase the monitoring costs faced by firms, and hence would reduce the likelihood that firms offer piece-rate systems in the first place.

Many workers also dislike piece-rate systems because their salaries might fluctuate a lot over time. For example, the daily earnings of a strawberry picker will depend on weather conditions, and the earnings of a salesperson working on commission will be influenced by the aggregate unemployment rate. If workers are risk-averse, they dislike such fluctuations in their weekly or monthly incomes. Workers will instead prefer a pay system where they can feel "insured" against these events and can be guaranteed a steady salary stream. Risk-averse workers, therefore, prefer to work in firms that offer time-rate systems. In order to attract workers, piece-rate firms will have to compensate workers for the disutility caused by fluctuations in salaries. This compensating differential reduces the firm's profits, and fewer firms will choose to offer piece rates.

Finally, workers in piece-rate firms fear the well-known **ratchet effect.** Suppose that a piece-rate worker produces more output than the firm expected. The firm's managers might interpret the high level of production as evidence that the job was not quite as difficult as they thought and that they are paying too much for the production of a unit of output. In the next period, therefore, the piece rate is lowered and workers have to work harder just to keep even. For example, Soviet managers who posted high levels of productivity in response to a particular set of worker incentives were often accused of being lazy or "counterrevolutionary" in earlier years, with dire consequences. The ratchet effect discourages workers from accepting piece-rate jobs.

The ratchet effect also discourages piece-rate workers from adopting more efficient production techniques. As the worker learns on the job, she might realize that she can produce even more output by making some adjustments in the manufacturing method. The firm, however, may interpret this increase in output as evidence that the piece rate is too high, and the firm will cut the piece rate. The worker, in turn, will refrain from adopting new production techniques.

Recent research shows that credible promises by the firm not to cut piece rates can induce the workforce to become very efficient and to outperform its competitors.[8] Lincoln Electric, founded in 1895, is a manufacturing company that develops and manufactures arc welding products and robotic welding systems. It has long used a piece-rate system for compensation in most factory jobs and is considered to be one of the world's most successful manufacturing firms. The firm also guarantees employment for all its workers, so total earnings can fall dramatically during an economic downturn, but no worker will be laid off. On average, Lincoln's workers earn twice what they can earn elsewhere. The company can afford to do this because it faces very low costs of production, relative to the norm in the industry. These efficient production methods are the result of incremental, worker-sponsored improvements in the manufacturing process and are known to the workers. But the secrets do not leave the firm; turnover rates are substantially lower at Lincoln than they

[8] H. Lorne Carmichael and W. Bentley MacLeod, "Worker Cooperation and the Ratchet Effect," *Journal of Labor Economics* 18 (January 2000): 1–19.

are in the rest of manufacturing. In short, Lincoln's workforce is composed of workers who prefer working in a piece-rate system and who earn high salaries.

Bonuses, Profit Sharing, and Team Incentives

Firms often reward high-productivity workers not simply through piece rates and sales commissions, but also through bonuses. Bonuses are payments awarded to workers above and beyond the base salary and are typically linked to the worker's (or to the firm's) performance during a specified time period. Bonuses are common among senior executives in the United States: 94 percent of senior executives in manufacturing, 90 percent of those in construction, and 67 percent of those in banking receive bonuses. These bonuses can be substantial; the typical manager receives a bonus that is nearly 10 percent of the annual salary.[9]

Many bonus programs are not tied to a particular worker's performance in the firm, but to the firm's performance in the marketplace. In these cases, the bonus is effectively a form of **profit sharing.** A profit-sharing plan redistributes part of the firm's profits back to the workers. We can interpret the income from these profit-sharing plans as a piece rate on the output of a group of workers. Unlike piece-rate systems applied to individual workers, however, profit-sharing programs suffer from the incentive problems that afflict all team efforts, particularly the **free-riding problem.** Because a single worker's pay is only distantly related to her productivity, a single worker does not have much incentive to allocate effort to her job and will instead depend on the "kindness of others." If all workers behave in this fashion, the workforce will not be very productive and there will be few profits to share.

A survey of 500 publicly traded U.S. companies indicated that nearly 38 percent of workers who were *not* in top management were covered by profit-sharing plans.[10] Profit-sharing contracts are even more widespread in other countries. Workers in Japanese and Korean manufacturing typically receive an annual payment equivalent to one-month's or two-months' pay as profit sharing. The evidence also suggests that profit-sharing plans increase productivity. A study of U.S. firms revealed that the adoption of a profit-sharing scheme increased the productivity of the firm by about 4 to 5 percent, with the productivity effect being larger when the firm adopted cash plans (rather than deferred-payment plans).[11]

[9] Arthur Blakemore, Stuart Low, and Michael Ormiston, "Employment Bonuses and Labor Turnover," *Journal of Labor Economics* 5 (October 1987, Part 2): S124–S135.

[10] Douglas L. Kruse, "Employee Stock Ownership and Corporate Performance among Public Companies," *Industrial and Labor Relations Review* 50 (October 1996): 60–79; see also Takatoshi Ito and Kyoungsik Kang, "Bonuses, Overtime and Employment: Korea vs. Japan," *Journal of the Japanese and International Economies* 3 (December 1989): 424–450; and Omar Azfar and Stephan Danninger, "Profit-Sharing, Employment Stability, and Wage Growth," *Industrial and Labor Relations Review* 54 (April 2001): 619–630.

[11] Kruse, "Employee Stock Ownership and Corporate Performance among Public Companies." Some studies also indicate that incentive pay systems are more effective when they are implemented alongside other innovative pay practices such as flexible job assignments and employment security; see Casey Ichniowski, Kathryn Shaw, and Giovanna Prennushi, "The Effects of Human Resource Management Practices on Productivity: A Study of Steel Finishing Lines," *American Economic Review* 87 (June 1997): 291–313. It has been noted that the increasing use of various forms of incentive pay (including bonuses and commissions) in the U.S. labor market is likely to increase wage inequality, because differences in pay are now more closely tied to differences in personal productivity; see Thomas Lemieux, W. Bentley MacLeod, and Daniel Parent, "Performance Pay and Wage Inequality," *Quarterly Journal of Economics* 124 (February 2009): 1–49.

Most of us would have little trouble accepting the validity of findings that persons who work harder in private-sector firms and bring in more business are compensated more handsomely. We all know from experience that is what makes the world go round. Remarkably, there is evidence that hard work and effort—and bringing in business—has monetary rewards in situations where one would think such considerations would be too crass to consider.

Consider, for example, how Methodist ministers are paid. The United Methodist Church has roughly 8 million members in the United States, including such luminaries as George W. Bush and Hillary Clinton, and is known for its mainstream Christian beliefs.

A recent study was able to examine a 43-year time series (from 1961 to 2003) of all financial and hiring data for every local parish in the United Methodist Church's Oklahoma Annual Conference. This conference, led by a bishop and officials, controls the hiring and assignment of individual ministers for the parishes within its jurisdiction. A minister usually serves a local congregation for a few years and then rotates on a mandatory basis across parishes within the conference.

Local parishes and potential ministers cannot screen or select each other, because this sorting is done at the conference level. But officials at the local parish, through the Pastor Parish Relations Committee, meet annually with the minister and set pay for the next year. Median minister compensation in the parishes of the Oklahoma Annual Conference was around $37,000 (in 2008 dollars).

Among a pastor's many responsibilities, of course, is attracting new members to the parish. For example, a pastor may devote some effort to identifying nonbelieving members of the community who may be receptive to the Methodist beliefs and traditions, or perhaps even compete for membership with other Christian denominations by stressing the benefits accruing from membership in the Methodist church.

The examination of the Oklahoma data reveals a systematic relationship between a minister's salary and the size of the membership of the local congregation. When a new member joins the congregation, the minister's annual salary increases by $15, while if a member leaves a congregation the salary falls by $7. The implied elasticity between a minister's salary and membership is about 0.2, about half the pay-size elasticity of CEOs in the private sector..

Source: Jay C. Hartzell, Christopher A. Parsons, and David L. Yermack, "Is A Higher Calling Enough? Incentive Compensation in the Church," *Journal of Labor Economics* 28 (July 2010): 509–539.

11-2   Tournaments

Throughout much of this book, we have assumed that the worker is paid according to an *absolute* measure of performance on the job. For example, if the worker's value of marginal product is $15 an hour, the worker's wage equals $15. In some situations, however, the labor market does not reward workers according to an absolute measure of productivity. Rather, the rewards are based on what the worker produced *relative* to other workers in the firm. In effect, the firm holds a **tournament,** or a contest, to rank the workers in the firm according to their productivity. The rewards are then distributed according to rank, with the winner receiving a sizable reward and the losers receiving much smaller payoffs.

The reward structure in amateur and professional sports illustrates this type of labor market. The winner of the 2010 British Open (Louis Oosthuizen) received $1.4 million, while the golfer ending up in second place (Lee Westwood) got only $800,000. The wage gap between the two players had nothing to do with the difference in the quality of play.

Instead, the compensation is determined solely by the relative standing of the players; one player ended up in first place, the other in second. Similarly, the financial rewards in the competitive world of ice skating are determined mainly by the color of the medal won in the Olympics. A popular winner of an Olympic gold medal can earn millions of dollars annually by endorsing products, charging fees for personal appearances, and participating in touring ice shows.[12] In contrast, the winner of the bronze medal will take home only $500,000 annually. The actual difference in productivity between the gold and bronze medal winners is hard to discern. In fact, the judges often disagree substantially over the ranking. Nevertheless, to the winner go the spoils.

Competitive sports are not the only setting where rewards are allocated according to relative performance. Typically, the senior vice presidents of large corporations compete fiercely for promotion to president or chief executive officer (CEO). It is instructive to view the competition among vice presidents as a tournament. The vice presidents compete against each other for the chance to move to the presidential suite and receive the financial rewards and perks of this higher position, whereas the losers remain vice presidents at much lower vice presidential salaries. A survey of 200 large American firms indicated that the promotion from vice president to CEO involved a pay increase of 142 percent.[13] It is hard to believe that a worker's value of marginal product increases that much overnight. The salary structure of vice presidents and CEOs is probably best understood as a compensation package where salaries are determined by relative performance, rather than by absolute performance.

Why do some firms offer tournament-type contracts, as opposed to piece-rate or time-rate systems? It is sometimes easier for the firm to observe a worker's rank in the "pecking order" than to measure the worker's actual contribution to the firm. A game will decide quickly which football team is better (at least on that particular day). It is difficult, however, to determine how much better the winning team is. Similarly, a tournament among vice presidents will determine which of them should be promoted to CEO, but the actual contribution of each vice president to the firm's output is much more difficult to assess.

How Much Effort Do Tournaments Elicit?

This approach to the labor market raises a number of interesting questions.[14] For example, why do some firms choose tournaments to determine promotions and salaries, but other firms pay workers according to their actual value of marginal product? Why do the winners of these tournaments earn many times the salary of the losers, even though the difference

---

[12] "How They Bring in the Gold," *U.S. News & World Report,* January 31, 1994, p. 16.

[13] Brian G. M. Main, Charles A. O'Reilly III, and James Wade, "Top Executive Pay: Tournament or Team Work?" *Journal of Labor Economics* 4 (October 1993): 606–628; see also Taye Mengistae and Lixin Colin Xu, "Agency Theory and Executive Compensation: The Case of Chinese State-Owned Enterprise," *Journal of Labor Economics* 22 (July 2004): 615–637.

[14] Edward P. Lazear and Sherwin Rosen, "Rank-Order Tournaments as Optimum Labor Contracts," *Journal of Political Economy* 89 (October 1981): 841–864; Sherwin Rosen, "Prizes and Incentives in Elimination Tournaments," *American Economic Review* 76 (September 1986): 701–715; Clive Bull, Andrew Schotter, and Keith Weigelt, "Tournaments and Piece Rates: An Experimental Study," *Journal of Political Economy* 95 (February 1987): 1–32; and Charles R. Knoeber and Walter N. Thurman, "Testing the Theory of Tournaments: An Empirical Analysis of Broiler Production," *Journal of Labor Economics* 12 (April 1994): 155–179.

in marginal product between winners and losers is often negligible? As we will see, tournaments exist because they elicit the "right" amount of effort from workers when it is difficult to measure a worker's actual productivity, but it is easier to contrast the productivity of one worker with that of another. Because the players in these contests know that winning the tournament entails fame and fortune, whereas losing entails obscurity and low salaries, both parties will try very hard to win.

To illustrate how the tournament elicits work effort, consider a situation in which two workers, Andrea and Bea, are competing for one of two prizes. The firm announces that the first-prize winner will receive a substantial financial reward of Z_1 dollars, whereas the second-prize winner gets only Z_2 dollars. Workers in this tournament know that they are more likely to win if they allocate a lot of effort to the job.

Figure 11-3 illustrates how Andrea decides how much effort to allocate to the contest by comparing the marginal cost of allocating effort to the marginal revenue. The marginal cost of effort curve is upward sloping (as illustrated by the curve MC in the figure) so each additional unit of effort causes more "pain" than earlier units. The marginal revenue of a unit of effort depends on the difference in rewards between the first and second prize, or the spread $Z_1 - Z_2$. When this difference is relatively small, the marginal revenue received from allocating an additional unit of effort is low (as in MR_{LOW} in the figure). A worker

FIGURE 11-3   The Allocation of Effort in a Tournament

The marginal cost curve gives the "pain" of allocating an additional unit of effort to a tournament. If the prize spread between first and second place is large, the marginal revenue to an additional unit of effort is very high (MR_{HIGH}) and the worker allocates a lot of effort to the tournament.

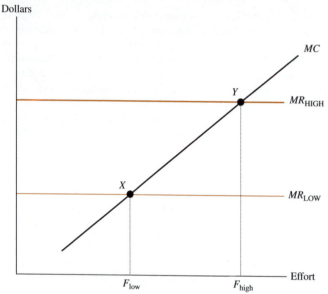

will choose the level of effort where the marginal cost of the effort allocated equals the marginal gain, or point X. The worker would then allocate F_{low} units of effort to the tournament. In contrast, if the prize spread is very high, the marginal revenue of allocating effort is substantial (as in MR_{HIGH}), and the worker will try very hard to win by allocating F_{high} units of effort to the job.

We assumed earlier that both Andrea and Bea have the same underlying ability, so that the winner would be determined partly by the amount of effort that each player allocated to the job. Bea also will choose the level of effort where the marginal revenue equals the marginal cost of allocating that extra effort. Suppose both workers "suffer" equally from allocating effort to the job (so that both players have the same marginal cost curve). Andrea and Bea will then behave in exactly the same way and allocate the same amount of effort to the contest. As a result, they have an equal chance of winning the tournament. The winner will be determined by random events at the time the game is played, and will depend on such factors as locale of the game (Are the fans rooting wildly for the home-team player?) or the personalities of the participants (Do key members on the board of directors particularly like Andrea or Bea?).

Perhaps a deeper understanding of this equilibrium might be obtained by describing more precisely the setting where the game takes place. Suppose that Andrea and Bea are playing a tennis tournament in which the winner takes home $500,000 and the loser takes home nothing. Each will play very hard to make sure that she is the one with the large prize at the end of the game. Because they are both equally adept at playing tennis, however, the outcome of the game will eventually be decided by random factors—perhaps a small wind gust slightly changing the direction and speed of the ball during a crucial play. But both Andrea and Bea know that if they do not give it their all, the other player will win. So they both work very hard at winning the game, even though that allocation of effort only helps them keep up with the other player.

The model also implies that factors that increase the disutility of playing the game (for example, a higher risk of serious injury or the possibility of burn-out) raise the marginal costs of allocating effort and reduce the level of effort that workers devote to the tournament. It is also clear that the prize spread is a key determinant of the amount of effort that players devote to this game: A very large prize spread elicits a very high level of effort—and keeps the game interesting. This explains why there is usually a large disparity in prizes between winners and losers in sports tournaments. Consumers of these contests like to watch a good game. If both sides do not give it their all, many spectators will leave the stadium or turn off the television before the game ends. If both sides play at their peak ability, however, the game will be close throughout much of the contest, with the final outcome being determined by random events in the last few minutes or even seconds of play. A large prize spread motivates both sides to play to their limit until the very end of the game.

The theory also predicts that the amount of effort exerted by workers may increase as the tournament reaches its final conclusion.[15] If, for example, a race is very tight at the half-point mark and if a player believes that a little extra effort can make the difference, the player will work harder in the second half. There is evidence, for instance, that a large prize gap between ending up in first and in second place leads to jockeys who have a realistic chance of winning to race much faster, leading to a significant decline in their race times in the second-half of a horse race.[16]

Disadvantages of Using Tournaments

Despite these favorable properties of tournaments, there are also important disadvantages. Suppose, for example, that two tennis players are competing for a particularly large prize. The winner will earn $10 million for her efforts; the loser gets only $1 million. These players have participated in many prior tournaments and have learned that they are roughly of equal ability. No matter how hard they play, the winner is typically determined by purely random events.

Both players quickly realize that they can get together prior to the tournament and agree to split the prize. They would then go through the motions of a game during the actual tournament and afterward each would take home $5.5 million. Because workers can collude, tournaments may not elicit the right level of work effort.[17] A related example of this type of corruption occurred in France, where soccer championships are taken very seriously and where membership in a championship team can lead to sizable rewards.[18] The local soccer team in Marseilles, the Olympique Marseilles, allegedly paid $42,000 to players of

[15] Rosen, "Prizes and Incentives in Elimination Tournaments."

[16] James G. Lynch, "The Effort Effects of Prizes in the Second Half of Tournaments," *Journal of Economic Behavior and Organization* 57 (May 2005): 115–129.

[17] This colluding solution, however, is not very stable. After they decide to split the prize and not to play "very hard," each of the players realizes that by putting in just a tiny bit of effort, she can win the game, renege on the agreement, and keep the entire $10 million.

[18] Roger Cohen, "A Soccer Scandal Engulfs All France," *New York Times*, September 6, 1993, p. 4.

There were 45 tournaments in the 1984 Professional Golf Association (PGA) tour in the United States. Each of these tournaments divided a specific pool of money among the players. Even though the size of the "pot" varied significantly among the tournaments, the way the prize money was allocated among players was essentially the same. About 18 percent of the pot was awarded to the winner of the tournament; 10.8 percent was awarded to the second-ranked player; and 6.8 percent was awarded to the third-ranked player. If a golfer did not rank among the top players, the prize was relatively small and was not greatly affected by the player's rank. For example, 1.1 percent of the pot was awarded to the player who ranked 22nd, and 1.0 percent to the player who ranked 23rd.

The reward structure used by the PGA suggests that professional golfers should work harder to win in those tournaments that have bigger pots. In other words, scores should be lower in tournaments with larger pots of money (in golf, a lower score means that the player hit the ball fewer times and hence is a better player). The reward structure also implies that there is a big financial gain to moving up the ranks for a player who is near the top, but that there is little gain for a less-successful player. As a result, golfers will allocate more effort to the game when they have a chance of winning (for example, a player who ranks second or third toward the end of the tournament), than when it is almost impossible to win (for example, a player who ranks 23rd after a few rounds). A study of scores in PGA tournaments reports that golfers do respond to the financial incentives provided by the tournaments. Increasing the total prize money available in the tournament by $100,000 reduces each player's score by 1.1 strokes.

Source: Ronald G. Ehrenberg and Michael L. Bognanno, "Do Tournaments Have Incentive Effects?" *Journal of Political Economy* 98 (December 1990): 1307–1324.

a competing team, the Valenciennes. In return, the Valenciennes would throw the game so that Marseilles could save its strength for an even bigger match that was scheduled within a week. The Marseilles team indeed won the match against the Valenciennes and then went on to capture the European Club Championship in 1993.

Tournaments also can encourage "too much" competition among the participants. The larger the prize spread, the higher the incentives of a player to take actions that *reduce* the chances that other players win the prize. A commonly heard story around college dorms, for instance, is that premed students often contaminate or destroy the experiments of other premed students in their chemistry and biology classes. Because the number of entry slots to medical schools is tightly rationed by the American Medical Association, the financial rewards to a medical degree can be considerable. The "winner" of a medical school slot is assured financial comfort and professional prestige.

Therefore, a large prize spread can be a double-edged sword. It not only elicits substantial work effort from the participants but also encourages participants to sabotage the work of others.[19] As a result, compensation systems that encourage pay equity (rather than a sizable prize spread) will arise naturally in organizations where workers can easily damage each other's output. This compression in the wage gap between winners and losers reduces the effort that each worker provides to the job, but might lower the costs of sabotage by an even greater amount.

[19] Edward P. Lazear, "Pay Equity and Industrial Politics," *Journal of Political Economy* 97 (June 1989): 561–580.

11-3 Policy Application: The Compensation of Executives

There has been a lot of interest in recent years in the salaries of high-level executives, such as chief executive officers, or CEOs.[20] Table 11-1 lists the highest-paid CEOs in the United States. The salaries of some of these CEOs reached dizzying heights. A few of the CEOs on the list earned in excess of $100 million annually.

The Principal-Agent Problem

Our interest in CEO salaries is due only partly to our fascination with persons who earn what most of us would consider to be extravagant salaries. The analysis of CEO compensation also raises a number of important questions in labor economics. In particular, *what should be the compensation package of a person who runs the firm, yet does not own it?*

The CEO is an "agent" for the owners of the firm (the owners are also called the *principals*). The owners of the firm, who are typically the shareholders, want the CEO to conduct the firm's business in a way that increases their wealth. The CEO instead might want to decorate her office with expensive Impressionist originals. The purchase of these paintings reduces shareholder wealth but increases the CEO's utility. The inevitable conflict between the interests of the principals and the interests of the agent is known as the **principal-agent problem.**

We suggested earlier that the structure of executive compensation can be interpreted in terms of a tournament in which the vice presidents compete for promotion, and in which the winner runs the company. Among large U.S. firms, persons promoted to CEO get an average 142 percent wage increase, whereas the promotion from one level of vice president to the next-higher level involves a much lower pay increase, on the order of 43 percent.[21] In other words, the "prize spread" is larger when executives are promoted to CEO than when executives are promoted from junior- to middle-level management. This is precisely the compensation structure suggested by the theory of tournaments. Suppose there are three levels of management: the CEO, senior vice presidents, and junior vice presidents. Junior vice presidents compete among themselves for promotion to one of the senior vice president slots, who in turn compete among themselves for promotion to CEO. Executives who won the first-level tournament and were promoted to high-paying jobs as senior vice presidents may find that the compensation in their current position "meets all their needs," and therefore, may not want to compete for promotion to CEO. In order to elicit work effort from the senior vice presidents, the prize associated with becoming a CEO must be even larger than the prize associated with becoming a senior vice president.[22]

The tournament approach also implies that the wage gap between first and second place would be larger when there are many senior vice presidents vying for the top spot. If there are too many senior vice presidents and if the gain from the promotion to CEO is small, the players

---

[20] A good survey of the literature is given by Kevin J. Murphy, "Executive Compensation," in Orley C. Ashenfelter and David Card, editors, *Handbook of Labor Economics,* vol. 3B, Amsterdam: Elsevier, 1999, pp. 2485–2563.

[21] Main, O'Reilly, and Wade, "Top Executive Pay: Tournament or Team Work?"

[22] Rosen, "Prizes and Incentives in Elimination Tournaments."

TABLE 11-1 The Highest Paid CEOs in the United States, 2009

Source: "Special Report: CEO Compensation," *Forbes*, April 28, 2010, www.forbes.com/lists/2010/12/boss-10_CEO-Compensation_Rank.html.

Rank	Name	Company	Total Compensation (millions)
1.	H. Lawrence Culp Jr.	Danaher	$141.4
2.	Lawrence J. Ellison	Oracle	130.2
3.	Aubrey K. McClendon	Chesapeake Energy	114.3
4.	Ray R. Irani	Occidental Petroleum	103.1
5.	David C. Novak	Yum Brands	76.5
6.	John C. Martin	Gilead Sciences	60.4
7.	Sol J. Barer	Celgene	59.3
8.	Keith A. Hutton	XTO Energy	54.8
9.	Richard C. Adkerson	Freeport Copper	48.8
10.	Jen-Hsun Huang	Nvidia	31.4
11.	Ivan G. Seidenberg	Verizon Communications	30.9
12.	Louis C. Camilleri	Philip Morris International	30.1
13.	Ralph Lauren	Polo Ralph Lauren	30.1
14.	Howard D. Schultz	Starbucks	29.2
15.	Robert W. Selander	MasterCard	29.0
16.	Laurence D. Fink	BlackRock	28.2
17.	J. Wayne Leonard	Entergy	27.3
18.	Leslie Moonves	CBS	26.5
19.	Hugh Grant	Monsanto	26.1
20.	Gregg L. Engles	Dean Foods	25.5
21.	Samuel J. Palmisano	IBM	25.2
22.	John H. Hammergren	McKesson	25.2
23.	David B. Snow Jr.	Medco Health	25.1
24.	William H. Swanson	Raytheon	24.9
25.	James C. Mullen	Biogen Idec	24.8

may decide that the probability of winning is too small and that it is not worth it to exert a lot of effort in the game. As the number of players increases, therefore, the prize gap also should increase to motivate the many players despite the low probability of promotion. It turns out that the structure of CEO pay in the United States exhibits this property—the wage gap between first and second place is larger as the number of potential competitors increases.[23]

The Link between CEO Compensation and Firm Performance

To continuously elicit the correct incentives from the person who wins the tournament, the CEO's compensation will have to be tied to the firm's economic performance. The CEO would then be restrained from taking actions that reduce shareholder wealth—because those actions also would reduce her wealth. The evidence indicates that there is indeed a positive correlation between firm performance and CEO compensation, although the elasticity of CEO pay with respect to the rate of return to shareholders is small. In particular, a 10-percentage-point increase in the shareholder's rate of return increases the pay of CEOs

[23] Michael L. Bognanno, "Corporate Tournaments," *Journal of Labor Economics* 19 (April 2001): 290–315.

Many studies in psychology reveal that men prefer competition more than women. Beginning in childhood, boys like to spend their time at competitive games, while girls tend to select activities where there is no clear winner or loser. The differences get accentuated at puberty, and by adulthood men are much more likely to describe themselves as competitive.

This type of behavioral difference clearly can have important labor market implications—particularly if the reward structure for top-level jobs is determined by a tournament. After all, if women tend to shy away from competition, they will be less likely to enter tournaments. This obviously implies that fewer women will win tournaments, seriously constraining the number of promotions and top-level jobs available to them. In fact, women fill only 2.5 percent of the five-highest-paid executive positions in U.S. firms.

Experimental evidence does indeed suggest that women are much less likely to enter tournaments. In a series of experiments, women and men were asked to perform a task—specifically, adding up sets of five two-digit numbers for five minutes. There is little reason to expect a gender difference in performance.

The participants in the experiment were first asked to perform the addition under a piece-rate compensation system—the payment depending on the number of correct sums the participant performed. All of the participants were then asked to perform the exercise again under tournament conditions, with the person who carried out the largest number of correct sums receiving all the rewards. Finally, the participants were asked to conduct the five-minute addition exercise again—but this time they were told that they could choose whichever compensation scheme they preferred, piece rates or tournaments.

In this third trial, 73 percent of the men preferred the tournament, as compared to only 35 percent of the women. This gender gap in choice of compensation scheme persists even after adjusting for differences in "skills" between men and women. Put differently, low-ability men tend to enter the tournament "too much" and high-ability women tend to enter it "too little."

Source: Muriel Niederle and Lise Vesterlund, "Do Women Shy Away from Competition? Do Men Compete Too Much?" *Quarterly Journal of Economics* 122 (August 2007): 1067–1101.

by only 1 percent. Put differently, the CEO's salary increases by only 2 cents for every $1,000 increase in shareholder wealth.[24]

It has been argued that this elasticity is much too small to impose real constraints on the CEO's behavior. Consider a CEO who wants to decorate her office with an Impressionist painting valued at $10 million. The purchase of this luxury good has no impact whatsoever on the firm's productivity and sales, and serves simply to further enlarge the CEO's ego. As a result, it is a redistribution of wealth from the firm's owners to the CEO. The weak correlation between firm performance and CEO salaries implies that a $10 million reduction in shareholder wealth reduces the CEO's salary by only $200 a year. In effect, the CEO is giving up the equivalent of a few minutes' pay when purchasing the Impressionist painting.

[24] Michael C. Jensen and Kevin J. Murphy, "Performance Pay and Top-Management Incentives," *Journal of Political Economy* 98 (April 1990): 225–264. Some recent research has begun to investigate if the finding of a small positive correlation between CEO compensation and firm performance is sensitive to how one defines the CEO's compensation. The increasing use (and dollar value) of stock options as part of the typical CEO's employment package seems to have considerably increased the size of the correlation; see Brian J. Hall and Jeffrey B. Liebman, "Are CEOs Really Paid Like Bureaucrats?" *Quarterly Journal of Economics* 113 (August 1998): 653–692.

A study of 16,000 managers at 250 large American corporations suggests that increasing the sensitivity of salary and bonuses to performance would improve the profitability of the firm.[25] The evidence indicates that when executives receive a bonus for good performance, the rate of return to the stockholders increases in future years.

11-4 Work Incentives and Delayed Compensation

Worker shirking, the allocation of employee time and effort to activities other than work, can generate large financial losses in many industries. As much as 80 percent of shipping losses in the freight and airport cargo-handling industries arise from employee theft; 30 percent of retail employees steal merchandise from the workplace or misuse discount privileges; 27 percent of hospital employees steal hospital supplies; 9 percent of workers in manufacturing falsify their time cards; and employees of the U.S. federal government abuse the government's long-distance phone system to the tune of $100 million a year.[26] In view of these costs, employers clearly want to structure compensation packages that discourage the worker from misbehaving.

It has been noted that upward-sloping age-earnings profiles can perform the very useful role of discouraging workers from shirking.[27] The intuition behind this hypothesis is illustrated in Figure 11-4. Suppose that the worker's value of marginal product over the life cycle is constant. The age-earnings profile in a spot labor market where the worker's effort can be measured easily would then be horizontal, as illustrated by the line *VMP* in the figure.

In fact, the worker's effort and output are hard to observe, and it is very expensive for the firm to monitor the worker continuously. At best, the firm can make only random observations of the worker's performance and take appropriate action if and when the worker is

[25] John M. Abowd, "Does Performance-Based Management Compensation Affect Corporate Performance," *Industrial and Labor Relations Review* 43 (February 1990, Special Issue): 52S–73S; see also Jonathan S. Leonard, "Executive Pay and Firm Performance," *Industrial and Labor Relations Review* 43 (February 1990, Special Issue): 13S–29S; Ulrike Malmendier and Geoffrey Tate, "Superstar CEOs," *Quarterly Journal of Economics* 124 (November 2009): 1593–1638; and Nancy L. Rose and Catherine Wolfram, "Regulating Executive Pay: Using the Tax Code to Influence Chief Executive Officer Compensation," *Journal of Labor Economics* 20 (April 2002, Part 2): S138–S175. For international evidence on the link between firm performance and CEO compensation, see Xianming Zhou, "CEO Pay, Firm Size, and Corporate Performance: Evidence from Canada," *Canadian Journal of Economics* 33 (February 2000): 213–251; and Takao Kato and Katsuyuki Kubo, "CEO Compensation and Firm Performance in Japan: Evidence from New Panel Data on Individual CEO Pay," *Journal of the Japanese and International Economies* 20 (March 2006): 1–19.

[26] William T. Dickens, Lawrence F. Katz, Kevin Lang, and Lawrence H. Summers, "Employee Crime and the Monitoring Puzzle," *Journal of Labor Economics* 7 (July 1989): 331–347.

[27] Edward P. Lazear, "Why Is There Mandatory Retirement?" *Journal of Political Economy* 87 (December 1979): 1261–1264. See also Gary S. Becker and George J. Stigler, "Law Enforcement, Malfeasance and Compensation of Enforcers," *Journal of Legal Studies* 3 (January 1974): 1–18; and Edward P. Lazear, "Agency, Earnings Profiles, Productivity, and Hours Restrictions," *American Economic Review* 71 (September 1981): 606–620. A good survey of the evidence is given by Robert M. Hutchens, "Seniority, Wages, and Productivity: A Turbulent Decade," *Journal of Economic Perspectives* 3 (Fall 1989): 49–64. An interesting discussion of the link between the model of delayed compensation and age discrimination is given by David Neumark and Wendy A. Stock, "Age Discrimination Laws and Labor Market Efficiency," *Journal of Political Economy* 107 (October 1999): 1081–1125.

FIGURE 11-4 **The Worker Is Indifferent between a Constant Wage and an Upward-Sloping Age-Earnings Profile**
If the firm could monitor a worker easily, she would get paid her constant value of marginal product (*VMP*) over the
life cycle. If it is difficult to monitor output, workers will shirk. An upward-sloping age-earnings profile (such as *AC*)
discourages workers from shirking. Workers get paid less than their value of marginal product during the first few years
on the job, and this "loan" is repaid in later years.

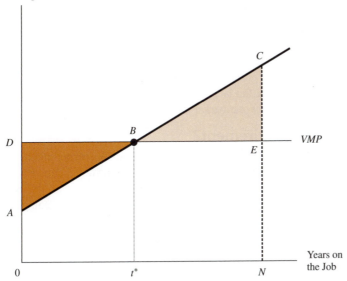

caught shirking. The worker stealing supplies from her employer knows that the chances
of getting caught and fired are remote. Therefore, she will behave in ways that limit her
productivity below her potential (so that the worker's actual contribution to the firm is less
than *VMP*).

It turns out, however, that the firm can set up a contract where the worker will *voluntarily*
produce the right level of output (that is, her *VMP*) even if the firm cannot constantly monitor the worker. Suppose the firm offered the worker a contract under which the wage during
the initial years on the job was below her value of marginal product but the wage in the later
years was above her value of marginal product. The curve *AC* in Figure 11-4 gives this alternative contract. The worker would be indifferent between this **delayed-compensation
contract** and a contract that paid *VMP* in each time period as long as the present value of
the two earnings streams was the same. In other words, the worker would be indifferent
between a constant wage of *VMP* and an upward-sloping age-earnings profile as long as the
triangle *DBA* in Figure 11-4 has the same present value as the triangle *BCE*. The relatively
low wage that the worker would receive initially is compensated by the high wage that the
worker would earn in later years.

These two contracts, however, have a very different impact on work incentives. If the
worker is offered a constant wage equal to *VMP* in each period, the worker knows that the
firm cannot monitor her activities constantly, so she has an incentive to shirk. At worst,
the worker gets caught shirking, is fired, and moves on to another job paying exactly the
same competitive wage.

In contrast, if the firm offers the upward-sloping profile *AC*, the worker will refrain from shirking. She knows that there is some monitoring of her activities and that there is a probability that if she shirks she will be caught and fired. Shirking activities now carry the risk of a substantial loss in income. For example, if the worker is fired prior to year *t**, the worker has contributed much more to the firm's output than she has received in compensation. In a sense, the worker made a loan to the firm, and if she gets fired, the loan is lost with no chance of its being repaid. Exactly the same logic applies if the worker is caught shirking anytime between year *t** and year *N*. Even though the worker is getting paid more than her value of marginal product, the firm still owes her money. By delaying compensation into the future, the firm elicits greater work effort and higher productivity from the worker. In a sense, the worker posts a bond with the firm during the initial years on the job, and the bond is repaid during the later years. *An upward-sloping age-earnings profile, therefore, elicits more effort from the worker and discourages shirking.*

Why Is There Mandatory Retirement?

The delayed compensation contract illustrated by the age-earnings profile *AC* in Figure 11-4 also has implications for the firm's retirement policy. In particular, the firm will not want the employment relationship to continue beyond year *N*. At year *N*, the firm has paid off the loan, and there is no further financial gain from employing the worker at a wage exceeding her value of marginal product. The firm, therefore, will want the worker to leave the firm. The worker will not wish to do so because she is getting "overpaid." This conflict might explain the origin of mandatory retirement clauses in employment contracts. It is important to note that although employment contracts containing a mandatory retirement clause have been illegal in the United States since the mid-1980s, they are still common in other countries.[28]

Without the delayed compensation model, it would be difficult to explain why such clauses are observed in the labor market. Why would a firm be willing to hire a worker aged 64 years and 364 days at a relatively high wage but be unwilling to hire that same worker one day later? In a spot labor market, the response to any decrease in productivity that might occur as a worker ages would be an immediate wage cut. There is no need to resort to mandatory retirement programs to terminate the labor market contract.

Even when mandatory retirement is not a legal option, firms go to great lengths to ensure that workers retire at a particular age. In the typical "defined-benefit" pension program, the worker's annual pension depends on her average salary as well as on the number of years she was employed at the firm. A careful study of the largest 250 private pension programs in the United States suggests that employers structure the defined benefit programs so as to encourage workers to retire at a particular age.[29] In many of these plans, the present value of the retirement benefits (that is, the discounted sum of the pension benefits over the expected length of the retirement years) is maximized if a worker retires earlier

[28] Robert M. Hutchens, "Delayed Payment Contracts and a Firm's Propensity to Hire Older Workers," *Journal of Labor Economics* 4 (October 1986): 439–457; Duane Leigh, "Why Is There Mandatory Retirement? An Empirical Reexamination," *Journal of Human Resources* 19 (Fall 1984): 512–531; Steven G. Allen, Robert L. Clark, and Ann A. McDermed, "Pensions, Bonding, and Lifetime Jobs," *Journal of Human Resources* 28 (Summer 1993): 463–481; and Steven Stern, "Promotion and Optimal Retirement," *Journal of Labor Economics* 5 (October 1987, Part 2): S107–S123.

[29] Edward P. Lazear, "Pensions as Severance Pay," in Zvi Bodie and John B. Shoven, editors, *Financial Aspects of the United States Pension System,* Chicago: University of Chicago Press, 1983, pp. 57–85.

than the "normal" age of retirement. If a worker chooses to delay retirement, the financial gains from this delay (a higher yearly pension benefit) do not compensate the worker sufficiently for the fact that he or she will collect benefits over a much shorter period. The firm is giving the worker a substantial financial incentive for a *voluntary* early end to the employment contract.

Do Delayed-Compensation Contracts Elicit More Effort?

There are a number of potential problems with the hypothesis that the firm elicits higher productivity from the worker by using a delayed-compensation employment contract. A worker would be willing to accept such jobs, for example, only if she knows that she would not be fired after accumulating t^* years of seniority. As shown in Figure 11-4, this is the point at which the firm begins to repay the loan. Once the worker has put in t^* years on the job, the firm may want to renege on the employment contract and fire the worker. This type of firm misbehavior, however, may not occur very often. After all, the firm is in the labor market for the long haul. If it becomes known that this firm exploits workers by paying them less than their lifetime value of marginal product, the firm will have a hard time recruiting workers and will be unable to compete in the marketplace. The value that the firm attaches to its reputation, therefore, keeps the firm's behavior in line.

Even if the firm is willing to keep its word and pay back the loan, there is always the chance that the firm will go out of business and that the worker will end up on the losing side of the deal. A delayed-compensation contract, therefore, is more likely to be offered by firms where the chances of bankruptcy are remote. As a result, delayed-compensation contracts, if they are observed at all, will tend to be observed in large and established firms.

There is some evidence in support of the delayed-compensation model. This framework, for example, is not relevant for workers who are employed in jobs where it is easy to monitor output. Workers employed in easy-to-monitor jobs find it difficult to shirk and firms do not have to tilt the age-earnings profiles to induce them to behave properly. As a result, workers in these jobs will have less wage growth, will not face mandatory retirement, and will tend to have little seniority.

It seems plausible that jobs that consist of repetitive tasks (such as addressing envelopes, peeling vegetables, or operating a truck crane) are easier to monitor because both the supervisor and the worker know precisely the nature and the value of the task that is being conducted.[30] During the 1970s (prior to the repeal of the mandatory retirement clause in labor contracts), older workers who did repetitive tasks were 9 percent less likely to have pensions (a form of delayed compensation), were 8 percent less likely to face mandatory retirement, and had 18 percent less seniority.

It is worth noting that the delayed-compensation model provides an explanation of why the age-earnings profile is upward sloping *within a job*. In other words, earnings grow over time as long as the worker stays in the same firm because this type of compensation system elicits work effort and reduces shirking. The model, therefore, provides an alternative story to the one told by the human capital model; namely, that the accumulation of general or specific training is responsible for the rise in earnings as workers accumulate job

---

[30] Robert M. Hutchens, "A Test of Lazear's Theory of Delayed Payment Contracts," *Journal of Labor Economics* 5 (October 1987, Part 2): S153–S170.

seniority. There is still a debate over whether wage growth within the job is correlated with objective measures of on-the-job training. Some studies report little correlation between training and wage growth, whereas other studies report a sizable correlation.[31]

Delayed-compensation contracts also provide an alternative explanation for the long-term "marriage" that often exists between firms and workers. As with specific training, delayed-compensation contracts reinforce the value of a particular employer-worker relationship. The worker will not want to quit because she will lose her loan to the firm, and the firm will not want to lay her off because it will be costly in terms of the firm's reputation. Employment relationships, therefore, will tend to be stable, and high levels of seniority will be the rule rather than the exception.

11-5 Efficiency Wages

Up to this point, the models linking work effort and compensation are based on the idea that it is profitable to induce workers to provide more effort *within the financial constraints imposed by a competitive market.* For example, the optimal piece rate or commission rate set by firms is the one ensuring that firms earn normal profits; a too-high or too-low piece rate would encourage the exit and entry of firms, driving profits back to their normal levels. The prize structure in tournaments is set in much the same way. If firms offer prizes below the competitive "wage," additional firms enter the industry and eat away at the firms' profits.

As we will see, however, some firms might be able to improve worker productivity by paying a wage that is *above* the wage paid by other firms. A well-known example of the gains from this type of wage setting is found in less-developed economies.[32] At the subsistence competitive wage, workers might not get the nutrition necessary to stay healthy. There is a link between the nutrition of workers and their productivity in the labor market. A 10 percent increase in caloric intake among farm workers in Sierra Leone, for example, increases productivity by about 3.4 percentage points.[33] As a result, it is possible for a firm to enhance worker productivity by paying workers a wage above the subsistence wage. The firm's workforce could then afford a more nutritious diet and would be better nourished, healthier, stronger, and more productive.

If firms pay the subsistence level, they attract a workforce composed of undernourished workers who are not very productive. If the firm sets its wage too high above the subsistence level, however, the firm would not be making any money. The increase in labor costs would probably exceed the value of the increased productivity of its workforce. There exists a wage, however, that has come to be known as the **efficiency wage,** where the marginal cost of increasing the wage exactly equals the marginal gain in the productivity of the firm's workers.

---

[31] David I. Levine, "Worth Waiting For? Delayed Compensation, Training, and Turnover in the United States and Japan," *Journal of Labor Economics* 11 (October 1993): 724–752; Jacob Mincer, "Job Training, Wage Growth, and Labor Turnover," in Jacob Mincer, *Studies in Human Capital,* Brookfield, VT: Edward Elgar Publishing, 1993, pp. 239–281; and James Brown, "Why Do Wages Increase with Tenure?" *American Economic Review* 79 (December 1989): 971–991.

[32] Harvey Leibenstein, "The Theory of Underemployment in Backward Economies," *Journal of Political Economy* 65 (April 1957): 91–103.

[33] John Strauss, "Does Better Nutrition Raise Farm Productivity?" *Journal of Political Economy* 94 (April 1986): 297–320.

Setting the Efficiency Wage

Many studies have adapted this argument to explain a number of important phenomena in modern, industrialized labor markets.[34] It is easy to illustrate the firm's choice of the profit-maximizing efficiency wage. For a given level of employment, the relationship between the firm's output and the firm's wage is given by the total product curve in Figure 11-5. The fact that this total product curve is upward sloping indicates that—for a given level of employment—the workers produce more output the better they are paid. In short, this total product curve embodies the notion that a worker's productivity and work effort depend on the wage. The firm's output might first rise very rapidly as the wage increases. Eventually, the firm encounters diminishing returns as it keeps increasing the wage, and the total product curve becomes concave. The slope of the total product curve is the marginal product of a wage increase, or MP_w. The concavity of the total product curve implies that this marginal product eventually declines.

What wage should the firm pay to maximize profits? Consider the straight line in Figure 11-5 that emanates from the origin and that is tangent to the total product curve at point X. It is easy to calculate the slope of this straight line. Recall that the slope of a line equals the change in the variable plotted on the vertical axis divided by the change in the variable plotted on the horizontal axis. Let's calculate the change that occurs as we move from the origin (where output and wages are both equal to zero) to point X, where the firm produces q^e units of output and pays a wage equal to w^e dollars. The slope is given by

$$\text{Slope of straight line} = \frac{\Delta \text{ in vertical axis}}{\Delta \text{ in horizontal axis}} = \frac{q^e - 0}{w^e - 0} = \frac{q^e}{w^e} \quad (11\text{-}1)$$

The slope of the straight line emanating from the origin, therefore, is equal to the average product of a dollar paid to workers. For example, suppose that, at point X, the firm produces 100 units of output and pays a wage of $5. The slope of the straight line is then equal to 20 at that point. On average, each dollar paid out to workers yields 20 units of output.

It turns out that the efficiency wage is the wage at which the slope of the total product curve (that is, $\Delta q/\Delta w$, or marginal product) equals the slope of the straight line emanating from the origin, or the average product. We can write the equilibrium condition as

$$\frac{\Delta q}{\Delta w} = \frac{q}{w} \quad (11\text{-}2)$$

The efficiency wage, therefore, is w^e. The intuition behind this condition is better understood if we rewrite as an elasticity, or

$$\frac{\Delta q}{\Delta w} \times \frac{w}{q} = \frac{\%\Delta q}{\%\Delta w} = 1 \quad (11\text{-}3)$$

[34] The literature began with a study by Robert Solow, "Another Possible Source of Wage Stickiness," *Journal of Macroeconomics* 1 (Winter 1979): 79–82. For a survey of this literature, see Andrew Weiss, *Efficiency Wages: Models of Unemployment, Layoffs, and Wage Dispersion*, Princeton, NJ: Princeton University Press, 1990.

FIGURE 11-5   The Determination of the Efficiency Wage

The total product curve indicates how the firm's output depends on the wage the firm pays its workers. The efficiency wage is given by point X, where the marginal product of the wage (the slope of the total product curve) equals the average product of the wage (the slope of the line from the origin). The efficiency wage maximizes the firm's profits.

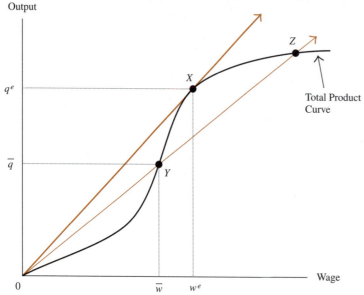

The efficiency wage, therefore, is the wage at which a 1 percent increase in the wage increases output by exactly 1 percent. To see why this is the wage at which the firm maximizes profits, suppose the firm chose to offer its workers another wage in Figure 11-5, such as wage $\bar{w}$ at point Y. At that wage, the slope of the total product curve is steeper than the slope of the straight line emanating from the origin. In other words, the marginal product of an increase in the wage exceeds the average product, so that $\Delta q/\Delta w > q/w$. If we rewrite this condition as an elasticity, we get that, at point Y,

$$\frac{\Delta q}{\Delta w} \times \frac{w}{q} = \frac{\%\Delta q}{\%\Delta w} > 1 \qquad (11\text{-}4)$$

In other words, a 1-percentage-point increase in the wage leads to an even larger increase in the firm's output. Therefore, the firm is better off by granting the wage increase. If the firm were to set the wage "too high," such as choosing point Z, the opposite restriction would hold: A 1 percent increase in the wage would increase output by less than 1 percent. In other words, the firm should refrain from granting that large a wage increase.

The efficiency wage, therefore, is the wage at which the elasticity of output with respect to the wage is exactly equal to 1. *A profit-maximizing firm will set this wage regardless of the value of the competitive wage determined outside the firm.* Because the efficiency wage will have to exceed the competitive wage (otherwise the firm would attract no workers), the firm has an oversupply of labor. At the efficiency wage, therefore, more workers want to work at the firm than the firm is willing to hire. The firm, however, will not want to reduce the wage. After all, the efficiency wage w^e is *the* profit-maximizing wage. A reduction in the wage would reduce worker effort by more than it reduces the payroll, lowering profits. Because efficiency wages attract an oversupply of workers, some workers will be involuntarily unemployed. This important implication of the model will be discussed in detail in Chapter 12.

In sum, the efficiency wage model indicates that the behavior of a profit-maximizing competitive firm is no longer confined to simply deciding how many workers to hire. A firm also must now decide what wage to pay. If the firm sets the wage too low, it saves on labor costs, but it will have an unproductive workforce. If the firm sets the wage too high, it will have high payroll costs but also a higher level of output. Note that in choosing the efficiency wage, the profit-maximizing firm will ignore the labor market conditions existing outside the firm. Instead, the firm considers how a wage increase in *this* firm influences worker effort and chooses the wage accordingly. Because different firms have different effort and production functions, different firms may choose to pay different efficiency wages.

Why Is There a Link between Wages and Productivity?

The link between wages and productivity illustrated by the total product curve in Figure 11-5 might arise for a number of distinct reasons.[35] A high wage makes it costly for workers to shirk. If a shirking worker is caught and fired, she loses her high-paying job and may become unemployed. The fear of unemployment, therefore, keeps the worker in line.

Second, higher wages might influence the "sociology" of the workplace. In particular, people who are well paid might work harder even if there is no threat of dismissal. Workers in these firms view the high wage as a gift from the employer and feel obligated to repay the gift by working harder.

Third, high-wage workers are less likely to quit. The lower turnover rates in firms paying efficiency wages reduce turnover costs and minimize the disruption that occurs when trained workers leave a production line and new workers are trained. Efficiency wages, therefore, reduce the quit rate and increase output and profits.[36]

Finally, firms paying efficiency wages might get a select pool of workers. Consider a firm offering the low competitive wage. Only workers who have reservation wages below this wage will accept job offers from this firm. High-ability workers will tend to have higher reservation wages and, hence, will reject job offers from this firm. Low wages,

[35] Carl Shapiro and Joseph E. Stiglitz, "Equilibrium Unemployment as a Worker Discipline Device," *American Economic Review* 74 (June 1984): 433–444; George A. Akerlof, "Labor Contracts as a Partial Gift Exchange," *Quarterly Journal of Economics* 97 (November 1982): 543–569; and Gary Charness and Peter Kuhn, "Does Pay Inequality Affect Worker Effort? Experimental Evidence," *Journal of Labor Economics* 25 (October 2007): 693–723. A critical survey of the arguments used to motivate efficiency wage models is given by H. Lorne Carmichael, "Efficiency Wage Models of Unemployment—One View," *Economic Inquiry* 28 (April 1990): 269–295. For a more sympathetic appraisal, see Lawrence F. Katz, "Efficiency Wage Theories: A Partial Evaluation," *NBER Macroeconomics Annual* (1986): 235–276. Experimental evidence on the link between wages and effort is given by Ernst Fehr and Lorenz Goette, "Do Workers Work More if Wages Are High? Evidence from a Randomized Field Experiment," *American Economic Review* 97 (March 2007): 298–317.

[36] The evidence suggests that high-wage firms are also the firms where turnover can be potentially very costly; see Carl M. Campbell III, "Do Firms Pay Efficiency Wages? Evidence with Data at the Firm Level," *Journal of Labor Economics* 11 (July 1993): 442–470.

The Ford Motor Company was founded in 1903. In 1908, it employed 450 employees and produced 10,607 automobiles. For the most part, Ford's initial workforce was composed of skilled craftsmen. Automobile parts were often produced by outside shops and the Ford craftsmen devoted a lot of time to assembling those parts into a finished automobile. Between 1908 and 1914, the character of the Ford Motor Company changed drastically. The first assembly-built car, the Model T, was introduced and the Ford Motor Company produced little else. Model T parts were made with sufficiently high precision that they could be fitted together by workers with little skill. By 1913, Ford employed 14,000 workers and produced 250,000 cars. The workforce became three-quarters foreign born, mostly from the rural regions of southern and eastern Europe.

A contemporary description of the tasks conducted by these workers is revealing: "Division of labor has been carried on to such a point that an overwhelming majority of the jobs consist of a very few simple operations. In most cases a complete mastery of the movements does not take more than five to ten minutes." The boredom and drudgery took its toll on the workers. Annual turnover at the Ford plant was nearly 370 percent in 1913. Put differently, Ford had to hire 50,448 persons to maintain an average labor force of 13,623 workers. In addition, the absenteeism rate was nearly 10 percent daily.

On January 5, 1914, the Ford Motor Company decided to disregard the wage and employment conditions that had been presumably set in the competitive labor market and unilaterally reduced the length of the workday from nine to eight hours and more than doubled the wage from $2.34 to $5.00 per day. Immediately following the announcement, over 10,000 people lined up outside the Ford plants looking for work. The outcome of this "new-and-improved" employment contract was immediate and dramatic. By 1915, the turnover rate had dropped to 16 percent, the absenteeism rate had dropped to 2.5 percent, productivity per worker had increased between 40 and 70 percent, and profits had increased by about 20 percent. It seems, therefore, that the Ford Motor Company benefited greatly by "discovering" efficiency wages.

Source: Daniel M. G. Raff and Lawrence H. Summers, "Did Henry Ford Pay Efficiency Wages?" *Journal of Labor Economics* 5 (October 1987, Part 2): S57–S86.

therefore, lead to adverse selection. A firm that pays efficiency wages attracts a more qualified pool of workers, increasing the productivity and profits of the firm.[37]

Evidence on Efficiency Wages

A lot of evidence indicates that there exist permanent wage differentials across firms, with some firms paying above-average wages and other firms paying below-average wages to workers of comparable skills. A case study of the fast-food industry argues that wage differentials across firms in this industry can be explained by the efficiency wage hypothesis.[38] Fast-food restaurants in the United States are usually owned by local franchises, but the national company also owns a substantial number. For example, 15 percent of Burger King restaurants and 25 percent of McDonald's restaurants are company owned. It turns out that workers employed in company-owned fast-food restaurants earn about 9 percent more than workers employed in restaurants that are locally franchised. This result can be

[37] The case for the positive relation between wages and productivity may be weakened if workers have a "vocation" for a particular line of work; see Anthony Heyes, "The Economics of Vocation or 'Why is a Badly Paid Nurse a Good Nurse'?" *Journal of Health Economics* 24 (May 2005): 561–569.

[38] Alan B. Krueger, "Ownership, Agency and Wages: An Examination of Franchising in the Fast-Food Industry," *Quarterly Journal of Economics* 106 (February 1991): 75–101.

interpreted in terms of the efficiency wage model: It is easier for the owners of the local franchise to supervise their employees, so there is less need to "buy" worker cooperation through higher wages.

There is also evidence that shirking-related employee problems are reduced when firms pay higher wages. A study of a large manufacturing firm in the United States indicates that fewer workers are dismissed for disciplinary reasons when the firm pays a higher wage.[39] In particular, a 10 percent increase in the wage reduced the rate at which workers were dismissed for disciplinary reasons by about 5 percent.

Interindustry Wage Differentials

The efficiency wage hypothesis also has been used to explain the huge interindustry wage differentials that exist among comparable workers.[40] Table 11-2 reports the log wage differential (which is approximately the percentage wage differential) between the typical person in an industry and the typical worker in the labor market who has the same socioeconomic background (such as age, sex, race, and education). Workers employed in metal mining or railroads earn around 30 percent more than the average worker in the economy, whereas workers employed in hardware stores or child care services earn around 25 percent less. It also has been found that these interindustry wage differentials are very persistent over time, so that industries that paid high wages in the early 1970s also paid high wages in the 1990s.

The competitive model argues that these interindustry wage differentials must reflect either differences in job characteristics or differences in unobserved worker traits. For example, it might be that jobs in some industries are more pleasant or safer. The "worse" jobs would then have to pay higher wages to attract workers who dislike high levels of pollution or risk. Workers also might sort themselves across industries on the basis of their abilities. If firms in the motor vehicle industry really do pay about 50 percent more than hardware retail stores, employers in the auto industry can sift through the job applicants. Workers in high-wage industries, therefore, would be more able and more productive. As a result, the ability sorting of workers across industries generates interindustry wage differentials, and these differentials may have nothing to do with efficiency wages.

In contrast to these competitive explanations, the efficiency wage model stresses that the interindustry wage differentials are "real." In other words, the differentials do not reflect the compensation paid to workers who are working in unpleasant or risky jobs or who are more productive. Rather, efficiency wages exist because firms in some industries find it

[39] Peter Cappelli and Keith Chauvin, "An Interplant Test of the Efficiency Wage Hypothesis," *Quarterly Journal of Economics* 106 (August 1991): 769–788. Additional evidence of efficiency wages is reported in Enrico Moretti and Jeffrey M. Perloff, "Wages, Deferred Payments, and Direct Incentives in Agriculture," *American Journal of Agricultural Economics* 84 (November 2002): 1144–1155; and Magnus Allgulin and Tore Ellingsen, "Monitoring and Pay," *Journal of Labor Economics* 20 (April 2002): 201–216.

[40] Alan B. Krueger and Lawrence H. Summers, "Efficiency Wages and the Inter-Industry Wage Structure," *Econometrica* 56 (March 1988): 259–293. See also Erica L. Groshen, "Sources of Intra-Industry Wage Dispersion: How Much Do Employers Matter?" *Quarterly Journal of Economics* 106 (August 1991): 869–884; Steven G. Allen, "Updated Notes on the Interindustry Wage Structure, 1890–1990," *Industrial and Labor Relations Review* 48 (January 1995): 305–321; and Paul Chen and Per-Anders Edin, "Efficiency Wages and Industry Wage Differentials: A Comparison across Methods of Pay," *Review of Economics & Statistics* 84 (November 2002): 617–631.

TABLE 11-2   The Interindustry Wage Structure

Source: Alan B. Krueger and Lawrence H. Summers, "Efficiency Wages and the Inter-Industry Wage Structure," *Econometrica* 56 (March 1988): 281–287.

Industry	Log Wage Differential between the Typical Worker in an Industry and a Comparably Skilled Worker in the Economy
Mining	
Metal mining	0.296
Crude petroleum, natural gas extraction	0.256
Construction	0.129
Manufacturing	
Meat products	−0.028
Dairy products	0.176
Apparel and accessories	−0.137
Tires and inner tubes	0.306
Motor vehicles	0.244
Transportation	
Railroads	0.268
Taxicab services	−0.203
Wholesale trade	
Electrical goods	0.123
Farm products	−0.109
Retail trade	
Hardware stores	−0.304
Department stores	−0.190
Finance, insurance, and real estate	
Banking	0.048
Real estate	0.004
Business and repair services	
Advertising	0.092
Automotive-repair shops	−0.058
Professional and related services	
Offices of physicians	−0.076
Child care services	−0.275

profitable to pay more than the competitive wage (perhaps because it is hard to monitor output or because there are high turnover costs), and firms in other industries do not.

Many studies have attempted to determine if the interindustry wage differentials can be attributed to differences in job and worker characteristics. The evidence, however, is mixed and confusing.[41] It seems that the interindustry wage differentials remain even if we

---

[41] See Krueger and Summers, "Efficiency Wages and the Inter-Industry Wage Structure"; Kevin M. Murphy and Robert Topel, "Efficiency Wages Reconsidered: Theory and Evidence," in Y. Weiss and G. Fishelson, editors, *Advances in the Theory and Measurement of Unemployment*, New York: Macmillan, 1990, pp. 204–240.

compare jobs that are equally risky or pleasant, so the theory of compensating wage differentials cannot account for the sizable wage gaps documented in Table 11-2. Moreover, if the interindustry wage differentials were solely due to differences in worker ability, we would not observe workers in low-wage industries quitting more often than workers in high-wage industries. After all, it would be very unlikely that a low-ability worker could get a job in the high-wage sector. In fact, workers in low-wage industries *do* have higher quit rates, suggesting that they perceive the high wages available in other firms as potential employment opportunities.

At the same time, however, it seems that workers *do* sort themselves across industries. Some studies, for example, have tracked the earnings of workers as they switch jobs across industries. If efficiency wages explain the interindustry wage differentials, workers who move from a low-wage industry to a high-wage industry should experience a sizable wage increase. If the interindustry wage differentials reflect differences in worker ability, a low-ability worker moving from a low-wage to a high-wage industry should not get much of a wage increase. One influential study, which "tracked" workers across industries, concluded that perhaps as much as 70 percent of interindustry wage differentials might be due to the sorting of able workers in high-wage industries.[42]

Efficiency Wages and Dual Labor Markets

Suppose that there are two sectors in the economy. In one sector, a worker's output is hard to observe and monitoring is costly. This sector might be composed of workers in software development teams or of professionals whose daily output is not easily measurable. This sector will tend to consist of jobs where workers have a lot of responsibility and take many independent actions. Firms in this sector will probably want to set up a compensation system that elicits the "right" effort from the workers, and these firms might choose to pay efficiency wages. The other sector in the economy consists of firms where workers perform repetitive and monotonous tasks. As a result, these workers can be supervised easily and their productivity monitored constantly. Firms need not pay high wages to discourage worker shirking in these jobs. Any type of worker misbehavior is immediately detected, and the worker is fired.

The efficiency wage hypothesis, therefore, generates an economy with **dual labor markets** or segmented labor markets.[43] One sector, called the primary sector, offers high wages, good working conditions, employment stability, and chances for promotion. The other sector, called the secondary sector, offers low wages, poor working conditions, high turnover, and few chances for promotion. In a competitive model, the differences between the two sectors would eventually vanish as workers move from the low-wage sector to the high-wage sector. Efficiency wages, however, prevent this equilibrating process. Firms in the high-wage sector will lose money if they lower the wage because output in that sector is hard to monitor and workers would then shirk their responsibilities.

As we showed earlier, there is evidence that some sectors of the economy pay relatively high wages, whereas other sectors pay lower wages. There is also evidence supporting the

[42] Murphy and Topel, "Efficiency Wages Reconsidered: Theory and Evidence."

[43] Jeremy I. Bulow and Lawrence H. Summers, "A Theory of Dual Labor Markets with Application to Industrial Policy, Discrimination, and Keynesian Unemployment," *Journal of Labor Economics* 3 (July 1986): 376–414; see also Peter Doeringer and Michael Piore, *Internal Labor Markets and Manpower Analysis,* Lexington, MA: DC Heath, 1971.

hypothesis that the characteristics of jobs in the high-wage industries resemble the characteristics we would expect to find in the primary sector, whereas the characteristics of jobs in low-wage industries resemble those we would expect to find in the secondary sector.[44] However, the debate over whether these differences are best understood in terms of a two-sector labor market (with little worker mobility occurring across sectors) or in terms of a competitive framework has not been resolved.

The Bonding Critique

The key implications of the efficiency wage model depend on the assumption that there are *permanent* wage differentials across firms, despite the fact that low-wage (or unemployed) workers would rather hold high-wage jobs. An important criticism of this assumption is known as the **bonding critique**.[45]

Firms can use many types of compensation schemes, such as tournaments, upward-sloping age-earnings profiles, and piece rates, to encourage workers not to shirk on the job. All of these mechanisms operate within the confines of a competitive market. Industries that pay too small a piece rate or award too small a first prize to the winner of a tournament encourage other entrepreneurs to enter the industry, increasing the demand for and salaries of workers and forcing the industry back to a normal level of profits. If the industry pays too high a piece rate or offers too big a prize, firms lose money and the compensation of workers falls.

Efficiency wages also provide incentives for workers not to shirk. The efficiency wage model, however, differs fundamentally from the tournaments and piece-rate models. In particular, *firms determine the efficiency wage without regard to market conditions.* As a result, firms that choose to pay very high wages will have too many job applicants. Critics of the efficiency wage hypothesis argue that this cannot be the end of the story. The job seekers should be willing to take actions that would "buy" them a job at the firm. In other words, workers who want a job in high-wage industries should be willing to pay employers for the right to be employed in such jobs. Job applicants, for instance, could post a bond at the time of hiring. If firms caught the workers shirking, the firm could dismiss the worker and keep the bond. If the employment relationship worked out, the firm would return the bond to the worker (plus interest) at the time of retirement. The competitive market would set the amount of the bond such that workers, in the end, would be indifferent between a job in a high-wage industry and a job in a low-wage industry. In a sense, the efficiency wage model works because it introduces a "sticky wage" assumption into the labor market.

In fact, workers seldom put up bonds to get jobs. As we saw earlier, however, upward-sloping age-earnings profiles or other forms of delayed-compensation schemes can play exactly the same role. Workers would accept wages lower than their value of marginal

[44] See William T. Dickens and Kevin Lang, "A Test of Dual Labor Market Theory," *American Economic Review* 75 (December 1985): 792–805.

[45] A good exposition of the bonding critique is given by Carmichael, "Efficiency Wage Models of Unemployment—One View"; see also Edward P. Lazear, "Compensation, Productivity, and the New Economics of Personnel," in David Lewin, Olivia S. Mitchell, and Peter D. Sherer, editors, *Research Frontiers in Industrial Relations and Human Resources,* Madison, WI: Industrial Relations and Research Association, 1992, pp. 341–380.

product during the initial years on the job and would be repaid in later years. As workers compete for jobs in high-wage industries, the wage profile in high-wage industries would tilt and become steeper. In the end, workers would again be indifferent between jobs in high-wage and low-wage industries because the present value of earnings in all jobs would be equalized. The bonding critique, therefore, suggests that efficiency wage models would self-destruct in the long run.

Labor economists are still debating the relevance of efficiency wage models and the validity of the bonding critique. As a result, we do not yet know if the bonding critique makes efficiency wages much less relevant in real-world labor markets.

Summary

- Piece rates are used by firms when it is cheap to monitor the output of the workers.

- Piece-rate compensation systems attract the most-able workers and elicit high levels of effort from these workers. Workers in these firms, however, may stress quantity over quality and may dislike the possibility that incomes fluctuate significantly over time.

- Some firms award promotions on the basis of the relative ranking of the workers. A tournament might be used when it is cheaper to observe the relative ranking of a worker than the absolute level of the worker's productivity.

- Workers allocate more effort to the firm when the prize spread between winners and losers in the tournament is very large. A large prize spread, however, also creates incentives for workers to sabotage the efforts of other players.

- There is a positive correlation between the compensation of CEOs and the performance of the firm, but the correlation is weak. It is unlikely, therefore, that CEOs have the "right" incentives to take only those actions that benefit the owners of the firm.

- Upward-sloping age-earnings profiles might arise because delaying the compensation of workers until later in the life cycle encourages them to allocate more effort to the firm. A delayed-compensation contract also implies that, at some point in the future, the contract must be terminated, thus explaining the existence of mandatory retirement in the labor market.

- Some firms might want to pay wages above the competitive wage in order to motivate the workforce to be more productive. The efficiency wage is set such that the elasticity of output with respect to the wage is equal to 1.

- Efficiency wages create a pool of workers who are involuntarily unemployed.

Key Concepts

Review Questions

1. What factors determine whether a firm offers a piece-rate or a time-rate compensation system?

2. Discuss how workers who differ in their innate abilities sort themselves across piece-rate and time-rate jobs. Also describe how the two compensation systems elicit different levels of effort from the workers.

3. If piece rates elicit more effort from workers, why do firms not use this method of compensation more often?

4. Show how a large prize spread in a tournament elicits a higher level of work effort from the participants.

5. Discuss some of the problems encountered when firms allocate sizable rewards to the winner of the tournament.

6. Why is the principal-agent problem relevant to understanding how CEOs should be compensated?

7. Discuss how upward-sloping age-earnings profiles can elicit more effort from workers.

8. Why is there mandatory retirement in many countries?

9. Describe how the firm sets an efficiency wage above the competitive level. Why are there no market forces forcing the profit-maximizing firm to reduce the wage to the competitive level?

10. What factors create the link between wages and productivity that is at the heart of efficiency wage models?

11. What is the bonding critique of efficiency wage models?

Problems

11-1. Suppose there are 100 workers in an economy with two firms. All workers are worth $35 per hour to firm A but differ in their productivity at firm B. Worker 1 has a value of marginal product of $1 per hour at firm B, worker 2 has a value of marginal product of $2 per hour at firm B, and so on. Firm A pays its workers a time-rate of $35 per hour, while firm B pays its workers a piece rate. How will the workers sort themselves across firms? Suppose a decrease in demand for both firms' output reduces the value of every worker to either firm by half. How will workers now sort themselves across firms?

11-2. Taxicab companies in the United States typically own a large number of cabs and licenses; taxicab drivers then pay a daily fee to the owner to lease a cab for the day. In return, the drivers keep their fares (so that, in essence, they receive a 100 percent commission on their sales). Why did this type of compensation system develop in the taxicab industry?

11-3. A firm hires two workers to assemble bicycles. The firm values each assembly at $12. Charlie's marginal cost of allocating effort to the production process is $MC = 4N$, where N is the number of bicycles assembled per hour. Donna's marginal cost is $MC = 6N$.

   a. If the firm pays piece rates, what will be each worker's hourly wage?

   b. Suppose the firm pays a time rate of $15 per hour and fires any worker who does not assemble at least 1.5 bicycles per hour. How many bicycles will each worker assemble in an eight-hour day?

11-4. All workers start working for a particular firm when they are 20 years old. The value of each worker's marginal product is $18 per hour. In order to prevent shirking on the job, a delayed-compensation scheme is imposed. In particular, the wage level at every level of seniority is determined by

$$\text{Wage} = \$10 + (0.4 \times \text{Years in the firm})$$

Suppose also that the discount rate is zero for all workers. What will be the mandatory retirement age under the compensation scheme? (Hint: Use a spreadsheet.)

11-5. Suppose a firm's technology requires it to hire 100 workers regardless of the wage level. The firm, however, has found that worker productivity is greatly affected by its wage. The historical relationship between the wage level and the firm's output is given by

Wage Rate	Units of Output
$ 8.00	65
$10.00	80
$11.25	90
$12.00	97
$12.50	102

What wage level should a profit-maximizing firm choose? What happens to the efficiency wage if there is an increase in the demand for the firm's output?

11-6. Consider three firms identical in all aspects except their monitoring efficiency, which cannot be changed. Even though the cost of monitoring is the same across the three firms, shirkers at Firm A are identified almost for certain; shirkers at Firm B have a slightly greater chance of not being found out; and shirkers at Firm C have the greatest chance of avoiding identification. If all three firms pay efficiency wages to keep their workers from shirking, which firm will pay the greatest efficiency wage? Which firm will pay the smallest efficiency wage?

11-7. Consider three firms identical in all aspects (including the probability with which they discover a shirker), except that monitoring costs vary across the firms. Monitoring workers is very expensive at Firm A, less expensive at Firm B, and cheapest at Firm C. If all three firms pay efficiency wages to keep their workers from shirking, which firm will pay the greatest efficiency wage? Which firm will pay the smallest efficiency wage?

11-8. a. The analysis of Figure 11-5 does not mention the price of output. What is implicitly being assumed about the product market in the analysis?

b. Instead of thinking of output as depending on the wage level, the analysis in Figure 11-5 can be altered to think of revenue as depending on the wage level. Redraw Figure 11-5 under this approach. Demonstrate the optimal efficiency wage in your graph. Characterize in words the optimal efficiency wage.

11-9. Consider a firm that offers the following employee benefit. When a worker turns 60 years old, she is given a one-time opportunity to quit her job, and in return the firm will pay her a bonus of 1.5 times her annual salary and pay her health insurance premiums until she is eligible for Medicare.

a. What problem is the firm trying to solve by offering this benefit?

b. Why is the health insurance premium portion of the benefit important in the United States?

c. For what industries might one expect such opportunities to be presented to workers?

11-10. a. Why would a firm ever choose to offer profit-sharing to its employees in place of paying piece rates?

b. Describe the free-riding problem in a profit-sharing compensation scheme. How might the workers of a firm "solve" the free-riding problem?

11-11. a. How does the offering of stock options to CEOs attempt to align CEO incentives with shareholder incentives?

b. Enron was a company that was ruined in part because of the stock options offered to upper management. Explain.

c. In addition to accounting reforms, how might stock options be changed to try to prevent situations like what happened at Enron from occurring in the future?

11-12. a. Personal injury lawyers typically do not charge a client unless they obtain a monetary award on their client's behalf. Why?

b. What would happen to the number of lawsuits if lawyers had to charge an hourly rate and could not charge a fixed percentage of the award?

11-13. The relationship between a worker's daily wage, w, and her daily output, q, is $q = 0.1w^2 - 0.0005w^3$ so that the worker's marginal product with respect to her wage is $MP_w = 0.2w - 0.0015w^2$. What is the optimal efficiency daily wage for the firm to pay? How much output will the worker produce each day? How much profit does the firm earn on the worker's output each day if the price of output is fixed at $0.80 per unit?

11-14. Economists and psychologists have long wondered how worker effort relates to wages. Specifically, the question is whether worker effort responds to increased wages alone or whether effort also responds to relative wages.

a. Design a classroom experiment that would allow you to quantify the relationship between effort, reward, and relative reward.

b. Explain how the data you collect can be used to identify both relationships. What do you think you would find?

c. Suppose a consulting firm intends to estimate the following regression for a firm:

$$output_i = \beta_0 + \beta_1 wage_i + \beta_2 relwage_i$$

where $output_i$ is worker i's hourly production, $wage_i$ is worker i's hourly wage, and $relwage_i$ is the ratio of worker i's wage to the publicly known average wage at the firm. How can the results of the regression be used to determine the importance of wage levels and relative wages in the production process?

11-15. Some compensation schemes include a signing bonus while others include the potential to receive annual year-end bonuses.

a. From the firm's perspective, what are the benefits of offering a signing bonus? What are the benefits of offering a year-end bonus?

b. If a firm pays its sales staff a piece rate and a year-end bonus, why will it be the case that the rate of pay per piece is less than the market value? Why will the sales staff willingly accept such an arrangement?

c. How does the existence of year-end bonuses support the bonding critique?

Selected Readings

Brian J. Hall and Jeffrey B. Liebman, "Are CEOs Really Paid Like Bureaucrats?" *Quarterly Journal of Economics* 113 (August 1998): 653–692.

Michael C. Jensen and Kevin J. Murphy, "Performance Pay and Top-Management Incentives," *Journal of Political Economy* 98 (April 1990): 225–264.

Alan B. Krueger and Lawrence H. Summers, "Efficiency Wages and the Inter-Industry Wage Structure," *Econometrica* 56 (March 1988): 259–293.

Edward P. Lazear, "Why Is There Mandatory Retirement?" *Journal of Political Economy* 87 (December 1979): 1261–1264.

Edward P. Lazear, "Performance Pay and Productivity," *American Economic Review* 90 (December 2000): 1346–1361.

Edward P. Lazear and Sherwin Rosen, "Rank-Order Tournaments as Optimum Labor Contracts," *Journal of Political Economy* 89 (October 1981): 841–864.

Jay C. Hartzell, Christopher A. Parsons, and David L. Yermack, "Is A Higher Calling Enough? Incentive Compensation in the Church," *Journal of Labor Economics* 28 (July 2010): 509–539.

Thomas Lemieux, W. Bentley MacLeod and Daniel Parent, "Performance Pay and Wage Inequality," *Quarterly Journal of Economics* 124 (February 2009): 1–49.

Daniel M. G. Raff and Lawrence H. Summers, "Did Henry Ford Pay Efficiency Wages?" *Journal of Labor Economics* 5 (October 1987, Part 2): S57–S86.

Beck A. Taylor and Justin G. Trogdon, "Losing to Win: Tournament Incentives in the National Basketball Association," *Journal of Labor Economics* 20 (January 2002): 23–41.

Web Links

Forbes **Magazine publishes various lists that include the "Best Places for Singles," the "Best Beach Resorts," and an annual summary of executive pay that compares CEO pay with firm performance: www.forbes.com/lists.**

The Web site of Lincoln Electric describes their incentive pay system: www.lincolnelectric.com/corporate/career/default.asp.

Chapter 12

Unemployment

It's a recession when your neighbor loses his job; it's a depression when you lose your own.

—*Harry S. Truman*

Why are some workers unemployed? This fundamental question raises some of the thorniest issues in economics. As we have seen, a competitive equilibrium equates the supply of workers with the demand for workers. The equilibrium wage clears the market, and all persons looking for work can find jobs.

Despite this implication of equilibrium, unemployment can be a widespread phenomenon in some labor markets. Although the unemployment rate in the United States had been relatively low for one or two decades (for instance, it stood at 4 percent in 2000), it began to rise rapidly as economic conditions deteriorated in 2008. By 2010, the U.S. unemployment rate had risen to 9.6 percent. Moreover, the length of unemployment spells increased rapidly. By 2010, nearly 43.3 percent of the unemployed had been without work for at least 27 weeks.

In fact, the unemployment rate had been substantially higher in many European countries in recent decades. In 2000, for instance, the unemployment rate stood at 9.1 percent in France and 7.8 percent in Germany. However, the severity and differential impact of the current recession dramatically changed the relative rankings, with the unemployment rate in the United States now reaching and often surpassing European levels. In 2010, the unemployment rate in France was 9.4 percent in France and 7.2 percent in Germany.

It is difficult to understand the existence and persistence of large pools of unemployed workers in terms of the typical model of supply and demand unless (1) firms pay wages that are above the equilibrium level and there is an excess supply of labor and (2) wages are "sticky" and cannot be driven down to the equilibrium level.

Workers are unemployed for many reasons, and policymakers usually worry more about some types of unemployment than about other types. At any time, for instance, many persons are "in between" jobs. They have either just quit or been laid off, or they have just entered (or reentered) the labor market. It takes time to learn about and locate available job opportunities. Therefore, even a well-functioning market economy, where the number of available jobs equals the number of persons looking for work, will exhibit some unemployment as workers search for jobs.

Put differently, the equilibrium level of unemployment will not be zero. This type of "frictional" unemployment, however, cannot explain why nearly 25 percent of the

U.S. workforce was unemployed at the nadir of the Great Depression in 1933 or why the unemployment rate hit 9.6 percent in 2010. Many workers seem to be unemployed not because they are in between jobs but because of a fundamental imbalance between the supply and the demand for workers.

This chapter shows how job search activities generate unemployment in a competitive economy and identifies some of the factors that can prevent the market from clearing— even after job search activities are accounted for. Economists have been particularly ingenious at creating stories of how unemployment arises in competitive markets. Each particular theory can explain certain aspects of the unemployment problem. No single theory, however, provides a convincing explanation of why unemployment sometimes afflicts a large fraction of the workforce, of why unemployment targets some groups more than others, and of why some workers remain unemployed for a very long time.

12-1   Unemployment in the United States

Figure 12-1 shows the historical trend in the U.S. unemployment rate since 1900. The unemployment rate has fluctuated dramatically over time; it reached a peak of about 25 percent in 1933 and lows of about 1 percent in 1906 and 1944. The unemployment rate gives the fraction of labor force participants looking for work. Many persons who would like to work might have withdrawn from the labor force because they could not find jobs. The count of the unemployed misses these discouraged workers. As a result, the official unemployment rate may underestimate the true scope of the unemployment problem, particularly during severe economic downturns when a large pool of discouraged workers might be "waiting out" the recession.

The data summarized in Figure 12-1 also reveal that from the 1950s through the 1980s, there was a slight upward drift in the unemployment rate. In the 1950s, the average

FIGURE 12-1   **Unemployment in the United States, 1900–2010**

Sources: The pre-1948 unemployment rates are reported in Stanley Lebergott, "Annual Estimates of Unemployment in the United States, 1900–1950," *The Measurement and Behavior of Unemployment,* NBER Special Committee Conference Series No. 8, Princeton, NJ: Princeton University Press, 1957, pp. 213–239. The post-1948 rates are from U.S. Bureau of Labor Statistics, "Historical Data for the 'A' Tables of the Employment Situation Release," Table A-15, "Alternative Measures of Labor Underutilization," http://stats.bls.gov/cps/cpsatabs.htm. The unemployment rate refers to the population of persons aged 16 and over.

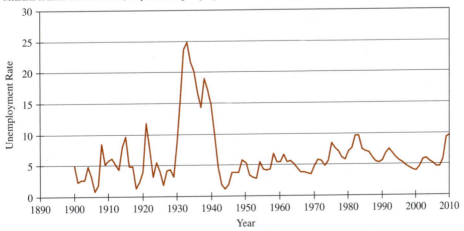

FIGURE 12-2 **Unemployment Rates by Education, 1970–2010**

Sources: U.S. Bureau of Labor Statistics, *Labor Force Statistics Derived from the Current Population Survey, 1948–87,* Bulletin 2307, Washington, DC: Government Printing Office, 1988, pp. 848–849; U.S. Bureau of the Census, *Statistical Abstract of the United States,* Washington, DC: Government Printing Office, various issues. The post-1992 data are from U.S. Bureau of Labor Statistics, "Historical Data for the 'A' Tables of the Employment Situation Release," Table A-4, "Labor Force Status of the Civilian Population 25 Years and Over by Educational Attainment," http://stats.bls.gov/cps/cpsatabs.htm. The unemployment rates refer to the population of persons aged 25 and over.

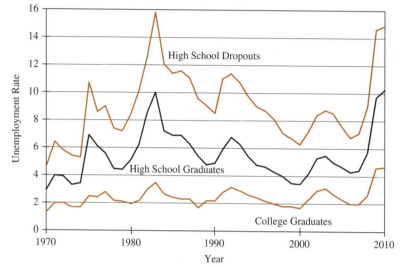

unemployment rate was 4.5 percent; during the 1960s it was 4.8 percent; during the 1970s it rose to 6.2 percent; and during the 1980s it rose further to 7.3 percent. This trend broke in the 1990s, when the unemployment rate fell to levels not seen in about 30 years. In 1998, the unemployment rate was just 4 percent.

The downward drift in the unemployment rate, however, abruptly stopped in 2008 when the United States entered a deep recession after a serious financial crisis. The very rapid rise in the unemployment rate after the financial crisis was remarkable, from 4.6 percent in 2007 to 9.6 percent in 2010, more than doubling the unemployment rate in just three years.

It is important to emphasize that the large jump in the unemployment rate was totally unexpected, among financial experts, policymakers, and economists. It is ironic to point out that a popular topic in macroeconomic research just prior to the financial crisis of 2008 was the attempt to understand how the United States had been able to "moderate" the volatility of business cycle activity, leading to a period that became known as the "Great Moderation." In a 2004 lecture, for example, Ben Bernanke (who would become the chairman of the U.S. Federal Reserve in 2006) noted that "one of the most striking features of the economic landscape over the past twenty years or so has been a substantial decline in macroeconomic volatility."

Who Are the Unemployed?

The fact that the unemployment rate in 2010 was 9.6 percent does not imply that each labor market participant had a 9.6 percent probability of being unemployed at a point in time during that calendar year. Unemployment is not an equal-opportunity employer. Instead, unemployment is concentrated among particular demographic groups and among workers in specific sectors of the economy. Figure 12-2 illustrates one key feature of unemployment in the United States: The unemployment rate is much higher for less-educated workers. In 2007, the unemployment rate of college graduates was 4.7 percent, as compared to 10.3 percent for high school graduates and 14.9 percent for high school dropouts.

Prior to the current recession, the "unemployment gap" between high-educated and low-educated workers first widened and then narrowed substantially. In 1970, for example, the unemployment rate of high school dropouts exceeded that of college graduates by only 3.3 percentage points. By 1985, however, the unemployment gap was 9 percentage points. By 2007, the gap had narrowed again to 5.1 percentage points. The current recession again led to a sizable widening of the gap, to 10.2 percentage points in 2010.

Education lowers unemployment rates for two distinct reasons. First, educated workers invest more in on-the-job training. Because specific training "marries" firms and workers, firms are less likely to lay off educated workers when they face adverse economic conditions. In addition, when educated workers switch jobs, they typically make the switch without suffering an intervening spell of unemployment. It seems as if educated workers are better informed or have better networks for learning about alternative job opportunities.

Table 12-1 reports unemployment rates by age, race, gender, and industry of employment. Younger workers are more likely to be unemployed than older workers.[1] The unemployment rate of teenagers is now 24 percent as compared to about 7 percent for workers aged 45 to 64. As we noted in the discussion of the economic impact of the minimum wage legislation, part of the higher unemployment rate of teenagers may be due to the adverse employment impact of the minimum wage.[2]

TABLE 12-1

Unemployment Rates in 2009, by Demographic Group and Industry

Source: U.S. Department of Commerce, *Statistical Abstract of the United States, 2011,* Washington, DC: Government Printing Office, 2011, Tables 621, 624.

Age:		Industry:	
16–19	24.3	Agriculture	14.3
20–24	14.7	Mining	11.6
25–34	9.9	Construction	19.0
35–44	7.9	Manufacturing	12.1
45–54	7.2	Information	9.2
55–64	6.6	Transportation and public utilities	8.9
		Retail trade	9.5
Race:		Finance, insurance, and real estate	6.4
White	8.5	Leisure and hospitality	11.7
Black	14.8	Professional and business services	10.8
Hispanic	12.1	Government	3.6
Gender:		All workers	4.6
Male	10.3		
Female	8.1		

[1] An interesting study of the link between the increase in the number of persons enrolled in the federal disability program and trends in unemployment is given by David H. Autor and Mark G. Duggan, "The Rise in the Disability Rolls and the Decline in Unemployment," *Quarterly Journal of Economics* 118 (February 2003): 157–205.

[2] An analysis of the consequences of youth unemployment is given by Thomas A. Mroz and Timothy H. Savage, "The Long-Term Effects of Youth Unemployment," *Journal of Human Resources* 41 (Spring 2006): 259–293.

The data also indicate that whites have lower unemployment rates than either blacks or Hispanics. The current recession has had a severe effect on the unemployment of minorities: 12.1 percent of Hispanics and 14.8 percent of African Americans are unemployed. The large black-white differential cannot be attributed to the lower schooling level of blacks. Historically, the racial gap in unemployment rates remains even if we compare black and white workers who have the same observable skills and who live in the same area.[3]

Until recently, women had higher unemployment rates than men. In 1983, for example, 9.8 percent of men and 15.3 percent of women were unemployed. It was typically argued that women had a higher unemployment rate because they were much more likely to be "on the move" either in between jobs or in and out of the labor market. These transition periods require women to look for work and increase their unemployment rate. By 2007, the gender gap in unemployment had disappeared; both groups had an unemployment rate of 4.6 percent. However, the current economic crisis, which has been labeled a "mancession" in some of the popular media, has broken with the historical pattern and led to a situation where men are more likely to be unemployed than women. In 2010, the unemployment rate was 10.3 percent for men and 8.1 percent for women. The reasons for this historic reversal in the gender unemployment gap are not known, although they may be partly caused by the declining fortunes of the manufacturing industry (which historically employs more men) and the growth of service industries (which employ more women).

Finally, the table shows that the unemployment rate varies greatly across industries. The unemployment rate for workers in construction is 19.0 percent, for workers in manufacturing it is 12.1 percent, and for workers in transportation and public utilities it is 8.9 percent.

There are four ways in which a worker can end up unemployed: Some workers lose their jobs due to layoffs or plant closings (or job losers); some workers leave their jobs (job leavers); some job seekers reenter the labor market after spending some time in the non-market sector (reentrants); and some job seekers are new to the job market, such as recent high school or college graduates (new entrants). As Figure 12-3 shows, the fraction of workers who are unemployed because they have lost their jobs (that is, the first category, job losers) hovered around 50 percent (with up-and-down blips) between 1980 and 2005. Because of the severity of the recent recession, this statistic now stands above 60 percent.

Figure 12-4 documents the fact that a larger fraction of the unemployed are likely to be in long-term unemployment spells. Even prior to the current recession, there had been an upward drift in the fraction of the unemployed who had been without work more than 26 weeks. In the early 1950s, for instance, only about 5 to 10 percent of unemployed workers were in spells lasting more than 26 weeks. By 2007, about 18 percent of the unemployed workers were in these long spells. The current recession led to a dramatic explosion in this number. By 2010, 43.3 percent of the unemployed are in long-term spells. Conversely, the notion that unemployment is best described by a short-term in-between jobs period is becoming increasingly irrelevant. Even prior to the current recession, there had been a noticeable downward drift in the fraction of unemployed persons who had been unemployed fewer than five weeks.

---

[3] Leslie S. Stratton, "Racial Differences in Men's Unemployment," *Industrial and Labor Relations Review* 46 (April 1993): 451–463.

FIGURE 12-3 **Unemployed Persons by Reason for Unemployment, 1967–2010 (as a percent of total unemployment)**

Source: U.S. Bureau of Labor Statistics, "Historical Data for the 'A' Tables of the Employment Situation Release," Table A-11, "Unemployed Persons by Reason of Unemployment," http://stats.bls.gov/cps/cpsatabs.htm. The population of unemployed includes all unemployed persons aged 16 or over.

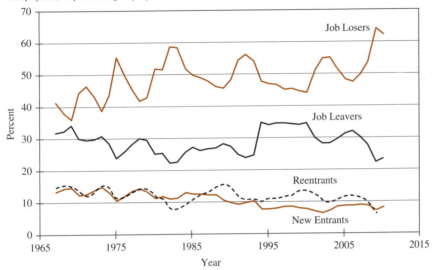

FIGURE 12-4 **Unemployed Persons by Duration of Unemployment, 1948–2010 (as a percent of total unemployment)**

Source: U.S. Bureau of Labor Statistics, "Historical Data for the 'A' Tables of the Employment Situation Release," Table A-12, "Unemployed Persons by Duration of Unemployment," http://stats.bls.gov/cps/cpsatabs.htm. The population of unemployed includes all unemployed persons aged 16 or over.

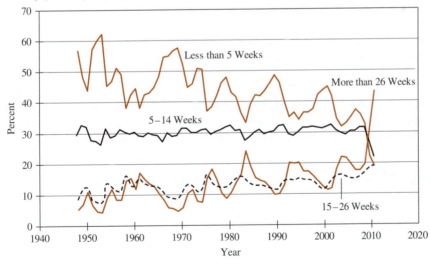

FIGURE 12-5   **Trends in Alternative Measures of the Unemployment Rate, 1994–2010**

Source: U.S. Bureau of Labor Statistics, "Historical Data for the 'A' Tables of the Employment Situation Release," Table A-15, "Alternative Measures of Labor Underutilization," http://stats.bls.gov/cps/cpsatabs.htm. The unemployment rate refers to the population of persons aged 16 and over.

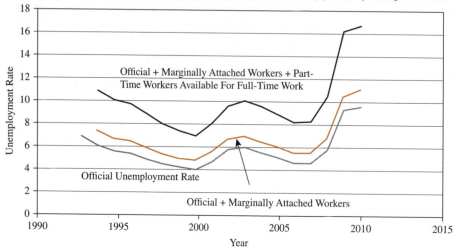

Finally, the unemployment rate gives the proportion of the labor force that is unemployed and looking for work. There also may be some discouraged workers—workers who gave up on their job search because they could not find any employment. The Bureau of Labor Statistics also publishes an alternative statistic that includes in the pool of unemployed any "marginally attached persons . . . who currently are neither working nor looking for work but indicate that they want and are available for a job and have looked for work sometime in the recent past." Figure 12-5 shows that the unemployment rate goes up by about 1 percentage point when the marginally attached are counted as unemployed.

A more sizable group is the "underemployed"—persons who "want and are available for full-time work but have had to settle for a part-time schedule." The inclusion of the underemployed in the numerator of the unemployment rate raises the unemployment rate by another 3 or 4 percentage points. In 2007, the official unemployment rate was 4.6 percent. The inclusion of the marginally attached and the underemployed increased the unemployment rate to 8.3 percent. The current recession, however, led to a particularly dramatic increase in the number of persons who are either marginally attached or underemployed. By 2010, 16.7 percent of workers could be classified as unemployed in this more general sense.

Residential Segregation and Black Unemployment

As we have seen, the unemployment rate of blacks is substantially higher than that of whites. Recent research has concluded that part of the racial gap in unemployment rates can be attributed to the very high levels of residential segregation experienced by blacks in the United States. Even though blacks make up only 11 percent of the population, the average black lives in a neighborhood that is 57 percent black. The spatial isolation of blacks

Theory at Work
THE LONG-TERM EFFECTS OF GRADUATING IN A RECESSION

Some of us are quite lucky. We somehow manage to time our birth so that the labor market is burning hot the year we happen to graduate from college. It's a seller's market—employers are actively trying to outbid each other to get our services. The wine-and-dining never ends. Some of us, however, are far less lucky. Our parents somehow conceived us without thinking of the fact that a couple of decades down the road we would be graduating from college under very poor economic conditions. Jobs are scarce, and we would be lucky to have a couple of job interviews and extremely lucky to have even one job offer.

It turns out that the harmful consequences of graduating during a recession do not end there, with the hardships of trying to find a paying job after graduation. It is easy to see why the labor market conditions at the time of college graduation might affect long-run outcomes. On the one hand, many young graduates may find that accepting any available offer, but continuing their job search and shifting into slightly different career paths, can easily overcome the initial disadvantage. On the other hand, it may be that labor market experience right after college graduation may provide valuable training and networking opportunities that yield substantial rewards in later years.

Recent research documents that the adverse consequences of graduating in a bad economy dominate the data both in the United States and abroad. A 1-percentage point increase in the national unemployment rate at the time of college graduation is associated with about a 6 percent wage loss initially for American workers. In other words, the initial job that the college graduate will get pays about 6 percent less than the first job offered to other graduation cohorts. Although this large wage effect gets weaker over time, it is still sizable even after 15 years. The wage loss associated with graduating in an economy that has a 1-percentage point higher unemployment rate is still 2.5 percent.

A study of the labor market experience of Canadian college graduates finds roughly similar results. College graduates who enter the labor market during a recession suffer an initial wage loss of about 9 percent; half of this wage loss remains even after 5 years, and eventually disappears after a decade. Finally, a study of the Japanese labor market finds that the initial wage loss associated with graduating in a recession is about 5 percent, with the wage loss eventually dropping to around 2 percent.

The implication is clear: Recessions are bad for young college graduates' long-term economic health.

Source: Lisa B. Kahn, "The Long-Term Labor Market Consequences of Graduating from College in a Bad Economy," *Labour Economics*, forthcoming 2011; Phil Oreopoulos, Till von Wachter, and Andrew Heisz, "The Short- and Long-Term Career Effects of Graduating in a Recession: Hysteresis and Heterogeneity in the Market for College Graduates," IZA Working Paper 3578, June 2008; and Yuji Genda, Ayako Kondo, and Souichi Ohta, "Long-Term Effects of a Recession at Labor Market Entry in Japan and the United States," *Journal of Human Resources* 45 (Winter 2010): 157–196.

from jobs and from the economic mainstream has led many to argue that residential segregation causes many of the social and economic problems faced by the black underclass.[4]

Table 12-2 uses the difference-in-differences methodology to show how the clustering of blacks into a relatively small number of geographic areas contributes to a higher rate of "idleness" among young blacks, a person being considered idle if he or she is neither employed nor in school. It turns out that 15.4 percent of young blacks living in the group of cities that have low levels of racial residential segregation are idle. In contrast, 21.6 percent of blacks living in cities that have high levels of residential segregation are idle. In short,

[4] William Julius Wilson, *The Truly Disadvantaged: The Inner City, the Underclass, and Public Policy,* Chicago: University of Chicago Press, 1987.

TABLE 12-2   Relation between Black Residential Segregation and Percentage of Blacks Who Are Idle, 1990

Source: David M. Cutler and Edward L. Glaeser, "Are Ghettos Good or Bad?" *Quarterly Journal of Economics* 112 (August 1997): 842.

Group	City Is Not Very Segregated	City Is Very Segregated	Difference
Blacks aged 20–24	15.4	21.6	6.2
Whites aged 20–24	7.0	6.6	−0.4
Difference-in-differences	—	—	**6.6**

the data seem to suggest that living in highly segregated cities raises the idleness rate of young blacks by 6.2 percentage points.

Before one attributes this increase in the rate of idleness to the harmful effects of residential segregation, it is important to note that other factors may be at work. For instance, the industrial composition of the labor market may differ significantly between the two types of cities. Employment in highly segregated cities may be concentrated in declining industries, such as manufacturing. It would not then be surprising to find that persons living in high-segregation cities have higher idleness rates, *regardless* of their race.

As Table 12-2 also shows, the idleness rates for white workers are not all that different across the two types of cities. In fact, it turns out that there is *less* idleness among whites living in the group of highly segregated cities: 7.0 percent of whites living in low-segregation cities are idle, as compared to only 6.6 percent of whites living in high-segregation cities. The difference-in-differences methodology then suggests that racial residential segregation increased the idleness rate of blacks by 6.6 percentage points. Therefore, the evidence indicates that the segregation of blacks into a small number of geographic areas may be partly responsible for the less-beneficial labor market opportunities faced by black workers.[5]

12-2   Types of Unemployment

The labor market is in constant flux. Some workers quit their jobs; other workers are laid off. Some firms are cutting back; other firms are expanding. New workers enter the market after completing their education, and other workers reenter after spending some time in the nonmarket sector. At any time, therefore, many workers are in between jobs. If workers looking for jobs and firms looking for workers could find each other immediately, there would be no unemployment. **Frictional unemployment** arises because both workers and firms need time to locate each other and to digest the information about the value of the job match.

The existence of frictional unemployment does not suggest that there is a fundamental structural problem in the economy, such as an imbalance between the number of workers

---

[5] See also Richard W. Martin, "Can Black Workers Escape Spatial Mismatch? Employment Shifts, Population Shifts, and Black Unemployment in American Cities," *Journal of Urban Economics* 55 (January 2004): 179–194.

looking for work and the number of jobs available. As a result, frictional unemployment is not viewed with alarm by policymakers. By its very nature, frictional unemployment leads to short unemployment spells. Moreover, frictional unemployment is "productive" because the search activities of workers and firms improve the allocation of resources. There are also easy policy solutions for reducing frictional unemployment, such as providing workers with information about job openings and providing firms with information about unemployed workers.

Many workers also experience **seasonal unemployment.** Workers in both the garment and the auto industries are laid off regularly because new models are introduced with clockwork regularity, and firms shut down so that they can be retooled. Spells of seasonal unemployment are usually very predictable. As a result, seasonal unemployment, like frictional unemployment, is not what the unemployment problem is about. After all, most of the unemployed workers will return to their former employer once the employment season starts.

The type of unemployment that causes the most concern is **structural unemployment.** Suppose the number of workers looking for work equals the number of jobs available; there is no imbalance between the total numbers being supplied and demanded. Structural unemployment can still arise if the kinds of persons looking for work do not "fit" the jobs available. At any time, some sectors of the economy are growing and other sectors are declining. If skills were perfectly transferable across sectors, the laid-off workers could quickly move to the growing sectors. Skills, however, might be specific to the worker's job or industry, and laid-off workers lack the qualifications needed in the expanding sector. As a result, the unemployment spells of the displaced workers might last for a long time because they must retool their skills. Structural unemployment thus arises because of a mismatch between the skills that workers are supplying and the skills that firms are demanding.

The policy prescriptions for this type of structural unemployment are very different from those that would reduce frictional or seasonal unemployment. The problem is skills; the unemployed are stuck with human capital that is no longer useful. To reduce this type of unemployment, therefore, the government would have to provide training programs that would "inject" the displaced workers with the types of skills that are now in demand.

There also may be a structural imbalance between the number of workers looking for jobs and the number of jobs available—even if skills were perfectly portable across sectors. This imbalance may arise because the economy has moved into a recession. Firms now require a smaller workforce to satisfy the shrinking consumer demand and employers lay off many workers, generating **cyclical unemployment.** There is an excess supply of workers, and the market does not clear because the wage is sticky and cannot adjust downward. We have already seen that union-mandated wage increases or government-imposed minimum wages introduce rigid wages into the labor market and prevent the market from clearing. As we will see below, economists have developed a number of models that can generate sticky wages and unemployment even in the absence of minimum wages and unions. The policy prescriptions for cyclical unemployment have little to do with helping workers find jobs or with retooling workers' skills. To reduce this type of unemployment, the government will have to stimulate aggregate demand and reestablish market equilibrium at the sticky wage.

FIGURE 12-6   Flows between Employment and Unemployment

Suppose a person is either working or unemployed. At any point in time, some workers lose their jobs and unemployed workers find jobs. If the probability of losing a job equals ℓ, there are $\ell \times E$ job losers. If the probability of finding a job equals h, there are $h \times U$ job finders.

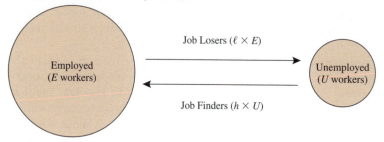

12-3   The Steady-State Rate of Unemployment

The flows of workers across jobs and in and out of the market generate some unemployment. It is easy to calculate the steady-state rate of unemployment, the unemployment rate that will be observed in the long run as a result of these labor flows. To keep things simple, suppose a worker can be either employed or unemployed. In reality, some persons also will be in the nonmarket sector, but we will ignore initially the nonmarket sector to simplify the presentation.

Figure 12-6 describes the labor flows in an economy where workers are either employed or unemployed. There are a total of E employed workers and U unemployed workers. In any given period, let ℓ be the fraction of the employed workers who lose their jobs and become unemployed, and let h be the fraction of the unemployed workers who find work and get hired. In a steady state, where the economy has reached a long-run equilibrium, the unemployment rate would be constant over time. In the steady state, therefore, we require that the number of workers who lose jobs equal the number of unemployed workers who find jobs. This implies that

$$\ell E = hU \tag{12-1}$$

The labor force is defined as the sum of persons who are either employed or unemployed, so $LF = E + U$. Substituting the definition into equation (12-1) yields

$$\ell(LF - U) = hU \tag{12-2}$$

By rearranging terms, we can solve for the steady-state unemployment rate:

$$\text{Unemployment rate} = \frac{U}{LF} = \frac{\ell}{\ell + h} \tag{12-3}$$

Equation (12-3) makes it clear that the steady-state unemployment rate is determined by the transition probabilities between employment and unemployment (ℓ and h). Policies designed to reduce steady-state unemployment must alter either or both of these probabilities.

As an example, suppose the probability that employed workers lose their jobs in any given month is .01, implying that the average job lasts 100 months. Suppose also the probability that unemployed workers find work in any given month is .10, implying the average unemployment spell lasts 10 months. The steady-state unemployment rate is 9.1 percent, or .01/(.01 + .10). The example illustrates that the unemployment rate is smaller when jobs are more stable and larger when unemployment spells last longer. In other words, two key factors determine the unemployment rate: the incidence of unemployment (that is, the likelihood that an employed worker loses his or her job, or ℓ) and the duration of unemployment spells (which equals $1/h$).

The steady-state rate of unemployment derived in equation (12-3) is sometimes called the **natural rate of unemployment**.[6] We will provide a more detailed discussion of the factors that determine the natural rate later in the chapter.

Of course, the simple model of labor force dynamics presented in this section does not accurately describe the actual flows observed in real-world labor markets. There are also flows in and out of the labor force, so a person can be in one of three states: employed, unemployed, and the nonmarket sector. Figure 12-7 illustrates the magnitude of these flows for the average month between 1990 and 2006. There were 130.0 million persons employed, 7.4 million persons unemployed, and 69.3 million persons in the nonmarket sector. During the typical month, about 1.8 million workers became unemployed and an additional 1.8 million persons who were out of the labor force entered the labor market to look for jobs. At the same time, however, 2.0 million of the unemployed found jobs and an additional 1.6 million left the labor force.[7]

Duration of Unemployment

Suppose there are 100 unemployed workers in the economy, and that 99 of these workers are in an unemployment spell that lasts only 1 week. The remaining worker, however, is in an unemployment spell that lasts 101 weeks. Most unemployment spells in this economy would then be short-term spells because most unemployed workers are unemployed for only 1 week. At the same time, however, there are a total of 200 weeks of unemployment in this economy (99 weeks for each of the workers with a 1-week spell, plus 101 weeks for the worker with the long spell). Most of the time spent unemployed, therefore, is attributable to a single worker (101/200). In other words, most unemployment spells might be short, yet most of the weeks that workers spend unemployed might be attributable to a very few workers with very long spells.

---

[6] John Haltinwanger, "The Natural Rate of Unemployment," in John Eatwell, Murray Milgate, and Peter Newman, editors, *The New Palgrave,* New York: Stockton Press, 1987, pp. 610–612.

[7] A reformulation of the algebraic model permits the calculation of the steady-state rate of unemployment when there are flows between the market and nonmarket sectors and when there is a continual flow of new labor market entrants. The steady-state rate of unemployment will then depend on the rate of job loss, on the average length of unemployment spells, and on the transition rates between unemployment and the nonmarket sector. See Stephen T. Marston, "Employment Instability and High Unemployment Rates," *Brookings Papers on Economic Activity* (1976): 169–203.

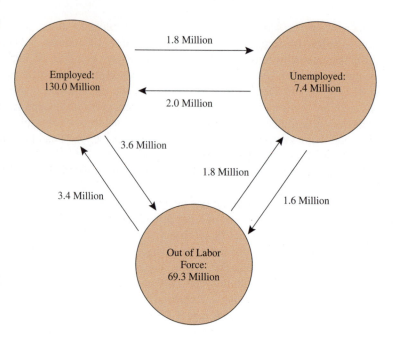

FIGURE 12-7
Dynamic Flows in the U.S. Labor Market, Monthly Average, 1990–2006

Source: Zhi Boon, Charles M. Carson, R. Jason Faberman, and Randy E. Ilg, "Studying the Labor Market Using BLS Labor Dynamics Data," *Monthly Labor Review* (February 2008): 3–16.

The evidence suggests that this numerical example summarized the structure of unemployment in the United States in the 1970s and 1980s.[8] In the mid-1970s, for instance, 2.4 percent of persons in the labor force were unemployed for at least six months. This 2.4 percent of the labor force participants accounted for 42 percent of all weeks unemployed! A small subset of the population, therefore, bears most of the burden of unemployment.

12-4   Job Search

Many theories claim to explain why unemployment exists and persists in competitive markets. We begin our discussion of these alternative stories by reemphasizing that we would observe frictional unemployment even if there were no fundamental imbalance between the supply of and demand for workers. Because different firms offer different job opportunities and because workers are not fully informed about where the "best" jobs are located, it takes time to find the available opportunities.

In fact, any given worker can choose from among many different job offers. Just as gas stations that are one block apart charge different prices for a gallon of gas, different firms make different offers to the same worker.[9] These wage differentials for the same

[8] Kim B. Clark and Lawrence H. Summers, "Labor Market Dynamics and Unemployment: A Reconsideration," *Brookings Papers on Economic Activity* (1979): 13–60.

[9] See Jonathan S. Leonard, "Carrots and Sticks: Pay, Supervision, and Turnover," *Journal of Labor Economics* 4 (October 1987, Part 2): S136–S152. There is also evidence that the same firm pays different wages to workers employed in the same job; see John E. Buckley, "Wage Differences among Workers in the Same Job and Establishment," *Monthly Labor Review* 108 (March 1985): 11–16.

There are many ways of looking for work, and some ways are more successful than others. Among unemployed young workers, nearly 85 percent used references provided by friends or relatives in their job search activities, 80 percent applied directly to an employer without referral, and about 50 percent used contacts provided by state employment agencies or newspaper ads. (These percentages do not add to 100 percent because unemployed workers typically use more than one method of search.)

Not surprisingly, the outcome of the search activity depends on how the contact between worker and firm was initiated. If a job contact was made through a friend or relative or through direct application, the contact resulted in a job offer about 18 percent of the time, as opposed to only about 10 percent when the job contact was recommended by a state employment agency or came from a newspaper ad. Moreover, job offers resulting from contacts initiated through friends or relatives are more likely to be accepted than other types of job offers. The most commonly used form of initiating contacts between workers and firms, therefore, is also the most productive in terms of generating job offers and job acceptances.

Source: Harry J. Holzer, "Search Method Use by Unemployed Youth," *Journal of Labor Economics* 6 (January 1988): 1–20.

type of work encourage an unemployed worker to "shop around" until he or she finds a superior job offer. Because it takes time to learn about the opportunities provided by different employers, search activities prolong the duration of the unemployment spell. The worker, however, is willing to endure a longer unemployment spell because it might lead to a higher-paying job. In effect, search unemployment is a form of human capital investment; the worker is investing in information about the labor market.[10]

The Wage Offer Distribution

To simplify the analysis, we assume that only unemployed workers conduct search activities. Workers might keep on searching for a better job even after they accept a particular job offer.[11] However, it is easier to analyze the main implications of the search model if we restrict our attention to unemployed workers. The wage offer distribution gives the frequency distribution describing the various offers available to a particular unemployed worker in the labor market. Figure 12-8 illustrates a typical **wage offer distribution.** As drawn, the worker can end up in a job paying anywhere from $5 to $25 per hour.

[10] Technical surveys of job search models include Dale T. Mortensen, "Job Search and Labor Market Analysis," in Orley C. Ashenfelter and Richard Layard, editors, *Handbook of Labor Economics,* vol. 2, Amsterdam: Elsevier, 1986, pp. 849–919; and Dale T. Mortensen and Christopher A. Pissarides, "New Developments in Models of Search in the Labor Market," in Orley C. Ashenfelter and David Card, editors, *Handbook of Labor Economics,* vol. 3B, Amsterdam: Elsevier, 1999, pp. 2567–2627.

[11] Joseph R. Meisenheimer II and Randy E. Ilg, "Looking for a 'Better' Job: Job-Search Activity of the Employed," *Monthly Labor Review* 123 (September 2000): 3–14.

FIGURE 12-8   The Wage Offer Distribution

The wage offer distribution gives the frequency distribution of potential job offers. A given worker can get a job paying anywhere from $5 to $25 per hour.

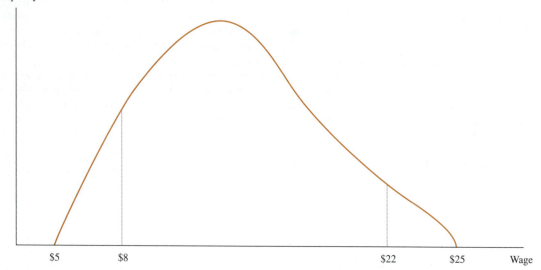

We will assume that the unemployed worker knows the shape of the wage offer distribution. In other words, he knows that there is a high probability that his search activities will locate a job paying between $8 and $22 per hour and that there is a small probability that he might end up with a job paying less than $8 or more than $22 per hour.

If search activities were free, the worker would keep on knocking from door to door until he finally hit the firm that paid the $25 wage. Search activities, however, are costly. Each time the worker applies for a new job, he incurs transportation costs and other types of expenses, such as a fee with a private employment agency. There is also an opportunity cost: He could have been working at a lower-paying job. The worker's economic trade-offs are clear: The longer he searches, the more likely he will get a high wage offer; the longer he searches, however, the more it costs to find that job.

Nonsequential and Sequential Search

When should the worker stop searching and settle for the job offer at hand? There are two approaches to answering this question.[12] Each approach gives a "stopping rule" telling the worker when to end his search activities. The worker could follow a strategy of **nonsequential search.** In this approach, the worker decides before he begins his search that he will randomly visit, say, 20 firms in the labor market and accept the job that pays the highest wage (which will not necessarily be the job paying $25 an hour). This search strategy is *not* optimal. Suppose that on his first try, the worker just happens to hit the firm

---

[12] The nonsequential search model was introduced by George J. Stigler, "Information in the Labor Market," *Journal of Political Economy* 70 (October 1962): 94–104; the sequential search model was introduced by John J. McCall, "Economics of Information and Job Search," *Quarterly Journal of Economics* 84 (February 1970): 113–126.

that pays $25 an hour. A nonsequential search strategy would force this worker to visit another 19 firms knowing full well that he could never do better. It does not make sense, therefore, for the worker to commit himself to a predetermined number of searches regardless of what happens while he is searching.

A better strategy is one of **sequential search.** Before the worker sets out on the search process, he decides which job offers he is willing to accept. For instance, he might decide that he is not willing to work for less than, say, $12 an hour. The worker will then visit one firm and compare the wage offer to his desired $12 wage. If the wage offer exceeds $12, he will accept the job, stop searching, and end the unemployment spell. If the wage offer is less than $12, he will reject the job offer and start the search process over again (that is, he will visit a new firm, compare the new wage offer to his desired wage, and so on). The sequential search strategy implies that if a worker is lucky enough to find the $25 job on the first try, he will immediately recognize that he lucked out and stop the search process.

The Asking Wage

The **asking wage** is the threshold wage that determines if the unemployed worker accepts or rejects incoming job offers.[13] There is a clear link between a worker's asking wage and the length of the unemployment spell the worker will experience. Workers who have low asking wages will find acceptable jobs very quickly and the unemployment spell will be short. Workers with high asking wages will take a long time to find an acceptable job and the unemployment spell will be very long. To summarize, *the unemployment spell will last longer the larger is the asking wage.*

It is easy to illustrate how the worker determines his asking wage. Consider again the wage offer distribution in Figure 12-8. Suppose the unemployed worker goes out and samples a particular job at random. By pure chance, he happens to visit the firm that pays the lowest wage possible, $5 per hour. The worker has obviously been very unlucky in his search, and he knows it. He must decide whether to accept or reject this offer by comparing the expected gain from one additional search (by how much would the wage offer increase?) with the costs of the search. If the offer at hand is only $5 per hour, the gains to searching one more time are very high. After all, even if the worker instantly forgets which firm he visited today, the odds of hitting the $5 firm again tomorrow are very low. An additional search, therefore, will probably generate a wage offer higher than $5 per hour. The marginal gain from one additional search, therefore, is substantial.

Suppose the worker visits another firm, and this time he gets a $10 wage offer. The incentive to continue searching will again depend partly on the marginal gain from one more search. Given the wage offer distribution illustrated in Figure 12-8, there is still a good chance that an additional search will generate a higher wage offer. The marginal gain to this additional search, however, is not as high as when the wage offer at hand was only $5. After all, there is a chance that if he searches one more time, he might hit a firm offering less than $10 per hour.

[13] The asking wage is called the *reservation wage* in many studies. We use the term *asking wage* to differentiate the threshold that determines whether an unemployed person accepts a job offer from the *reservation wage* defined in Chapter 2, which determines whether a person enters the labor market. The intuition underlying the threshold wage in both contexts is the same; it is the wage that makes a worker indifferent between two alternative actions.

Suppose the worker decides to try his luck one more time. This time he hits the jackpot, getting a wage offer of $25. At this point, the marginal gain from further search is zero. The worker cannot get a higher wage offer.

Our discussion indicates that the marginal gains from search are lower if the worker has a good wage offer at hand. As a result, the marginal revenue curve (that is, the marginal gain from one additional search) is downward sloping, as illustrated by the *MR* curve in Figure 12-9.

Of course, the asking wage is determined not only by the marginal gains from searching, but also by the marginal cost of searching. As noted above, there are two types of search costs. The first is the direct costs of search, including transportation costs and the cost of preparing résumés. Search activities are also time-consuming. Even if the wage offer at hand is the $5 wage offer, the worker who rejects this offer and searches again incurs a $5 opportunity cost. As a result, the marginal cost of search is high if the worker has a good wage offer at hand. Therefore, the marginal cost curve (or *MC* in Figure 12-9) is upward sloping.

The intersection of the marginal cost curve and the marginal revenue curve gives the asking wage, or $\tilde{w}$. Consider what would happen if the worker gets a wage offer of only $10, which is less than the asking wage $\tilde{w}$ in the figure. The marginal revenue from search

FIGURE 12-9 **The Determination of the Asking Wage**
The marginal revenue curve gives the gain from an additional search. It is downward sloping because the better the offer at hand, the less there is to gain from an additional search. The marginal cost curve gives the cost of an additional search. It is upward sloping because the better the job offer at hand, the greater the opportunity cost of an additional search. The asking wage equates the marginal revenue and the marginal cost of the search.

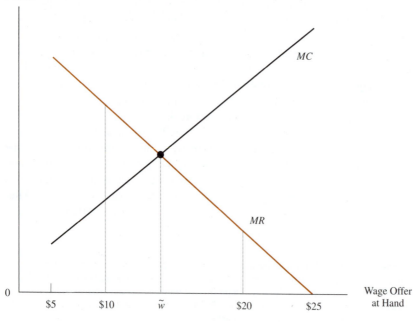

exceeds the marginal cost, and the worker should continue searching. If the wage offer at hand was $20 per hour (above the asking wage), the worker should accept the job because the expected benefits from additional search are lower than the marginal cost of search. The asking wage, therefore, makes the worker indifferent between continuing and ending his search activities.

Determinants of the Asking Wage

The worker's asking wage will respond to changes in the benefits and costs of search activities. As with all human capital investments, the benefits from search are collected in the future, so they depend on the worker's discount rate. Workers with high discount rates are present oriented, and, hence, perceive the future benefits from search to be low. As illustrated in Figure 12-10a, workers who have high discount rates have lower marginal revenue curves (shifting the marginal revenue curve from MR_0 to MR_1), and hence will have lower asking wages (from $\tilde{w}_0$ to $\tilde{w}_1$). Because these workers do not have the patience to wait until a better offer comes along, they accept lower wage offers and have short unemployment spells.

A major component of search costs is the opportunity cost resulting from rejecting a job offer and continuing the search. The unemployment insurance (UI) system, which we will discuss in greater detail below, compensates workers who are unemployed and who are actively engaging in search activities. Suppose that the worker has a wage offer at hand of $10 per hour (or $400 per week). If he qualifies for UI benefits of $200 per week, the worker is only giving up $200 by rejecting the job offer. Unemployment insurance benefits, therefore, reduce the marginal cost of search.

FIGURE 12-10 **Discount Rates, Unemployment Insurance Benefits, and the Asking Wage**
A "present-oriented" worker has a high discount rate and has less to gain from additional searches, so the marginal revenue curve shifts to MR_1 and the asking wage falls. Unemployment insurance benefits reduce the marginal cost of search and shift the marginal cost curve to MC_1. A reduction in search costs increases the asking wage.

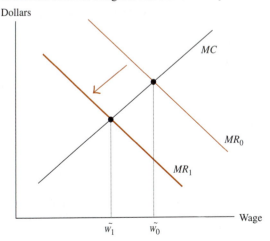

(*a*) Increase in Discount Rates

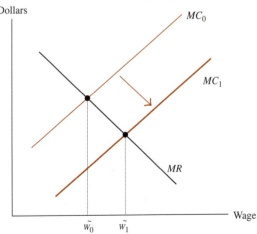

(*b*) Increase in Unemployment Benefits

As illustrated in Figure 12-10*b,* a reduction in the marginal cost of search (from MC_0 to MC_1) raises the asking wage from $\widetilde{w}_0$ to $\widetilde{w}_1$ The UI system, therefore, has three important effects on the labor market: (1) It leads to longer unemployment spells, (2) it increases the unemployment rate, and (3) it leads to higher postunemployment wages.

In sum, the job search model has two key predictions about the length of unemployment spells: Unemployment spells will last longer when the cost of searching falls and unemployment spells will last longer when the benefits from searching rise.

Although the asking wage is not observed directly, a number of surveys have attempted to determine a worker's asking wage by asking such questions as "What type of work are you looking for?" and "At what wage would you be willing to take this job?" In 1980, white unemployed youth in the United States reported that their asking wage was $4.30 an hour, and black unemployed youth reported an asking wage of $4.22 an hour.[14] The worker's self-reported asking wage was strongly correlated with the worker's unemployment experience. Workers who reported higher asking wages had longer unemployment spells. Moreover, higher asking wages led to higher postunemployment wages; a 10 percent increase in the asking wage increased the postunemployment wage by 5 percent for young whites and by 3 percent for young blacks. In the United Kingdom, where similar surveys have been conducted, a 10 percent increase in the asking wage increases the length of the unemployment spell by at least 5 percent.[15]

Is the Asking Wage Constant over Time?

If the marginal revenue and marginal cost of search were constant over time, the asking wage also would be constant. Put differently, an unemployed worker would have the same chance of finding a job in the 1st week of an unemployment spell as in the 30th week. However, it is unlikely that the probability of escaping unemployment is independent of the length of the unemployment spell. After all, search is costly. The unemployed worker has limited means and will hit a "liquidity constraint" at some point; put simply, he will no longer have the cash required to keep his search activities going. The liquidity constraint forces the worker to recognize that he cannot spend the rest of his life searching for the best job possible and that he will have to settle for less. As the worker's cash runs out, therefore, the asking wage falls. The worker will then be willing to accept job offers that were rejected at the beginning of the unemployment spell. This argument suggests that the probability of escaping unemployment rises the longer the worker has been unemployed.

---

[14] Harry J. Holzer, "Reservation Wages and Their Labor Market Effects for Black and White Male Youth," *Journal of Human Resources* 21 (Spring 1986): 157–177; see also Harry J. Holzer, "Job Search by Employed and Unemployed Youth," *Industrial and Labor Relations Review* 40 (July 1987): 601–611.

[15] Stephen R. G. Jones, "The Relationship between Unemployment Spells and Reservation Wages as a Test of Search Theory," *Quarterly Journal of Economics* 103 (November 1988): 741–765; and Kristen Keith and Abagail McWilliams, "The Returns to Mobility and Job Search by Gender," *Industrial and Labor Relations Review* 52 (April 1999): 460–477.

Job Search and the Internet

The information revolution can greatly reduce the costs associated with job search—both for workers looking for jobs as well as for firms looking to fill a vacancy. As early as 2000, for example, 25 percent of unemployed persons in the United States reported that they used the Internet in their job search (and 11 percent of *working* persons also conducted job search activities on the Web). It is widely believed that such a technological shift in the technology of job search could have a substantial (and presumably beneficial) impact on the speed with which unemployed workers find jobs and on the quality of the jobs acquired through this type of search.

However, an empirical study finds that this hope may be misplaced.[16] Superficially, the data seem to indicate that unemployed workers who use the Internet find jobs faster: In 2000, the typical job searcher who used the Internet took 3.4 months to find a job, as compared to 3.7 months for a worker who avoided the Web. It turns out, however, that this difference can be entirely accounted for by differences in observed characteristics, such as educational attainment, gender, and age. Once one controls for the underlying differences between the two groups, the advantage of Internet search activities completely disappears. This finding is consistent with one of two hypotheses. It may be, for instance, that Internet job search is completely ineffective. Or it may be that persons who search on the Internet are negatively selected in terms of underlying unobserved characteristics. The unemployed persons who use the Internet, for instance, may be the subset of people who do not put in the time and effort required to pound the pavement in order to find a job.

This preliminary evidence is unlikely to be the last word on the topic. The rapidly growing access to the Internet and the growing sophistication of job search activities on the Web (by *both* sides of the market) may easily lead to very different correlations as the digital revolution matures.

12-5 Policy Application: Unemployment Compensation

The UI system in the United States is run mainly at the state level. In 2008, the system distributed $40.7 billion in benefits. The basic parameters of the system are roughly similar across states.[17] When a worker becomes unemployed, he may become eligible for unemployment benefits depending on how long he has been employed and the reason for the job

[16] Peter Kuhn and Mikal Skuterud, "Internet Job Search and Unemployment Durations," *American Economic Review* 94 (March 2004): 218–232; see also David Autor, "Wiring the Labor Market," *Journal of Economic Perspectives* 15 (Winter 2001): 25–40.

[17] U.S. Bureau of the Census, *Statistical Abstract of the United States*, Washington, DC: Government Printing Office, 2011, Table 556. For a complete description of the parameters of the UI system, see Committee on Ways and Means, U.S. House of Representatives, *2004 Green Book: Overview of Entitlement Programs*, Washington, DC: Government Printing Office, 2004, section 4; available at http://waysandmeans.house.gov/Documents.asp?section=813. Unfortunately, the *Green Book* has not been updated since 2004. The U.S. Department of Labor maintains a Web site that contains reports summarizing many aspects of the financing of the Unemployment Insurance system for each state; see www.ows.doleta.gov/unemploy/sig_measure.asp.

separation. Workers who are laid off from their jobs typically qualify for unemployment benefits if they have worked for at least two quarters in the year prior to the layoff and if they have had some minimum level of earnings during that year (on the order of $1,000 to $3,000 for the year). Workers who quit their jobs, who were fired for just cause, or who are on strike are usually not eligible for unemployment benefits. New labor market entrants or reentrants are also not eligible for benefits. Because of these eligibility requirements, only 44 percent of unemployed workers in 2002 received UI benefits.[18]

Eligible workers can collect UI benefits after a waiting period of one week. The level of benefits depends on the worker's weekly wage: The higher the weekly wage, the higher the level of benefits to which the worker is entitled. However, there is both a minimum and a maximum level of weekly benefits. In 2010, the minimum level of benefits is $45 in Alabama, $40 in California, and $24 in West Virginia; the maximum level is $265 in Alabama, $450 in California, and $424 in West Virginia.

Because benefits are capped both from below and from above, the **replacement ratio,** the proportion of weekly earnings that are replaced by UI benefits, may be very high for low-income workers but will be low for high-income workers. On average, the replacement ratio is about 38 percent. The ratio, however, varies widely across states and skill levels. In the early 1990s, the replacement ratio for low-wage workers was 60 percent in Colorado and Michigan but only 47 percent in California. The replacement ratio for high-wage workers was 26 percent in New York and Connecticut but only 10 percent in Indiana.

The unemployed worker receives UI benefits as long as he actively seeks work, up to a specified number of weeks. The maximum number of benefit weeks is typically 26, but the benefit period is lengthened if the national or state economy faces particularly adverse conditions. In 2010, for instance, unemployed workers could have collected UI benefits for a much longer period. In Massachusetts, as a result of the increased benefits at both the state and federal levels, an unemployed worker could receive benefits for up to 99 weeks. Once a worker exhausts his UI benefits, he no longer qualifies to receive benefits unless he finds another job, works the required number of quarters, and becomes unemployed once again.

The Impact of Unemployment Insurance on the Duration of Unemployment Spells

The structure of the UI system has important implications for the duration of unemployment spells. There should be a positive correlation between the replacement ratio and the duration of the unemployment spell (because higher replacement ratios lower search costs). This prediction of search theory has been confirmed by many studies.[19] A 25 percent

---

[18] It is also the case that about a quarter of the workers who qualify for UI benefits do not file their application with the appropriate agency; see Patricia M. Anderson and Bruce D. Meyer, "Unemployment Insurance Takeup Rates and the After-Tax Value of Benefits," *Quarterly Journal of Economics* 112 (August 1997): 913–937.

[19] Good surveys of the literature are given by Gary Burtless, "Unemployment Insurance and Labor Supply: A Survey," in W. Lee Hansen and James F. Byers, editors, *Unemployment Insurance: The Second Half-Century,* Madison, WI: University of Wisconsin Press, 1990, pp. 69–107; and Anthony B. Atkinson and John Micklewright, "Unemployment Compensation and Labor Market Transitions: A Critical Review," *Journal of Economic Literature* 29 (December 1991): 1679–1727.

Theory at Work
CASH BONUSES AND UNEMPLOYMENT

Because of the disincentive effects of UI, there are many calls for reform of the system, and some states have conducted experiments to see if various policy changes shorten the duration of unemployment spells. In these experiments, some of the workers applying for UI benefits are offered a cash bonus if they find jobs relatively quickly. This random sample of unemployed workers forms "the treatment group." The remaining group of unemployed workers (that is, "the control group") participates in the typical UI program.

In Illinois, for example, workers in the treatment group who found a job within 11 weeks (and who kept that job for at least four months) were given a cash bonus of $500, or about four times the average weekly benefit. In Pennsylvania, unemployed workers in the treatment group who found a job within six weeks were entitled to a bonus equal to six times the weekly benefit amount.

The evidence provided by the experiments is clear. Unemployed workers who are offered cash bonuses have shorter unemployment spells than workers in the control group (the difference in the duration of the average unemployment spell between the two groups is about one week). Surprisingly, workers who participated in the cash bonus experiments did not end their unemployment spells quickly by accepting lower-paying jobs. In other words, workers in the treatment group had essentially the same postunemployment wage as workers in the control group. Offering workers cash incentives to find jobs quickly, therefore, seems to speed up the transition out of unemployment without a corresponding decline in the postunemployment economic status of workers.

Sources: Stephen Woodbury and Robert Spiegelman, "Bonuses to Workers and Employers to Reduce Unemployment: Randomized Trials in Illinois," *American Economic Review* 77 (September 1987): 513–550; and Bruce D. Meyer, "Lessons from the U.S. Unemployment Insurance Experiments," *Journal of Economic Literature* 33 (March 1995): 91–131.

rise in the replacement ratio (from, say, 0.4 to 0.5) increases the average duration of an unemployment spell by about 15 to 25 percent.[20] In 1996, the typical unemployed worker in the United States was unemployed for 13.8 weeks. The evidence thus suggests that reducing the replacement ratio from 0.4 to 0.3 (or a 25 percent cut in the replacement ratio) would reduce the average length of an unemployment spell by three to four weeks. The UI system, therefore, has a numerically important impact on the duration of unemployment.[21]

It is also worth recalling that low-wage workers have high replacement ratios and high-wage workers have low replacement ratios. Because the UI system provides a large subsidy for the search activities of low-wage workers, these workers will have the longest

---

[20] Kathleen P. Classen, "The Effect of Unemployment Insurance on the Duration of Unemployment and Subsequent Earnings," *Industrial and Labor Relations Review* 30 (July 1977): 438–444; Daniel S. Hamermesh, *Jobless Pay and the Economy,* Baltimore: John Hopkins University Press, 1977; Patricia M. Anderson and Bruce D. Meyer, "The Effects of the Unemployment Insurance Payroll Tax on Wages, Employment, Claims and Denials," *Journal of Public Economics* 78 (October 2000): 81–106.

[21] There is also evidence suggesting that eligibility for UI encourages workers to have shorter jobs; see Stepan Jurajda, "Estimating the Effect of Unemployment Insurance Compensation on the Labor Market Histories of Displaced Workers," *Journal of Econometrics* 108 (June 2002): 227–252; Orley Ashenfelter, David Ashmore, and Olivier Deschênes, "Do Unemployment Insurance Recipients Actively Seek Work? Evidence from Randomized Trials in Four U.S. States," Princeton University, June 2001; and Audrey Light and Yoshiaki Omori, "Unemployment Insurance and Job Quits," *Journal of Labor Economics* 22 (January 2004): 159–188.

FIGURE 12-11   **The Relationship between the Probability of Finding a New Job and UI Benefits**

Source: Lawrence F. Katz and Bruce D. Meyer, "Unemployment Insurance, Recall Expectations, and Unemployment Outcomes," *Quarterly Journal of Economics* 105 (November 1990): 973–1002, Figure IV.

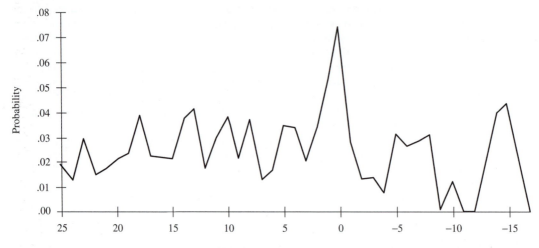

unemployment spells.[22] Therefore, the observation that low-skill workers have longer unemployment spells need not imply that these workers have a particularly difficult time finding new jobs.

After collecting UI benefits for a specified time period (typically 26 weeks), an unemployed worker in the United States does not qualify for additional benefits. The benefit cut in the 26th week, therefore, substantially raises the cost of search. The worker will likely reduce his asking wage at that point. Thus, we should expect to see a noticeable increase in the escape rate from unemployment at that point. The evidence indeed shows that a job-seeking worker's chance of finding a job improves dramatically the week the benefits run out. Figure 12-11 illustrates how the probability that unemployed workers find a new job depends on the number of weeks remaining until exhaustion of benefits. A worker with 5 to 10 weeks of UI benefits left has a probability of finding a job (on any given week) of about 3 percent. The week the benefits run out, the probability of finding a job "spikes" to almost 8 percent. It is important to note that the data summarized in Figure 12-11 refer to the probability that unemployed workers find new jobs. As we shall see below, the UI system also encourages employers to end temporary layoffs and recall their workers when UI benefits are exhausted.

The UI system not only lengthens the duration of unemployment spells, but also leads to a higher postunemployment wage. A 10 percent increase in the replacement ratio increases

[22] Bruce D. Meyer, "Unemployment Insurance and Unemployment Spells," *Econometrica* 58 (July 1990): 757–782; see also Olympia Bover, Manuel Arellano, and Samuel Bentolila, "Unemployment Duration, Benefit Duration and the Business Cycle," *Economic Journal* 112 (April 2002): 223–265.

the subsequent wage of male workers by 7 percent and of women by 1.5 percent.[23] The evidence, therefore, strongly supports the implications of the search model of unemployment: Lower search costs increase both the duration of spells and the postunemployment wage.

A number of recent studies have analyzed situations in which the parameters of the UI system have changed either in an experiment or through idiosyncratic legislative change. An interesting example is the New Jersey case. In a peculiar deal that was struck to gain the support of labor unions, New Jersey extended UI benefits for 13 additional weeks mainly to persons who exhausted their regular UI benefits between June 2 and November 24 of 1996. This legislative change allows us to analyze if those targeted by this particular legislation had longer unemployment spells than either those who exhausted benefits before June 2 or those who exhausted benefits after November 24. Despite the very short-run nature of this UI benefit extension, and despite the fact that many of those affected probably began looking for work prior to June 2, persons in this "notch" actually had a higher probability of exhausting benefits and qualified for the additional 13 weeks. The evidence suggests that a permanent extension of the 26-week limit to a 39-week limit would likely increase the number of long-term unemployed (those who exhaust the 26-week limit) by 7 percent.[24]

There is also strong evidence that a tightening of the eligibility rules of the UI system has strong effects on unemployment duration in many European countries. In Switzerland, for example, government authorities are required to inform an unemployed person that he is going to be investigated for noncompliance with the eligibility requirements. Not surprisingly, this warning has a sizable impact on the speed with which unemployed workers find jobs.[25]

Temporary Layoffs

Nearly 70 percent of laid-off workers return to their former employer at the end of the unemployment spell.[26] To understand the nature of unemployment, therefore, it is crucial to know why **temporary layoffs** are so prevalent. It turns out that the way in which the UI system is financed encourages employers to "overuse" temporary layoffs.

---

[23] Ronald G. Ehrenberg and Ronald Oaxaca, "Unemployment Insurance, Duration of Unemployment, and Subsequent Wage Gain," *American Economic Review* 66 (December 1976): 754–766.

[24] David Card and Phillip B. Levine, "Extended Benefits and the Duration of UI Spells: Evidence from the New Jersey Extended Benefit Program," *Journal of Public Economics* 78 (October 2000): 107–138; see also Peter Dolton and Donal O'Neill, "The Long-Run Effects of Unemployment Monitoring and Work-Search Programs: Experimental Evidence from the United Kingdom," *Journal of Labor Economics* 20 (April 2002): 381–403.

[25] Rafael Lalive, Jan C. van Ours, and Josef Zweimuller, "The Effect of Benefit Sanctions on the Duration of Unemployment," *Journal of the European Economic Association* 3 (December 2005): 1386–1417. For a study of the Slovenia case, see Jan C. van Ours and Milan Vodopivec, "How Shortening the Potential Duration of Unemployment Benefits Affects the Duration of Unemployment: Evidence from a Natural Experiment," *Journal of Labor Economics* 24 (April 2006): 351–378; for a study of the Norwegian case, see Knut Roed and Tao Zhang, "Does Unemployment Compensation Affect Unemployment Duration?" *Economic Journal* 113 (January 2003): 190–206.

[26] Martin Feldstein, "The Importance of Temporary Layoffs: An Empirical Analysis," *Brookings Papers on Economic Activity* 3 (1975): 725–744; and Lawrence F. Katz and Bruce D. Meyer, "Unemployment Insurance, Recall Expectations, and Unemployment Outcomes," *Quarterly Journal of Economics* 105 (November 1990): 973–1002.

Unemployment insurance is funded by a payroll tax on employers. Typically, a state decides on a taxable wage base, indicating the maximum worker's salary that is subject to the UI payroll tax. There is a great deal of variation in this cap across states. In 2010, the taxable wage base in California was $7,000; in Massachusetts, $14,000; and in Oregon, $32,100. If the government imposes a tax rate of t on the firm's payroll to fund the UI system and if the taxable wage base in the state is $7,000, the firm has to pay a tax equal to t times the first $7,000 of a worker's salary each year.

The tax rate t depends on a number of variables, including the general state of the economy, the layoff history of firms in that industry, and the firm's own layoff history. As Figure 12-12 shows, firms that have had high layoff rates in the past are typically assessed higher tax rates. The maximum tax rate a firm can be assessed, however, is capped at some rate t_{MAX}. If the firm rarely uses layoffs, it is assessed a low tax rate, but this tax rate is no lower than some rate t_{MIN} (which in some states is zero). In California, for example, the minimum tax rate is 1.5 percent and the maximum is 6.2 percent. In Michigan, the minimum and maximum tax rates are 0.06 and 10.3 percent, respectively; and in Massachusetts, 1.26 and 12.27 percent.

Although this method of determining an employer's tax rate is guided by the belief that employers who use the UI system should pay for it, the system does not perfectly impose the tax burden on employers who initiate the most layoffs. Because the tax rate is capped at t_{MAX}, employers who lay off many workers do not pay their "fair share" of the costs and are instead subsidized by other firms. The determination of the employer's tax rate, therefore, uses an **imperfect experience rating.**

FIGURE 12-12   Funding the UI System: Imperfect Experience Rating
If the firm has very few layoffs (below threshold ℓ_0), the firm is assessed a very low tax rate to fund the UI system. If the firm has had many layoffs in the past (above some threshold ℓ_1), the firm is assessed a tax rate, but this tax rate is capped at t_{MAX}.

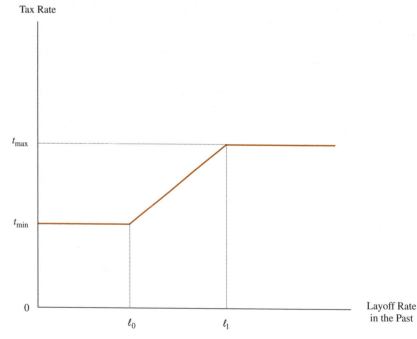

To see how this imperfect experience rating encourages some employers to rely on temporary layoffs, consider a labor market where workers and firms are engaged in long-term contracts, perhaps because of the existence of specific training.[27] Suppose economic conditions worsen temporarily. The financing of the UI system implies that employers who lay off many workers do not pay the entire costs of the worker's "salary" during the unemployment spell (that is, the unemployment benefits). The firm can then lay off many workers and shift part of the payroll to other taxpayers during the period of economic hardship. The bond between worker and firm implies that both parties find it worthwhile to continue the employment relationship. As a result, workers do not want to look for alternative employment because they expect to be recalled to their jobs, and firms do not want to look for other workers because the existing pool of workers is valuable to the firm. Imperfect experience rating, therefore, allows firms to use taxpayer funds to "ride over" some of the rough waves in the economy.

The evidence indicates that imperfect experience rating has a substantial impact on the layoff behavior of firms. The probability that an unemployed worker is recalled to his job increases substantially the week that unemployment benefits are exhausted. In the weeks prior to the exhaustion of benefits, the probability of being recalled is only about 1 to 2 percent per week. In the week when benefits are exhausted, the probability of recall rises to more than 5 percent.[28] In other words, many employers use the taxpayer subsidy for as long as they can. It has been estimated that the unemployment rate would fall by about 30 percent (from, say, 6 to 4.2 percent) if the UI system used a perfect experience rating method of financing.[29]

A particularly striking example of the correlation between temporary layoffs and UI is the pattern of seasonal unemployment exhibited by many industries. As noted earlier, there is a lot of variation in how states finance the UI system. Some states have high marginal tax rates, and firms located in those states face a substantial increase in payroll taxes when they lay off additional workers; other states have low marginal tax rates, and the firm's payroll tax does not increase much when the firm lays off workers. Not surprisingly, firms located in states with low marginal tax rates make heavy use of temporary layoffs during the slow season: 6 percent of construction workers in states with low marginal tax rates are on temporary layoff in the off-season, as compared to only 3 percent of workers in states with high marginal tax rates.[30]

---

[27] Martin Feldstein, "Temporary Layoffs in the Theory of Unemployment," *Journal of Political Economy* 84 (October 1976): 937–958; and Robert H. Topel, "On Layoffs and Unemployment Insurance," *American Economic Review* 73 (September 1983): 541–559.

[28] Katz and Meyer, "Unemployment Insurance, Recall Expectations, and Unemployment Outcomes."

[29] Robert H. Topel, "Financing Unemployment Insurance: History, Incentives, and Reform," in W. Lee Hansen and James F. Byers, editors, *Unemployment Insurance: The Second Half-Century,* Madison, WI: University of Wisconsin Press, 1990, pp. 108–135; see also Anderson and Meyer, "The Effects of the Unemployment Insurance Payroll Tax on Wages, Employment, Claims and Denials."

[30] David Card and Phillip B. Levine, "Unemployment Insurance Taxes and the Cyclical and Seasonal Properties of Unemployment," *Journal of Public Economics* 53 (January 1994): 1–30. There is also a link between UI and the growth of seasonal unemployment in the agriculture industry. Prior to 1975, workers in the agricultural sector were excluded from the UI system. When the UI program was expanded to cover agricultural workers, the unemployment rate rose by 2 percentage points during the off-season months; see Barry R. Chiswick, "The Effect of Unemployment Compensation on a Seasonal Industry: Agriculture," *Journal of Political Economy* 84 (June 1976): 591–602.

Much of the empirical literature examining the impact of unemployment compensation focuses on the distortionary effects of the program: UI leads to more and longer-lasting unemployment spells. Workers search longer because UI reduces search costs, and employers lay off more workers because UI uses an imperfect experience rating.

In contrast, few studies measure the *benefits* resulting from unemployment compensation. Presumably, the social goal of providing unemployment benefits to the unemployed is to smooth out consumption during the unemployment spells. In other words, persons suffering a spell of unemployment need not fear that the spell will completely disrupt their financial standing; they will still be able to pay their bills and provide for their families. It turns out that the UI system does a very good job of helping the unemployed achieve this goal.

A recent study estimates that, *in the absence of UI,* household consumption would fall by about 22 percent when the head of household becomes unemployed. This sizable decline in consumption is greatly attenuated by UI benefits. Each 10-percentage-point increase in the replacement ratio reduces the drop in consumption that would have otherwise occurred by 3 percentage points. The typical replacement ratio is around 0.4, implying that UI reduces the consumption loss for the typical household from 22 percent to about 10 percent. A replacement ratio of around 80 percent would fully smooth consumption during the unemployment spell.

These findings suggest that the unemployment compensation program substantially improves the well-being of the targeted households. A complete assessment of this program, therefore, requires that we contrast the distortionary effects that have dominated our attention with the potential benefits that UI imparts to the unemployed.

Source: Jonathan Gruber, "The Consumption Smoothing Benefits of Unemployment Insurance," *American Economic Review* 87 (March 1997): 192–205; see also Robert Shimer and Ivan Werning, "Reservation Wages and Unemployment Insurance," *Quarterly Journal of Economics* 122 (August 2007): 1145–1185.

12-6   The Intertemporal Substitution Hypothesis

Job search models provide an important explanation for the existence of frictional unemployment. This type of unemployment is voluntary in the sense that workers invest in information so as to get higher wages in the postunemployment period. Some studies have proposed that even the large increase in unemployment observed during a severe economic downturn (which probably has little to do with job search activities) might have a voluntary component.[31]

In our discussion of life cycle labor supply in Chapter 2, we noted that workers have an incentive to allocate their time to work activities during those periods of the life cycle when the wage is high and to consume leisure when the wage is low and leisure is cheap. The intertemporal substitution hypothesis also has important implications for how workers allocate their time over the business cycle. Suppose that the real wage fluctuates over the business cycle and that this fluctuation is procyclical; in other words, the real

[31] This influential hypothesis was first proposed by Robert E. Lucas and Leonard Rapping, "Real Wages, Employment, and Inflation," *Journal of Political Economy* 77 (September/October 1969): 721–754.

wage rises when the economy expands and declines when the economy contracts. Because it is cheap to consume leisure when the real wage is low, workers are more than willing to reduce their labor supply during recessions; they can become unemployed and collect UI benefits, or perhaps leave the labor force altogether. As a result, part of the unemployment observed during economic downturns might be voluntary because workers are taking advantage of the decline in the real wage to consume leisure.

The intertemporal substitution hypothesis makes two key assumptions: (1) The real wage is procyclical and (2) labor supply responds to shifts in the real wage. The question of whether real wages are sticky over the business cycle is one of the oldest questions in macroeconomics and has not yet been settled. Although there is a growing consensus that wages are indeed procyclical, we are still unsure about the strength of the correlation between the real wage and the business cycle.[32]

The movement of the real wage over the business cycle is difficult to calculate because the composition of the labor force changes over the cycle. Unemployment typically has a particularly adverse effect on low-skill workers. When we calculate the average wage of workers during an economic expansion, we use a very different sample than when we calculate the average wage of workers during a recession. In other words, because unemployment targets low-skill workers, they are less likely to be included in the calculation during an economic contraction than during an economic expansion. The changing sample mix biases the calculation of the cyclical trend in the real wage. Although it was widely believed for many years that real wages were sticky, studies that try to correct for the "composition" bias suggest that the real wage may be procyclical.

Even if real wages are procyclical, it is doubtful that the large pool of unemployed workers during severe recessions are "voluntarily unemployed" in the sense implied by the intertemporal substitution hypothesis. After all, the hypothesis also assumes that labor supply is responsive to changes in the real wage over the business cycle.

The evidence presented in Chapter 2 indicated that labor supply curves—particularly for men—tend to be inelastic, that labor supply is not very responsive to changes in the wage. A well-known study concluded that we need a labor supply elasticity that is at least 10 times the "consensus estimates" to explain the intertemporal shifts in labor supply.[33] The evidence, therefore, does not suggest that much of the unemployment increase observed during an economic downturn can be interpreted as a rational reallocation of the worker's time.

---

[32] Mark J. Bils, "Real Wages over the Business Cycle: Evidence from Panel Data," *Journal of Political Economy* 93 (August 1985): 666–689; Gary Solon, Robert Barsky, and Jonathan A. Parker, "Measuring the Cyclicality of Real Wages: How Important Is Composition Bias?" *Quarterly Journal of Economics* 109 (February 1994): 1–25; Kenneth J. McLaughlin, "Rigid Wages," *Journal of Monetary Economics* 34 (December 1994): 383–414; Paul J. Devereux, "The Cyclicality of Real Wages within Employer-Employee Matches," *Industrial and Labor Relations Review* 54 (July 2001): 835–850; and Dongguyn Shin and Gary Solon, "New Evidence on Real Wage Cyclicality within Employer-Employee Matches," National Bureau of Economic Research Working Paper No. 12262, May 2006.

[33] The consensus estimate of the labor supply elasticity measuring how workers respond to a wage increase over the life cycle is on the order of 0.1. The observed procyclical movement of the real wage requires a labor supply elasticity of at least 1.0 in order to explain the huge shifts in labor supply over the business cycle; see Solon, Barsky, and Parker, "Measuring the Cyclicality of Real Wages."

12-7   The Sectoral Shifts Hypothesis

Although job search activities can help us understand the presence of frictional unemployment, they do not explain the existence and persistence of long-term unemployment.[34] As a result, a number of alternative models have been proposed to explain why structural unemployment might arise in a competitive market.

One important explanation stresses the possibility that workers who are searching for jobs do not have the qualifications to fill the available vacancies. It is well known that shifts in demand do not affect all sectors of the economy equally. At any point in time, some sectors of the economy are growing rapidly and other sectors are in decline. To see how these sectoral shocks might create structural unemployment, suppose the manufacturing industry is hit by an adverse shock. Because of the reduced demand for their output, manufacturers lay off many of their workers. Favorable shocks to other sectors (such as the computer industry) increase the demand for labor by computer firms. If the laid-off manufacturing workers have skills that can be easily transferred across industries, the adverse conditions in the manufacturing sector would not lead to long-term unemployment. The laid-off workers would leave the manufacturing sector and move on to jobs in the now-thriving computer industry. There would be frictional unemployment as workers learned about and sampled the various job opportunities available in the computer industry.

Manufacturing workers, however, probably have skills that are partly specific to the manufacturing sector, so that their skills may not be very useful to computer firms. Long-term unemployment arises because it will take time for these workers to acquire the skills that are now in demand in the computer industry. The **sectoral shifts hypothesis** suggests that there will be a pool of workers who are unemployed for long spells because of a *structural* imbalance between the skills of unemployed workers and the skills that employers are looking for.[35]

There is disagreement about whether sectoral shifts contribute to the unemployment problem in the United States and other advanced economies. The typical empirical analysis relates the aggregate unemployment rate at a particular time to the dispersion in employment growth rates across industries. The sectoral shifts hypothesis implies that the unemployment rate rises when there is a lot of dispersion in employment growth rates across industries (in other words, when some industries are growing and some are declining). The evidence documents a positive correlation between measures of dispersion in employment growth rates and the aggregate unemployment rate.[36] Some recent studies also have tested the sectoral shifts hypothesis by noting that sectoral shocks have an impact on stock

---

[34] A study of the link between structural unemployment and business cycles is given by Robert Shimer, "The Cyclical Behavior of Equilibrium Unemployment and Vacancies," *American Economic Review* 95 (March 2005): 25–49.

[35] David M. Lilien, "Sectoral Shifts and Cyclical Unemployment," *Journal of Political Economy* 90 (August 1982): 777–793.

[36] A critical appraisal of this evidence is given by Katharine G. Abraham and Lawrence F. Katz, "Cyclical Unemployment: Sectoral Shifts or Aggregate Disturbances," *Journal of Political Economy* 94 (June 1986): 507–522.

market prices, with stock prices rising when firms are hit by favorable shocks and declining when firms are hit by adverse shocks. The dispersion in the change in stock prices across industries, therefore, provides information about the importance of sectoral shocks in the economy. It turns out that there is also a positive correlation between the dispersion in movements in stock prices and the unemployment rate.

It has been estimated that sectoral shifts might explain about 25 to 40 percent of unemployment, although in some time periods the sectoral shifts might explain substantially more. The sectoral shifts resulting from the oil-price shock of 1973, for example, may have accounted for about 60 percent of the 3.5-percentage-point increase in the unemployment rate between 1973 and 1975.[37]

12-8 Efficiency Wages Revisited

As we saw in the last chapter, when firms find it expensive to monitor the worker's output, they might use efficiency wages to "buy" the worker's cooperation. Because the firm pays above-market wages, efficiency wage models generate involuntary unemployment. There are no pressures on the firm to lower the wage because the efficiency wage *is* the profit-maximizing wage; if the firm lowers the wage, the payroll savings are more than outweighed by the productivity losses caused by worker shirking.

The No-Shirking Supply Curve

We can interpret the unemployment caused by the efficiency wage as the "stick" that keeps the lucky workers who have highly paid jobs in line.[38] To see why, consider first the wage-employment outcome in a competitive labor market where worker shirking is not a problem (perhaps because workers can be monitored at a very low cost). There are E workers in this labor market, and the labor supply curve is inelastic. Point P in Figure 12-13 gives the traditional competitive equilibrium, where the vertical supply curve S intersects the downward-sloping labor demand curve D. The market-clearing competitive wage, therefore, is w^*.

Suppose now that firms cannot easily monitor the output of workers, so monitoring activities are expensive. To simplify the discussion, let's assume that workers who shirk spend all their time reading the newspaper comics or uselessly surfing the Web, so that shirking workers are completely unproductive. The firm, therefore, will want to offer a wage-employment package that encourages its workers not to shirk at all.

Let's derive the wage that firms must pay to ensure that workers do not shirk. Suppose the unemployment rate is very high. It is then costly to shirk because once a shirking worker gets caught and fired, he faces a long unemployment spell. As a result, firms will be able to attract workers who will not shirk even if they pay a relatively low wage. If the unemployment rate is very low, however, shirking workers who are caught and fired face only a short

[37] S. Lael Brainard and David M. Cutler, "Sectoral Shifts and Cyclical Unemployment Reconsidered," *Quarterly Journal of Economics* 108 (February 1993): 219–243.

[38] Carl Shapiro and Joseph E. Stiglitz, "Equilibrium Unemployment as a Worker Discipline Device," *American Economic Review* 74 (June 1984): 433–444.

FIGURE 12-13   The Determination of the Efficiency Wage

If shirking is not a problem, the market clears at wage w^* (where supply S equals demand D). If monitoring is expensive, the threat of unemployment can keep workers in line. If unemployment is high (point F), firms can attract workers who will not shirk at a very low wage. If unemployment is low (point G), firms must pay a very high wage to ensure that workers do not shirk. The efficiency wage w_{NS} is given by the intersection of the no-shirking supply curve (NS) and the demand curve.

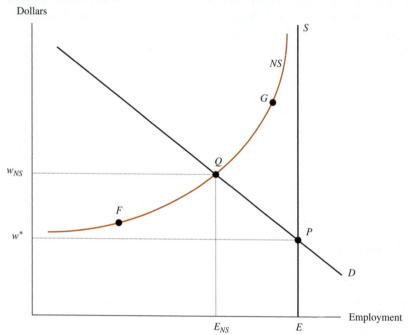

unemployment spell. To make shirking costly and to make even the short unemployment spell unprofitable, firms will have to offer the worker a relatively high wage.

The discussion generates an upward-sloping **no-shirking supply curve** (labeled NS in Figure 12-13), which gives the number of nonshirking workers that firms can hire at each wage. The no-shirking supply curve states that when firms employ few workers out of the total E (point F), they can attract nonshirking workers at a low wage because a layoff leads to a long and costly unemployment spell. If firms hire a large number of workers (point G), they must pay higher wages to encourage workers not to shirk. The no-shirking supply curve, therefore, gives the number of workers that the market can attract at any given wage and who will not shirk.

Note that the no-shirking supply curve NS will never touch the perfectly inelastic supply curve at E workers and that the difference between the two curves gives the number of workers who are unemployed. If the market employs all the workers at a particular wage, a shirking worker who gets fired can walk across the street and get another job. In other words, there is no penalty for shirking. The key insight provided by the efficiency wage model is clear: Some unemployment is necessary to keep the employed workers in line.

Efficiency Wages and Unemployment

The equilibrium wage is given by the intersection of the no-shirking supply curve and the labor demand curve (at point Q). The wage w_{NS} is the efficiency wage and firms will employ E_{NS} workers, so that $(E - E_{NS})$ workers will be unemployed. A number of properties of this equilibrium are worth noting.

1. There are no market pressures forcing the efficiency wage w_{NS} downward toward the competitive wage w^*. If firms were to pay less than w_{NS}, there would be fewer workers who are willing to work and not shirk than are being demanded by firms in the industry, and the wage would rise. If the wage was higher than the efficiency wage w_{NS}, there would be more workers willing to work and not shirk than are being demanded, and the wage would fall. Therefore, the efficiency wage w_{NS} is above the market-clearing competitive wage.

2. Workers do not shirk in this labor market. The efficiency wage w_{NS} is the wage that encourages the E_{NS} employed workers to behave.

3. There is involuntary unemployment. The $(E - E_{NS})$ unemployed workers want to work at the going wage but cannot find jobs. Firms in this market, however, do not wish to employ these workers because full employment encourages workers to shirk.

The structural unemployment generated by efficiency wages is very different from the frictional unemployment generated by job search. Search unemployment is productive; it is an investment in information that leads to a higher-paying job. The unemployment that is due to efficiency wages is involuntary and unproductive (from the worker's point of view). The worker would like a job but cannot find one. Further, the worker has nothing to gain from being in a long spell of unemployment. From the firm's point of view, however, the involuntary unemployment is productive. It keeps the employed workers honest, thereby increasing output.

The efficiency wage model also implies that wages will be relatively sticky over the business cycle. Suppose that output demand falls because of a sudden downturn in economic activity. In a competitive market, the labor demand curve shifts down from D_0 to D_1 and the competitive wage drops from w_0^* to w_1^* (see Figure 12-14). If firms paid an efficiency wage, the same decline in demand reduces the wage from w_0^{NS} to w_1^{NS}. Therefore, the efficiency wage is less responsive to changes in demand than the competitive wage. Moreover, employment falls from E_0^{NS} to E_1^{NS} during the contraction and the unemployment rate rises.

The Wage Curve

Recent empirical work suggests that efficiency wages may play an important role in generating unemployment in many countries. In particular, this research has documented the existence of a downward-sloping curve that summarizes the relation between wage levels and unemployment.[39] It turns out that—within each country—the wage tends to be high in regions where the unemployment rate is low and the wage tends to be low in regions where the unemployment rate is high. This relationship, which has been called the **wage curve,** is illustrated in Figure 12-15.

[39] David G. Blanchflower and Andrew J. Oswald, *The Wage Curve,* Cambridge, MA: MIT Press, 1994. See also Lutz Bellmann and Uwe Blien, "Wage Curve Analyses of Establishment Data from Western Germany," *Industrial and Labor Relations Review* 54 (July 2001): 851–863; and David Card, "The Wage Curve: A Review," *Journal of Economic Literature* 33 (June 1995): 285–299.

FIGURE 12-14   The Impact of an Economic Contraction on the Efficiency Wage

A fall in output demand shifts the labor demand curve from D_0 to D_1. The competitive wage falls from w_0^* to w_1^*. If firms pay an efficiency wage, the contraction in demand also reduces the efficiency wage but by a smaller amount. The efficiency wage, therefore, is less responsible to demand fluctuations than the competitive wage.

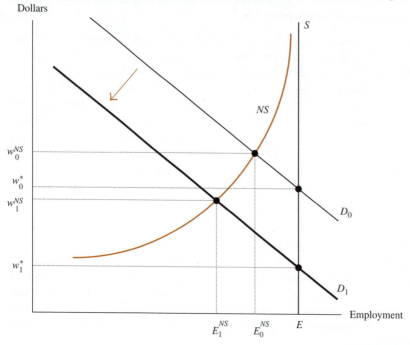

FIGURE 12-15   The Wage Curve: The Relation between Wage Levels and Unemployment across Regions

Geographic regions (such as B) that offer higher wage rates also tend to have lower unemployment rates.

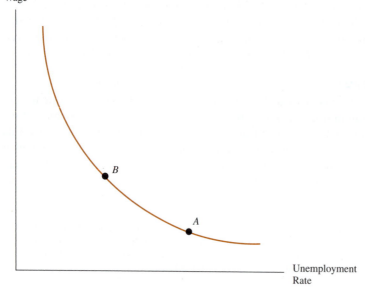

The downward-sloping shape of the wage curve is difficult to explain in the context of a competitive supply and demand framework. The intuition of the supply-demand framework tells us that unemployment arises only when the wage is relatively high—above the competitive wage. This excess supply of labor would then put a downward pressure on the wage. As long as the wage is relatively "sticky," there will be some unemployment. Note that it is *high* wages that are associated with unemployment, precisely the opposite of what is implied by the downward-sloping wage curve.

The efficiency wage model provides one possible explanation for the wage curve. Firms located in regional labor markets where there is a great deal of unemployment need not offer high wage rates to prevent workers from shirking. The high unemployment rates do the job of keeping workers in line. In contrast, firms located in tight regional labor markets where there is little unemployment must pay high wages in order to encourage workers not to shirk.

12-9   Implicit Contracts

The long-term nature of labor contracts (perhaps resulting from specific training) introduces opportunities for workers and firms to bargain over both wages and layoff probabilities.[40] The bargaining leads to a contract that specifies both the wage and the number of hours of work for any given set of aggregate economic conditions. Because these contracts will exist even if the workers are not represented by a formal institution like a union, these labor market contracts are called **implicit contracts.** In real-world labor markets, these implicit contracts are often unwritten and unspoken, yet workers within a particular firm have a good understanding of how employment conditions will vary over time and over the business cycle.

There are many types of feasible implicit contracts between workers and firms. Consider, in particular, two extreme types of contracts. The first is a "fixed-employment" contract, under which the person works the same number of hours per year (say, 2,000 hours) regardless of the economic conditions facing the firm. The second is a "fixed-wage" contract, where the worker receives the same hourly wage, again regardless of the economic conditions facing the firm.

Over the business cycle, the firm will face very different market conditions for its product. During an expansion, the firm typically finds that product demand is strong and growing; during a contraction, the demand for the firm's output weakens. If the firm and the worker settled on a fixed-employment contract, the firm would respond to these changes in market conditions by varying the worker's wage. The worker would get paid a high wage during an economic expansion and would have to accept substantial wage cuts during a recession. As a result of these wage cuts and wage increases, the worker's income would probably fluctuate greatly over the business cycle.

In contrast, if the firm and the worker settled on a fixed-wage contract, the firm would respond to changes in the product market by changing the worker's hours so the worker

---

[40] This literature began with the work of Costas Azariadis, "Implicit Contracts and Underemployment Spells," *Journal of Political Economy* 83 (December 1975): 1183–1202, and Martin N. Baily, "Wages and Employment under Uncertain Demand," *Review of Economic Studies* 41 (January 1974): 37–50. An excellent survey of the literature is given by Sherwin Rosen, "Implicit Contracts: A Survey," *Journal of Economic Literature* 23 (September 1985): 1144–1175.

works fewer hours during a recession (when he has less to contribute to the firm's profits). In a fixed-wage contract, for instance, the worker might work 2,000 hours per year during the expansion, but only 1,000 hours per year during a recession. Even though the worker's annual income would be lower during a recession, his loss might be offset by the fact that the additional leisure hours the worker would have to consume during a recession have some value (after all, workers like leisure) and by the possibility that unemployment compensation might replace some of the lost earnings. As a result, the worker's "real" income may be relatively constant over the business cycle in a fixed-wage contract.

Many studies have argued that workers, in general, prefer fixed-wage contracts and willingly "accept" layoffs as part of the long-term employment relationship. In other words, workers willingly enter implicit contracts where their incomes are relatively stable over the business cycle, even if their hours of work are not.

The reason is that workers are typically assumed to be risk-averse. The utility function of a risk-averse worker exhibits diminishing marginal utility of income. In other words, the utility gain associated with the first $1,000 of income exceeds the utility gain associated with the second $1,000, and so on. Because workers are assumed to be risk-averse, the increase in utility resulting from the higher incomes paid during an expansion is not enough to offset the loss in utility resulting from the lower incomes paid during a recession. Firms that offer fixed-wage contracts, in effect, offer "insurance" against wage declines during recessions and hence can attract risk-averse workers at lower average wages. The typical implicit contract in the labor market would then be a fixed-wage contract—implying that the wage is sticky over the business cycle and that unemployment increases during a recession.

Note, however, that the unemployment generated by this type of implicit contract is "voluntary." Workers are better off with the fixed-wage contract and therefore they have accepted layoffs in return for a more stable consumption path. A number of empirical studies have examined various aspects of the implicit contracts approach, such as the implication that wage contracts are not renegotiated as aggregate economic conditions change. Some of the evidence tends to suggest that implicit contracts may play a role in the labor market.[41]

12-10   Policy Application: The Phillips Curve

In 1958, A. W. H. Phillips published a famous study documenting a negative correlation between the rate of inflation and the rate of unemployment in the United Kingdom from 1861 to 1957.[42] The negative relationship between these two variables, illustrated in Figure 12-16, is now known as the **Phillips curve.**

---

[41] Paul Beaudry and John DiNardo, "The Effect of Implicit Contracts on the Movement of Wages over the Business Cycle: Evidence from Micro Data," *Journal of Political Economy* 99 (August 1991): 665–688; James N. Brown, "How Close to an Auction Is the Labor Market?" *Research in Labor Economics* 5 (1982): 189–235; Paul Beaudry and John DiNardo, "Is the Behavior of Hours Worked Consistent with Implicit Contract Theory," *Quarterly Journal of Economics* 110 (August 1995): 743–768; John C. Ham and Kevin T. Reilly, "Testing Intertemporal Substitution, Implicit Contracts and Hours Restriction Models of the Labor Market Using Micro Data," *American Economic Review* 92 (September 2002): 905–927; and Darren Grant, "The Effect of Implicit Contracts on the Movement of Wages over the Business Cycle: Evidence from the National Longitudinal Surveys," *Industrial and Labor Relations Review* 56 (April 2003): 393–408.

[42] A. W. H. Phillips, "The Relation between Unemployment and the Rate of Change of Money Wage Rates in the United Kingdom, 1861–1957," *Economica* 25 (November 1958): 283–299.

FIGURE 12-16 The Phillips Curve

The Phillips curve describes the negative correlation between the inflation rate and the unemployment rate. The curve may imply that an economy faces a trade-off between inflation and unemployment.

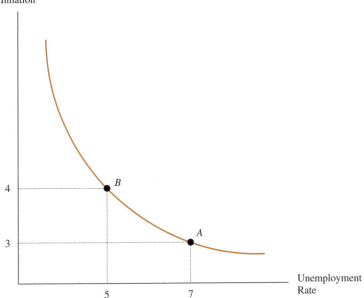

The Phillips curve is significant because it suggests that there might be a trade-off between inflation and unemployment. Suppose, for instance, that the unemployment rate is 7 percent and that the inflation rate is 3 percent, as at point *A* in the figure. The Phillips curve implies that the government could pursue expansionary policies that would move the economy to point *B,* where the unemployment rate falls to 5 percent and the inflation rate rises to 4 percent. Depending on what the government perceives to be in the national interest, it might then be worthwhile to pursue fiscal and monetary policies that would lower the unemployment rate at the cost of a higher rate of inflation. The belief that this trade-off provided a real opportunity to policymakers to permanently solve the problem of unemployment is vividly illustrated by an observation made by (future) Nobel Prize–winning economist William Vickrey: "If unemployment could be brought down to, say, 2 percent at the cost of an assured steady rate of inflation of 10 percent per year, or even 20 percent, this would be a good bargain."

The experience of the U.S. economy during the 1960s seemed to confirm the hypothesis that there was a trade-off between inflation and unemployment. Figure 12-17 illustrates the various inflation-unemployment outcomes observed between 1961 and 2005; remarkably, the experience between 1961 and 1969 suggested that the United States was moving up a stable Phillips curve. As the figure makes clear, however, the confidence of policymakers in the inflation-unemployment trade-off was shattered during the 1970s. The data points simply refused to cooperate and lie along a stable Phillips curve. Instead, the relationship between inflation and unemployment went "out of kilter." If anything, there seem to be a number of different Phillips curves generated by the data points. For example, the

FIGURE 12-17   Inflation and Unemployment in the United States, 1961–2005

Sources: The unemployment rate data are drawn from U.S. Bureau of Labor Statistics, "Historical Data for the 'A' Tables of the Employment Situation Release," Table A-12, "Alternative Measures of Labor Underutilization," http://stats.bls.gov/cps/cpsatabs.htm. The inflation rate is drawn from U.S. Bureau of Labor Statistics, "Table Containing History of CPI-U U.S. All Items Indexes and Annual Percent Changes from 1913 to Present," http://stats.bls.gov/cpi/home.htm#tables.

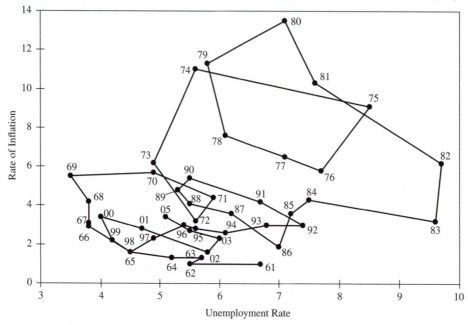

data between 1976 and 1979 lie on a different Phillips curve than the one traced by the 1980–1983 points and from the one traced by the 2000–2002 points.

The Natural Rate of Unemployment

At the same time that the inflation-unemployment experience of the 1970s was demolishing the notion of a stable Phillips curve, some economists began to argue that a long-run trade-off between inflation and unemployment did not make theoretical sense.[43] Instead, they argued, economic theory implies that the long-run Phillips curve must be vertical. Put differently, there exists an equilibrium unemployment rate, now called the *natural rate of unemployment,* that persists regardless of the rate of inflation.

There are many ways of deriving the long-run Phillips curve, but one particularly simple way uses the search model that we presented earlier in this chapter.[44] Suppose that the economy is in a noninflationary long-run equilibrium, with an unemployment rate of 5 percent and zero inflation, as at point *A* in Figure 12-18. Unemployed workers have an asking wage that makes them indifferent between accepting a job and continuing their search activities. Since the economic environment is not changing over time, the asking

[43] Milton Friedman, "The Role of Monetary Policy," *American Economic Review* 58 (March 1968): 1–17; and Edmund S. Phelps, "Phillips Curves, Expectations of Inflation, and Optimal Unemployment over Time," *Economica* 34 (August 1968): 254–281.

[44] Dale T. Mortensen, "Job Search, the Duration of Unemployment and the Phillips Curve," *American Economic Review* 60 (December 1970): 847–862.

FIGURE 12-18 The Short-Run and Long-Run Phillips Curves

The economy is initially at point *A;* there is no inflation and a 5 percent unemployment rate. If monetary policy increases the inflation rate to 7 percent, job searchers will suddenly find many jobs that meet their reservation wage and the unemployment rate falls in the short run, moving the economy to point *B*. Over time, workers realize that the inflation rate is higher and will adjust their reservation wage upward, returning the economy to point *C*. In the long run, the unemployment rate is still 5 percent, but there is now a higher rate of inflation. In the long run, therefore, there is no trade-off between inflation and unemployment.

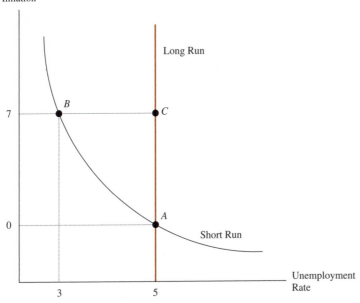

wage is constant. As a result, the unemployment rate is also constant at 5 percent, the natural rate.

Suppose the government unexpectedly pursues a monetary policy (perhaps by printing money) that pushes the inflation rate up to 7 percent. It takes time for unemployed workers to learn that inflation has increased, so even though the wage offer distribution shifted to the right by 7 percent, workers still believe there is no inflation. In other words, workers do not adjust the asking wage upward to account for the unanticipated inflation. As a result, the asking wage is too low relative to the new level of nominal wage offers. Workers will now encounter many job offers that meet the asking wage, and the unemployment rate falls. A high rate of unanticipated inflation, therefore, reduces the unemployment rate.

Our discussion has generated a downward-sloping short-run Phillips curve as the economy moves from point *A* to point *B* in Figure 12-18.[45] In particular, the behavior of job seekers moves the economy to a new point on the Phillips curve, where the inflation rate has risen to 7 percent and the unemployment rate has fallen to, say, 3 percent. Workers, however, do not remain ignorant forever. Once they try to spend their newly found "wealth," they quickly realize that a dollar does not go as far as it used to. Workers will then revise the asking wage

---

[45] In other words, workers suffer from "money illusion" in the short run; they accept too many job offers because they perceive the real wage to have increased when, in fact, it did not.

upward to account for the now-observed 7 percent rate of inflation. The asking wage thus goes up by 7 percent, and the unemployment rate shifts back up to the 5 percent natural rate of unemployment. At the end of the process, therefore, the economy ends up at point C in Figure 12-18. The unemployment rate is back at the natural rate, but the economy has a higher rate of inflation.

The relation between inflation and unemployment during the 1960s gave the false hope that government fine-tuning of the economy could lead policymakers to choose from the menu of inflation-unemployment trade-offs implied by a downward-sloping Phillips curve. The experience of many developed countries has taught the hard lesson that there is no long-run trade-off. Increases in the inflation rate do not reduce the natural rate of unemployment. They simply lead to higher prices.

What Is the Natural Rate of Unemployment?

The upward drift in the unemployment rate between 1960 and 1990 suggested that the natural rate of unemployment could easily change over time. In the 1960s, it was not uncommon to think of the natural rate of unemployment as being on the order of 4 percent; by the 1980s, the natural rate of unemployment was believed to be around 6 or 7 percent.

The trend toward an increasing natural rate of unemployment was shattered in the 1990s, when unemployment in the U.S. economy fell to levels that were previously thought impossible without an accompanying increase in the rate of inflation. By 2000, the annual rate of inflation was 3.4 percent and the unemployment rate was 4 percent. We do not yet know if the much higher unemployment rate since 2008 represents a new "normal" or if the natural rate has remained unchanged since the financial crisis.

As we saw earlier, the natural rate of unemployment is partly determined by transition probabilities indicating the rate of job loss among workers, the rate of job finding among the unemployed, and the magnitude of the flows between the market and nonmarket sectors. It is inevitable, for instance, that demographic shifts influence the natural rate of unemployment. For example, the baby boom cohorts that entered the labor market in the 1970s and 1980s probably increased the natural rate. Young workers are much more likely to be in between jobs as they locate and try out alternative job opportunities. In contrast, the aging of the baby boomers in the 1990s should have had a moderating impact on the natural rate because they are now settled into long-term jobs. We also have witnessed a steady rise in the labor force participation rate of women. As women enter and reenter the labor market, it is inevitable that some unemployment arises. It is believed that these demographic shifts increased the natural rate of unemployment by over 1 percentage point between the 1950s and the 1980s.[46]

Structural economic changes also affect the natural rate of unemployment. For example, the 1980s witnessed a substantial deterioration in the labor market status of less-skilled workers. The evidence suggests that part of the observed increase in the natural rate of unemployment during the 1980s can be attributed to the economic experiences of less-skilled workers.[47] However, we do not yet have a good understanding of the factors that led to such a large reduction in the natural rate of unemployment during the 1990s.

---

[46] Michael Darby, John Haltinwanger, and Mark Plant, "Unemployment Rate Dynamics and Persistent Unemployment under Rational Expectations," *American Economic Review* 75 (September 1985): 614–637.

[47] Chinhui Juhn, Kevin M. Murphy, and Robert H. Topel, "Why Has the Natural Rate of Unemployment Increased over Time?" *Brookings Papers on Economic Activity* 2 (1991): 75–142.

12-11 Policy Application: The Unemployment Gap between Europe and the United States

Until about 1980, the United States had substantially higher unemployment rates than most western European countries (see Figure 12-19). In 1970, the unemployment rate in the United States was 4.9 percent, as compared to 2.5 percent in France and 0.7 percent in Germany. By 2001, however, the unemployment rate in the United States was 4.7 percent, as compared to 8.8 percent in France and 10.3 percent in Germany. The much lower unemployment rate in the United States motivated a great deal of research that attempted to isolate the source of the European disadvantage. This research, however, was clearly unaware of what would happen after the economic upheaval of 2008. The unemployment rates of the United States and many other developed countries not only converged, but, in fact, the U.S. unemployment rate suddenly became the highest among the set of countries illustrated in Figure 12-19. By 2010, the 9.6 percent unemployment rate in the United States exceeded that of the United Kingdom (7.9 percent), Sweden (8.3 percent), Italy (8.6 percent), and France (9.4 percent).

Moreover, it used to be the case that the European unemployment problem—unlike the American case—consisted mainly of persons who were in very long unemployment spells. As Table 12-3 shows, a sizable proportion of the unemployed in many European countries have been unemployed for more than a year! As recently as 2006, for example, the proportion of the unemployed who had been out of work for at least 12 months was 57.2 percent in Germany, 44.0 percent in France, and 52.9 percent in Italy. In contrast, only 10.0 percent of the unemployed in the United States were in these very long unemployment spells at the time.

FIGURE 12-19   **Unemployment in Western Europe, 1960–2010**

Source: U.S. Bureau of Labor Statistics, "Foreign Labor Statistics," Table 1-2, "Civilian Labor Force, Employment and Unemployment Approximating U.S. Concepts, 1960–2006," http://stats.bls.gov/fls/home.htm.

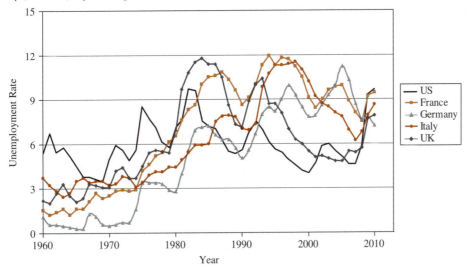

TABLE 12-3 **Percentage of Unemployed Workers in Spells Lasting at Least 12 Months**

Source: *OECD Employment Outlook*, Statistical Annex, Paris: OECD, 2010, Table H.

Country	1990	2006	2009
Belgium	68.7	56.6	44.2
Denmark	29.9	20.4	9.1
Germany	46.8	57.2	45.5
France	38.0	44.0	34.7
Ireland	66.0	34.3	29.0
Italy	69.8	52.9	44.4
Netherlands	49.3	45.2	24.8
Spain	54.0	29.5	30.2
United Kingdom	34.4	22.1	24.6
United States	5.5	10.0	16.3

The situation changed dramatically after 2008. The proportion of unemployed workers in spells longer than a year either remained constant or declined in all of the countries listed in Table 12-3, *except* the United States. In Germany, for instance, the fraction of unemployed workers in spells longer than a year dropped from 57.2 to 45.5 percent between 2006 and 2009, while in France it dropped from 44.0 to 34.7 percent. In the United States, in contrast, it rose from 10.0 to 16.3 percent. It seems as if in the aftermath of the financial crisis the U.S. unemployment problem has become much like the European problem of the 1990s and early 2000s.

As noted above, there has been a great deal of study attempting to understand the Europe-U.S. unemployment gap, but all of this research deals with the world as it used to be, rather than the world as it now is.[48] As in the related discussion regarding the causes of the increase in U.S. wage inequality in the 1980s and 1990s, there was no consensus over which factor was most important in creating the European unemployment problem. Instead, most studies conclude that a number of variables jointly contributed to the problem.

Most studies emphasize the importance of the unemployment insurance system in Europe. Unemployment insurance tends to be much more generous in western European countries than in the United States, in terms of both the level and the duration of benefits. In 1994, for example, the replacement ratio for a single unemployed person during the first year of the spell was 79 percent in France, 66 percent in Germany, and 81 percent in Sweden, as compared to 34 percent in the United States. By the second year of the spell, the replacement

---

[48] Lars Ljungqvist and Thomas J. Sargent, "The European Unemployment Dilemma," *Journal of Political Economy* 106 (June 1998): 514–550; Olivier Blanchard and Justin Wolfers, "The Role of Shocks and Institutions in the Rise of European Unemployment: The Aggregate Evidence," *Economic Journal* 110 (March 2000): C1–C33; and Ghazala Azmat, Maia Ghazala, and Alan Manning, "Gender Gaps in Unemployment Rates in OECD Countries," *Journal of Labor Economics* 24 (January 2006): 1–37. Good overviews of the problem are given by Horst Siebert, "Labor Market Rigidities: At the Root of Unemployment in Europe," *Journal of Economic Perspectives* 11 (Summer 1997): 37–54; Stephen Nickell, "Unemployment and Labor Market Rigidities," *Journal of Economic Perspectives* 11 (Summer 1997): 55–74; and Christopher A. Pissarides, "Public Influences on Unemployment: The European Experience," *Scottish Journal of Political Economy* 46 (September 1999): 389–418.

ratio had fallen to 9 percent in the United States, but remained at 63 percent in France, 63 percent in Germany, and 76 percent in Sweden.[49] The available evidence indicates that the countries that had the most generous unemployment insurance benefits in 1981 were also the countries that had the largest increases in unemployment subsequently.

Many European countries also have enacted strict employment protection regulations that restrict the right of employers to fire workers at will or that require employers to pay sizable severance pay at the time of layoff. The Organization for Economic Cooperation and Development (OECD) has constructed an index that measures the extent of employer restrictions in 20 advanced economies. According to this index, the United States ranks first in this index, offering the least-restrictive labor markets; France and Germany rank 14th and 15th; and Italy ranks last. Because European firms know that it is expensive to lay off workers, they do not want to hire new workers or recall their previously laid-off workers unless they expect favorable economic conditions to persist for a long time. The firm's reluctance to expand inevitably generates long spells of unemployment.

In addition, payroll taxes are very high in many European countries. It is estimated that the "tax wedge," the difference between total labor costs and take-home pay, is 63.8 percent in France, 53.0 percent in Germany, and 62.9 percent in Italy, as compared to 43.8 percent in the United States.[50] It was argued that the relatively high tax burden in European labor markets further reduced employment and contributed to the unemployment gap between Europe and the United States.

It is also the case that wages in the United States are more flexible than wages in Europe. As a response to the various shocks that occurred in the 1980s and 1990s, such as the information revolution and increasing globalization, the U.S. economy adjusted in ways that greatly increased inequality between low-wage and high-wage workers. Because of the restrictions placed on labor market adjustments in some European countries, however, the wage in many of those markets was relatively fixed and this would have led to higher unemployment rates. This argument raises the possibility that, at least in recent years, there may have been an "inequality-unemployment" trade-off. In the United States, the shocks led to a substantial decline in the relative wage of low-skill workers.[51] In much of Europe, those same shocks led to large employment losses.

The rigidity of wages in some European labor markets may be partly due to the very high rate of unionization in these economies. The unionized workers who hold jobs gain substantially from the union, while the "outsiders"—the workers who are unlucky enough to have lost their jobs—can do little to foster more competition in the labor market. The above-market union wage, combined with the additional restrictions on the nature of the employment contract that the union inevitably introduces into the workplace, creates further disincentives for employers to hire and expand, and large levels of unemployment persist.[52]

[49] John P. Martin, "Measures of Replacement Rates for the Purpose of International Comparisons," *OECD Economic Studies* (1996): 99–115.

[50] Nickell, "Unemployment and Labor Market Rigidities."

[51] Paul Krugman, "Past and Prospective Causes of High Unemployment," in *Reducing Unemployment: Current Issues and Policy Options,* Proceedings of a Symposium in Jackson Hole, Wyoming, Kansas City, MO: Federal Reserve Bank of Kansas City, 1995.

[52] Assar Lindbeck and Dennis Snower, "Wage Setting, Unemployment, and Insider-Outsider Relations," *American Economic Review* 76 (May 1986): 235–239.

None of these arguments, however, would help us understand why there was a great reversal in the direction of the European-U.S. unemployment gap after 2008. Almost surely there will be a great deal of theoretical and empirical research on this question for years to come. It is worth emphasizing, however, that the recent experience should make us more than a bit skeptical about the theories that were put forward to explain why the U.S. labor market outperformed the European labor market in the 1990s and early 2000s. A consistent conceptual framework would imply that the recent reversal could be traced back to changes in these fundamental factors, such as the different tax systems in Europe or the different extent of wage flexibility. However, it is unlikely that any of these factors changed sufficiently in recent years to create the "European" unemployment problem now facing the United States.

Summary

- Although the unemployment rate in the United States drifted upward between 1960 and 1990, the economic expansion of the 1990s reduced the unemployment rates substantially.

- Even a well-functioning competitive economy experiences frictional unemployment because some workers will unavoidably be "in between" jobs. Structural unemployment arises when there is an imbalance between the supply of workers and the demand for workers.

- The steady-state rate of unemployment depends on the transition probabilities among employment, unemployment, and the nonmarket sector.

- Although most spells of unemployment do not last very long, most weeks of unemployment can be attributed to workers who are in very long spells.

- The asking wage makes the worker indifferent between continuing his search activities and accepting the job offer at hand. An increase in the benefits from search raises the asking wage and lengthens the duration of the unemployment spell; an increase in search costs reduces the asking wage and shortens the duration of the unemployment spell.

- Unemployment insurance lengthens the duration of unemployment spells and increases the probability that workers are laid off temporarily.

- The intertemporal substitution hypothesis argues that the huge shifts in labor supply observed over the business cycle may be the result of workers reallocating their time so as to purchase leisure when it is cheap (that is, during recessions).

- The sectoral shifts hypothesis argues that structural unemployment arises because the skills of workers cannot be easily transferred across sectors. The skills of workers laid off from declining industries have to be retooled before they can find jobs in growing industries.

- Efficiency wages arise when it is difficult to monitor workers' output. The above-market efficiency wage generates involuntary unemployment.

- Implicit contract theory argues that workers prefer employment contracts under which incomes are relatively stable over the business cycle, even if such contracts imply reductions in hours of work during recessions.

- A downward-sloping Phillips curve can exist only in the short run. In the long run, there is no trade-off between inflation and unemployment.
- The combination of high unemployment insurance benefits, employment protection restrictions, and wage rigidity probably accounts for the high levels of unemployment observed in Europe in the 1980s and 1990s.

Key Concepts

asking wage, *513*
cyclical unemployment, *507*
frictional
   unemployment, *506*
imperfect experience
   rating, *522*
implicit contracts, *531*
intertemporal substitution
   hypothesis, *524*

natural rate of
   unemployment, *509*
nonsequential search, *512*
no-shirking
   supply curve, *528*
Phillips curve, *532*
replacement ratio, *518*
seasonal
   unemployment, *507*

sectoral shifts
   hypothesis, *526*
sequential search, *513*
structural
   unemployment, *507*
temporary layoffs, *521*
wage curve, *529*
wage offer distribution, *511*

Review Questions

1. Discuss some of the basic patterns of unemployment in the United States since 1960.

2. What are the differences between frictional and structural unemployment? Should we be equally concerned with all types of unemployment? Do the same policies help alleviate both frictional and structural unemployment?

3. Derive the steady-state rate of unemployment. Show how it depends on the transition probabilities between employment and unemployment.

4. Discuss how it is simultaneously possible for "most" unemployment to be due to short spells and for "most" unemployment to be accounted for by a few persons in very long spells.

5. Should a job seeker pursue a nonsequential or a sequential search strategy? Derive a job seeker's asking wage. Discuss why the asking wage makes a worker indifferent between searching and not searching.

6. Discuss the impact of the UI system on a job seeker's search behavior. Discuss the impact of the UI system on the firm's layoff behavior.

7. What is the intertemporal substitution hypothesis? Does this argument provide a convincing account of the cyclical trend in the unemployment rate?

8. What is the sectoral shifts hypothesis?

9. Why do implicit contracts generate unemployment?

10. Why do efficiency wages generate involuntary unemployment? What factors prevent the market from clearing in efficiency wage models?

11. Why is the Phillips curve vertical in the long run?

12. Discuss some of the factors that may be responsible for the higher unemployment rates observed in many European countries.

Problems   12-1. Suppose 25,000 persons become unemployed. You are given the following data about the length of unemployment spells in the economy:

Duration of Spell (in months)	Exit Rate
1	0.60
2	0.20
3	0.20
4	0.20
5	0.20
6	1.00

where the exit rate for month t gives the fraction of unemployed persons who have been unemployed t months and who "escape" unemployment at the end of the month.

a. How many unemployment-months will the 25,000 unemployed workers experience?

b. What fraction of persons who are unemployed are "long-term unemployed" in that their unemployment spells will last five or more months?

c. What fraction of unemployment months can be attributed to persons who are long-term unemployed?

d. What is the nature of the unemployment problem in this example: too many workers losing their jobs or too many long spells?

12-2. Consider Table 610 of the 2008 *U.S. Statistical Abstract*.

a. How many workers aged 20 or older were unemployed in the United States during 2006? How many of these were unemployed less than 5 weeks, 5 to 14 weeks, 15 to 26 weeks, and 27 or more weeks?

b. Assume that the average spell of unemployment is 2.5 weeks for anyone unemployed for less than 5 weeks. Similarly, assume the average spell is 10 weeks, 20 weeks, and 35 weeks for the remaining categories. How many weeks did the average unemployed worker remain unemployed? What percent of total months of unemployment are attributable to the workers that remained unemployed for at least 15 weeks?

12-3. Suppose the marginal revenue from search is

$$MR = 50 - 1.5w$$

where w is the wage offer at hand. The marginal cost of search is

$$MC = 5 + w$$

a. Why is the marginal revenue from search a negative function of the wage offer at hand?

b. Can you give an economic interpretation of the intercept in the marginal cost equation; in other words, what does it mean to say that the intercept equals $5? Similarly, what does it mean to say that the slope in the marginal cost equation equals one dollar?

c. What is the worker's asking wage? Will a worker accept a job offer of $15?

d. Suppose UI benefits are reduced, causing the marginal cost of search to increase to $MC = 20 + w$. What is the new asking wage? Will the worker accept a job offer of $15?

12-4. a. How does the exclusion of nonworking welfare recipients affect the calculation of the unemployment rate? Use Tables 525 and 569 of the 2008 *U.S. Statistical Abstract* to estimate what the 2005 unemployment rate would have been if welfare recipients had been included in the calculation.

b. How does the exclusion of workers in the underground economy affect the calculation of the unemployment rate? Estimate, the best you can, what the 2005 unemployment rate would have been if workers in the underground economy had been included in the calculation.

12-5. Compare two unemployed workers: one is 25 years old while the other is 55 years old. Both workers have similar skills and face the same wage offer distribution. Suppose that both workers also incur similar search costs. Which worker will have a higher asking wage? Why? Can search theory explain why the unemployment rate of young workers differs from that of older workers?

12-6. Suppose the government proposes to increase the level of UI benefits for unemployed workers. A particular industry is now paying efficiency wages to its workers in order to discourage them from shirking. What is the effect of the proposed legislation on the wage and on the unemployment rate for workers in that industry?

12-7. During the debate over a federal spending bill, Senator A proposed changing the schedule for paying out unemployment benefits to be one where benefits were doubled but offered for half the current duration (so that UI benefits would expire after 13 weeks). In contrast, Senator B proposed cutting UI benefits in half but to pay benefits for twice as long (so that UI benefits would not expire until after 52 weeks). Comparing to the status quo, contrast both plans along the following dimensions: overall unemployment rate, average duration of unemployment spells, and the distribution of wages accepted by workers coming out of a spell of unemployment.

12-8. Suppose a country has 100 million inhabitants. The population can be divided into the employed, the unemployed, and the persons who are out of the labor force (OLF). In any given year, the transition probabilities among the various categories are given by

		Moving into:		
		Employed	Unemployed	OLF
Moving from:	Employed	0.94	0.02	0.04
	Unemployed	0.20	0.65	0.15
	OLF	0.05	0.03	0.92

These transition probabilities are interpreted as follows. In any given year, 2 percent of the workers who are employed become unemployed; 20 percent of the unemployed find jobs, and so on. What will be the steady-state unemployment rate?

12-9. Consider a small island economy in which almost all jobs are in the tourism industry. A law is passed mandating that all workers in the tourism industry be paid the same national hourly wage, even though workers differ in their skills and effort. In fact, some workers simply cannot produce enough output to be worth the national wage.

    a. How will a worker's optimal job search strategy differ from that discussed in the text? What is the essential difference between this example and the general case discussed in the text?

    b. Despite the law, workers become more productive with experience. How might firms compete over workers when all workers must be paid the same wage?

    c. After the law has been enforced for several years, an economist looks at the data and finds that the duration of unemployment spells is significantly longer when unemployment rates are low and significantly shorter when unemployment rates are high. How can this behavior be explained?

12-10. Consider an economy with three types of jobs. The table below shows the jobs, the frequency with which vacancies open up on a yearly basis, and the income associated with each job. Searching for a job costs $C per year and generates at most one job offer. There is a 20 percent chance of not receiving an offer in a year. (Note: The expected search duration for a job with probability p of appearing is $1/p$ year.)

Job Type	Frequency	Income
A	30 percent	$ 60,000
B	20 percent	$100,000
C	30 percent	$ 80,000

As a function of C, specify the optimal job search strategy if the worker maximizes her expected income net of search costs.

12-11. Consider Figure 12-19 in the text. What happened to the unemployment rate in France, Germany, and Italy from 1970 to 2000? What do you think explains this pattern?

12-12. a. Use Table 571 of the 2008 *U.S. Statistical Abstract* to describe how unemployment rates have changed for males, females, whites, blacks, and Hispanics since 1970.

    b. Now use Table 609 of the 2008 *U.S. Statistical Abstract* to describe how educational status is related to unemployment rates for each of these groups. For which racial groups is a college education an equalizer in terms of unemployment rates compared to whites?

12-13. Suppose the current UI system pays $500 per week for up to 15 weeks. The government considers changing to a UI system that requires someone to be unemployed for five weeks before receiving any benefits. After five weeks, the person receives a lump-sum payment of $2,500. He then receives no benefits for another five weeks. If he is still unemployed then, he receives a second lump-sum payment of $2,500. He again receives no benefits for another five weeks. If he is still unemployed then, he receives a third and final lump-sum payment of $2,500. Provide a graph similar to Figure 12-11 showing how the probability of finding a job over time is likely to be different under the status quo and the proposed scheme.

12-14. Unemployment insurance automatically stimulates the economy during an economic contraction, which is good from the workers' point of view. From the firm's point of view, however, the UI system can be overbearing on business during prolonged contractions.

    a. What is it about the UI system that generates these opposing views?

    b. How could the UI system be changed to also assist firms during economic contractions while not removing the benefits available to laid-off workers?

12-15. Consider the standard job search model as described in the text.

    a. Why are the asking wage and expected unemployment duration positively related?

    b. Can the standard job search model explain why unemployment duration is longer, on average, for secondary workers when compared to primary workers? Discuss.

    c. In the context of the standard search model, explain how the economy-wide average asking wage and unemployment duration are affected by an expanded underground (cash) economy. What is the effect on the equilibrium unemployment rate?

    d. In the context of the standard search model, explain how the economy-wide average asking wage and unemployment duration are affected by federal policy that greatly restricts mortgage-holding companies from pursuing foreclosures. What is the effect on the equilibrium unemployment rate?

Selected Readings

Katharine G. Abraham and Lawrence F. Katz, "Cyclical Unemployment: Sectoral Shifts or Aggregate Disturbances," *Journal of Political Economy* 94 (June 1986): 507–522.

Paul Beaudry and John DiNardo, "The Effect of Implicit Contracts on the Movement of Wages over the Business Cycle: Evidence from Micro Data," *Journal of Political Economy* 99 (August 1991): 665–688.

Lawrence F. Katz and Bruce D. Meyer, "Unemployment Insurance, Recall Expectations, and Unemployment Outcomes," *Quarterly Journal of Economics* 105 (November 1990): 973–1002.

Peter Kuhn and Mikal Skuterud, "Internet Job Search and Unemployment Durations," *American Economic Review* 94 (March 2004): 218–232.

David M. Lilien, "Sectoral Shifts and Cyclical Unemployment," *Journal of Political Economy* 90 (August 1982): 777–793.

Robert E. Lucas and Leonard Rapping, "Real Wages, Employment, and Inflation," *Journal of Political Economy* 77 (September/October 1969): 721–754.

Sherwin Rosen, "Implicit Contracts: A Survey," *Journal of Economic Literature* 23 (September 1985): 1144–1175.

Carl Shapiro and Joseph E. Stiglitz, "Equilibrium Unemployment as a Worker Discipline Device," *American Economic Review* 74 (June 1984): 433–444.

Gary Solon, Robert Barsky, and Jonathan A. Parker, "Measuring the Cyclicality of Real Wages: How Important Is Composition Bias?" *Quarterly Journal of Economics* 109 (February 1994): 1–25.

Web Links

The U.S. Department of Labor collects detailed information on various aspects of the state-run unemployment insurance program: http://workforcesecurity.doleta.gov/unemploy/aboutui.asp.

The OECD reports unemployment statistics for many advanced economies and frequently publishes reports comparing the unemployment situation in different countries: www.oecd.org.

Mathematical Appendix

Some Standard Models in Labor Economics

This appendix presents the mathematics behind some of the basic models in labor economics. None of the material in the appendix is required to follow the discussion in the text, but it does provide additional insight to students who have the mathematical ability (in particular, calculus) and who wish to see the models derived in a more technical way. Because the text discusses the economic intuition behind the various models in depth, the presentation in this appendix focuses solely on the mathematical details.

1.   The Neoclassical Labor-Leisure Model (Chapter 2)

Suppose an individual has a utility function $U(C, L)$, where C is consumption of goods measured in dollars and L is hours of leisure. The partial derivatives of the utility function are $U_C = \partial U/\partial C > 0$ and $U_L = \partial U/\partial L > 0$.

The individual's budget constraint is given by:

$$C = w\,(T - L) + V \qquad \text{(A-1)}$$

where T is total hours available in the time period under analysis (and assumed constant), w is the wage rate, and V is other income. Note that equation (A-1) can be rewritten as:

$$wT + V = C + wL \qquad \text{(A-2)}$$

An individual's full income, given by $wT + V$, gives how much money the individual would have if he or she were to work every available hour. Full income is spent either on consumption or on leisure. This rewriting of the budget constraint shows that each hour of leisure requires the expenditure of w dollars. Hence, the price of leisure is w.

The maximization of equation (A-1) subject to the constraint in equation (A-2) is a standard problem in calculus. We solve it by maximizing the Lagrangian:

$$\max \Omega = U(C, L) + \lambda\,(wT + V - C - wL) \qquad \text{(A-3)}$$

where λ is the Lagrange multiplier. The first-order conditions are:

$$\frac{\partial\Omega}{\partial C} = U_C - \lambda = 0$$

$$\frac{\partial\Omega}{\partial L} = U_L - \lambda w = 0$$

$$\frac{\partial\Omega}{\partial\lambda} = wT + V - C - wL = 0 \qquad \text{(A-4)}$$

The last condition simply restates the budget constraint. If the equality holds, the optimal choice of C and L must lie on the budget line. The ratio of the first two equations gives the familiar condition that an internal solution to the neoclassical labor-leisure model requires that the ratio of marginal utilities $U_L/U_C = w$.

The Lagrange multiplier λ has a special interpretation in a constrained optimization models. Let F be full income. It can then be shown that $\lambda = \partial\Omega/\partial F = \partial U/\partial F$. In other words, the Lagrange multiplier equals the worker's marginal utility of income.

2.   The Slutsky Equation: Income and Substitution Effects (Chapter 2)

The *Slutsky equation* decomposes the change in hours of work resulting from a change in the wage into a substitution and an income effect. It can be derived by combining the restrictions implied by the first-order conditions in equation (A-4) with the second-order conditions to the constrained maximization problem. That derivation, however, is somewhat messy.

This section presents a simpler (and more economically intuitive) approach. Although the neoclassical labor-leisure model has two choice variables (C and L), it can be rewritten as a standard one-variable calculus maximization problem. We will assume there is an interior solution to the problem throughout. We can write the individual's maximization problem as:

$$\max Y = U(wT - wL + V, L) \qquad \text{(A-5)}$$

where we have simply solved out the variable C from the utility function. An individual maximizes Y by choosing the right amount of leisure. This maximization yields the first-order condition:

$$\frac{\partial Y}{\partial L} = U_C(-w) + U_L = 0 \qquad \text{(A-6)}$$

Note that equation (A-6) can be rearranged so that it becomes the familiar expression that the ratio of marginal utilities (U_L/U_C) equals the wage.

Because this is a standard one-variable maximization problem, the second-order condition is relatively trivial. In particular, a maximum requires that the second derivative $\partial^2 Y/\partial L^2$ be negative. After some algebra, it can be shown that:

$$\frac{\partial^2 Y}{\partial L^2} = -w[U_{CC}(-w) + U_{CL}] - wU_{CL} + U_{LL} = \Delta < 0 \qquad \text{(A-7)}$$

Note that we will use the simpler notation of Δ to denote the expression that must be negative according to the second-order condition.

We can now derive the Slutsky equation in three separate steps. First, let's find out what happens to leisure when other income V changes, *holding the wage constant.* This is done by totally differentiating the first-order condition in equation (A-6). The total differential of the first-order condition resulting from a change in V is:

$$-wU_{CC}[-wdL + dV] - wU_{CL}dL + U_{LC}[-wdL + dV] + U_{LL}dL = 0 \quad \text{(A-8)}$$

Rearranging terms in this equation yields:

$$\frac{\partial L}{\partial V} = \frac{wU_{CC} - U_{LC}}{\Delta} \quad \text{(A-9)}$$

Note that even though the denominator is negative, we still cannot sign the derivative in equation (A-9). We instead define leisure to be a normal good if $dL/dV > 0$.

We now want to determine what happens to leisure when the wage changes, *holding other income constant.* Note that this type of conceptual experiment must inevitably move the worker to a different indifference curve. An increase in the wage makes the worker better off, while a decrease in the wage makes the worker worse off. To derive the expression for dL/dw, we return to the first-order condition in equation (A-6) and totally differentiate this equation, holding V constant. After some algebra, we can show that:

$$\frac{\partial L}{\partial w} = \frac{U_C}{\Delta} + h\frac{wU_{CC} - U_{CL}}{\Delta}$$

$$= \frac{U_C}{\Delta} + h\frac{\partial L}{\partial V} \quad \text{(A-10)}$$

The impact of a change in the wage on the quantity of leisure consumed can be written as the sum of two terms. The first of these terms must be negative (because $U_C > 0$ and $\Delta < 0$), while the second term is positive under our assumption that leisure is a normal good. We will now show that the first term in equation (A-10) captures the substitution effect, while the second term captures the income effect.

The substitution effect measures what happens to the demand for leisure if the wage changes and the individual is "forced" to remain in the same indifference curve at utility U^*. The only way a worker can remain on the same indifference curve after a change in the wage is if somehow the worker is compensated in some other fashion. For instance, a fall in the wage will shrink the size of the opportunity set so that the only way the worker can remain on the same indifference curve is if there is a compensation for the lost wages through an increase in other income. In other words, V has to change as the wage changes in order to maintain utility constant at U^*. This type of change in the quantity of leisure consumed is called a *compensated* change.

It is easy to figure out the amount of compensation required to hold utility constant. Consider the question: by how much must V change after the change in the wage in order for the individual to remain on the same indifference curve? Let both w and V change, and hold utility constant. Differentiation of equation (A-5) then yields:

$$U_C[h\,dw + dV] = 0 \quad \text{(A-11)}$$

Hence, the compensating change in V is given by $dV = -h\,dw$.

Equation (A-9) shows what happens to leisure when other income changes, and equation (A-10) shows what happens to leisure when the wage changes. We now want to know what happens to leisure when there is a compensated change in the wage—in other words, what happens to leisure when the wage increases but the individuals' utility is held constant. This exercise, of course, would measure exactly the substitution effect.

The substitution effect is calculated by again totally differentiating the first-order condition and by letting both w and V change. This total differential equals:

$$\Delta dL - [U_C + wU_{CC}h - U_{LC}h]dw - [wU_{CC} - U_{LC}]dV = 0 \qquad \text{(A-12)}$$

The worker will remain in the same indifference curve if $dV = -h\,dw$. Imposing this restriction in equation (A-12) implies that:

$$\left.\frac{\partial L}{\partial w}\right|_{U=U^*} = \frac{U_C}{\Delta} \qquad \text{(A-13)}$$

Note that the substitution effect implies that a compensated increase in the wage must lower the quantity consumed of leisure because the denominator in equation (A-13) is negative. Finally, note that $h = T - L$. By combining the various expressions, we can rewrite equation (A-10) as:

$$\frac{\partial h}{\partial w} = \left.\frac{\partial h}{\partial w}\right|_{U=U^*} + h\frac{\partial h}{\partial V} \qquad \text{(A-14)}$$

Equation (A-14) is known as the Slutksy equation.

3. Labor Demand (Chapter 3)

The firm's production function is given by $q = f(K, E)$, where q is the firm's output, K is capital, and E is employment. The marginal product of capital and labor are given by $f_K = \partial q/\partial K$ and $f_E = \partial Q/\partial E$, respectively, and are positive. The firm's objective is to maximize profits, which can be written as:

$$\pi = p\,f(K, E) - rK - wE \qquad \text{(A-15)}$$

where p is the price of a unit of output, r is the rental rate of capital, and w is the wage rate. The firm is assumed to be competitive in the output and input markets. From the firm's perspective, therefore, prices p, w, and r are constants.

In the short run, capital is fixed at level $\overline{K}$. The firm's maximization problem can then be written as:

$$\pi = p\,f(\overline{K}, E) - r\overline{K} - wE \qquad \text{(A-16)}$$

The competitive firm's maximization problem is simple: choose the level of E that maximizes profits. The first- and second-order conditions to the problem are:

$$\frac{\partial \pi}{\partial E} = pf_E - w = 0$$

$$\frac{\partial^2 \pi}{\partial E^2} = pf_{EE} < 0 \qquad \text{(A-17)}$$

The first equation gives the familiar condition that the wage equals the value of marginal product, while the second-order condition requires that the law of diminishing returns hold at the optimal employment.

We can use the results in equation (A-17) to show that the labor demand curve must be downward sloping in the short run. In particular, totally differentiate the first-order condition as the wage w changes:

$$pf_{EE}dE - dw = 0 \qquad \text{(A-18)}$$

It follows that $dE/dw = 1/pf_{EE}$, which must be negative because of the second-order condition.

In the long run, the firm can choose the optimal amount of both capital and labor. The first-order conditions to the maximization problem in equation (A-15) are:

$$\frac{\partial \pi}{\partial K} = pf_K - r = 0$$

$$\frac{\partial \pi}{\partial E} = pf_E - w = 0 \qquad \text{(A-19)}$$

The second-order conditions for the two-variable unconstrained maximization problem are a bit harder to derive, but they require that $f_{KK} < 0, f_{EE} < 0$, and $(f_{KK}f_{EE} - f_{KE}^2) > 0$.

It is easy to show that the labor demand curve must also be downward sloping in the long run. In particular, suppose that there is a wage shift. Totally differentiate the two first-order conditions in equation (A-19) to capture the response to this wage shift. This differentiation yields:

$$pf_{KK}dK + pf_{KE}dE = 0$$

$$pf_{EK}dK + pf_{EE}dE = dw \qquad \text{(A-20)}$$

where the rental rate of capital is being held constant. The first of these equations implies that $dK = \dfrac{-f_{KE}}{f_{KK}} dE$. Substituting this fact into the second of the equations in (A-20) implies:

$$\frac{\partial E}{\partial w} = \frac{f_{KK}}{p(f_{KK}f_{EE} - f_{KE}^2)} < 0 \qquad \text{(A-21)}$$

The second-order conditions to the maximization problem imply this derivative is negative and the labor demand curve in the long run must be downward sloping.

As an exercise, it is instructive to prove the truly remarkable theoretical implication that:

$$\frac{\partial E}{\partial r} = \frac{\partial K}{\partial w} \qquad \text{(A-22)}$$

This prediction, known as the *symmetry restriction,* states that the change in employment resulting from a $1 increase in the rental price of capital must be identical to the change in the capital stock resulting from a $1 increase in the wage. These types of symmetry implications of the model are almost always rejected by the data.

5.   Marshall's Rules of Derived Demand (Chapter 3)

We will now prove the first three of Marshall's rules of derived demand and, in doing so, also derive a Slutsky-type equation that decomposes the industry-level elasticity of demand into scale and substitution effects. The proof of Marshall's fourth rule is much messier, and little is learned from the added complexity.

Labor economists often assume a specific functional form for the production function. A common assumption in modern labor economics is that the industry can be characterized in terms of a constant elasticity of substitution (CES) production function. This industry-level production function is given by:

$$Q = [\alpha K^{\delta} + (1 - \alpha)E^{\delta}]^{1/\delta} \qquad \text{(A-23)}$$

As an exercise, it is worth showing that the CES production function has constant returns to scale (that is, a doubling of all inputs doubles output).

The CES functional form is useful because it allows for a wide array of possibilities that describe the extent of substitution between labor and capital. The parameter δ is less than or equal to one (and can be negative). If $\delta = 1$, it is easy to see that the CES production function is linear, and that is the case where labor and capital are perfectly substitutable (so that the isoquants are straight lines). It can be shown that if δ goes to minus infinity, the isoquants associated with the CES production function become right-angled isoquants, so that there is no substitution possible between labor and capital. The elasticity of substitution between labor and capital is defined by $\sigma = 1/(1 - \delta)$. Note that if $\delta = 1$, the elasticity of substitution goes to infinity (perfect substitution), and if $\delta = -\infty$, the elasticity of substitution goes to zero (perfect complements).

If the industry is competitive, the price of labor and capital must equal the respective values of marginal product. It is easy to verify that these conditions can be written as:

$$r = p\,\alpha\,Q^{1-\delta}K^{\delta-1}$$
$$w = p(1 - \alpha)Q^{1-\delta}E^{\delta-1} \qquad \text{(A-24)}$$

As an exercise, it is instructive to derive:

$$s_K = \frac{rK}{pQ} = \frac{\alpha K^{\delta}}{Q^{\delta}}$$

$$s_E = \frac{wE}{pQ} = \frac{(1 - \alpha)E^{\delta}}{Q^{\delta}} \qquad \text{(A-25)}$$

where s_K gives the share of industry income that goes to capital and s_E gives the share that goes to labor.

By totally differentiating the production function in equation (A-23) and rearranging terms, it follows that:

$$d \log E = d \log Q - s_K(d \log K - d \log E) \qquad \text{(A-26)}$$

Changes in the scale of the industry ($d \log Q$) depend on the demand for the industry's output. Define the absolute value of the elasticity of demand for the output as:

$$\eta = \left| \frac{d \log Q}{d \log p} \right| \tag{A-27}$$

Note that although the demand curve for the output is downward sloping, the elasticity η is defined to be a positive number. Equation (A-26) can then be rewritten as:

$$d \log E = -\eta \, d \log p - s_K (d \log K - d \log E) \tag{A-28}$$

We now need to find out by how much the price of the output changes when the wage changes (note that we are holding r constant throughout the exercise). In a competitive industry, the output price must equal the marginal cost, which must equal the average cost (there are zero profits). We can write the zero-profit condition as:

$$p = \frac{rK + wE}{Q} \tag{A-29}$$

Note that equation (A-23) implies that $d \log Q = s_K \, d \log K + s_E \, d \log E$. By totally differentiating equation (A-29) and rearranging terms, we can derive that:

$$d \log p = s_E d \log w \tag{A-30}$$

Finally, the ratio of first-order conditions in equation (A-24) implies that:

$$\frac{w}{r} = \frac{(1 - \alpha)E^{\delta - 1}}{\alpha K^{\delta - 1}} \tag{A-31}$$

Totally differentiating equation (A-31) implies that the (percent) change in the capital/labor ratio is:

$$d \log K - d \log E = (1 - \delta)d \log w$$

$$= \sigma d \log w \tag{A-32}$$

Substituting equations (A-30) and (A-32) into equation (A-28) yields:

$$\frac{d \log E}{d \log w} = -[s_E \eta + (1 - s_E)\sigma] \tag{A-33}$$

The elasticity of demand for labor can be written as a weighted average of the elasticity of product demand and the elasticity of substitution between capital and labor. The first term of equation (A-33) gives the scale effect that depends on the elasticity of demand for the industry's output, while the second term gives the substitution effect that depends on how easily substitutable labor and capital are along a single isoquant.

The first three of Marshall's rules of derived demand state that:

1. The labor demand curve is more elastic the greater the elasticity of substitution.
2. The labor demand curve is more elastic the greater the elasticity of demand for the output.

3. The labor demand curve is more elastic the greater labor's share in total costs (but this holds only when the absolute value of the elasticity of product demand exceeds the elasticity of substitution).

As an exercise, it is worth verifying these rules directly from equation (A-33).

6. Immigration in a Cobb-Douglas Economy (Chapter 4)

A single aggregate good is produced using a production function that combines capital and labor. The aggregate production function is Cobb-Douglas with constant returns to scale, so that $Q = AK^{\alpha}E^{1-\alpha}$. If the labor market were competitive, the input prices are each equal to their value of marginal product. Setting the price of the output Q at unity, we obtain:

$$r = \alpha AK^{\alpha-1}E^{1-\alpha}$$
$$w = (1 - \alpha)AK^{\alpha}E^{-\alpha} \tag{A-34}$$

The number of native workers in the labor market is assumed to be perfectly inelastic. Suppose an influx of immigrants enters the labor market. By taking logs and totally differentiating the second of the equations in (A-34), we obtain the change in the log wage:

$$d \log w = \alpha \, d \log K - \alpha \, d \log E \tag{A-35}$$

Consider two alternative scenarios: the short run and the long run. In the short run, the capital stock is fixed, and hence, the elasticity giving the change in the wage resulting from an immigration-induced increase in labor supply is:

$$\left. \frac{d \log w}{d \log E} \right|_{dK=0} = -\alpha \tag{A-36}$$

As an exercise, it is worth showing that the parameter α is simply equal to capital's share of income in the economy ($\alpha = rK/Q$). It is well known that labor's share of income in the United States is around 0.7, implying that capital's share of income is around 0.3. Hence, the short-run wage elasticity is -0.3. As an exercise, it is instructive to derive the prediction that although immigration lowers the wage in the short run, it raises the rental rate to capital, r.

In the long run, we assume that the rental rate to capital, r, is constant. The higher profitability of capital attracts a flow of capital, and this flow will continue until the rental rate of capital returns to its global equilibrium level. The question is: how much additional capital will flow into the economy? The answer is obtained by totally differentiating the first-order condition equating the price of capital to its value of marginal product. This differentiation yields:

$$d \log r = (\alpha - 1)(d \log K - d \log E) = 0 \tag{A-37}$$

If the rental rate of capital r is constant in the long run, equation (A-37) implies that $d \log K = d \log E$. Hence, if immigration increases labor supply by 10 percent, capital must also eventually go up by 10 percent. It is evident from equation (A-35) that the wage impact of immigration in the long run must be given by:

$$\left. \frac{d \log w}{d \log E} \right|_{dr=0} = 0 \tag{A-38}$$

The assumption of a Cobb-Douglas production function not only gives us qualitative predictions about the wage impact of immigration in a competitive labor market, but *quantitative* predictions as well. In short, one would expect the wage elasticity to lie between 0.0 and -0.3, depending on the extent to which capital has adjusted to the presence of the immigrant influx.

7. Monopsony (Chapter 4)

A firm has monopsony power when it is not a price-taker in the labor market. In other words, the labor supply curve is upward sloping and the only way the firm can hire more workers is to increase the wage. Suppose the labor supply function facing the firm is:

$$E = S(w) \tag{A-39}$$

with $S' > 0$. It is easier to derive the model using the inverse supply function—that is, the function that defines the wage that the firm must pay to attract a particular number of workers, or $w = s(E)$, with $s' > 0$. For simplicity, suppose the firm's capital stock is fixed so that we can effectively ignore the role of capital in the model and write the production function as $f(E)$. The firm's profit maximization problem is then given by:

$$\pi = p\,f(E) - wE = p\,f(E) - s(E)\,E \tag{A-40}$$

The first-order condition to this maximization problem is given by:

$$\frac{d\pi}{dE} = pf_E - s(E) - s'(E)E = 0 \tag{A-41}$$

Note that this equation can be rewritten as:

$$pf_E = w + \frac{dw}{dE}E$$

$$= w\left(1 + \frac{dw}{dE}\frac{E}{w}\right)$$

$$= w\left(1 + \frac{1}{\sigma}\right) \tag{A-42}$$

where σ is the labor supply elasticity, or $d \log E / d \log w$. Note that if the firm were perfectly competitive, the labor supply elasticity would equal infinity, and the condition in equation (A-42) reduces to the standard result that the wage must equal the value of marginal product.

8. The Rosen Schooling Model (Chapter 6)

The wage-schooling locus, $y(A, s)$, describes how much a person with innate ability A earns as a result of having accrued s years of schooling. Let's assume that (1) the only cost of schooling is the foregone earnings associated with being in school, (2) individuals choose the level of schooling that maximizes the present value of the lifetime earnings stream, and (3) individuals live forever.

It is easier to derive the model in terms of continuous time, rather than discrete year-by-year accounting. In continuous time, the present value of a payment of $1 paid in each period henceforth is given by:

$$\int_0^\infty 1 \cdot e^{-rt}dt = \frac{1}{r} \tag{A-43}$$

where r is the rate of discount. Note that the exponential function e^{-rt} plays the same role as the $[1/(1 + r)^t]$ terms when we calculate present values in discrete time. The present value of the earnings stream for a person who lives forever is then given by:

$$V(A, s) = \int_s^\infty y(A, s), e^{-rt}dt = \frac{y(A, s)e^{-rs}}{r} \tag{A-44}$$

where r is the person's rate of discount. Note that the assumption that the only costs associated with schooling are foregone earnings is built into equation (A-44) by starting the addition of positive earnings when the individual leaves school after s years.

There is nothing the person can do about his or her innate ability. A person instead maximizes the present value of earnings by picking the optimal level of s. The first-order condition to this maximization problem is:

$$\frac{\partial V(A, s)}{\partial s} = \frac{\partial y(A, s)}{\partial s} - ry(A, s) = 0 \tag{A-45}$$

which can be written as:

$$\frac{y_s}{y} = r \tag{A-46}$$

For a given individual, the percentage change in earnings associated with going to school one more year must equal the rate of discount. As an exercise, it is instructive to examine the relationship between ability and the optimal level of schooling: will more able people get more schooling?

9.　The Becker Model of Taste Discrimination (Chapter 9)

Employers care not only about profits, but also about the racial composition of their workforce. Suppose a competitive employer wishes to maximize a utility function given by:

$$V = U(E_w, E_b, \pi) \tag{A-47}$$

where E_w gives the number of white workers, E_b gives the number of black workers, and π gives profits. An employer who is nepotistic toward white workers will have $U_w = \partial V/\partial E_w > 0$. An employer who discriminates against black workers will have $U_b = \partial V/\partial E_b < 0$. The employer's profit is given by:

$$\pi = pf(L_w + L_b) - w_w E_w - w_b E_b \tag{A-48}$$

where p is the price of the output, and w_i gives the wage of workers in group i. We assume that $U_\pi > 0$. Note that the labor input in the production function f is the sum of the number of white and black workers, so that the two groups are assumed to be perfect substitutes in production. For simplicity, we ignore the role of capital. The first-order conditions to the maximization problem are:

$$\frac{\partial V}{\partial E_w} = U_w + U_\pi(pf' - w_w) = 0$$

$$\frac{\partial V}{\partial E_b} = U_b + U_\pi(pf' - w_b) = 0 \qquad \text{(A-49)}$$

We can rewrite these first-order conditions as:

$$pf' = w_w - \frac{U_w}{U_\pi} = w_w - d_w$$

$$pf' = w_b - \frac{U_b}{U_\pi} = w_b + d_b \qquad \text{(A-50)}$$

where the discrimination coefficients d_w and d_b are both defined as positive numbers, and are given by the ratio of the marginal utilities of employment in a particular race group and profits. Equation (A-50) shows that employers who care about the race of their workforce will hire up to the point where the value of marginal product of workers in a particular group equals the utility-adjusted price of that type of worker (that is, the sum of the wage rate and the discrimination coefficient).

Name Index

DiNardo, John, 302n, 303n, 304n, 316n, 347n, 426n, 444n, 445n, 450n, 532n, 545n
Disney, Richard, 132n
Doeringer, Peter, 491n
Dolton, Peter, 521n
Dominitz, Jeff, 187n
Doms, Mark, 302n
Donahue, John J. III, 130n
Donald, Stephen G., 184n
Donal O'Neill, 521n
Donohue, John J., 393n
Dou, Thomas, 406n
Dreze, Jean, 467n
Duflo, Esther, 63n, 254n
Duggan, Mark G., 75n, 83n, 501n
Duncan, Greg, 47n, 223n, 447n, 450n
Duncan, Greg J., 404n
Dunn, Thomas A., 311n
Dunne, Timothy, 302n
Dustmann, Christian, 305n, 322n
Dynarski, Susan M., 247n

E

Eatwell, John, 509n
Eberts, Randall, 222n, 438n
Edin, Per-Anders, 337n, 404n, 489n
Edwards, Linda N., 53n
Ehrenberg, Ronald G., 130n, 131n, 132n, 197n, 259n, 476n, 521n
Eide, Eric R., 259n
Eisenhower, Dwight D., 444
Eissa, Nada, 61n, 63n, 83n
Eliason, Marcus, 353n
Ellingsen, Tore, 489n
Ellison, Lawrence J., 478
Ellwood, David, 54n, 425n
Enchautegui, Maria E., 343n
England, Paula, 406n, 407n
Engles, Gregg L., 478
Erling, Brath, 171n
Estes, Eugena, 347n
Evans, William N., 52n, 278n, 349n

F

Faberman, R. Jason, 510n
Fair, Ray, 129n
Fairlie, Robert W., 378n

Falch, Torberg, 194n
Fallick, Bruce C., 426n
Fama, Eugene F., 464n
Farber, Henry S., 69n, 194n, 202N, 269n, 352n, 353n, 356n, 357n, 358n, 359n, 365n, 422n, 426n, 428n, 442n, 448n, 455n, 462n
Farkas, George, 406n
Farrell, John, 448n
Fay, Jon, 129n
Feenstra, Robert C., 300n
Fehr, Ernst, 487n
Feldstein, Martin, 46n, 58n, 83n, 131n, 273n, 521n, 523n
Feliciano, Zadia M., 120n
Field-Hendrey, Elizabeth, 53n
Filer, Randall, 175n
Fine, Glenn, 425n
Fink, Laurence D., 478
Fishback, Price V., 177n
Fishelson, G., 490n
Fitzsimons, Emla, 280n
Ford, Henry, 488n
Fortin, Nicole, 177n, 304n, 316n, 405n
Fraundorf, Martha, 448n
Fredrikksson, Peter, 337n
Freeman, Richard B., 32n, 114n, 124n, 143n, 157n, 169n, 175n, 176n, 179n, 185n, 299n, 300n, 301n, 304n, 305n, 343n, 393n, 395n, 417n, 418n, 421n, 426n, 427n, 428n, 430n, 447n, 448n, 449n, 450n, 451n, 453n, 462n, 465n
French, Eric, 125n
Friedberg, Leora, 77n
Friedberg, Rachel, 169n, 171n, 335n, 336n
Friedman, John N., 249n, 287n
Friedman, Milton, 239n, 449, 449n, 534n
Fryer, Roland, 386n
Fuess, Scott, 450n

G

Garen, John, 215n, 262n
Genda, Yuji, 505n
Gertler, Paul, 226n
Ghazala, Maia, 538n
Gibbons, Robert, 269n, 358n, 464n
Giuliano, Laura, 387n

Glaeser, Edward, 48n, 378n, 506n
Glenn, Andrew J., 125n
Goette, Lorenz, 487n
Goldberg, Matthew S., 371n, 416n
Goldfarb, Robert, 111n
Goldin, Claudia, 50n, 53n, 113n, 135n, 143n, 405n, 406n
Goldsmith, Arthur H., 398n
Gompers, Samuel, 428
Gonzalez-Chapela, Jorge, 73n
Goodman, Alissa, 280n
Gordon, M. S., 72n
Gordon, R. A., 72n
Gordon, Robert, 349n
Gottschalk, Peter, 157n, 304n
Gramm, Cynthia, 441n
Grant, Darren, 532n
Grant, Hugh, 478
Grant, Kenneth E., 322n
Gray, Wayne B., 221n
Green, David, 46n
Greenstone, Michael, 218n, 234n
Greenwood, Michael, 320n
Gregory, Robert, 409n
Griffin, Peter, 109n
Griliches, Zvi, 113n, 251n, 302n
Grogger, Jeffrey, 58n, 59n, 83n, 179n, 257n, 338n, 398n
Gronau, Reuben, 404n
Groshen, Erica L., 489n
Grossman, Jean B., 169n
Grosso, Jean-Luc, 130n
Gruber, Jonathan, 73n, 76n, 155n, 202n, 223n, 524n
Gunderson, Morley, 215n
Gupta, Indrani, 225n
Guryan, Jonathan, 370n, 416n
Gustavsson, Magnus, 404n
Gustman, Alan, 74n
Gwartney, James, 395n

H

Haider, Steven J., 77n
Haim, Bradley T., 53n
Hall, Brian J., 479n, 497n
Hall, Robert E., 273n, 352n
Hallock, Kevin F., 444n
Haltinwanger, John, 133n, 302n, 509n, 536n
Ham, John C., 532n

Subject Index